KU-433-230

THE ⟨crest⟩ TIMES
ATLAS
OF THE
WORLD
MINI EDITION

Times Books, 77-85 Fulham Palace Road,
London W6 8JN

First published 1991
First published as The Times Atlas
of the World Mini Edition 1994
Second Edition 1999

Printed and bound in the UK

ISBN 0 7230 0992 9

KH9204

www.fireandwater.com
visit the book lover's website

THE TIMES
ATLAS
OF THE
WORLD

2000
MINI EDITION

TIMES BOOKS
London

CONTENTS

THE EARTH TODAY

Title	Pages

IMAGES OF EARTH

OCEANIA	8-9
ASIA	10-11
EUROPE	12-13
AFRICA	14-15
NORTH AMERICA	16-17
SOUTH AMERICA	18-19
ANTARCTICA	20-21

THE WORLD IN 2000

CLIMATE	22-23
LAND COVER	24-25
POPULATION	26-27
URBANIZATION	28-29
CITIES	30-31

GEOGRAPHICAL INFORMATION

STATES AND TERRITORIES OF THE WORLD	32-37
CONTINENTS, ISLANDS AND MOUNTAINS	38-39
OCEANS, SEAS, LAKES AND RIVERS	40-41

 # CONTENTS

ATLAS OF THE WORLD

Pages	Title	Scale
44-45	INTRODUCTION TO THE ATLAS	
46-47	SYMBOLS AND ABBREVIATIONS	
48-49	**OCEANIA**	1:70 000 000
50-51	**AUSTRALIA**	1:25 000 000
52-53	**AUSTRALIA** SOUTHEAST	1:10 000 000
54	**NEW ZEALAND**	1:10 000 000
55	**ANTARCTICA**	1:60 000 000
56-57	**ASIA**	1:70 000 000
58-59	**SOUTHEAST ASIA**	1:30 000 000
60-61	**MALAYSIA AND INDONESIA WEST**	1:15 000 000
62-63	**CONTINENTAL SOUTHEAST ASIA**	1:15 000 000
64	**PHILIPPINES**	1:15 000 000
65	**NORTH KOREA AND SOUTH KOREA**	1:9 000 000
66-67	**JAPAN**	1:10 000 000
68-69	**CHINA AND MONGOLIA**	1:30 000 000
70-71	**CHINA** CENTRAL	1:15 000 000
72-73	**SOUTH ASIA**	1:20 000 000
74-75	**PAKISTAN, INDIA AND BANGLADESH**	1:15 000 000
76-77	**CENTRAL ASIA**	1:20 000 000
78-79	**ARABIAN PENINSULA**	1:15 000 000

CONTENTS

Pages	Title	Scale
80-81	**EAST MEDITERRANEAN**	1:15 000 000
82-83	**RUSSIAN FEDERATION**	1:42 000 000
84-85	**EUROPE**	1:40 000 000
86-87	**EUROPEAN RUSSIAN FEDERATION**	1:20 000 000
88-89	**NORTHEAST EUROPE**	1:8 000 000
90-91	**UKRAINE AND MOLDOVA**	1:8 000 000
92-93	**SCANDINAVIA AND ICELAND**	1:10 000 000
94-95	**BRITISH ISLES**	1:8 000 000
96	**SCOTLAND**	1:4 000 000
97	**IRELAND**	1:4 000 000
98-99	**ENGLAND AND WALES**	1:4 000 000
100-101	**NORTHWEST EUROPE**	1:4 000 000
102-103	**CENTRAL EUROPE**	1:8 000 000
104-105	**FRANCE AND SWITZERLAND**	1:8 000 000
106-107	**SPAIN AND PORTUGAL**	1:8 000 000
108-109	**ITALY AND THE BALKANS**	1:8 000 000
110-111	**GREECE, ROMANIA AND BULGARIA**	1:8 000 000
112-113	**AFRICA**	1:60 000 000
114-115	**NORTHWEST AFRICA**	1:26 000 000
116-117	**NORTHEAST AFRICA**	1:26 000 000
118-119	**CENTRAL AFRICA**	1:20 000 000
120-121	**SOUTHERN AFRICA**	1:20 000 000
122-123	**REPUBLIC OF SOUTH AFRICA**	1:10 000 000

CONTENTS

Pages	Title	Scale
124-125	**NORTH AMERICA**	1:70 000 000
126-127	**CANADA**	1:30 000 000
128-129	**CANADA** WEST	1:15 000 000
130-131	**CANADA** EAST	1:15 000 000
132-133	**UNITED STATES OF AMERICA**	1:25 000 000
134-135	**USA** WEST	1:11 000 000
136-137	**USA** NORTH CENTRAL	1:11 000 000
138-139	**USA** SOUTH CENTRAL	1:11 000 000
140-141	**USA** NORTHEAST	1:11 000 000
142-143	**USA** SOUTHEAST	1:11 000 000
144-145	**MEXICO**	1:15 000 000
146-147	**CARIBBEAN**	1:20 000 000
148-149	**SOUTH AMERICA**	1:70 000 000
150-151	**SOUTH AMERICA** NORTH	1:25 000 000
152-153	**SOUTH AMERICA** SOUTH	1:25 000 000
154-155	**BRAZIL** SOUTHEAST	1:10 000 000
	OCEANS	
156-157	**PACIFIC OCEAN**	1:120 000 000
158	**ATLANTIC OCEAN**	1:120 000 000
159	**INDIAN OCEAN**	1:120 000 000
160	**ARCTIC OCEAN**	1:60 000 000
	INDEX	161-256

OCEANIA

Australia and the vast expanse of the Pacific Ocean
dominate this satellite image of Oceania. The
islands of Indonesia lie to the northwest of
Australia and New Guinea to the north, with the
islands of the Solomon Islands chain, Vanuatu and
New Caledonia stretching southeast from New
Guinea towards New Zealand. The Hawaiian
Islands appear top right of the image.

© Bartholomew Ltd

Data from the 1 km AVHRR Global Land dataset project by ESA, CEOS, IGBP, NASA, NOAA, USGS.
IONIA processed by ESA/ESRIN distributed by Eurimage S.p.A.

ASIA

This image shows the continent of Asia from the
Mediterranean Sea and the distinctive shape of
The Gulf in the west, to Japan in the east, and
from snow-covered Siberia in the north to the
tropical islands of Indonesia in the south. The
shapes of the Caspian and Aral Seas appear in
the northwest.

© Bartholomew Ltd

Data from the 1 km AVHRR Global Land dataset project by ESA, CEOS, IGBP, NASA, NOAA, USGS,
IONIA processed by ESA/ESRIN distributed by Eurimage S.p.A.

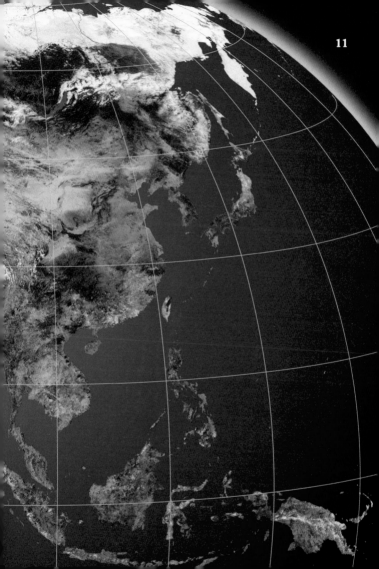

EUROPE

The distinctive shapes of Scandinavia, the British
Isles, Spain and Italy can be clearly seen on this
image; Greenland lies to the northwest with
Svalbard top centre. The huge land mass of the
Russian Federation stretches from the Gulf of
Bothnia and the Black Sea in the centre right of the
image, northeast into Asia and beyond the horizon.

© Bartholomew Ltd

AFRICA

—

This view of Africa looks north, with South America just appearing in the southwest, the island of Madagascar to the southeast and Arabia and Asia to the northeast.

© Bartholomew Ltd

Data from the 1 km AVHRR Global Land dataset project by ESA, CEOS, IGBP, NASA, NOAA, USGS, IONIA processed by ESA/ESRIN distributed by Eurimage S.p.A.

NORTH AMERICA

This image views North America from above the centre of the continent and includes most of the Arctic Ocean. The Aleutian Islands in the northwest stretch in an arc toward the Kamchatka Peninsula in eastern Asia, and western Europe and northwest Africa appear to the northeast. The islands of the Caribbean lie east and south of Florida in the bottom right of the image.

© Bartholomew Ltd

Data from the 1 km AVHRR Global Land dataset project by ESA, CEOS, IGBP, NASA, NOAA, USGS, IONIA processed by ESA/ESRIN distributed by Eurimage S.p.A.

SOUTH AMERICA

South and Central America appear in the centre
of this image with the Pacific Ocean to the west
and the Atlantic Ocean to the east, and Africa
appearing on the northeast and southeast
horizons. The Galapagos Islands lie off the coast
of Ecuador and the Falkland Islands, South
Georgia and the Antarctic Peninsula off the
southern tip of the continent.

© Bartholomew Ltd

Data from the 1 km AVHRR Global Land dataset project by ESA, CEOS, IGBP, NASA, NOAA, USGS, IONIA processed by ESA/ESRIN distributed by Eurimage S.p.A.

ANTARCTICA

This image positions the Antarctic continent with the Greenwich meridian to the top centre. The distinctive shape of the Antarctic Peninsula lies to the top left and the prominent Ross Ice Shelf can be identified to the bottom of the image, below the Transantarctic Mountains range.

CLIMATE

MAJOR CLIMATIC REGIONS AND SUB-TYPES

Winkel Tripel Projection
scale 1:200 000 000

Polar

| EF | Ice cap |
| ET | Tundra |

Cooler humid

Dc Dd	Subarctic
Db	Continental cool summer
Da	Continental warm summer

Warmer humid

Cb Cc	Temperate
Ca	Humid subtropical
Cs	Mediterranean

Dry

| BS | Steppe |
| BW | Desert |

Tropical humid

| Aw As | Savanna |
| Af Am | Rain forest |

A Rainy climate with no winter: coolest month above 18°C (64.4°F).

B Dry climates; limits are defined by formulae based on rainfall effectiveness:
- **BS** Steppe or semi-arid climate.
- **BW** Desert or arid climate.

*C Rainy climates with mild winters: coolest month above 0°C (32°F), but below 18°C (64.4°F); warmest month above 10°C (50°F).

*D Rainy climates with severe winters: coldest month below 0°C (32°F) warmest month above 10°C (50°F).

E Polar climates with no warm season: warmest month below 10°C (50°F).
- **ET** Tundra climate: warmest month below 10°C (50°F) but above 0°C (32°F).
- **EF** Perpetual frost: all months below 0°C (32°F).

a   Warmest month above 22°C (71.6°F).

b   Warmest month below 22°C (71.6°F).

c   Less than four months over 10°C (50°F).

d   As 'c', but with severe cold: coldest
    month below -38°C (-36.4°F).

f   Constantly moist rainfall throughout the year.

*h Warmer dry: all months above 0°C (32°F).

*k Cooler dry: at least one month below
    0°C (32°F).

m   Monsoon rain: short dry season, compensated
    by heavy rains during rest of the year.

n   Frequent fog.

s   Dry season in summer.

w   Dry season in winter.

*   Modification of Köppen definition.

WORLD WEATHER EXTREMES

Highest shade temperature	57.8°C/136°F Al 'Azīzīyah, Libya (13th September 1922)
Hottest place — Annual mean	34.4°C/93.9°F Dalol, Ethiopia
Driest place — Annual mean	0.1 mm/0.004 inches Desierto de Atacama, Chile
Most sunshine — Annual mean	90% Yuma, Arizona, USA (over 4 000 hours)
Least sunshine	Nil for 182 days each year, South Pole
Lowest screen temperature	-89.2°C/-128.6°F Vostok Station, Antarctica (21st July 1983)
Coldest place — Annual mean	-56.6°C/-69.9°F Plateau Station, Antarctica
Wettest place — Annual mean	11 873 mm/467.4 inches Meghalaya, India
Highest surface wind speed High altitude	372 km per hour/231 miles per hour Mount Washington, New Hampshire, USA, (12th April 1934)
Low altitude	333 km per hour/207 miles per hour Qaanaaq (Thule), Greenland (8th March 1972)
Tornado	512 km per hour/318 miles per hour Oklahoma City, Oklahoma, USA (3rd May 1999)
Greatest snowfall	31 102 mm/1 224.5 inches Mount Rainier, Washington, USA (19th February 1971 — 18th February 1972)

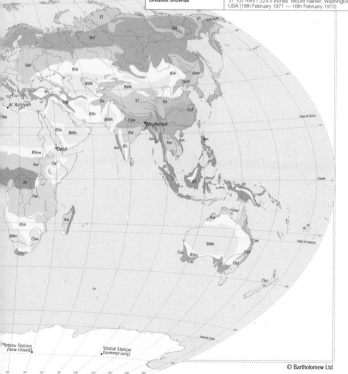

© Bartholomew Ltd

LAND COVER

WORLD LAND COVER

Goode Interrupted Homolosine Projection
scale: approximately 1:200 000 000

- 1. Evergreen needleleaf forest
- 2. Evergreen broadleaf forest
- 3. Deciduous needleleaf forest
- 4. Deciduous broadleaf forest
- 5. Mixed forest
- 6. Closed shrublands
- 7. Open shrublands

LAND COVER GRAPHS - CLASSIFICATION

Class description	Map classes (IGBP/DISCover)
Forest/Woodland	1 Evergreen needleleaf forest
	2 Evergreen broadleaf forest
	3 Deciduous needleleaf forest
	4 Deciduous broadleaf forest
	5 Mixed forest
Shrubland	6 Closed shrublands
	7 Open shrublands
Grass/Savanna	8 Woody savannas
	9 Savannas
	10 Grasslands
Wetland	11 Permanent wetlands
Crops/Mosaic	12 Croplands
	14 Cropland/Natural vegetation mosaic
Urban	13 Urban and built-up
Snow/Ice	15 Snow and Ice
Barren	16 Barren or sparsely vegetated

- 8. Woody savannas
- 9. Savannas
- 10. Grasslands
- 11. Permanent wetlands
- 12. Croplands
- 13. Urban and built-up
- 14. Cropland/Natural vegetation mosaic
- 15. Snow and Ice
- 16. Barren or sparsely vegetated
- 17. Water bodies

Map courtesy of IGBP, JRC and USGS

CONTINENTAL LAND COVER COMPOSITION

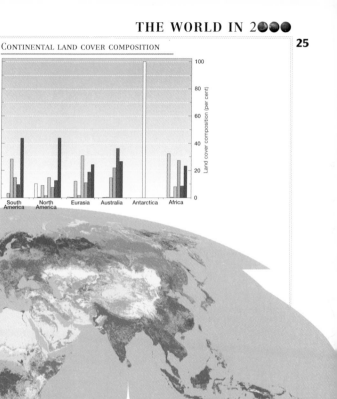

Land cover composition (per cent)

South America North America Eurasia Australia Antarctica Africa

GLOBAL LAND COVER COMPOSITION

Wetland 0.9%
Snow/Ice 11.4%
Urban 0.2%
Barren 12.6%
Forest/Woodland 27.5%
Grass/Savanna 14.0%
Shrubland 14.2%
Crops/Mosaic 19.2%

© Bartholomew Ltd

POPULATION

WORLD POPULATION DISTRIBUTION

Winkel Tripel Projection
scale 1:190 000 000

POPULATION DENSITY

per sq mile

500	100	25	5	0

inhabitants

Uninhabited

200	40	10	2	0

per sq km

WORLD POPULATION GROWTH BY CONTINENT 1750 - 2050

KEY POPULATION STATISTICS FOR MAJOR REGIONS

	Population 1998 (millions)	Growth (per cent)	Infant mortality rate	Total fertility rate	Life expectancy
World	5 901	1.33	57	2.7	65
More developed regions	1 182	0.28	9	1.6	75
Less developed regions	4 719	1.59	63	3.0	63
Africa	749	2.37	87	5.1	51
Asia	3 585	1.38	57	2.6	66
Europe	729	0.03	12	1.4	73
Latin America and the Caribbean	504	1.57	36	2.7	69
North America	305	0.85	7	1.9	77
Oceania	30	1.30	24	2.4	74

Except for population (1998), the data are annual averages projected for the period 1995-2000.

URBANIZATION

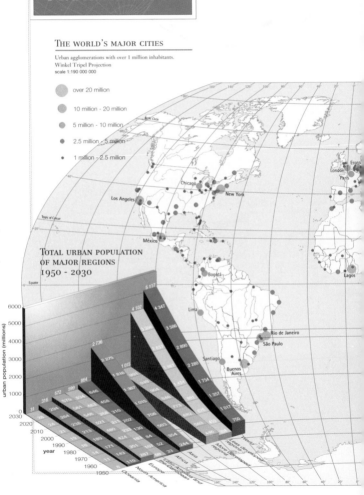

THE WORLD'S MAJOR CITIES

Urban agglomerations with over 1 million inhabitants.
Winkel Tripel Projection
scale 1:190 000 000

- over 20 million
- 10 million - 20 million
- 5 million - 10 million
- 2.5 million - 5 million
- 1 million - 2.5 million

TOTAL URBAN POPULATION OF MAJOR REGIONS 1950 - 2030

urban population (millions)

LEVEL OF URBANIZATION BY MAJOR REGION 1970-2030

Urban population as a percentage of total population

	1970	2000	2030
World	36.7	47.4	61.1
More developed regions[1]	67.7	76.1	83.7
Less developed regions[2]	25.1	40.5	57.3
Africa	23.0	37.8	54.4
Asia	23.4	37.6	55.2
Europe[3]	64.5	74.9	82.9
Latin America and the Caribbean[4]	57.4	75.4	83.2
North America	73.8	77.2	84.4
Oceania	70.8	70.0	74.5

1. Europe, North America, Australia, New Zealand and Japan.

2. Africa, Asia (excluding Japan), Latin America and the Caribbean, and Oceania (excluding Australia and New Zealand).

3. Includes Russian Federation.

4. South America, Central America (including Mexico) and all Caribbean Islands.

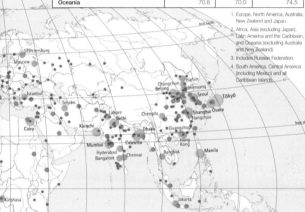

© Bartholomew Ltd

Cities

The world's largest cities 2000

Figures are for the urban agglomeration, defined as the population contained within the contours of a contiguous territory inhabited at urban levels without regard to administrative boundaries. They incorporate the population within a city plus the suburban fringe lying outside of, but adjacent to, the city boundaries.

Tōkyō Japan	28 025 000
México Mexico	18 131 000
Mumbai India	18 042 000
São Paulo Brazil	17 711 000
New York USA	16 626 000
Shanghai China	14 173 000
Lagos Nigeria	13 488 000
Los Angeles USA	13 129 000
Calcutta India	12 900 000
Buenos Aires Argentina	12 431 000
Seoul South Korea	12 215 000
Beijing China	12 033 000
Karachi Pakistan	11 774 000
Delhi India	11 680 000
Dhaka Bangladesh	10 979 000
Manila Philippines	10 818 000
Cairo Egypt	10 772 000
Ōsaka Japan	10 609 000
Rio de Janeiro Brazil	10 556 000
Tianjin China	10 239 000
Jakarta Indonesia	9 815 000
Paris France	9 638 000
Istanbul Turkey	9 413 000
Moscow Russian Federation	9 299 000
London United Kingdom	7 640 000
Lima Peru	7 443 000
Tehrān Iran	7 380 000
Bangkok Thailand	7 221 000
Chicago USA	6 945 000
Bogotá Colombia	6 834 000
Hyderabad India	6 833 000
Chennai India	6 639 000
Essen Germany	6 559 000
Hangzhou China	6 389 000
Hong Kong China	6 097 000
Lahore Pakistan	6 030 000
Shenyang China	5 681 000
Changchun China	5 566 000
Bangalore India	5 544 000
Harbin China	5 475 000
Chengdu China	5 293 000

Santiago Chile	5 261 000
Guangzhou China	5 162 000
St. Petersburg Russian Federation	5 132 000
Kinshasa Dem. Rep. Congo	5 068 000
Baghdād Iraq	4 796 000
Jinan China	4 789 000
Wuhan China	4 750 000
Toronto Canada	4 657 000
Yangôn Myanmar	4 458 000
Algiers Algeria	4 447 000
Philadelphia USA	4 398 000
Qingdao China	4 376 000
Milan Italy	4 251 000
Pusan South Korea	4 239 000
Belo Horizonte Brazil	4 160 000
Ahmadabad India	4 154 000
Madrid Spain	4 072 000
San Francisco USA	4 051 000
Alexandria Egypt	3 995 000
Washington USA	3 927 000
Dallas USA	3 912 000
Guadalajara Mexico	3 908 000
Chongqing China	3 896 000
Medellín Colombia	3 831 000
Detroit USA	3 785 000
Handan China	3 763 000
Frankfurt Germany	3 700 000
Porto Alegre Brazil	3 699 000
Ha Nôi Vietnam	3 678 000
Sydney Australia	3 665 000
Santo Domingo Dominican Republic	3 601 000
Singapore Singapore	3 587 000
Casablanca Morocco	3 535 000
Katowice Poland	3 488 000
Pune India	3 485 000
Bandung Indonesia	3 420 000
Monterrey Mexico	3 416 000
Montréal Canada	3 401 000
Nagoya Japan	3 377 000
Nanjing China	3 375 000
Houston USA	3 365 000
Abidjan Côte d'Ivoire	3 359 000
Xi'an China	3 352 000
Berlin Germany	3 337 000
Riyadh Saudi Arabia	3 328 000
Recife Brazil	3 307 000
Düsseldorf Germany	3 251 000
Ankara Turkey	3 190 000
Melbourne Australia	3 188 000
Salvador Brazil	3 180 000
Dalian China	3 153 000
Caracas Venezuela	3 153 000
Addis Ababa Ethiopia	3 112 000
Athens Greece	3 103 000
Cape Town South Africa	3 092 000
Cologne Germany	3 067 000
Maputo Mozambique	3 017 000
Naples Italy	3 012 000

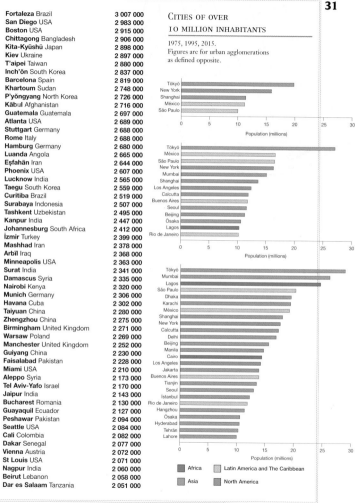

City	Population
Fortaleza Brazil	3 007 000
San Diego USA	2 983 000
Boston USA	2 915 000
Chittagong Bangladesh	2 906 000
Kita-Kyūshū Japan	2 898 000
Kiev Ukraine	2 897 000
T'aipei Taiwan	2 880 000
Inch'ŏn South Korea	2 837 000
Barcelona Spain	2 819 000
Khartoum Sudan	2 748 000
P'yŏngyang North Korea	2 726 000
Kābul Afghanistan	2 716 000
Guatemala Guatemala	2 697 000
Atlanta USA	2 689 000
Stuttgart Germany	2 688 000
Rome Italy	2 688 000
Hamburg Germany	2 680 000
Luanda Angola	2 665 000
Eşfahān Iran	2 644 000
Phoenix USA	2 607 000
Lucknow India	2 565 000
Taegu South Korea	2 559 000
Curitiba Brazil	2 519 000
Surabaya Indonesia	2 507 000
Tashkent Uzbekistan	2 495 000
Kanpur India	2 447 000
Johannesburg South Africa	2 412 000
İzmir Turkey	2 399 000
Mashhad Iran	2 378 000
Arbīl Iraq	2 368 000
Minneapolis USA	2 363 000
Surat India	2 341 000
Damascus Syria	2 335 000
Nairobi Kenya	2 320 000
Munich Germany	2 306 000
Havana Cuba	2 302 000
Taiyuan China	2 280 000
Zhengzhou China	2 275 000
Birmingham United Kingdom	2 271 000
Warsaw Poland	2 269 000
Manchester United Kingdom	2 252 000
Guiyang China	2 230 000
Faisalabad Pakistan	2 228 000
Miami USA	2 210 000
Aleppo Syria	2 173 000
Tel Aviv-Yafo Israel	2 170 000
Jaipur India	2 143 000
Bucharest Romania	2 130 000
Guayaquil Ecuador	2 127 000
Peshawar Pakistan	2 094 000
Seattle USA	2 084 000
Cali Colombia	2 082 000
Dakar Senegal	2 077 000
Vienna Austria	2 072 000
St Louis USA	2 071 000
Nagpur India	2 060 000
Beirut Lebanon	2 058 000
Dar es Salaam Tanzania	2 051 000

CITIES OF OVER 10 MILLION INHABITANTS

1975, 1995, 2015.
Figures are for urban agglomerations as defined opposite.

Africa
Asia
Latin America and The Caribbean
North America

STATES AND TERRITORIES
OF THE WORLD

State/Territory Name	Population	Capital	Area sq km	Area sq miles
A				
AFGHANISTAN	21 354 000	Kābul	652 225	251 825
ALBANIA	3 119 000	Tirana (Tiranë)	28 748	11 100
ALGERIA	30 081 000	Algiers (Alger)	2 381 741	919 595
American Samoa	63 000	Fagatogo	197	76
ANDORRA	72 000	Andorra la Vella	465	180
ANGOLA	12 092 000	Luanda	1 246 700	481 354
Anguilla (U.K.)	8 000	The Valley	155	60
ANTIGUA AND BARBUDA	67 000	St John's	442	171
ARGENTINA	36 123 000	Buenos Aires	2 766 889	1 068 302
ARMENIA	3 536 000	Yerevan (Erevan)	29 800	11 506
Aruba (Netherlands)	94 000	Oranjestad	193	75
AUSTRALIA	18 520 000	Canberra	7 682 300	2 966 153
AUSTRIA	8 140 000	Vienna (Wien)	83 855	32 377
AZERBAIJAN	7 669 000	Baku (Bakı)	86 600	33 436
Azores (Portugal)	243 600	Ponta Delgada	2 300	888
B				
THE BAHAMAS	296 000	Nassau	13 939	5 382
BAHRAIN	595 000	Manama (Al Manāmah)	691	267
BANGLADESH	124 774 000	Dhaka (Dacca)	143 998	55 598
BARBADOS	268 000	Bridgetown	430	166
BELARUS	10 315 000	Minsk	207 600	80 155
BELGIUM	10 141 000	Brussels (Bruxelles)	30 520	11 784
BELIZE	230 000	Belmopan	22 965	8 867
BENIN	5 781 000	Porto-Novo	112 620	43 483
Bermuda (U.K.)	64 000	Hamilton	54	21
BHUTAN	2 004 000	Thimphu	46 620	18 000
BOLIVIA	7 957 000	La Paz/Sucre	1 098 581	424 164
BOSNIA-HERZEGOVINA	3 675 000	Sarajevo	51 130	19 741
BOTSWANA	1 570 000	Gaborone	581 370	224 468
BRAZIL	165 851 000	Brasília	8 547 379	3 300 161
BRUNEI	315 000	Bandar Seri Begawan	5 765	2 226
BULGARIA	8 336 000	Sofia (Sofiya)	110 994	42 855
BURKINA	11 305 000	Ouagadougou	274 200	105 869
BURUNDI	6 457 000	Bujumbura	27 835	10 747
C				
CAMBODIA	10 716 000	Phnum Pénh (Phnom Penh)	181 000	69 884
CAMEROON	14 305 000	Yaoundé	475 442	183 569
CANADA	30 563 000	Ottawa	9 970 610	3 849 674

State/Territory Name	Population	Capital	Area sq km	Area sq miles
Canary Islands (Spain)	1 606 522	Santa Cruz de Tenerife	7 447	2 875
CAPE VERDE	408 000	Praia	4 033	1 557
Cayman Islands (U.K.)	36 000	George Town	259	100
CENTRAL AFRICAN REPUBLIC	3 485 000	Bangui	622 436	240 324
CHAD	7 270 000	Ndjamena	1 284 000	495 755
CHILE	14 824 000	Santiago	756 945	292 258
CHINA	1 262 817 000	Beijing (Peking)	9 584 492	3 700 593
Christmas Island (Australia)	2 195	The Settlement	135	52
Cocos Islands (Australia)	637	Home Island	14	5
COLOMBIA	40 803 000	Bogotá	1 141 748	440 831
COMOROS	658 000	Moroni	1 862	719
CONGO	2 785 000	Brazzaville	342 000	132 047
CONGO, DEMOCRATIC REPUBLIC OF	49 139 000	Kinshasa	2 345 410	905 568
Cook Islands (N.Z.)	19 000	Avarua	293	113
COSTA RICA	3 841 000	San José	51 100	19 730
CÔTE D'IVOIRE	14 292 000	Yamoussoukro	322 463	124 504
CROATIA	4 481 000	Zagreb	56 538	21 829
CUBA	11 116 000	Havana (La Habana)	110 860	42 803
CYPRUS	771 000	Nicosia (Lefkosia)	9 251	3 572
CZECH REPUBLIC	10 282 000	Prague (Praha)	78 864	30 450

D

DENMARK	5 270 000	Copenhagen (København)	43 075	16 631
DJIBOUTI	623 000	Djibouti	23 200	8 958
DOMINICA	71 000	Roseau	750	290
DOMINICAN REPUBLIC	8 232 000	Santo Domingo	48 442	18 704

E

ECUADOR	12 175 000	Quito	272 045	105 037
EGYPT	65 978 000	Cairo (El Qâhira)	1 000 250	386 199
EL SALVADOR	6 032 000	San Salvador	21 041	8 124
EQUATORIAL GUINEA	431 000	Malabo	28 051	10 831
ERITREA	3 577 000	Asmara	117 400	45 328
ESTONIA	1 429 000	Tallinn	45 200	17 452
ETHIOPIA	59 649 000	Addis Ababa (Ādīs Ābeba)	1 133 880	437 794

F

Falkland Islands (U.K.)	2 000	Stanley	12 170	4 699
Faroe Islands (Denmark)	43 000	Tórshavn (Thorshavn)	1 399	540
FIJI	796 000	Suva	18 330	7 077
FINLAND	5 154 000	Helsinki (Helsingfors)	338 145	130 559
FRANCE	58 683 000	Paris	543 965	210 026
French Guiana	167 000	Cayenne	90 000	34 749
French Polynesia	227 000	Papeete	3 265	1 261

G

GABON	1 167 000	Libreville	267 667	103 347
THE GAMBIA	1 229 000	Banjul	11 295	4 361
GAZA	1 036 000	Gaza	363	140
GEORGIA	5 059 000	T'bilisi	69 700	26 911

State/Territory Name	Population	Capital	Area sq km	Area sq miles
GERMANY	82 133 000	Berlin	357 028	**137 849**
GHANA	19 162 000	Accra	238 537	**92 100**
Gibraltar (U.K.)	25 000	Gibraltar	7	**3**
GREECE	10 600 000	Athens (Athina)	131 957	**50 949**
Greenland (Denmark)	56 000	Nuuk (Godthåb)	2 175 600	**840 004**
GRENADA	93 000	St George's	378	**146**
Guadeloupe (France)	443 000	Basse-Terre	1 780	**687**
Guam (U.S.A.)	161 000	Agana	541	**209**
GUATEMALA	10 801 000	Guatemala (Guatemala City)	108 890	**42 043**
Guernsey (U.K.)	64 555	St Peter Port	78	**30**
GUINEA	7 337 000	Conakry	245 857	**94 926**
GUINEA-BISSAU	1 161 000	Bissau	36 125	**13 948**
GUYANA	850 000	Georgetown	214 969	**83 000**

H

HAITI	7 952 000	Port-au-Prince	27 750	**10 714**
HONDURAS	6 147 000	Tegucigalpa	112 088	**43 277**
HUNGARY	10 116 000	Budapest	93 030	**35 919**

I

ICELAND	276 000	Reykjavík	102 820	**39 699**
INDIA	982 223 000	New Delhi	3 065 027	**1 183 414**
INDONESIA	206 338 000	Jakarta	1 919 445	**741 102**
IRAN	65 758 000	Tehrān	1 648 000	**636 296**
IRAQ	21 800 000	Baghdād	438 317	**169 235**
IRELAND, REPUBLIC OF	3 681 000	Dublin (Baile Átha Cliath)	70 282	**27 136**
Isle of Man (U.K.)	77 000	Douglas	572	**221**
ISRAEL	5 984 000	Jerusalem (Yerushalayim) (El Quds)	20 770	**8 019**
ITALY	57 369 000	Rome (Roma)	301 245	**116 311**

J

JAMAICA	2 538 000	Kingston	10 991	**4 244**
JAPAN	126 281 000	Tōkyō	377 727	**145 841**
Jersey (U.K.)	89 136	St Helier	116	**45**
JORDAN	6 304 000	'Ammān	89 206	**34 443**

K

KAZAKHSTAN	16 319 000	Astana (Akmola)	2 717 300	**1 049 155**
KENYA	29 008 000	Nairobi	582 646	**224 961**
KIRIBATI	81 000	Bairiki	717	**277**
KUWAIT	1 811 000	Kuwait (Al Kuwayt)	17 818	**6 880**
KYRGYZSTAN	4 643 000	Bishkek (Frunze)	198 500	**76 641**

L

LAOS	5 163 000	Vientiane (Viangchan)	236 800	**91 429**
LATVIA	2 424 000	Rīga	63 700	**24 595**
LEBANON	3 191 000	Beirut (Beyrouth)	10 452	**4 036**
LESOTHO	2 062 000	Maseru	30 355	**11 720**

State/Territory Name	Population	Capital	Area sq km	Area sq miles
LIBERIA	2 666 000	Monrovia	111 369	**43 000**
LIBYA	5 339 000	Tripoli (Ṭarābulus)	1 759 540	**679 362**
LIECHTENSTEIN	32 000	Vaduz	160	**62**
LITHUANIA	3 694 000	Vilnius	65 200	**25 174**
LUXEMBOURG	422 000	Luxembourg	2 586	**998**

M

State/Territory Name	Population	Capital	Area sq km	Area sq miles
MACEDONIA (Former Yugoslav Republic of Macedonia - F.Y.R.O.M.)	1 999 000	Skopje	25 713	**9 928**
MADAGASCAR	15 057 000	Antananarivo	587 041	**226 658**
Madeira (Portugal)	259 000	Funchal	779	**301**
MALAWI	10 346 000	Lilongwe	118 484	**45 747**
MALAYSIA	21 410 000	Kuala Lumpur	332 965	**128 559**
MALDIVES	271 000	Male	298	**115**
MALI	10 694 000	Bamako	1 240 140	**478 821**
MALTA	384 000	Valletta	316	**122**
MARSHALL ISLANDS	60 000	Delap-Uliga-Darrit	181	**70**
Martinique (France)	389 000	Fort-de-France	1 079	**417**
MAURITANIA	2 529 000	Nouakchott	1 030 700	**397 955**
MAURITIUS	1 141 000	Port Louis	2 040	**788**
Mayotte (France)	144 944	Dzaoudzi	373	**144**
MEXICO	95 831 000	México (Mexico City)	1 972 545	**761 604**
MICRONESIA, FEDERATED STATES OF	114 000	Palikir	701	**271**
MOLDOVA	4 378 000	Chişinău (Kishinev)	33 700	**13 012**
MONACO	33 000	Monaco-Ville	2	**1**
MONGOLIA	2 579 000	Ulaanbaatar (Ulan Bator)	1 565 000	**604 250**
Montserrat (U.K.)	11 000	Plymouth	100	**39**
MOROCCO	27 377 000	Rabat	446 550	**172 414**
MOZAMBIQUE	18 880 000	Maputo	799 380	**308 642**
MYANMAR (Burma)	44 497 000	Yangôn (Rangoon)	676 577	**261 228**

N

State/Territory Name	Population	Capital	Area sq km	Area sq miles
NAMIBIA	1 660 000	Windhoek	824 292	**318 261**
NAURU	11 000	Yaren	21	**8**
NEPAL	22 847 000	Kathmandu	147 181	**56 827**
NETHERLANDS	15 678 000	Amsterdam/The Hague ('s-Gravenhage)	41 526	**16 033**
Netherlands Antilles	213 000	Willemstad	800	**309**
New Caledonia (France)	206 000	Nouméa	19 058	**7 358**
NEW ZEALAND	3 796 000	Wellington	270 534	**104 454**
NICARAGUA	4 807 000	Managua	130 000	**50 193**
NIGER	10 078 000	Niamey	1 267 000	**489 191**
NIGERIA	106 409 000	Abuja	923 768	**356 669**
Niue (N.Z.)	2 000	Alofi	258	**100**
Norfolk Island (Australia)	2 000	Kingston	35	**14**
Northern Mariana Islands (U.S.A.)	70 000	Saipan	477	**184**
NORTH KOREA	23 348 000	P'yôngyang	120 538	**46 540**
NORWAY	4 419 000	Oslo	323 878	**125 050**

O

State/Territory Name	Population	Capital	Area sq km	Area sq miles
OMAN	2 382 000	Muscat (Masqaṭ)	309 500	**119 499**

36

State/Territory Name	Population	Capital	Area sq km	Area sq miles

P

PAKISTAN	148 166 000	Islamabad	803 940	310 403
PALAU	19 000	Koror	497	192
PANAMA	2 767 000	Panamá (Panama City)	77 082	29 762
PAPUA NEW GUINEA	4 600 000	Port Moresby	462 840	178 704
PARAGUAY	5 222 000	Asunción	406 752	157 048
PERU	24 797 000	Lima	1 285 216	496 225
PHILIPPINES	72 944 000	Manila	300 000	115 831
Pitcairn Islands (U.K.)	46	Adamstown	45	17
POLAND	38 718 000	Warsaw (Warszawa)	312 683	120 728
PORTUGAL	9 869 000	Lisbon (Lisboa)	88 940	34 340
Puerto Rico (U.S.A.)	3 810 000	San Juan	9 104	3 515

Q

QATAR	579 000	Doha (Ad Dawḥah)	11 437	4 416

R

Réunion (France)	682 000	St-Denis	2 551	985
ROMANIA	22 474 000	Bucharest (Bucureşti)	237 500	91 699
RUSSIAN FEDERATION	147 434 000	Moscow (Moskva)	17 075 400	6 592 849
RWANDA	6 604 000	Kigali	26 338	10 169

S

St Helena and Dependencies (U.K.)	5 644	Jamestown	121	47
ST KITTS AND NEVIS	39 000	Basseterre	261	101
ST LUCIA	150 000	Castries	616	238
St Pierre and Miquelon (France)	7 000	St-Pierre	242	93
ST VINCENT AND THE GRENADINES	112 000	Kingstown	389	150
SAMOA	174 000	Apia	2 831	1 093
SAN MARINO	26 000	San Marino	61	24
SÃO TOMÉ AND PRÍNCIPE	141 000	São Tomé	964	372
SAUDI ARABIA	20 181 000	Riyadh (Ar Riyāḍ)	2 200 000	849 425
SENEGAL	9 003 000	Dakar	196 720	75 954
SEYCHELLES	76 000	Victoria	455	176
SIERRA LEONE	4 568 000	Freetown	71 740	27 699
SINGAPORE	3 476 000	Singapore	639	247
SLOVAKIA	5 377 000	Bratislava	49 035	18 933
SLOVENIA	1 993 000	Ljubljana	20 251	7 819
SOLOMON ISLANDS	417 000	Honiara	28 370	10 954
SOMALIA	9 237 000	Muqdisho (Mogadishu)	637 657	246 201
SOUTH AFRICA, REPUBLIC OF	39 357 000	Pretoria/Cape Town	1 219 090	470 693
SOUTH KOREA	46 109 000	Seoul (Sŏul)	99 274	38 330
SPAIN	39 628 000	Madrid	504 782	194 897
SRI LANKA	18 455 000	Sri Jayewardenepura Kotte	65 610	25 332
SUDAN	28 292 000	Khartoum	2 505 813	967 500
SURINAME	414 000	Paramaribo	163 820	63 251
Svalbard (Norway)	2 591	Longyearbyen	61 229	23 641
SWAZILAND	952 000	Mbabane	17 364	6 704
SWEDEN	8 875 000	Stockholm	449 964	173 732

State/Territory Name	Population	Capital	Area sq km	Area sq miles
SWITZERLAND	7 299 000	Bern (Berne)	41 293	15 943
SYRIA	15 333 000	Damascus (Dimashq)	185 180	71 498

T

State/Territory Name	Population	Capital	Area sq km	Area sq miles
TAIWAN	21 908 135	T'aipei	36 179	13 969
TAJIKISTAN	6 015 000	Dushanbe	143 100	55 251
TANZANIA	32 102 000	Dodoma	945 087	364 900
THAILAND	60 300 000	Bangkok (Krung Thep)	513 115	198 115
TOGO	4 397 000	Lomé	56 785	21 925
Tokelau (N.Z.)	1 000	none	10	4
TONGA	98 000	Nuku'alofa	748	289
TRINIDAD AND TOBAGO	1 283 000	Port of Spain	5 130	1 981
TUNISIA	9 335 000	Tunis	164 150	63 379
TURKEY	64 479 000	Ankara	779 452	300 948
TURKMENISTAN	4 309 000	Ashgabat (Ashkhabad)	488 100	188 456
Turks and Caicos Islands (U.K.)	16 000	Grand Turk (Cockburn Town)	430	166
TUVALU	11 000	Vaiaku	25	10

U

State/Territory Name	Population	Capital	Area sq km	Area sq miles
UGANDA	20 554 000	Kampala	241 038	93 065
UKRAINE	50 861 000	Kiev (Kyiv)	603 700	233 090
UNITED ARAB EMIRATES	2 377 453	Abu Dhabi (Abū Ẓabī)	83 600	32 278
UNITED KINGDOM	58 649 000	London	244 082	94 241
UNITED STATES OF AMERICA	274 028 000	Washington	9 809 378	3 787 422
URUGUAY	3 289 000	Montevideo	176 215	68 037
UZBEKISTAN	23 574 000	Tashkent	447 400	172 742

V

State/Territory Name	Population	Capital	Area sq km	Area sq miles
VANUATU	182 000	Port Vila	12 190	4 707
VATICAN CITY	480	Vatican City	0.5	0.2
VENEZUELA	23 242 000	Caracas	912 050	352 144
VIETNAM	77 562 000	Ha Nôi (Hanoi)	329 565	127 246
Virgin Islands (U.K.)	20 000	Road Town	153	59
Virgin Islands (U.S.A.)	94 000	Charlotte Amalie	352	136

W

State/Territory Name	Population	Capital	Area sq km	Area sq miles
Wallis and Futuna Islands (France)	14 000	Mata-Utu	274	106
Western Sahara	275 000	Laâyoune	266 000	102 703

Y

State/Territory Name	Population	Capital	Area sq km	Area sq miles
YEMEN	16 887 000	Şan'ā'	527 968	203 850
YUGOSLAVIA	10 635 000	Belgrade (Beograd)	102 173	39 449

Z

State/Territory Name	Population	Capital	Area sq km	Area sq miles
ZAMBIA	8 781 000	Lusaka	752 614	290 586
ZIMBABWE	11 377 000	Harare	390 759	150 873

38

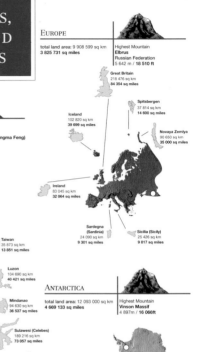

CONTINENTS, ISLANDS AND MOUNTAINS

ASIA

total land area: 45 036 492 sq km
17 388 686 sq miles

Highest Mountain
Mt Everest
(Sagarmatha/Qomolangma Feng)
China/Nepal
8 848 m / **29 028 ft**

Hokkaidō
78 073 sq km
30 144 sq miles

Honshū
227 414 sq km
87 805 sq miles

Shikoku
18 256 sq km
7 049 sq miles

Kyūshū
36 554 sq km
14 114 sq miles

Sakhalin
76 400 sq km
29 498 sq miles

Taiwan
35 873 sq km
13 851 sq miles

Luzon
104 690 sq km
40 421 sq miles

Mindanao
94 630 sq km
36 537 sq miles

Sri Lanka
65 610 sq km
25 332 sq miles

Sulawesi (Celebes)
189 216 sq km
73 057 sq miles

Borneo
745 561 sq km
287 863 sq miles

Sumatera (Sumatra)
473 606 sq km
182 860 sq miles

Jawa (Java)
132 188 sq km
51 038 sq miles

EUROPE

total land area: 9 908 599 sq km
3 825 731 sq miles

Highest Mountain
Elbrus
Russian Federation
5 642 m / **18 510 ft**

Great Britain
218 476 sq km
84 354 sq miles

Spitsbergen
37 814 sq km
14 600 sq miles

Novaya Zemlya
90 650 sq km
35 000 sq miles

Iceland
102 820 sq km
39 699 sq miles

Ireland
83 045 sq km
32 064 sq miles

Sardegna (Sardinia)
24 090 sq km
9 301 sq miles

Sicilia (Sicily)
25 426 sq km
9 817 sq miles

ANTARCTICA

total land area: 12 093 000 sq km
4 669 133 sq miles

Highest Mountain
Vinson Massif
4 897m / **16 066ft**

HIGHEST MOUNTAINS IN THE WORLD

Mt Everest
China/Nepal
8 848m / 29 028ft

K2
China/J. and K.
8 611m / 28 251ft

Kangchenjunga
India/Nepal
8 586m / 28 169ft

Lhotse
China/Nepal
8 516m / 27 939ft

Makalu
China/Nepal
8 463m / 27 760ft

Cho Oyu
China/Nepal
8 201m / 26 906ft

Dhaulagiri
Nepal
8 167m / 26 794ft

Manaslu
Nepal
8 163m / 26 781ft

Nanga Parbat
Jammu and Kashmir
8 126m / 26 660ft

Annapurna I
Jammu and Kashmir/Nepal
8 091m / 26 545ft

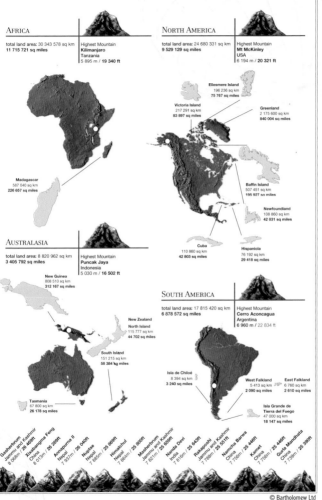

AFRICA

total land area: 30 343 578 sq km
11 715 721 sq miles

Highest Mountain
Kilimanjaro
Tanzania
5 895 m / **19 340 ft**

Madagascar
587 040 sq km
226 657 sq miles

NORTH AMERICA

total land area: 24 680 331 sq km
9 529 129 sq miles

Highest Mountain
Mt McKinley
USA
6 194 m / **20 321 ft**

Ellesmere Island
196 236 sq km
75 767 sq miles

Victoria Island
217 291 sq km
83 897 sq miles

Greenland
2 175 600 sq km
840 004 sq miles

Baffin Island
507 451 sq km
195 927 sq miles

Newfoundland
108 860 sq km
42 031 sq miles

Cuba
110 860 sq km
42 803 sq miles

Hispaniola
76 192 sq km
29 418 sq miles

AUSTRALASIA

total land area: 8 820 962 sq km
3 405 792 sq miles

Highest Mountain
Puncak Jaya
Indonesia
5 030 m / **16 502 ft**

New Guinea
808 510 sq km
312 167 sq miles

New Zealand
North Island
115 777 sq km
44 702 sq miles

South Island
151 215 sq km
58 384 sq miles

Tasmania
67 800 sq km
26 178 sq miles

SOUTH AMERICA

total land area: 17 815 420 sq km
6 878 572 sq miles

Highest Mountain
Cerro Aconcagua
Argentina
6 960 m / **22 834 ft**

Isla de Chiloé
8 394 sq km
3 240 sq miles

West Falkland
5 413 sq km
2 090 sq miles

East Falkland
6 760 sq km
2 610 sq miles

Isla Grande de
Tierra del Fuego
47 000 sq km
18 147 sq miles

Gasherbrum
Jammu and Kashmir
8 068m / **26 469ft**

Xixabangma Feng
China
8 013m / **26 289ft**

Annapurna II
Nepal
7 937m / **26 040ft**

Nuptse
Nepal
7 885m / **25 869ft**

Himalchuli
Nepal
7 864m / **25 800ft**

Masherbrum
Jammu and Kashmir
7 821m / **25 659ft**

Nanda Devi
India
7 816m / **25 643ft**

Rakaposhi
Jammu and Kashmir
7 788m / **25 551ft**

Namcha Barwa
China
7 756m / **25 446ft**

Kamet
China
7 756m / **25 446ft**

Gurla Mandhata
China
7 739m / **25 390ft**

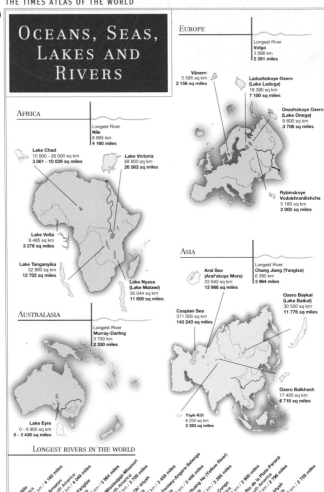

OCEANS, SEAS, LAKES AND RIVERS

EUROPE

Longest River
Volga
3 688 km
2 291 miles

Vänern
5 585 sq km
2 156 sq miles

**Ladozhskoye Ozero
(Lake Ladoga)**
18 390 sq km
7 100 sq miles

**Onezhskoye Ozero
(Lake Onega)**
9 600 sq km
3 706 sq miles

**Rybinskoye
Vodokhranilishche**
5 180 sq km
2 000 sq miles

AFRICA

Longest River
Nile
6 695 km
4 160 miles

Lake Chad
10 000 - 26 000 sq km
3 861 - 10 039 sq miles

Lake Victoria
68 800 sq km
26 563 sq miles

Lake Volta
8 485 sq km
3 276 sq miles

Lake Tanganyika
32 900 sq km
12 702 sq miles

**Lake Nyasa
(Lake Malawi)**
30 044 sq km
11 600 sq miles

ASIA

Longest River
Chang Jiang (Yangtze)
6 380 km
3 964 miles

**Aral Sea
(Aral'skoye More)**
33 640 sq km
12 988 sq miles

**Ozero Baykal
(Lake Baikal)**
30 500 sq km
11 776 sq miles

Caspian Sea
371 000 sq km
143 243 sq miles

Ozero Balkhash
17 400 sq km
6 718 sq miles

Ysyk-Köl
6 200 sq km
2 393 sq miles

AUSTRALASIA

Longest River
Murray-Darling
3 750 km
2 330 miles

Lake Eyre
0 - 8 900 sq km
0 - 3 436 sq miles

LONGEST RIVERS IN THE WORLD

Nile
Africa
6 695 km / 4 160 miles

Amazon
South America
6 516 km / 4 049 miles

Yangtze
Asia
6 380 km / 3 964 miles

Mississippi-Missouri
North America
5 969 km / 3 709 miles

Ob'-Irtysh
Asia
5 568 km / 3 459 miles

Yenisey-Angara-Selenga
Asia
5 550 km / 3 448 miles

Huang He (Yellow River)
Asia
5 464 km / 3 395 miles

Congo
Africa
4 667 km / 2 900 miles

Rio de la Plata-Paraná
South America
4 500 km / 2 796 miles

Irtysh
Asia
4 440 km / 2 759 miles

GEOGRAPHICAL INFORMATION

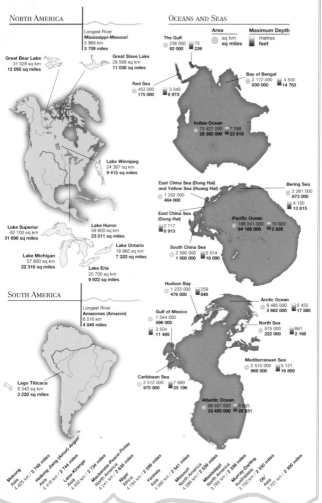

North America

Longest River
Mississippi-Missouri
5 969 km
3 709 miles

Great Bear Lake
31 328 sq km
12 095 sq miles

Great Slave Lake
28 568 sq km
11 030 sq miles

Lake Winnipeg
24 387 sq km
9 415 sq miles

Lake Superior
82 100 sq km
31 698 sq miles

Lake Huron
59 600 sq km
23 011 sq miles

Lake Ontario
18 960 sq km
7 320 sq miles

Lake Michigan
57 800 sq km
22 316 sq miles

Lake Erie
25 700 sq km
9 922 sq miles

South America

Longest River
Amazonas (Amazon)
6 516 km
4 049 miles

Lago Titicaca
8 340 sq km
3 220 sq miles

Oceans and Seas

Area
sq km
sq miles

Maximum Depth
metres
feet

The Gulf 238 000 / 92 000 ▪ 73 / 239

Bay of Bengal 2 172 000 / 839 000 ▪ 4 500 / 14 763

Red Sea 453 000 / 175 000 ▪ 3 040 / 9 973

Indian Ocean 73 427 000 / 28 350 000 ▪ 7 288 / 23 910

East China Sea (Dong Hai) and Yellow Sea (Huang Hai) 1 202 000 / 464 000

Bering Sea 2 261 000 / 873 000 ▪ 4 150 / 13 615

East China Sea (Dong Hai) ▪ 2 717 / 8 913

Pacific Ocean 166 241 000 / 64 186 000 ▪ 10 920 / 5 826

South China Sea 2 590 000 / 1 000 000 ▪ 5 514 / 18 090

Hudson Bay 1 233 000 / 476 000 ▪ 259 / 849

Arctic Ocean 9 485 000 / 3 662 000 ▪ 5 450 / 17 880

Gulf of Mexico 1 544 000 / 596 000 ▪ 3 504 / 11 495

North Sea 575 000 / 222 000 ▪ 661 / 2 168

Mediterranean Sea 2 510 000 / 969 000 ▪ 5 121 / 16 800

Caribbean Sea 2 512 000 / 970 000 ▪ 7 680 / 25 196

Atlantic Ocean 88 557 000 / 33 420 000 ▪ 8 605 / 28 231

Mekong
4 425 km / 2 749 miles
Asia

Heilong Jiang (Amur)-Argun'
4 416 km / 2 744 miles
Asia

Lena-Kirenga
4 400 km / 2 734 miles
Asia

Mackenzie-Peace-Finlay
4 241 km / 2 635 miles
North America

Niger
4 184 km / 2 599 miles
Africa

Yenisey
4 090 km / 2 541 miles
Asia

Missouri
4 086 km / 2 539 miles
North America

Mississippi
3 765 km / 2 339 miles
North America

Murray-Darling
3 750 km / 2 330 miles
Australasia

Ob'
3 701 km / 2 300 miles
Asia

ATLAS
OF THE
WORLD

INTRODUCTION TO THE ATLAS

In the tradition of The Times Atlas of the World, the map sequence in this edition starts at the International Date Line in the Pacific Ocean and broadly works westwards, moving from Oceania through Asia, Europe, Africa, North America and finally to South America. Each continent is introduced by a politically coloured map on the same projection as the satellite images on pages 8-19 at the beginning of the atlas.

The map pages include a key to the relief layer-colouring and scale bars. The measurements on the relief key are given in both metric and imperial units and there are separate metric and imperial scale bars. The symbols and place name abbreviations used on the maps are fully explained on pages 46-47. The alphanumeric reference system used in the index is based on latitude and longitude, and the number and letter for each graticule square is shown along the sides, top and bottom of each map, within the map frame, in red.

PROJECTIONS

The creation of new computer-generated maps presented the opportunity to review the map projections used and to select projections specifically for the area and scale of each map, or suite of maps. As the only way to show the Earth with absolute accuracy is on a globe, all map projections are compromises. Some projections seek to maintain correct area relationships (equal area projections), true distances and bearings from a point (equidistant projections) or correct angles and shapes (conformal projections); others attempt to achieve a balance between these properties. The choice of projections used in this atlas has been made on an individual continental and regional basis. Projections used, and their individual parameters, have been defined to minimize distortion and to reduce scale errors as much as possible.

The selection of projections for the series of regional maps within each continent has been made on an individual basis for that region. The Albers Conic Equal Area projection has been selected for Asia; in Europe the Conic Equidistant projection has been used and the Lambert Azimuthal Equal Area projection has been employed in North America, South America, Africa and Australia. The projection used is indicated at the bottom left of each map page.

PLACE NAMES

The spelling of place names on maps has always been a matter of great complexity, because of the variety of the world's languages and the systems used to write them down. There is no standard way of spelling names or of converting them from one alphabet, or symbol set, to another. Instead, conventional ways of spelling have evolved in each of the world's major languages, and the results often differ significantly from the name as it is spelled in the original language. Familiar examples of English conventional names include Munich (München), Florence (Firenze) and Moscow (from the transliterated form, Moskva).

In this atlas, local name forms are used where these are in the Roman alphabet, though for major cities, and main physical features, conventional English names are given first. The local forms are those which are officially recognized by the government of the country concerned, usually as represented by its official mapping agency. This is a basic principle laid down by the United Kingdom government's Permanent Committee on Geographical Names (PCGN) and the equivalent United States Board on Geographic Names, (BGN).

The names of continents, oceans, seas and under-water features in international waters

BOUNDARIES

The status of nations, their names and their boundaries, are shown in this atlas as they are at the time of going to press, as far as can be ascertained. Where an international boundary symbol appears in the sea or ocean it does not necessarily infer a de jure maritime boundary, but shows which off-shore islands belong to which country. The extent of island nations is shown by a short boundary symbol at the extreme limits of the area of sea or ocean within which all land is part of that nation.

Where international boundaries are the subject of dispute it may be that no portrayal of them will meet with the approval of any of the countries involved, but it is not seen as the function of this atlas to try to adjudicate between the rights and wrongs of political issues. Although reference mapping at atlas scales is not the ideal medium for indicating the claims of many separatist and irredentist movements, every reasonable attempt is made to show where an active territorial dispute exists, and where there is an important difference between 'de facto' (existing in fact, on the ground) and 'de jure' (according to law) boundaries. This is done by the use of a different symbol where international boundaries are disputed, or where the alignment is unconfirmed, to that used for settled international boundaries. Cease-fire

lines are also shown by a separate symbol. For clarity, disputed boundaries and areas are annotated where this is considered necessary. The atlas aims to take a strictly neutral viewpoint of all such cases, based on advice from expert consultants.

JAMMU AND KASHMIR

The territory is de facto divided between India and Pakistan along a cease-fire line established following hostilities in 1948 and formalized in 1972 as the Line of Control. It terminates at a grid reference known as NJ9842: between that point and the Chinese border there is no agreed dividing line. The area known as Aksai Chin is regarded by India as an integral part of Jammu and Kashmir and therefore of Indian territory, but is de facto controlled by China.

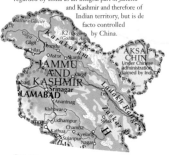

SCALE

appear in English throughout the atlas, as do those of other international features where such an English form exists and is in common use. International features are defined as features crossing one or more international boundary.

Country names are shown in conventional English form, but include changes promulgated by national governments and adopted by the United Nations – Myanmar (replacing Burma), Belarus (replacing Belorussia and a variety of other versions including the traditional White Russia), Kyrgyzstan (for Kirghizia or Kirgizia), Moldova (Moldavia), and Côte d'Ivoire (Ivory Coast).

In order to directly compare like with like throughout the world it would be necessary to maintain a single scale throughout the atlas. However, the desirability of mapping the more densely populated areas of the world at larger scales, and other geographical considerations, such as the need to fit a homogeneous physical region within a uniform rectangular page format, mean that a range of scales have been used. Scales for continental maps range between 1:40 000 000 and 1:70 000 000, depending on the size of the continental land mass being covered. Scales for regional maps are typically in the range 1:20 000 000 to 1:30 000 000. Mapping for most countries is at scales between 1:8 000 000 and 1:15 000 000.

SYMBOLS AND ABBREVIATIONS

Map symbols used on the map pages are explained here. The depiction of relief follows the tradition of layer-colouring, with colours depicting altitude bands. Ocean pages have a different contour interval. Settlements are classified in terms of both population and administrative significance. The abbreviations listed are those used in place names on the map pages and within the index.

LAND AND WATER FEATURES

Lake	———— River
Impermanent lake	- - - - Impermanent river
Salt lake or lagoon	Ice cap / Glacier
Impermanent salt lake	123 Pass — height in metres
Dry salt lake or salt pan	∴ Site of special interest
	ᴧᴧᴧᴧ Wall

RELIEF

Contour intervals used in layer-colouring for land height and sea depth

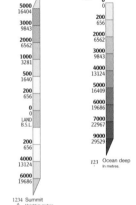

METRES FEET		Ocean pages METRES FEET
5000 16404		0 0
3000 9843		200 656
2000 6562		2000 6562
1000 3281		3000 9843
500 1640		4000 13124
200 656		5000 16409
0 0		6000 19686
LAND B.S.L.		7000 22967
200 656		9000 29529
4000 13124		123 Ocean deep In metres.
6000 19686		

1234 Summit
△ Height in metres

BOUNDARIES

▬▬▬	International boundary
·▬■◆	Disputed international boundary or alignment unconfirmed
⌐	Undefined international boundary in the sea. All land within this boundary is part of state or territory named.
▬▬▬	Administrative boundary Shown for selected countries only.
●●●●	Ceasefire line or other boundary described on the map

TRANSPORT

═══	Motorway
———	Main road
- - -	Track
———	Main railway
⊥⊥⊥⊥	Canal
✈	Main airport

CITIES AND TOWNS

Population	National Capital	Administrative Capital Shown for selected countries only	Other City or Town
over 1 million	**BEIJING** □	Sydney ⊙	New York ⊙
500 000 to 1 million	**BANGUI** □	Edmonton ⊙	Jeddah ⊙
100 000 to 500 000	WELLINGTON □	Edinburgh ⊙	Apucarana ⊙
50 000 to 100 000	PORT OF SPAIN □	Bismarck ⊙	Invercargill ⊙
under 50 000	MALABO ▫	Charlottetown ○	Ceres ○
	Built-up area Scale 1:4 000 000 only		

STYLES OF LETTERING

Cities and towns are explained separately

		Physical features	
Country	**FRANCE**	Island	*Gran Canaria*
Overseas Territory/Dependency	**Guadeloupe**	Lake	*Lake Erie*
Disputed Territory	AKSAI CHIN	Mountain	*Mt Blanc*
Administrative name Shown for selected countries only.	**SCOTLAND**	River	*Thames*
Area name	PATAGONIA	Region	*LAPPLAND*

CONTINENTAL MAPS

BOUNDARIES

——— International boundary

------ Disputed international boundary

••••••• Ceasefire line

CITIES AND TOWNS

Over 1 million	**Beijing** □	**New York** ○
500 000 to 1 million	**Bangui** □	**Irkutsk** ○
100 000 to 500 000	Wellington □	Iquitos ○
under 100 000	Malabo □	Inuvik ○

ABBREVIATIONS

Abbr.	Name	Language	Meaning
Arch.	Archipelago		
B.	Bay Bahía, Baía Bahía Baie	Portuguese Spanish French	bay bay bay bay
C.	Cape Cabo Cap	Portuguese, Spanish French	cape, headland cape, headland
Co	Cerro	Spanish	hill, peak, summit
E.	East, Eastern		
Est.	Estrecho	Spanish	strait
G.	Gebel	Arabic	hill, mountain
Gt	Great		
I.	Island, Isle Ilha Isla	Portuguese Spanish	island island
Is	Islands, Isles Islas	Spanish	islands
Khr.	Khrebet	Russian	mountain range
L.	Lake Loch Lough Lac Lago	(Scotland) (Ireland) French Portuguese, Spanish	lake lake lake lake lake
M.	Mys	Russian	cape, point
Mt	Mount Mont	French	hill, mountain
Mt.	Mountain		

Abbr.	Name	Language	Meaning
Mte	Monte	Portuguese, Spanish	hill, mountain
Mts	Mountains Monts	French	hills, mountains
N.	North, Northern		
O.	Ostrov	Russian	island
Pt	Point		
Pta	Punta	Italian, Spanish	cape, point
R.	River Rio Río Rivière	Portuguese Spanish French	river river river
Ra.	Range		
S.	South, Southern Salar, Salina, Salinas	Spanish	salt pan, salt pans
Sa	Serra Sierra	Portuguese Spanish	mountain range mountain range
Sd	Sound		
S.E.	Southeast, Southeastern		
St	Saint Sankt Sint	German Dutch	saint
Sta	Santa	Italian, Portuguese, Spanish	saint
Ste	Sainte	French	saint
Str.	Strait		
W.	West, Western Wadi, Wādī, Wâdi	Arabic	watercourse

A S I A

East China Sea

Tropic of Cancer

Luzon

South China Sea

Mindanao

Palau Islands

Northern Mariana Islands
Saipan (U.S.A.)

Guam (U.S.A.) Agaña

Caroline Islands

FEDERATED STAT

New Ireland

Bismarck Sea Rabaul

New Britain Solomon

PAPUA NEW GUINEA

Port Moresby

Halmahera

Borneo

Sulawesi

Banda Sea

Java Sea

Flores Sea

Timor

Arafura Sea

Coral Sea Islands Territory (Austr.)

Great Barrier Reef

Coral Sea

Bali

Java (Jawa)

Timor Sea

Gulf of Carpentaria

Darwin

Townsville

Sumatera

Christmas Island (Austr.)

Broome

NORTHERN TERRITORY

Alice Springs

QUEENSLAND

Brisbane

Gold Coast

Cocos Islands (Austr.)

INDIAN OCEAN

AUSTRALIA

WESTERN AUSTRALIA

SOUTH AUSTRALIA

NEW SOUTH WALES

Newcastle

Port Pirie

Sydney

Canberra

Equator

Geraldton

Perth

Great Australian Bight

Adelaide

Albany

VICTORIA

Geelong Melbourne

Bass Strait

TASMANIA

Hobart

SOUTHERN OCEAN

Tropic of Capricorn

30° 75°   90°   45° 105°   120°   135°   150°

Orthographic Projection

1 : 70 000 000   MILES 0   500   1000

0   500   1000   1500 KILOMETRES

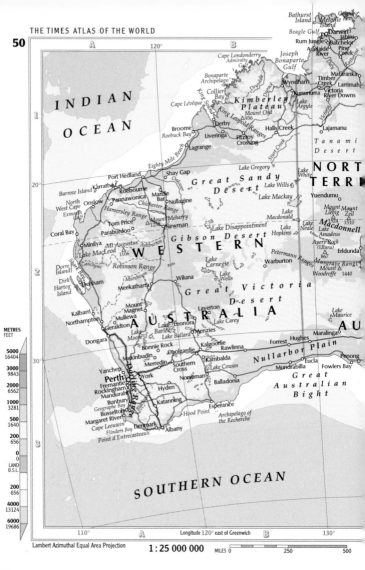

A · 120° · B

INDIAN

OCEAN

NORT
TERR

Bathurst Island · *Melville Pen. Island* · Croker
Beagle Gulf · Darwin · Jabiru
Rum Jungle · Adelaide · Batchelor · Pine Creek
Adelaide River

Cape Londonderry
Admiralty G. · *Joseph Bonaparte Gulf*
Bonaparte Archipelago · *Drysdale* · Wyndham · Kununurra · Timber Creek · Larrimah · Victoria River Downs · Matara
Collier Bay · Kimberley Plateau · *Mount Ord* 936
Cape Lévêque · *King Leopold Ranges* · Halls Creek · Lake Argyle
King Sound · Derby · Fitzroy Crossing · Sturt Creek · Lajamanu
Broome · Liveringa
Roebuck Bay · *Tanami Desert*
Lagrange

Eighty Mile Beach

Shay Gap · Lake Gregory · Lake White

Port Hedland · *Great Sandy Desert* · Lake Wills · Yuendumu

Barrow Island · Karratha · Roebourne · Marble Bar · Nullagine · Lake Mackay · *Mount Liebig* 1524 · *Mount Zeil* 1510 · Macdonnell
North West Cape · Onslow · Pannawonica · *Chichester Range* · Lake Macdonald · *Macdonnell*
Exmouth Gulf · *Hamersley Range* · Mount Meharry 1250 · Lake Disappointment · Lake Neale · Lake Amadeus · *Ayers Rock (Uluru)* 867 · Erlunda
Coral Bay · Tom Price · Paraburdoo · Newman · *Gibson Desert* · Lake Hopkins · *Petermann Ranges* · *Musgrave Ranges* Mount Woodroffe 1440

WESTERN

Minilya · *Mt Augustus* 1106 · *Ashburton* · Warburton
Lake MacLeod · *Cascoyne* · *Robinson Range* · Lake Carnegie
Dorre Island · *Murchison* · Lake Wells
Dirk Hartog Island · Denham · Meekatharra · *Great Victoria* · Lake Maurice

AUSTRALIA · Desert · AU

Wiluna

Kalbarri · Mount Magnet · Laverton
Northampton · Mullewa · Leonora · Lake Carey · Maralinga
Geraldton · Lake Barlee · Menzies · Forrest · Hughes
Dongara · Bonnie Rock · Coolgardie · Kalgoorlie · Rawlinna · *Nullarbor Plain* · Penong
· Lake Moore · Kambalda · Mundrabilla · Eucla · Fowlers Bay
Yanchep · Mukinbudin · Merredin · Southern Cross · Lake Cowan · Norseman · Balladonia · *Great Australian Bight*
Perth · York
Fremantle · Hyden
Rockingham · *Avon R.* · Esperance
Mandurah · Katanning · *Hood Point* · *Archipelago of the Recherche*
Bunbury · Busselton
Margaret River · *Geographe Bay*
Cape Leeuwin · Denmark · Albany
Flinders Bay
Point d'Entrecasteaux

SOUTHERN OCEAN

Lambert Azimuthal Equal Area Projection

1:25 000 000

MILES 0 · 250 · 500

METRES / FEET
5000 / 16404
3000 / 9843
2000 / 6562
1000 / 3281
500 / 1640
200 / 656
0 / 0
LAND / B.S.L.
200 / 656
4000 / 13124
6000 / 19686

A · 110° · *Longitude 120° east of Greenwich* · B · 130°

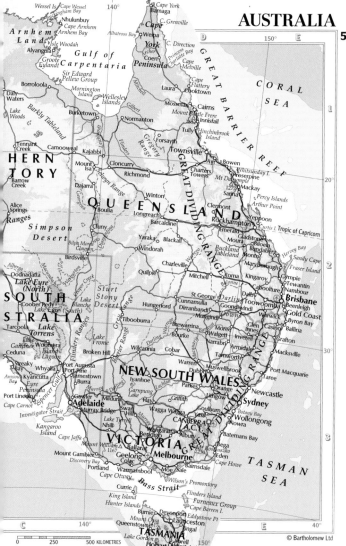

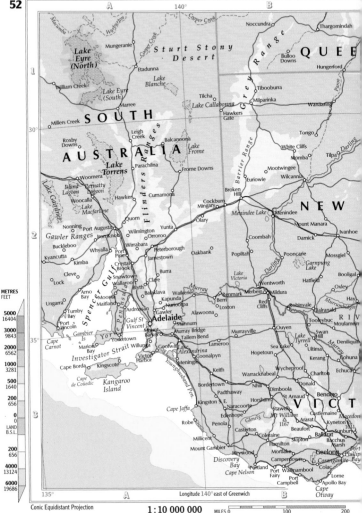

A   140°   B

Macumba

Warburton

Lake
Eyre
(North)

Mungeranie

Etadunna

Sturt Stony
Desert

Coopers Creek

Noccundra

Thargomindah

QUEE

Grey Range

Bulloo
Downs

Hungerford

William Creek

Lake
Blanche

Lake Eyre
(South)

Marree

Tilcha

Lake Callabonna

Tibooburra

Milparinka

Wanaaring

Paroo

30°

Millers Creek

SOUTH

Leigh
Creek

Balcanoona

Hawkers
Gate

Tongo

White Cliffs

Momba

Tilpa

Darling

Roxby
Downs

Lake
Frome

Barrier Range

AUSTRALIA

Lake
Torrens

Parachilna

Frome Downs

Euriowie

Wilcannia

NEW

Woomera

Pernatty Lagoon

Flinders Ranges

Curnamona

Cockburn

Broken
Hill

Mingary

Olary

Menindee Lake

Menindee

Mount Manara

Island
Lagoon

Lake
Gairdner

Woocalla

Lake
Macfarlane

Nonning

Port Augusta

Iron Knob

Hawker

Quorn

Wilmington

Yunta

Coombah

Darnick

Ivanhoe

Gawler Ranges

Buckleboo

Whyalla

Orroroo

Popiltah

Pooncarie

Mossgiel

Garnpung
Lake

Kyancutta

Kimba

Port
Pirie

Wirrabara

Peterborough

Oakbank

Hatfield

Booligal

Lock

Cleve

Crystal
Brook

Jamestown

Lake
Victoria

Wentworth

Oxley

Snowtown

Burra

Ungarra

Arno
Bay

Maitland

Blyth

Balaklava

Clare

Waikerie

Renmark

Merbein

Mildura

Red
Cliffs

Robinvale

Balranald

Murrumbidgee

RIV

Tumby
Bay

Spencer Gulf

Moonta

Ardrossan

Kapunda

Nuriootpa

Berri

Loxton

Tooleybuc

Moulamein

Port y
Lincoln

Gambier
Is

Yorke Pen.

Gawler

Adelaide

Mannum

Alawoona

Swan
Hill

Cape
Carnot

Marion
Bay

Gulf St
Vincent

Mount
Barker

Murray Bridge

Tailem Bend

Murrayville

Ouyen

Lake
Tyrrell

Ultima

Murray

Gohuna

Investigator Strait

Willunga

Lameroo

Sea
Lake

Kerang

Echuca

Cape Borda

Kingscote

Victor
Harbor

Goolwa

Lake
Alexandrina

Goolamyn

Meningie

Hopetoun

Wycheproof

Charlton

Bendigo

Cape
de Couedic

Kangaroo
Island

Keith

Bordertown

Padthaway

Nhill

Warracknabeal

Dimboola

Donald

St Arnaud

Macedon

Kyneton

Sunbury

Cape Jaffa

Kingston S.E.

Naracoorte

Horsham

Stawell

Ararat

Beaufort

Ballarat

Bacchus
Marsh

Robe

Edenhope

Penola

Glenelg

Mt William
1167

VICT

Castlemaine

Geelong

Millicent

Mount Gambier

Casterton

Coleraine

Hamilton

Skipton

Port
Phillip
Bay

Discovery
Bay

Heywood

Portland

Mortlake

Camperdown

Colac

Lake
Corangamite

Lorne

Cape Nelson

Port
Fairy

Warrnambool

Port
Campbell

Cape
Otway

Apollo Bay

135°   Longitude 140° east of Greenwich   A   B

Conic Equidistant Projection   1:10 000 000   MILES 0   100   200

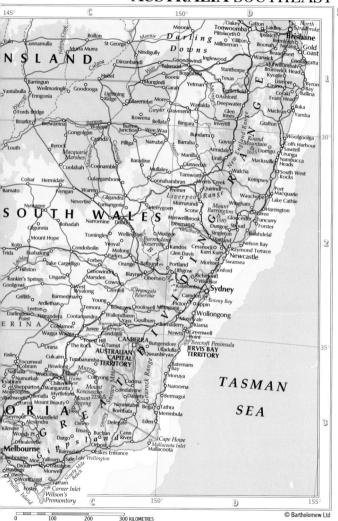

145°   C   150°   D   155°

Eulo Cunnamulla Bollon St George Moonie Oakey Gatton Laidley North Stradbroke
Nebine Creek Moonie Toowoomba Ipswich Brisbane
Pittsworth Clifton Gold Coast
Murra Murra Nindigully Millmerran Boonah Beaudesert Coolangatta

Darling Downs

NSLAND Barringun Weilmoringle Goodooga Hebel Dirranbandi Talwood Goondiwindi Inglewood Stanthorpe Warwick Williamburgh Kyogle Lismore
Yantabulla Enngonia Lightning Boomi Texas Emmerville Casino Byron Bay
Ridge Garah Yetman Deepwater Coraki Ballina
Fords Bridge Collarenebri Moree Wallada Ashford Glen Maclean Iluka
Bourke Brewarrina Rowena Bellata Bingara Inverell Grafton Yamba
Gongolgon Burren Wee Waa Barraba Guyra Round Woolgoolga
Junction Narrabri Mountain Coffs Harbour
Louth Byrock Catinda Pilliga Manilla 1615 Dorrigo Sawtell
Macquarie Coonamble Baradine Gunnedah Armidale Uralla Macksville Nambucca
Coolabah Marshes Mullaley Tamworth Walcha South West
Cobar Hermidale Oulgambanna Coonabarabran Werris Creek Kempsey Rocks
Barnato Nyngan Warren Premier Quirindi Wauchope Port Macquarie
Nymagee Gilgandra Liverpool Range Wingham Lake Cathie
Gulgunnia Nevertire Tumingerie Merrygoen Murrurundi Mount Gloucester Taree
Mount Hope Narromine Dubbo Muswellbrook Barrington Stroud Tuncurry
Roto Bobadah Tomingley Wellington Mudgee Scone 1585 Dungog Bulahdelah
Trida Euabalong Condobolin Yeoval Burrendong Denman Singleton Nelson Bay
Lake Cargelligo Molong Reservoir Kandos Cessnock Glen Davis Raymond Terrace
Hillston Ungarie Forbes Parkes Orange Bathurst Portland Morisset Swansea
Rankin's Springs Marsden Canowindra Blayney Oberon Lithgow Gosford
Goolgowi Cowra Richmond Katoomba Windsor **Sydney**
Griffith West Grenfell Wyangala Picton Camden Botany Bay
Leeton Wyalong Young Reservoir Katoomba Appin
Ardlethan Temora Boorowa Crookwell Mittagong Mossvale Wollongong
Darlington Narrandera Cootamundra Wallendbeen Yass Goulburn Bowral Kiama
Point Coolamon Junee Gundagai Bungendore Nowra Greenwell
ERINA Wagga Wagga Harden Burrinjuck Point
Urana The Rock Cootamundra Reservoir **CANBERRA** Jervis Bay
Finley Culcairn Tumbarumba Tumut **AUSTRALIAN** Queanbeyan Ulladulla **JERVIS BAY**
Tocumwal Howlong **CAPITAL** **TERRITORY**
Cobram Albury Murray Cooma Batemans Bay
Nathalia Numurkah Wodonga Corryong Kosciuszko Bombala Moruya
Kyabram Shepparton Wangaratta Mount Jindabyne Narooma
Mooroopna Benalla Myrtleford Kosciuszko Dalgety Bermagui
Rushworth Euroa Mount Beauty Mount Bega Merimbula
Bogong Nimmitabel Tathra
ORIA Mansfield 1986 Bombala
Seymour Alexandra Omeo Delegate Eden
Goulburn Cann
Kilmore Woods Pt Ensay Buchan River
Healesville Dargo Bairnsdale Orbost Cape Howe
Cranbourne Moe Yallourn Lake Wellington Lakes Entrance Mallacoota Inlet
Melbourne Sale Mallacoota
Hastings Drouin Traralgon Morwell
Dandenong Worthington Ninety Mile Beach
Phillip Island Foster Yarram Corner Inlet
Wilson's Promontory

TASMAN SEA

30°
1
2
35°
3

0   100   200   300 KILOMETRES

© Bartholomew Ltd

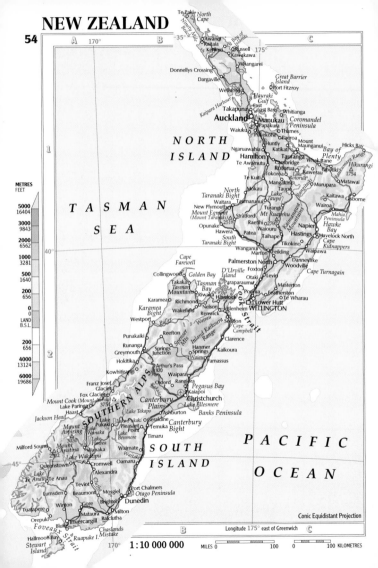

NEW ZEALAND

METRES / FEET

METRES	FEET
5000	16404
3000	9843
2000	6562
1000	3281
500	1640
200	656
0	LAND B.S.L.
200	656
4000	13124
6000	19686

TASMAN SEA

NORTH ISLAND

SOUTH ISLAND

PACIFIC OCEAN

Te Paki · North Cape
Ninety Mile Beach
-35°
Awanui
Kaitaia
Kerikeri
Russell
Kawakawa
Bay of Islands
Whangarei
Donnellys Crossing
Dargaville
Great Barrier Island
Port Fitzroy
Wellsford
Kaipara Harbour
Hauraki Gulf
Takapuna
East Coast Bays
Whitianga
Auckland
Manukau
Papakura
Coromandel Peninsula
Waiuku
Thames
Pukekohe
Paeroa
Huntly
Ngaruawahia
Katikati
Mount Maunganui
Hamilton
Tauranga
Hicks Bay
Te Awamutu
Cambridge
Whakatane
Bay of Plenty
Tokoroa
Rotorua
Kawerau
Hikurangi 1754
Te Kuiti
Mangakino
Lake Rotorua
Murupara
Matawai
Mokau
Taupo
Kaitawa
Lake Taupo
Wairoa
Gisborne
North Taranaki Bight
Waitara
Turangi
Mahia Peninsula
New Plymouth
Taumarunui
Mt Ruapehu
Napier
Mount Egmont (Mount Taranaki) 2518
Stratford
Raetihi 2797
Hastings
Opunake
Hawera
Taihape
Havelock North
Cape Kidnappers
South Taranaki Bight
Patea
Tikokino
Wanganui
Waipawa
Marton
Feilding
Danneyirke
Cape Farewell
Palmerston North
Woodville
Collingwood
Golden Bay
Foxton
Levin
Waipukurau
Takaka
D'Urville Island
Otaki
Cape Turnagain
Tasman Mountains
Tasman Bay
Paraparaumu
Masterton
Karamea
Riwaka
Porirua
Featherston
Richmond
Nelson
Te Wharau
Karamea Bight
Wakefield
Havelock
WELLINGTON
Westport
Renwick
Blenheim
Lower Hutt
Cook Strait
Punakaiki
Reefton
Wairau
Seddon
Buller
Spenser Mts
Inland Kaikoura Range
Cape Campbell
Runanga
Springs Junction
Hanmer Springs
Kaikoura
Greymouth
Clarence
Hokitika
Arthur's Pass 920
Waiau
Parnassus
Kowhitirangi
Waipara
Pegasus Bay
Oxford
Rangiora
Kaiapoi
Franz Josef Glacier
Christchurch
Fox Glacier
Lake Tekapo
Canterbury Plains
Lake Ellesmere
Mount Cook (Mount) 3754
Banks Peninsula
SOUTHERN ALPS
Ashburton
Jackson Head
Haast
Lake Pukaki
Geraldine
Canterbury Bight
Mount Aspiring 3030
Pleasant Point
Temuka
Lake Hawea
Lake Wanaka
Timaru
Milford Sound
Mount Christina 2502
Wanaka
Waimate
Lake Wakatipu
Cromwell
Oamaru
Waitaki
Queenstown
Alexandra
Lake Te Anau
Teviot
Clutha
Port Chalmers
Lumsden
Beaumont
Mosgiel
Otago Peninsula
Winton
Gore
Brighton
Dunedin
Tuatapere
Mataura
Balclutha
Orepuki
Milton
Invercargill
Chaslands Mistake
Foveaux Strait
Bluff
Ruapuke I.
Halfmoon Bay
Stewart Island

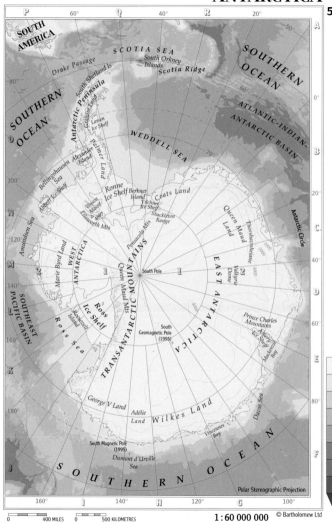

South America

SCOTIA SEA
South Orkney Islands
Scotia Ridge

SOUTHERN OCEAN

Drake Passage

SOUTHERN OCEAN

ATLANTIC-INDIAN-ANTARCTIC BASIN

South Shetland Is
Antarctic Peninsula
Graham Land
Larsen Ice Shelf
Palmer Land

WEDDELL SEA

Bellingshausen Sea
Abbot Ice Shelf
Alexander Island

Ronne Ice Shelf
Vinson Massif 4892
Ellsworth Mts

Berkner Island
Filchner Ice Shelf
Shackleton Range

Coats Land

Queen Maud Land

Thurstonheime

Antarctic Circle

Amundsen Sea

Pensacola Mts

Queen Maud Mts

South Pole

EAST ANTARCTICA

Valkyrie Dome

WEST ANTARCTICA

Marie Byrd Land

Ross Ice Shelf
Roosevelt Island

TRANSANTARCTIC MOUNTAINS

South Geomagnetic Pole (1995)

Prince Charles Mountains
Amery Ice Shelf
Mackenzie Bay

SOUTHEAST PACIFIC BASIN

Ross Sea

George V Land

Adélie Land
Wilkes Land

Darvis Sea

South Magnetic Pole (1995)

Dumont d'Urville Sea

Vincennes Bay

SOUTHERN OCEAN

Polar Stereographic Projection

METRES FEET
METRES	FEET
0	0
200	656
2000	6562
3000	9843
4000	13124
5000	16409
6000	19686
7000	22967
9000	29529

0   400 MILES   0   500 KILOMETRES

1 : 60 000 000   © Bartholomew Ltd

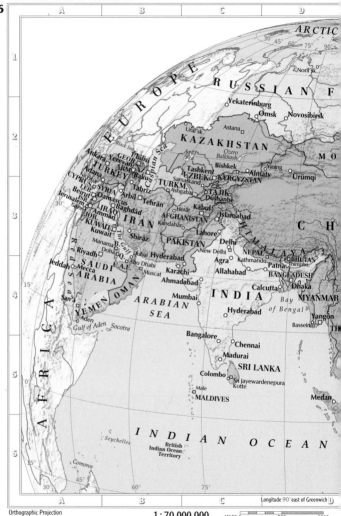

ARCTIC

EUROPE

RUSSIAN F

Noril'sk

Yekaterinburg
Omsk
Novosibirsk

Ural'sk
Astana

KAZAKHSTAN

Black Sea

Ozero
Balkhash

MO

Ankara
Yerevan
GEOR.
Tbilisi
ARM.
AZ.
Bishkek
Yining
Almaty
Ürümqi

TURKEY
Baku
Tashkent
UZBEK.
KYRGYZSTAN

Adana
Samarkand

CYPRUS
SYRIA
Tabriz
TURKM.
Ashgabat
TAJIK.

LEB.
Beirut
Arbil
Dushanbe

Jerusalem
Damascus
Tehran
Herãt
Kãbul
Islamabad

IRAQ
Baghdad
AFGHANISTAN

JOR.
Amman
IRAN
Kandahãr

KUWAIT
Lahore
Delhi

Kuwait
Shiraz
PAKISTAN
New Delhi

The Gulf
B.Gulf
Manama
Dubai
Hyderabad
Agra
Kathmandu
Patna
BHUTAN
Thimphu

Riyadh
Doha
Q.
Abu Dhabi
U.A.E.
Muscat
Karachi
Allahabad
BANGLADESH

Jeddah
Mecca
SAUDI
ARABIA
Ahmadabad
Calcutta
Dhaka
MYANMAR

San'a
OMAN
Mumbai
INDIA
Bay
of Bengal
Yangôn

YEMEN
ARABIAN
Hyderabad
Bassein
TH

Aden
Gulf of Aden
Socotra
SEA

Bangalore
Chennai

Madurai

Colombo
SRI LANKA

Male
Sri Jayewardenepura
Kotte

MALDIVES
Medan

Seychelles
INDIAN OCEAN

British
Indian
Territory

Comoros

Red Sea

AFRICA

KAZAKHSTAN

Caspian Sea

HIMALAYA

CH

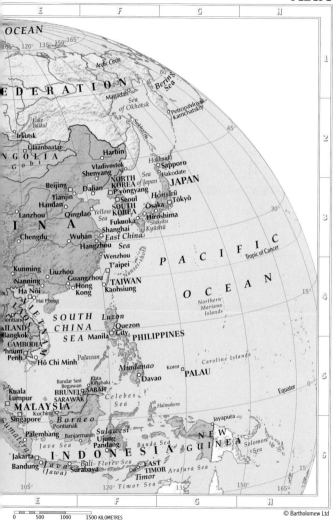

OCEAN

165° 120° 135° 150° 165°

Arctic Circle

60°

EDERATION

Magadan

Bering Sea

Sea of Okhotsk

Lake Baikal

Petropavlovsk-Kamchatskiy

Irkutsk

Sakhalin

45°

Ulaanbaatar

Harbin

NGOLIA

Gobi

Vladivostok

Hokkaido

Sapporo

Shenyang

NORTH KOREA

Sea of Japan

Hakodate

JAPAN

Beijing

Dalian

P'yŏngyang

Honshū

Tianjin

Seoul

Handan

SOUTH KOREA

Ōsaka

Tōkyō

Lanzhou

Qingdao

Yellow Sea

Fukuoka

Hiroshima

30°

INA

Shikoku

Chengdu

Wuhan

Shanghai

East China

Kyūshū

Hangzhou

Sea

Wenzhou

Nansei-shotō

PACIFIC

Kunming

Liuzhou

T'aipei

Tropic of Cancer

Nanning

Guangzhou

TAIWAN

OCEAN

Ha Nôi

Hong Kong

Kaohsiung

15°

Hai Phong

Northern Mariana Islands

AOS

SOUTH

Luzon

ientiane

CHINA

Quezon City

AILAND

SEA

Manila

PHILIPPINES

Bangkok

CAMBODIA

Palawan

hnum Penh

Hô Chi Minh

Mindanao

Koror

Caroline Islands

Davao

PALAU

Kuala Lumpur

Bandar Seri Begawan

Kota Kinabalu

BRUNEI

SABAH

Celebes Sea

Halmahera

Equator

Singapore

SARAWAK

MALAYSIA

Kuching

Borneo

Jayapura

Palembang

Pontianak

Sulawesi

NEW

Banjarmasin

Ujung Pandang

Banda Sea

Solomon Sea

Jakarta

Java Sea

INDONESIA

GUINEA

Bandung

Java (Jawa)

Surabaya

Bali

Flores Sea

EAST

Dili

Timor

TIMOR

Arafura Sea

105°

120°

Timor Sea

135°

150°

165°

15°

Sumatra

VIETNAM

0 500 1000 1500 KILOMETRES

© Bartholomew Ltd

PHILIPPINE

SEA

PACIFIC

OCEAN

Northern
Mariana
Islands
(U.S.A.)

Pagan

Saipan
Tinian

15°

Guam
(U.S.A.)

Rota

Polillo
Islands

PHILIPPINES

Catanduanes

Daet
Sorsogon
rosit Catarman
Samar
Catbalogan
Tacloban
Bacolod
Cebu
Iloilo
Aghilaran
Bohol Sea Surigao
Butuan
Cagayan de Oro
Oroquieta
Pagadian Mindanao
Cotabato Davao
Mati
General Santos
Moro
Gulf

Ulithi

Fais

Yap
Ngulu

FEDERATED STATES
OF MICRONESIA

Sorol

Faraulip

Caroline Islands

2°

PALAU
KOROR

ebes

Kepulauan
Talaud

a

Kepulauan
Sangir

Minahasa
Tondano
Gorontalo

Manado

Togian
tuwuk
Peleng
Taliabu Mangoli
Banggai Sula
Manui
Raha
Wowoni
Buton
aubau Tukangbesi

Kepulauan
Togian

Kendari

Tobelo

Ternate
Sao-Siu

Morotai

Halmahera

Waigeo

Bacan
Obi

Molucca Sea

Salawati
Misool Jafanlap
Seram
Namlea
Buru Kepulauan
Amboina
Ambon Kepulauan
Banda

Sili Damar Kiwoka
Sorong Jamrah Manokwari
Ransiki Numfoor
Jafanlap Inanwatan

Pk Jaya Trikora
5030 4730

Biak

Sarmi Jayapura

Teluk
Cenderawasih

Yapen
Nabire

Pegunungan Van Rees
Taritatu

Jayapura

Pegunungan Maoke
4700

Vanimo

Sepik

Wewak

Aitape

Schouten Islands

Hermit Is

Equator

Pelleluhu Is

0°

Manam I.

PAPUA

Madang

Long
Island

Umboi

Banda Sea

Kepulauan
Barat Daya
Kepulauan
Alor Roma
Huaki Kaiwatu
Manatuto Leti Wetar Kepulauan
Sermata

Faktak
Kaimana
Kepulauan
Watubela

Fakfak

Kepulauan
Kai
Tual Dobo
Kai Kecil
Kai Besar
Benjina
Saumlakki
Kepulauan Tanimbar
Larat Trangan

Amamapare

Enarotali

NEW
GUINEA

Central Rg. 4000
Mendi Mount
Hagen
Kikori

P. Dolak

Tg Deyong
Digul

Merauke

4509

Goroka
Mount Hagen

4073

NEW GUINEA

Kerema

Baimuru

Morehead

Daru

Gulf
of Papua

Lae

Mt
Victoria

Wau
Bereina

Morobeo

PORT
MORESBY

Kepulauan
Tanimbar

Damar
Wuliaru
Selaru

Tg Vals

SIA

Kepulauan
Sermata

EAST
TIMOR

Dili
Kupang

Kelamenanu
Saparua

Rote

Savu
Sea

Timor
Sea

Melville
Island

Bathurst Island

Beagle Gulf

AUSTRALIA

Van Dieman
Gulf

Darwin
Jabiru

C. Wessel

Wessel Is

Croker I.
C. Arnhem

Nhulunbuy

Arafura Sea

Gulf
of
Carpentaria

Coen

Weipa

Bamaga

C. York

135°

135°

0   500   1000 KILOMETRES

© Bartholomew Ltd

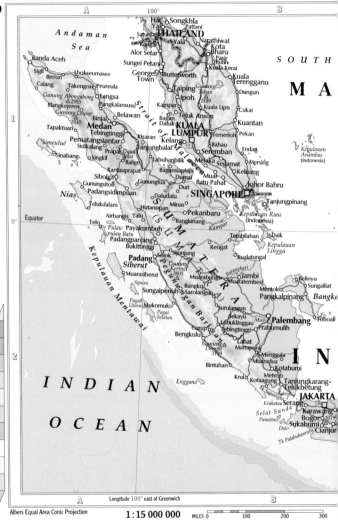

A   100°   B

Andaman Sea

Banda Aceh
Sigli
Bireun
Calang
Lhokseumawe
Takengon
Peureula
Gunung Abongabong △2985
Blangkejeren
Tangsa
Pangkalansusu
Gunung Leuser △3145
Binjai
Belawan
Medan
Tapaktuan
Tebingtinggi
Simeuluë
Pematangsiantar
Prapat   *Danau Toba*
Sidikalang
Baligé
Sinabang
Singkil
Nias
Sibolga
Rantauprapat
Gunungsitoli
Padangsidimpuan
Telukdalam

Hat
Yai   Songkhla
Pattani
Satun   Yala   Narathiwat
Kanian
Alor Setar   Kota Bharu
Pasir
Sungei Petani   Kuala Kerai
George   Butterworth   Kuala Terengganu
Town   Taiping
Gunung Tahan △2189   Dungun
Ipoh
Kampar   Kuala Lipis   Cukai
Teluk Anson
Bagan   Kuantan
Datuk
Kisaran   Kelang   Temerloh   Pekan
Tanjungbalai   KUALA
LUMPUR   Bahau   Endau
Labuhanbilik   Seremban
Melaka   *Kepulauan Anambas (Indonesia)*
Baganapiapi   Segamat   Mersing
Dumai   Muar
Gunungtua   Batu Pahat   Keluang
Daludalu   Duri   SINGAPORE   Johor Bahru
Hutanopan   Minas   Tanjungpinang
Airbangis   Talu   Pekanbaru
Equator   Bangkinang   *Kepulauan Riau (Indonesia)*
Telo   *Kampar*   Daik
Pulau   Payakumbuh   Tembilahan
pulau Batu   Bukittinggi   Rengat   *Kepulauan Lingga*
Padangpanjang   Solok   Kualatungal
Padang   Sijunjung
Siberut   *Gunung Kerinci* △3805
Muarasiberut   Muarabungo   Jambi   Belinyu
Sipura   Bangko   Muaratembesi   Sungailiat
Sungaipenuh   Sarolangun   Mentok   Pangkalpinang   *Bangka*
Pagai Utara   Mukomuko   Surulangun   Toboali
Pagai Selatan   Sekayu   *Musi*   Palembang
Lubuklinggau   Prabumulih
Curup   Tebingtinggi
Bengkulu   Lahat
Gunung Dempo △3159   Martapura
Menggala
Muaradua
Bintuhan   Kotabumi
Enggano   Kruio   Metro
Kotaagung   Tanjungkarang-
Telukbetung
Krakatau   JAKARTA
Serang
Selat Sunda   Karawang
Panaitan   Bogor   △3019
Deli   Sukabumi
Tk Palabuhanratu   Cianjur

SOUTH

M A

I N

INDIAN

OCEAN

METRES
FEET

5000   16404
3000   9843
2000   6562
1000   3281
500   1640
200   656
0   0   LAND
B.S.L.
200   656
4000   13124
6000   19686

A   Longitude 100° east of Greenwich   B

Albers Equal Area Conic Projection

1 : 15 000 000   MILES 0   100   200   300

110°

Banggi

Kundat

SULU SEA

CHINA SEA

Kota Belud

Gunung
Kinabalu
4094

Kota
Kinabalu

Ranau

Sandakan

LAYSIA

Natuna Besar
(Indonesia)

Panarik

Beaufort

Labuan

BANDAR SERI
BEGAWAN

Kuala Belait

Lutong

Miri

BRUNEI

Seria

Lamag

Kuamut

SABAH

Lahad
Datu

Pensiangan

Lumbis

Semporna

Tawau

Tumindao

Kepulauan
Natuna
(Indonesia)

Bintulu

Igan Mukah

Sarikei

Sibu

Belaga

Kapit

Long
Akah

Kubuang

Tanjungredeb

CELEBES

SEA

Tarakan

Tanjungselor

Sepinang

Sambaliung

Liku

Sematan

Kuching
Kota
Samarahan
Sri Aman
Serian

Saratok

Debak

Rajang

SARAWAK

Datadian

2988

Sangkulirang

Sambas

Pemangkat

Singkawang

Lubuk
Antu

Putusibau

Pegunungan Müller

Mahakam

Bontang

Kepulauan
Tambelan

Bengkayang

Ngabang

Sanggau

Semitau

Sintang

Kapuas

BORNEO

Samarinda

Tenggarong

0°

Mempawah

Pontianak

Nangahpinoh
Balaiberkuak

Telukbatang

Muaralaung

Pegunungan Schwaner

Muarateweh

Barito

Balikpapan

Macassar Strait

Babana

Pulau-pulau
Karimata

Sukadana

Nangatayap

Rantaupanjang

KALIMANTAN

Kahayan

Tanahgrogot

Mamuju

Ketapang

Kendawangan

Belangiran
Pangkalanbuun

Sampit

Palangkaraya

Amuntai

Bukit
Gandadiwata
3074

Tanjungpandan

Manggar

Belitung

Tanjung
Sambar

Kualapembuang

Tanjung
Puting

Banjarmasin

Kandangan

Martapura

Pagatan

Kotabaru

Polewali

Majene

Selat Karimata

Tanjung
Selatan

Laut

DONESIA

JAVA SEA

Kepulauan
Laut Kecil

Sabalana

Pulau-pulau
Karimunjawa

Bawean

Tanjung
Indramayu

Kemujan

Tanjung
Bugel

Kepulauan
Kangean

urwakarta

irebon

Tegal

Semarang

Kudus

Pati

Tuban

Bangkalan

Madura

Sumenep

Kepulauan
Tengah

Bandung

Garut

Pekalongan

Temanggung

Surakarta

Jombang

Surabaya

Pasuruan

Selat Madura

Situbondo

Bali Sea

Sumbawa

Ciamis

Cilacap

Kebumen

Madiun

Yogyakarta

Malang

3676

G. Raung

Banyuwangi

Raas

Alas

Dompu

Raba

JAVA
(JAWA)

3428

Lumajang

Jember

Barung

3142

Singaraja

Bali

Denpasar

Giawar

Selat Lombok

Mataram

Praya

Lombok

Taliwang

Sumbawa

110°

0   250   500 KILOMETRES

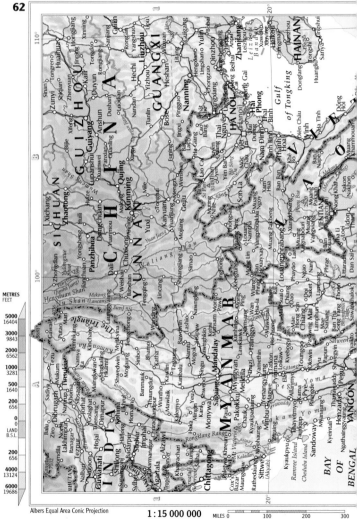

METRES
FEET

5000
16404

3000
9843

2000
6562

1000
3281

500
1640

200
656

0
0
LAND
B.S.L.

200
656

4000
13124

6000
19686

Albers Equal Area Conic Projection

1 : 15 000 000

MILES 0   100   200   300

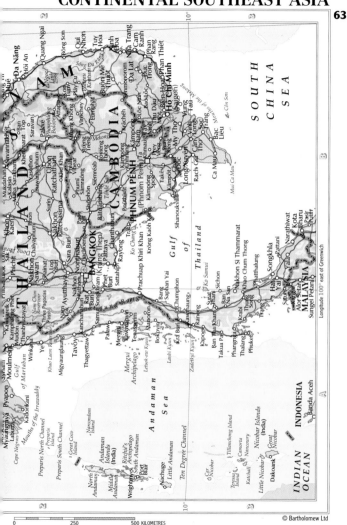

0   250   500 KILOMETRES

PHILIPPINES

120°

A   B

Babuyan
Calayan Babuyan
Islands
Fuga Camiguin

Laoag Aparri

PHILIPPINE

Bangued Tuguegarao
Vigan Mount Chico
Tagudin Bontoc Sapocoy Ilagan
San Fernando Palanan
La Trinidad Mount Santiago
Baguio Pulog 2929
Dagupan Bayombong
Lingayen San Carlos LUZON
Tarlac San Jose
Iba Cabanatuan
Angeles San Fernando
Olongapo Valenzuela Polillo Islands
Balanga Quezon City
MANILA
Tagaytay City Santa Cruz Lubo
San Pablo Daet
Batangas Lucena Naga Catanduanes
Calapan Bibac Oas Virac
Mount
Halcon Legaspi Sorsogon
2585 Irosin Catarman
Mindoro Masbate Calbayog
San Jose Roxas Sibuyan Samar
Romblon Catbalogan
Busuanga Sibuyan Sea Masbate Tacloban
Calamian Pandan Guiuan
Group Roxas Visayan Sea
Culion Panay Ormoc
El Nido Linapacan Sea Cebu Leyte
Cuyo Pototan Guiuan
Taytay Islands Ilolo Dinagat
San Jose de Cebu Siargao
Buenavista Negros Talisay
Dumaran Bohol
Roxas Cauayan Tagbilaran Surigao
Palawan Puerto Princesa Tanjay Bohol Sea
Bayawan Tandag
Quezon Aborlan Dumaguete
Mount Cagayan Butuan
Mantalingahan Dipolog de Oro
2054 Brooke's Point Roxas
Oroquieta Iligan Malaybalay
SULU SEA Liloy Ozamiz
Bugsuk Pagadian MINDANAO
Balabac Mount
Balabac Kagang Tagum
Cotabato 2815 Davao
Balabac Strait Mapin Mount Digos Mati
Zamboanga Datu Piang Apo Davao
Banggi Peninsula Moro 2954 Gulf
Kota Belud Zamboanga Gulf Banga
Gunung Basilan General Santos
Kinabalu Isabela
4094 Jolo
Ranau Sandakan Jolo
MALAYSIA Sulu
SABAH Lamag Archipelago Sarangani Islands Kepulauan
Kuamut Lahad Nanusa
Datu
Pensiangan Tumindao
Tawitawi Kepulauan
Sempoma Talaud
Tawau CELEBES Karakelong
INDONESIA SEA INDONESIA
Sangir Kaburuang

PHILIPPINE SEA

PHILIPPINES

SOUTH

CHINA

SEA

Scarborough
Shoal

Mindoro Strait

Cordillera Range
2450

Zamboanga

SULU SEA

Scale

METRES
FEET

METRES	FEET
5000	16404
3000	9843
2000	6562
1000	3281
500	1640
200	656
0	0
LAND	B.S.L.
200	656
4000	13124
6000	19686

10°

Longitude 120° east of Greenwich

A   B

Albers Equal Area Conic Projection

1:15 000 000 MILES 0 100 0 250 KILOMETRES

Siping Yingchengzu Huadian Songhua Hu Laotougou Wangqing Tumen
Kangping Liaoyuan Xin Handa Lin Panshi Zengfeng Yanji Hunchun
Faku Kaiyuan Meihekou Huinan Jingyu Fusong Baihe Helong Musan Unggi Najin
Fushun Tonghua Baishan Chan Samjiyon Ch'ongjin
Tieling Qingyuan Huanren Laoling Ji'an Chasong Puksubaek Orang
Shenyang Kanggye san Myonggan
LIAONING Guanshui Ch'osan Kilchu
Liaoyang Benxi Kuandian Yalu Jiang Sakchu Changjin Kimch'aek
Anshan Hengcheng Pukchin Hongwon Tanch'on
Dandong Sinuiju Kujang Changjin Sinp'o
Gushan Chongju Anju Hamhung Hungnam
Zhuanghe Donggang Sinanju Sunch'on Tongjoson man
Korea Bay Namp'o Kaedong Yangdok Wonsan
Songnim Chinghwa P'yong'yang Hoeyang
Sariwon Namch'on Ich'on Ch'ango
Chaeryong Kumch'on P'aro-ho
Pyoksong Haeju Tongduch'on Ch'unch'on
Ongjin Kaesong Uijongbu Kangnung

JILIN
CHINA
Liao
Xinmin
Huan
Maokui Shan
1110
Paektu-san
2750
Kwanmo-bong
2541
P'ungsan
P'ungan
NORTH
KOREA
SEA
OF
JAPAN
SEOUL (Soul)
SOUTH
KOREA
YELLOW
SEA
(HUANG HAI)
Ullung-do
(S.Korea)
Tonghae
Samch'ok
T'aebaek
Ulchin

Puch'on SEOUL (Soul)
Inch'on Anyang Songnam Wonju Chech'on
Suwon Ch'onan
Sosan Andong Yongdok
Yesan Kongju Sangju Uisong
Poryong Nonsan Kumch'on P'ohang
Soch'on Taejon Kumi Taegu Kyongju
Kunsan Iksan Muju Koryong Miryang Ulsan
Chongup Chonju Ch'angwon
Namwon Chiri-san Masan Pusan
Changsong 1915 Chinju Chinhae
Kwangju Saeho'un
Mokp'o Sunch'on Tongyong Korea Strait
Chang-hung (Tsushima-kaikyo)
Haenam Tsushima
Chin-do Chindo

Paengnyong-do
(S.Korea)
Haeju-man
Cheju-haehyop
Cheju-do
(S.Korea)
Cheju
Halla-san
1950
Taejong
Iki
Nagato
Shimonoseki
Kita-Kyushu
Fukuoka
JAPAN
Karatsu
Imari
Saga Kurume
Sasebo

METRES	FEET
5000	16404
3000	9843
2000	6562
1000	3281
500	1640
200	656
0	0
LAND	B.S.L.
200	656
4000	13124
6000	19686

MILES 0   50   100   0   100   200 KILOMETRES   1 : 9 000 000

© Bartholomew Ltd

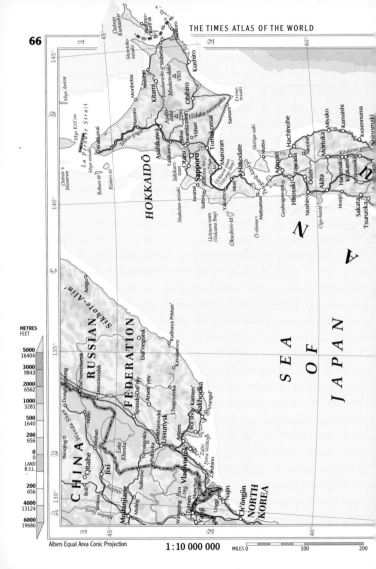

Map labels

Ostrov Kunashir

Sirětoko-misaki

Kushiro

Mys Aniva

Monbetsu
Kitami
Abashiri
Meakan-dake 1503
Obihiro
Erimo-misaki

Nayoro
Asahi-dake
Hidaka-sanmyaku
Samani

La Pérouse Strait

Sōya-misaki
Wakkanai
Teshio-gawa
Asahikawa
Ishikari-zan
Iwamizawa
Yubari
Tomakomai

HOKKAIDŌ

Rishiri-tō
Rebun-tō
Ishikari-wan
Otaru
Sapporo
Uchiura-wan
(Volcano Bay)
Noboribetsu
Muroran
Esashi
Hakodate

Ostrov Moneron

Shakotan-misaki
Iwanai
Satsu
Yakumo
Mori
Shiriya-zaki
Mutsu

Uchiura-wan
(Volcano Bay)
Ōshima-tō
Matsumae
Ōkushiri-tō

Kitakami-gawa

Mikro
Kamaishi
Kesennuma
Ishinomaki

Hachinohe
Ninohe
Morioka

Aomori
Towada
Odate
Oga-hantō
Akita
Hanamaki
Kitakami
Ichinoseki

Goshogawara
Hirosaki
Noshiro
Honjō
Sakata

HONSHŪ

Tsuruoka

SEA
OF
JAPAN

Sikhote-Alin'

Amgu

Dongning
Angu

RUSSIAN
FEDERATION

Dal'nerechensk
Dal'negorsk

Rudnaya Pristan'

Lesozavodsk

Spassk-Dal'niy
Arsen'yev
Kavalerovo

Baoqing
Hulin

Boli
Mishan
Chuguyevka

Qitaihe

Lake
Khanka

Jixi

Yaroslavskiy
Pogranichnyy
Ussuriysk
Bol'shoy Kamen'
Nakhodka

Muling
Suifenhe
Artem
Vrangel'

Mudanjiang
Wangqing
Zaliv
Petra Velikogo
Zarubino

Wanda Shan
Hunchun
Vladivostok

Tumen
Najin

CHINA
Tumen
Ling
Ch'ŏngjin
Unggi
Tuman

NORTH
KOREA

METRES
FEET

5000
16404

3000
9843

2000
6562

1000
3281

500
1640

200
656

0
0
LAND
B.S.L.

200
656

4000
13124

6000
19686

1 : 10 000 000

MILES 0   100   200

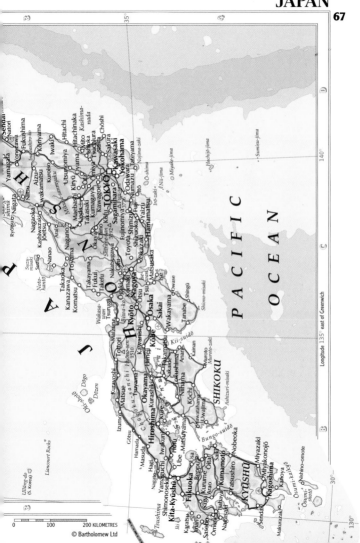

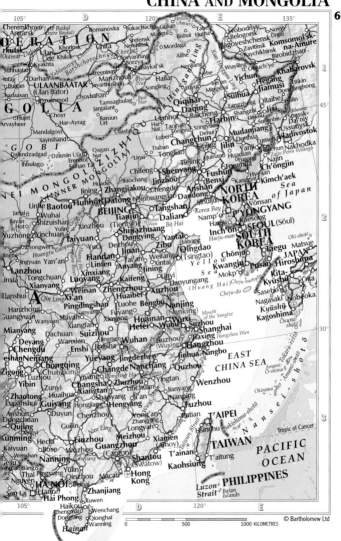

105°   D   120°   E   135°

Cheremkhovo Lake Baikal (ozero Baykal) Romanovka Bukachacha Gulian Heilong (Amur) Tahe Bishui Huma Svobodnyy Belogorsk Novyy Urgal Komsomol'sk-na-Amure
Angarsk Khamar-Daban Khrebet Chita Sretensk Nerchinsk Maguli Alihe Zavitinsk Shimanovsk Birobidzhan
Irkutsk Ulan-Ude Khilok Shilka Chernyshevsk Zeya Xiao Hinggan Ling Wuyiling Yichun Hegang Jiamusi Khabarovsk
Suhbaatar Kyakhta Yablonovyy Borzya Olovyannaya Nenjiang Bei'an Mingshui Suihua Qitaihe Bikin Dongning
Jutaj Bulgan ULAANBAATAR (Ulan Bator) Darhan Javarhlustaru Manzhouli Hailar Hulun Nur Songling Fuyu Harbin Mudanjiang Suifenhe Dal'niy Ussuriysk Vladivostok
Hadaasan Zuunmod Choybalsan Tamsagbulag Buir Nur Qiqihar Daqing Baicheng Dehui Jilin Huadian Dunhua Tumen Zaliv Petra Velikogo Najin
GOLIA Choyr Har-Ayrag Baruun Urt Ulanhot Taonan Songyuan Changchun Siping Tieling Tonghua Ch'ongjin
Hujirt Arvayheer Mandalgovi Saynshand Ullastai Lubei Linxi Daban Tongliao Shenyang Fushun Benxi Kangayng Hyesan Kimch'aek
GOBI Dalandzadgad Dzamin Uüd Qagan Nur Erenhot Saihan Tal Chifeng Baochang Huade Jinzhou Chengde Anshan Dandong Sinuiju Korea Bay NORTH KOREA Sea of Japan
Inbulago Zhangjiakou Qinhuangdao Huludao Kangye Wonsan
NEI MONGOL ZIZHIQU (INNER MONGOLIA) Jining Huhhot Datong BEIJING Tangshan Tianjin (Tientsin) Bo Hai PYONGYANG Haeju Namp'o Kaesong Inch'on SEOUL (Sŏul) Kangnŭng Oki-shotō
Jartai Bayan Hot Linhe Baotou Wuhai Shizuishan Xinzhou Bohai Wan Dalian Yantai Weifang Haeju-man SOUTH KOREA Taegu Matsue JAPAN
Wuzhong Yinchuan Zhongwei Yinchuan Yulin Taiyuan Yuci Dezhou Jinan Zibo Qingdao (Tsingtao) Chŏnju Kwangju Pusan Hiroshima Kyūshū Ōta
Lanzhou Tianshui Lingyuan Yan'an Huangtu Gaoyuan Handan Linfen Anyang Tai'an Weifang Xintai Yellow Sea Mokp'o Cheju-haehyŏp Sasebo Kita-Kyūshū
Tongchuan Xianyang Xinxiang Zhengzhou Kaifeng Jining Linyi Lianyungang (Huang Hai) Cheju-do Nagasaki Nobeoka Kagoshima Osumi-shotō
A Qin Ling Xi'an Weinan Luoyang Huaibei Xuzhou Hongze Hu
Hanzhong Pingdingshan Luohe Bengbu
Guangyuan Wanyuan Shiyan Xiangfan Fuyang Huainan Nanjing (Nanking) Mouth of the Yangtze
Mianyang Dachuan Suizhou Xinyang Hefei Wuhu Wuxi Suzhou Shanghai
Deyang Wanxian Jingmen Wuhan Huzhou Jiaxing Hangzhou Wan
Chengdu Enshi Jingshan (Wuxing) Hangzhou
eshan Neijiang Yueyang Jingdezhen Jinhua Ningbo EAST CHINA SEA
Zigong Luzhou Chongqing (Chungking) Changde Nanchang Quzhou Amami-ō-shima
Zhaotong Zunyi Huaihua Changsha Zhuzhou Yingtan Jianyang Wenzhou Okinawa
Lupanshui Guiyang Hongjiang Hengyang Ji'an Nanping Nansei-shotō
Anshun Dongchuan Duyun Chenzhou Yong'an Fuzhou Okinawa-shotō
Qujing Zhangzhou Longyan Putian Sakishima-shotō Tropic of Cancer
KUNMING Guilin Nan Ling Meizhou Hsinchu T'AIPEI
Kaiyuan Hechi Bose Wuzhou Guangzhou (Canton) Xiamen (Amoy) TAIWAN PACIFIC OCEAN
eju Wenshan NANNING Xunjiang Shantou (Swatow) T'ainan T'aitung
Cao Bang Thai Pingxiang Yulin Qinzhou Macau Hong Kong Kaohsiung Luzon Strait Batan Islands PHILIPPINES
Son La HÀ NỘI (Hanoi) Beihai Zhanjiang Xuwen
Hai Phong Haikou Wenchang Dongfang Qionghai Wanning Hainan

0   500   1000 KILOMETRES

© Bartholomew Ltd

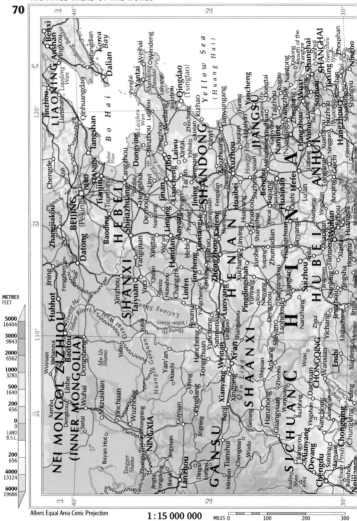

METRES
FEET

5000 16404
3000 9843
2000 6562
1000 3281
500 1640
200 656
0 0
LAND B.S.L.
200 656
4000 13124
6000 19686

Albers Equal Area Conic Projection

1 : 15 000 000

MILES 0   100   200   300

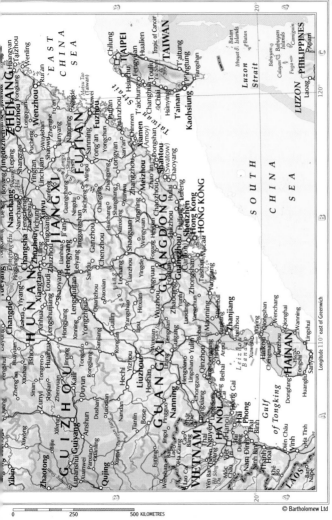

0   250   500 KILOMETRES

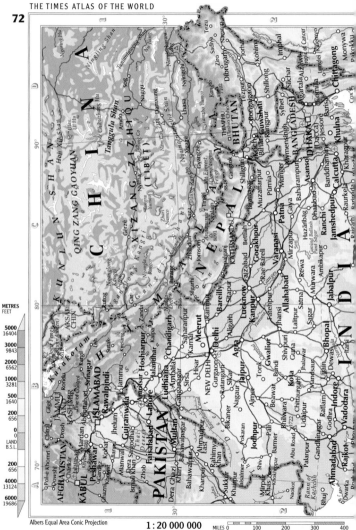

METRES
FEET

5000	16404
3000	9843
2000	6562
1000	3281
500	1640
200	656
0	
LAND	
B.S.L.	
200	656
4000	13124
6000	19686

Albers Equal Area Conic Projection

1 : 20 000 000

MILES 0   100   200   300   400

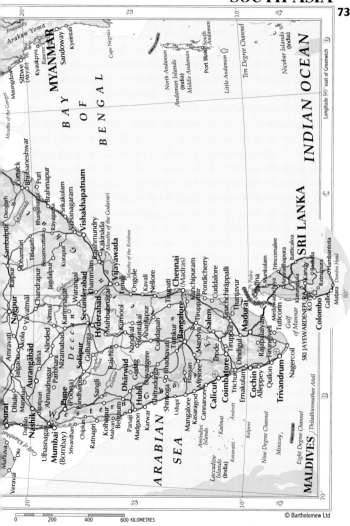

0   200   400   600 KILOMETRES

Gushgy
Dowshi
Pol-e Khomri
Bathra Glacier
Tirich Mir 7690
K2 (Qogir Feng) 8611 Godwin Austen

Murghab
Chitral
Gilgit
Karakoram

Hari Rud
Chaghcharan
Barikot
Drosh
Dir
Astor
Skardu

Hindu Kush
Jalalabad
Dargai
Chilas
Line of Control
JAMMU
AND KASHMIR

Koh-e Baba
Charikar
KABUL
Mardan
Abbottabad
Srinagar

5143
Shah Foladi
Mardan
Haripur
Anantnag

AFGHANISTAN
Gardez
PESHAWAR
Nowshera
ISLAMABAD

Ghazni
Khowst
Kohat
Rawalpindi
Kishwar

HAZARAJAT
Daud
Khel
Talagang
Jhelum
Jammu
Udhampur

Delaram
Gereshk
Arghandab
Bannu
Mianwali
Khushab
Gujrat
Sialkot
Chamba

Kandahar
Qalat
Lakki
Tank
Sargodha
Wazirabad
Gujranwala
Hoshiarpur

Toba and Kakar Ranges
Ismail Khan
Thal Jhang
Chiniot
Lahore
Amritsar
Jalandhar

Chaman
Muslimbagh
Leiah
Ahmadpur Sial
Faisalabad
Ferozpur
Chandigarh

30°
Quetta
Loralai
Khanewal
Ravi
Okara
Fazilka
Ambala

Karnal
Mastung
Mach
Dera Ghazi Khan
Mandi Burewala
Abohar
Sirsa
Tohana
Panipat

Chagai
Nushki
Kalat
Sibi
Muzaffargarh
Multan
Ganganagar
Hanumangarh
Hisar

Nok Kundi
Dalbandin
Ras Koh 3007
Lahri
Rajanpur
Bahawalpur
Suratgarh
Mahajan
Bhiwani

PAKISTAN
Dera Bugti
Uch
Fort Abbas
Anupgarh
Rajgarh
NEW DELHI

Qila Ladgasht
Washuk
Nushki
Khuzdar
Shikarpur
Kashmor
Khanpur
Rahimyar Khan
Barsalpur
Pugal
Sardarshahr
Churu
Narnaul
Gurgaon

Kamarod
Nagha Kalat
Jacobabad
Larkana
Kandhkot
Ghotki
Sukkur
Jaisalmer
Bikaner
Nokha
Sujangarh
Sikar
Alwar

Panjgur
Sorab
Wad
Khairpur
Ramgarh
Pokaran
Phalodi
Nagaur
Bharatpur

Hoshab
Bazdar
Dadu
Nawabshah
Merta
Ajmer
Jaipur

Turbat
Bela
Tatta
Adam
Klupro
Shiv
Balotra
Jodhpur
Tonk
Sawai Madhopur

Pasni
Ormara
Sonmiani
Thano
Bula Khan
Hyderabad
Mirpur Khas
Barmer
Pali
Beawar
Devli
Bundi
Kota

Gwadar
Karachi
Badin
Tando Muhammad Khan
Nagar Parkar
Sirohi
Deogarh
Bhilwara
Jhalawar

Jati
Rann of Kachchh
Radhanpur
Abu Road
Palanpur
Udaipur
Chittaurgarh
Bundi

Tropic of Cancer
Lakhpat
Bhuj
Mahesana
Dungarpur
Banswara
Ratlam
Mandsaur
Bhopal

ARABIAN
Rapur
Kandla
Gandhidham
Siddhpur
Gandhinagar
Ahmadabad
Godhra
Dahod
Ujjain
Dewas
Indore

Okha
Dwarka
Morbi
Surendranagar
Nadiad
Vadodara
Mhow
Harda Khas

SEA
Jamnagar
Rajkot
Dhasa
Khambhat
Narmada
Bharuch
Khandwa

Porbandar
Junagadh
Bhavnagar
Burhanpur

20°
Keshod
Veraval
Mahuva
Diu
Gulf of Khambhat
Surat
Valsad
Dhule
Nashik

Daman
Nandurbar
Jalgaon
Bhusawal
Akola

Dahanu
Igatpuri
Kalyan
Manmad
Aurangabad
Jalna

METRES FEET
5000 16404
3000 9843
2000 6562
1000 3281
500 1640
200 656
0 0
LAND B.S.L.
200 656
4000 13124
6000 19686

Albers Equal Area Conic Projection

1:15 000 000

MILES 0 100 200 300

PAKISTAN, INDIA AND BANGLADESH

XINJIANG UYGUR ZIZHIQU (SINKIANG)

Hoh Xil Shan

AKSAI CHIN Under Chinese administration, claimed by India

Minteng
Gozha Co

Dogai Coring

Ulan Ul Hu

C H I N A

QING ZANG GAOYUAN (PLATEAU OF TIBET)

Lumajangdong Co

XIZANG ZIZHIQU (TIBET)

Tanggula Shan

Chibzhang Hu

Nganglong Kangri 6596

Gangdisê Shan

Ngang'ons Kangri

Gêrzê

Nyima

Siling Co

Nam Co

Damxung

Ge'gyai

Gar

Ngangla Ringco

Chabyêr Caka

Zhari Namco

Tangra Yumco

Ngangzê

Gyaring Co

Nyainqêntanglha

Feng 7114

Nyainqêntanglha Shan

Zanda

Kalpa

Mapam Yumco

Zhabdun

Ngamring

Paiku Co

Yarlung Zangbo

Xigazê

Lhasa

Yamzho Yumco

Nanda Devi

Burang

Zhabdun

Nyainqêntanglha

Dehra Dun 7816
Saharanpur
Roorkee
Almora
Pithoragarh
Jumla
Sangsang
Gyangzê
Kangmar
Kula Kangri 7554

Nagina
Haldwani
Sigarhi
Jomsom
Tingri
Lhagoi Kangri
Dinggyê
Yadong
Kangmar
THIMPHU
Kangto 7102

Meerut
Moradabad
Rampur
Bisalpur
Jajarkot
Salyana
Pokhara
Mt Everest (Qomolangma) 8848
Kangchenjunga 8580
Gangtok
Bomdila

Delhi
Bareilly
Budaun
Mailani
Nanpara
Tansen
Butwal
Nyalam
KATHMANDU
Darjiling
BHUTAN
Tezpur
Nalbari
Nagaon

Aligarh
Shahjahanpur
Bahraich
Patan
Okhaldhunga
Dhankuta
Shiliguri
Bongaigaon
Goalpara
Guwahati

Mathura
Fatehgarh
Sitapur
Balrampur
Birganj
Janakpur
Biratnagar
Kishanganj
Koch Bihar
Rangpur
Khasi Hills

Agra
Firozabad
Lucknow
Faizabad
Basti
Gorakhpur
Betiah
Darbhanga
Katihar
Purnia
Rangpur
Jamalpur
Silchar

Etawah
Kanpur
Rae Bareli
Jaunpur
Chhapra
Muzaffarpur
Saharsa
Bihar Sharif
Rajshahi
Mymensingh
Agartala

Gwalior
Kalpi
Fatehpur
Ghazipur
Ara
Patna
Munger
Bhagalpur
Ingraj Bazar
Pabna
DHAKA (Dacca)

Jhansi
Banda
Varanasi
Sasaram
Gaya
Bihar Sharif
Deoghar
Baharampur
Comilla

Shivpuri
Chhatarpur
Allahabad
Mirzapur
Dehri
Kodarma
Raishahi
Krishnanagar
Kushtia

Lalitpur
Panna
Hanumana
Renukut
Daltenganj
Hazaribag
Dhanbad
Asansol
Barddhaman
Jessore
Khulna

I N D I A
Satna
Rewa
Beohari
Govind Ballash Pant Sagar
Pairatu
Purulia
Bankura
Ranaghat
Barisal

Sagar
Damoh
Murwara
Shahdol
Ambikapur
Hazaribagh Range 1255
Gumla
Ranchi
Ghatal
Chittagong

Jabalpur
Kareli
Mandla
Raigarh
Jharsuguda
Jamshedpur
Chaibasa
Baripada
Kharagpur
Calcutta
Cox's Bazar

Itarsi
Betul
Seoni
Pandaria
Bilaspur
Raipur
Dharmjaygarh
Raurkela
Meghasani 1165
Kendujhargarh
Baleshwar

Nagpur
Gondia
Dhamtari
Balangir
Sambalpur
Anugul
Bhadrakh

Amravati
Wardha
Hinganghat
Kanker
Titlagarh
Baliguda
Bhanjanagar
Cuttack
BAY OF BENGAL

Yavatmal
Chandrapur
Garhchiroli
Kondagaon
Bhawanipatna
Chilka Lake
Puri
Bhubaneshwar

Mouths of the Ganges

A 50° B 60°

Jobol
Komsomolets
Kostanay
Magnitogorsk
Balashov • Atkarsk Vol'sk Pugachev Buzuluk Kumertau Baymak
Saratov Balakovo Sorochinsk Lubenka Tyul'gan Kartaly
Novoanninskiy Kotovsk Engel's yershov Ozinki Novosergiyevka Orenburg Saraktash Zhitikara Kushmurun
Kamyshin Kamenka Ural'sk Aksay Sol'- Mednogorsk Orsk
Frolovo Dzhanybek Zhalpaktal Iletsk Akbulak Khromtau
RUS. FED. Chapayevo Khobda Aktyubinsk Karabutak Tūrga
Volzhskiy Akhtubinsk Dzhangala Kandyagash Akshiganak Irgiz
Volgograd Inderborskiy Shubarkuduk Embá
(Stalingrad) Aybas Makhambet Martuk
Kotel'nikovo Prikaspiyskaya Nizmennost' Makat Chelkar
Tsimlyanskoye Kharabali Atyrau Kul'sary Karakalpakiya Aral'sk
Vodokhranilishche Utta -12 Balykshi Peski KAZA
Elista Burynshyk Opornyy Kulandy
Astrakhan' Lagan' Mys Tyub- Mertvyy Kultuk Ayteke Bi
Divnoye Ulan- Karagan Beyneu Baykonur
Budennovsk Khol Komsomol'skiy Fort-Shevchenko Ustyurt Dzhusaly
Nal'chik Kochubey Mangistau Plateau Muynak UZBEKISTAN
Grozny Kizlyar Shetpe Zhanaozen Kungrad KYZY
Vladikavkaz Khasav'yurt Aktau Khodzheyli DES
Makhachkala Zaliv Nukus
GEORGIA Derbent Kara-Bogaz Ozero Dashkhovuz
T'BILISI Buzdyag Karabogazkel' Gol Urgench Gaz-Achak
ARMENIA Şäki Qoba Chagyl Bukhara
YEREVAN Mingäçevir Sumqayit Turkmenbashi TURKMENISTAN Chardzhev
AZERBAIJAN BAKU Nebitdag KARAKUM
Marand Yankandi (Bakı) Gazandzhyk DESERT Mary
Tabriz Astara Gumdag Gyzylarbat ASHGABAT Tejen
Ardabil Gonbad-e Bakherden
Saqqez Zanjān Bandar-e Anzali Kavus Bojnūrd Mashhad Meymaneh
As Sulaymaniyah Rasht Behshahr Sabzevār Neyshabūr Qala
Sanandaj Qazvīn Bābol Sārī Gorgān Kāshmar Morghab
Hamadān Amol Alborz Semnān Torbat-e Heydariyeh Torbat- Herāt
Kermānshāh Karaj Dasht-e Kavīr Jām
Borūjerd TEHRĀN Qom AFGHA
Ilām Khorramābad Arāk Kāshān Tabas Bīrjand
Aligudarz Ardestān
Eşfahān
Dezfūl (Isfahan) Nā'īn Farāh
IRAQ Shahr-e Yazd Dasht-e Lūt
Ahvāz IRAN Kord Zarand
Ash Shatrah Abādeh Zābol Dasht-e Margo
An Nāşirīyah Abarqū Bāfq Zaranj
Basra Abādān Rafsanjān Kermān Helmand
(Al Başrah) KUWAIT

METRES FEET
5000 16404
3000 9843
2000 6562
1000 3281
500 1640
200 656
0 0
LAND B.S.L.
200 656
4000 13124
6000 19686

Albers Equal Area Conic Projection

1 : 20 000 000 MILES 0 100 200

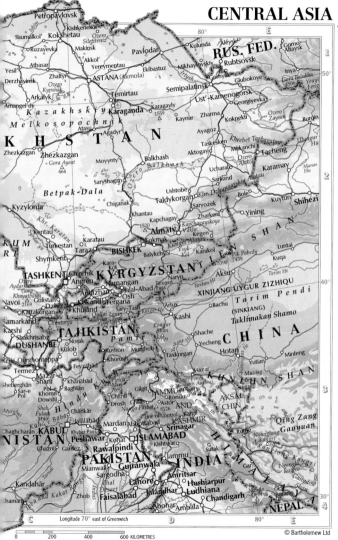

0   200   400   600 KILOMETRES

© Bartholomew Ltd

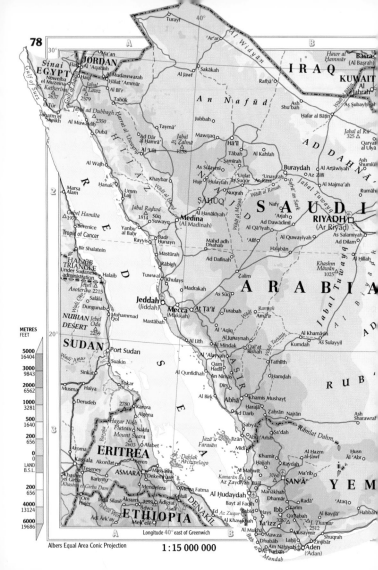

METRES
FEET

5000
16404

3000
9843

2000
6562

1000
3281

500
1640

200
656

0
0
LAND
B.S.L.

200
656

4000
13124

6000
19686

Albers Equal Area Conic Projection

Longitude 40° east of Greenwich

1:15 000 000

A   40°   B

30°

EGYPT
Sinai
el Katherina
2637

JORDAN
Ma'an
'Aqaba
Mudawwarah
Halat 'Ammār
Elat
Haql
Nuweiba
el Muzeini
et Tūr
Jebel Katherîna
Et Tûr
Ras
el Sheikh
Jabal ad Dubbagh
2350
Farrat el 'Uwayrid

Al Jawf

Sakākah

IRAQ

Hawr al
Hammār (Al Basrah)
Basra

KUWAIT
Al
Jahrah

Al Widyan
'Ar'ar

Rafhā

An Nafūd
Ash
Shu'bah

Hafar al Bāṭin

Aş Şubayḥiyah

Jabal al Ka
325

Qaryat
al Ulyā

Ad Dār
al Hamrā'
Tabūk
2579
Al Muwaylih
Dubā
Al Muwaylih

Taymā'

Mawqaq

Jubbah

Ḥā'il

Tābah
Al Kahfah
Samirah

A D   D A H N Ā

Ash
Shumlūl

Al Wajh

Khaybar
Hanak
Umm
Lajj

As Sulaymi
Ḥulayfah
Ḥujr
'Uqlat
aş Şuqūr

Nuqrah
Uqlat

As Ras

Buraydah
Al Artāwīyah
Az Zilfī
Al Majma'ah

Rumāh

Marsa
Alam
Gebel Hamáta
1977
Berenice
Tropic of Cancer
Bir Shalatein

Jabal Radwā
1814
Sūq
Suwayq
Medina
(Al Madīnah)

Yanbu'
al Bahr
Rayyis

Badr
Ḥunayn
Mastūrah

Mahd adh
Dhahab

Al Ḥanākīyah

Nafy

Ad Dawādimī

Ṣafrā as Sark
Jabal Tuwayq

Arjah

'Afīf

RIYADH
(Ar Riyāḍ)

As Salamīyah
Ad Dilam

Al Quwayīyah

Halabān

Khashm
Māwān
1025

Al Hillah

N A J D

S A U D I

Rābigh
Tuwwal
Khulays

Ad Dafīnah

Zalim

Al 'Āqiq

Al Mindak

'Unayzah
As Sulayyil

SUDAN
NUBIAN
DESERT
Jebel Oda
2259
Muhammad
Qol

Madrakah
Mastābah

As Sūq

Turabah
Rānyah
Wadi
Amaq
Wadi Tathilth

Al Khamāsīn
Kumdah

A R A B I A

Port Sudan
Suakin

Jeddah
(Jiddah)
Mecca
(Makkah)
Al Ṭā'if

J A B A L
Al Līth
Al 'Alayyah
Qam
Ḥadil

Jazā'ir

Tathlīth

R U B '

Sinkat
Derudeb
2780
Karora
Algena

**HALAIB
TRIANGLE**
Under Sudanese
administration
Halaib
Jebel
Asoteriba 2215
Salāla
Dungunab

Al Qunfidhah
An Nimāṣ
Dīs
Al Birk

'A S I R

Ḥamdān

Ash
Sharawrah

AD

Musmar
Haiya
Tokar

Hagar Nish
Plateau
2603
Mount Suara
Nakfa

Abhā
Khamis Mushayt
Harajah

Najrān
Ramlat Dahm

Sabyā

Afrema
Kassala
Akordat
Barentu

ERITREA

ASMARA
Keren
Dekemhare
Mendefera

Massawa
Dahlak
Archipelago

Jīzān
Midī
Jazā'ir
Farasān

Al Hazm
al-Jawf
Husn
Āl 'Abr

'Arīsh

Al Dar'b
Zahrān

Sa'dah
Khamir
Raydah

Al Malwīt
Ma'rib

Khashm
el Girba
Khashm el Girba Dam

Teseney
Adi Silase
Aksum
3293
Adigrat

Mereb Fatma
Keluli

DENAKIL

Hajjah
Az Zaydīyah
Bājil

ṢAN'Ā

Manākhah
Dhamār
Radā'

YEM

'Atāq

Habban

Om
Hager
Indu Silasé
Adi Ark'ay

Mek'elé

ETHIOPIA

Ed Az Zuqur
Zabid
Al Khawkhah

Bayt al Faqih
Al Ḥudaydah

'Ataq

Al Bayda'

Dahūb
Am Nābiyah

Ibb
Qa'tabah

Ta'izz
2512

Shuqrah
Zinjibār

Aden
('Adan)

Al Mukhā
Mawza
Al Thamar
3760
Karīm
Husn

Lahij
Musaymir
Turbah

Bab al
Mandab

MILES 0   100   200   0   250   500 KILOMETRES

© Bartholomew Ltd

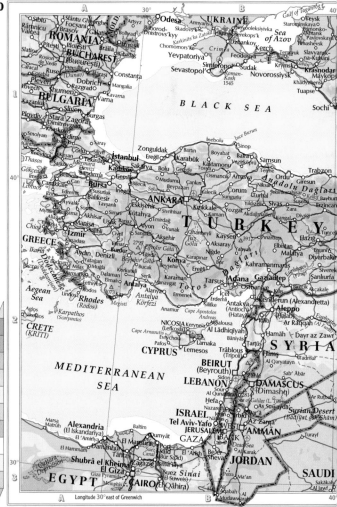

METRES
FEET

5000
16404

3000
9843

2000
6562

1000
3281

500
1640

200
656

0
0
LAND
B.S.L.

200
656

4000
13124

6000
19686

Albers Equal Area Conic Projection

1 : 15 000 000

MILES 0   100   200   300

Map labels (reading across the map):

Gulf of Taganrog
UKRAINE
Odesa
Armyans'k
Skadovs'k
Novooleksiyivka
Sea of Azov
Yeysk
Primorsko-Akhtarsk
Slavyansk-na-Kubani
Artsyz
Bilhorod-Dnistrovs'kyy
Karkinits'ka Zatoka
Dzhankoy
Kerch
Temryuk
Krasnodar
Maykop
Sfântu Gheorghe
Brăila
Izmayil
Chornomors'ke
Crimea
Simferopol'
Feodosiya
Kryms'k
Khadyzhensk
Răhnicu Vâlcea
Focşani
Galaţi
Bolhrad
Yevpatoriya
Sudak
Krymsk
Tuapse
ROMANIA
Piteşti
Ploieşti
Roman-Kosh 1545
Sevastopol'
Novorossiysk
Sibiu
Braşov
BUCHAREST
(Bucureşti)
Slatina
Rosioni de Vede
Dunărea
Constanţa
BLACK SEA
Sochi
Caracal
Corabia
Ruse
Tărasi
Dobrich
Razgrad
Mangalia
Lovech
Pleven
Shumen
Kavarna
BULGARIA
Kazanlŭk
Varna
Smolyan
Stara Zagora
Sliven
Burgas
Plovdiv
Dimitrovgrad
Khaskovo
Sandanski
Edirne
Kŭrdzhali
Xanthi
Kesan
Silivri
Çorlu
Tekirdağ
Saray
Zonguldak
Bartın
Inebolu
İnce Burun
Sinop
Samsun
Terme
Ordu
Giresun
Trabzon
Thasos
Gökçeada
İmroz
Ereğli
Karabük
Boyabat
Bafra
Yazıköprü
Anadolu Dağları
Komotini
Gelibolu
İstanbul
Adapazarı
Sakarya
Bolu
Gerede
Tosya
Osmancık
Amasya
Çorum
Niksar
Reşadiye
Kelkit
Bayburt
Erzincan
Limnos
Çanakkale
Bursa
Gemlik
Bilecik
Mudurnu
Beypazarı
Çankırı
Kalecik
Sungurlu
Turhal
Sivas
Zara
Divriği
Lesbos
Ayvacık
Balıkesir
İnegöl
Eskişehir
ANKARA
Kırıkkale
Yozgat
Akdağmadeni
Kangal
Mytilini
Bergama
Susurluk
Sıma
Sivrihisar
Kaman
Yıldızeli
Çıkaralarbaşı
Chios
Aliağa
Akhisar
Salihli
Kütahya
Afyon
Emirdağ
Yunak
Cihanbeyli
Kayseri
Pınarbaşı
Hazro
Elazığ
Malatya
Engani
Diyarbakır
İzmir
Manisa
Uşak
Banaz
Civril
Akşehir
Tuz Gölü
Aksaray
Niğde
Yalvaç
Elbistan
Silvereki
Şanlıurfa
Aydın
Denizli
Burdur
Isparta
Eğirdir Gölü
Eğirdir
Karapınar
Kahramanmaraş
Gaziantep
Nazilli
Beyşehir Gölü
Konya
Ereğli
Toros Dağları
Adana
Osmaniye
Akçakale
Ar Raqqah (Ar Raqqa)
Milas
Yatağan
Elmalı
Bucak
Serik
Karaman
Tarsus
İçel
Erdemli
İskenderun (Alexandretta)
Aleppo (Halab)
Bodrum
Muğla
Dalaman
Fethiye
Antalya
Manavgat
Alanya
Anamur
Silifke
Antakya (Antioch) (Hatay)
İdlib
Euphrates
Rhodes (Rodos)
Meğisti
Antalya Körfezi
Cape Apostolos Andreas
Ḥamāh
Dayr az Zawr
GREECE
Aegean Sea
Kos
Dodecanese
Cape Arnaouti
Kyrenia (Lefkoşa)
Agialousa
NICOSIA (Lefkoşa)
Al Lādhiqīyah
Banias
Ḥimṣ
Tadmur
Agios Nikolaos
Karpathos (Scarpanto)
Evrychou
Larnaka
Tartūs
Al Qaryatayn
Lindos
CYPRUS
Lemesos
Trâblous (Tripoli)
Sab' Ābār
CRETE (KRITI)
MEDITERRANEAN SEA
BEIRUT (Beyrouth)
Sidon
Zahlé
DAMASCUS (Dimashq)
Ar Rutbah
SYRIA
Soûr
Al Qunayṭirah
Sea of Galilee (L. Tiberias)
As Suwaydā'
Syrian Desert (Bādiyat ash Shām)
Ḥefa
Nazareth
Irbid
Az Zarqā'
Turayf
LEBANON
ISRAEL
Tel Aviv-Yafo
JERUSALEM
GAZA
WEST BANK
AMMAN
Marsa Matrûh
Alexandria (El Iskandarīya)
El 'Amrīya
Baltim
Dumyāt
Dead Sea
Al Karak
JORDAN
El Hammam
Damanhûr
El Mansûra
El 'Arîsh
Beer Sheva
SAUDI
El Giza
Zagazig
Shubrâ el Kheima
Port Said (Bûr Sa'îd)
Isma'ilîya
Ma'ān
Sakākah
Al Jawf
Qattâra Depression
Memphis
Giza Pyramids
CAIRO (El Qâhira)
Suez Canal
Suez (El Suweis)
Sinai
Petra
EGYPT
Al 'Aqabah
Al Mudawwarah

Longitude 30° east of Greenwich

0   250   500 KILOMETRES

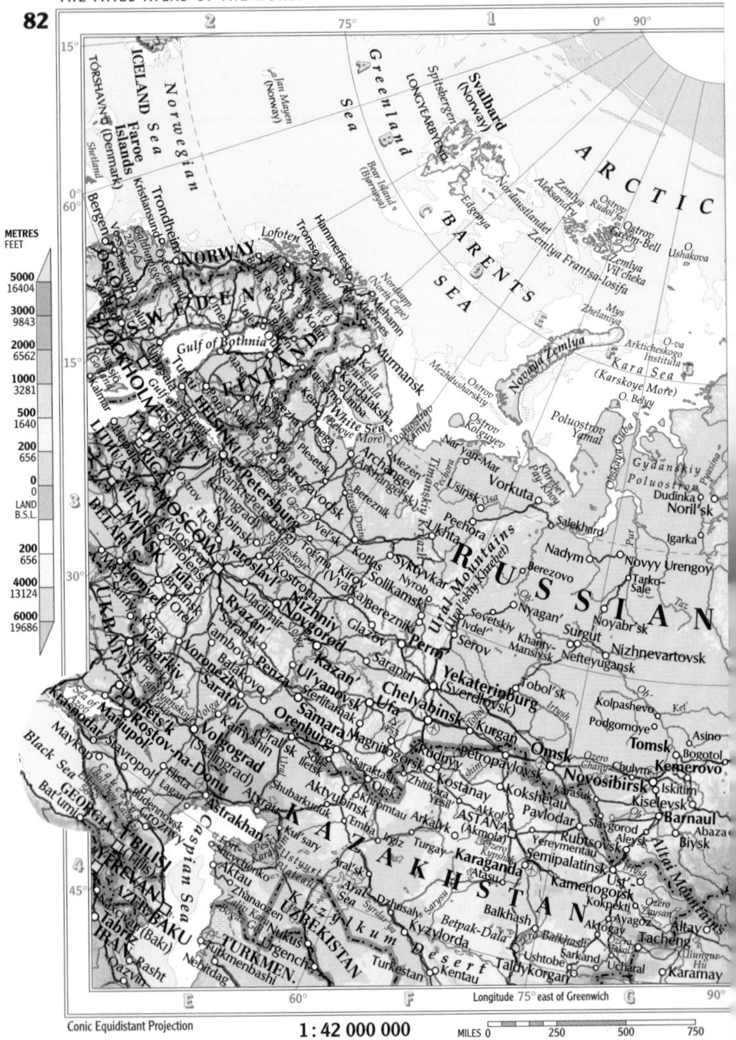

METRES
FEET
5000
16404
3000
9843
2000
6562
1000
3281
500
1640
200
656
0
0
LAND
B.S.L.
200
656
4000
13124
6000
19686
ARCTIC
BARENTS SEA
Norwegian Sea
Greenland Sea
Jan Mayen (Norway)
Svalbard (Norway)
Spitsbergen
LONGYEARBYEN
Bear Island (Bjørnøya)
Nordaustlandet
Edgeøya
Zemlya Aleksandry
Ostrov Rudol'fa
Ostrov Greem-Bell
O. Ushakova
Zemlya Frantsa-Iosifa
Zemlya Vil'cheka
Mys Zhelaniya
Novaya Zemlya
O-va Arkticheskogo Instituta
Kara Sea (Karskoye More)
O. Belyy
Ostrov Mezhdusharskiy
Ostrov Kolguyev
Poluostrov Yamal
Obskaya Guba
Gydanskiy Poluostrov
ICELAND
TÓRSHAVN
Faroe Islands (Denmark)
Shetland
NORWAY
SWEDEN
FINLAND
Lofoten
Tromsø
Hammerfest
Nordkapp (North Cape)
Kirkenes
Murmansk
Kola Peninsula
Kandalaksha
Umba
White Sea (Beloye More)
Gulf of Bothnia
Gulf of Finland
Trondheim
Kristiansund
Bergen
OSLO
STOCKHOLM
Uppsala
Turku
HELSINKI
Kalmar
ESTONIA
LATVIA
LITHUANIA
RIGA
VILNIUS
MINSK
BELARUS
UKRAINE
MOSCOW
St Petersburg
Petrozavodsk
Plesetsk
Archangel (Arkhangel'sk)
Mezen'
Nar'yan-Mar
Vorkuta
Usinsk
Pechora
Ukhta
Salekhard
Nadym
Novyy Urengoy
Noril'sk
Dudinka
Igarka
Syktyvkar
Kotlas
Vel'sk
Tver'
Rybinsk
Yaroslavl'
Kostroma
Vologda
Kirov (Vyatka)
Solikamsk
Berezniki
Perm'
Ural Mountains
RUSSIAN
Berezovo
Nyagan'
Sovetskiy
Ivdel'
Serov
Khanty-Mansiysk
Surgut
Nefteyugansk
Noyabr'sk
Nizhnevartovsk
Tarko-Sale
Smolensk
Tula
Bryansk
Homyel'
Orel
Kursk
Kharkiv (Khar'kov)
Voronezh
Ryazan'
Vladimir
Nizhniy Novgorod
Glazov
Kazan'
Sarapul
Saransk
Penza
Tambov
Saratov
Balakovo
Ul'yanovsk
Samara
Sterlitamak
Ufa
Yekaterinburg (Sverdlovsk)
Chelyabinsk
Tobol'sk
Kurgan
Omsk
Kolpashevo
Podgornoye
Tomsk
Asino
Bogotol
Kemerovo
Novosibirsk
Iskitim
Kiselevsk
Barnaul
Biysk
Abaza
Donets'k
Mariupol'
Rostov-na-Donu
Krasnodar
Maykop
Stavropol'
Elista
Volgograd (Stalingrad)
Kamyshin
Orenburg
Magnitogorsk
Orsk
Rudnyy
Kostanay
Petropavlovsk
Kokshetau
Pavlodar
Slavgorod
Rubtsovsk
Aleysk
Altai Mountains
Black Sea
Sea of Azov
GEORGIA
T'BILISI
YEREVAN
AZERBAIJAN
BAKU
Caspian Sea
Astrakhan'
Atyrau
Aktyubinsk
Shubarkuduk
Emba
Arkalyk
Turgay
ASTANA (Akmola)
KAZAKHSTAN
Karaganda
Semipalatinsk
Ust'-Kamenogorsk
Kokpekti
Ayagoz
Aktogay
Balkhash
Ozero Balkhash
Sarkand
Ucharal
Ushtobe
Taldykorgan
Tacheng
Karamay
Altay
Aral Sea
Aral'sk
Kyzylorda
Turkestan
Kentau
Kyzyl kum Desert
Betpak-Dala
UZBEKISTAN
TURKMEN.
Nukus
Urgench
Turkmenbashi
Nebitdag
Aktau
Zhanaozen
Kul'sary
Ustyurt Plateau
Tabriz
IRAN
Rasht
Qazvin
Bat'umi
Groznyy
Budennovsk
75°
0°
90°
15°
60°
30°
45°
Longitude 75° east of Greenwich

Conic Equidistant Projection

1 : 42 000 000

MILES 0 250 500 750

0   500   1000   1500 KILOMETRES

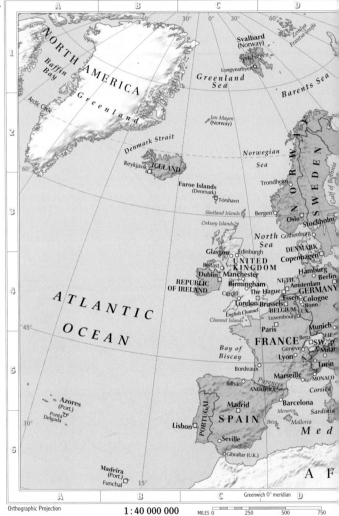

NORTH AMERICA

Baffin Bay

Greenland

Arctic Circle

Svalbard
(Norway)

Spitsbergen

Longyearbyen

Greenland Sea

Barents Sea

Zemlya
Frantsa-Josifa

Jan Mayen
(Norway)

Norwegian Sea

Denmark Strait

Reykjavik ICELAND

Trondheim

NORWAY

SWEDEN

Gulf of Bothnia

Faroe Islands
(Denmark)

Tórshavn

Bergen

Oslo

Stockholm

Shetland Islands

Orkney Islands

North Sea

Gothenburg

Glasgow   Edinburgh

DENMARK

Copenhagen

Belfast

UNITED
KINGDOM

Manchester

Hamburg

Berlin

Dublin

REPUBLIC
OF IRELAND

Birmingham

NETH.   Amsterdam

GERMANY

Cardiff

The Hague

Essen   Cologne

London

Brussels

Bonn

BELGIUM LUX.

English Channel

Luxembourg

Channel Islands

Paris

FRANCE

Munich

Bern   SW.

Milan

ATLANTIC

OCEAN

Bay of
Biscay

Genève

Lyon

Turin

Bordeaux

Marseille

MONACO

Corsica

Bilbao

Pyrenees

ANDORRA

Azores
(Port.)

Ponta
Delgada

Madrid

Barcelona

Menorca

Sardinia

SPAIN

Ibiza   Mallorca

Lisbon

PORTUGAL

Med

Seville

Gibraltar (U.K.)

Madeira
(Port.)

Funchal

A F

Greenwich 0° meridian

Orthographic Projection

1 : 40 000 000

MILES 0   250   500   750

B.H.   BOSNIA-HERZEGOVINA
CR.   CROATIA
CZ.R.   CZECH REPUBLIC
HUN.   HUNGARY
LIE.   LIECHTENSTEIN
LUX.   LUXEMBOURG
M.   MACEDONIA
NETH.   NETHERLANDS
RUS.FED. RUSSIAN FEDERATION
SL.   SLOVENIA
SLA.   SLOVAKIA
SW.   SWITZERLAND
YU.   YUGOSLAVIA

0   500   1000 KILOMETRES

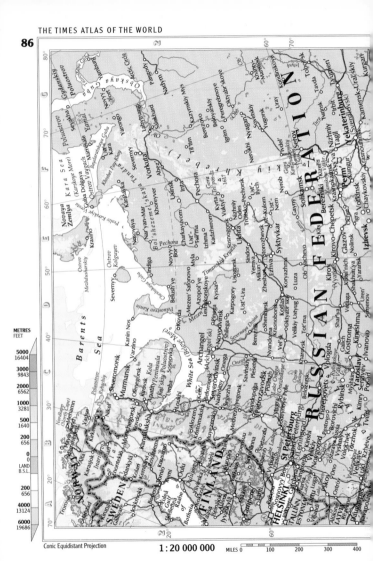

1:20 000 000

MILES 0   100   200   300   400

METRES
FEET

5000
16404

3000
9843

2000
6562

1000
3281

500
1640

200
656

0
0

LAND
B.S.L.

200
656

4000
13124

6000
19686

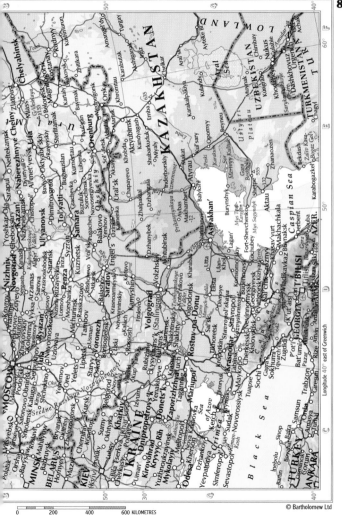

0   200   400   600 KILOMETRES

STOCKHOLM

SWEDEN

Gotland

GULF OF FINLAND

TALLINN

ESTONIA

Tartu

Lake
Peipus

Lake
Pskov

Pskov

Saaremaa

Gulf
of
Riga

LATVIA

RIGA

Liepāja

LITHUANIA

Klaipėda

Panevėžys

Kaunas

VILNIUS

RUSSIAN
FEDERATION

Kaliningrad

MINSK

POLAND

WARSAW
(Warszawa)

BELARUS

Brest

Pinsk

UKRAINE

METRES
FEET

5000
16404

3000
9843

2000
6562

1000
3281

500
1640

200
656

0
0

LAND
B.S.L.

200
656

4000
13124

6000
19686

Conic Equidistant Projection

1 : 8 000 000

MILES 0   50   100   150

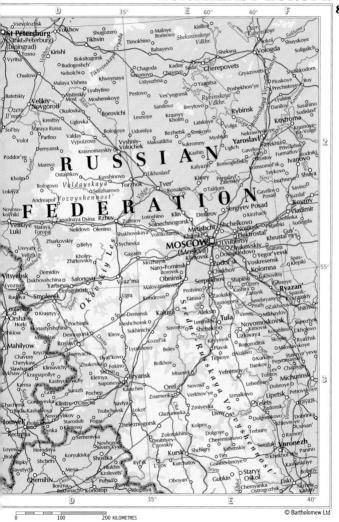

0   100   200 KILOMETRES

Ostrów Mazowiecka · Vawkavysk · Baranavichy · Slonim · Lyakhavichy · Klyetsk · Kapyl' · Slutsk · Asipovichy · Babruysk · Karma

Białystok · Ivatsevichy · Hantsavichy · Mal'kavichy · Lyuban' · Staryya Darohi · Rahachow · Zhlobin · Chachersk

WARSAW (Warszawa) · Kamyanyets · Byaroza · Kobryn · Drahichyn · Ivanava · Luninyets · Pinsk · Stolin · Zarichne · Lyel'chytsy · Pyetrykaw · Narowlya · Loyew

Siedlce · Biała Podlaska · Brest · Pripyats (Pripet) · Mazyr · Yel'sk · Brahin · Slavutych

BELARUS

POLAND · Radom · Pionki · Lubartów · Kamin'-Kashyrs'kyy · Dubrovytsya · Rokytne · Ovruch · Polis'ke

Lublin · Chelm · Turiys'k · Manevychi · Berezne · Luhyny · Narodychi · Ivankiv

Ostrowiec Świętokrzyski · Sandomierz · Zamość · Volodymyr-Volyns'kyy · Luts'k · Kostopil' · Olevs'k · Korosten'

Stalowa Wola · Tarnobrzeg · Mielec · Bogoraj · Sokal · Horokhiv · Mlyniv · Rivne · Zdolbuniv · Slavuta · Novohrad-Volyns'kyy · Radomyshl' · Borodyanka · Vyshhorod

Rzeszów · Tomaszów Lubelski · Radyvyliv · Dubno · Pochayiv · Polonne · Baranivka · Chervonohrad · KIEV (Kyïv) · Boryspil'

Jarosław · Przemyśl · Kam'yanka-Buz'ka · Brody · Zolochiv · Shepetivka · Chudniv · Zhytomyr · Fastiv · Okhukhiv

Jasło · Krosno · Sanok · Horodok · L'viv (L'vov) · Peremyshlyany · Bilohir'ya · Izyaslav · Starokostyantyniv · Berdychiv · Kozyatyn · Bila Tserkva · Kaharlyk · Myronivka

SLA · Humenné · Michalovce · Trebišov · Uzhhorod · Drohobych · Boryslav · Stryy · Zhydachiv · Kalush · Krasyliv · Volochys'k · Khmel'nyts'kyy · Vinnytsya · UKRA

UKRA · Ternopil' · Berezhany · Terebovlya · Horodok · Tetyiv · Zvenyhorodka · Monastyryshche

HUNGARY · Nyíregyháza · Mukacheve · Berehove · Khust · Mizhhir'ya · Verkhovyna · Kolomyya · Sniatyn · Horodenka · Borshchiv · Dunaivtsi · Zhmerynka · Nemyriv · Illintsi · Khrystynivka · Uman' · Tal'ne

Ivano-Frankivs'k · Nadvirna · Kam'yanets'-Podil's'kyy · Sharhorod · Tul'chyn

Chernivtsi · Sokyryany · Dnister · Mohyliv-Podil's'kyy · Bershad' · Kodyma · Pervomays'k

Satu Mare · Baia Mare · Sighetu Marmaţiei · Rădăuţi · Dorohoi · Briceni · Yampil' · Balta

Carei · Zalău · Borşa · Pietrosa 2305 · Storozhynets' · Dorohoi · Soroca · Rîbniţa · Anan'yiv

Şimleu Silvaniei · Baia Mare · Suceava · Botoşani · Fălticeni · MOLDOV · Kotovs'k · Berezivka

Alesd · Oradea · Cluj-Napoca · Gherla · Bistriţa · Vatra Dornei · Roman · Iaşi · CHIŞINĂU (Kishinev) · Tiraspol · Rozdil'na · Kominternivs'ke

Turda · Târgu Mureş · Reghin · Piatra Neamţ · Vaslui · Tighina · Bilyayivka · Illichivs'k · Odesa

Huedin · Aiud · Alba Iulia · Mediaş · Sighişoara · Bacău · Huşi · Cimişlia · Comrat · Bilhorod-Dnistrovs'kyy · Sarata

Deva · Hunedoara · Orăştie · Agnita · Miercurea-Ciuc · Oneşti · Bârlad · Ciadâr-Lunga · Artsyz · Tatarbunary

ROMANIA · Sibiu · Făgăraş · Sfântu Gheorghe · Tecuci · Cahul · Bolhrad · Kiliya · Vylkove

Caransebeş · Petroşani · Braşov · Focşani · Galaţi · Reni · Izmayil · Tulcea

Târgu Jiu · Râmnicu Vâlcea · Câmpulung · Buzău · Râmnicu Sărat · Brăila · Măcin · Babadag · Lacul Razim

Drobeta-Turnu Severin · Strehaia · Drăgăşani · Piteşti · Târgovişte · Ploieşti · Slobozia · Cernavodă · Hârşova · Năvodari

Craiova · Balş · Caracal · Costeşti · Găeşti · Titu · Buftea · Urziceni · BUCHAREST (Bucureşti)

METRES / FEET

5000	16404
3000	9843
2000	6562
1000	3281
500	1640
200	656
0	0
LAND B.S.L.	
200	656
4000	13124
6000	19686

Conic Equidistant Projection

1 : 8 000 000

MILES 0   50   100   150

© Bartholomew Ltd

0   100   200 KILOMETRES

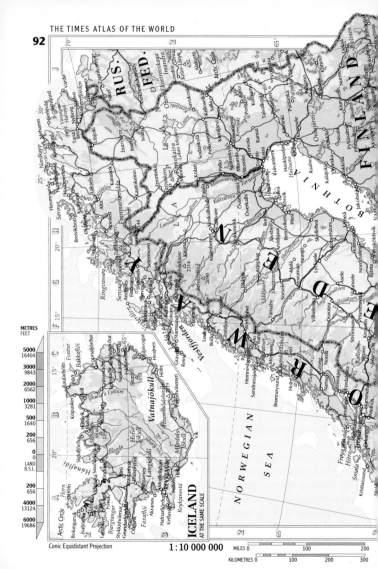

RUS. FED.

FINLAND

70°

65°

Arctic Circle

30°

25°

20°

15°

BOTHNIA

N

S W E D E N

N O R W A Y

N O R W E G I A N

S E A

METRES FEET

5000	16404
3000	9843
2000	6562
1000	3281
500	1640
200	656
0	0
LAND	B.S.L.
200	656
4000	13124
6000	19686

Vatnajökull

Arctic Circle

ICELAND

AT THE SAME SCALE

REYKJAVÍK

Conic Equidistant Projection

1 : 10 000 000

MILES 0 — 100

KILOMETRES 0 — 100 — 200 — 300

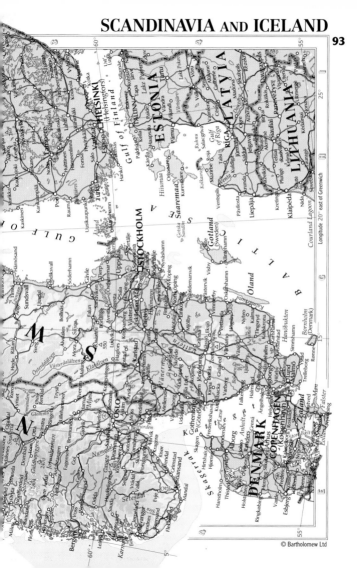

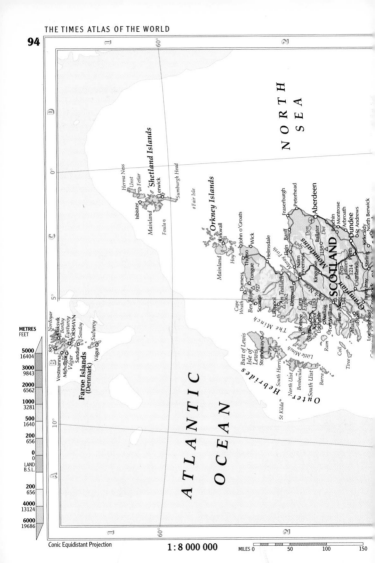

METRES
FEET

5000
16404

3000
9843

2000
6562

1000
3281

500
1640

200
656

0
0

LAND
B.S.L.

200
656

4000
13124

6000
19686

Conic Equidistant Projection

1 : 8 000 000

MILES 0   50   100   150

NORTH SEA

ATLANTIC OCEAN

Shetland Islands
Herma Ness
Unst
Fetlar
Isbister
Mainland
Lerwick
Foula
Sumburgh Head
Fair Isle

Orkney Islands
Mainland
Kirkwall
Hoy
John o'Groats
Wick
Helmsdale
Thurso
Tongue
Durness
Scourie
Cape Wrath
Ben TSaidhbh
Ullapool
Lairg

SCOTLAND
Fraserburgh
Peterhead
Aberdeen
Banff
Elgin
Nairn
Inverness
Grampian Mountains
Montrose
Arbroath
Dundee
St Andrews
North Berwick
Kirkcaldy
Stirling
Perth
Crieff
Callander
Grampian
Ballater
Dee

The Minch
Little Minch
Stornoway
Butt of Lewis
Isle of Lewis
South Harris
North Uist
Benbecula
South Uist
Barra
St Kilda
Outer Hebrides

Coll
Tiree
Mull
Rum
Skye
Portree

Faroe Islands
(Denmark)
Nordragøy
Vestmanna
Miðvágur
Vágar
TÓRSHAVN
Eysturøy
Bordøy
Klaksvik
Sandur
Sandoy
Vágur
Suðuroy

UNITED KINGDOM

FRANCE

Berwick-upon-Tweed
Coldstream
Alnwick
Amble
Morpeth
Newcastle upon Tyne
South Shields
Sunderland
Durham
Hartlepool
Middlesbrough
Darlington
Whitby
Scarborough
Bridlington

Calais
Dunkirk (Dunkerque)
Boulogne
Le Touquet-Paris-Plage
Berck
St-Valery
Abbeville
Amiens
Dieppe
Neufchâtel-en-Bray
Fécamp
Le Havre
Honfleur
Caen
Coutances
Granville

PENNINE

Carlisle

Kingston upon Hull
Grimsby
Cromer
Great Yarmouth
Lowestoft
Norwich

SOUTHERN UPLANDS

York
Leeds
Huddersfield
Manchester
Sheffield
Lincoln
Boston
King's Lynn
Thetford
Bury St Edmunds
Ipswich
Felixstowe
Harwich
Clacton-on-Sea

ENGLAND

Liverpool
Blackpool
Preston
Bolton
Stockport
Crewe
Stoke
Derby
Nottingham
Leicester
Peterborough
Ely
Cambridge
Colchester
Chelmsford
Southend-on-Sea
Isle of Sheppey

Isle of Man
DOUGLAS
(U.K.)

St Helens
Shrewsbury
Telford
Wolverhampton
Birmingham
Coventry
Northampton
Milton Keynes
Bedford
Luton
St Albans
London
Dartford
Canterbury
Dover
Folkestone
Hastings

Strait of Dover
(Pas de Calais)

WALES

Colwyn Bay
Caernarfon
Pwllheli
Cambrian Mts
Aberystwyth
Cardigan Bay
Llandovery
Merthyr Tydfil
Swansea
Cardiff
Newport
Bristol
Bath
Swindon
Oxford
Banbury
Gloucester
Worcester
Hereford

Worthing
Brighton
Portsmouth
Bournemouth
Poole
Southampton
Winchester
Basingstoke
Reading
Slough
Isle of Wight

English Channel
(La Manche)

Channel Islands
(Îles Normandes)
Guernsey
(U.K.)
ST HELIER
Jersey
(U.K.)
Alderney
Cherbourg
Cap de la Hague
Baie de Seine
PETER PORT
ST PETER PORT

REPUBLIC OF IRELAND

NORTHERN IRELAND

DUBLIN
Dún Laoghaire
Wicklow
Arklow
Wexford
Waterford
Dungarvan

St George's Channel

Holyhead
Anglesey
Pembroke
Haverfordwest
Fishguard

Bristol Channel
Exmoor
Barnstaple
Ilfracombe
Bideford
Bude
Newquay
St Ives
Penzance
Land's End
Isles of Scilly
Lizard Point

Taunton
Exeter
Dartmoor
Plymouth
Falmouth
Torquay
Lyme Bay
Start Point

CELTIC SEA

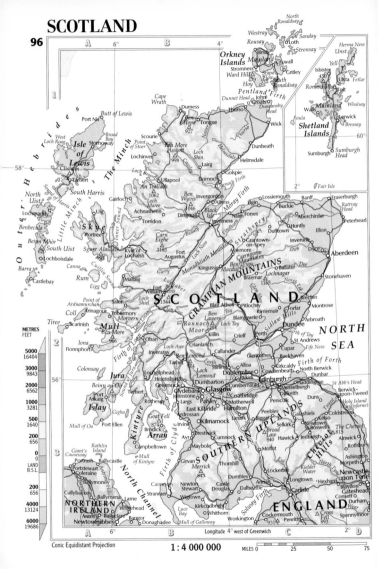

SCOTLAND

North Ronaldsay
Westray
Rousay · Sanday
Orkney · Uyea · Stronsay
Islands · Mainland · Herma Ness
Stromness · Kirkwall · Unst
Ward Hill · Stapa · Gritley · Isbister
479 · Hoy · South Ronaldsay · Uista · Fetlar
Pentland Firth · Walls · Mainland · Whalsay
Cape · Dunnet Head · John · Foula · Lerwick
Wrath · Durness · o'Groats · Bressay
Ben · Tongue · Thurso · Wick · Shetland
Hope · 927 · Dunbeath · Islands
Butt of Lewis · Scourie · Loch · 60°
Port Nis · Ben More · Shin · Helmsdale · Sumburgh
Stornoway · Assynt · Lairg · Sumburgh Head
West · Broad · 998 · Golspie
Loch Roag · Bay · Lochinver · Point · Loch · Dornoch · Fair Isle
Isle · of Stoer · Ullapool · Dornoch Firth
of · Loch Broom · An Teallach · Invergordon · Lossiemouth · Banff · Fraserburgh
Lewis · 1062 · Ben · Alness · Elgin · Buckie · Rattray
Clisham · An Teallach · Wyvis · Black · Moray Firth · Forres · Dufftown · Head
Tarbert · Gairloch · Loch · 1046 · Dingwall · Isle · Keith · Huntly · Ellon · Peterhead
South Harris · Maree · Torridon · Beauly · Inverness · Strathspey · Inverurie · Dyce · Aberdeen
North · Sound of Harris · Carn · Loch Ness · Grantown- · Aviemore · Dee · Stonehaven
Uist · Skye · Eighe · Fort · on-Spey · Braemar · Ballater · Lochnagar
Lochmaddy · 1183 · Augustus · Monadhliath Mountains · Macdui · 1155 · Brechin
Benbecula · Portree · Garry · Kingussie · Cairngorms · GRAMPIAN MOUNTAINS · Forfar
South Uist · Sgurr Alasdair · Loch · Ben Nevis · Dalwhinnie · Blair Atholl · Pitlochry · Sidlaw · Montrose
Lochboisdale · 993 · Canna · Mallaig · 1344 · Rannoch · Blairgowrie · Kirriemuir · Hills · Arbroath
Barra · Rum · Eigg · Fort · Loch · Moor · Tay · Perth · Dundee
Castlebay · Point of · William · Ben · Lawers · Blair · Firth of Tay · NORTH
Ardnamurchan · Salen · Loch Shiel · Killin · Loch Tay · St Andrews · SEA
Coll · Arinagour · Morvern · Rannoch · Crieff · Fife Ness
Tiree · Mull · Tobermory · Moor · Killin · Glenrothes · Cupar
Iona · Ben More · Oban · Loch Awe · Crianlarich · Callander · Kirkcaldy · North Berwick
Fionnphort · Loch · Inveraray · Callander · Stirling · Dunfermline · Firth of Forth
Colonsay · Tarbet · Ben Lomond · Alloa · Cowdenbeath · Dunbar
Jura · Lochgilphead · Loch · Dumbarton · Cumbernauld · Edinburgh · St Abb's Head
Islay · Beinn an Oir · Helensburgh · Lomond · Clydebank · Glasgow · Haddington · Berwick-
Port · 785 · Greenock · Paisley · Coatbridge · Penicuik · Dalkeith · Duns · upon-Tweed
Askaig · Tarbert · Rothesay · Johnstone · Motherwell · Holy Island
Gigha · Largs · East Kilbride · Hamilton · Lanark · Galashiels · (Lindisfarne)
Port Ellen · Goat Fell · Ardrossan · Kilmarnock · Biggar · Selkirk · Kelso
Mull of Oa · 874 · Irvine · Coldstream
Giant's · Brodick · Prestwick · Broad · Hawick · Jedburgh · Cheviot
Causeway · Arran · Ayr · Cumnock · Law · 815 · Alnwick
Portrush · Ballycastle · Maybole · 840 · SOUTHERN UPLANDS · Rothbury
Portstewart · Coleraine · Girvan · Thornhill · Moffat · Lockerbie · Ashington
Ballymoney · Mull of · Merrick · Dumfries · Longtown · Morpeth
NORTHERN · Ballymena · Kintyre · 843 · Newton · Castle · Annan · Hexham · Newcastle
IRELAND · Antrim · Larne · Stewart · Douglas · Dalbeattie · Solway Firth · Carlisle · upon Tyne
Cullybackey · Stranraer · Wigtown · Kirkcudbright · Blaydon · Gateshead
Ballyclare · Whithorn · Cockermouth · Penrith · Durham · Spennymoor
Newtownabbey · Donaghadee · Luce · Mull of Galloway · ENGLAND · Cross · Fell
Bangor · Bay · 977 · 893

METRES · FEET
5000 · 16404
3000 · 9843
2000 · 6562
1000 · 3281
500 · 1640
200 · 656
0
LAND · B.S.L.
200 · 656
4000 · 13124
6000 · 19686

Conic Equidistant Projection

1 : 4 000 000

MILES 0 · 25 · 50 · 75

Longitude 4° west of Greenwich

A 10° B 8° C 6° D

ATLANTIC

OCEAN

Islay
Mull of Oa Gigha
Port Ellen
Campbeltown
Mull of Kintyre

Malin Head
West Town *Tory Island*
Bloody Foreland *Inishowen* Carndonagh
Gweedore Errigal Buncrana
Burtonport Letterkenny Rathlin Island
Aran Island Gweebarra Bay Lifford
Glenties Londonderry Limavady Coleraine
Malin More Donegal Strabane Dungiven Ballymoney
Rossan Point Killybegs Castlederg Cullybackey Ballymena Larne
Ballyshannon Omagh Cookstown Newtownstewart Magherafelt Antrim Ballyclare Whitehead
Bundoran Lower Dungannon Belfast Donaghadee
Benwee Head Lough Erne Portadown Lisburn Newtownards
Erris Head Killala Sligo Bay Sligo Enniskillen Armagh Banbridge Downpatrick
Belmullet Ballycastle Ballina Colloney Upper Lisnaskea Monaghan Clones Slieve Donard Newcastle
Blacksod Bay Lough Boyle Carrick- Cavan Castleblayney Warrenpoint Dundrum Bay
Achill Island Crough Castlebar on-Shannon Carrickmacross Dundalk Kilkeel
Clare Island Patrick Ballaghaderreen Longford Kells Dundalk Bay
Louisburgh Westport Claremorris Castlerea Lough Drogheda
Inishbofin CONNAUGHT Roscommon Sheelin Navan Balbriggan
Clifden Ballinrobe Lough Mask Tuam Lough Trim Skerries
Connemara Lough Ree Mullingar Swords
Gorumna Corrib Ballinasloe Athlone LEINSTER DUBLIN
Island Galway Loughrea Edenderry Leixlip Lucan Dún Laoghaire
Inishmore Galway Bay Portumna Tullamore Bog of Allen Naas Bray
Aran Islands Burren Shannon Birr Newbridge Greystones
Hag's Head Ennistymon Lough Portlaoise Athy Lugnaquilla Wicklow
Liscannor Bay REPUBLIC Derg Roscrea Mountain 926 Wicklow Head
Spanish Point Ennis Killaloe Nenagh Templemore Carlow Arklow
Kilkee OF Thurles Kilkenny Gorey
Loop Head Kilrush Limerick Tipperary Thomastown Enniscorthy
Mouth of the Shannon IRELAND Golden Vale Cashel Muine Bheag Wexford
Brandon Listowel Glanaruddery Mts Newcastle Galtymore Clonmel Carrick-on-Suir Rosslare
Mountain 953 West MUNSTER 920 Cahir New Ross Waterford
Tralee Newtown Comeragh Carnsore Point
Dingle Castleisland Mitchelstown Fermoy Mountains Tramore
Dingle Bay Kanturk Blackwater Dungarvan Helvick Head
Caherciveen Killarney Mallow Midleton Youghal
Magillycuddy's Lough Leane Macroom Cork Waterford Harbour St George's Channel
Reeks Carrauntoohil 1041 Bandon Cóbh
Sneem Kenmare Kinsale Clonakilty
Cahermore Bantry Bay Skibbereen Old Head of Kinsale
Dursey Island
Mizen Head Cape Clear

North Channel

Longitude 8° west of Greenwich

METRES	FEET
5000	16404
3000	9843
2000	6562
1000	3281
500	1640
200	656
0	0
LAND	B.S.L.
200	656
4000	13124
6000	19686

0 50 100 KILOMETRES

1 : 4 000 000

© Bartholomew Ltd

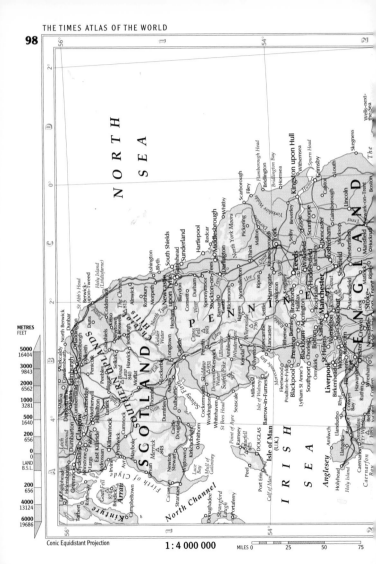

N O R T H S E A

Wells-next-the-Sea

Flamborough Head
Bridlington Bay
Bridlington
Skegness
The

Holy Island
(Lindisfarne)
Berwick-upon-Tweed
St Abb's Head

Scarborough
Filey
Hornsea
Kingston upon Hull
Withernsea
Spurn Head
Grimsby
Cleethorpes
Mablethorpe

Whitby
Redcar
Hartlepool
North York Moors
Pickering
Malton
Beverley
Selby
Market Weighton
Scunthorpe
Gainsborough
Lincoln
Boston

North Shields
South Shields
Sunderland
Gateshead
Middlesbrough
Stockton-on-Tees
Tees
Darlington
Northallerton
Thirsk
York
Doncaster
Retford
Newark-on-Trent

Alnwick
Rothbury
Morpeth
Newcastle upon Tyne
Consett
Durham
Spennymoor
Barnard Castle
Richmond
Ripon
Harrogate
Knaresborough
Leeds
Wakefield
Barnsley
Rotherham
Sheffield
Worksop
Mansfield
Chesterfield
Matlock

Kirkcaldy
Dunfermline
Edinburgh
Dunbar
North Berwick
Haddington
Coldstream
Kelso
Galashiels
Jedburgh
Hexham
Hawes
Wensleydale
Settle
Skipton
Keighley
Bradford
Halifax
Huddersfield
Dewsbury
Manchester
Stockport
Macclesfield
Stoke-on-Trent

E N G L A N D

Alloa
Stirling
Falkirk
Coatbridge
Motherwell
Hamilton
Lanark
Peebles
Selkirk
Moffat
Longtown
Carlisle
Penrith
Appleby
Cross Fell 893
Kirkby Stephen
Leyburn
Ingleborough 723

S C O T L A N D
S O U T H E R N U P L A N D S

P E N N I N E S

Greenock
Paisley
Glasgow
Dumbarton
Clydebank
Largs
Kilmarnock
Dumfries
Annan
Lockerbie
Gretna
Dalbeattie
Cockermouth
Workington
Whitehaven
Skiddaw 931
Derwent Water
Keswick
Ullswater
Windermere
Ambleside
Kendal
Sedbergh

Helvellyn 950
Scafell Pike 978
Lancaster
Morecambe
Fleetwood
Poulton-le-Fylde
Blackpool
Lytham St Anne's
Southport
Formby
Ormskirk
Preston
Chorley
Blackburn
Burnley
Accrington
Bolton
St Helens
Liverpool
Birkenhead
Chester
Crewe
Nantwich

Ayr
Prestwick
Troon
Kilmarnock
Maybole
East Kilbride
Cumnock
Newton Stewart
Wigtown
Stranraer
Kirkcudbright
Castle Douglas
Dalbeattie
Whithorn
Solway Firth
St Bees Head
Isle of Walney
Barrow-in-Furness
Ulverston
Millom
Seascale

I R I S H   S E A

Kintyre
Campbeltown
Arran
Firth of Clyde
Ailsa Craig
Merrick 842
Cairnsmore
of Fleet 711
Mull of Galloway
Luce Bay

North Channel

Isle of Man
(U.K.)
DOUGLAS
Ramsey
Peel
Port Erin
Calf of Man
Point of Ayre

Llandudno
Anglesey
Amlwch
Holyhead
Holy Island
Caernarfon
Caernarfon Bay

Strangford Lough

METRES
FEET

5000 / 16404
3000 / 9843
2000 / 6562
1000 / 3281
500 / 1640
200 / 656
0 / 0
LAND
B.S.L.
200 / 656
4000 / 13124
6000 / 19686

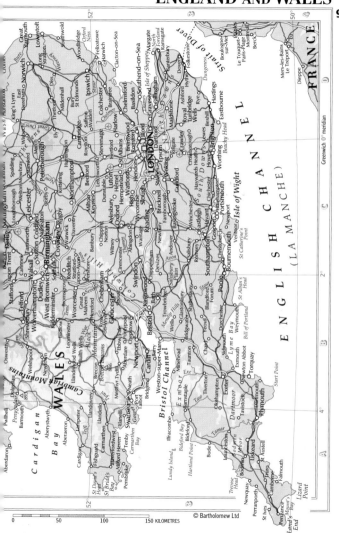

ENGLAND AND WALES

FRANCE

Strait of Dover

ENGLISH CHANNEL (LA MANCHE)

Greenwich 0° meridian

WALES

Cambrian Mountains

Cardigan Bay

Bristol Channel

Isle of Wight

LONDON

0   50   100   150 KILOMETRES

© Bartholomew Ltd

A   4°   B   6°   C   8°

NORTH SEA

East Frisian Islands
Spiekeroog Wangerooge
Langeoog Mellum
Norderney Juist Langeoog
Baltrum
Borkum Norderney Westerholt Wittmund
Norden
Wilhelmshaven

Waddeneilanden West-Terschelling Schiermonnikoog
Terschelling Ameland
West-Terschelling Oost-Vlieland Ferwerd Lauwersmeer Uithuizen Aurich Wiesmoor Westerstede
Vlieland Holwerd Birdaard Emden Ostfriesland
Waddenzee Dokkum Bedum Delfzijl Leer (Ostfriesland) Bad Zwischenahn
Texel Witmarsum Harlingen Damwoude Groningen Loppersum Strückhausen
Den Burg Bolsward Leeuwarden Hoogezand- Winschoten Papenburg Friesoythe
Den Helder Sneek Drachten Sappemeer Veendam Haren Oldenburg
Schagen Heerenveen Assen Stadskanaal Meppen Cloppenburg
Nieuwe-Niedorp Wolvega Beilen Emmen Haren (Ems) Lingen Bersenbrück
Heerhugowaard Urk Steenwijk Meppel Hoogeveen Quakenbrück (Ems) Fürstenau
Alkmaar Enkhuizen Emmeloord Hardenberg Groß-Hesepe Ibbenbüren
Castricum Berkhout Markermeer Kampen Zwolle Kloosterhaar Nordhorn Rheine Ibbenbüren
Beverwijk Purmerend Flevoland Ommen Gronau Ibbenbüren Osnabrück
IJmuiden Zaanstad **NETHERLANDS** Raalte Almelo Westfalen Greven
Haarlem **AMSTERDAM** Harderwijk Deventer Enschede Steinfurt
Katwijk aan Zee Amstelveen Hilversum Apeldoorn Gronau Ahaus **Münster**
Leiden Amersfoort Barneveld Zutphen Tilburg Coesfeld **Münsterland**
THE HAGUE Woerden Utrecht Ede Arnhem Hoog- Winterswijk Borken Dülmen Ahlen
('s-Gravenhage) Waddinxveen Barneveld Keppel Doetinchem Coesfeld Aschenberg Ahlen
(Den Haag) Gouda Veenendaal Wageningen Anholt Bocholt Dülmen Recklinghausen
Hoek van Holland Delft Capelle aan d'Ussel Nijmegen Kleve Wesel Marl Dortmund
(Hook of Holland) **Rotterdam** Maas Kranenburg Geldern Gelsenkirchen Bottrop Lünen
Hellevoetsluis Dordrecht 's-Hertogenbosch Goch Kevelaer Duisburg Bochum
Scharendijke Oosterhout Waalwijk Uden Wanroij Krefeld Moers Mülheim an der Ruhr Essen Iserlohn
Burgh Breda Tilburg Helmond St-Anthonis Viersen Mönchengladbach Düsseldorf Hagen
Middelburg Roosendaal Eindhoven Venray Straelen Neuss Remscheid Attendorn
Knokke- Bergen op Zoom Valkenswaard Weert Venlo Grevenbroich Leverkusen Plettenberg
Heist Philippine Kapellen Lommel Maaseik Herkenbosch Bergisch Gladbach Gummersbach
Zeebrugge Terneuzen St-Niklaas Geel Beringen Genk **Cologne** Wiehl Siegen
Ostend Maldegem **Antwerpen** Aarschot Hasselt Maastricht Bergheim (Köln) Kreuztal
(Oostende) Brugge (Anvers) Mechelen Tongeren Aachen Eschweiler Bonn Neuwied
Nieuwpoort Tielt Deinze Wichelen Aalst **BRUSSELS** Leuven Oupeye Düren Stolberg Euskirchen Siegburg
Veurne Torhout Gent Anderlecht **Bruxelles** Liège Kreuzau Bonn Altenkirchen
Diksmuide Wingene (Gand) Oudenaarde Nivelles Verviers Zülpich Mechernich Rennerod
Roeselare Mouscron **BELGIUM** Soignies Ottignies Braives Raeren Blankenheim Bad Neuenahr-Ahrweiler Westerburg
Ieper Ath Lens Tournai Charleroi Namur Andenne Malmedy Adenau Neuwied Timburg
Kortrijk Valenciennes Mons Thuin Assesse Ciney Marche- Vielsalm St-Vith Dahlem Hillesheim Koblenz Lahn
Aulnoye- Maubeuge Châtelet en-Famenne Prüm Kelberg Cochem
Aymeries Beaumont Philippeville La Roche- Bastogne Arzfeld Mayen
Caudry Avesnes- Couvin Rochefort en-Ardenne St-Hubert Bitburg Wittlich Manderscheid Blankenrath
La Capelle sur-Helpe Humay Wiltz Manderscheid Boppard
Hirson Rocroi St-Quentin Bogny-sur-Meuse Fleuze **LUXEMBOURG** Mersch Salmtal am Rhein
Vervins Rozoy-sur-Serre Charleville- Bouillon Neufchâteau Echternach Bernkastel-Kues Bad Kreuznach
Marle Mézières Vresse Mersch Morbach Idar-Oberstein
FRANCE Rethel Sedan **LUXEMBURG** Trier Birkenfeld Wolstein
Laon d'Ablaye Aymont Mouzon Virton Arlon **LUXEMBOURG** Reinsfeld Merzig St-Wendel
Soissons Guignicourt Vouziers Longuyon Mettlach

Conic Equidistant Projection

1:4 000 000

MILES 0   25   50   75

Longitude 6° east of Greenwich

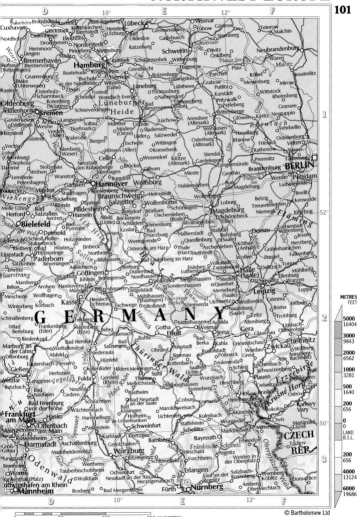

METRES	FEET
5000	16404
3000	9843
2000	6562
1000	3281
500	1640
200	656
0	0
	LAND B.S.L.
200	656
4000	13124
6000	19686

0   50   100   150 KILOMETRES

A   5°   B   10°   C

NORTH
SEA

Helgoländer
Bucht
Helgoland

East Frisian Islands

BALTIC

Kap Arkona

Zatoka
Pomorsk

NETHERLANDS

AMSTERDAM

Hamburg

Bremen

Hannover

BERLIN

GERMANY

Leipzig

Dresden

PRAGUE
(Praha)

CZECH

BEL

Cologne
(Köln)

Bonn

Frankfurt
am Main

Wiesbaden
Mainz

Mannheim
Heidelberg

LUXEMBOURG

Trier

Saarbrücken

Nürnberg

Regensburg

FRANCE

Strasbourg

Baden
Baden

Stuttgart

Ulm

Augsburg

Munich
(München)

AUS

Nancy

Mulhouse

Freiburg
im Breisgau

Zürich

Innsbruck

Salzburg

BERN

SWITZERLAND

LIECHTEN-
STEIN

ITALY

Bolzano

Trento

SLO

LJUBLJANA

METRES
FEET

5000
16404

3000
9843

2000
6562

1000
3281

500
1640

200
656

0
0
LAND
B.S.L.

200
656

4000
13124

6000
19686

Conic Equidistant Projection

B   Longitude 10° east of Greenwich   C

1 : 8 000 000

MILES 0   50   100   150

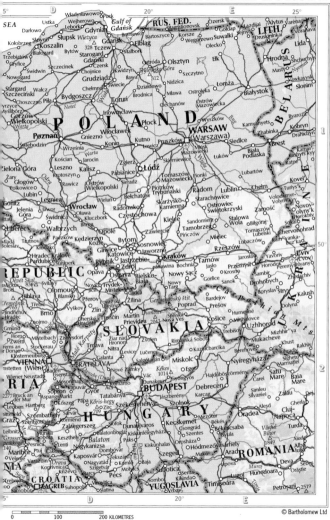

0   100   200 KILOMETRES

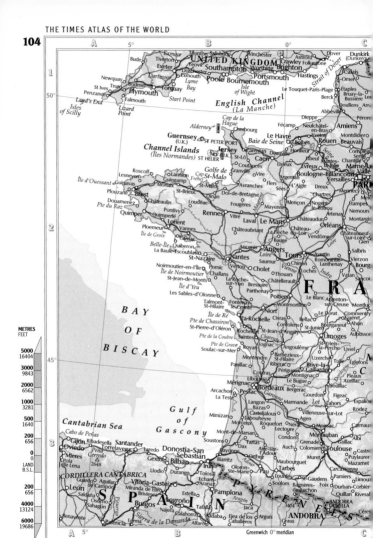

THE TIMES ATLAS OF THE WORLD

UNITED KINGDOM

Exmoor · Taunton · Salisbury · Winchester · Ashford · Dover · Dunkirk (Dunkerque)
Bude · Tiverton · Yeovil · Southampton · Worthing · Brighton · Hastings · Folkestone · Calais
Newquay · Honiton · Dorchester · Poole · Bournemouth · Portsmouth · St-Omer
St Ives · Truro · Bodmin · Dartmoor · Exmouth · Lyme · Isle of Wight · Le Touquet-Paris-Plage · Étaples · Bruay-la-Bussière
Penzance · Plymouth · Torquay · Bay · Start Point · English Channel (La Manche) · Berck · Doullens · Arras
Land's End · Falmouth · Lizard Point · Cap de la Hague · Cherbourg · Dieppe · Neufchâtel-en-Bray · Abbeville · Péronne
Isles of Scilly · Alderney · Fécamp · Amiens
Guernsey (U.K.) · ST PETER PORT · Baie de Seine · Le Havre · Montdidier
Channel Islands (Îles Normandes) · Jersey (U.K.) · ST HELIER · Carentan · Caen · Honfleur · Bolbec · Rouen · Beauvais
St-Lô · Coutances · Lisieux · Évreux · Les Andelys · Compiègne · Senlis
Roscoff · Lannion · St-Malo · Granville · Vire · Argentan · L'Aigle · Dreux · Chantilly · Marne-la-Vallée
Lesneven · Guingamp · Fréhel · Dol-de-Bretagne · Flers · Sées · Chartres · Mantes · Versailles · PARIS
Île d'Ouessant · Guipavas · Morlaix · St-Brieuc · Fougères · Mayenne · Alençon · Nogent-le-Rotrou · Montlhéry
Plouzané · Brest · Châteaulin · Dinan · Loudéac · Laval · Le Mans · Châteaudun · Étampes · Nemours
Douarnenez · Quimperlé · Pontivy · Rennes · Vitré · La Flèche · Vendôme · Orléans · Montargis
Pte du Raz · Quimper · Ploemeur · Lorient · Vannes · Châteaubriant · Baugé · Château-du-Loir · Châteauneuf-sur-Loire · Gien
Île de Groix · Ancenis · Angers · Saumur · Tours · Avertin · Romorantin-Lanthenay · Salbris · Vierzon · Bourges
Belle-Île · Quiberon · La Baule-Escoublac · St-Nazaire · Nantes · Cholet · Chinon · Loches · Indre · Vatan · Sancoi
Noirmoutier-en-l'Île · Pornic · Vertou · Vienne · Thouars · Loudun · Poitiers · Le Blanc · Argenton-sur-Creuse · Montluç
Île de Noirmoutier · St-Jean-de-Monts · Challans · La Roche-sur-Yon · Bressuire · Parthenay · Montmorillon · Bélabre · Le Dorat · Commentry · Guéret
Île d'Yeu · Les Sables-d'Olonne · Talmont-St-Hilaire · Fontenay-le-Comte · Niort · Civray · St-Junien · Limoges · La Souterraine · Ahun · Aubusson

FRANCE

Île de Ré · Pte de Chassiron · La Rochelle
St-Pierre-d'Oléron · Rochefort · St-Jean-d'Angély · Bellac · Bourganeuf · Ussel
Pte de la Coubre · Saintes · Cognac · Angoulême · St-Yrieix-la-Perche · Uzerche · Egletons
Royan · Barbezieux-St-Hilaire · Ribérac · Brive-la-Gaillarde · Tulle · Pleaux · Aurillac
Soulac-sur-Mer · Pte de Grave · Montendre · Périgueux · Montignac · Souillac
Pauillac · Coutras · Libourne · Bergerac · Gourdon · Espalion
Arcachon · Mérignac · Pessac · BORDEAUX · Le Bugue · Dordogne
La Teste · Langon · Marmande · Lot · Cahors · Rodez
Mimizan · Bazas · Casteljaloux · Villeneuve-sur-Lot · Agen · Caussade
Labouheyre · Nérac · Moissac · Carmaux
Mont-de-Marsan · Lectoure · Condom · Montauban · Albi
Soustons · Tartas · Auch · Colomiers · Gaillac · Castre
Dax · Aire-sur-l'Adour · TOULOUSE · Puylaurens · Mazamet
Bayonne · Orthez · Pau · Maubourguet · Muret · Carcassonne
Biarritz · Oloron-Ste-Marie · Tarbes · Lourdes · St-Gaudens · Pamiers · Quillan
Irún · Bagnères-de-Luchon · St-Girons · Foix · Durban-Corbières
PYRÉNÉES · ANDORRA LA VELLA · Rivesal
ANDORRA · Céret

Cabo de Peñas · Ribadesella · Santander
Gijón · Oviedo · Torrelavega · Laredo · Donostia-San Sebastián
Mieres · Peña Cerredo 2648 · Bilbao · Gexto · Bayonne
Pola de Lena · Llodio · Durango · Tolosa · Echarri-Aranaz
CORDILLERA CANTÁBRICA · Vitoria-Gasteiz · Irún · Pamplona
Guardo · Aguilar de Campóo · Miranda de Ebro · Estella
León · Saldaña · Briviesca · Logroño · Aragón · Jaca
Osorno · Sahagún · Burgos · Nájera · Calahorra · Alsasua · Ejea de los Caballeros · Graus
Benavente · Palencia · Lerma · Sierra de la Demanda · Aranda · Alfaro · Zaragoza

SPAIN

Cantabrian Sea

BAY OF BISCAY

Gulf of Gascony

Greenwich 0° meridian

Conic Equidistant Projection

1:8 000 000

MILES 0 · 50 · 100 · 150

METRES / FEET
5000 / 16404
3000 / 9843
2000 / 6562
1000 / 3281
500 / 1640
200 / 656
0 / 0
LAND B.S.L.
200 / 656
4000 / 13124
6000 / 19686

FRANCE AND SWITZERLAND

Brugge • Antwerpen
BRUSSELS • Genk • Düsseldorf • Remscheid • Eisenach • Gotha
(Bruxelles) • Hasselt • Maastricht • Cologne • Siegen • Bad Hersfeld • Bad Salzungen • Suhl • Hof • Gera • Zwickau
Roeselare • Liège • Aachen (Köln) • Leverkusen • Schwarzenberg
Roubaix • BELGIUM • Bonn • Wetzlar • Bad Salzungen • Suhl • Coburg • Kulmbach • Karlovy
Lille • Charleroi • Namur • Andenne • Malmédy • Koblenz • Neuwied • Gießen • GERMANY • Bamberg • Bayreuth • Plauen
Douai • Cambrai • Dinant • Bastogne • Bitburg • Frankfurt am Main • Offenbach • Schweinfurt • Würzburg • Bamberg • in der Oberpfalz
St-Quentin • Hirson • Fumay • Bouillon • Arlon • Trier • Idar-Oberstein • Darmstadt • Würzburg • Erlangen • Amberg • Schwandorf
Noyon • Charleville- • LUXEMBOURG • Merzig • Ludwigshafen • Mannheim • Ansbach • Nürnberg • Regensburg
Soissons • Mézières • Thionville • Saarbrücken • am Rhein • Heidelberg • Mosbach • Speyer • Roth • Straubing
Reims • Metz • Pont-à- • Saarlouis • Karlsruhe • Heilbronn • Nördlingen • Ingolstadt • Landshut • Isar
Château- • Châlons-en- • Freyming- • Merlebach • Bitche • Pforzheim • Ludwigsburg • Göppingen • Donauwörth • Augsburg • Freising
Thierry • Champagne • Bar-le-Duc • Nancy • Sarreguemines • Baden- • Stuttgart • Ulm • Günzburg • Dachau
Sézanne • Vitry-le- • St-Dizier • Joinville • Lunéville • Saverne • Baden • Offenburg • Reutlingen • Tübingen • Biberach an der Riß • MUNICH
Sens • François • Bar-sur- • Vittel • Remiremont • Colmar • Villingen • Balingen • Memmingen • Kempten (München) • Rosenheim
Troyes • Aube • Chaumont • Épinal • Luxeuil- • Mulhouse • Freiburg • Rottweil • Sigmaringen • (Allgäu) • Garmisch- • Kufstein
Auxerre • Chatillon- • Langres • les-Bains • im Breisgau • Schaffhausen • Konstanz • Ravensburg • Partenkirchen • Wörgl
Clamecy • Avallon • sur-Seine • Gray • Vesoul • BASEL • Winterthur • Friedrichshafen • Landeck • AUSTRIA
Cosne- • Semur-en- • Baume-les- • (Basle) • St.Gallen • Bregenz • Bludenz • Merano • Brixen
Cours- • Auxois • Dijon • Dames • Delémont • ZÜRICH • LIECHTEN- • Chur • Brenner-paß • Bolzano
sur-Loire • Saulieu • Nuits-St- • Dole • Biel • STEIN • Davos • Scuol
Nevers • Autun • Georges • Besançon • BERN • Luzern • Zug • Schwyz • St.Moritz • DOLOMITI
Chalon- • Pontarlier • Neuchâtel • Altdorf • Chiavenna • Tirano • Trento
sur-Saône • Lausanne • Thun • SWITZERLAND • Passo del • Feltre
N • C • E • Louhans • Frutigen • Interlaken • Jungfrau • San Gottardo • Lago di Como • Bellinzona
St-Pourcain- • Digoin • Tournus • Montreux • Brig • Biasca • Como • Bergamo • Brescia • Vicenza • Verona • Padua
sur-Sioule • Paray-le- • Mâcon • St-Claude • Sion • Zermatt • Locarno • Lugano • Monza • ITALY • (Padova) • Rovigo
Vichy • Monial • Bourg-en- • Montreux • Matterhorn • Lago • MILAN • Treviglio • Brescia • Cremona • Mantova
Riom • Thiers • Roanne • Bresse • Cluses • Mont- • di Garda • (Milano) • Vercelli • Piacenza • Parma • Ferrara
Clermont- • Villeurbanne • Annecy • Blanc • Borgosesia • Biella • Pavia • Modena • Bologna
Ferrand • LYON • Givors • Aix-les- • Ivrea • Novara • Alessandria • Reggio nell'Emilia • Imola
Issoire • Montbrison • Chambéry • Bains • Cuorgnè • Cirié • TURIN • Acqui • Novi Ligure • Monte • Pistoia • Prato
A S S I F • Firminy • St-Étienne • Voiron • St-Jean-de- • Modane • (Torino) • Terme • Savona • Carrara • Cimone • FLORENCE
N T R A L • Le Puy- • Yssingeaux • Grenoble • Oulx • Moncalieri • Asti • Fossano • Mondovi • La Spezia • Viareggio • Pisa • (Firenze) • Siena
Saugues • en-Velay • St-Bonnet- • Briançon • Cuneo • Sestri • Carrara • Livorno
Flour • Mende • Aubenas • Montélimar • en-Champsaur • Gap • Barcelonnette • GENOA • Levante • Cecina
Séverac-le- • Villefort • Vans • Bollène • Valréas • Digne-les- • Tende • San Remo • (Genova) • Empoli • San Vincenzo
Château • Millau • Uzès • Orange • Carpentras • Sisteron • Bains • Imperia • Albenga • Ligurian • Isola
Lodève • Ganges • Avignon • Manosque • Grasse • MONACO • Capo Mele • di Capraia
Montpellier • Nîmes • Arles • Aix-en- • Cannes • Nice • Sea • Cap Corse • Grosseto
Béziers • Vauvert • Marignane • Provence • Antibes • Capo • Castiglione • della Pescaia
Narbonne • Châteauneuf-les- • Martigues • St-Tropez • Corse • Orbetello
Étang de Leucate • Montpellier • Marseille • La Ciotat • Cap de St-Tropez • L'Île-Rousse • Bastia
Perpignan • Six-Fours-les-Plages • Toulon • Îles d'Hyères • Calvi • Vescovato
Port-Vendres • Cap • Sicié • Hyères • Corsica • Porte • Cervione
Figueres • Cap de Creus • (Corse) • (France) • Corte • Isola di Pianosa
MEDITERRANEAN SEA • Capo Rosso • Monte • Prunelli-di-Fiumorbo
Ajaccio • Rotondo • Ghisonaccia
2622 • Sartène • Porto-Vecchio
Capo di Feno • Bonifacio • Ozzana

0 ——— 100 ——— 200 KILOMETRES

© Bartholomew Ltd

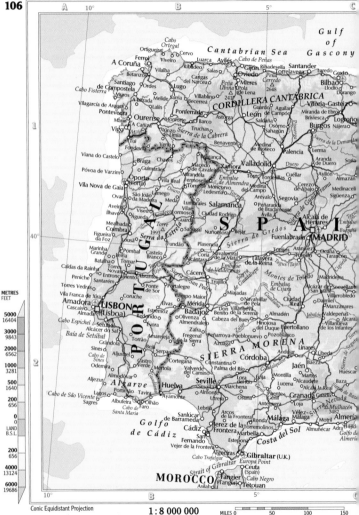

Gulf
of
Gascony

Cantabrian Sea

Cabo
Ortegal
Ortigueira   Cervo
Ferrol   Viveiro   Luarca   Avilés   Cabo de Peñas   Santander
A Coruña   Ribadeo   Gijón   Ribadesella   Torrelavega   Laredo Gexto
Betanzos   Vilalba   Salas   Oviedo   Peña   Bilbao   Llodio
Santiago   Ordes   Cangas   Mieres   Cerredo   Durango
de Compostela   Lugo   del Narcea   Pola   △2648
Muros   Melide   Sarria   Becerreá   Villablino   de Lena   2417   Vitoria-Gasteiz   Miranda de Ebro
Vilagarcía de Arousa   A Estrada   CORDILLERA CANTÁBRICA   Logroño
Pontevedra   Ourense   Ponferrada   León   de Campóo   Burgos   Nájera
Marín   A Cañiza   Monforte   Astorga   Saldaña   Sahagún   Sierra de la Demanda
Vigo   Xinzo de Limia   Barco   Truchas   Benavente   Medina   Lerma   Aranda
Tui   Verín   Sierra de la Cabrera   de Rioseco   Palencia   de Duero
Fondevila   Puebla   Bragança   Zamora   Valladolid   Duero   Ayllón
Viana do Castelo   Chaves   Macedo   Toro   Tordesillas   Cuéllar   Medinaceli
Braga   Guimarães   de Cavaleiros   Medina   Arévalo   Segovia   Sigüenza
Póvoa de Varzim   Vila Real   Fermoselle   del Campo   Peñaranda   Embalse
Oporto   Mirandela   Torre de Moncorvo   de Bracamonte   de Burguillo
Vila Nova de Gaia   (Porto)   São João   Lamego   Salamanca   MADRID
Ovar   da Madeira   Meda   Lumbrales   Ciudad Rodrigo   Béjar   Fuenlabrada
Aveiro   Viseu   Vilar Formoso   Guarda   SPAIN   Alcalá de Henares
Ílhavo   Mealhada   Sabugal   Nuñomoral   Sierra de Gredos   Aranjuez   Ocaña   Tarancón
Coimbra   Torre   Plasencia   Navalmoral   Torrijos   Toledo
Figueira da Foz   1993   Fundão   Coria   de la Mata   Talavera   Montes de Toledo   Madridejos
Lousã   Castelo Branco   Navalvillar   de la Reina   Embalse   Alcázar de San Juan
Marinha Grande   Pombal   Alcántara   Cáceres   de Pela   de Cíjara   Villarrobledo
Batalha   Tomar   Abrantes   Trujillo   Ciudad   Manzanares
Torres Novas   Entroncamento   Ponte   Cáceres   Real   Valdepeñas
Caldas da Rainha   Santarém   de Sor   Portalegre   Miajadas   Navalvillar de Pela
Torres Vedras   Coruche   Elvas   Campo Maior   Valverde   Almadén   Alcaraz
Vila Franca de Xira   Amadora   Estremoz   Mérida   Badajoz   Cabeza del Buey   Puertollano   Pozoblanco   Villanueva de los Infantes
Cascais   (Lisboa)   Olivenza   Almendralejo   San Benito de la Serena   Peñarroya-Pueblonuevo   Andújar
LISBON   Évora   Zafra   Fregenal   Hinojosa   Azuaga   Linares   Úbeda   Huéscar
Setúbal   Amareleja   de la Sierra   del Duque   Córdoba   Jaén   Baza
Alcácer do Sal   SIERRA MORENA   Martos   Baza
Baía de Setúbal   Torrão   Constantina   Palma del Río   Montilla   Alcaudete   Alcalá la Real
Sines   Beja   Guadalquivir   Lucena   Granada   Guadix
Cabo de Sines   Aljustrel   Valverde   Lora   Écija   Antequera   Vélez-   Sierra Nevada   Almería
Odemira   Almodôvar   del Camino   Seville   Osuna   Rubio   Mulhacén   △3482
Aljezur   Castro Verde   (Sevilla)   Marchena   Ronda   Málaga   Motril   Golfo de
Algarve   Mértola   Huelva   Utrera   Fuengirola   Costa del Sol   Almuñécar
Lagos   Portimão   Tavira   Ayamonte   Lebrija   Arcos de la Frontera
Cabo de São Vicente   Albufeira   Olhão   Sanlúcar   Jerez de la   Marbella   Estepona
Sagres   Cabo de Faro   de Barrameda   Frontera   Algeciras   Gibraltar (U.K.)
Santa Maria   Cádiz   San   Europa Point
Golfo   Fernando   Ceuta
de Cádiz   Vejer de la Frontera   (Spain)   Cabo Negro
Cabo Trafalgar   Strait of Gibraltar   MOROCCO   Tangier   Tetouan
Asilah   Tanger

PORTUGAL

Serra da Estrela

Sierra de San Pedro

METRES
FEET

5000   16404
3000   9843
2000   6562
1000   3281
500   1640
200   656
0   0
LAND   B.S.L.
200   656
4000   13124
6000   19686

METRES
FEET

5000
16404

3000
9843

2000
6562

1000
3281

500
1640

200
656

0
0
LAND
B.S.L.

200
656

4000
13124

6000
19686

Conic Equidistant Projection   1 : 8 000 000

MILES 0   50   100   150

Longitude 10° east of Greenwich

ITALY

ROME (Roma)
VATICAN CITY

Naples (Napoli)

Florence (Firenze)

Genoa (Genova)

Milan (Milano)

Turin (Torino)

SAN MARINO

MONACO

MONTE-CARLO

Nice
Antibes
Cannes
Grasse

Venice (Venezia)

Trieste

LJUBLJANA

SLO

Sardinia (Sardegna) (Italy)

Cagliari

Sassari

Oristano

Corsica (Corse) (France)

Ajaccio
Bastia

Sicily (Sicilia)

Palermo

Marsala
Trapani
Agrigento

Ligurian
Sea

TYRRHENIAN

SEA

ADRIATIC

MEDITERRANEAN   SEA

Sicilian Channel

0   100   200 KILOMETRES

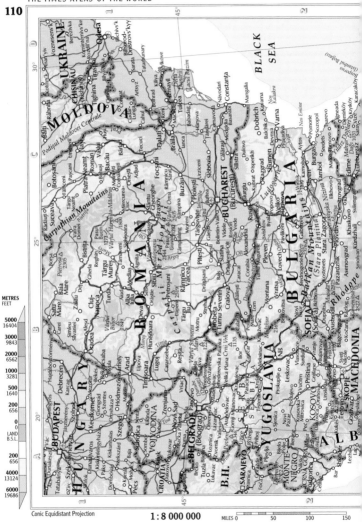

METRES
FEET

5000	16404
3000	9843
2000	6562
1000	3281
500	1640
200	656
0	0
LAND	
B.S.L.	
200	656
4000	13124
6000	19686

Conic Equidistant Projection

1 : 8 000 000

MILES 0   50   100   150

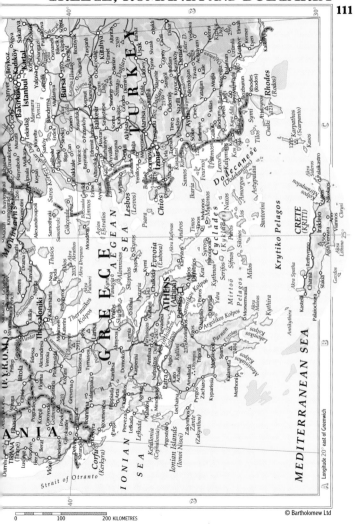

0   100   200 KILOMETRES

112

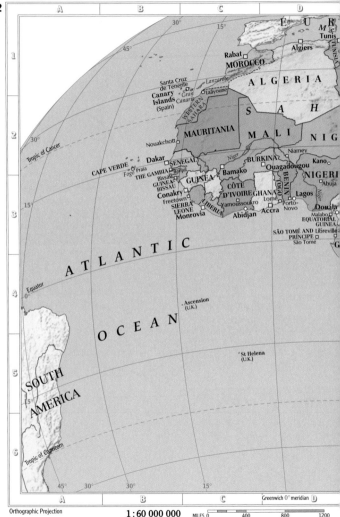

Tunis

Algiers

Rabat
MOROCCO

ALGERIA

Santa Cruz
de Tenerife   Lanzarote
Canary   Gran   Laâyoune
Islands   Canaria
(Spain)   WESTERN SAHARA   S A H A

MAURITANIA   M A L I   N I G

Nouakchott

Niamey   Kano

Tropic of Cancer

Dakar   SENEGAL   BURKINA   NIGERI
CAPE VERDE   Niger   Ouagadougou
Fogo Praia   THE GAMBIA Banjul   Bamako   Abuja
Bissau   BENIN
GUINEA-   Lagos
Conakry   BISSAU   GUINEA   CÔTE   GHANA   TOGO   Porto-
Freetown   D'IVOIRE   Lomé   Novo
SIERRA   LIBERIA   Yamoussoukro   Accra   Douala
LEONE   Malabo
Monrovia   Abidjan   EQUATORIAL
                                               GUINEA
                        SÃO TOMÉ AND Libreville
                        PRÍNCIPE
A T L A N T I C   São Tomé   G

O C E A N   Ascension
                      (U.K.)

Equator

St Helena
(U.K.)

SOUTH

AMERICA

Tropic of Capricorn

1 : 60 000 000   MILES 0   400   800   1200

Greenwich 0° meridian

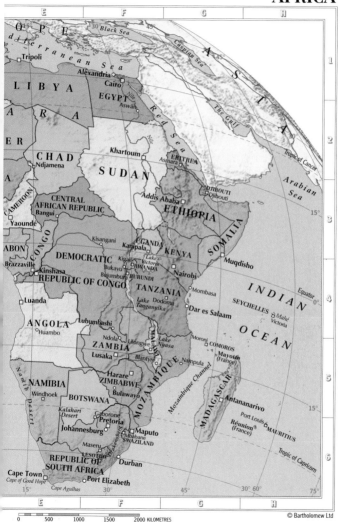

0   500   1000   1500   2000 KILOMETRES

114

20° A 10°

ATLANTIC OCEAN

SPAIN
Cartagena
Almería
Ech
Gibraltar (U.K.)
Málaga
Mostaganem
Strait of Gibraltar
Oran
Tangier
Ceuta (Spain)
Sidi Bel
Tetouan
Melilla
Abbès
Tlemcen
Larache
Ksar el Kebir
Faza
Kenitra
Oujda
RABAT
Meknès
Fès (Fez)
Sidi Kacem
Casablanca
El Jadida
Settat
MOROCCO
Safi
Marrakech
Haut Atlas (High Atlas)
Bou Arfa
Aïn Sefra
Essaouira
ATLAS
Ksar
Béchar
Madeira (Portugal)
FUNCHAL
Agadir
Taroudannt
4167
Ouarzazate
Rachidia
Abadla
Grand Erg
Anti Atlas
Beni-
Occidental
Tiznit
Sidi Ifni
Guelmine
Hammada du Drâa
Tabelbala
El Homr

Lanzarote
SANTA
CRUZ DE
TENERIFE
La Palma
Tenerife
Gran
Canaria
Fuerteventura
La Gomera
El Hierro
Canary Islands
(Islas Canarias)
(Spain)
LAS PALMAS
DE GRAN
CANARIA
LAAYOUNE
Es Semara
ALGE
Ksabi
Timimoun
El Eglab
Reggane
In Salah
Sebkha
Mekerrhane
Boujdour
Tindouf
Bir
Moghrein
Galtat
Zemmour
Aïn
Ben Tili
Chegga
Sebkha Azzel
Matti
Tropic of Cancer
Ad Dakhla
WESTERN
SAHARA
El Hammâmi
CHECH
Taoudenni
Taouzrout
Tichla
Zouérat
Fdérik
Choûm
OURÂNE
ERG
S A H
Nouâdhibou
Atâr
Nouâmghâr
Akjoujt
Araouane
Adrar
des
Ifoghas
NOUAKCHOTT
Boutilimit
Tidjikja
Tichît
Anéfis
Kidal
MAURITANIA
Oualâta
MALI
Rosso
Aleg
HÔD
Ayoûn el
Atroûs
Néma
Gourma-
Rharous
St Louis
Dagana
Kaédi
Kiffa
IRÎGUI
Lac
Faguibine
Bourem
Louga
Linguère
Matam
Sélibaby
Nioro
Bassikounou
Timbédgha
Timbouctou
Goundam
Gao
DAKAR
Diourbel
Bakel
Yélimané
Nara
Nampala
Mopti
Hombori
Ansongo
Mbour
Kaolack
Koungheul
Tambacounda
Diéma
Ténenkou
Bandiagara
Gorom-
Gorom
Tillabéri
SENEGAL
Kédougou
Kita
Bafoulabé
Kayes
Nono
Massina
Koro
Ouahigouya
Djibo
NIAMEY
BANJUL
THE GAMBIA
Ziguinchor
Kolda
Kolokani
Ségou
Bla
Koutiala
San
Toma
Yako
Kaya
Bogandé
Dosso
Cacheu
GUINEA-
BISSAU
Gabú
Labé
Dabola
Koulikoro
BAMAKO
Koudougou
Fada-Ngourma
Diapaga
Kandi
CONAKRY
Kindia
Kissidougou
Kankan
Sikasso
Bobo-
Dioulasso
OUAGADOUGOU
BURKINA
Manga
Tenkodogo
Dapaong
Natitingou
Djougou
BENIN
Parakou
FREETOWN
SIERRA
LEONE
GUINEA
Macenta
Man
Odienné
Korhogo
Banfora
Tawra
Bolgatanga
Yendi
GHANA
CÔTE
D'IVOIRE
Bouaké
Sunyani
Tamale
Kumasi
Savé
PORTO-NOVO
Lagos
MONROVIA
LIBERIA
YAMOUSSOUKRO
Abidjan
Aboisso
Cape Coast
ACCRA
Abeokuta
Slave Coast
Buchanan
Greenville
Harper
San-Pédro
Tabou
Cape Palmas
GULF OF GUINEA
Gold Coast
Bight of Benin

Lambert Azimuthal
Equal Area Projection

METRES
FEET
5000 16404
3000 9843
2000 6562
1000 3281
500 1640
200 656
0 0
LAND
B.S.L.
200 656
4000 13124
6000 19686

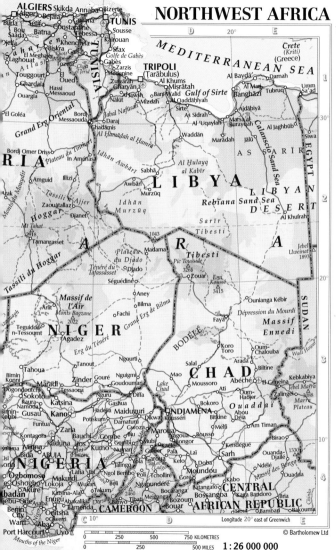

ALGIERS Skikda Annaba Bizerte
Algér Béjaïa Sétif Guelma TUNIS
Blida Bou Constantine Sousse
Saâda Batna Tébessa
Djelfa Khenchela Kairouan
Laghouat Biskra Gafsa Sfax
El Meghaier Golfe de Gabès
Touggourt Gabès
El Zarzis
Oued Médenine
Ghardaïa Hassi Zuwārah
Ouargla Messaouda Gharyān Al Khums Miṣrātah
El Goléa Bordj Nālūt Banī Walīd Qaddāḥiyah
Messaouda Ghadāmis Mizdah
Daraj As Sidrah
Bordj Omer Driss Al Ḥumaydah al Ḥamrā Al 'Uqaylah
In Amenas Ajdābiyā
Amguid Sabhā Marādah Jālū
Illizi Awbārī Al Khufrah
Zaouatallaz Murzūq Rebiana
Djanet Idhān Sand
Murzūq Sea
Plateau du Djado Madama Tibesti
Ténéré du Djado Pic Toussīde
Tafassâsset Zouar
Séguédine Aney
Massif de Bilma
l'Aïr Fachi Grand Erg de Bilma
Arlit Faya
Teguidda Agadez Erg du Ténéré
n-Tessoumt Koro
Tahoua Tanout Ngourti Toro
Birnin Zinder Nguigmi Salal Arada Biltine
Konni Maradi Gouré Goudoumaria Mao
Dogondoutchi Tessaoua Diffa Moussoro Ati
Sokoto Nguru Gashua Oum-
Katsina Hadejia Maiduguri Hadjer Abéché El Geneina
Gusau Kano Potiskum Damaturu Dikwa NDJAMÉNA Bokoro Bitkine Abou
Funtua Bauchi Gombe Gwoza Maroua Mora Bongor Melfi Am Timan
Zaria Kaduna Jos Biu Numan Guider Kélo Doba Kendégué Birao
Kontagora Bida Minna Kumo Garoua Pala Laï Sarh Ouanda-
Lafia Ngol Bembo Poli Moundou Djallé
Ogbomosho Makurdi Wukari Takum Ngaoundéré Kabo Massif des Bongo
Oshogbo Oyo Lokoja Katsina-Ala Banyo Meiganga Batangafo Bossangoa Bouar CENTRAL Ouadda
Ibadan Enugu Abakaliki Bamenda Bozoum
Jebu-Ode Asaba Onitsha CAMEROON Bocaranga AFRICAN REPUBLIC
Benin Owerri
City Aba Uyo
Port Harcourt
Mouths of the Niger

A L G E R I A

TUNISIA

MEDITERRANEAN SEA

Crete
(Kriti)
(Greece)

TRIPOLI
(Ṭarābulus)

Gulf of Sirte

Al Baydā' Darnah
Al Marj Tubruq
Banghāzī Umm
Saʿad

L I B Y A

Sirte
Marsā al
Burayqah

Al Jaghbūb
Siwa

Waddān

EGYPT

L I B Y A N
D E S E R T

A S   S A R Ī R
Sand Sea

Jebel
Uweinat
1893

S A H A R A

Sarīr
Tibesti

Emi
Koussi
3415

Ounianga Kébir

Dépression du Mourdi

Massif
Ennedi

BODÉLÉ

Oum-
Chalouba

Wadi Howar

SUDAN

Lake
Chad

C H A D

Ouaddai

Jebel Marra
Jebel Marra
Marra
Plateau

Kebkabiya

Zalingei

1330

Longitude 20° east of Greenwich

© Bartholomew Ltd

0   250   500   750 KILOMETRES
0   250   500 MILES

1 : 26 000 000

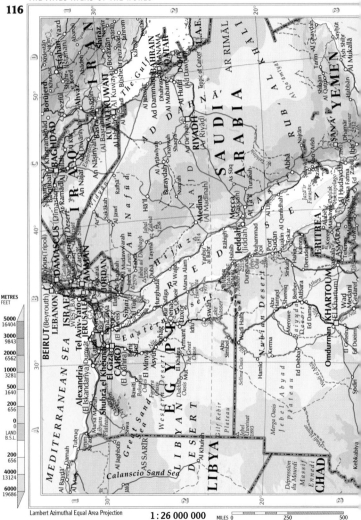

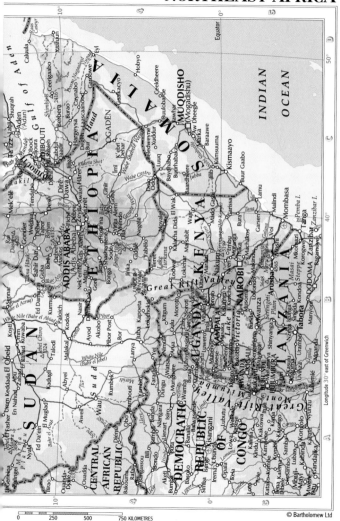

0   250   500   750 KILOMETRES

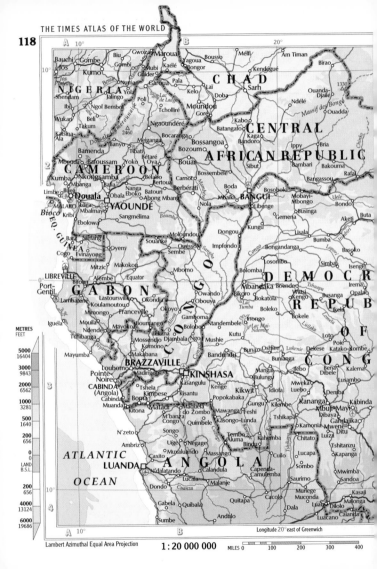

CENTRAL AFRICA

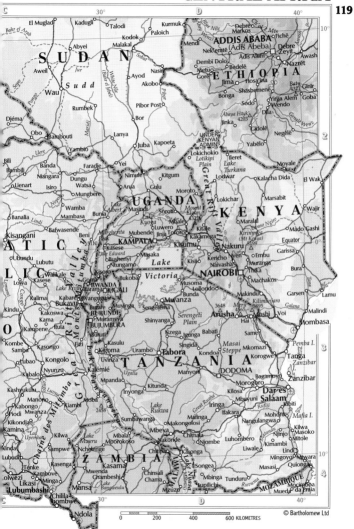

119

0   200   400   600 KILOMETRES

© Bartholomew Ltd

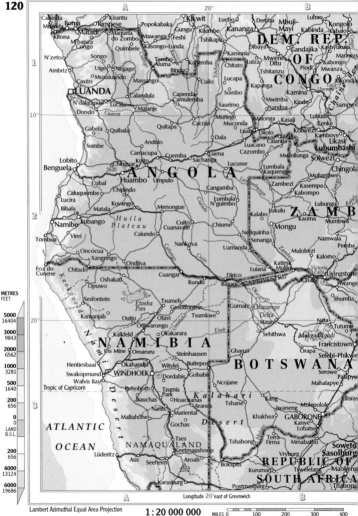

METRES
FEET

5000	16404
3000	9843
2000	6562
1000	3281
500	1640
200	656
0	0
LAND	B.S.L.
200	656
4000	13124
6000	19686

Lambert Azimuthal Equal Area Projection

Longitude 20° east of Greenwich

1 : 20 000 000

MILES 0   100   200   300   400

INDIAN OCEAN

COMOROS

MORONI · Grande Comore

Mayotte (France)

TANZANIA

MALAWI

MOZAMBIQUE

ZIMBABWE

ZAMBIA

LUSAKA

HARARE

MADAGASCAR

ANTANANARIVO

MAPUTO

SWAZILAND

PRETORIA

Johannesburg

INDIAN OCEAN

Tropic of Capricorn

© Bartholomew Ltd

0   200   400   600 KILOMETRES

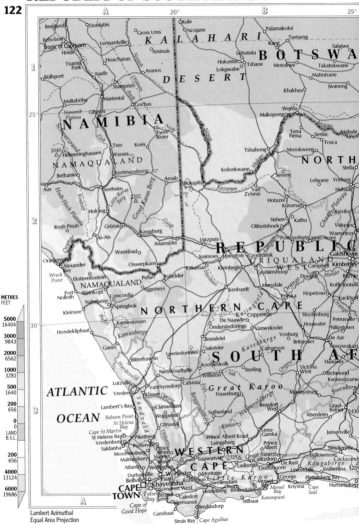

20°   A   B   25°

METRES
FEET

5000
16404

3000
9843

2000
6562

1000
3281

500
1640

200
656

0
0
**LAND
B.S.L.**

200
656

4000
13124

6000
19686

Lambert Azimuthal
Equal Area Projection

Berglund · Dordabis · Gross Ums · Kule · Palamakoloi
Rehoboth · Leopardville · Ncojane · Kang · Tsetseng · Salajwe
Tropic of Capricorn · Heide · Aminuis · Lehututu · BOTSWA
Tsumis · Hoachanas · Hukuntsi · Tshane · Motokwe · Takatokwane
Park · Narib · Lokgwabe · Mabutsane · Jwaneng
Büllsport · Khakhea

Nanami · Stampriet · DESERT
Plateau · Mariental · Werda
Maltahöhe · Gibeon · Gochas · Makopong
25° · NAMIBIA · Terra Firma · Senlac · Mabule
Tses · Tweer · Rivier · Tshabong · Morokweng · Tosca
2040 · Helmeringhausen · Wasser · Koës · NORTH
NAMAQUALAND · Keetmanshoop · Kolonkwane · Stella
Bethanie · Aroab · Severn · Lolwane · Vryburg
Aus · Seeheim · 1202 · Bokspits · Van · Huhudi
Holoog · Grünau · Karasburg · Ariamsvlei · Zylsrus · Hotazel · Sishen · Kuruman · Reivilo · Valspan
Rosh Pinah · Ai-Ais · Warmbad · Lutzputs · Keimoes · Upington · Groottrink · Olifantshoek · Kathu · Warrenton
Orangemund · Alexander · Onseepkans · Kakamas · Grootdrink · Groblershoop · Priska · REPUBLIC
Bay · Eksteenfontein · Pella · Pofadder · Kleinbegin · GRIQUALAND · Galeshewe
Wreck · Aggeneys · Kenhardt · WEST · Kimberley
Point · Port · Concordia · Marydale · Douglas · Ritchie
Nolloth · Nababeep · Springbok · Hopetown · Koffiefontein
Kleinsee · Kamieskroon · De Naawte · Coppeton · Strydenburg · Luckhoff
Hondeklipbaai · Kamiesberg · Onderstedorings · Vanwyksvlei · Vosburg · Houwater · Petrusville
30° · Garies · Brandvlei · Carnarvon · Britstown · De Aar · Philipstown · Nonzwakazi
NORTHERN CAPE · Sakrivier · SOUTH · Hanover
Bitterfontein · Loeriesfontein · Kootjieskolk · Williston · Sterling · Victoria · Richmond · AF
ATLANTIC · Lutzville · Nieuwoudtville · Sak · West · Kwanonzame
Vredendal · Vanrhynsdorp · Calvinia · Fraserburg · Murraysburg · Graaf-
OCEAN · Klawer · Great Karoo · Beaufort · Reinet · Sneuberg
Baboon Point · Lambert's Bay · Sutherland · West · Aberdeen · Jansenville
St Helena Bay · Clanwilliam · Komsberg · Kougabe...
Cape St Martin · Citrusdal · Wuppertal · Prince · Willowmore
St Helena Bay · Piketberg · Laingsburg · Albert · Joubertina
Vredenburg · Porterville · Touwsrivier · Ladismith · Oudtshoorn · Cockscomb
Saldanha · Moorreesburg · WESTERN · Montagu · De Rust · Humansdorp
Atlantis · Malmesbury · Prince · Ladismith · Uniondale
Durbanville · Wellington · Worcester · Robertson · Mossel · Knysna · Cape
Bellville · Paarl · Montagu · Swellendam · Bay · Seal
CAPE · Khayelitsha · Somerset West · Heidelberg · Riversdale · George
TOWN · False Bay · Strand · Caledon · Mossel
Cape of · Gansbaai · Bredasdorp · Stilbaai · Kanonpunt
Good Hope · Struis Bay · Cape Agulhas

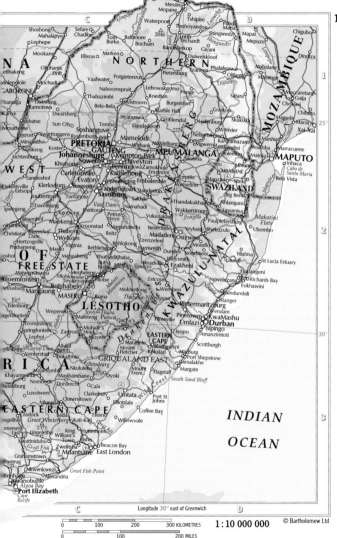

INDIAN

OCEAN

0   100   200   300 KILOMETRES

0   100   200 MILES

1 : 10 000 000

© Bartholomew Ltd

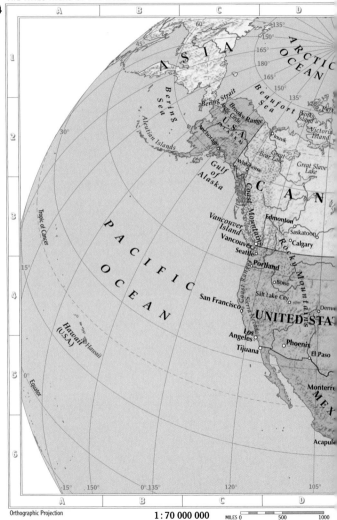

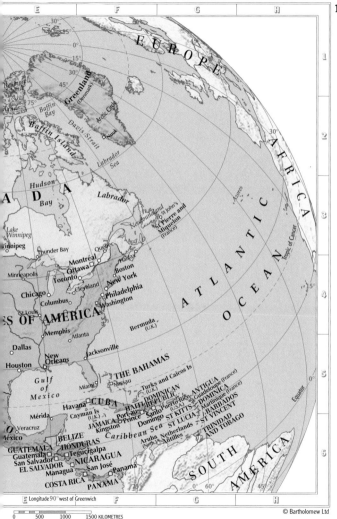

EUROPE

AFRICA

Greenland
(Denmark)

Baffin
Bay

Davis Strait

Arctic Circle

Nuuk

Baffin Island

Labrador
Sea

Hudson
Bay

Labrador

Newfoundland

St John's

St Pierre and
Miquelon
(France)

Azores

Tropic of Cancer

Lake
Winnipeg

Winnipeg

Thunder Bay

Québec

Minneapolis

Montréal
Ottawa   Halifax
Toronto
Cleveland   Boston
New York

Chicago

Columbus

Philadelphia
Washington

St Louis

ES OF AMERICA

Memphis

Atlanta

Bermuda
(U.K.)

ATLANTIC

OCEAN

Dallas

New
Orleans

Jacksonville

Houston

Gulf
of
Mexico

Miami

THE BAHAMAS

Nassau

Turks and Caicos Is
(U.K.)

Equator

Mérida

Havana   CUBA

Cayman Is
(U.K.)

HAITI   DOMINICAN
REPUBLIC

Port-au-   Santo
JAMAICA Prince   Domingo

Kingston

Puerto Rico ANTIGUA
(USA)   Guadeloupe (France)

ST KITTS   DOMINICA

ST LUCIA   Martinique (France)

BARBADOS

Veracruz

O

México

BELIZE

GUATEMALA   HONDURAS

Guatemala   Tegucigalpa

San Salvador   NICARAGUA

EL SALVADOR   Managua   San José

COSTA RICA   PANAMA

Panama

Caribbean Sea

Aruba Netherlands
(Neth.) Antilles

ST VINCENT

TRINIDAD
AND TOBAGO

SOUTH

AMERICA

E Longitude 90° west of Greenwich   F   G   H

0   500   1000   1500 KILOMETRES

© Bartholomew Ltd

150° B 75° 135° C

105°

BEAUFORT SEA

QUEEN ELIZABETH ISLANDS

Cape Prince Alfred

Prince Patrick Island

Melville Island

Banks Island

Parry Islands

Heiberg

Prudhoe

Kaktovik

Brooks Range

U.S.A.

ALASKA

YUKON TERRITORY

NORTHWEST TERRITORIES

Victoria Island

Sachs Harbour

Tuktoyaktuk

Inuvik

Mackenzie

Fort McPherson

Great Bear Lake

NUNA

Resolute

Somerset Island

Prince of Wales Island

Boothia Peninsula

Dawson

Mayo

Whitehorse

Mackenzie Mountains

Fort Good Hope

Norman Wells

Déline

Yellowknife

Great Slave Lake

Rankin Inlet

Whale Cove

Baker Lake

Arviat

C A N A D A

BRITISH COLUMBIA

ALBERTA

SASKATCHEWAN

MANITOBA

Fort Nelson

Fort St John

Prince George

Edmonton

Calgary

Saskatoon

Regina

Prince Albert

Lake Athabasca

Reindeer Lake

Lake Winnipeg

Winnipeg

Churchill

Vancouver

Vancouver Island

Victoria

Kamloops

Kelowna

Medicine Hat

Lethbridge

Swift Current

Brandon

Portage la Prairie

Selkirk

WASHINGTON

Seattle

Tacoma

Spokane

OREGON

Portland

Salem

Eugene

IDAHO

Boise

Idaho Falls

MONTANA

Helena

Butte

Billings

Great Falls

WYOMING

N. DAKOTA

Bismarck

Fargo

Jamestown

S. DAKOTA

Minneapolis

MINNESOTA

U S A

Missouri

120° D Longitude 105° west of Greenwich E

METRES FEET

5000	16404
3000	9843
2000	6562
1000	3281
500	1640
200	656
0	0
LAND B.S.L.	
200	656
4000	13124
6000	19686

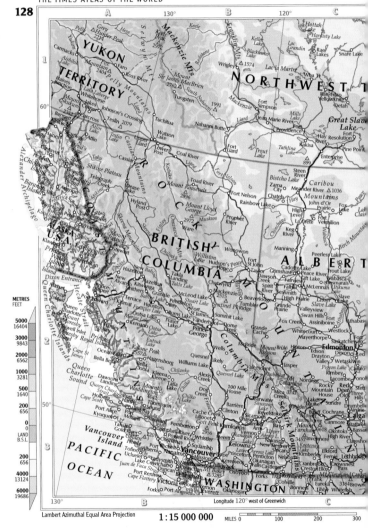

METRES FEET

5000	16404
3000	9843
2000	6562
1000	3281
500	1640
200	656
0	0
LAND	B.S.L.
200	656
4000	13124
6000	19686

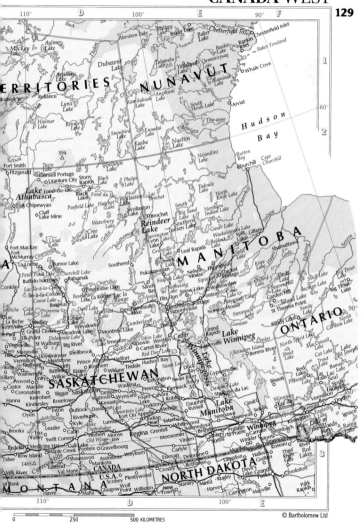

110° · 100° · 90°

TERRITORIES · **NUNAVUT**

Back
McKay Lake
Aylmer Lake
Mallery Lake
Baker Lake
Baker Lake
Chesterfield Inlet
Chesterfield Inlet
Rankin Inlet
Baker Foreland

Aberdeen Lake
Thelon
Banks Lake
Qamanirjuaq Lake
Whale Cove

Dubawnt Lake
Artillery Lake
Reliance
Lynx Lake
Kamilukuak Lake
Angikuni Lake
South Henik Lake
Tha-anne
Arviat

Lutsek'e'e
Snowdrift
Hjalmar Lake
Rennie Lake
Snowbird Lake
Ennadai Lake
Nueltin Lake
Kasba Lake
Tlogaga
Nejanilini Lake

Hudson
Bay

60°

Taltson
Fort Smith
Fitzgerald
594
Tazin Lake
Selwyn Lake
Button Bay
Cape Churchill

Slave
Gamsell Portage
Uranium City
Stony Rapids
Black Lake
Phelps Lake
Churchill
Seal

Fort Chipewyan
Lake Athabasca
Fond-du-Lac
Fond du Lac
Wollaston Lake
Brochet
Tadoule Lake
North Knife Lake

Cluff Lake Mine
Pasfield Lake
Hatchet Lake
Wollaston Lake
Big Sand Lake
Northern Indian Lake
Churchill

Fort Mackay
Fort McMurray
Lloyd Lake
Clearwater
Waterbury Lake
Cree Lake
Reindeer Lake
Barrington Lynn Lake
Southern Indian Lake
Waskaiowaka Lake
Split Lake
Gillam

Conklin
La Loche
Turnor Lake
Peter Pond Lake
Churchill Lake
Patuanak
Granville Lake
Leaf Rapids
MANITOBA
Knee Lake
Gods Lake
Shamattawa

Buffalo Narrows
Pinehouse Lake
Churchill
Pukatawagan
Nelson
Thompson
Split Lake
Oxford Lake
Gods Lake
Red Sucker Lake

A
Lac Île-à-la-Crosse
Île-à-la-Crosse
Besnard Lake
Lac La Ronge
La Ronge
Sandy Bay
Sisipuk Lake
Snow Lake
Wabowden
Garden Hill
Big Trout Lake
Big Trout Lake

laBiche
Canoe Lake
Beauval
Dore Lake
Deschambault Lake
Nississing
Flin Flon
Cranberry Portage
Pikwitonei
Playgreen Lake
St Theresa Point
Sachigo Lake

La Biche
Medley
Primrose Lake
Green Lake
Montreal Lake
Cumberland Lake
Simonhouse
The Pas
Norway House
Sandy Lake
ONTARIO

bonnyville
Grand Centre
Meadow Lake
Montreal Lake
Tobin Lake
Cedar Lake
Grand Rapids
Stevenson
Gunisao
North Spirit Lake
North Caribou Lake
90°

St Paul
Elk Point
Weyakwin
Nipawin
Westray
Squaw Rapids
Lake Winnipeg
Poplar
Reinder Island
Berens River
Deer Lake
MacDowell Lake

Vegreville
St Walburg
Big River
Shellbrook
Carrot River
Easterville
Cat Lake
Trout Lake
Lake St Joseph

viking
Vermilion
Lloydminster
Prince Albert
Melfort
Hudson Bay
Swan River
Duck Bay
Gypsumville
Stout Lake
Bamaji Lake
Slate Falls

Wainwright
Maidstone
Battleford
Tisdale
Preeceville
Kamsack
Lake Manitoba
Fisher River
North Spirit Lake
Red Lake
Ear Falls
Lac Seul

Castor
Wilkie
Blaine Lake
Rosthern
Wadena
Preeceville
Swan River
Dauphin
Gimli
Berens River
Vermilion
Dryden

Coronation
Kerrobert
SASKATCHEWAN
Wynyard
Foam Lake
Roblin
Russell
Neepawa
Stonewall
Beausejour
Keewatin
Eagle Lake
Ignace

Hanna
Biggar
Saskatoon
Watrous
Wynyard
Yorkton
Melville
Dauphin
Manitoba
Selkirk
Winnipeg
Falcon Lake
Rainy

Kindersley
Rosetown
Eston
Outlook
Davidson
Nokomis
Esterhazy
Whitewood
Brandon
Carman
Steinbach
Lake of the Woods

Oyen
Leader
Kyle
Riverhurst
Lumsden
Indian Head
Grenfell
Portage la Prairie
Morden
Winkler
Morris
Roseau River
Rainy River

Brooks
Fox Valley
Cabri
Dinsmore
Moose Jaw
Regina
Grenfell
Moosomin
Virden
Souris
Wawanesa
Altona
Emerson
Vermilion
Red Lake

Redcliff
Medicine Hat
Swift Current
Gull Lake
Old Wives Lake
Carlyle
Deloraine
Langdon
Halloes
Grand Forks
Crookston

Maple Creek
Cypress Hills
Ponteix
Gravelbourg
Assiniboia
Weyburn
Estevan
Bottineau
Devil's Lake
Thief River Falls

Taber
Bow Island
1465△
Eastend
Val Marie
Shaunavon
Minton
CANADA
Crosby
NORTH DAKOTA
Grand Forks
Park Rapids

Milk River
MONTANA
U.S.A.
Plentywood
Scobey
Wolf Point
Williston
New Town
Stanley
Minot
Rugby
Harvey
Carrington
Valley City

Havre
Malta
Glasgow
New Town

110° · 100° · 90°

0 · 250 · 500 KILOMETRES

© Bartholomew Ltd

90° 80°

A B C

MANITOBA

H u d s o n
B a y

Inukjuak

Lac
Le Roy

Lac
Chavigny

Lac
Bacqueville

Nelson
Gillam
Hayes
Shamattawa
Gods
Oxford
Lake
Cook
Lake
Shut Lake
Sachigo Lake
Big Trout
Lake
Fort
Severn
Winisk

Sleeper Islands

North Belcher
Islands

King George
Islands

Sanikiluaq

Belcher
Islands

Flaherty Island

Nastapoca Islands

Lac
Minto

Île du
Gros
Mécatina

Lac
Guillaume-Delisle

Cape Henrietta
Maria

Poste-de-
la-Baleine

Long
Island

Grande Rivière de la
Baleine

Le
Biennial

North Spirit
Lake
Sandy Lake
Stout
Lake
Red
Lake
Pakwash
Far
Falls
Vermillion
Sioux
Lookout
Drayton
Pickle Lake
Pledger
Lake

Big Trout
Lake
Wunnummin
Lake
Kasabonika
Lake
Webequie
Winisk
Lake
Ekwan
Attawapiskat
Akimiski
Island
Fort Albany

J a m e s
B a y

North
Twin I.
South
Twin I.

Charlton
Island

Fort George
Radisson
Wemindji
Eastmain

QUÉ

Réservoir
La Grande 2

Réservoir
La Grande 3

Lac Burton

Réservoir
Opinaca
Eastmain

O N T A R I O

St Joseph
Lake
Ogoki
Reservoir
Caribou Lake
Albany
Nakina
Ogoki
Albany
Kapiskau
Missisa
Lake
Attawapiskat
Lake

Moosonee
Moose
Factory
Rupert
Waskaganish
Fort
Rupert

Lac Evans

Lac au Goéland

Lac Matagami

Mistassini

Lac
Mistassini

Lac
Albanel

Lac
Opataca

Chibougamau

Lac de la Biche
Lac
Bienville

Longlac
Beardmore
Nakina
Hearst
Opasatika
Kapuskasing
Fraserdale
Smooth Rock
Falls
Cochrane
Iroquois
Falls
Timmins
La Sarre
Amos
Noranda
Rouyn
Senneterre
Val-d'Or

Thunder
Bay
Nipigon
Terrace
Bay
Marathon

Longlac

Foleyet
Chapleau
Biscotasi
Lake
New Liskeard
Kirkland
Lake

Réservoir
Gouin
Obedjiwan

Réservoir
Baskatong

Mont-
Laurier
Mt Tremblant

Réservoir
Cabonga

Réservoir
Dozois

METRES
FEET

5000
16404
3000
9843
2000
6562
1000
3281
500
1640
200
656
0
0
LAND
B.S.L.
200
656
4000
13124
6000
19686

L a k e   S u p e r i o r

Isle Royale
Keweenaw
Peninsula
Houghton
Hancock
Marquette
Escanaba
Ishpeming

M I C H I G A N

W I S C O N S I N

Green Bay

Milwaukee
Racine
Kenosha
Waukegan

Chicago

I N D I A N A

South Bend
Fort
Wayne

Gary

Sault Ste Marie

L a k e   H u r o n

Georgian
Bay

Sudbury
Espanola
North
Bay
Sturgeon
Falls
Mattawa
Pembroke

Ottawa

Hull

Montréal

OTTAWA

Huntsville
Barrie
Bracebridge
Gravenhurst

L a k e   M i c h i g a n

Traverse City
Cadillac
Manistee
Big Rapids
Midland
Bay City
Saginaw
Flint

Detroit

Windsor

Toledo

O H I O

Cleveland
Lorain
Sandusky

L a k e   E r i e

Buffalo
St Catharines
Hamilton
Kitchener
Guelph
Toronto
Oshawa
Peterborough
Kingston

L a k e   O n t a r i o

Rochester
Syracuse
Oswego
Auburn

N E W
Y O R K

Utica
Albany
Schenectady
Binghamton
Elmira
Corning
Ithaca

Longitude 80° west of Greenwich

Lambert Azimuthal Equal Area Projection

1 : 15 000 000

MILES 0 100 200 300

0   250   500 KILOMETRES

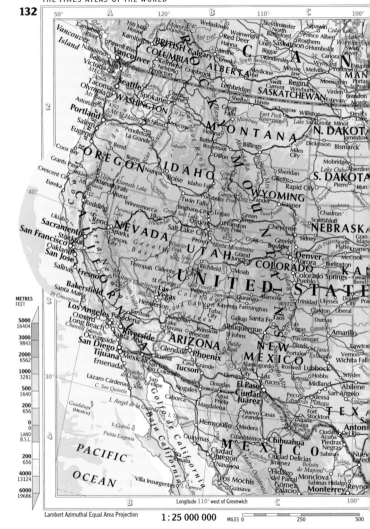

0   250   500   750 KILOMETRES

© Bartholomew Ltd

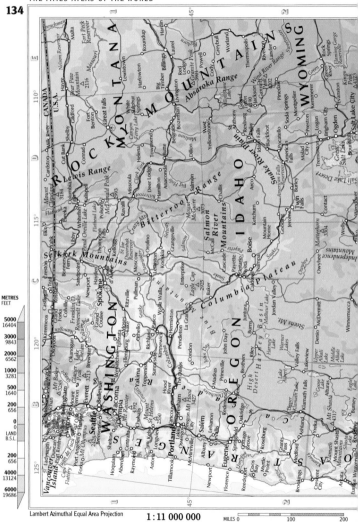

0   100   200   300 KILOMETRES

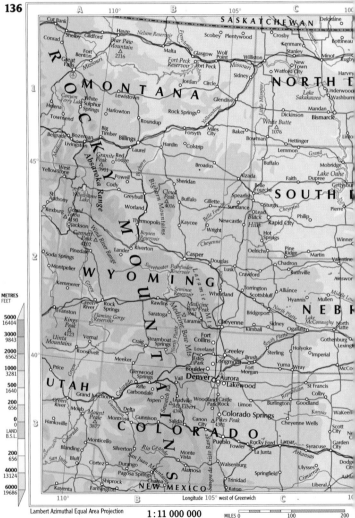

SASKATCHEWAN

Cut Bank
Conrad, Shelby Galdford
Havre Nelson Reservoir Fronteau
Scobey Plentywood Crosby Deloraine
Kenmare Bottineau
Great Falls Bear Paw Mountain △ 2116 Malta Glasgow Wolf Point Williston Stanley New Town Minot Rugby
Fort Benton Fort Peck Reservoir Fort Peck Sidney Watford City Harvey
Canyon Ferry Lake Lewistown Jordan Circle Glendive Dickinson Mandan Underwood Washburn NORTH D
Helena White Sulphur Springs Harlowton Roundup Forsyth Miles City Baker Bowman White Butte △ 1076 Hettinger Lemmon Lake Sakakawea Bismarck Lint
Townsend Big Timber Billings Hardin Colstrip Mobridge
Belgrade Bozeman Livingston Granite Peak △ 3901 Red Lodge Laurel Broadus Alzada Belle Fourche Faith Dupree Lake Oahe Gettysbur
West Yellowstone Absaroka Range Powell Cody Sheridan Spearfish Sturgis O'Leary Black Hills Philip Pierre
St Anthony Yellowstone Lake Greybull Cloud Peak △ 4016 Buffalo Gillette Sundance Rapid City Winner
Rexburg Grand Teton △ 4190 Jackson Worland Kaycee Newcastle Hot Springs Pine Ridge Martin Valentine
Soda Springs Gannett Peak △ 4202 Wind River Range Thermopolis Boysen Reservoir Riverton Lander Casper Douglas Lusk Crawford Oelrichs Chadron Rushville Middle Lou
Montpelier Pinedale Sweetwater Pathfinder Reservoir Laramie Torrington Alliance Hyannis Mullen NEBR
Kemmerer Green Rock Springs Seminoe Reservoir Rawlins Wheatland Scottsbluff Bridgeport North Platte Lake McConaughy North Platte Gothenburg Lexing
Evanston Green River Flaming Gorge Reservoir Saratoga Medicine Bow Peak △ 3661 Medicine Bow Mts Laramie Cheyenne Kimball Sidney Ogallala
Kings Peak △ 4123 Uinta Mountains Vernal Craig Steamboat Springs Fort Collins Greeley Brush Sterling Holyoke Imperial McCo
Price Roosevelt Meeker Loveland Longmont Fort Morgan Yuma Wray
Grand Junction Glenwood Springs Vail Boulder Estes Park Denver Aurora Lakewood St Francis
UTAH Green River Moab Rifle Carbondale Aspen Leadville Woodard Castle Rock Limon Burlington Goodland Colby Kansas WaKee
Hanksville Mount Peale △ 3877 Delta Gunnison Mt Elbert △ 4399 Salida Canon City Colorado Springs Cheyenne Wells Scott City Garden City Ne
Monticello Montrose Pikes Peak △ 4301 Pueblo Rocky Ford Lamar Syracuse
Blanding Silverton Rio Grande Monte Vista Fowler La Junta Arkansas Dodge City
Cortez Durango Pagosa Springs Chama Walsenburg Springfield Ulysses Ashl
Kayenta Shiprock Farmington San Juan Mountains Alamosa Sangre de Cristo Mts Trinidad Liberal

R O C K Y   M O U N T A I N S
M O N T A N A
W Y O M I N G
C O L O R A D O
U T A H
NEW MEXICO
SOUTH D

Lambert Azimuthal Equal Area Projection 1:11 000 000 MILES 0 100 200

METRES FEET

5000	16404
3000	9843
2000	6562
1000	3281
500	1640
200	656
0	0
LAND B.S.L.	
200	656
4000	13124
6000	19686

45°

40°

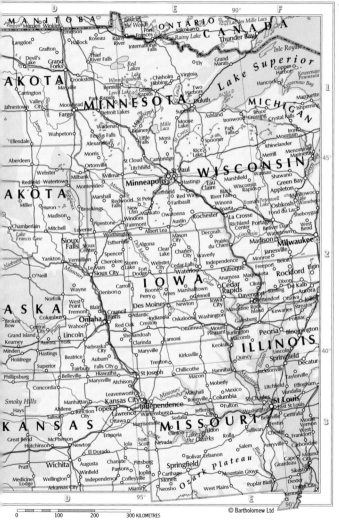

0   100   200   300 KILOMETRES

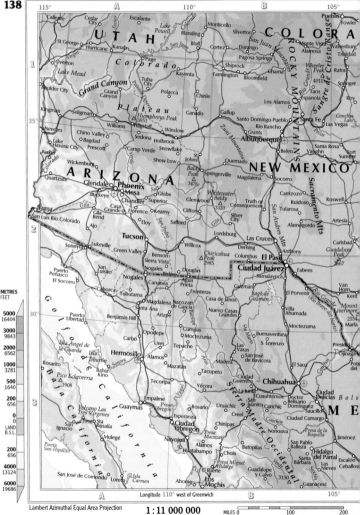

Lambert Azimuthal Equal Area Projection

1:11 000 000

METRES
FEET

5000
16404

3000
9843

2000
6562

1000
3281

500
1640

200
656

0
0

LAND
B.S.L.

200
656

4000
13124

6000
19686

MILES 0   100   200

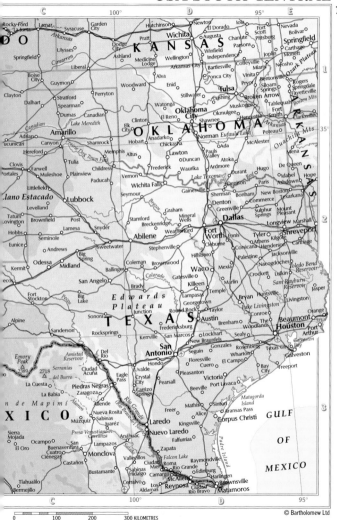

Lambert Azimuthal Equal Area Projection

1:11 000 000

MILES 0   100   200

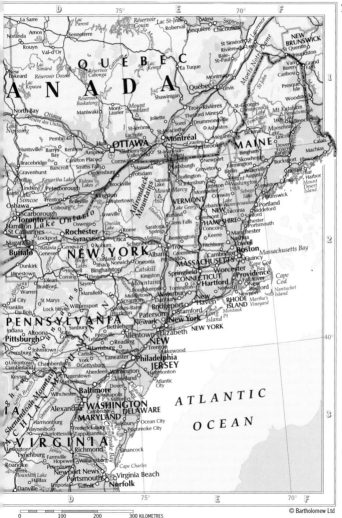

0   100   200   300 KILOMETRES

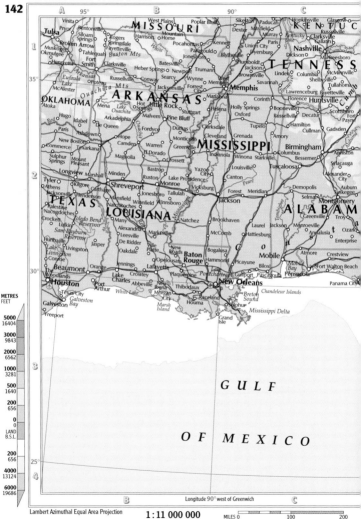

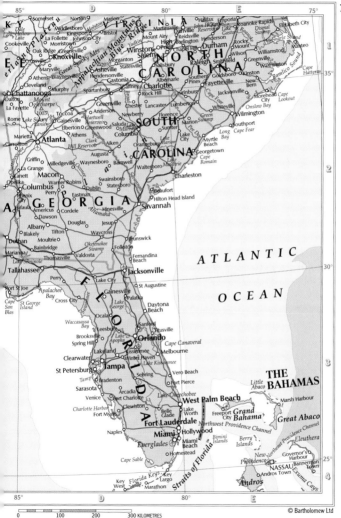

METRES
FEET

5000 16404
3000 9843
2000 6562
1000 3281
500 1640
200 656
0 0
LAND B.S.L.
200 656
4000 13124
6000 19686

Lambert Azimuthal Equal Area Projection

Longitude 110° west of Greenwich

1:15 000 000

MILES 0   100   200   300

PACIFIC OCEAN

STATES OF AMERICA

Snyder, Abilene, Weatherford, Fort Worth, Longview, Marshall, Monroe, Winnsboro, Jackson, **ALABAMA**
Sweetwater, Stephenville, Cleburne, Athens, Tyler, Henderson, Jonesboro, Laurel, Jackson
Ballinger, Brownwood, Gatesville, Waco, Marlin, Palestine, Natchez, McComb, Hattiesburg, Atmore
San Angelo, **T E X A S**, Temple, Crockett, Toledo Bend Res., Many, Alexandria, Raleville, Bogalusa, Picayune, **Mobile**
Sonora, Junction, Georgetown, Bryan, Huntsville, Lufkin, Jasper, **LOUISIANA**, Hammond, Gulfport, Biloxi, Pascagoula
Eduards, Fredericksburg, San Marcos, Taylor, Brenham, Conroe, Lake Charles, Lafayette, **Baton Rouge**, **New Orleans**, Mobile Bay
Rocksprings, Kerrville, **Austin**, **Houston**, Orange, Abbeville, Morgan, Houma, Breton Islands
Del Rio, **San Antonio**, New Braunfels, Lockhart, Rosenberg, Port Arthur, Thibodaux, Race, Grand Sound
Zaragoza, Uvalde, Hondo, Seguin, Gonzales, Texas City, **Galveston**, Morgan City, Mississippi Delta
Piedras Negras, Crystal City, Pearsall, Floresville, El Campo, Wharton, Bay City, Galveston Bay
Allende, Carrizo Springs, Pleasanton, Victoria, Freeport
Nueva Rosita, Sabinas, Mathis, Beeville, Simton, Matagorda Island, Aransas Pass
Juarez, Alice, Corpus Christi, Kingsville
Anahuac, Zapata, Falfurrias, Padre Island
Lampazos, Vallecillos, Rio Grande, Raymondville
Sabinas Hidalgo, Ciudad Camargo, McAllen, Harlingen
Cerralvo, Reynosa, Brownsville
Garza Garcia, **Monterrey**, China, Ciudad Rio Bravo, Matamoros
Saltillo, Cadereyta, Valle Hermoso
Montemorelos, Mendez, Laguna Madre
Galeana, Linares, Burgos, San Fernando
El Salvador, Villagran, Hidalgo, El Temascal
Matehuala, Jimenez, La Pesca
Nevada, Ciudad Soto la Marina
Doctor Arroyo, Palmillas, Xicotencatl, Aldama

Tropic of Cancer

G U L F
O F
M E X I C O

Charcas, Ciudad Victoria, Gonzales, **Cabo Catoche**
Moctezuma, Ciudad Mante, Ebano, Río Lagartos, Telchac Puerto, Tizimin, Cancún
Cerritos, Tampico, Progreso, Motul, Izamal, Valladolid
San Luis Potosi, Rayon, El Higo, Panuco, Laguna de Tamiahua, Sisal, Celestún, **Mérida**, Piste, Cozumel
Arroyo Seco, Ciudad de Valles, Tempoal, Calkini, Muna, Tekax, Tenabo, Peto
Valle Verde, San Felipe, Arroyo, Tamazunchale, Cerro Azul, Naranjos, Campeche, **YUCATÁN**, Felipe C. Puerto, Banco Chinchorro
San Luis de la Paz, Jalpan, Zimapan, Molango, Tuxpan, Champotón, Escárcega, Chetumal
Salamanca, **Querétaro**, Zacualtipán, Poza Rica, Tihuatlán, Nautla, **BAHÍA DE CAMPECHE**, Ciudad del Carmen, Laguna de Términos
Celaya, Amealco, Tula, Tulancingo, Martinez, Frontera, Candelaria, Carmelita
Morelia, **Toluca**, **MÉXICO**, Pachuca, Zacatlán, Chignahuapan, Perote, **Veracruz**, Paraíso, **Villahermosa**, Balancan, Tenosique
Zitacuaro, Popocatépetl, **Puebla**, Huatusco, **Córdoba**, Alvarado, Ciudad del Carmen, Macuspana, Palenque, Flores
Tejupilco, **Cuernavaca**, Cuautla, Orizaba, Tlacotalpan, San Andrés Tuxtla, Comalcalco, Teapa, Jesús Carranza, Emiliano Zapata, Ocosingo
Ciudad Altamirano, Arcelia, Iguala, Tehuacán, Acatlán, Tuxtepec, Cosamaloapan, Acayucan, **Coatzacoalcos**, Cárdenas, Las Casas, Nezahualcóyotl, San Cristóbal de las Casas, **BELIZE**
SIERRA MADRE DEL SUR, Chilpancingo, Chiapa, Huajuapan de León, **Oaxaca**, Jaltepec, Juan Bautista Tuxtepec, Nudo de Zempoaltepec, Jesús Carranza, Palomares, Copainalá, Teopisca, Tila, Sta. Cruz Barillas
Acapulco, Coyuca de Benitez, Tierra Colorada, Ayutla, Zacatepec, Tlaxiaco, Istmo de Tehuantepec, Tapanatepec, Cintalapa, **Tuxtla Gutiérrez**, Comitán de Domínguez, Libertad
Copala, Ometepec, San Miguel, Sola de Vega, Ciudad Ixtepec, Juchitán, Villa Flores, La Concordia, **GUATEMALA**
Pinotepa Nacional, Puerto Escondido, Puerto Ángel, Miahuatlán, Salina Cruz, Tonalá, Mapastepec, Presa de la Angostura
Golfo de Tehuantepec, Pijijiapan, Huixtla, Tapachula, Cd Hidalgo

0   250 KILOMETRES

© Bartholomew Ltd

METRES
FEET

5000
16404

3000
9843

2000
6562

1000
3281

500
1640

200
656

0
0

LAND
B.S.L.

200
656

4000
13124

6000
19686

Lambert Azimuthal Equal Area Projection

1 : 20 000 000

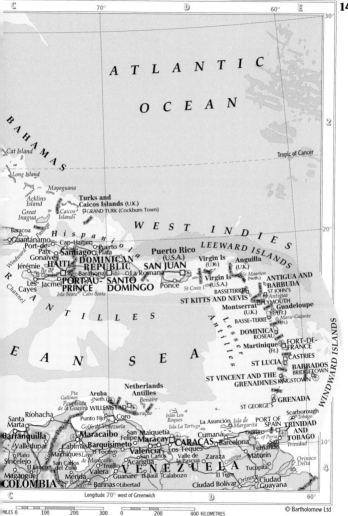

C 70° D 60° E

30°

ATLANTIC

OCEAN

2

Tropic of Cancer

BAHAMAS

Cat Island

Long Island

Mayaguana

Acklins Island

Turks and Caicos Islands (U.K.)

Great Inagua

Caicos Islands

☐ GRAND TURK (Cockburn Town)

W E S T I N D I E S

20°

Baracoa

Hispaniola

LEEWARD ISLANDS

Guantánamo

Cap-Haïtien

Puerto Rico

Virgin Is

Anguilla

Port-de-Paix

Puerto Plata

(U.S.A.)

(U.K.)

Windward Passage

Gonaïves

Santiago

(U.K.)

St Maarten

ANTIGUA AND

Jérémie

HAITI

DOMINICAN

SAN JUAN

Virgin Is

(Neth.)

BARBUDA

REPUBLIC

La Romana

ST JOHN'S

Les

Jacmel

PORT-AU-

Barahona

Ponce

St Croix I.

Antigua

Cayes

PRINCE

SANTO

(U.S.A.)

BASSETERRE

R

DOMINGO

ST KITTS AND NEVIS

A

Isla Beata Cabo Beata

Montserrat

PLYMOUTH

Guadeloupe

N

(U.K.)

(Fr.)

T

BASSE-TERRE

Marie-Galante

I

(Fr.)

L

DOMINICA

L

E

ROSEAU

Martinique

FORT-DE-

E

S

(Fr.)

FRANCE

A

Lesser

CASTRIES

N

ST LUCIA

BARBADOS

Antilles

BRIDGETOWN

S E A

ST VINCENT AND THE

Kingstown

GRENADINES

ST GEORGE'S

GRENADA

Netherlands

Antilles

Aruba

(Neth.)

Scarborough

Tobago

Bonaire

(Neth.)

WILLEMSTAD

Curaçao

ST GEORGE'S

PORT OF

TRINIDAD

Islas Los Roques

La Asunción *Isla de Margarita*

SPAIN

AND

Ríohacha

Punto Fijo

Coro

Isla La Tortuga

TOBAGO

Santa Marta

Golfo de Venezuela

Cumaná

G. of Paria

Trinidad

10°

Barranquilla

Maracaibo

San Felipe

Maiquetía

CARACAS

Barcelona

San Fernando

Valledupar

Cabimas

Barquisimeto

Los Teques

Maturín

Plato

Lago de Maracaibo

Valencia

Valle de

Zaraza

Tucupita

El Banco

Machiques

San Carlos

Acarigua

la Pascua

Guanipa

Orinoco Delta

Sincelejo

San Carlos del Zulia

Tocuyo

Guanare

El Tigre

Magangué

Trujillo

San

Barinas

El Baúl

Calabozo

Ciudad

COLOMBIA

Mérida

Valera

Guayana

Pico Bolívar

VENEZUELA

Barinas

Ciudad Bolívar

Orinoco

60°

Longitude 70° west of Greenwich

D

MILES 0 100 200 300 0 200 400 KILOMETRES

© Bartholomew Ltd

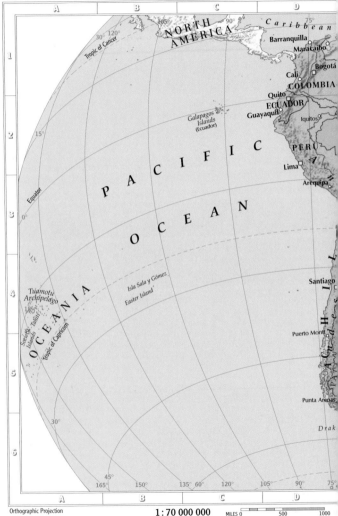

Sea

Caracas

Valencia

VENEZUELA

Georgetown

Paramaribo

Cayenne

SUR. French Guiana

Manaus

Belém

Fortaleza

B R A Z I L

Recife

La Paz

BOLIVIA

Santa Cruz

Sucre

Brasília

Salvador

Equator

Ascension

0°

PARAGUAY

São Paulo

Curitiba

Asunción

Rio de Janeiro

A T L A N T I C

St Helena

Córdoba

Porto Alegre

Buenos **URUGUAY**

Aires Montevideo

O C E A N

ARGENTINA

Rio de la Plata

Mar del Plata

Tristan da Cunha

Cape of Good Hope

Tropic of Capricorn

15°

AFRICA

Falkland

Islands

Stanley

Isla Grande

de Tierra del Fuego

Cape Horn

Passage

South

Shetland

Islands

South Georgia

South Orkney

Islands

South Georgia

and

South Sandwich

Islands

(U.K.)

South

Sandwich

Islands

Antarctic

Peninsula

60°

Antarctic Circle 30°

15°

60°

0°

15°

45°

30°

Tropic of Cancer

15°

AFRICA

Longitude 45° west of Greenwich

F

G

H

© Bartholomew Ltd

0   500   1000   1500 KILOMETRES

ATLANTIC

OCEAN

GEORGETOWN
New
Amsterdam
Linden Nieuw
Nickerie
Professor van
Blommestein Mee
SURINAME
Kourou
French
Guiana
Pontoetoe

Serra Tumucumaque

PARAMARIBO
St-Laurent-du-Maroni
CAYENNE
Oiapoque

Lourenço Calçoene
Amapá Ilha de Maracá

Equator

Porto
Santana Macapá Mouths of the Amazon
Mazagão Chaves Cabo
Arere Para Ilha de Marajó Baía de Marajó

Oriximiná Óbidos Almeirim Breves
Urucara Parintins Monte Breves Portel Belém
Uricurituba Santarém Alegre Xingu Sãopolis Bragança
Itaituba Altamira Cametá Viseu
Tucuruí Castanhal
Represa Pinheiro São Luís Camocim
Jacareacanga Tucuruí Jacundá Viana Fortaleza
Maraba Capim Itapicuru Mirim Tianguá Sobral Caucaia
Manuelzinho Imperatriz Grajaú Bacabal Codó Parnaiba Aracati
Araras São Barra Caxias Campo Maior Caninde Quixadá
Félix do Corda Timon Crateús Iguatu Mossoró
B R A Z I L Tocantinópolis Araguaína Balsas Jerumenha Floriano Picos Oeiras Crato Juazeiro Natal
Serra Conceição Carolina Canto do Burití Petrolina do Norte João
Porto do Araguaia Santa Maria Pedro São Raimundo Nonato Floresta Salgueiro Pessoa
dos Gaúchos Óbidos das Barreiras Afonso Caracol Paulistana Caruaru Olinda
Porto Ilha do Porto Barragem de Senhor do Bonfim Jaboatão Recife
Artur Bananal Nacional Sobradinho Afonso Maceió
Diamantino Rosário Oeste São Félix Dianópolis Corrente Xique Santo Arapiraca
Cuiabá Natividade Barreiras Ibotirama Jacobina Aracaju
Cáceres Barra do Porangatu Santana Bom Jesus Feira de Estância
Garças Cavalcante Posse da Lapa Itaberaba Santana Alagoinhas
Diamantino Uruaçu Correntina Itabuna Salvador
Alto Garças Niquelândia Sto Antônio Ubaitaba Ilhéus
Puerto Rondonópolis Iporá Formosa de Jesus Una
Coxim BRASÍLIA Anápolis Januária Vitória/da Itapetinga
Itiquira Goiás Goiânia Unaí Montes Claros Conquista Porto Seguro
Rio Verde Vianópolis Salinas Almenara
Jataí Itumbiara Paracatu Jequitaí Alcobaça
Rio Verde de Mato Grosso Araguari de Minas Patos Teófilo Otoni

0   250   500   750 KILOMETRES

© Bartholomew Ltd

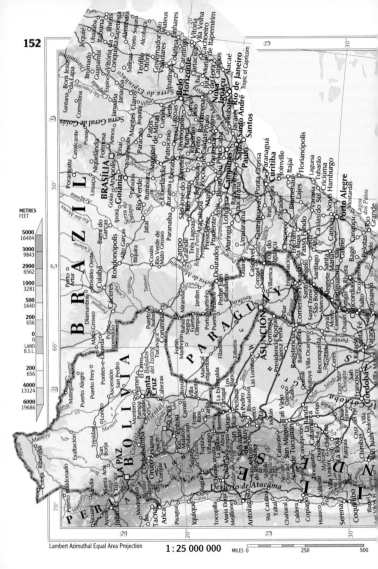

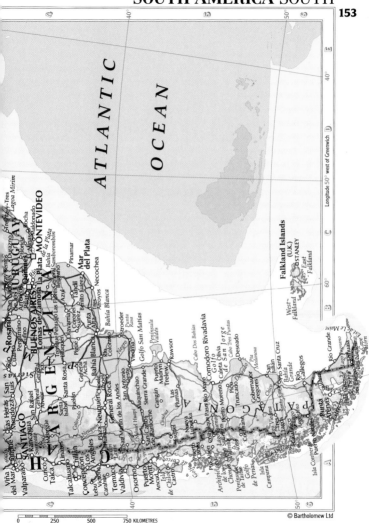

ATLANTIC

OCEAN

Longitude 50° west of Greenwich

Falkland Islands
(U.K.)
STANLEY
East
Falkland

West
Falkland

MONTEVIDEO
URUGUAY

Rosario
BUENOS AIRES
Mar del Plata

Bahía Blanca

A R G E N T I N A

Comodoro Rivadavia

P A T A G O N I A

SANTIAGO
Valparaíso

C H I L E

Punta Arenas

Río Grande

Ushuaia

0   250   500   750 KILOMETRES

© Bartholomew Ltd

Rio das Mortes
Planalto do
Mato Grosso
Poxoréu
Rondonópolis
Anhumas
Itiquira
Correntes
Pedro
Gomes
Coxim
Rio Verde de
Mato Grosso
Camapuã
Rochedo
Jaraguari
Campo
Grande
Sidrolândia
Dourados
Caarapó
Amambai
Iguatemi
Salto de Guaíra
Umuarama
Guaíra
Porto Mendes
Toledo
Cascavel
Catanduvas
Foz do
Iguaçu
Wanda
Dionísio
Cerqueira
ARG.

Batoví
Tesouro
Guiratinga
Alto Garças
Sta Rita
do Araguaia
Alto
Araguaia
Mineiros
Taquari
Costa Rica
Baús
Paraíso
Alto
Sucuriú
Água
Clara
Ribas do
Rio Pardo
Três
Lagoas
Panorama
Bataguaçu
Rio
Brilhante
Ivinhema
Represa
Ilha Grande
Nova
Londrina
Querência
do Norte
Nova Esperança
Maringá
Cianorte
Goio-
Erê
Telêmaco Borba
Prudentópolis
Guarapuava
Laranjeiras
do Sul
Chapimzinho
Pato Branco
Palmas

Barra do Garças
Aragarças
Piranhas
Iporá
Calapônia
Aurilândia
Jataí
Serra do Caiapó
Serra do Verdinho
Rio
Verde
Caçu
Cachoeira
Alta
São Simão
Barragem de
São Simão
Gurinhatã
Itumbiara

Ceres
Rianópolis Brasilândia
Itapuranga
Goiás
Jaraguá
Anicuns
Trindade
Goiânia
Hidrolândia
Paraúna
Edéia
Pontalina
Morrinhos
Caldas
Novas
Santa Helena
de Goiás
Goiandira
Catalão
Itumbiara
Tupaciguara
Prata
Ituiutaba
Campo
Florido
Iturama
Itapagipe
Colômbia
Planaltina
Formosa
Unaí
BRASÍLIA
Gamá
Nempolis
Anápolis
Luziânia
Vianópolis
Cristalina
Pires do Rio
Paracatu
Guarda
Mor
Coromandel
Represa de
Emborcação
Araguari
Patrocínio
Uberlândia
Uberaba
Araxá
Ibiá

B R A Z

Campo
Verde
Indianópolis
Votuporanga
Nova
Granada
Olímpia
Barretos
Colina
Franca
Orlândia Cássia
São Joaquim
da Barra
Pedregulho
Igarapava
São Sebastião
do Paraíso

Paranaíba
Inocência
Cassilândia
Itumara
Aparecida
do Tabuado
Jales
Fernandópolis
São José do
Rio Preto
Bebedouro
Sertãozinho
Ribeirão
Preto
Mococa
Casa Branca
Piraçununga

Andradina
Araçatuba
Birigui
Penápolis
Catanduva
Taquaritinga
Jaboticabal
Araraquara
São Carlos
Rio Claro
Limeira
Mogi
Mirim
Campinas
Jundiaí
Itu
Sorocaba
Capão
Bonito
Itanhaém
Juquiá
Peruíbe
Cananéia
Iguape
Jacupiranga
Guaraqueçaba
Antonina
Paranaguá
São Francisco do Sul
Ilha de São Francisco
Joinville
Araquari

Mirandópolis
Valparaíso
Dracena
Lucélia
Presidente
Epitácio
Teodoro
Sampaio
Represa
Porto Primavera
Presidente
Prudente
Iepê
Tupã
Lins
Novo
Horizonte
Pirajuí
Garça
Marília
Bauru
São Manuel
Piracicaba
Botucatu
Conchas
Tietê
Itapetininga
Tatuí

Assis
Ourinhos
Avaré
Santo Antônio
da Platina
Cornélio
Procópio
Paranavaí
Iguatemi
Paranapanema
Rolândia
Arapongas
Apucarana
Londrina
Jaguapitã
Ibiporã
Venceslau Bráz
Itapeva
Itararé
Apiaí
Ribeira
Cerro Azul
Rio/Branco do Sul
Curitiba
São José
dos Pinhais
Lapa
Rio Negro
Mafra

Campo
Mourão
Pitanga
Reserva
Castro
Ponta
Grossa
Palmeira
Pirá
do Sul
Ipiranga
Prudentópolis
Irati
União da
Vitória
Canoinhas
Mangueirinha

METRES
FEET

5000
16404
3000
9843
2000
6562
1000
3281
500
1640
200
656
0
0
LAND
B.S.L.
200
656
4000
13124
6000
19686

MILES 0 · 100 · 200

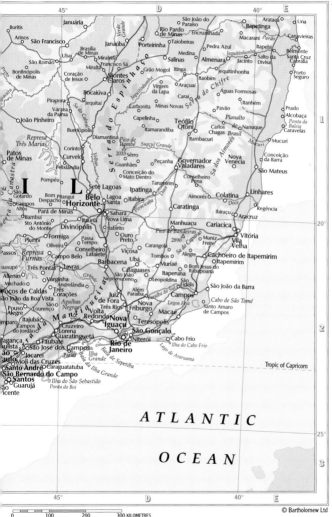

0   100   200   300 KILOMETRES

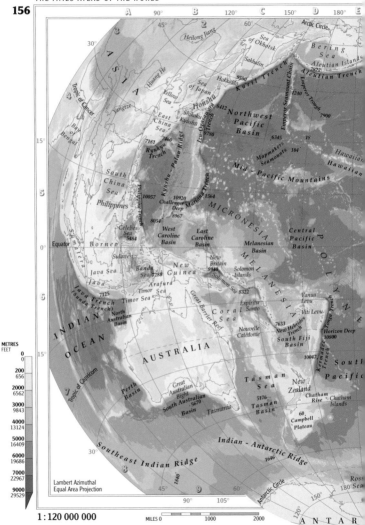

A 90° B 120° C 150° D 180° E

45° 60° Arctic Circle

30° *Heilong Jiang*

Sea of Okhotsk

Bering Sea

Aleutian Islands

Aleutian Trench

Huang He Sakhalin

A S I A Hokkaido 9550 Kuril Trench 7822

Yellow Sea Emperor Seamount Chain 1240 7900

Yangtze Sea of Japan Honshu

Tropic of Cancer East China Sea Shikoku 8412 Northwest Pacific Basin

460 Kyushu Izu-Ogasawara Trench

Bay of Bengal 9780 6345 18

15° 7181 Ryukyu Trench Kyushu-Palau Ridge Mapmakers Seamounts 104 Hawaii

Mid - Pacific Mountains Hawaiian

South China Sea 10057 10920 Challenger 1564 Mariana Trench

Philippines Deep 8967 M I C R O N E S I A

8054 P O L

Philippine Trench West Caroline Basin East Caroline Basin Central Pacific Basin

Sumatra Celebes Sea 5484 Melanesian Basin Y N E

0° Equator Borneo

Sulawesi New Britain Solomon

Java Sea New 8940 Islands

Java Banda Sea 7288 Guinea Solomon Sea 8322 M E L A N E S I A

Timor Sea Arafura Great Barrier Reef Espiritu Vanua Levu

Java Trench Sea Santo Viti Levu

(Sunda Trench) Timor Sea North Australian Basin Coral Sea 7633 New Hebrides Horizon Deep

15° I N D I A N Nouvelle Trench 10800

Calédonie South Fiji Basin

O C E A N 10047

AUSTRALIA S o u t h

METRES Tropic of Capricorn T a s m a n Pacific

FEET Perth Sea New

0 Basin Great Zealand

0 Australian Chatham Rise Chatham

200 Bight 5176 Islands

656 South Australian Tasman

2000 Basin 5670 Tasmania Basin 60

6562 Campbell

2000 Plateau

6562

3000 Indian - Antarctic Ridge

9843

4000 Southeast Indian Ridge 1646

13124

5000 1840 Ross

16409 90° 105° Sea

6000 Lambert Azimuthal Antarctic Circle 150°

19686 Equal Area Projection 45° 180°

7000 90° 105° A N T A R

22967

9000 **1 : 120 000 000** MILES 0 1000 2000

29529

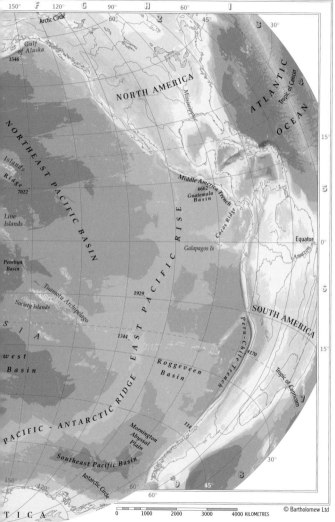

Arctic Circle

Gulf of Alaska
1546

NORTH AMERICA

Mississippi

ATLANTIC

OCEAN

Tropic of Cancer

NORTHEAST PACIFIC BASIN

Islands
Ridge
7022

Line
Islands

Penrhyn
Basin

Middle America Trench
6662
Guatemala
Basin

Cocos Ridge

Galapagos Is

Equator

Amazon

Tuamotu Archipelago

Society Islands

1929

SOUTH AMERICA

S I A

1344

Peru-Chile Trench

8170

w e s t

Basin

EAST PACIFIC RISE

Roggeveen
Basin

Tropic of Capricorn

PACIFIC - ANTARCTIC RIDGE

Mornington
Abyssal
Plain

114

Southeast Pacific Basin

Antarctic Circle

T I C A

0   1000   2000   3000   4000 KILOMETRES

120° A 90° B 60° C 30° D 0° E 30° F 60°

Arctic Circle

Davis Strait

Greenland

Iceland

Norwegian Basin

Norwegian Sea

Baltic Sea

1

Hudson Bay

Labrador Sea

Reykjanes Ridge

Iceland Basin

Rockall Bank

North Sea

NORTH

AMERICA

St Lawrence

Newfoundland

Grand Banks of Newfoundland

13

British Isles

EUROPE

45°

Celtic Shelf 38

MID-ATLANTIC RIDGE

4938

5943

Azores

Mediterranean Sea

5121

2

4556

Bermuda

Monaco Basin

Canary Is.

AFRICA

Tropic of Cancer

30°

Nares Deep

5508

Sargasso Sea

8605 Milwaukee Deep

Puerto Rico Trench

5491

6690

3

Cayman Trench 7535

Greater Antilles

Caribbean Sea

5523

Lesser Antilles

Cape Verde

Cape Verde Basin

15°

Niger

Guiana Basin

Amazon Cone

Gulf of Guinea

Guinea Basin

5212

4

Equator

Amazon

0°

Congo

SOUTH

AMERICA

Brazil Basin

Ascension

MID-ATLANTIC RIDGE

3391

St Helena

Angola Basin

5

Tropic of Capricorn

Parana

5460

Rio Grande Rise

Walvis Ridge

24

Orange Cone

Cape of Good Hope

Cape Basin

6

30°

Tristan da Cunha

5520

PACIFIC

OCEAN

6681

Argentine Basin

Falkland Islands

Agulhas Basin

6195

7

Cape Horn

Scotia Ridge

South Georgia

Drake Passage

Scotia Sea

8325

1530

Atlantic-Indian Ridge

Antarctic Peninsula

5750

Atlantic-Indian Antarctic Basin

8

Antarctic Circle

60°

90° 60° 30° 0° 30°

METRES
FEET

METRES	FEET
0	0
200	656
2000	6562
3000	9843
4000	13124
5000	16409
6000	19686
7000	22967
9000	29529

Lambert Azimuthal Equal Area Projection

1 : 120 000 000

MILES 0 ____ 1000 ____ 2000

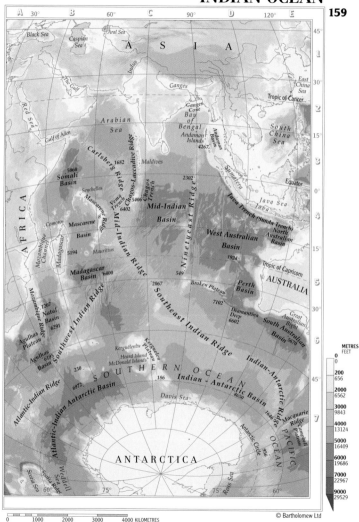

Black Sea
Caspian Sea
Aral Sea

A S I A

Indus

The Gulf

Ganges

Red Sea

Gulf of Aden

Arabian Sea

Ganges
Ganges Cone
Bay of Bengal

Andaman Islands
4267

East China Sea

Tropic of Cancer

South China Sea

Carlsberg Ridge   1682

Chagos-Laccadive Ridge

Maldives

Somali Basin   5060

Seychelles

2302

Chagos Trench

Mascarene Ridge

Vema Trench
5406
5402

Mid-Indian Basin

Mid-Indian Ridge

Ninetyeast Ridge

Sumatra

Java Trench (Sunda Trench)

Java

Java Sea

Equator

North Australian Basin

Comoros

Mascarene Basin

5194

AFRICA

Mozambique Channel

Madagascar

Mauritius

Madagascar Basin   6400

549

West Australian Basin   1924

Tropic of Capricorn

AUSTRALIA

2067

Broken Plateau

7102

Perth Basin

Mozambique Ridge

Natal Basin   1207

6291

Agulhas Plateau

Agulhas Basin   5193

Southwest Indian Ridge

Southeast Indian Ridge

Diamantina Deep   6602

South Australian Basin   5670

Great Australian Bight

Indian-Antarctic Ridge

METRES
FEET

0 | 0
200 | 656
2000 | 6562
3000 | 9843
4000 | 13124
5000 | 16409
6000 | 19686
7000 | 22967
8000 | 26247
9000 | 29529

Kerguelen
Kerguelen
Heard Island
McDonald Islands

230

S O U T H E R N   O C E A N

186

Indian - Antarctic Basin   4650

Indian-Antarctic Basin

Atlantic-Indian Ridge

Atlantic Antarctic Basin   6972

Davis Sea

1646.5

Macquarie Ridge

Campbell Plateau

PACIFIC

Weddell Sea

Scotia Ridge

75°

Antarctic Circle

956

Ross Sea

60°

A N T A R C T I C A

© Bartholomew Ltd

0   1000   2000   3000   4000 KILOMETRES

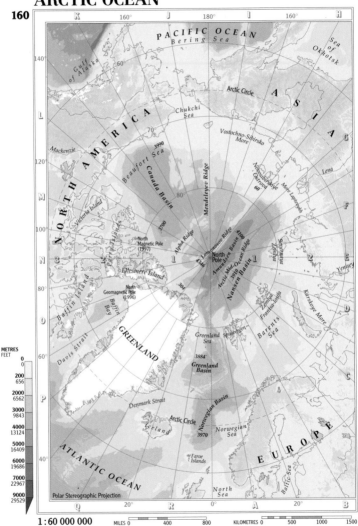

PACIFIC OCEAN
Bering Sea

Sea of Okhotsk

Gulf of Alaska

Arctic Circle

A S I A

Chukchi Sea

NORTH AMERICA

Mackenzie

Vostochno-Sibirsko More

Beaufort Sea

3990

Canada Basin

Novosibirskiye Ostrova

Lena

More Laptevykh

Mendeleyev Ridge

3700

80

Lomonosov Ridge

Amundsen Basin

4100

Victoria Island

Alpha Ridge

4346

Lomonosov Ridge

North Pole

Arctic Mid-Ocean Ridge

3810

Nansett Basin

Yenisey

North Magnetic Pole (1997)

Parry Islands

304

Ellesmere Island

North Geomagnetic Pole (1996)

Baffin Island

Baffin Bay

Zemlya Frantsa-Iosifa

Barents Sea

Karskoye More

Davis Strait

GREENLAND

Greenland Sea

Spitsbergen

3884

Greenland Basin

Denmark Strait

Norwegian Basin

Arctic Circle

Iceland

3970

Norwegian Sea

EUROPE

ATLANTIC OCEAN

Faroe Islands

North Sea

Baltic Sea

Polar Stereographic Projection

METRES
FEET

METRES	FEET
0	0
200	656
2000	6562
3000	9843
4000	13124
5000	16409
6000	19686
7000	22967
9000	29529

1 : 60 000 000

MILES 0 ——— 400 ——— 800

KILOMETRES 0 ——— 500 ——— 1000 ——— 1500

INTRODUCTION TO THE INDEX

The index includes all names shown on the maps in the Atlas of the World. Names are referenced by page number and by a grid reference. The grid reference correlates to the alphanumeric values which appear within each map frame. Each entry also includes the country or geographical area in which the feature is located. Entries relating to names appearing on insets are indicated by a small box symbol: □, followed by a grid reference if the inset has its own alphanumeric values.

Name forms are as they appear on the maps, with additional alternative names or name forms included as cross-references which refer the user to the entry for the map form of the name. Names beginning with Mc or Mac are alphabetized exactly as they appear. The terms Saint, Sainte, etc, are abbreviated to St, Ste, but alphabetized as if in the full form.

Names of physical features beginning with generic, geographical terms are permuted – the descriptive term is placed after the main part of the name. For example, Lake Superior is indexed as Superior, Lake; Mount Everest as Everest, Mount. This policy is applied to all languages.

Entries, other than those for towns and cities, include a descriptor indicating the type of geographical feature. Descriptors are not included where the type of feature is implicit in the name itself.

Administrative divisions are included to differentiate entries of the same name and feature type within the one country. In such cases, duplicate names are alphabetized in order of administrative division. Additional qualifiers are also included for names within selected geographical areas.

INDEX ABBREVIATIONS

admin. div.	administrative division	for.	forest	Pol.	Poland
Afgh.	Afghanistan	g.	gulf	Port.	Portugal
Alg.	Algeria	Ger.	Germany	prov.	province
Arg.	Argentina	Guat.	Guatemala	reg.	region
Austr.	Australia	hd	headland	Rep.	Republic
aut. reg.	autonomous region	Hond.	Honduras	Rus. Fed.	Russian Federation
aut. rep.	autonomous republic	imp. l.	impermanent lake	S.	South
		Indon.	Indonesia	Switz.	Switzerland
Azer.	Azerbaijan	isth.	isthmus	Tajik.	Tajikistan
Bangl.	Bangladesh	Kazakh.	Kazakhstan	Tanz.	Tanzania
Bol.	Bolivia	Kyrg.	Kyrgyzstan	terr.	territory
Bos.-Herz.	Bosnia Herzegovina	lag.	lagoon	Thai.	Thailand
Bulg.	Bulgaria	Lith.	Lithuania	Trin. and Tob.	Trinidad and Tobago
Can.	Canada	Lux.	Luxembourg		
C.A.R.	Central African Republic	Madag.	Madagascar	Turkm.	Turkmenistan
Col.	Colombia	Maur.	Mauritania	U.A.E.	United Arab Emirates
Czech Rep.	Czech Republic	Mex.	Mexico	U.K.	United Kingdom
Dem. Rep.	Democratic	Moz.	Mozambique	Ukr.	Ukraine
Congo	Republic of Congo	mun.	municipality	Uru.	Uruguay
depr.	depression	N.	North	U.S.A.	United States of America
des.	desert	Neth.	Netherlands		
Dom. Rep.	Dominican Republic	Nic.	Nicaragua	Uzbek.	Uzbekistan
		N.Z.	New Zealand	val.	valley
esc.	escarpment	Pak.	Pakistan	Venez.	Venezuela
est.	estuary	Para.	Paraguay	Yugo.	Yugoslavia
Eth.	Ethiopia	Phil.	Philippines		
Fin.	Finland	plat.	plateau		
		P.N.G.	Papua New Guinea		

A

100 C2 Aachen Ger.
100 B2 Aalst Belgium
100 B2 Aarschot Belgium
88 C2 Aba China
115 C4 Aba Nigeria
81 C2 Ābādān Iran
81 D2 Ābādeh Iran
114 B1 Abadla Alg.
115 C4 Abakaliki Nigeria
83 H3 Abakan Rus. Fed.
150 A3 A'bancay Peru
81 D2 Abarqū Iran
66 D2 Abashiri Japan
117 B4 Abaya Hāyk' l. Eth.
         Abay Wenz r. Eth./Sudan see
         Blue Nile
82 G3 Abaza Rus. Fed.
108 A2 Abbasanta Sardinia Italy
104 C1 Abbeville France
142 B3 Abbeville U.S.A.
74 B1 Abbottabad Pak.
55 C0 Abbott Ice Shelf Antarctica
115 E3 Abéché Chad
114 B4 Abengourou Côte d'Ivoire
93 E4 Åbenrå Denmark
114 C4 Abeokuta Nigeria
99 A2 Aberaeron U.K.
96 C2 Aberchirder U.K.
99 B3 Aberdare U.K.
99 A2 Aberdaron U.K.
122 B3 Aberdeen S. Africa
96 C2 Aberdeen U.K.
141 D3 Aberdeen MD U.S.A.
137 D1 Aberdeen SD U.S.A.
134 B1 Aberdeen WA U.S.A.
129 E1 Aberdeen Lake Can.
134 B2 Abert, Lake U.S.A.
99 A2 Aberystwyth U.K.
86 F2 Abez' Rus. Fed.
78 B3 Abhā Saudi Arabia
         Abiad, Bahr el r.
         Sudan/Uganda see White Nile
114 B4 Abidjan Côte d'Ivoire
137 D3 Abilene KS U.S.A.
139 D2 Abilene TX U.S.A.
99 C3 Abingdon U.K.
91 D3 Abinsk Rus. Fed.
130 B2 Abitibi, Lake Can.
         Åbo Fin. see Turku
74 B1 Abohar India
114 C4 Abomey Benin
60 A1 Abongabong, Gunung
         mt. Indon.
118 B2 Abong Mbang Cameroon
64 A2 Aborlan Phil.
115 D3 Abou Déia Chad
106 B2 Abrantes Port.
152 B3 Abra Pampa Arg.
136 A2 Absaroka Range mts U.S.A.
81 C1 Abşeron Yarımadası
         pen. Azer.
78 B3 Abū 'Arīsh Saudi Arabia
79 C2 Abu Dhabi U.A.E.
116 B3 Abu Hamed Sudan
115 C4 Abuja Nigeria
81 C2 Abū Kamāl Syria
152 B1 Abunã r. Bol.
150 B2 Abunã Brazil
74 B2 Abu Road India
116 B2 Abu Simbel Egypt
117 A3 Abu Zabad Sudan
         Abū Zabī U.A.E. see
         Abu Dhabi
117 A4 Abyei Sudan
145 B2 Acambaro Mex.
106 B1 A Cañiza Spain
144 B2 Acaponeta Mex.
145 C3 Acapulco Mex.
151 D2 Acará Brazil
150 B1 Acarigua Venez.
145 C3 Acatlan Mex.
145 C3 Acayucan Mex.
114 B4 Accra Ghana
98 B2 Accrington U.K.
74 B2 Achalpur India
97 A2 Achill Island Rep. of Ireland
101 D1 Achim Ger.
96 B2 Achnasheen U.K.
91 D2 Achuyevo Rus. Fed.
111 C3 Acıpayam Turkey
109 C3 Acireale Sicily Italy
147 C2 Acklins Island Bahamas
153 B4 Aconcagua, Cerro mt. Arg.
106 B1 A Coruña Spain
108 A2 Acqui Terme Italy
103 D2 Ács Hungary
145 C2 Actopán Mex.
139 D2 Ada U.S.A.
79 C2 Adam Oman
         'Adan Yemen see Aden
80 B2 Adana Turkey
         Adapazarı Turkey see
         Sakarya
108 A1 Adda r. Italy
78 B2 Ad Dafinah Saudi Arabia
78 B2 Ad Dahnā' des. Saudi Arabia
78 B2 Ad Dahnā' des. Saudi Arabia
114 A2 Ad Dakhla Western Sahara
79 C2 Ad Dammām Saudi Arabia
78 A2 Ad Dār al Ḥamrā'
         Saudi Arabia
78 B3 Ad Darb Saudi Arabia
78 B2 Ad Dawādimī Saudi Arabia
         Ad Dawḥah Qatar see Doha
78 B2 Ad Dilam Saudi Arabia
116 C2 Ad Dir'īyah Saudi Arabia
117 B4 Addis Ababa Eth.
81 C2 Ad Dīwānīyah Iraq
52 A2 Adelaide Austr.
101 D2 Adelbach Ger.
55 J2 Adélie Land reg. Antarctica
117 C3 Aden Yemen
117 C3 Aden, Gulf of Somalia/Yemen
100 C2 Adenau Ger.
79 C2 Adh Dhayd U.A.E.
59 C3 Adi i. Indon.
78 A3 Ādī Ārk'ay Eth.
116 B3 Adīgrat Eth.
75 B3 Adilabad India
141 E2 Adirondack Mountains
         U.S.A.
         Ādīs Ābeba Eth. see
         Addis Ababa
117 B4 Ādīs Ālem Eth.
110 C1 Adjud Romania
50 B1 Admiralty Gulf Austr.
128 A2 Admiralty Island U.S.A.
104 B3 Adour r. France
106 C2 Adra Spain
114 B2 Adrar Alg.
140 C2 Adrian MI U.S.A.
139 C1 Adrian TX U.S.A.
108 B2 Adriatic Sea Europe
116 B3 Adwa Eth.
83 K3 Adycha r. Rus. Fed.
91 D3 Adygeysk Rus. Fed.
114 B4 Adzopé Côte d'Ivoire
111 B3 Aegean Sea Greece/Turkey
101 D1 Aerzen Ger.
106 B1 A Estrada Spain
116 B3 Afabet Eritrea
76 C3 Afghanistan country Asia
78 B2 'Afīf Saudi Arabia
80 B2 Afyon Turkey
115 C3 Agadez Niger

114 B1 Agadir Morocco
77 D2 Agapa? Kazakh.
74 B2 Agar India
75 D2 Agartala India
81 C2 Ağdam Azer.
105 C3 Agde France
104 C3 Agen France
111 C3 Agia Vervara Greece
111 C3 Agios Dimitrios Greece
111 C3 Agios Efstratios i. Greece
111 C3 Agios Nikolaos Greece
110 B1 Agnita Romania
75 B2 Agra India
81 C2 Ağrı Turkey
108 B3 Agrigento Sicily Italy
111 B3 Agrinio Greece
109 B2 Agropoli Italy
154 B2 Água Clara Brazil
146 B4 Aguadulce Panama
144 B2 Aguanaval r. Mex.
144 B1 Agua Prieta Mex.
144 B2 Aguascalientes Mex.
154 C1 Águas Formosas Brazil
155 D1 Águas Formosas Brazil
106 B1 Águeda Port.
106 C1 Aguilar de Campóo Spain
107 C2 Águilas Spain
144 B3 Aguililla Mex.
122 B3 Agulhas, Cape S. Africa
155 D2 Agulhas Negras mt. Brazil
111 C2 Ağva Turkey
81 C2 Ahar Iran
100 C1 Ahaus Ger.
81 C2 Ahlat Turkey
100 C2 Ahlen Ger.
74 B2 Ahmadabad India
73 B3 Ahmadnagar India
74 B2 Ahmadpur East Pak.
74 B1 Ahmadpur Sial Pak.
144 B2 Ahome Mex.
79 C2 Ahram Iran
101 E1 Ahrensburg Ger.
104 C2 Ahun France
81 C2 Ahvāz Iran
122 A2 Ai-Ais Namibia
80 B2 Aigialousa Cyprus
111 B3 Aigio Greece
143 D2 Aiken U.S.A.
155 D1 Aimorés Brazil
155 D1 Aimorés, Serra dos hills
         Brazil
114 B2 'Aïn Ben Tili Maur.
107 D2 Aïn Defla Alg.
114 B1 Aïn Sefra Alg.
136 D2 Ainsworth U.S.A.
         Aintab Turkey see
         Gaziantep
107 D2 Aïn Taya Alg.
107 D2 Aïn Tédélès Alg.
60 A1 Airbangis Indon.
128 C2 Airdrie Can.
104 B3 Aire-sur-l'Adour France
101 E3 Aisch r. Ger.
128 A1 Aishihik Lake Can.
100 A3 Aisne r. France
59 D3 Aitape P.N.G.
110 B1 Aiud Romania
105 D3 Aix-en-Provence France
105 D2 Aix-les-Bains France
62 A1 Aizawl India
88 C2 Aizkraukle Latvia
67 C3 Aizu-wakamatsu Japan
105 D3 Ajaccio Corsica France
115 E1 Ajdābiyā Libya
74 B2 Ajmer India
138 A2 Ajo U.S.A.
87 E3 Akbulak Rus. Fed.
80 B2 Akçakale Turkey
80 B2 Akdağmadeni Turkey
88 A2 Åkersberga Sweden

118 C2 **Aketi** Dem. Rep. Congo
87 D4 **Akhal'alak'i** Georgia
79 C2 **Akhḍar, Jabal** mts Oman
111 C3 **Akhisar** Turkey
87 D4 **Akhtubinsk** Rus. Fed.
130 B1 **Akimiski Island** Can.
66 D3 **Akita** Japan
114 A3 **Akjoujt** Maur.
77 D1 **Akkol'** Kazakh.
88 B2 **Akmenrags** pt Latvia
　　 Akmola Kazakh. see Astana
117 B4 **Akobo** Sudan
74 B2 **Akola** India
78 A3 **Akordat** Eritrea
127 G2 **Akpatok Island** Can.
92 □A3 **Akranes** Iceland
111 B2 **Akrathos, Akra** pt Greece
140 C2 **Akron** U.S.A.
75 B1 **Aksai Chin** terr. Asia
80 B2 **Aksaray** Turkey
76 B1 **Aksay** Kazakh.
91 D2 **Aksay** Rus. Fed.
80 B2 **Akşehir** Turkey
76 C2 **Akshiganak** Kazakh.
77 E2 **Aksu** China
78 A3 **Aksum** Eth.
76 B2 **Aktau** Kazakh.
77 D2 **Aktogay** Kazakh.
88 C3 **Aktsyabrski** Belarus
76 B1 **Aktyubinsk** Kazakh.
115 C4 **Akure** Nigeria
92 □B2 **Akureyri** Iceland
　　 Akyab Myanmar see Sittwe
142 C2 **Alabama** r. U.S.A.
142 C2 **Alabama** state U.S.A.
111 C3 **Alaçatı** Turkey
81 C1 **Alagir** Rus. Fed.
151 E3 **Alagoinhas** Brazil
107 C1 **Alagón** Spain
79 B2 **Al Aḥmadī** Kuwait
77 E2 **Alakol', Ozero** salt l. Kazakh.
92 J2 **Alakurtti** Rus. Fed.
78 B3 **Al 'Alayyah** Saudi Arabia
81 C2 **Al 'Amādīyah** Iraq
135 C3 **Alamo** U.S.A.
138 B2 **Alamogordo** U.S.A.
144 A2 **Alamos** Sonora Mex.
144 B2 **Alamos** Sonora Mex.
144 B2 **Alamos** r. Mex.
136 B3 **Alamosa** U.S.A.
93 G3 **Åland** is Fin.
80 B2 **Alanya** Turkey
80 B3 **Al 'Aqabah** Jordan
78 B2 **Al 'Aqiq** Saudi Arabia
107 C2 **Alarcón, Embalse de** resr Spain
78 B2 **Al Arṭāwīyah** Saudi Arabia
61 C2 **Alas** Indon.
111 C3 **Alaşehir** Turkey
128 A2 **Alaska** state U.S.A.
124 C2 **Alaska, Gulf of** U.S.A.
81 C2 **Alāt** Azer.
87 D3 **Alatyr'** Rus. Fed.
150 A2 **Alausí** Ecuador
93 H3 **Alavus** Fin.
52 B2 **Alawoona** Austr.
108 A2 **Alba** Italy
107 C2 **Albacete** Spain
110 B1 **Alba Iulia** Romania
109 C2 **Albania** country Europe
50 A3 **Albany** Austr.
130 B1 **Albany** r. Can.
143 D2 **Albany** GA U.S.A.
141 E2 **Albany** NY U.S.A.
134 B2 **Albany** OR U.S.A.
　　 Al Başrah Iraq see Basra
51 D1 **Albatross Bay** Austr.
115 E1 **Al Bayḍā'** Libya
78 B3 **Al Bayḍā'** Yemen

143 D1 **Albemarle** U.S.A.
143 E1 **Albemarle Sound** sea chan. U.S.A.
108 A2 **Albenga** Italy
51 C2 **Alberga** watercourse Austr.
119 D2 **Albert, Lake** Dem. Rep. Congo/Uganda
128 C2 **Alberta** prov. Can.
100 B2 **Albert Kanaal** canal Belgium
137 E2 **Albert Lea** U.S.A.
104 C3 **Albi** France
78 A2 **Al Bi'r** Saudi Arabia
78 B3 **Al Birk** Saudi Arabia
78 B2 **Al Biyāḍh** reg. Saudi Arabia
93 E4 **Ålborg** Denmark
78 B2 **Alborz, Reshteh-ye** mts Iran
106 B2 **Albufeira** Port.
138 B1 **Albuquerque** U.S.A.
79 C2 **Al Buraymī** Oman
53 C3 **Albury** Austr.
106 B2 **Alcácer do Sal** Port.
106 C1 **Alcalá de Henares** Spain
106 C2 **Alcalá la Real** Spain
108 B3 **Alcamo** Sicily Italy
107 C1 **Alcañiz** Spain
106 B2 **Alcántara** Spain
106 C2 **Alcaraz** Spain
106 C2 **Alcaraz, Sierra de** mts Spain
106 C2 **Alcaudete** Spain
106 C2 **Alcázar de San Juan** Spain
90 D2 **Alchevs'k** Ukr.
155 E1 **Alcobaça** Brazil
107 C1 **Alcora** Spain
107 C2 **Alcoy** Spain
107 D2 **Alcúdia** Spain
145 C2 **Aldama** Mex.
83 J3 **Aldan** Rus. Fed.
83 J2 **Aldan** r. Rus. Fed.
95 C4 **Alderney** i. Channel Is
114 A3 **Aleg** Maur.
155 D2 **Alegre** Brazil
152 C3 **Alegrete** Brazil
83 K3 **Aleksandrovsk-Sakhalinskiy** Rus. Fed.
91 D1 **Alekseyevka** Belgorodskaya Oblast' Rus. Fed.
91 D1 **Alekseyevka** Belgorodskaya Oblast' Rus. Fed.
89 E3 **Aleksin** Rus. Fed.
109 D2 **Aleksinac** Yugo.
118 B3 **Alèmbé** Gabon
155 D2 **Além Paraíba** Brazil
93 F3 **Ålen** Norway
104 C2 **Alençon** France
80 B2 **Aleppo** Syria
150 A3 **Alerta** Peru
128 B2 **Alert Bay** Can.
105 C3 **Alès** France
110 B1 **Aleşd** Romania
108 A2 **Alessandria** Italy
93 E3 **Ålesund** Norway
124 B2 **Aleutian Islands** U.S.A.
83 L3 **Alevina, Mys** c. Rus. Fed.
128 A2 **Alexander Archipelago** is U.S.A.
122 A2 **Alexander Bay** S. Africa
142 C2 **Alexander City** U.S.A.
55 O2 **Alexander Island** Antarctica
53 C3 **Alexandra** Austr.
54 A3 **Alexandra** N.Z.
111 B2 **Alexandreia** Greece
　　 Alexandretta Turkey see İskenderun
116 A1 **Alexandria** Egypt
110 C2 **Alexandria** Romania
123 C3 **Alexandria** S. Africa
142 B2 **Alexandria** LA U.S.A.
137 D1 **Alexandria** MN U.S.A.
141 D3 **Alexandria** VA U.S.A.

52 A3 **Alexandrina, Lake** Austr.
111 C2 **Alexandroupoli** Greece
131 E1 **Alexis** r. Can.
128 B2 **Alexis Creek** Can.
77 E1 **Aleysk** Rus. Fed.
107 C1 **Alfaro** Spain
81 C2 **Al Fāw** Iraq
101 D2 **Alfeld (Leine)** Ger.
155 C2 **Alfenas** Brazil
　　 Al Furāt r. Iraq/Syria see Euphrates
106 B2 **Algeciras** Spain
107 C2 **Algemesí** Spain
78 A3 **Algena** Eritrea
　　 Alger Alg. see Algiers
114 C1 **Algeria** country Africa
79 C3 **Al Ghaydah** Yemen
108 A2 **Alghero** Sardinia Italy
79 B2 **Al Ghwaybīyah** Saudi Arabia
115 C1 **Algiers** Alg.
123 C3 **Algoa Bay** S. Africa
137 E2 **Algona** U.S.A.
81 C2 **Al Ḥadīthah** Iraq
79 C2 **Al Ḥajar al Gharbī** mts Oman
115 D2 **Al Ḥamādah al Ḥamrā'** plat. Libya
107 C2 **Alhama de Murcia** Spain
78 B2 **Al Ḥanākīyah** Saudi Arabia
81 C2 **Al Ḥasakah** Syria
81 C2 **Al Ḥayy** Iraq
78 B3 **Al Ḥazm al-Jawf** Yemen
79 C3 **Al Ḥibāk** des. Saudi Arabia
81 C2 **Al Ḥillah** Iraq
78 B2 **Al Ḥillah** Saudi Arabia
79 B2 **Al Ḥinnāh** Saudi Arabia
78 B3 **Al Ḥudaydah** Yemen
79 B2 **Al Ḥufūf** Saudi Arabia
115 D2 **Al Ḥulayq al Kabīr** hills Libya
79 C2 **'Aliābād** Iran
111 C3 **Aliağa** Turkey
111 B2 **Aliakmonas** r. Greece
107 C2 **Alicante** Spain
139 D3 **Alice** U.S.A.
109 C3 **Alice, Punta** pt Italy
51 C2 **Alice Springs** Austr.
75 B2 **Aligarh** India
81 C2 **Alīgūdarz** Iran
69 E1 **Alihe** China
118 B3 **Alima** r. Congo
71 C2 **Aliova** r. Turkey
117 C3 **Ali Sabieh** Djibouti
123 C3 **Aliwal North** S. Africa
115 E2 **Al Jaghbūb** Libya
78 B2 **Al Jahrah** Kuwait
79 C2 **Al Jamalīyah** Qatar
78 B2 **Al Jawf** Saudi Arabia
115 D1 **Al Jawsh** Libya
106 B2 **Aljezur** Port.
79 B2 **Al Jubayl** Saudi Arabia
78 B2 **Al Junaynah** Saudi Arabia
106 B2 **Aljustrel** Port.
78 B2 **Al Kahfah** Saudi Arabia
79 C2 **Al Kāmil** Oman
80 B2 **Al Karak** Jordan
79 C2 **Al Khābūrah** Oman
78 B2 **Al Khamāsīn** Saudi Arabia
79 C2 **Al Khaṣab** Oman
78 B3 **Al Khawkhah** Yemen
79 C2 **Al Khawr** Qatar
115 E2 **Al Khufrah** Libya
115 D1 **Al Khums** Libya
78 B2 **Al Khunn** Saudi Arabia
79 C2 **Al Kir'ānah** Qatar
100 B1 **Alkmaar** Neth.
81 C2 **Al Kūt** Iraq
　　 Al Kuwayt Kuwait see Kuwait
80 B2 **Al Lādhiqīyah** Syria
75 C2 **Allahabad** India

83 K2 Allakh-Yun' Rus. Fed.
62 A2 Allanmyo Myanmar
141 D2 Allegheny r. U.S.A.
140 C3 Allegheny Mountains U.S.A.
97 B1 Allen, Lough l.
　　　Rep. of Ireland
145 B2 Allende Coahuila Mex.
145 B2 Allende Nuevo León Mex.
141 D2 Allentown U.S.A.
73 B4 Alleppey India
101 D1 Aller r. Ger.
136 C2 Alliance NE U.S.A.
140 C2 Alliance OH U.S.A.
78 B2 Al Lith Saudi Arabia
96 C2 Alloa U.K.
131 C2 Alma Can.
　　　Alma-Ata Kazakh. see
　　　Almaty
106 B2 Almada Port.
106 C2 Almadén Spain
　　　Al Madīnah Saudi Arabia see
　　　Medina
116 B1 Al Mafraq Jordan
78 B3 Al Maḥwīt Yemen
78 B2 Al Majma'ah Saudi Arabia
135 B2 Almanor, Lake U.S.A.
107 C2 Almansa Spain
78 B2 Al Mariyyah U.A.E.
115 E1 Al Marj Libya
77 D2 Almaty Kazakh.
81 C2 Al Mawṣil Iraq
106 C1 Almazán Spain
151 C2 Almeirim Brazil
100 C1 Almelo Neth.
155 D1 Almenara Brazil
106 B1 Almendra, Embalse de resr
　　　Spain
106 B2 Almendralejo Spain
106 C2 Almería Spain
106 C2 Almería, Golfo de b. Spain
87 E3 Al'met'yevsk Rus. Fed.
78 B2 Al Mindak Saudi Arabia
79 B2 Al Mish'āb Saudi Arabia
106 B2 Almodôvar Port.
106 B2 Almonte Spain
75 B2 Almora India
79 B2 Al Mubarraz Saudi Arabia
79 C2 Al Muḍaibī Oman
80 B3 Al Mudawwarah Jordan
79 B3 Al Mukallā Yemen
78 B3 Al Mukhā Yemen
106 C2 Almuñécar Spain
78 A2 Al Muwayliḥ Saudi Arabia
111 B3 Almyros Greece
96 B2 Alness U.K.
98 C1 Alnwick U.K.
111 B3 Alonnisos i. Greece
59 C3 Alor i. Indon.
59 C3 Alor, Kepulauan is Indon.
60 B1 Alor Setar Malaysia
　　　Alost Belgium see Aalst
86 C2 Alozero Rus. Fed.
140 C1 Alpena U.S.A.
139 C2 Alpine U.S.A.
84 D3 Alps mts Europe
79 B3 Al Qa'āmīyāt reg.
　　　Saudi Arabia
115 D1 Al Qaddāḥīyah Libya
78 B2 Al Qā'iyah Saudi Arabia
81 C2 Al Qāmishlī Syria
80 B2 Al Qaryatayn Syria
79 B3 Al Qaṭn Yemen
80 B2 Al Qunayṭirah Syria
78 B3 Al Qunfidhah Saudi Arabia
78 B2 Al Quwayīyah Saudi Arabia
101 D2 Alsfeld Ger.
92 H2 Alta Norway
92 H2 Altaelva r. Norway
68 B1 Altai Mountains Asia
143 D2 Altamaha r. U.S.A.

151 C2 Altamira Brazil
109 C2 Altamura Italy
68 B1 Altay China
68 C1 Altay Mongolia
105 D2 Altdorf Switz.
107 C2 Altea Spain
101 F2 Altenburg Ger.
100 C2 Altenkirchen (Westerwald)
　　　Ger.
111 C3 Altınoluk Turkey
111 D3 Altıntaş Turkey
152 B2 Altiplano plain Bol.
154 B1 Alto Araguaia Brazil
107 C1 Alto del Moncayo mt. Spain
154 B1 Alto Garças Brazil
121 C2 Alto Molócuè Moz.
129 E3 Altona Can.
141 D2 Altoona U.S.A.
154 B1 Alto Sucuriú Brazil
102 C2 Altötting Ger.
68 B2 Altun Shan mts China
134 B2 Alturas U.S.A.
139 D2 Altus U.S.A.
88 C2 Alūksne Latvia
78 A2 Al 'Ulā Saudi Arabia
115 D1 Al 'Uqaylah Libya
91 C3 Alushta Ukr.
139 D1 Alva U.S.A.
145 C3 Alvarado Mex.
93 F3 Älvdalen Sweden
93 F3 Älvdalen val. Sweden
92 H1 Älvsbyn Sweden
78 A2 Al Wajh Saudi Arabia
74 B2 Alwar India
81 C2 Al Widyān plat.
　　　Iraq/Saudi Arabia
　　　Alxa Youqi China see
　　　Ehen Hudag
　　　Alxa Zuoqi China see
　　　Bayan Hot
51 C1 Alyangula Austr.
88 B3 Alytus Lith.
136 C1 Alzada U.S.A.
100 D3 Alzey Ger.
50 C2 Amadeus, Lake salt flat Austr.
127 G2 Amadjuak Lake Can.
106 B2 Amadora Port.
78 B3 Amā'ir Saudi Arabia
93 F4 Åmål Sweden
111 B3 Amaliada Greece
59 D3 Amamapare Indon.
154 A2 Amambaí Brazil
154 B2 Amambaí r. Brazil
69 E3 Amami-Ō-shima i. Japan
69 E3 Amami-shotō is Japan
77 C1 Amangel'dy Kazakh.
109 C3 Amantea Italy
123 D3 Amanzimtoti S. Africa
151 C1 Amapá Brazil
106 B2 Amareleja Port.
139 C1 Amarillo U.S.A.
108 B2 Amaro, Monte mt. Italy
80 B1 Amasya Turkey
150 C1 Amazon r. S. America
151 D1 Amazon, Mouths of the
　　　Brazil
　　　Amazonas r. S. America see
　　　Amazon
74 B1 Ambala India
121 D3 Ambalavao Madag.
121 D2 Ambanja Madag.
150 A2 Ambato Ecuador
121 D2 Ambato Boeny Madag.
121 D3 Ambato Finandrahana
　　　Madag.
121 D3 Ambatolampy Madag.
121 D2 Ambatondrazaka Madag.
101 E3 Amberg Ger.
146 B3 Ambergris Cay i. Belize
75 C2 Ambikapur India

121 D2 Ambilobe Madag.
98 B1 Ambleside U.K.
121 D3 Amboasary Madag.
121 D2 Ambohimahasoa Madag.
59 C3 Ambon Indon.
59 C3 Ambon i. Indon.
121 D3 Ambositra Madag.
121 D3 Ambovombe Madag.
135 C4 Amboy U.S.A.
120 A1 Ambriz Angola
68 C2 Amdo China
145 B2 Amealco Mex.
144 B2 Ameca Mex.
100 B1 Ameland i. Neth.
134 D2 American Falls U.S.A.
134 D2 American Falls Reservoir
　　　U.S.A.
135 D2 American Fork U.S.A.
49 G4 American Samoa terr.
　　　S. Pacific Ocean
143 D2 Americus U.S.A.
100 B1 Amersfoort Neth.
55 E2 Amery Ice Shelf Antarctica
137 E2 Ames U.S.A.
111 B3 Amfissa Greece
83 J2 Amga Rus. Fed.
66 C1 Amgu Rus. Fed.
115 C2 Amguid Alg.
83 K3 Amgun' r. Rus. Fed.
131 D2 Amherst Can.
104 C2 Amiens France
73 B3 Amindivi Islands India
122 A1 Aminuis Namibia
74 A2 Amir Chah Pak.
129 D2 Amisk Lake Can.
139 C3 Amistad Reservoir
　　　Mex./U.S.A.
98 A2 Amlwch U.K.
80 B2 'Ammān Jordan
127 I2 Ammassalik Greenland
78 B3 Am Nābiyah Yemen
81 D2 Amol Iran
111 C3 Amorgos i. Greece
142 C2 Amory U.S.A.
130 C2 Amos Can.
　　　Amoy China see Xiamen
155 C2 Amparo Brazil
107 D1 Amposta Spain
75 B2 Amravati India
74 B1 Amritsar India
100 B1 Amstelveen Neth.
100 B1 Amsterdam Neth.
103 C2 Amstetten Austria
115 E3 Am Timan Chad
76 B2 Amudar'ya r. Asia
126 E1 Amund Ringnes Island Can.
126 C2 Amundsen Gulf Can.
55 M2 Amundsen Sea Antarctica
61 C2 Amuntai Indon.
　　　Amur r. China/Rus. Fed. see
　　　Heilong Jiang
78 A3 'Amur, Wadi watercourse
　　　Sudan
83 J2 Anabar r. Rus. Fed.
83 J2 Anabarskiy Zaliv b.
　　　Rus. Fed.
134 D1 Anaconda U.S.A.
139 D1 Anadarko U.S.A.
80 B1 Anadolu Dağları mts Turkey
83 M2 Anadyr' r. Rus. Fed.
81 C2 'Ānah Iraq
145 B2 Anáhuac Mex.
60 B1 Anambas, Kepulauan is
　　　Indon.
137 E2 Anamosa U.S.A.
80 B2 Anamur Turkey
67 B4 Anan Japan
73 B3 Anantapur India
74 B1 Anantnag
　　　Jammu and Kashmir

90 B2 Anan'yiv Ukr.
91 D3 Anapa Rus. Fed.
154 C1 Anápolis Brazil
152 B3 Añatuya Arg.
65 B2 Anbyon N. Korea
104 B2 Ancenis France
108 B2 Ancona Italy
153 A5 Ancud Chile
Anda China see Daqing
93 E3 Andalsnes Norway
142 C2 Andalusia U.S.A.
73 D3 Andaman Islands India
63 A2 Andaman Sea Indian Ocean
121 □D2 Andapa Madag.
100 B2 Andelst Neth.
92 G2 Andenes Norway
100 B2 Andenne Belgium
100 B2 Anderlecht Belgium
126 C2 Anderson r. Can.
126 B2 Anderson AK U.S.A.
140 E2 Anderson IN U.S.A.
143 D2 Anderson SC U.S.A.
148 D2 Andes mts S. America
121 □D2 Andilamena Madag.
121 □D2 Andilanatoby Madag.
77 D2 Andizhan Uzbek.
121 □D2 Andoany Madag.
Andong China see Dandong
65 B2 Andong S. Korea
107 D1 Andorra country Europe
107 D1 Andorra la Vella Andorra
99 C3 Andover U.K.
154 B1 Andradina Brazil
89 D2 Andreapol' Rus. Fed.
155 D2 Andrelândia Brazil
139 C2 Andrews U.S.A.
109 C2 Andria Italy
121 □D3 Androka Madag.
146 C2 Andros i. Bahamas
111 B3 Andros i. Greece
143 E4 Andros Town Bahamas
73 B3 Andrott i. India
90 B1 Andrushivka Ukr.
92 G2 Andselv Norway
106 C2 Andújar Spain
120 A2 Andulo Angola
114 C3 Anéfis Mali
115 D3 Aney Niger
83 H3 Angara r. Rus. Fed.
69 C1 Angarsk Rus. Fed.
93 G3 Ange Sweden
144 A2 Angel de la Guarda, Isla i. Mex.
64 B1 Angeles Phil.
150 B1 Angel Falls waterfall Venez.
93 F4 Ängelholm Sweden
92 G3 Ångermanälven r. Sweden
104 B2 Angers France
129 E1 Angikuni Lake l. Can.
98 A2 Anglesey i. U.K.
121 C2 Angoche Moz.
79 C2 Angohrān Iran
120 A2 Angola country Africa
140 C2 Angola U.S.A.
128 A2 Angoon U.S.A.
104 C2 Angoulême France
77 D2 Angren Uzbek.
147 D3 Anguilla terr. West Indies
93 F4 Anholt i. Denmark
71 B3 Anhua China
72 D2 Anhui prov. China
154 B1 Anhumas Brazil
154 C1 Anicuns Brazil
66 D1 Aniva, Mys c. Rus. Fed.
65 B2 Anjū N. Korea
70 A2 Ankang China
80 B2 Ankara Turkey
71 B3 Anlu China
91 E1 Anna Rus. Fed.
115 C1 Annaba Alg.

101 F2 Annaberg-Buchholtz Ger.
78 B2 An Nafūd des. Saudi Arabia
81 C2 An Najaf Iraq
96 C3 Annan U.K.
141 D3 Annapolis U.S.A.
75 C2 Annapurna I mt. Jammu and Kashmir/Nepal
140 C2 Ann Arbor U.S.A.
150 C1 Anna Regina Guyana
81 C2 An Nāşirīyah Iraq
105 D2 Annecy France
78 B3 An Nimāş Saudi Arabia
62 B1 Anning China
142 C2 Anniston U.S.A.
105 C2 Annonay France
79 B2 An Nu'ayrīyah Saudi Arabia
121 □D2 Anorontany, Tanjona hd Madag.
111 C3 Ano Viannos Greece
71 B3 Anpu China
70 B2 Anqing China
102 C2 Ansbach Ger.
70 C1 Anshan China
71 A3 Anshun China
150 A3 Ansongo Mali
150 A3 Antabamba Peru
80 B2 Antakya Turkey
121 □E2 Antalaha Madag.
80 B2 Antalya Turkey
80 B2 Antalya Körfezi g. Turkey
121 □D2 Antananarivo Madag.
55 Q3 Antarctic Peninsula Antarctica
96 B2 An Teallach mt. U.K.
106 C2 Antequera Spain
138 B2 Anthony U.S.A.
114 B2 Anti Atlas mts Morocco
105 D3 Antibes France
131 D2 Anticosti, Île d' i. Can.
131 D2 Antigonish Can.
147 D3 Antigua i. Antigua
147 D3 Antigua and Barbuda country West Indies
145 C2 Antiguo-Morelos Mex.
111 B3 Antikythira i. Greece
Antioch Turkey see Antakya
152 A3 Antofagasta Chile
154 C3 Antonina Brazil
97 C1 Antrim U.K.
97 C1 Antrim Hills U.K.
121 □D2 Antsalova Madag.
121 □D2 Antsirabe Madag.
121 □D2 Antsirañana Madag.
121 □D2 Antsohihy Madag.
100 B2 Antwerpen Belgium
An Uaimh Rep. of Ireland see Navan
75 C2 Anugul India
74 B2 Anupgarh India
73 C4 Anuradhapura Sri Lanka
Anvers Belgium see Antwerpen
68 C2 Anxi China
51 C3 Anxious Bay Austr.
70 B2 Anyang China
65 B2 Anyang S. Korea
108 B2 Anzio Italy
66 D2 Aomori Japan
Aoraki mt. N.Z. see Cook, Mount
108 A1 Aosta Italy
143 D3 Apalachee Bay U.S.A.
150 B2 Apaporis r. Col.
154 B2 Aparecida do Tabuado Brazil
64 B1 Aparri Phil.
86 C2 Apatity Rus. Fed.
144 B3 Apatzingán Mex.
100 B1 Apeldoorn Neth.
100 C1 Apen Ger.

154 C2 Apiaí Brazil
64 B2 Apo, Mount vol. Phil.
101 E2 Apolda Ger.
52 B3 Apollo Bay Austr.
143 D3 Apopka, Lake U.S.A.
154 B1 Aporé Brazil
154 B1 Aporé r. Brazil
80 B2 ·Apostolos Andreas, Cape Cyprus
133 E3 Appalachian Mountains U.S.A.
108 A2 Appennino mts Italy
53 D2 Appin Austr.
140 B2 Appleton U.S.A.
108 B2 Aprilia Italy
91 D3 Apsheronsk Rus. Fed.
154 B2 Apucarana Brazil
154 B2 Apucarana, Serra da hills Brazil
78 A2 Aqaba, Gulf of Asia
154 A1 Aquidauana r. Brazil
75 C2 Ara India
77 A4 Arab, Bahr el watercourse Sudan
56 B4 Arabian Sea Indian Ocean
151 E3 Aracaju Brazil
151 E2 Aracati Brazil
154 B2 Araçatuba Brazil
155 D1 Aracruz Brazil
155 D1 Araçuaí Brazil
110 B1 Arad Romania
115 E3 Arada Chad
156 C6 Arafura Sea Austr./Indon.
154 B1 Aragarças Brazil
107 C1 Aragón r. Spain
151 D2 Araguaia r. Brazil
151 D2 Araguaína Brazil
154 C1 Araguari Brazil
67 C3 Arai Japan
115 C2 Arak Alg.
81 C2 Arāk Iran
62 A1 Arakan Yoma mts Myanmar
81 C1 Araks r. Armenia/Turkey
76 C2 Aral Sea salt l. Kazakh./Uzbek.
76 C2 Aral'sk Kazakh.
Aral'skoye More salt l. Kazakh./Uzbek. see Aral Sea
106 C1 Aranda de Duero Spain
109 C2 Arandelovac Yugo.
97 B1 Aran Island Rep. of Ireland
97 B2 Aran Islands Rep. of Ireland
107 C1 Aranjuez Spain
122 A1 Aranos Namibia
139 D3 Aransas Pass U.S.A.
67 B4 Arao Japan
114 B3 Araouane Mali
151 E2 Arapiraca Brazil
154 B2 Arapongas Brazil
154 B2 Arapoti Brazil
78 B1 'Ar'ar Saudi Arabia
154 C3 Araraquara Brazil
151 C2 Araras Brazil
154 B3 Araras, Serra das mts Brazil
52 B3 Ararat Austr.
155 D2 Araruama, Lago de lag. Brazil
155 E1 Arataca Brazil
Aratürük China see Yiwu
150 A1 Arauca Col.
154 C1 Araxá Brazil
81 C2 Arbīl Iraq
96 C2 Arbroath U.K.
74 A2 Arbu Lut, Dasht-e des. Afgh.
104 B3 Arcachon France
140 C3 Arcadia U.S.A.
134 B2 Arcata U.S.A.
145 B3 Arcelia Mex.
86 D2 Archangel Rus. Fed.
51 D1 Archer r. Austr.

134 D2 Arco U.S.A.
106 B2 Arcos de la Frontera Spain
127 F2 Arctic Bay Can.
160   Arctic Ocean
126 C2 Arctic Red r. Can.
81 C2 Ardabil Iran
81 C1 Ardahan Turkey
93 E3 Árdalstangen Norway
81 D2 Ardestán Iran
53 C2 Ardlethan Austr.
139 D2 Ardmore U.S.A.
96 A2 Ardnamurchan, Point of U.K.
52 A2 Ardrossan Austr.
96 B3 Ardrossan U.K.
135 B3 Arena, Point U.S.A.
93 E4 Arendal Norway
101 E1 Arendsee (Altmark) Ger.
150 A3 Arequipa Peru
151 C2 Arere Brazil
108 B2 Arezzo Italy
104 B2 Argentan France
153 C3 Argentina country S. America
153 A6 Argentino, Lago l. Arg.
104 C2 Argenton-sur-Creuse France
110 C2 Argeş r. Romania
74 A1 Arghandab r. Afgh.
111 B3 Argolikos Kolpos b. Greece
111 B3 Argos Greece
111 B3 Agostoli Greece
107 C1 Arguis Spain
69 E1 Argun' r. China/Rus. Fed.
50 B1 Argyle, Lake Austr.
93 F4 Århus Denmark
122 A2 Ariamsvlei Namibia
152 A2 Arica Chile
96 A2 Arinagour U.K.
155 C1 Arinos Brazil
150 C3 Aripuaná Brazil
150 B2 Aripuaná r. Brazil
150 B2 Ariquemes Brazil
154 B1 Arianhã r. Brazil
138 A2 Arizona state U.S.A.
144 A1 Arizpe Mex.
78 B2 'Arjah Saudi Arabia
92 G2 Arjeplog Sweden
142 B2 Arkadelphia U.S.A.
77 C1 Arkalyk Kazakh.
142 B2 Arkansas r. U.S.A.
142 B1 Arkansas state U.S.A.
137 D3 Arkansas City U.S.A.
       Arkhangel'sk Rus. Fed. see Archangel
97 C2 Arklow Rep. of Ireland
102 C1 Arkona, Kap c. Ger.
82 G1 Arkticheskogo Instituta, Ostrova is Rus. Fed.
105 C3 Arles France
115 C3 Arlit Niger
100 B3 Arlon Belgium
97 C1 Armagh U.K.
81 C1 Armant Egypt
81 C1 Armavir Rus. Fed.
81 C1 Armenia country Asia
150 A1 Armenia Col.
144 B3 Armería Mex.
53 D2 Armidale Austr.
130 B1 Armstrong Can.
80 B1 Armyans'k Ukr.
80 B2 Arnaoutis, Cape Cyprus
100 B2 Arnhem Neth.
51 C1 Arnhem, Cape Austr.
51 C1 Arnhem Bay Austr.
51 C1 Arnhem Land reg. Austr.
108 B2 Arno r. Italy
52 A2 Arno Bay Austr.
130 C2 Arnprior Can.

100 D2 Arnsberg Ger.
101 E2 Arnstadt Ger.
122 A2 Aroab Namibia
101 D2 Arolsen Ger.
78 A3 Aroma Sudan
108 A1 Arona Italy
144 B2 Aros r. Mex.
81 C2 Ar Ramadi Iraq
96 B3 Arran i. U.K.
80 B2 Ar Raqqah Syria
104 C1 Arras France
78 B2 Ar-Rass Saudi Arabia
145 C3 Arriagá Mex.
79 C2 Ar Rimãl reg. Saudi Arabia
       Ar Riyad Saudi Arabia see Riyadh
145 C2 Arroyo Seco Mex.
79 C2 Ar Rustaq Oman
80 C2 Ar Rutbah Iraq
81 D3 Arsenaján Iran
66 B2 Arsen'yev Rus. Fed.
111 B3 Arta Greece
144 B3 Arteaga Mex.
66 B2 Artem Rus. Fed.
91 D2 Artemivs'k Ukr.
104 C2 Artenay France
138 C2 Artesia U.S.A.
51 E2 Arthur Point Austr.
152 C4 Artigas Uru.
129 D1 Artillery Lake Can.
90 B2 Artsyz Ukr.
77 D3 Artux China
81 C1 Artvin Turkey
59 C3 Aru, Kepulauan is Indon.
119 D2 Arua Uganda
147 D3 Aruba terr. West Indies
119 D3 Arusha Tanz.
69 C1 Arvayheer Mongolia
129 E1 Arviat Can.
92 G2 Arvidsjaur Sweden
93 F4 Arvika Sweden
87 D3 Arzamas Rus. Fed.
107 C2 Arzew Alg.
101 F2 Arzfeld Ger.
101 F2 Aš Czech Rep.
115 C4 Asaba Nigeria
66 D2 Asahi-dake vol. Japan
66 D2 Asahikawa Japan
78 B3 Āsalē l. Eth.
75 C2 Asansol India
131 C2 Asbestos Can.
109 C2 Ascea Italy
152 B2 Ascensión Bol.
112 C4 Ascension i. S. Atlantic Ocean
101 D3 Aschaffenburg Ger.
100 C2 Ascheberg Ger.
101 E2 Aschersleben Ger.
108 B2 Ascoli Piceno Italy
92 G3 Åsele Sweden
110 B2 Asenovgrad Bulg.
50 A2 Ashburton watercourse Austr.
54 B2 Ashburton N.Z.
142 B2 Ashdown U.S.A.
143 D1 Asheville U.S.A.
53 D1 Ashford Austr.
99 D3 Ashford U.K.
76 B3 Ashgabat Turkm.
66 D3 Ashikaga Japan
98 C2 Ashington U.K.
67 B4 Ashizuri-misaki pt Japan
       Ashkhabad Turkm. see Ashgabat
136 D3 Ashland KS U.S.A.
140 C3 Ashland KY U.S.A.
140 C2 Ashland OH U.S.A.
134 B2 Ashland OR U.S.A.
140 A1 Ashland WI U.S.A.
88 C3 Ashmyany Belarus

78 B3 Ash Sharawrah Saudi Arabia
81 C2 Ash Sharqat Iraq
81 C2 Ash Shatrah Iraq
79 B3 Ash Shihr Yemen
79 C2 Ash Shinãs Oman
78 B2 Ash Shu'bah Saudi Arabia
78 B2 Ash Shumlul Saudi Arabia
140 C2 Ashtabula U.S.A.
131 D1 Ashuanipi Lake Can.
106 B2 Asilah Morocco
108 A2 Asinara, Golfo dell' b. Sardinia Italy
82 G3 Asino Rus. Fed.
88 C3 Asipovichy Belarus
78 B2 'Asir reg. Saudi Arabia
93 F4 Askim Norway
68 C1 Askiz Rus. Fed.
116 B3 Asmara Eritrea
93 F4 Åsnen l. Sweden
116 B2 Asoteriba, Jebel mt. Sudan
103 D2 Aspang-Markt Austria
136 B3 Aspen U.S.A.
54 A2 Aspiring, Mount N.Z.
117 C3 Assab Eritrea
78 B2 As Salamiyah Saudi Arabia
81 C2 As Samawah Iraq
79 C2 Aş Şanam reg. Saudi Arabia
115 E2 As Sarir reg. Libya
100 C1 Assen Neth.
100 B2 Assesse Belgium
115 D1 As Sidrah Libya
129 D3 Assiniboia Can.
128 C2 Assiniboine, Mount Can.
154 B2 Assis Brazil
78 B2 Aş Şubayhiyah Kuwait
81 C2 As Sulaymaniyah Iraq
78 B2 As Sulaymi Saudi Arabia
78 B2 As Sulayyil Saudi Arabia
78 B2 As Süq Saudi Arabia
80 B2 As Suwayda' Syria
79 C2 As Suwayq Oman
111 B3 Astakos Greece
77 D1 Astana Kazakh.
81 C2 Astara Iran
108 A2 Asti Italy
74 B1 Astor Jammu and Kashmir
106 B1 Astorga Spain
134 B1 Astoria U.S.A.
87 D4 Astrakhan' Rus. Fed.
88 C3 Astravyets Belarus
111 C3 Astypalaia i. Greece
152 C3 Asunción Para.
116 B2 Aswân Egypt
116 B2 Asyût Egypt
152 B3 Atacama, Desierto de des. Chile
152 B3 Atacama, Salar de salt flat Chile
114 C4 Atakpamé Togo
111 B3 Atalanti Greece
150 A3 Atalaya Peru
78 B3 'Ataq Yemen
114 A2 Atâr Maur.
135 B3 Atascadero U.S.A.
77 D2 Atasu Kazakh.
116 B3 Atbara Sudan
116 B3 Atbara r. Sudan
77 C1 Atbasar Kazakh.
137 D3 Atchison U.S.A.
108 B2 Aterno r. Italy
108 B2 Atessa Italy
100 A2 Ath Belgium
128 C2 Athabasca Can.
129 C2 Athabasca r. Can.
129 D2 Athabasca, Lake Can.
111 B3 Athens Greece
143 D2 Athens GA U.S.A.
140 C3 Athens OH U.S.A.
143 D1 Athens TN U.S.A.

139 D2 Athens TX U.S.A.
Athina Greece see Athens
97 C2 Athlone Rep. of Ireland
111 B2 Athos mt. Greece
97 C2 Athy Rep. of Ireland
115 D3 Ati Chad
130 A2 Atikokan Can.
87 D3 Atkarsk Rus. Fed.
143 D2 Atlanta U.S.A.
137 D2 Atlantic U.S.A.
141 E3 Atlantic City U.S.A.
158 Atlantic Ocean
122 A3 Atlantis S. Africa
114 B1 Atlas Mountains mts Africa
114 C1 Atlas Saharien mts Alg.
128 A2 Atlin Can.
128 A2 Atlin Lake Can.
142 C2 Atmore U.S.A.
139 D2 Atoka U.S.A.
75 C2 Atrai r. India
78 B2 Aṭ Ṭā'if Saudi Arabia
63 B2 Attapu Laos
111 C3 Attavyros mt. Greece
130 B1 Attawapiskat Can.
130 B1 Attawapiskat r. Can.
130 B1 Attawapiskat Lake Can.
100 C2 Attendorn Ger.
78 B3 At Turbah Yemen
76 B2 Atyrau Kazakh.
105 C3 Aubenas France
126 C2 Aubry Lake Can.
142 C2 Auburn AL U.S.A.
135 B3 Auburn CA U.S.A.
137 D2 Auburn NE U.S.A.
141 D2 Auburn NY U.S.A.
104 C2 Aubusson France
104 C3 Auch France
54 B1 Auckland N.Z.
101 F2 Aue Ger.
102 C2 Augsburg Ger.
109 C3 Augusta Sicily Italy
143 D2 Augusta GA U.S.A.
137 D3 Augusta KS U.S.A.
141 F2 Augusta ME U.S.A.
50 A2 Augustus, Mount Austr.
100 A2 Aulnoye-Aymeries France
122 B2 Auob watercourse
Namibia/S. Africa
74 B3 Aurangābād India
100 C1 Aurich Ger.
154 B1 Aurilândia Brazil
104 C3 Aurillac France
136 C3 Aurora CO U.S.A.
140 B2 Aurora IL U.S.A.
137 D2 Aurora NE U.S.A.
122 A2 Aus Namibia
137 E2 Austin MN U.S.A.
135 C3 Austin NV U.S.A.
139 D2 Austin TX U.S.A.
50 B2 Australia country Oceania
53 C3 Australian Capital Territory
admin. div. Austr.
102 C2 Austria country Europe
144 B3 Autlán Mex.
105 C2 Autun France
105 C2 Auxerre France
105 C2 Auxonne France
105 C3 Avallon France
131 E2 Avalon Peninsula Can.
154 C2 Avaré Brazil
91 D2 Avdiyivka Ukr.
106 B1 Aveiro Port.
109 B2 Avellino Italy
100 A2 Avesnes-sur-Helpe France
93 G3 Avesta Sweden
108 B2 Avezzano Italy
96 C2 Aviemore U.K.
108 B2 Avigliano Italy
105 C3 Avignon France
106 C1 Ávila Spain

106 B1 Avilés Spain
109 C3 Avola Sicily Italy
99 C3 Avon r. England U.K.
99 B3 Avon r. England U.K.
104 B2 Avranches France
54 B1 Awanui N.Z.
117 C4 Āwash Eth.
117 C4 Āwash r. Eth.
115 D2 Awbārī Libya
117 C4 Aw Dheegle Somalia
96 B2 Awe, Loch l. U.K.
117 A4 Aweil Sudan
126 E1 Axel Heiberg Island Can.
114 B4 Axim Ghana
150 A3 Ayacucho Peru
77 E2 Ayagoz Kazakh.
68 C2 Ayakkum Hu salt l. China
106 B2 Ayamonte Spain
83 K3 Ayan Rus. Fed.
150 A3 Ayaviri Peru
76 A2 Aybas Kazakh.
91 D2 Aydar r. Ukr.
77 C2 Aydarkul', Ozero l. Uzbek.
111 C3 Aydın Turkey
77 C2 Ayeat, Gora hill Kazakh.
50 C2 Ayers Rock hill Austr.
99 C3 Aylesbury U.K.
106 C1 Ayllón Spain
129 D1 Aylmer Lake Can.
117 B4 Ayod Sudan
83 M2 Ayon, Ostrov i. Rus. Fed.
114 B3 'Ayoûn el 'Atroûs Maur.
51 D1 Ayr Austr.
96 B3 Ayr U.K.
98 A1 Ayre, Point of Isle of Man
76 C2 Ayteke Bi Kazakh.
110 C2 Aytos Bulg.
145 C3 Ayutla Mex.
63 B2 Ayutthaya Thai.
111 C3 Ayvacık Turkey
111 C3 Ayvalık Turkey
114 C3 Azaouagh, Vallée de
watercourse Mali/Niger
Azbine mts Niger see
L'Aïr, Massif de
81 C1 Azerbaijan country Asia
86 D2 Azopol'ye Rus. Fed.
84 A5 Azores aut. reg.
N. Atlantic Ocean
91 D2 Azov Rus. Fed.
91 D2 Azov, Sea of Rus. Fed./Ukr.
Azraq, Bahr el r. Eth./Sudan
see Blue Nile
106 B2 Azuaga Spain
146 B4 Azuero, Península de pen.
Panama
153 C4 Azul Arg.
80 B2 Az Zarqā' Jordan
78 B3 Az Zaydīyah Yemen
114 C2 Azzel Matti, Sebkha
salt pan Alg.
78 B2 Az Zilfī Saudi Arabia
78 B3 Az Zuqur i. Yemen

B

117 C4 Baardheere Somalia
77 C3 Bābā, Kūh-e mts Afgh.
110 C2 Bacabal Romania
111 C2 Babaeski Turkey
117 C3 Bāb al Mandab str.
Africa/Asia
61 C2 Babana Indon.
59 C3 Babar i. Indon.
119 D3 Babati Tanz.
89 E2 Babayevo Rus. Fed.
128 B2 Babine r. Can.

128 B2 Babine Lake Can.
59 C3 Babo Indon.
81 D2 Bābol Iran
122 A3 Baboon Point S. Africa
88 C3 Babruysk Belarus
64 B1 Babuyan i. Phil.
64 B1 Babuyan Islands Phil.
151 D2 Bacabal Brazil
59 C3 Bacan i. Indon.
110 C1 Bacău Romania
52 B3 Bacchus Marsh Austr.
77 D3 Bachu China
129 E1 Back r. Can.
109 C1 Bačka Palanka Yugo.
62 B1 Bac Lac Vietnam
63 B3 Bac Liêu Vietnam
64 B1 Bacolod Phil.
130 C1 Bacqueville, Lac l. Can.
106 B2 Badajoz Spain
62 A1 Badarpur India
101 E2 Bad Berka Ger.
101 D2 Bad Berleburg Ger.
101 E1 Bad Bevensen Ger.
100 C2 Bad Ems Ger.
103 D2 Baden Austria
102 B2 Baden-Baden Ger.
101 E2 Bad Harzburg Ger.
101 D2 Bad Hersfeld Ger.
102 C2 Bad Hofgastein Austria
101 D2 Bad Homburg vor der Höhe
Ger.
74 A2 Badin Pak.
80 B2 Bādiyat ash Shām des. Asia
101 D2 Bad Kissingen Ger.
100 C2 Bad Kreuznach Ger.
101 E2 Bad Lauterberg im Harz
Ger.
101 D2 Bad Lippspringe Ger.
101 D3 Bad Mergentheim Ger.
101 D2 Bad Nauheim Ger.
100 C2 Bad Neuenahr-Ahrweiler
Ger.
101 E2 Bad Neustadt an der Saale
Ger.
101 E1 Bad Oldesloe Ger.
101 D2 Bad Pyrmont Ger.
78 A2 Badr Ḥunayn Saudi Arabia
101 D1 Bad Salzuflen Ger.
101 E2 Bad Salzungen Ger.
102 C1 Bad Schwartau Ger.
101 E1 Bad Segeberg Ger.
73 C4 Badulla Sri Lanka
100 D1 Bad Zwischenahn Ger.
106 B2 Baeza Spain
114 A3 Bafatá Guinea-Bissau
160 O2 Baffin Bay sea
Can./Greenland
127 G2 Baffin Island Can.
118 B2 Bafia Cameroon
114 A3 Bafing r. Guinea/Mali
114 A3 Bafoulabé Mali
118 B2 Bafoussam Cameroon
76 B3 Bāfq Iran
80 B1 Bafra Turkey
79 C2 Bāft Iran
119 C2 Bafwasende
Dem. Rep. Congo
119 D3 Bagamoyo Tanz.
60 B1 Bagan Datuk Malaysia
120 B2 Bagani Namibia
60 B1 Bagansiapiapi Indon.
138 A2 Bagdad U.S.A.
152 C4 Bagé Brazil
81 C2 Baghdād Iraq
77 C3 Baghlān Afgh.
104 C3 Bagnères-de-Luchon
France
88 B3 Bagrationovsk Rus. Fed.
Bagrax China see Bohu
64 B1 Baguio Phil.

115	C3	Bagzane, Monts *mts* Niger
		Bahamas *country* West
		Indies *see* The Bahamas
75	C2	Baharampur India
116	A2	Bahariya Oasis Egypt
60	B1	Bahau Malaysia
72	B2	Bahawalnagar Pak.
74	B2	Bahawalpur Pak.
153	B4	Bahía Blanca Arg.
144	A2	Bahía Kino Mex.
152	C3	Bahía Negra Para.
144	A2	Bahía Tortugas Mex.
117	B3	Bahir Dar Eth.
75	C2	Bahraich India
79	C2	Bahrain *country* Asia
79	D2	Bāhū Kālāt Iran
110	B1	Baia Mare Romania
69	E1	Baicheng China
131	D2	Baie-Comeau Can.
		Baie-du-Poste Can. *see*
		Mistissini
131	C2	Baie-St-Paul Can.
65	B1	Baihe China
69	D1	Baikal, Lake Rus. Fed.
110	B2	Băileşti Romania
68	C2	Baima China
75	C2	Bainang China
143	D2	Bainbridge U.S.A.
		Bairin Youqi China *see*
		Daban
53	C3	Bairnsdale Austr.
65	B1	Baishan *Jilin* China
65	B1	Baishan *Jilin* China
70	A2	Baiyin China
116	B3	Baiyuda Desert Sudan
103	D2	Baja Hungary
144	A1	Baja California *pen.* Mex.
78	B3	Bājil Yemen
114	A3	Bakel Senegal
135	C3	Baker *CA* U.S.A.
136	C1	Baker *MT* U.S.A.
134	C2	Baker *OR* U.S.A.
134	B1	Baker, Mount *vol.* U.S.A.
129	E1	Baker Foreland Can.
129	E1	Baker Lake Can.
129	E1	Baker Lake *l.* Can.
135	C3	Bakersfield U.S.A.
91	C1	Bakhchysaray Ukr.
76	B3	Bakherden Turkm.
91	C1	Bakhmach Ukr.
		Bākhtarān Iran *see*
		Kermānshāh
		Baku Azer. *see* Baku
111	C3	Bakırköy Turkey
92	□C2	Bakkaflói *b.* Iceland
118	C2	Bakouma C.A.R.
81	C1	Baku Azer.
64	A2	Balabac Phil.
64	A2	Balabac *i.* Phil.
64	A2	Balabac Strait Malaysia/Phil.
61	C2	Balaiberkuak Indon.
52	A2	Balaklava Austr.
91	C3	Balaklava Ukr.
91	D2	Balakliya Ukr.
87	D3	Balakovo Rus. Fed.
76	C3	Bālā Morghāb Afgh.
145	C3	Balancán Mex.
111	C3	Balan Dağı *hill* Turkey
64	B1	Balanga Phil.
75	C2	Balāngīr India
87	D3	Balashov Rus. Fed.
103	D2	Balaton *l.* Hungary
103	D2	Balatonboglár Hungary
150	C2	Balbina, Represa de *resr* Brazil
97	C2	Balbriggan Rep. of Ireland
52	A2	Balcanoona Austr.
110	C2	Balchik Bulg.
54	A3	Balclutha N.Z.
129	E2	Baldock Lake Can.

129	D2	Baldy Mountain Can.
138	B2	Baldy Peak U.S.A.
		Baleares, Islas *is* Spain *see* Balearic Islands
107	D2	Balearic Islands *is* Spain
155	E1	Baleia, Ponta da *pt* Brazil
75	C2	Bāleshwar India
61	C2	Bali *i.* Indon.
60	A1	Balige Indon.
75	C2	Baliguda India
111	C3	Balıkesir Turkey
61	C2	Balikpapan Indon.
59	D3	Balimo P.N.G.
102	B2	Balingen Ger.
61	C2	Bali Sea Indon.
110	B2	Balkan Mountains Bulg./Yugo.
77	D2	Balkhash Kazakh.
77	D2	Balkhash, Ozero *l.* Kazakh.
50	B3	Balladonia Austr.
97	B2	Ballaghaderreen Rep. of Ireland
92	G2	Ballangen Norway
52	B3	Ballarat Austr.
50	B2	Ballard, Lake *salt flat* Austr.
96	C2	Ballater U.K.
114	B3	Ballé Mali
53	D1	Ballina Austr.
97	B1	Ballina Rep. of Ireland
97	B2	Ballinasloe Rep. of Ireland
139	D2	Ballinger U.S.A.
97	B2	Ballinrobe Rep. of Ireland
97	B1	Ballycastle U.K.
97	C1	Ballycastle U.K.
97	D1	Ballyclare U.K.
97	C1	Ballymena U.K.
97	C1	Ballymoney U.K.
97	D1	Ballynahinch U.K.
97	B1	Ballyshannon Rep. of Ireland
95	B2	Ballyvoy U.K.
51	D2	Balonne *r.* Austr.
74	B2	Balotra India
75	C2	Balrampur India
52	B2	Balranald Austr.
110	B2	Balş Romania
151	D2	Balsas Brazil
145	C3	Balsas Mex.
90	B2	Balta Ukr.
90	B2	Bălţi Moldova
93	G4	Baltic Sea *g.* Europe
80	B2	Baltim Egypt
123	C1	Baltimore S. Africa
141	D3	Baltimore U.S.A.
88	B2	Baltiysk Rus. Fed.
62	A1	Balu India
88	C2	Balvi Latvia
77	D2	Balykchy Kyrg.
87	E4	Balykshi Kazakh.
79	C2	Bam Iran
51	D1	Bamaga Austr.
130	A1	Bamaji Lake Can.
114	B3	Bamako Mali
118	C2	Bambari C.A.R.
101	E3	Bamberg Ger.
118	C2	Bambili Dem. Rep. Congo
119	C2	Bambouti C.A.R.
155	C2	Bambuí Brazil
118	B2	Bamenda Cameroon
74	A1	Bāmīān Afgh.
152	B2	Bañados del Izozog *swamp* Bol.
119	C2	Banalia Dem. Rep. Congo
151	C3	Bananal, Ilha do *i.* Brazil
74	B2	Banas *r.* India
111	C3	Banaz Turkey
62	B2	Ban Ban Laos
99	D3	Banbridge U.K.
99	C2	Banbury U.K.
130	C2	Bancroft Can.
119	C2	Banda Dem. Rep. Congo

75	C2	Banda India
59	C3	Banda, Kepulauan *is* Indon.
60	A1	Banda Aceh Indon.
79	C2	Bandar-e ‘Abbās Iran
81	C2	Bandar-e Anzalī Iran
79	C2	Bandar-e Chārak Iran
81	C2	Bandar-e Emām Khomeynī Iran
79	C2	Bandar-e Lengeh Iran
79	C2	Bandar-e Maqām Iran
61	C1	Bandar Seri Begawan Brunei
59	C3	Banda Sea Indon.
155	D2	Bandeiras, Pico de *mt.* Brazil
123	C1	Bandelierkop S. Africa
144	B2	Banderas, Bahía de *b.* Mex.
114	B3	Bandiagara Mali
111	C2	Bandırma Turkey
97	B3	Bandon Rep. of Ireland
118	B3	Bandundu Dem. Rep. Congo
61	B2	Bandung Indon.
128	C2	Banff Can.
96	C2	Banff U.K.
114	B3	Banfora Burkina
64	B2	Banga Phil.
73	B3	Bangalore India
118	C2	Bangassou C.A.R.
59	C3	Banggai Indon.
59	C3	Banggai, Kepulauan *is* Indon.
61	C1	Banggi *i.* Sabah Malaysia
115	E1	Banghāzī Libya
60	B2	Bangka *i.* Indon.
61	C2	Bangkalan Indon.
60	B1	Bangkinang Indon.
60	B2	Bangko Indon.
63	B2	Bangkok Thai.
75	C2	Bangladesh *country* Asia
97	D1	Bangor *Northern Ireland* U.K.
98	A2	Bangor *Wales* U.K.
141	F2	Bangor U.S.A.
63	A2	Bang Saphan Yai Thai.
64	B1	Bangued Phil.
118	B2	Bangui C.A.R.
121	B2	Bangweulu, Lake Zambia
62	B1	Ban Houayxay Laos
115	D1	Banī Walīd Libya
80	B2	Bāniyās Syria
109	C2	Banja Luka Bos.-Herz.
61	C2	Banjarmasin Indon.
114	A3	Banjul Gambia
128	A2	Banks Island *B.C.* Can.
126	C2	Banks Island *N.W.T.* Can.
129	E1	Banks Lake *l.* Can.
54	B2	Banks Peninsula N.Z.
75	C2	Bankura India
62	A1	Banmauk Myanmar
62	B2	Ban Mouang Laos
97	C1	Bann *r.* U.K.
62	B2	Ban Napè Laos
63	A3	Ban Na San Thai.
143	E4	Bannerman Town Bahamas
74	B1	Bannu Pak.
74	B2	Banswara India
63	B2	Ban Tha Kham Thai.
62	A2	Ban Tha Song Yang Thai.
63	B2	Ban Tôp Laos
97	B3	Bantry Rep. of Ireland
97	B3	Bantry Bay Rep. of Ireland
118	B2	Banyo Cameroon
107	D1	Banyoles Spain
61	C2	Banyuwangi Indon.
		Bao'an China *see* Shenzhen
69	D2	Baochang China
70	B2	Baoding China
70	A2	Baoji China
63	B2	Bao Lôc Vietnam
66	B1	Baoqing China
62	A1	Baoshan China

70 B1 **Baotou** China
81 C2 **Ba'qūbah** Iraq
109 C2 **Bar** Yugo.
117 C4 **Baraawe** Somalia
147 C2 **Baracoa** Cuba
53 C2 **Baradine** Austr.
147 C3 **Barahona** Dom. Rep.
116 B3 **Baraka** *watercourse*
    Eritrea/Sudan
61 C1 **Baram** *r. Sarawak* Malaysia
88 C3 **Baranavichy** Belarus
90 B1 **Baranivka** Ukr.
128 A2 **Baranof Island** U.S.A.
59 C3 **Barat Daya, Kepulauan** *is*
    Indon.
155 D2 **Barbacena** Brazil
147 E3 **Barbados** *country*
    West Indies
107 D1 **Barbastro** Spain
104 B2 **Barbezieux-St-Hilaire**
    France
51 D2 **Barcaldine** Austr.
107 D1 **Barcelona** Spain
150 B1 **Barcelona** Venez.
105 D3 **Barcelonnette** France
150 B2 **Barcelos** Brazil
    Barcoo Creek *watercourse*
    Austr. *see* Cooper Creek
103 D2 **Barcs** Hungary
75 C2 **Bardhaman** India
103 E2 **Bardejov** Slovakia
79 C2 **Bardsīr** Iran
75 B2 **Bareilly** India
160 B2 **Barents Sea** Arctic Ocean
78 A3 **Barentu** Eritrea
75 C2 **Barh** India
141 F2 **Bar Harbor** U.S.A.
109 C2 **Bari** Italy
74 B1 **Barikot** Afgh.
150 A1 **Barinas** Venez.
75 C2 **Baripada** India
75 D2 **Barisal** Bangl.
60 B2 **Barisan, Pegunungan**
    mts Indon.
61 C2 **Barito** *r.* Indon.
79 C2 **Barkā** Oman
88 C2 **Barkava** Latvia
51 C1 **Barkly Tableland** *reg.* Austr.
64 B2 **Barkol** China
110 C1 **Bârlad** Romania
105 D2 **Bar-le-Duc** France
50 A2 **Barlee, Lake** *salt flat* Austr.
109 C2 **Barletta** Italy
53 C2 **Barmedman** Austr.
74 B2 **Barmer** India
99 A2 **Barmouth** U.K.
101 D1 **Barmstedt** Ger.
98 C1 **Barnard Castle** U.K.
53 B2 **Barnato** Austr.
82 G3 **Barnaul** Rus. Fed.
127 G2 **Barnes Icecap** Can.
100 B1 **Barneveld** Neth.
98 C2 **Barnsley** U.K.
99 A3 **Barnstaple** U.K.
143 D2 **Barnwell** U.S.A.
    Baroda India *see* Vadodara
150 B1 **Barquisimeto** Venez.
96 A2 **Barra** *i.* U.K.
53 D2 **Barraba** Austr.
151 D2 **Barra do Corda** Brazil
154 B1 **Barra do Garças** Brazil
150 C2 **Barra de São Manuel** Brazil
150 A3 **Barranca** *Lima* Peru
150 A2 **Barranca** *Loreto* Peru
152 C3 **Barranqueras** Arg.
150 A1 **Barranquilla** Col.
151 D3 **Barreiras** Brazil
154 C2 **Barretos** Brazil
130 C2 **Barrie** Can.
128 B2 **Barrière** Can.

52 B2 **Barrier Range** *hills* Austr.
53 D2 **Barrington, Mount** Austr.
129 D2 **Barrington Lake** Can.
53 C1 **Barringun** Austr.
97 C2 **Barrow** *r.* Rep. of Ireland
51 C2 **Barrow Creek** Austr.
98 B1 **Barrow-in-Furness** U.K.
50 A2 **Barrow Island** Austr.
126 E2 **Barrow Strait** Can.
99 B3 **Barry** U.K.
130 C2 **Barrys Bay** Can.
74 B2 **Barsalpur** India
135 C4 **Barstow** U.S.A.
105 C2 **Bar-sur-Aube** France
80 B1 **Bartın** Turkey
51 D1 **Bartle Frere, Mount** Austr.
139 D1 **Bartlesville** U.S.A.
103 E1 **Bartoszyce** Pol.
61 C2 **Barung** *i.* Indon.
69 D1 **Baruun Urt** Mongolia
91 D2 **Barvinkove** Ukr.
53 C2 **Barwon** *r.* Austr.
88 C3 **Barysaw** Belarus
110 C2 **Basarabi** Romania
105 D2 **Basel** Switz.
91 C2 **Bashtanka** Ukr.
64 B2 **Basilan** *i.* Phil.
99 D3 **Basildon** U.K.
99 C3 **Basingstoke** U.K.
81 C2 **Başkale** Turkey
130 C2 **Baskatong, Réservoir**
    resr Can.
    Basle Switz. *see* Basel
118 C3 **Basoko** Dem. Rep. Congo
81 C2 **Basra** Iraq
128 C2 **Bassano** Can.
114 C4 **Bassar** Togo
63 A2 **Bassein** Myanmar
147 D3 **Basse-Terre** Guadeloupe
147 D3 **Basseterre**
    St Kitts and Nevis
114 B3 **Bassikounou** Maur.
51 D3 **Bass Strait** Austr.
79 C2 **Bastak** Iran
101 E2 **Bastheim** Ger.
75 C2 **Basti** India
105 D3 **Bastia** *Corsica* France
100 B2 **Bastogne** Belgium
142 B2 **Bastrop** U.S.A.
    Basuo China *see* Dongfang
118 A2 **Bata** Equat. Guinea
83 J2 **Batagay** Rus. Fed.
154 B2 **Bataguaçu** Brazil
106 B2 **Batalha** Port.
71 C3 **Batan** *i.* Phil.
118 B2 **Batangafo** C.A.R.
64 B1 **Batangas** Phil.
60 B2 **Batanghari** *r.* Indon.
71 C3 **Batan Islands** Phil.
141 D2 **Batavia** U.S.A.
91 D2 **Bataysk** Rus. Fed.
130 B2 **Batchawana Mountain**
    Can.
50 C1 **Batchelor** Austr.
63 B2 **Bâtdâmbâng** Cambodia
53 D3 **Batemans Bay** Austr.
142 B1 **Batesville** U.S.A.
89 D2 **Batetskiy** Rus. Fed.
99 B3 **Bath** U.K.
74 B1 **Bathinda** India
53 C2 **Bathurst** Austr.
131 D2 **Bathurst** Can.
126 D2 **Bathurst Inlet** Can.
126 D2 **Bathurst Inlet** *inlet* Can.
50 C1 **Bathurst Island** Austr.
126 E1 **Bathurst Island** Can.
78 B1 **Bāṭin, Wādī al** *watercourse*
    Asia
81 C2 **Batman** Turkey
115 C1 **Batna** Alg.

142 B2 **Baton Rouge** U.S.A.
144 B2 **Batopilas** Mex.
118 B2 **Batouri** Cameroon
154 B1 **Batovi** Brazil
92 I1 **Båtsfjord** Norway
73 C4 **Batticaloa** Sri Lanka
109 B2 **Battipaglia** Italy
129 D2 **Battle** *r.* Can.
140 B2 **Battle Creek** U.S.A.
135 C2 **Battle Mountain** U.S.A.
74 B1 **Battura Glacier**
    Jammu and Kashmir
117 B4 **Batu** *mt.* Eth.
60 A2 **Batu, Pulau-pulau** *is* Indon.
81 C1 **Batumi** Georgia
60 B1 **Batu Pahat** Malaysia
59 C3 **Baubau** Indon.
115 C3 **Bauchi** Nigeria
104 B2 **Baugé** France
105 D2 **Baume-les-Dames** France
154 C2 **Bauru** Brazil
102 C1 **Bautzen** Ger.
144 B2 **Bavispe** *r.* Mex.
87 E3 **Bavly** Rus. Fed.
62 A1 **Bawdwin** Myanmar
61 C2 **Bawean** *i.* Indon.
116 A2 **Bawiti** Egypt
114 B3 **Bawku** Ghana
146 C2 **Bayamo** Cuba
    Bayan Gol China *see*
    Dengkou
68 C1 **Bayanhongor** Mongolia
70 A2 **Bayan Hot** China
64 B2 **Bayawan** Phil.
80 C1 **Bayburt** Turkey
140 C2 **Bay City** *MI* U.S.A.
139 D3 **Bay City** *TX* U.S.A.
86 F2 **Baydaratskaya Guba** *b.*
    Rus. Fed.
117 C4 **Baydhabo** Somalia
81 C2 **Bayjī** Iraq
    Baykal, Ozero *l.* Rus. Fed.
    see Baikal, Lake
83 I3 **Baykal'skiy Khrebet** *mts*
    Rus. Fed.
76 C2 **Baykonur** Kazakh.
87 E3 **Baymak** Rus. Fed.
64 B1 **Bayombong** Phil.
104 B3 **Bayonne** France
111 C3 **Bayramiç** Turkey
101 E3 **Bayreuth** Ger.
78 B3 **Bayt al Faqīh** Yemen
106 C2 **Baza** Spain
106 C2 **Baza, Sierra de** *mts* Spain
76 A2 **Bazardyuzi, Gora** *mt.*
    Azer./Rus. Fed.
104 B3 **Bazas** France
74 A2 **Bazdar** Pak.
70 A2 **Bazhong** China
70 D3 **Bazmān** Iran
79 D2 **Bazmān, Kūh-e** *mt.* Iran
99 D3 **Beachy Head** *hd* U.K.
123 C3 **Beacon Bay** S. Africa
50 B1 **Beagle Gulf** Austr.
121 □D2 **Bealanana** Madag.
130 B2 **Beardmore** Can.
82 C2 **Bear Island** *i.* Arctic Ocean
134 E1 **Bear Paw Mountain** U.S.A.
147 C3 **Beata, Cabo** *c.* Dom. Rep.
147 C3 **Beata, Isla** *i.* Dom. Rep.
137 D2 **Beatrice** U.S.A.
135 C3 **Beatty** U.S.A.
53 D1 **Beaudesert** Austr.
53 C2 **Beaufort** Austr.
61 C1 **Beaufort** *Sabah* Malaysia
143 D2 **Beaufort** U.S.A.
160 L2 **Beaufort Sea** Can./U.S.A.
122 B3 **Beaufort West** S. Africa

96 B2 **Beauly** r. U.K.
100 B2 **Beaumont** Belgium
54 A3 **Beaumont** N.Z.
139 E2 **Beaumont** U.S.A.
105 C2 **Beaune** France
100 B2 **Beauraing** Belgium
129 E2 **Beauséjour** Can.
104 C2 **Beauvais** France
129 D2 **Beauval** Can.
129 D2 **Beaver** r. Can.
135 D3 **Beaver** U.S.A.
126 B2 **Beaver Creek** Can.
140 B2 **Beaver Dam** U.S.A.
129 E2 **Beaver Hill Lake** Can.
140 B1 **Beaver Island** U.S.A.
128 C2 **Beaverlodge** Can.
74 B2 **Beawar** India
154 C2 **Bebedouro** Brazil
101 C2 **Bebra** Ger.
106 B1 **Becerreá** Spain
114 B1 **Béchar** Alg.
140 C3 **Beckley** U.S.A.
117 B4 **Bedelē** Eth.
99 C2 **Bedford** U.K.
140 B3 **Bedford** U.S.A.
100 C1 **Bedum** Neth.
53 D2 **Beecroft Peninsula** Austr.
101 F1 **Beelitz** Ger.
53 D1 **Beenleigh** Austr.
80 B2 **Be'ér Sheva'** Israel
139 D3 **Beeville** U.S.A.
53 C3 **Bega** Austr.
107 D1 **Begur, Cap de** c. Spain
81 D2 **Behshahr** Iran
69 E1 **Bei'an** China
71 A3 **Beihai** China
70 B2 **Beijing** China
100 C1 **Beilen** Neth.
96 B3 **Beinn an Oir** hill U.K.
96 A2 **Beinn Mhòr** hill U.K.
121 C2 **Beira** Moz.
80 B2 **Beirut** Lebanon
123 C1 **Beitbridge** Zimbabwe
106 B2 **Beja** Port.
115 C1 **Bejaïa** Alg.
106 B1 **Béjar** Spain
74 A2 **Beji** r. Pak.
76 B2 **Bekdash** Turkm.
103 E2 **Békés** Hungary
103 E2 **Békéscsaba** Hungary
121 □D3 **Bekily** Madag.
74 A2 **Bela** Pak.
123 C1 **Bela-Bela** S. Africa
118 B2 **Bélabo** Cameroon
109 D2 **Bela Crkva** Yugo.
61 C1 **Belaga** Sarawak Malaysia
61 C2 **Belangiran** Indon.
88 C3 **Belarus** country Europe
Belau country
N. Pacific Ocean see Palau
123 D2 **Bela Vista** Moz.
60 A1 **Belawan** Indon.
83 M2 **Belaya** r. Rus. Fed.
103 D1 **Bełchatów** Pol.
130 C1 **Belcher Islands** Can.
117 C4 **Beledweyne** Somalia
151 D2 **Belém** Brazil
138 B2 **Belen** U.S.A.
89 E3 **Belev** Rus. Fed.
97 D1 **Belfast** U.K.
141 F2 **Belfast** U.S.A.
105 D2 **Belfort** France
73 B3 **Belgaum** India
100 B2 **Belgium** country Europe
91 D1 **Belgorod** Rus. Fed.
134 D1 **Belgrade** U.S.A.
109 D2 **Belgrade** Yugo.
115 C4 **Beli** Nigeria
60 B2 **Belinyu** Indon.
61 B2 **Belitung** i. Indon.

146 B3 **Belize** Belize
146 B3 **Belize** country
Central America
83 K1 **Bel'kovskiy, Ostrov** i.
Rus. Fed.
128 B2 **Bella Bella** Can.
104 C2 **Bellac** France
128 B2 **Bella Coola** Can.
53 C1 **Bellata** Austr.
136 C2 **Belle Fourche** U.S.A.
136 C2 **Belle Fourche** r. U.S.A.
143 D3 **Belle Glade** U.S.A.
104 B2 **Belle-Île** i. France
131 E1 **Belle Isle** i. Can.
131 E1 **Belle Isle, Strait of** Can.
130 C2 **Belleville** Can.
140 B3 **Belleville** IL U.S.A.
137 D3 **Belleville** KS U.S.A.
134 B1 **Bellevue** U.S.A.
134 B1 **Bellingham** U.S.A.
55 O2 **Bellingshausen Sea**
Antarctica
105 D2 **Bellinzona** Switz.
108 B1 **Belluno** Italy
122 A3 **Bellville** S. Africa
155 E1 **Belmonte** Brazil
146 B3 **Belmopan** Belize
97 B1 **Belmullet** Rep. of Ireland
69 E1 **Belogorsk** Rus. Fed.
121 □D3 **Beloha** Madag.
155 D1 **Belo Horizonte** Brazil
140 B2 **Beloit** U.S.A.
86 C2 **Belomorsk** Rus. Fed.
91 D3 **Belorechensk** Rus. Fed.
87 E3 **Beloretsk** Rus. Fed.
Belorussia country Europe
see Belarus
86 F2 **Beloyarskiy** Rus. Fed.
86 C2 **Beloye, Ozero** l. Rus. Fed.
Beloye More sea Rus. Fed.
see White Sea
86 C2 **Belozersk** Rus. Fed.
77 E2 **Belukha, Gora** mt.
Kazakh./Rus. Fed.
86 D2 **Belush'ye** Rus. Fed.
89 D2 **Belyy** Rus. Fed.
82 F2 **Belyy, Ostrov** i. Rus. Fed.
101 F1 **Belzig** Ger.
137 E1 **Bemidji** U.S.A.
118 C3 **Bena Dibele**
Dem. Rep. Congo
53 C3 **Benalla** Austr.
106 B1 **Benavente** Spain
96 A2 **Benbecula** i. U.K.
134 B2 **Bend** U.S.A.
123 C3 **Bendearg** mt. S. Africa
52 B3 **Bendigo** Austr.
121 C2 **Bene** Moz.
102 C2 **Benešov** Czech Rep.
109 B2 **Benevento** Italy
159 C2 **Bengal, Bay of** sea
Indian Ocean
70 B2 **Bengbu** China
61 B1 **Bengkayang** Indon.
60 B2 **Bengkulu** Indon.
120 A2 **Benguela** Angola
96 B1 **Ben Hope** hill U.K.
152 B2 **Beni** r. Bol.
119 C2 **Beni** Dem. Rep. Congo
114 B1 **Beni-Abbès** Alg.
107 C2 **Benidorm** Spain
114 B1 **Beni Mellal** Morocco
114 C4 **Benin** country Africa
114 C4 **Benin, Bight of** g. Africa
115 C4 **Benin City** Nigeria
116 B2 **Beni Suef** Egypt
153 C4 **Benito Juárez** Arg.
150 B2 **Benjamin Constant** Brazil
144 A1 **Benjamín Hill** Mex.
59 C3 **Benjina** Indon.

96 B2 **Ben Lawers** mt. U.K.
96 B2 **Ben Lomond** hill U.K.
96 C2 **Ben Macdui** mt. U.K.
96 A2 **Ben More** mt. U.K.
54 B2 **Benmore, Lake** N.Z.
96 B1 **Ben More Assynt** hill U.K.
128 A2 **Bennett** Can.
83 K1 **Bennetta, Ostrov** i.
Rus. Fed.
96 B2 **Ben Nevis** mt. U.K.
141 E2 **Bennington** U.S.A.
123 C2 **Benoni** S. Africa
101 D3 **Bensheim** Ger.
138 A2 **Benson** U.S.A.
58 C3 **Benteng** Indon.
140 B2 **Benton Harbor** U.S.A.
142 B1 **Bentonville** U.S.A.
115 C4 **Benue** r. Nigeria
97 B1 **Benwee Head** hd
Rep. of Ireland
96 B2 **Ben Wyvis** mt. U.K.
70 C1 **Benxi** China
Beograd Yugo. see Belgrade
75 C2 **Beohari** India
67 B4 **Beppu** Japan
109 C2 **Berane** Yugo.
109 C2 **Berat** Albania
59 C3 **Berau, Teluk** b. Indon.
116 B3 **Berber** Sudan
117 C3 **Berbera** Somalia
118 B2 **Berbérati** C.A.R.
104 C1 **Berck** France
91 D2 **Berdyans'k** Ukr.
90 C2 **Berdychiv** Ukr.
90 A2 **Berehove** Ukr.
59 D3 **Bereina** P.N.G.
78 A2 **Berenice** Egypt
129 E2 **Berens River** Can.
90 B2 **Berezhany** Ukr.
90 C2 **Berezivka** Ukr.
90 B1 **Berezne** Ukr.
86 D2 **Bereznik** Rus. Fed.
86 E3 **Berezniki** Rus. Fed.
86 F2 **Berezovo** Rus. Fed.
107 D1 **Berga** Spain
111 C3 **Bergama** Turkey
108 A1 **Bergamo** Italy
102 C1 **Bergen** Mecklenburg-
Vorpommern Ger.
101 D1 **Bergen** Niedersachsen Ger.
93 E3 **Bergen** Norway
100 B2 **Bergen op Zoom** Neth.
104 C3 **Bergerac** France
100 C2 **Bergheim (Erft)** Ger.
100 C2 **Bergisch Gladbach** Ger.
122 A1 **Bergland** Namibia
92 H2 **Bergsviken** Sweden
83 M3 **Beringa, Ostrov** i. Rus. Fed.
100 B2 **Beringen** Belgium
124 B1 **Bering Sea** N. Pacific Ocean
83 N2 **Bering Strait**
Rus. Fed./U.S.A.
135 B3 **Berkeley** U.S.A.
100 B1 **Berkhout** Neth.
55 Q2 **Berkner Island** Antarctica
110 B2 **Berkovitsa** Bulg.
92 I1 **Berlevåg** Norway
101 F1 **Berlin** Ger.
141 E2 **Berlin** U.S.A.
101 E2 **Berlingerode** Ger.
53 D3 **Bermagui** Austr.
144 B2 **Bermejillo** Mex.
152 B3 **Bermejo** Bol.
125 F4 **Bermuda** terr.
N. Atlantic Ocean
105 D2 **Bern** Switz.
101 E2 **Bernburg (Saale)** Ger.
127 F2 **Bernier Bay** Can.
100 C3 **Bernkastel-Kues** Ger.
121 □D3 **Beroroha** Madag.

52 B2 **Berri** Austr.
107 D2 **Berrouaghia** Alg.
146 C2 **Berry Islands** Bahamas
100 C1 **Bersenbrück** Ger.
90 B2 **Bershad'** Ukr.
131 D1 **Berté, Lac** l. Can.
118 B2 **Bertoua** Cameroon
150 B2 **Beruri** Brazil
98 B1 **Berwick-upon-Tweed** U.K.
91 C2 **Beryslav** Ukr.
121 □D2 **Besalampy** Madag.
105 D2 **Besançon** France
118 B2 **Besnard Lake** Can.
142 C2 **Bessemer** U.S.A.
76 B2 **Besshoky, Gora** hill Kazakh.
106 B1 **Betanzos** Spain
118 B2 **Bétaré Oya** Cameroon
122 A2 **Bethanie** Namibia
123 C2 **Bethlehem** S. Africa
141 D2 **Bethlehem** U.S.A.
121 □D3 **Betioky** Madag.
77 D2 **Betpak-Dala** plain Kazakh.
121 □D3 **Betroka** Madag.
131 D2 **Betsiamites** Can.
121 □D2 **Betsiboka** r. Madag.
137 E2 **Bettendorf** U.S.A.
75 C2 **Bettiah** India
75 B2 **Betul** India
75 B2 **Betwa** r. India
98 B3 **Betws-y-coed** U.K.
98 C2 **Beverley** U.K.
101 D2 **Beverungen** Ger.
100 B1 **Beverwijk** Neth.
99 D3 **Bexhill** U.K.
111 C2 **Beykoz** Turkey
114 B4 **Beyla** Guinea
76 B2 **Beyneu** Kazakh.
80 B1 **Beypazarı** Turkey
Beyrouth Lebanon see Beirut
80 B2 **Beyşehir** Turkey
80 B2 **Beyşehir Gölü** l. Turkey
91 D2 **Beysug** r. Rus. Fed.
88 C2 **Bezhanitsy** Rus. Fed.
89 E2 **Bezhetsk** Rus. Fed.
105 C3 **Béziers** France
75 C2 **Bhadrakh** India
73 B3 **Bhadravati** India
75 C2 **Bhagalpur** India
74 A2 **Bhairi Hol** mt. Pak.
74 B1 **Bhakkar** Pak.
62 A1 **Bhamo** Myanmar
75 B3 **Bhanjanagar** India
74 B2 **Bharatpur** India
74 B2 **Bharuch** India
73 B3 **Bhavnagar** India
75 C3 **Bhawanipatna** India
123 D2 **Bhekuzulu** S. Africa
74 B2 **Bhilwara** India
73 B3 **Bhima** r. India
74 B2 **Bhiwani** India
123 C3 **Bhongweni** S. Africa
74 B2 **Bhopal** India
75 C2 **Bhubaneshwar** India
74 A2 **Bhuj** India
74 B2 **Bhumiphol Dam** Thai.
74 B2 **Bhusawal** India
75 D2 **Bhutan** country Asia
62 B2 **Bia, Phou** mt. Laos
59 D3 **Biak** Indon.
59 D3 **Biak** i. Indon.
103 E1 **Biała Podlaska** Pol.
103 D1 **Białogard** Pol.
103 E1 **Białystok** Pol.
109 C3 **Bianco** Italy
104 B3 **Biarritz** France
105 D2 **Biasca** Switz.
66 D2 **Bibai** Japan
120 A2 **Bibala** Angola
102 B2 **Biberach an der Riß** Ger.
115 C4 **Bida** Nigeria

141 E2 **Biddeford** U.S.A.
99 A3 **Bideford** U.K.
99 A3 **Bideford Bay** U.K.
101 D2 **Biedenkopf** Ger.
105 D2 **Biel** Switz.
101 D1 **Bielefeld** Ger.
108 A1 **Biella** Italy
103 D2 **Bielsko-Biała** Pol.
63 B2 **Biên Hoa** Vietnam
130 C1 **Bienville, Lac** l. Can.
100 B3 **Bièvre** Belgium
118 B3 **Bifoun** Gabon
111 C2 **Biga** Turkey
123 D2 **Big Bend** Swaziland
129 D2 **Biggar** Can.
96 C3 **Biggar** U.K.
134 D1 **Big Hole** r. U.S.A.
136 B1 **Bighorn** r. U.S.A.
136 B2 **Bighorn Mountains** U.S.A.
139 C2 **Big Lake** U.S.A.
140 B2 **Big Rapids** U.S.A.
129 D2 **Big River** Can.
129 E2 **Big Sand Lake** Can.
137 D2 **Big Sioux** r. U.S.A.
139 C2 **Big Spring** U.S.A.
134 E1 **Big Timber** U.S.A.
130 B1 **Big Trout Lake** Can.
130 A1 **Big Trout Lake** l. Can.
109 C2 **Bihać** Bos.-Herz.
75 C2 **Bihar Sharif** India
110 B1 **Bihor, Vârful** mt. Romania
114 A3 **Bijagós, Arquipélago dos** is Guinea-Bissau
81 C2 **Bījār** Iran
109 C2 **Bijeljina** Bos.-Herz.
109 C2 **Bijelo Polje** Yugo.
71 A3 **Bijie** China
74 B2 **Bikaner** India
69 E1 **Bikin** Rus. Fed.
118 B3 **Bikoro** Dem. Rep. Congo
79 C2 **Bilād Banī Bū 'Alī** Oman
90 C2 **Bilasuvar** India
90 C2 **Bila Tserkva** Ukr.
63 A2 **Bilauktaung Range** mts Myanmar/Thai.
106 C1 **Bilbao** Spain
111 C2 **Bilecik** Turkey
103 E1 **Biłgoraj** Pol.
90 C2 **Bilhorod-Dnistrovs'kyy** Ukr.
119 C2 **Bili** Dem. Rep. Congo
83 M2 **Bilibino** Rus. Fed.
134 E1 **Billings** U.S.A.
99 B3 **Bill of Portland** hd U.K.
115 D3 **Bilma** Niger
51 E2 **Biloela** Austr.
90 B1 **Bilohir"ya** Ukr.
91 C1 **Bilopillya** Ukr.
91 D2 **Bilovods'k** Ukr.
142 C2 **Biloxi** U.S.A.
51 C2 **Bilpa Morea Claypan** salt flat Austr.
101 E2 **Bilshausen** Ger.
115 E3 **Biltine** Chad
90 C2 **Bilyayivka** Ukr.
143 E3 **Bimini Islands** Bahamas
75 B2 **Bina-Etawa** India
59 C3 **Binaija, Gunung** mt. Indon.
118 B3 **Bindu** Dem. Rep. Congo
121 C2 **Bindura** Zimbabwe
107 D1 **Binefar** Spain
53 D1 **Bingara** Austr.
100 C3 **Bingen am Rhein** Ger.
141 F1 **Bingham** U.S.A.
141 D2 **Binghamton** U.S.A.
81 C2 **Bingöl** Turkey
60 A1 **Binjai** Indon.
60 B2 **Bintuhan** Indon.
61 C1 **Bintulu** Sarawak Malaysia
70 B2 **Binzhou** China

118 A2 **Bioco** i. Equat. Guinea
109 C2 **Biograd na Moru** Croatia
118 C1 **Birao** C.A.R.
75 C2 **Biratnagar** Nepal
128 C2 **Birch Mountains** Can.
100 B1 **Birdaard** Neth.
51 C2 **Birdsville** Austr.
80 B2 **Birecik** Turkey
60 A1 **Bireun** Indon.
75 C2 **Birganj** Nepal
117 B3 **Birhan** mt. Eth.
154 B2 **Birigüi** Brazil
76 B3 **Birjand** Iran
98 B2 **Birkenhead** U.K.
99 C2 **Birmingham** U.K.
142 C2 **Birmingham** U.S.A.
114 A2 **Bîr Mogreïn** Maur.
115 C3 **Birnin-Kebbi** Nigeria
115 C3 **Birnin Konni** Niger
69 E1 **Birobidzhan** Rus. Fed.
97 C2 **Birr** Rep. of Ireland
96 C1 **Birsay** U.K.
78 A2 **Bîr Shalatein** Egypt
82 G2 **Birˌžai** Lith.
75 B2 **Bisalpur** India
138 B2 **Bisbee** U.S.A.
104 A2 **Biscay, Bay of** sea France/Spain
102 C2 **Bischofshofen** Austria
130 B2 **Biscotasi Lake** Can.
77 D2 **Bishkek** Kyrg.
123 C3 **Bisho** S. Africa
135 C3 **Bishop** U.S.A.
69 E1 **Bishui** China
123 Col. **Bisinaca** Col.
115 C1 **Biskra** Alg.
136 C1 **Bismarck** U.S.A.
107 D2 **Bissa, Djebel** mt. Alg.
114 A3 **Bissau** Guinea-Bissau
129 E2 **Bissett** Can.
128 C2 **Bistcho Lake** Can.
110 B1 **Bistrița** Romania
110 C1 **Bistrița** r. Romania
100 C3 **Bitburg** Ger.
105 D2 **Bitche** France
115 D3 **Bitkine** Chad
109 D2 **Bitola** Macedonia
109 C2 **Bitonto** Italy
122 A3 **Bitterfontein** S. Africa
134 C1 **Bitterroot** r. U.S.A.
134 C1 **Bitterroot Range** mts U.S.A.
91 D1 **Bityug** r. Rus. Fed.
115 D3 **Biu** Nigeria
67 C3 **Biwa-ko** l. Japan
68 B1 **Biysk** Rus. Fed.
115 C1 **Bizerte** Tunisia
92 □A2 **Bjargtangar** hd Iceland
92 G2 **Bjästa** Sweden
92 G2 **Bjerkvik** Norway
Björneborg Fin. see Pori
Bjørnøya i. Arctic Ocean see Bear Island
118 B3 **Bla** Mali
137 E3 **Black** r. U.S.A.
141 D2 **Blackall** Austr.
98 B2 **Blackburn** U.K.
134 D2 **Blackfoot** U.S.A.
136 C2 **Black Hills** U.S.A.
96 B2 **Black Isle** pen. U.K.
129 D2 **Black Lake** Can.
129 D2 **Black Lake** l. Can.
98 B3 **Black Mountains** U.K.
98 B2 **Blackpool** U.K.
Black River r. Vietnam see Ða, Sông
140 A2 **Black River Falls** U.S.A.
140 C3 **Blacksburg** U.S.A.
80 B1 **Black Sea** Asia/Europe
97 A1 **Blacksod Bay** Rep. of Ireland

97 C2 **Blackstairs Mountains** Rep. of Ireland
114 B4 **Black Volta** r. Africa
97 C2 **Blackwater** r. Rep. of Ireland
128 B1 **Blackwater Lake** l. Can.
50 A3 **Blackwood** r. Austr.
76 A2 **Blagodarnyy** Rus. Fed.
110 B2 **Blagoevgrad** Bulg.
69 E1 **Blagoveshchensk** Rus. Fed.
129 D2 **Blaine Lake** Can.
137 D2 **Blair** U.K.
96 C2 **Blair Atholl** U.K.
96 C2 **Blairgowrie** U.K.
143 D2 **Blakely** U.S.A.
153 B4 **Blanca, Bahía** b. Arg.
52 A1 **Blanche, Lake** salt flat Austr.
152 B2 **Blanco** r. Bol.
131 E1 **Blanc-Sablon** Can.
92 □A2 **Blanda** r. Iceland
99 B3 **Blandford Forum** U.K.
135 E3 **Blanding** U.S.A.
107 D1 **Blanes** Spain
60 A1 **Blangkejeren** Indon.
100 C2 **Blankenheim** Ger.
100 C2 **Blankenrath** Ger.
103 D2 **Blansko** Czech Rep.
121 C2 **Blantyre** Malawi
98 C1 **Blaydon** U.K.
53 C2 **Blayney** Austr.
54 B2 **Blenheim** N.Z.
115 C1 **Blida** Alg.
130 B2 **Blind River** Can.
123 C2 **Bloemfontein** S. Africa
123 C2 **Bloemhof** S. Africa
123 C2 **Bloemhof Dam** S. Africa
92 □A2 **Blönduós** Iceland
97 B1 **Bloody Foreland** pt Rep. of Ireland
138 B3 **Bloomfield** U.S.A.
140 B2 **Bloomington** IL U.S.A.
140 B3 **Bloomington** IN U.S.A.
140 C3 **Bluefield** U.S.A.
146 B3 **Bluefields** Nic.
53 C2 **Blue Mountains** Austr.
134 C1 **Blue Mountains** U.S.A.
116 B3 **Blue Nile** r. Eth./Sudan
126 D2 **Bluenose Lake** Can.
140 C3 **Blue Ridge** mts U.S.A.
97 B1 **Blue Stack Mountains** Rep. of Ireland
54 A3 **Bluff** N.Z.
135 E3 **Bluff** U.S.A.
152 D3 **Blumenau** Brazil
52 A2 **Blyth** Austr.
98 C1 **Blyth** U.K.
135 D4 **Blythe** U.S.A.
142 C1 **Blytheville** U.S.A.
114 A4 **Bo** Sierra Leone
64 B1 **Boac** Phil.
151 D2 **Boa Esperança, Açude** resr Brazil
150 B1 **Boa Vista** Brazil
53 C2 **Bobadah** Austr.
71 B3 **Bobai** China
121 □D2 **Bobaomby, Tanjona** c. Madag.
114 B3 **Bobo-Dioulasso** Burkina
89 F3 **Bobrov** Rus. Fed.
91 C1 **Bobrovytsya** Ukr.
91 C2 **Bobrynets'** Ukr.
121 □D3 **Boby** mt. Madag.
150 B2 **Boca do Acre** Brazil
155 D1 **Bocaiúva** Brazil
118 B2 **Bocaranga** C.A.R.
103 E2 **Bochnia** Pol.
100 C2 **Bocholt** Ger.
100 C2 **Bochum** Ger.
123 C1 **Bochum** S. Africa
101 E1 **Bockenem** Ger.
118 B2 **Boda** C.A.R.

83 I3 **Bodaybo** Rus. Fed.
115 D3 **Bodélé** reg. Chad
92 H2 **Boden** Sweden
99 A3 **Bodmin** U.K.
99 A3 **Bodmin Moor** moorland U.K.
92 F2 **Bodø** Norway
111 C3 **Bodrum** Turkey
118 C3 **Boende** Dem. Rep. Congo
142 C2 **Bogalusa** U.S.A.
114 B3 **Bogandé** Burkina
68 B2 **Bogda Shan** mts China
53 D1 **Boggabilla** Austr.
97 B2 **Boggeragh Mountains** Rep. of Ireland
100 B3 **Bogny-sur-Meuse** France
97 C2 **Bog of Allen** reg. Rep. of Ireland
53 C3 **Bogong, Mount** Austr.
60 B2 **Bogor** Indon.
89 E3 **Bogoroditsk** Rus. Fed.
150 A1 **Bogotá** Col.
82 G3 **Bogotol** Rus. Fed.
83 H3 **Boguchany** Rus. Fed.
91 E2 **Boguchar** Rus. Fed.
70 B2 **Bo Hai** g. China
100 A3 **Bohain-en-Vermandois** France
70 B2 **Bohai Wan** b. China
123 C2 **Bohlokong** S. Africa
102 C2 **Böhmer Wald** mts Ger.
91 D1 **Bohodukhiv** Ukr.
64 B2 **Bohol** i. Phil.
64 B2 **Bohol Sea** Phil.
68 B2 **Bohu** China
155 C2 **Boi, Ponta do** pt Brazil
154 B1 **Bois** r. Brazil
126 C2 **Bois, Lac des** l. Can.
134 C2 **Boise** U.S.A.
139 C1 **Boise City** U.S.A.
123 C2 **Boitumelong** S. Africa
101 E1 **Boizenburg** Ger.
76 B3 **Bojnūrd** Iran
118 B3 **Bokatola** Dem. Rep. Congo
114 A3 **Boké** Guinea
118 C3 **Bokele** Dem. Rep. Congo
93 E4 **Boknafjorden** sea chan. Norway
115 D3 **Bokoro** Chad
63 A2 **Bokpyin** Myanmar
89 D2 **Boksitogorsk** Rus. Fed.
122 B2 **Bokspits** S. Africa
114 A3 **Bolama** Guinea-Bissau
104 C2 **Bolbec** France
77 E2 **Bole** China
118 B3 **Boleko** Dem. Rep. Congo
114 B3 **Bolgatanga** Ghana
90 B2 **Bolhrad** Ukr.
66 B1 **Boli** China
110 C2 **Bolintin-Vale** Romania
137 E3 **Bolivar** U.S.A.
150 A1 **Bolívar, Pico** mt. Venez.
152 B2 **Bolivia** country S. America
89 E3 **Bolkhov** Rus. Fed.
105 C3 **Bollène** France
93 G3 **Bollnäs** Sweden
53 C1 **Bollon** Austr.
101 E2 **Bollstedt** Ger.
93 F4 **Bolmen** l. Sweden
118 B3 **Bolobo** Dem. Rep. Congo
108 B2 **Bologna** Italy
89 D2 **Bologovo** Rus. Fed.
89 D2 **Bologoye** Rus. Fed.
118 B2 **Bolomba** Dem. Rep. Congo
63 B2 **Bolovens, Phouphieng** plat. Laos
83 H1 **Bol'shevik, Ostrov** i. Rus. Fed.
86 E2 **Bol'shezemel'skaya Tundra** lowland Rus. Fed.
83 L2 **Bol'shoy Aluy** r. Rus. Fed.

66 B2 **Bol'shoy Kamen'** Rus. Fed.
Bol'shoy Kavkaz mts Asia/Europe see Caucasus
83 K2 **Bol'shoy Lyakhovskiy, Ostrov** i. Rus. Fed.
100 B1 **Bolsward** Neth.
98 B2 **Bolton** U.K.
80 B1 **Bolu** Turkey
92 □A2 **Bolungarvík** Iceland
108 B1 **Bolzano** Italy
118 B3 **Boma** Dem. Rep. Congo
53 D2 **Bomaderry** Austr.
53 C3 **Bombala** Austr.
Bombay India see Mumbai
151 D3 **Bom Despacho** Brazil
75 D2 **Bomdila** India
151 D3 **Bom Jesus da Lapa** Brazil
155 D2 **Bom Jesus do Itabapoana** Brazil
115 D1 **Bon, Cap** c. Tunisia
147 D3 **Bonaire** i. Neth. Antilles
50 B1 **Bonaparte Archipelago** is Austr.
131 E2 **Bonavista** Can.
131 E2 **Bonavista Bay** Can.
118 C2 **Bondo** Dem. Rep. Congo
114 B4 **Bondoukou** Côte d'Ivoire
58 C3 **Bonerate, Kepulauan** is Indon.
155 C1 **Bonfinópolis de Minas** Brazil
117 B4 **Bonga** Eth.
75 D2 **Bongaigaon** India
118 C2 **Bongandanga** Dem. Rep. Congo
118 C2 **Bongo, Massif des** mts C.A.R.
115 D3 **Bongor** Chad
114 B4 **Bongouanou** Côte d'Ivoire
63 B2 **Bông Son** Vietnam
139 D2 **Bonham** U.S.A.
105 D3 **Bonifacio** Corsica France
108 A2 **Bonifacio, Strait of** France/Italy
100 C2 **Bonn** Ger.
134 C1 **Bonners Ferry** U.S.A.
50 A3 **Bonnie Rock** Austr.
129 C2 **Bonnyville** Can.
108 A2 **Bonorva** Sardinia Italy
61 C1 **Bontang** Indon.
64 B1 **Bontoc** Phil.
58 B3 **Bontosunggu** Indon.
123 C3 **Bontrug** S. Africa
52 B2 **Booligal** Austr.
53 C1 **Boomi** Austr.
53 D1 **Boonah** Austr.
137 E2 **Boone** U.S.A.
142 C2 **Booneville** U.S.A.
137 E3 **Boonville** U.S.A.
53 C2 **Boorowa** Austr.
126 F2 **Boothia, Gulf of** Can.
126 E2 **Boothia Peninsula** Can.
100 C2 **Boppard** Ger.
117 B4 **Bor** Sudan
80 B2 **Bor** Turkey
109 D2 **Bor** Yugo.
93 F4 **Borås** Sweden
79 C2 **Borāzjān** Iran
150 C2 **Borba** Brazil
104 B3 **Bordeaux** France
127 F2 **Borden Peninsula** Can.
52 B3 **Bordertown** Austr.
107 D2 **Bordj Bou Arréridj** Alg.
107 D2 **Bordj Bounaama** Alg.
115 C1 **Bordj Messaouda** Alg.
115 C2 **Bordj Omer Driss** Alg.
94 B1 **Borðoy** i. Faroe Is
92 □A3 **Borgarnes** Iceland
108 A1 **Borgosesia** Italy
87 D3 **Borisoglebsk** Rus. Fed.

89 E2 Borisoglebskiy Rus. Fed.
91 D1 Borisovka Rus. Fed.
100 D2 Borken Ger.
92 G2 Borkenes Norway
100 C1 Borkum Ger.
100 C1 Borkum i. Ger.
93 G3 Borlänge Sweden
101 F2 Borna Ger.
61 C1 Borneo i. Asia
93 F4 Bornholm i. Denmark
111 C3 Bornova Turkey
90 B1 Borodyanka Ukr.
89 D2 Borovichi Rus. Fed.
89 E2 Borovsk Rus. Fed.
51 C1 Borroloola Austr.
110 B1 Borşa Romania
90 B2 Borshchiv Ukr.
69 D1 Borshchovochnyy Khrebet
   mts Rus. Fed.
101 E1 Börßum Ger.
   Bortala China see Bole
81 C2 Borüjerd Iran
90 A2 Boryslav Ukr.
90 C1 Boryspil' Ukr.
91 C1 Borzna Ukr.
69 D1 Borzya Rus. Fed.
109 C1 Bosanska Dubica Bos.-Herz.
109 C1 Bosanska Gradiška
   Bos.-Herz.
109 C2 Bosanska Krupa Bos.-Herz.
109 C1 Bosanski Novi Bos.-Herz.
109 C2 Bosansko Grahovo
   Bos.-Herz.
71 A3 Bose China
123 C2 Boshof S. Africa
109 C2 Bosnia-Herzegovina country
   Europe
118 B2 Bosobolo Dem. Rep. Congo
110 C2 Bosporus str. Turkey
118 B2 Bossangoa C.A.R.
118 B2 Bossembélé C.A.R.
68 B2 Bosten Hu l. China
98 C2 Boston U.K.
141 E2 Boston U.S.A.
142 B1 Boston Mountains U.S.A.
53 D2 Botany Bay Austr.
110 B2 Botev mt. Bulg.
93 G3 Bothnia, Gulf of
   Fin./Sweden
110 C1 Botoşani Romania
123 C2 Botshabelo S. Africa
120 B3 Botswana country Africa
109 C3 Botte Donato, Monte
   mt. Italy
136 C1 Bottineau U.S.A.
100 C2 Bottrop Ger.
154 C2 Botucatu Brazil
114 B4 Bouaké Côte d'Ivoire
118 B2 Bouar C.A.R.
114 B1 Bouârfa Morocco
131 D2 Bouctouche Can.
107 E2 Bougaa Alg.
114 B3 Bougouni Mali
100 B3 Bouillon Belgium
107 D2 Bouira Alg.
114 A2 Boujdour Western Sahara
136 C2 Boulder U.S.A.
135 D3 Boulder City U.S.A.
51 C2 Boulia Austr.
104 C2 Boulogne-Billancourt
   France
99 D3 Boulogne-sur-Mer France
118 B3 Boumango Gabon
118 B2 Boumba r. Cameroon
107 D2 Boumerdes Alg.
114 B4 Bouna Côte d'Ivoire
114 B4 Boundiali Côte d'Ivoire
134 D2 Bountiful U.S.A.
114 B3 Bourem Mali
104 C2 Bourganeuf France

105 D2 Bourg-en-Bresse France
104 C2 Bourges France
53 C2 Bourke Austr.
99 C3 Bournemouth U.K.
115 C1 Bou Saâda Alg.
115 D3 Bousso Chad
114 A3 Boutilimit Maur.
129 C3 Bow r. Can.
51 D2 Bowen Austr.
129 C3 Bow Island Can.
140 B3 Bowling Green KY U.S.A.
140 C2 Bowling Green OH U.S.A.
136 C1 Bowman U.S.A.
101 D3 Boxberg Ger.
100 B2 Boxtel Neth.
80 B1 Boyabat Turkey
71 B3 Boyang China
97 B2 Boyle Rep. of Ireland
97 C2 Boyne r. Rep. of Ireland
136 B2 Boysen Reservoir U.S.A.
152 B3 Boyuibe Bol.
111 C3 Bozburun Turkey
111 C3 Bozcaada i. Turkey
111 C3 Bozdağ mt. Turkey
111 C3 Boz Dağları mts Turkey
111 C3 Bozdoğan Turkey
134 D1 Bozeman U.S.A.
118 B2 Bozoum C.A.R.
111 D3 Bozüyük Turkey
109 C2 Brač i. Croatia
130 C2 Bracebridge Can.
131 D2 Brachet, Lac au l. Can.
99 C3 Bracknell U.K.
109 C2 Bradano r. Italy
143 D3 Bradenton U.S.A.
98 C2 Bradford U.K.
141 D2 Bradford U.S.A.
139 D2 Brady U.S.A.
96 C2 Braemar U.K.
106 B1 Braga Port.
151 D2 Bragança Brazil
106 B1 Bragança Port.
155 C2 Bragança Paulista Brazil
89 D3 Brahin Belarus
73 C3 Brahmapur India
62 A1 Brahmaputra r. China/India
111 C1 Brăila Romania
137 E1 Brainerd U.S.A.
99 D3 Braintree U.K.
100 B2 Braives Belgium
101 D1 Brake (Unterweser) Ger.
100 D1 Bramsche Ger.
150 B2 Branco r. Brazil
101 F1 Brandenburg Ger.
129 E3 Brandon Can.
97 A2 Brandon Mountain
   Rep. of Ireland
122 B3 Brandvlei S. Africa
103 D1 Braniewo Pol.
130 B2 Brantford Can.
131 D2 Bras d'Or Lake Can.
155 D1 Brasil, Planalto do plat. Brazil
154 C1 Brasilândia Brazil
154 C1 Brasília Brazil
155 D1 Brasília de Minas Brazil
88 C2 Braslaw Belarus
110 C1 Braşov Romania
103 D2 Bratislava Slovakia
83 H3 Bratsk Rus. Fed.
102 C2 Braunau am Inn Austria
101 E1 Braunschweig Ger.
92 □A2 Brautarholt Iceland
   Bravo del Norte, Rio r.
   Mex./U.S.A. see Rio Grande
135 C4 Brawley U.S.A.
97 C2 Bray Rep. of Ireland
150 C2 Brazil country S. America
139 D3 Brazos r. U.S.A.
118 B3 Brazzaville Congo
109 C2 Brčko Bos.-Herz.

96 C2 Brechin U.K.
100 B2 Brecht Belgium
139 D2 Breckenridge U.S.A.
103 D2 Břeclav Czech Rep.
99 B3 Brecon U.K.
99 B3 Brecon Beacons reg. U.K.
100 B2 Breda Neth.
122 B3 Bredasdorp S. Africa
102 B2 Bregenz Austria
92 H1 Breivikbotn Norway
92 E3 Brekstad Norway
101 D1 Bremen Ger.
101 D1 Bremerhaven Ger.
134 B1 Bremerton U.S.A.
101 D1 Bremervörde Ger.
139 D2 Brenham U.S.A.
108 B1 Brennero Italy
102 C2 Brenner Pass Austria/Italy
99 D3 Brentwood U.K.
108 B1 Brescia Italy
108 B1 Bressanone Italy
96 □ Bressay i. U.K.
104 B2 Bressuire France
88 B3 Brest Belarus
104 B2 Brest France
142 C3 Breton Sound b. U.S.A.
151 C2 Breves Brazil
53 C1 Brewarrina Austr.
134 C1 Brewster U.S.A.
89 E2 Breytovo Rus. Fed.
109 C1 Brezovo Polje hill Croatia
118 C2 Bria C.A.R.
105 D3 Briançon France
90 B2 Briceni Moldova
99 B3 Bridgend U.K.
141 E2 Bridgeport CT U.S.A.
136 C2 Bridgeport NE U.S.A.
147 E3 Bridgetown Barbados
131 D2 Bridgewater Can.
99 B3 Bridgwater U.K.
98 C1 Bridlington U.K.
98 C1 Bridlington Bay U.K.
105 D2 Brig Switz.
134 D2 Brigham City U.S.A.
54 B3 Brighton N.Z.
99 C3 Brighton U.K.
105 D3 Brignoles France
101 D2 Brilon Ger.
109 C2 Brindisi Italy
53 D1 Brisbane Austr.
99 B3 Bristol U.K.
143 D1 Bristol U.S.A.
99 A3 Bristol Channel est. U.K.
128 B2 British Columbia prov. Can.
56 C6 British Indian Ocean
   Territory terr. Indian Ocean
123 C2 Brits S. Africa
122 B3 Britstown S. Africa
104 C2 Brive-la-Gaillarde France
106 C1 Briviesca Spain
103 D2 Brno Czech Rep.
143 D2 Broad r. U.S.A.
130 C1 Broadback r. Can.
96 A1 Broad Bay U.K.
96 C2 Broad Law hill U.K.
136 B1 Broadus U.S.A.
129 D2 Brochet Can.
129 D2 Brochet, Lac l. Can.
101 E1 Bröckel Ger.
126 D1 Brock Island Can.
130 C2 Brockville Can.
127 F2 Brodeur Peninsula Can.
96 B3 Brodick U.K.
103 D1 Brodnica Pol.
90 B1 Brody Ukr.
139 D1 Broken Arrow U.S.A.
137 D2 Broken Bow U.S.A.
52 B2 Broken Hill Austr.
99 B2 Bromsgrove U.K.
93 E4 Brønderslev Denmark

92 F2	**Brønnøysund** Norway	
64 A2	**Brooke's Point** Phil.	
142 B2	**Brookhaven** U.S.A.	
134 B2	**Brookings** *OR* U.S.A.	
137 D2	**Brookings** *SD* U.S.A.	
129 C2	**Brooks** Can.	
126 B2	**Brooks Range** *mts* U.S.A.	
143 D3	**Brooksville** U.S.A.	
96 B2	**Broom, Loch** *inlet* U.K.	
50 B1	**Broome** Austr.	
134 B2	**Brothers** U.S.A.	
	Broughton Island Can. *see*	
	Qikiqtarjuaq	
90 C1	**Brovary** Ukr.	
139 C2	**Brownfield** U.S.A.	
128 C3	**Browning** U.S.A.	
142 C1	**Brownsville** *TN* U.S.A.	
139 D3	**Brownsville** *TX* U.S.A.	
139 D2	**Brownwood** U.S.A.	
92 □A2	**Brú** Iceland	
104 C1	**Bruay-la-Bussière** France	
140 B1	**Bruce Crossing** U.S.A.	
103 D2	**Bruck an der Mur** Austria	
100 A2	**Bruges** Belgium	
	Brugge Belgium *see* **Bruges**	
128 C2	**Brûlé** Can.	
151 D3	**Brumado** Brazil	
93 F3	**Brumunddal** Norway	
61 C1	**Brunei** *country* Asia	
102 C2	**Brunico** Italy	
101 D1	**Brunsbüttel** Ger.	
143 D2	**Brunswick** *GA* U.S.A.	
141 F2	**Brunswick** *ME* U.S.A.	
53 D1	**Brunswick Head** Austr.	
136 C2	**Brush** U.S.A.	
100 B2	**Brussels** Belgium	
	Bruxelles Belgium *see*	
	Brussels	
139 D2	**Bryan** U.S.A.	
89 D3	**Bryansk** Rus. Fed.	
91 D2	**Bryn'kovskaya** Rus. Fed.	
91 D2	**Bryukhovetskaya** Rus. Fed.	
103 D1	**Brzeg** Pol.	
114 A3	**Buba** Guinea-Bissau	
80 B2	**Bucak** Turkey	
150 A1	**Bucaramanga** Col.	
53 C3	**Buchan** Austr.	
114 A4	**Buchanan** Liberia	
110 C2	**Bucharest** Romania	
101 D1	**Bucholz in der Nordheide** Ger.	
110 C1	**Bucin, Pasul** *pass* Romania	
101 D1	**Bückeburg** Ger.	
138 A2	**Buckeye** U.S.A.	
96 C2	**Buckhaven** U.K.	
96 C2	**Buckie** U.K.	
51 C1	**Buckingham Bay** Austr.	
51 D2	**Buckland Tableland** *reg.* Austr.	
52 A2	**Buckleboo** Austr.	
141 F2	**Bucksport** U.S.A.	
	Bucureşti Romania *see* **Bucharest**	
89 D3	**Buda-Kashalyova** Belarus	
103 D2	**Budapest** Hungary	
75 B2	**Budaun** India	
108 A2	**Buddusò** *Sardinia* Italy	
99 A3	**Bude** U.K.	
87 D4	**Budennovsk** Rus. Fed.	
89 D2	**Budogoshch'** Rus. Fed.	
108 A2	**Budoni** *Sardinia* Italy	
118 A2	**Buea** Cameroon	
144 B2	**Buenaventura** Mex.	
106 C1	**Buendia, Embalse de** *resr* Spain	
155 D1	**Buenópolis** Brazil	
153 C4	**Buenos Aires** Arg.	
153 A5	**Buenos Aires, Lago** *l.* Arg./Chile	
141 D2	**Buffalo** *NY* U.S.A.	
136 C1	**Buffalo** *SD* U.S.A.	
136 B2	**Buffalo** *WY* U.S.A.	
129 D2	**Buffalo Narrows** Can.	
122 A2	**Buffels** *watercourse* S. Africa	
110 C2	**Buftea** Romania	
103 E1	**Bug** *r.* Pol.	
61 C2	**Bugel, Tanjung** *pt* Indon.	
109 C2	**Bugojno** Bos.-Herz.	
64 A2	**Bugsuk** *i.* Phil.	
87 E3	**Buguruslan** Rus. Fed.	
110 C1	**Buhuşi** Romania	
99 B2	**Builth Wells** U.K.	
69 D1	**Buir Nur** *l.* Mongolia	
120 A3	**Buitepos** Namibia	
109 D2	**Bujanovac** Yugo.	
119 C3	**Bujumbura** Burundi	
69 D1	**Bukachacha** Rus. Fed.	
119 C3	**Bukavu** Dem. Rep. Congo	
76 C3	**Bukhara** Uzbek.	
60 B2	**Bukittinggi** Indon.	
119 D3	**Bukoba** Tanz.	
53 D2	**Bulahdelal** Austr.	
121 B3	**Bulawayo** Zimbabwe	
111 C3	**Buldan** Turkey	
123 D2	**Bulembu** Swaziland	
69 C1	**Bulgan** Mongolia	
110 C2	**Bulgaria** *country* Europe	
54 B2	**Buller** *r.* N.Z.	
52 B1	**Bulloo Downs** Austr.	
122 A1	**Büllsport** Namibia	
58 C3	**Bulukumba** Indon.	
118 B3	**Bulungu** Dem. Rep. Congo	
118 C2	**Bumba** Dem. Rep. Congo	
62 A1	**Bumhkang** Myanmar	
118 B3	**Buna** Dem. Rep. Congo	
50 A3	**Bunbury** Austr.	
97 C1	**Buncrana** Rep. of Ireland	
119 D3	**Bunda** Tanz.	
51 E2	**Bundaberg** Austr.	
53 D2	**Bundarra** Austr.	
74 B2	**Bundi** India	
97 B1	**Bundoran** Rep. of Ireland	
53 C3	**Bungendore** Austr.	
67 B4	**Bungo-suidō** *sea chan.* Japan	
119 D2	**Bunia** Dem. Rep. Congo	
118 C3	**Bunianga** Dem. Rep. Congo	
63 B2	**Buôn Mê Thuôt** Vietnam	
75 C1	**Bura** Kenya	
117 C4	**Burang** China	
78 B2	**Burao** Somalia	
78 B2	**Buraydah** Saudi Arabia	
100 D2	**Burbach** Ger.	
80 B2	**Burdur** Turkey	
117 B3	**Burë** Eth.	
99 D2	**Bure** *r.* U.K.	
110 C2	**Burgas** Bulg.	
101 E1	**Burg bei Magdeburg** Ger.	
101 E1	**Burgdorf** *Niedersachsen* Ger.	
101 E1	**Burgdorf** *Niedersachsen* Ger.	
131 E2	**Burgeo** Can.	
123 D1	**Burgersfort** S. Africa	
100 A2	**Burgh-Haamstede** Neth.	
145 C2	**Burgos** Mex.	
106 C1	**Burgos** Spain	
111 C3	**Burhaniye** Turkey	
74 B2	**Burhanpur** India	
101 D1	**Burhave (Butjadingen)** Ger.	
131 E2	**Burin** Can.	
151 D2	**Buriti Bravo** Brazil	
155 C1	**Buritis** Brazil	
51 C1	**Burketown** Austr.	
114 B3	**Burkina** *country* Africa	
134 D2	**Burley** U.S.A.	
136 C3	**Burlington** *CO* U.S.A.	
137 E2	**Burlington** *IA* U.S.A.	
143 E1	**Burlington** *NC* U.S.A.	
141 E2	**Burlington** *VT* U.S.A.	
	Burma *country* Asia *see* **Myanmar**	
134 B2	**Burney** U.S.A.	
51 D4	**Burnie** Austr.	
98 B2	**Burnley** U.K.	
134 C2	**Burns** U.S.A.	
128 B2	**Burns Lake** Can.	
77 E2	**Burqin** China	
52 A2	**Burra** Austr.	
109 D2	**Burrel** Albania	
97 B2	**Burren** *reg.* Rep. of Ireland	
	Burrendong Reservoir Austr.	
53 C2	**Burren Junction** Austr.	
107 C2	**Burriana** Spain	
53 C2	**Burrinjuck Reservoir** Austr.	
144 B2	**Burro, Serranías del** *mts* Mex.	
111 C2	**Bursa** Turkey	
116 B2	**Bûr Safâga** Egypt	
	Bûr Sa'îd Egypt *see* **Port Said**	
130 C1	**Burton, Lac** *l.* Can.	
97 B1	**Burtonport** Rep. of Ireland	
99 C2	**Burton upon Trent** U.K.	
59 C3	**Buru** *i.* Indon.	
119 C3	**Burundi** *country* Africa	
119 C3	**Bururi** Burundi	
91 C1	**Buryn'** Ukr.	
77 D2	**Burynshyk** Kazakh.	
99 D2	**Bury St Edmunds** U.K.	
118 C3	**Busanga** Dem. Rep. Congo	
79 C2	**Büshehr** Iran	
119 D3	**Bushenyi** Uganda	
118 C2	**Businga** Dem. Rep. Congo	
50 A3	**Busselton** Austr.	
144 B2	**Bustamante** Mex.	
64 A1	**Busuanga** Phil.	
118 C2	**Buta** Dem. Rep. Congo	
119 C3	**Butare** Rwanda	
123 C2	**Butha Buthe** Lesotho	
140 D2	**Butler** U.S.A.	
59 C3	**Buton** *i.* Indon.	
134 D1	**Butte** U.S.A.	
60 B1	**Butterworth** Malaysia	
96 A1	**Butt of Lewis** *hd* U.K.	
129 E2	**Button Bay** Can.	
64 B2	**Butuan** Phil.	
91 E1	**Buturlinovka** Rus. Fed.	
75 C2	**Butwal** Nepal	
101 D2	**Butzbach** Ger.	
117 C4	**Buulobarde** Somalia	
117 C5	**Buur Gaabo** Somalia	
117 C4	**Buurhakaba** Somalia	
101 E1	**Buxtehude** Ger.	
89 F2	**Buy** Rus. Fed.	
87 D4	**Buynaksk** Rus. Fed.	
111 C3	**Büyükmenderes** *r.* Turkey	
110 C1	**Buzău** Romania	
121 C2	**Búzi** Moz.	
89 E3	**Buzuluk** Rus. Fed.	
110 C2	**Byala** Bulg.	
88 C3	**Byalynichy** Belarus	
88 D3	**Byarezina** *r.* Belarus	
88 B3	**Byaroza** Belarus	
88 C3	**Bydgoszcz** Pol.	
88 C3	**Byerazino** Belarus	
88 C3	**Byeshankovichy** Belarus	
89 D3	**Bykhaw** Belarus	
127 F2	**Bylot Island** Can.	
53 C2	**Byrock** Austr.	
53 D1	**Byron Bay** Austr.	
83 J2	**Bytantay** *r.* Rus. Fed.	
103 D1	**Bytom** Pol.	
103 D1	**Bytów** Pol.	

C

154 B2	**Caarapó** Brazil	

64 B1 Cabanatuan Phil.
117 C3 Cabdul Qaadir Somalia
106 C2 Cabeza del Buey Spain
152 B2 Cabezas Bol.
150 A1 Cabimas Venez.
120 A1 Cabinda Angola
118 B3 Cabinda prov. Angola
155 D2 Cabo Frio Brazil
155 D2 Cabo Frio, Ilha do i. Brazil
130 C2 Cabonga, Réservoir resr Can.
51 E2 Caboolture Austr.
150 A2 Cabo Pantoja Peru
144 A1 Caborca Mex.
131 D2 Cabot Strait Can.
155 D1 Cabral, Serra de mts Brazil
107 D2 Cabrera i. Spain
129 D2 Cabri Can.
107 C2 Cabriel r. Spain
152 C3 Caçador Brazil
109 D2 Čačak Yugo.
108 A2 Caccia, Capo c. Sardinia Italy
151 C3 Cáceres Brazil
106 C2 Cáceres Spain
128 B2 Cache Creek Can.
114 A3 Cacheu Guinea-Bissau
151 C2 Cachimbo, Serra do hills Brazil
154 B1 Cachoeira Alta Brazil
155 D2 Cachoeiro de Itapemirim Brazil
114 A3 Cacine Guinea-Bissau
120 A2 Cacolo Angola
154 B1 Caçu Brazil
103 D2 Čadca Slovakia
101 D1 Cadenberge Ger.
145 B2 Cadereyta Mex.
140 B2 Cadillac U.S.A.
106 B2 Cádiz Spain
106 B2 Cádiz, Golfo de g. Spain
128 C2 Cadotte Lake Can.
104 B2 Caen France
98 A2 Caernarfon U.K.
98 A2 Caernarfon Bay U.K.
152 B3 Cafayate Arg.
64 B1 Cagayan de Oro Phil.
108 B2 Cagli Italy
108 A3 Cagliari Sardinia Italy
108 A3 Cagliari, Golfo di b. Sardinia Italy
97 B3 Caha Mountains Rep. of Ireland
97 A3 Cahermore Rep. of Ireland
97 A3 Cahersiveen Rep. of Ireland
97 C2 Cahir Rep. of Ireland
121 C2 Cahora Bassa, Lago de resr Moz.
97 C2 Cahore Point Rep. of Ireland
104 C3 Cahors France
121 D2 Caia Moz.
151 C3 Caiabis, Serra dos hills Brazil
120 B2 Caianda Angola
154 B1 Caiapó, Serra do mts Brazil
154 B1 Caiapônia Brazil
147 C2 Caicos Islands Turks and Caicos Is
96 C2 Cairngorm Mountains U.K.
98 A1 Cairnryan U.K.
51 D1 Cairns Austr.
116 B1 Cairo Egypt
98 C2 Caistor U.K.
120 A2 Caiundo Angola
150 A2 Cajamarca Peru
109 C1 Čakovec Croatia
123 C3 Cala S. Africa
150 B1 Calabozo Venez.
110 B2 Calafat Romania

153 A6 Calafate Arg.
107 C1 Calahorra Spain
104 C1 Calais France
141 F1 Calais U.S.A.
152 B3 Calama Chile
64 A1 Calamian Group is Phil.
107 C1 Calamocha Spain
120 A1 Calandula Angola
60 A1 Calang Indon.
115 E1 Calanscio Sand Sea des. Libya
64 B1 Calapan Phil.
110 C2 Călăraşi Romania
107 C1 Calatayud Spain
64 B1 Calayan i. Phil.
64 B1 Calbayog Phil.
151 E2 Calcanhar, Ponta do pt Brazil
151 C1 Calçoene Brazil
75 C2 Calcutta India
106 B2 Caldas da Rainha Port.
154 C1 Caldas Novas Brazil
152 A3 Caldera Chile
134 C2 Caldwell U.S.A.
123 C3 Caledon r. Lesotho/S. Africa
122 A3 Caledon S. Africa
153 B5 Caleta Olivia Arg.
98 A1 Calf of Man i. Isle of Man
128 C2 Calgary Can.
150 A1 Cali Col.
73 B3 Calicut India
135 D3 Caliente U.S.A.
135 B2 California state U.S.A.
144 A1 California, Golfo de g. Mex.
135 B3 California Aqueduct canal U.S.A.
122 B3 Calitzdorp S. Africa
145 C2 Calkini Mex.
52 B1 Callabonna, Lake salt flat Austr.
96 B2 Callander U.K.
150 A3 Callao Peru
108 B3 Caltagirone Sicily Italy
108 B3 Caltanissetta Sicily Italy
120 A2 Caluquembe Angola
117 D3 Caluula Somalia
105 D3 Calvi Corsica France
107 D2 Calvià Spain
145 B2 Calvillo Mex.
122 A3 Calvinia S. Africa
109 C2 Calvo, Monte mt. Italy
144 B2 Camacho Mex.
120 A2 Camacupa Angola
146 C2 Camagüey Cuba
150 A3 Camana Peru
154 B1 Camapuã Brazil
145 C2 Camargo Mex.
63 B3 Ca Mau Vietnam
63 B2 Cambodia country Asia
99 A3 Camborne U.K.
105 C1 Cambrai France
99 B2 Cambrian Mountains U.K.
54 C1 Cambridge N.Z.
99 D2 Cambridge U.K.
141 E2 Cambridge MA U.S.A.
141 D3 Cambridge MD U.S.A.
137 E1 Cambridge MN U.S.A.
140 C2 Cambridge OH U.S.A.
131 D1 Cambrien, Lac l. Can.
53 D2 Camden Austr.
142 B2 Camden AR U.S.A.
141 F2 Camden ME U.S.A.
118 B2 Cameroon country Africa
151 D2 Cametá Brazil
64 B1 Camiguin i. Phil.
152 B3 Camiri Bol.
151 D2 Camocim Brazil
51 C1 Camooweal Austr.
63 A3 Camorta i. India

153 A5 Campana, Isla i. Chile
122 B2 Campbell S. Africa
54 B2 Campbell, Cape N.Z.
128 B2 Campbell River Can.
140 B3 Campbellsville U.S.A.
131 D2 Campbellton Can.
96 B3 Campbeltown U.K.
145 C3 Campeche Mex.
145 C3 Campeche, Bahía de g. Mex.
52 B3 Camperdown Austr.
110 C1 Câmpina Romania
151 E2 Campina Grande Brazil
154 C2 Campinas Brazil
154 C1 Campina Verde Brazil
108 B2 Campobasso Italy
155 C2 Campo Belo Brazil
154 C1 Campo Florido Brazil
152 B3 Campo Gallo Arg.
154 B2 Campo Grande Brazil
151 D2 Campo Maior Brazil
106 B2 Campo Maior Port.
154 B2 Campo Mourão Brazil
155 D2 Campos Brazil
155 C1 Campos Altos Brazil
155 C2 Campos do Jordão Brazil
110 C1 Câmpulung Romania
138 A2 Camp Verde U.S.A.
63 B2 Cam Ranh Vietnam
129 C2 Camrose Can.
129 D2 Camsell Portage Can.
111 C2 Çan Turkey
126 F3 Canada country N. America
139 C1 Canadian U.S.A.
139 D1 Canadian r. U.S.A.
111 C2 Çanakkale Turkey
144 A1 Cananea Mex.
154 C2 Cananéia Brazil
Canarias, Islas terr. N. Atlantic Ocean see Canary Islands
114 A2 Canary Islands terr. N. Atlantic Ocean
155 C1 Canastra, Serra da mts Brazil
144 B2 Canatlán Mex.
143 D3 Canaveral, Cape U.S.A.
155 E1 Canavieiras Brazil
53 C3 Canberra Austr.
145 C3 Cancún Mex.
111 C3 Çandarlı Turkey
145 C3 Candelaria Mex.
129 D2 Candle Lake l. Can.
120 A2 Cangamba Angola
106 B1 Cangas del Narcea Spain
154 C2 Canguçu Brazil
70 B2 Cangzhou China
131 D1 Caniapiscau Can.
131 D1 Caniapiscau r. Can.
131 C1 Caniapiscau, Lac l. Can.
106 B2 Cañiza Spain
151 E2 Canindé Brazil
144 B2 Cañitas de Felipe Pescador Mex.
80 B1 Çankırı Turkey
128 C2 Canmore Can.
96 A2 Canna i. U.K.
73 B3 Cannanore India
105 D3 Cannes France
99 B2 Cannock U.K.
53 C3 Cann River Austr.
152 C3 Canoas Brazil
129 D2 Canoe Lake l. Can.
154 B3 Canoinhas Brazil
136 B3 Canon City U.S.A.
129 D2 Canora Can.
53 C2 Canowindra Austr.
106 B1 Cantabrian Sea sea Spain
106 C1 Cantábrica, Cordillera mts Spain

99 D3 Canterbury U.K.
54 B2 Canterbury Bight b. N.Z.
54 B2 Canterbury Plains N.Z.
63 B2 Cần Thơ Vietnam
151 D2 Canto do Buriti Brazil
Canton China see Guangzhou
142 C2 Canton MS U.S.A.
140 C2 Canton OH U.S.A.
139 C1 Canyon U.S.A.
134 D1 Canyon Ferry Lake U.S.A.
62 B1 Cao Bằng Vietnam
154 C2 Capão Bonito Brazil
155 D2 Caparaó, Serra do mts Brazil
51 D4 Cape Barren Island Austr.
52 A3 Cape Borda Austr.
131 D2 Cape Breton Island Can.
114 B4 Cape Coast Ghana
141 E2 Cape Cod Bay U.S.A.
127 F2 Cape Dorset Can.
143 E2 Cape Fear r. U.S.A.
137 F3 Cape Girardeau U.S.A.
155 D1 Capelinha Brazil
100 B2 Capelle aan de IJssel Neth.
120 A1 Capenda-Camulemba Angola
122 A3 Cape Town S. Africa
112 B2 Cape Verde country N. Atlantic Ocean
51 D1 Cape York Peninsula Austr.
147 C3 Cap-Haïtien Haiti
151 D2 Capim r. Brazil
109 C2 Čapljina Bos.-Herz.
109 B3 Capo d'Orlando Sicily Italy
108 A2 Capraia, Isola di i. Italy
108 A2 Caprara, Punta pt Sardinia Italy
108 B2 Capri, Isola di i. Italy
120 B2 Caprivi Strip reg. Namibia
150 B2 Caquetá r. Col.
110 B2 Caracal Romania
150 B1 Caracas Venez.
151 D2 Caracol Brazil
155 C2 Caraguatatuba Brazil
153 A4 Carahue Chile
155 D1 Caraí Brazil
155 D2 Carangola Brazil
110 B1 Caransebeş Romania
131 D2 Caraquet Can.
146 B3 Caratasca, Laguna lag. Hond.
155 D1 Caratinga Brazil
150 B2 Carauari Brazil
107 C2 Caravaca de la Cruz Spain
155 E1 Caravelas Brazil
129 E3 Carberry Can.
144 A2 Carbó Mex.
108 A3 Carbonara, Capo c. Sardinia Italy
136 B3 Carbondale CO U.S.A.
140 B3 Carbondale IL U.S.A.
131 E2 Carbonear Can.
155 D1 Carbonita Brazil
107 C2 Carcaixent Spain
104 C3 Carcassonne France
128 A1 Carcross Can.
145 C3 Cárdenas Mex.
99 B3 Cardiff U.K.
99 A2 Cardigan U.K.
99 A2 Cardigan Bay U.K.
128 C3 Cardston Can.
110 B1 Carei Romania
104 B2 Carentan France
50 B2 Carey, Lake salt flat Austr.
155 D2 Cariacica Brazil
146 B3 Caribbean Sea N. Atlantic Ocean
141 F1 Caribou U.S.A.
130 B1 Caribou Lake Can.

128 C2 Caribou Mountains Can.
144 B2 Carichic Mex.
100 B3 Carignan France
53 C2 Carinda Austr.
107 C1 Cariñena Spain
130 C2 Carleton Place Can.
123 C2 Carletonville S. Africa
97 C1 Carlingford Lough inlet Rep. of Ireland/U.K.
98 B1 Carlisle U.K.
141 D2 Carlisle U.S.A.
155 D1 Carlos Chagas Brazil
97 C2 Carlow Rep. of Ireland
135 C4 Carlsbad CA U.S.A.
138 C2 Carlsbad NM U.S.A.
129 D3 Carlyle Can.
128 A1 Carmacks Can.
129 E3 Carman Can.
99 A3 Carmarthen U.K.
99 A3 Carmarthen Bay U.K.
104 C3 Carmaux France
145 C3 Carmelita Guat.
144 A2 Carmen, Isla i. Mex.
104 B2 Carnac France
122 B3 Carnarvon S. Africa
97 C1 Carndonagh Rep. of Ireland
50 B2 Carnegie, Lake salt flat Austr.
96 B2 Carn Eighe mt. U.K.
63 A3 Car Nicobar i. India
118 B2 Carnot C.A.R.
52 A2 Carnot, Cape Austr.
97 C2 Carnsore Point Rep. of Ireland
151 D2 Carolina Brazil
59 D2 Caroline Islands N. Pacific Ocean
103 D2 Carpathian Mountains Europe
110 B1 Carpaţii Meridionali mts Romania
51 C1 Carpentaria, Gulf of Austr.
105 D3 Carpentras France
97 B3 Carrantuohill mt. Rep. of Ireland
105 E3 Carrara Italy
97 C2 Carrickmacross Rep. of Ireland
97 B2 Carrick-on-Shannon Rep. of Ireland
97 C2 Carrick-on-Suir Rep. of Ireland
137 D1 Carrington U.S.A.
139 D3 Carrizo Springs U.S.A.
138 B2 Carrizozo U.S.A.
137 E2 Carroll U.S.A.
143 C2 Carrollton U.S.A.
129 D2 Carrot River Can.
135 C3 Carson City U.S.A.
150 A1 Cartagena Col.
107 C2 Cartagena Spain
146 B4 Cartago Costa Rica
137 E3 Carthage MO U.S.A.
139 E2 Carthage TX U.S.A.
131 E1 Cartwright Can.
151 E2 Caruarú Brazil
114 B1 Casablanca Morocco
154 C2 Casa Branca Brazil
144 B1 Casa de Janos Mex.
138 A2 Casa Grande U.S.A.
108 A1 Casale Monferrato Italy
109 C2 Casarano Italy
134 C2 Cascade U.S.A.
134 B2 Cascade Range mts Can./U.S.A.
106 B2 Cascais Port.
154 B2 Cascavel Brazil
108 B2 Caserta Italy
117 D3 Caseyr, Raas c. Somalia
97 C2 Cashel Rep. of Ireland

53 D1 Casino Austr.
107 C1 Caspe Spain
136 B2 Casper U.S.A.
81 C1 Caspian Sea Asia/Europe
154 C2 Cássia Brazil
128 B2 Cassiar Can.
128 A2 Cassiar Mountains Can.
154 B1 Cassilândia Brazil
108 B2 Cassino Italy
96 B2 Cassley r. U.K.
151 D2 Castanhal Brazil
152 B4 Castaño r. Arg.
144 B2 Castaños Mex.
104 C3 Casteljaloux France
107 C2 Castelló de la Plana Spain
106 B2 Castelo Branco Port.
108 B3 Castelvetrano Sicily Italy
52 B3 Casterton Austr.
109 C3 Castiglione della Pescaia Italy
97 B2 Castlebar Rep. of Ireland
96 A2 Castlebay U.K.
97 C1 Castleblayney Rep. of Ireland
97 C1 Castlederg U.K.
96 C3 Castle Douglas U.K.
128 C3 Castlegar Can.
97 B2 Castleisland Rep. of Ireland
52 B3 Castlemaine Austr.
97 B2 Castlerea Rep. of Ireland
53 C2 Castlereagh r. Austr.
136 C3 Castle Rock U.S.A.
129 C2 Castor Can.
104 C3 Castres France
100 B1 Castricum Neth.
147 D3 Castries St Lucia
154 C2 Castro Brazil
153 A5 Castro Chile
106 B2 Castro Verde Port.
109 C3 Castrovillari Italy
150 A2 Catacaos Peru
155 D2 Cataguases Brazil
154 C1 Catalão Brazil
152 B3 Catamarca Arg.
64 B1 Catanduanes i. Phil.
154 C2 Catanduva Brazil
154 B3 Catanduvas Brazil
109 C3 Catania Sicily Italy
109 C3 Catanzaro Italy
64 B1 Catarman Phil.
64 B1 Catbalogan Phil.
145 C3 Catemaco Mex.
147 C2 Cat Island Bahamas
130 A1 Cat Lake l. Can.
145 D2 Catoche, Cabo c. Mex.
141 E2 Catskill Mountains U.S.A.
64 B2 Cauayan Phil.
150 A1 Cauca r. Col.
151 E2 Caucaia Brazil
81 C1 Caucasus mts Asia/Europe
100 A2 Caudry France
109 C3 Caulonia Italy
131 D2 Causapscal Can.
105 D3 Cavaillon France
151 D3 Cavalcante Brazil
97 C2 Cavan Rep. of Ireland
154 B3 Cavernoso, Serra do mts Brazil
151 D2 Caxias Brazil
152 C3 Caxias do Sul Brazil
120 A1 Caxito Angola
151 C1 Cayenne Fr. Guiana
146 B3 Cayman Islands terr. West Indies
117 C4 Caynabo Somalia
120 B2 Cazombo Angola
144 B2 Ceballos Mex.
64 B1 Cebu Phil.
64 B1 Cebu i. Phil.
108 B2 Cecina Italy

137 F2 Cedar *r.* U.S.A.
135 D3 Cedar City U.S.A.
137 E2 Cedar Falls U.S.A.
129 D2 Cedar Lake *l.* Can.
137 E2 Cedar Rapids U.S.A.
144 A2 Cedros, Isla *i.* Mex.
51 C3 Ceduna Austr.
117 C4 Ceeldheere Somalia
117 C3 Ceerigaabo Somalia
108 B3 Cefalù *Sicily* Italy
145 B2 Celaya Mex.
Celebes *i.* Indon. *see* Sulawesi
156 B5 Celebes Sea Indon./Phil.
145 C2 Celestún Mex.
101 E1 Celle Ger.
95 B3 Celtic Sea
Rep. of Ireland/U.K.
59 D3 Cenderawasih, Teluk *b.*
Indon.
150 A1 Central, Cordillera *mts* Col.
150 A3 Central, Cordillera *mts* Peru
64 B1 Central, Cordillera *mts* Phil.
118 C2 Central African Republic
country Africa
74 A2 Central Brahui Range
mts Pak.
137 D2 Central City U.S.A.
140 B3 Centralia *IL* U.S.A.
134 B1 Centralia *WA* U.S.A.
74 A2 Central Makran Range
mts Pak.
59 D3 Central Range *mts* P.N.G.
Central Siberian Plateau
Rus. Fed. *see* Sredne-
Sibirskoye Ploskogor'ye
Cephalonia *i.* Greece *see*
Kefallonia
152 B3 Ceres Arg.
154 E1 Ceres Brazil
122 A3 Ceres S. Africa
104 C2 Céret France
106 C1 Cerezo de Abajo Spain
109 C2 Cerignola Italy
110 C2 Cernavodă Romania
145 B2 Cerralvo Mex.
144 B2 Cerralvo, Isla *i.* Mex.
145 B2 Cerritos Mex.
154 C2 Cerro Azul Brazil
145 C2 Cerro Azul Mex.
150 A3 Cerro de Pasco Peru
105 D3 Cervione *Corsica* France
106 B1 Cervo Spain
108 B2 Cesena Italy
88 C2 Cēsis Latvia
102 C2 České Budějovice
Czech Rep.
101 F3 Český Les *mts*
Czech Rep./Ger.
111 C3 Çeşme Turkey
53 D2 Cessnock Austr.
109 C2 Cetinje Yugo.
109 C3 Cetraro Italy
106 B2 Ceuta N. Africa
105 C3 Cévennes *mts* France
Ceylon *country* Asia *see*
Sri Lanka
79 D2 Châbahar Iran
75 C1 Chabyêr Caka *salt l.* China
150 A2 Chachapoyas Peru
89 D3 Chachersk Belarus
63 B2 Chachoengsao Thai.
115 D3 Chad *country* Africa
115 D3 Chad, Lake Africa
69 C1 Chadaasan Mongolia
68 C1 Chadan Rus. Fed.
123 C1 Chadibe Botswana
136 C2 Chadron U.S.A.
65 B2 Chaeryŏng N. Korea
74 A2 Chagai Pak.
77 C3 Chaghcharān Afgh.

89 E2 Chagoda Rus. Fed.
76 B2 Chagyl Turkm.
75 C2 Chāibāsa India
63 B2 Chainat Thai.
63 B2 Chaiyaphum Thai.
152 C4 Chajarí Arg.
131 D1 Chakonipau, Lake Can.
150 A3 Chala Peru
74 A1 Chalap Dalan *mts* Afgh.
131 D2 Chaleur Bay *inlet* Can.
74 B2 Chalisgaon India
111 C3 Chalki *i.* Greece
111 B3 Chalkida Greece
104 B2 Challans France
134 D2 Challis U.S.A.
105 C2 Châlons-en-Champagne
France
105 C2 Chalon-sur-Saône France
138 B1 Chama U.S.A.
121 C2 Chama Zambia
74 A1 Chaman Pak.
74 B1 Chamba India
74 B2 Chambal *r.* India
137 D2 Chamberlain U.S.A.
141 D3 Chambersburg U.S.A.
105 D2 Chambéry France
121 C2 Chambeshi Zambia
140 B2 Champaign U.S.A.
141 E2 Champlain, Lake
Can./U.S.A.
145 C3 Champotón Mex.
152 A3 Chañaral Chile
126 B2 Chandalar *r.* U.S.A.
142 C3 Chandeleur Islands U.S.A.
74 B1 Chandigarh India
138 A2 Chandler U.S.A.
75 B3 Chandrapur India
63 B2 Chang, Ko *i.* Thai.
Chang'an China *see* Rong'an
121 C3 Changane *r.* Moz.
121 C2 Changara Moz.
65 B1 Changbai China
65 B1 Changbai Shan *mts*
China/N. Korea
69 E2 Changchun China
71 B3 Changde China
71 C3 Ch'angdo N. Korea
71 C3 Changhua Taiwan
65 B3 Changhŭng S. Korea
Chang Jiang *r.* China *see*
Yangtze
65 B1 Changjin N. Korea
65 B1 Changjin-gang *r.* N. Korea
71 B3 Changsha China
65 B2 Changsŏng S. Korea
71 B3 Changting China
65 B2 Ch'angwŏn S. Korea
70 B2 Changyuan China
70 B2 Changzhi China
70 C2 Changzhou China
111 B3 Chania Greece
95 C4 Channel Islands Europe
135 C4 Channel Islands U.S.A.
131 E2 Channel-Port-aux-Basques
Can.
63 B2 Chanthaburi Thai.
104 C2 Chantilly France
137 D3 Chanute U.S.A.
82 G3 Chany, Ozero *salt l.*
Rus. Fed.
71 B3 Chaoyang China
Chaoyang China *see* Huinan
71 B3 Chaozhou China
144 B2 Chapala, Laguna de *l.* Mex.
76 B1 Chapayevo Kazakh.
152 C3 Chapecó Brazil
143 E1 Chapel Hill U.S.A.
130 B2 Chapleau Can.
89 E3 Chaplygin Rus. Fed.
91 C2 Chaplynka Ukr.

145 B2 Charcas Mex.
99 B3 Chard U.K.
76 C3 Chardzhev Turkm.
104 B2 Charente *r.* France
77 C3 Chārīkār Afgh.
86 E2 Charkayuvom Rus. Fed.
100 B2 Charleroi Belgium
141 D3 Charles, Cape U.S.A.
137 E2 Charles City U.S.A.
140 B3 Charleston *IL* U.S.A.
143 E2 Charleston *SC* U.S.A.
140 C3 Charleston *WV* U.S.A.
135 C3 Charleston Peak U.S.A.
51 D2 Charleville Austr.
105 C2 Charleville-Mézières France
143 D1 Charlotte U.S.A.
143 D3 Charlotte Harbor *b.* U.S.A.
131 D2 Charlottesville U.S.A.
52 B3 Charlton Austr.
130 C1 Charlton Island Can.
51 D2 Charters Towers Austr.
104 C2 Chartres France
128 C2 Chase Can.
88 C3 Chashniki Belarus
54 A3 Chaslands Mistake *c.* N.Z.
65 B1 Chasŏng N. Korea
104 B2 Chassiron, Pointe de *pt*
France
104 B2 Châteaubriant France
104 C2 Château-du-Loir France
104 C2 Châteaudun France
104 B2 Châteaulin France
105 D3 Châteauneuf-les-Martigues
France
104 C2 Châteauneuf-sur-Loire
France
105 C2 Château-Thierry France
128 C2 Chateh Can.
100 B2 Châtelet Belgium
104 C2 Châtellerault France
131 D2 Chatham *N.B.* Can.
140 C2 Chatham *Ont.* Can.
105 C2 Châtillon-sur-Seine France
143 D2 Chattahoochee *r.* U.S.A.
143 C1 Chattanooga U.S.A.
63 B2 Châu Đôc Vietnam
62 A1 Chauk Myanmar
105 C2 Chaumont France
105 C2 Chauny France
151 D2 Chaves Brazil
106 B1 Chaves Port.
130 C1 Chavigny, Lac *l.* Can.
89 D3 Chavusy Belarus
89 E2 Chayevo Rus. Fed.
86 E3 Chaykovskiy Rus. Fed.
102 C1 Cheb Czech Rep.
87 D3 Cheboksary Rus. Fed.
140 C1 Cheboygan U.S.A.
65 B2 Chech'ŏn S. Korea
62 A2 Cheduba Island Myanmar
114 B2 Chegga Maur.
134 B1 Chehalis U.S.A.
65 B3 Cheju S. Korea
65 B3 Cheju-do *i.* S. Korea
65 B3 Cheju-haehyŏp *sea chan.*
S. Korea
89 E2 Chekhov Rus. Fed.
134 B1 Chelan, Lake U.S.A.
76 C3 Cheleken Turkm.
107 D2 Chélif, Oued *r.* Alg.
76 B2 Chelkar Kazakh.
103 E1 Chełm Pol.
99 D3 Chelmer *r.* U.K.
103 D1 Chełmno Pol.
99 D3 Chelmsford U.K.
99 B3 Cheltenham U.K.
87 F3 Chelyabinsk Rus. Fed.
101 F2 Chemnitz Ger.
114 B2 Chenachane Alg.

70 B1 **Chengde** China
70 A2 **Chengdu** China
71 B4 **Chengmai** China
Chengshou China *see*
Yingshan
70 A2 **Chengxian** China
Chengyang China *see* Juxian
Chennai India *see* Madras
71 B3 **Chenzhou** China
99 B3 **Chepstow** U.K.
104 B2 **Cherbourg** France
89 E3 **Cheremisinovo** Rus. Fed.
69 C1 **Cheremkhovo** Rus. Fed.
89 E2 **Cherepovets** Rus. Fed.
91 C2 **Cherkasy** Ukr.
87 D4 **Cherkessk** Rus. Fed.
91 C1 **Chernihiv** Ukr.
91 D2 **Cherninivka** Ukr.
90 B2 **Chernivtsi** Ukr.
90 B1 **Chernyakhiv** Ukr.
88 B3 **Chernyakhovsk** Rus. Fed.
89 E3 **Chernyanka** Rus. Fed.
83 I2 **Chernyshevskiy** Rus. Fed.
137 D2 **Cherokee** U.S.A.
83 K2 **Cherskogo, Khrebet** *mts*
Rus. Fed.
91 E2 **Chertkovo** Rus. Fed.
90 A1 **Chervonohrad** Ukr.
88 C3 **Chervyen'** Belarus
89 D3 **Cherykaw** Belarus
143 D3 **Chesapeake Bay** U.S.A.
86 D2 **Cheshskaya Guba** *b.*
Rus. Fed.
98 B2 **Chester** U.K.
140 B3 **Chester** *IL* U.S.A.
143 D2 **Chester** *SC* U.S.A.
98 C2 **Chesterfield** U.K.
129 E1 **Chesterfield Inlet** Can.
129 E1 **Chesterfield** *inlet* Can.
141 F1 **Chesuncook Lake** U.S.A.
131 D2 **Chéticamp** Can.
145 D3 **Chetumal** Mex.
128 B2 **Chetwynd** Can.
98 B1 **Cheviot Hills** U.K.
136 C2 **Cheyenne** U.S.A.
136 C2 **Cheyenne** *r.* U.S.A.
136 C3 **Cheyenne Wells** U.S.A.
75 C2 **Chhapra** India
75 B2 **Chhatarpur** India
71 C3 **Chiai** Taiwan
62 A2 **Chiang Dao** Thai.
62 A2 **Chiang Mai** Thai.
62 A2 **Chiang Rai** Thai.
108 A1 **Chiavenno** Italy
121 C2 **Chiboma** Moz.
130 C2 **Chibougamau** Can.
123 D1 **Chibuto** Moz.
75 D1 **Chibuzhang Hu** *l.* China
140 B2 **Chicago** U.S.A.
128 A2 **Chichagof Island** U.S.A.
99 C3 **Chichester** U.K.
50 A2 **Chichester Range** *mts*
Austr.
139 D1 **Chickasha** U.S.A.
150 A2 **Chiclayo** Peru
153 B5 **Chico** *r.* Arg.
135 B3 **Chico** U.S.A.
131 C2 **Chicoutimi** Can.
108 B2 **Chieti** Italy
69 D2 **Chifeng** China
155 C1 **Chifre, Serra do** *mts* Brazil
77 D2 **Chiganak** Kazakh.
145 C3 **Chignahuapán** Mex.
121 C3 **Chigubo** Moz.
144 B2 **Chihuahua** Mex.
88 C2 **Chikhachevo** Rus. Fed.
67 C3 **Chikuma-gawa** *r.* Japan
128 B2 **Chilanko** *r.* Can.
74 B1 **Chilas** Jammu and Kashmir
139 C2 **Childress** U.S.A.

153 A4 **Chile** *country* S. America
152 B3 **Chilecito** Arg.
75 C3 **Chilika Lake** India
121 B2 **Chililabombwe** Zambia
128 B2 **Chilko** *r.* Can.
128 B2 **Chilko Lake** Can.
153 A4 **Chillán** Chile
137 E3 **Chillicothe** *MO* U.S.A.
140 C3 **Chillicothe** *OH* U.S.A.
128 B3 **Chilliwack** Can.
153 A5 **Chiloé, Isla de** *i.* Chile
145 C3 **Chilpancingo** Mex.
53 C3 **Chiltern** Austr.
71 C3 **Chilung** Taiwan
119 D3 **Chimala** Tanz.
152 B4 **Chimbas** Arg.
87 E4 **Chimbay** Uzbek.
150 A2 **Chimborazo** *mt.* Ecuador
150 A2 **Chimbote** Peru
Chimkent Kazakh. *see*
Shymkent
121 C2 **Chimoio** Moz.
77 D3 **Chimtargha, Qullai** *mt.* Tajik.
68 B2 **China** *country* Asia
145 C2 **China** Mex.
150 A3 **Chincha Alta** Peru
128 C2 **Chinchaga** *r.* Can.
145 D3 **Chinchorro, Banco**
sea feature Mex.
121 C2 **Chinde** Moz.
65 B3 **Chindo** S. Korea
65 B3 **Chin-do** *i.* S. Korea
68 C2 **Chindu** China
62 A1 **Chindwin** *r.* Myanmar
65 B2 **Chinghwa** N. Korea
120 B2 **Chingola** Zambia
120 A2 **Chinguar** Angola
65 B2 **Chinhae** S. Korea
121 C2 **Chinhoyi** Zimbabwe
74 B1 **Chiniot** Pak.
144 B2 **Chinipas** Mex.
65 B2 **Chinju** S. Korea
118 C2 **Chinko** *r.* C.A.R.
138 B1 **Chinle** U.S.A.
71 B3 **Chinmen** Taiwan
67 C3 **Chino** Japan
104 C2 **Chinon** France
138 A2 **Chino Valley** U.S.A.
121 C2 **Chinsali** Zambia
108 B1 **Chioggia** Italy
111 C3 **Chios** Greece
111 C3 **Chios** *i.* Greece
121 C2 **Chipata** Zambia
120 A2 **Chipindo** Angola
121 C3 **Chipinge** Zimbabwe
73 B3 **Chiplun** India
99 B3 **Chippenham** U.K.
99 C3 **Chipping Norton** U.K.
77 C3 **Chirchik** Uzbek.
121 C3 **Chiredzi** Zimbabwe
138 B2 **Chiricahua Peak** U.S.A.
146 B4 **Chiriquí, Golfo de** *b.*
Panama
65 B2 **Chiri-san** *mt.* S. Korea
146 B4 **Chirripo** *mt.* Costa Rica
121 B2 **Chirundu** Zimbabwe
137 E1 **Chisholm** U.S.A.
90 B2 **Chişinău** Moldova
87 E3 **Chistopol'** Rus. Fed.
69 D1 **Chita** Rus. Fed.
120 A2 **Chitado** Angola
121 C2 **Chitambo** Zambia
120 B1 **Chitato** Angola
121 C1 **Chitipa** Malawi
73 B3 **Chitradurga** India
74 B1 **Chitral** Pak.
146 B4 **Chitré** Panama
75 D2 **Chittagong** Bangl.
74 B2 **Chittaurgarh** India
121 C2 **Chitungwiza** Zimbabwe

120 B2 **Chiume** Angola
121 C2 **Chivhu** Zimbabwe
153 B4 **Choele Choel** Arg.
144 B2 **Choix** Mex.
103 D1 **Chojnice** Pol.
117 B3 **Ch'ok'ē Mountains** Eth.
83 K2 **Chokurdakh** Rus. Fed.
121 C3 **Chókwè** Moz.
104 B2 **Cholet** France
102 C1 **Chomutov** Czech Rep.
83 I2 **Chona** *r.* Rus. Fed.
65 B1 **Ch'ŏnan** S. Korea
150 A2 **Chone** Ecuador
65 B1 **Ch'ŏngjin** N. Korea
65 B2 **Chŏngju** N. Korea
65 B2 **Chŏngp'yŏng** N. Korea
70 A3 **Chongqing** China
70 A2 **Chongqing** *mun.* China
71 A3 **Chongzuo** China
65 B2 **Chŏnju** S. Korea
154 B3 **Chopinzinho** Brazil
98 B2 **Chorley** U.K.
91 C2 **Chornomors'ke** Ukr.
90 B2 **Chortkiv** Ukr.
65 B2 **Ch'ŏrwŏn** S. Korea
65 B1 **Ch'osan** N. Korea
67 D3 **Chōshi** Japan
103 D1 **Choszczno** Pol.
114 A2 **Choûm** Maur.
69 D1 **Choybalsan** Mongolia
69 D1 **Choyr** Mongolia
54 B2 **Christchurch** N.Z.
99 C3 **Christchurch** U.K.
127 G2 **Christian, Cape** Can.
123 C2 **Christiana** S. Africa
54 A2 **Christina, Mount** N.Z.
48 B4 **Christmas Island** *terr.*
Indian Ocean
111 C3 **Chrysi** *i.* Greece
153 B5 **Chubut** *r.* Arg.
90 B1 **Chudniv** Ukr.
89 D2 **Chudovo** Rus. Fed.
Chudskoye Ozero *l.*
Estonia/Rus. Fed. *see*
Peipus, Lake
126 B2 **Chugach Mountains** U.S.A.
67 B4 **Chūgoku-sanchi** *mts* Japan
66 B2 **Chuguyevka** Rus. Fed.
91 D2 **Chuhuyiv** Ukr.
160 J3 **Chukchi Sea**
Rus. Fed./U.S.A.
83 N2 **Chukotskiy Poluostrov** *pen.*
Rus. Fed.
135 C4 **Chula Vista** U.S.A.
82 G3 **Chulym** Rus. Fed.
152 B3 **Chumbicha** Arg.
83 K3 **Chumikan** Rus. Fed.
63 A2 **Chumphon** Thai.
65 B2 **Ch'unch'ŏn** S. Korea
Chungking China *see*
Chongqing
83 H2 **Chunya** *r.* Rus. Fed.
150 A3 **Chuquibamba** Peru
152 B3 **Chuquicamata** Chile
105 D2 **Chur** Switz.
62 A1 **Churachandpur** India
129 E2 **Churchill** Can.
129 E2 **Churchill** *r. Man.* Can.
131 D1 **Churchill** *r. Nfld.* Can.
129 E2 **Churchill, Cape** Can.
131 D1 **Churchill Falls** Can.
129 D2 **Churchill Lake** Can.
74 B2 **Churu** India
131 C2 **Chute-des-Passes** Can.
62 B1 **Chuxiong** China
90 B2 **Ciadâr-Lunga** Moldova
61 B2 **Ciamis** Indon.
60 B2 **Cianjur** Indon.
154 B2 **Cianorte** Brazil
103 E1 **Ciechanów** Pol.

146 C2 Ciego de Avila Cuba
146 B2 Cienfuegos Cuba
107 C2 Cieza Spain
106 C2 Ciguela r. Spain
80 B2 Cihanbeyli Turkey
144 B3 Cihuatlán Mex.
106 C2 Cijara, Embalse de resr Spain
61 B2 Cilacap Indon.
139 C1 Cimarron r. U.S.A.
90 B2 Cimişlia Moldova
108 B2 Cimone, Monte mt. Italy
140 C3 Cincinnati U.S.A.
111 C3 Çine Turkey
100 B2 Ciney Belgium
145 C3 Cintalapa Mex.
126 B2 Circle AK U.S.A.
136 B1 Circle MT U.S.A.
58 B3 Cirebon Indon.
99 C3 Cirencester U.K.
108 A1 Ciriè Italy
109 C3 Cirò Marina Italy
109 C2 Čitluk Bos.-Herz.
122 A3 Citrusdal S. Africa
145 C2 Ciudad Acuña Mex.
145 B3 Ciudad Altamirano Mex.
150 B1 Ciudad Bolívar Venez.
144 B2 Ciudad Camargo Mex.
145 C3 Ciudad del Carmen Mex.
144 B2 Ciudad Delicias Mex.
145 C2 Ciudad de Valles Mex.
150 B1 Ciudad Guayana Venez.
138 B3 Ciudad Guerrero Mex.
144 B3 Ciudad Guzmán Mex.
145 C3 Ciudad Hidalgo Mex.
145 C3 Ciudad Ixtepec Mex.
144 B1 Ciudad Juárez Mex.
145 C2 Ciudad Mante Mex.
144 B2 Ciudad Obregón Mex.
106 C2 Ciudad Real Spain
145 C2 Ciudad Río Bravo Mex.
106 B1 Ciudad Rodrigo Spain
145 C2 Ciudad Victoria Mex.
107 D1 Ciutadella de Menorca Spain
111 C3 Çivan Dağ mt. Turkey
108 B1 Cividale del Friuli Italy
108 B2 Civitanova Marche Italy
108 B2 Civitavecchia Italy
104 C2 Civray France
111 C3 Çivril Turkey
70 C2 Cixi China
99 D3 Clacton-on-Sea U.K.
128 C2 Claire, Lake Can.
105 C2 Clamecy France
122 A3 Clanwilliam S. Africa
52 A2 Clare Austr.
97 A2 Clare Island Rep. of Ireland
141 E2 Claremont U.S.A.
97 B2 Claremorris Rep. of Ireland
54 B2 Clarence N.Z.
131 E2 Clarenville Can.
128 C2 Claresholm Can.
137 D2 Clarinda U.S.A.
123 C3 Clarkebury S. Africa
134 C1 Clark Fork r. U.S.A.
143 D2 Clark Hill Reservoir U.S.A.
140 C3 Clarksburg U.S.A.
142 B2 Clarksdale U.S.A.
142 B1 Clarksville AR U.S.A.
142 C1 Clarksville TN U.S.A.
154 B1 Claro r. Brazil
139 C1 Clayton U.S.A.
97 B3 Clear, Cape Rep. of Ireland
137 E2 Clear Lake U.S.A.
135 B3 Clear Lake I. U.S.A.
128 C2 Clearwater Can.
143 D3 Clearwater U.S.A.
128 C2 Clearwater r. Can.
143 D3 Clearwater r. U.S.A.

134 C1 Clearwater r. U.S.A.
139 D2 Cleburne U.S.A.
51 C2 Clermont Austr.
105 C2 Clermont-Ferrand France
52 A2 Cleve Austr.
142 B2 Cleveland MS U.S.A.
140 C2 Cleveland OH U.S.A.
143 D1 Cleveland TN U.S.A.
134 D1 Cleveland, Mount U.S.A.
143 D3 Clewiston U.S.A.
97 A2 Clifden Rep. of Ireland
53 D1 Clifton Austr.
138 B2 Clifton U.S.A.
128 B2 Clinton Can.
137 E2 Clinton IA U.S.A.
137 E3 Clinton MO U.S.A.
139 D1 Clinton OK U.S.A.
96 A2 Clisham hill U.K.
98 B2 Clitheroe U.K.
97 B3 Clonakilty Rep. of Ireland
51 D2 Cloncurry Austr.
97 C1 Clones Rep. of Ireland
97 C2 Clonmel Rep. of Ireland
100 D1 Cloppenburg Ger.
136 B2 Cloud Peak U.S.A.
139 C2 Clovis U.S.A.
129 D2 Cluff Lake Mine Can.
110 B1 Cluj-Napoca Romania
51 C2 Cluny Austr.
105 D2 Cluses France
54 A3 Clutha r. N.Z.
96 B3 Clyde r. U.K.
96 B3 Clyde, Firth of est. U.K.
96 B3 Clydebank U.K.
127 G2 Clyde River Can.
144 B3 Coalcomán Mex.
135 C3 Coaldale U.S.A.
128 B2 Coal River Can.
150 B2 Coari Brazil
150 B2 Coari r. Brazil
142 B2 Coastal Plain U.S.A.
128 B2 Coast Mountains Can.
135 B2 Coast Ranges mts U.S.A.
96 B3 Coatbridge U.K.
127 F2 Coats Island Can.
55 R2 Coats Land reg. Antarctica
145 C3 Coatzacoalcos Mex.
146 A3 Cobán Guat.
53 C2 Cobar Austr.
97 B3 Cobh Rep. of Ireland
152 B2 Cobija Bol.
141 D2 Cobourg Can.
50 C1 Cobourg Peninsula Austr.
53 C3 Cobram Austr.
101 E2 Coburg Ger.
152 B2 Cochabamba Bol.
100 C2 Cochem Ger.
73 B4 Cochin India
128 C2 Cochrane Alta Can.
130 B2 Cochrane Ont. Can.
153 A5 Cochrane Chile
52 B2 Cockburn Austr.
Cockburn Town Turks and Caicos Is see Grand Turk
98 B1 Cockermouth U.K.
122 B3 Cockscomb mt. S. Africa
146 B3 Coco r. Hond./Nic.
48 B4 Cocos Islands terr. Indian Ocean
144 B2 Cocula Mex.
150 A1 Cocuy, Sierra Nevada del mt. Col.
141 E2 Cod, Cape U.S.A.
108 B2 Codigoro Italy
131 D1 Cod Island Can.
151 D2 Codó Brazil
136 B2 Cody U.S.A.
51 D1 Coen Austr.
100 C2 Coesfeld Ger.

134 C1 Coeur d'Alene U.S.A.
123 C3 Coffee Bay S. Africa
137 D3 Coffeyville U.S.A.
53 D2 Coffs Harbour Austr.
104 B2 Cognac France
118 A2 Cogo Equat. Guinea
52 B3 Cohuna Austr.
146 B4 Coiba, Isla i. Panama
153 A5 Coihaique Chile
73 B3 Coimbatore India
106 B1 Coimbra Port.
52 B3 Colac Austr.
155 D1 Colatina Brazil
136 C3 Colby U.S.A.
99 D3 Colchester U.K.
129 C2 Cold Lake l. Can.
96 C3 Coldstream U.K.
52 B3 Coleman U.S.A.
52 B3 Coleraine Austr.
97 C1 Coleraine U.K.
123 C2 Colesberg S. Africa
144 B3 Colima Mex.
144 B3 Colima, Nevado de vol. Mex.
96 A2 Coll i. U.K.
53 C1 Collarenebri Austr.
50 B1 Collier Bay Austr.
54 B2 Collingwood N.Z.
97 B1 Collooney Rep. of Ireland
105 D2 Colmar France
100 C2 Cologne Ger.
154 C2 Colômbia Brazil
150 A1 Colombia country S. America
73 B4 Colombo Sri Lanka
104 C3 Colomiers France
152 C4 Colón Arg.
146 C4 Colón Panama
109 C3 Colonna, Capo c. Italy
96 A2 Colonsay i. U.K.
153 B4 Colorado r. Arg.
138 A2 Colorado r. Mex./U.S.A.
139 D3 Colorado r. U.S.A.
136 B3 Colorado state U.S.A.
135 E3 Colorado Plateau U.S.A.
136 C3 Colorado Springs U.S.A.
144 B2 Colotlán Mex.
136 B1 Colstrip U.S.A.
137 E3 Columbia MO U.S.A.
143 D2 Columbia SC U.S.A.
142 C1 Columbia TN U.S.A.
134 B1 Columbia r. U.S.A.
128 C2 Columbia, Mount Can.
134 D1 Columbia Falls U.S.A.
128 B2 Columbia Mountains Can.
134 C1 Columbia Plateau U.S.A.
143 D2 Columbus GA U.S.A.
140 B3 Columbus IN U.S.A.
142 C2 Columbus MS U.S.A.
137 D2 Columbus NE U.S.A.
138 B2 Columbus NM U.S.A.
140 C3 Columbus OH U.S.A.
134 C1 Colville U.S.A.
126 A2 Colville r. U.S.A.
126 C2 Colville Lake Can.
98 B2 Colwyn Bay U.K.
108 B2 Comacchio Italy
145 C3 Comalcalco Mex.
110 C1 Comăneşti Romania
130 C1 Comencho, Lac l. Can.
97 C2 Comeragh Mountains Rep. of Ireland
75 D2 Comilla Bangl.
108 A2 Comino, Capo c. Sardinia Italy
145 C3 Comitán de Dominguez Mex.
104 C2 Commentry France
139 D2 Commerce U.S.A.
127 F2 Committee Bay Can.
108 A1 Como Italy
108 A1 Como, Lago di l. Italy

153 B5 **Comodoro Rivadavia** Arg.
121 D2 **Comoros** *country* Africa
104 C2 **Compiègne** France
144 B2 **Compostela** Mex.
90 B2 **Comrat** Moldova
114 A4 **Conakry** Guinea
155 E1 **Conceição da Barra** Brazil
151 D2 **Conceição do Araguaia** Brazil
155 D1 **Conceição do Mato Dentro** Brazil
152 B3 **Concepción** Arg.
153 A4 **Concepción** Chile
144 B2 **Concepción** Mex.
146 B4 **Concepción** Panama
135 B4 **Conception, Point** U.S.A.
122 C2 **Conchas** Brazil
138 C1 **Conchas Lake** U.S.A.
144 B2 **Conchos** *r. Chihuahua* Mex.
145 C2 **Conchos** *r. Nuevo León/ Tamaulipas* Mex.
135 B3 **Concord** *CA* U.S.A.
141 E2 **Concord** *NH* U.S.A.
152 C4 **Concordia** Arg.
122 A2 **Concordia** S. Africa
137 D3 **Concordia** U.S.A.
53 C2 **Condobolin** Austr.
104 C3 **Condom** France
134 B1 **Condon** U.S.A.
108 B1 **Conegliano** Italy
104 C2 **Confolens** France
118 B3 **Congo** *country* Africa
118 B3 **Congo** *r.*
Congo/Dem. Rep. Congo
118 C3 **Congo, Democratic Republic of** *country* Africa
129 C2 **Conklin** Can.
97 B1 **Conn, Lough** *l.* Rep. of Ireland
97 B2 **Connaught** *reg.* Rep. of Ireland
141 E2 **Connecticut** *r.* U.S.A.
141 E2 **Connecticut** *state* U.S.A.
97 B2 **Connemara** *reg.* Rep. of Ireland
134 D1 **Conrad** U.S.A.
139 D2 **Conroe** U.S.A.
155 D2 **Conselheiro Lafaiete** Brazil
155 D1 **Conselheiro Pena** Brazil
98 C1 **Consett** U.K.
63 B3 **Côn Son** *i.* Vietnam
110 C2 **Constanța** Romania
106 B2 **Constantina** Spain
115 C1 **Constantine** Alg.
134 D2 **Contact** U.S.A.
150 A2 **Contamana** Peru
153 A6 **Contreras, Isla** *i.* Chile
126 D2 **Contwoyto Lake** Can.
142 B1 **Conway** *AR* U.S.A.
141 E2 **Conway** *NH* U.S.A.
51 C2 **Coober Pedy** Austr.
54 B2 **Cook, Mount** *mt.* N.Z.
143 C1 **Cookeville** U.S.A.
49 G4 **Cook Islands** S. Pacific Ocean
131 E1 **Cook's Harbour** Can.
97 C1 **Cookstown** U.K.
54 B2 **Cook Strait** N.Z.
51 D1 **Cooktown** Austr.
53 C2 **Coolabah** Austr.
53 C2 **Coolamon** Austr.
53 D1 **Coolangatta** Austr.
50 B3 **Coolgardie** Austr.
53 C3 **Cooma** Austr.
52 B2 **Coombah** Austr.
53 C2 **Coonabarabran** Austr.
52 A3 **Coonalpyn** Austr.
53 C2 **Coonamble** Austr.
52 A1 **Cooper Creek** *watercourse* Austr.

134 B2 **Coos Bay** U.S.A.
53 C2 **Cootamundra** Austr.
145 C3 **Copainalá** Mex.
145 C3 **Copala** Mex.
93 F4 **Copenhagen** Denmark
129 C2 **Copertino** Italy
152 A3 **Copiapó** Chile
140 B1 **Copper Harbor** U.S.A.
Coppermine Can. *see* Kugluktuk
126 D2 **Coppermine** *r.* Can.
122 B2 **Copperton** S. Africa
152 A3 **Coquimbo** Chile
110 B2 **Corabia** Romania
155 D1 **Coração de Jesus** Brazil
150 A3 **Coracora** Peru
53 D1 **Coraki** Austr.
50 A2 **Coral Bay** Austr.
127 F2 **Coral Harbour** Can.
156 D7 **Coral Sea** S. Pacific Ocean
52 B3 **Corangamite, Lake** Austr.
99 C2 **Corby** U.K.
153 A5 **Corcovado, Golfo de** *sea chan.* Chile
143 D2 **Cordele** U.S.A.
64 B1 **Cordilleras Range** *mts* Phil.
152 B4 **Córdoba** Arg.
145 C3 **Córdoba** Mex.
106 C2 **Córdoba** Spain
153 B4 **Córdoba, Sierras de** *mts* Arg.
111 A3 **Corfu** *i.* Greece
106 B2 **Coria** Spain
142 C2 **Corinth** Greece
155 D1 **Corinto** Brazil
97 B3 **Cork** Rep. of Ireland
111 C2 **Çorlu** Turkey
154 B2 **Cornélio Procópio** Brazil
131 E2 **Corner Brook** Can.
53 C3 **Corner Inlet** *b.* Austr.
135 B3 **Corning** *CA* U.S.A.
141 D2 **Corning** *NY* U.S.A.
Corn Islands *is* Nic. *see* Maíz, Islas del
108 B2 **Corno, Monte** *mt.* Italy
130 C2 **Cornwall** Can.
126 E1 **Cornwallis Island** Can.
150 C1 **Coro** Venez.
154 C1 **Coromandel** Brazil
54 C1 **Coromandel Peninsula** N.Z.
129 C2 **Coronation** Can.
126 D2 **Coronation Gulf** Can.
152 C3 **Coronel Oviedo** Para.
153 B4 **Coronel Suárez** Arg.
109 D2 **Çorovodë** Albania
139 D3 **Corpus Christi** U.S.A.
151 D3 **Corque** Bol.
151 D3 **Corrente** Brazil
151 D3 **Correntes** Brazil
151 D3 **Corrientina** Brazil
97 B2 **Corrib, Lough** *l.* Rep. of Ireland
152 C3 **Corrientes** Arg.
144 B2 **Corrientes, Cabo** *c.* Mex.
53 C3 **Corryong** Austr.
Corse *i.* France *see* Corsica
105 D3 **Corse, Cap** *c. Corsica* France
105 D3 **Corsica** *i.* France
139 D2 **Corsicana** U.S.A.
105 D3 **Corte** *Corsica* France
106 B2 **Cortegana** Spain
136 B3 **Cortez** U.S.A.
108 B1 **Cortina d'Ampezzo** Italy
141 D2 **Cortland** U.S.A.
108 B2 **Cortona** Italy
106 B2 **Coruche** Port.
Çoruh Turkey *see* Artvin
80 B1 **Çorum** Turkey
152 C2 **Corumbá** Brazil
154 C1 **Corumbá** *r.* Brazil

134 B2 **Corvallis** U.S.A.
98 B2 **Corwen** U.K.
144 B2 **Cosalá** Mex.
145 C3 **Cosamaloapan** Mex.
109 C3 **Cosenza** Italy
105 C2 **Cosne-Cours-sur-Loire** France
107 C2 **Costa Blanca** *coastal area* Spain
107 D1 **Costa Brava** *coastal area* Spain
106 B2 **Costa del Sol** *coastal area* Spain
146 B3 **Costa de Mosquitos** *coastal area* Nic.
154 B1 **Costa Rica** Brazil
146 B3 **Costa Rica** *country* Central America
144 B2 **Costa Rica** Mex.
110 B2 **Costeşti** Romania
64 B2 **Cotabato** Phil.
114 B4 **Côte d'Ivoire** *country* Africa
150 A2 **Cotopaxi, Volcán** *vol.* Ecuador
99 B3 **Cotswold Hills** U.K.
134 B2 **Cottage Grove** U.S.A.
102 C1 **Cottbus** Ger.
52 A3 **Côuedic, Cape de** Austr.
137 D2 **Council Bluffs** U.S.A.
88 B2 **Courland Lagoon** *b.* Lith./Rus. Fed.
128 B3 **Courtenay** Can.
104 B2 **Coutances** France
104 B2 **Coutras** France
100 B2 **Couvin** Belgium
99 C2 **Coventry** U.K.
140 C3 **Covington** U.S.A.
50 B3 **Cowan, Lake** *salt flat* Austr.
96 C2 **Cowdenbeath** U.K.
53 C3 **Cowes** Austr.
134 B1 **Cowlitz** *r.* U.S.A.
53 C2 **Cowra** Austr.
154 B1 **Coxim** Brazil
75 D2 **Cox's Bazar** Bangl.
145 B3 **Coyuca de Benítez** Mex.
145 C2 **Cozumel** Mex.
145 C2 **Cozumel, Isla de** *i.* Mex.
123 C3 **Cradock** S. Africa
136 B2 **Craig** U.S.A.
102 C2 **Crailsheim** Ger.
110 B2 **Craiova** Romania
129 D2 **Cranberry Portage** Can.
53 C3 **Cranbourne** Austr.
128 C3 **Cranbrook** Can.
151 D2 **Crateús** Brazil
151 E2 **Crato** Brazil
136 C2 **Crawford** U.S.A.
140 B2 **Crawfordsville** U.S.A.
99 C3 **Crawley** U.K.
134 D1 **Crazy Mountains** U.S.A.
129 D2 **Cree** *r.* Can.
144 B2 **Creel** Mex.
129 D2 **Cree Lake** Can.
100 B2 **Creil** Neth.
105 D2 **Crema** Italy
108 B1 **Cremona** Italy
108 B2 **Cres** *i.* Croatia
134 B2 **Crescent City** U.S.A.
128 C3 **Creston** Can.
137 E2 **Creston** U.S.A.
142 C2 **Crestview** U.S.A.
111 B3 **Crete** *i.* Greece
107 D1 **Creus, Cap de** *c.* Spain
98 B2 **Crewe** U.K.
96 B2 **Crianlarich** U.K.
152 D3 **Criciúma** Brazil
96 C2 **Crieff** U.K.
108 B1 **Crikvenica** Croatia
91 C2 **Crimea** *pen.* Ukr.

101 F2 **Crimmitschau** Ger.
154 C1 **Cristalina** Brazil
101 E1 **Crivitz** Ger.
 Crna Gora *aut. rep.* Yugo. *see* Montenegro
109 D2 **Crni Vrh** *mt.* Yugo.
109 C1 **Črnomelj** Slovenia
 97 B2 **Croagh Patrick** *hill* Rep. of Ireland
109 C1 **Croatia** *country* Europe
 61 C1 **Crocker, Banjaran** *mts* Malaysia
139 D2 **Crockett** U.S.A.
 59 C3 **Croker Island** Austr.
 99 D2 **Cromer** U.K.
 54 A3 **Cromwell** N.Z.
137 C1 **Crookston** U.S.A.
 53 C2 **Crookwell** Austr.
136 C1 **Crosby** U.S.A.
143 D3 **Cross City** U.S.A.
142 B2 **Crossett** U.S.A.
 98 B1 **Cross Fell** *hill* U.K.
129 E2 **Cross Lake** *l.* Can.
143 C1 **Crossville** U.S.A.
109 C3 **Crotone** Italy
 99 D3 **Crowborough** U.K.
142 B2 **Crowley** U.S.A.
128 C3 **Crowsnest Pass** Can.
146 C3 **Cruz, Cabo** *c.* Cuba
152 C3 **Cruz Alta** Brazil
152 B4 **Cruz del Eje** Arg.
155 C2 **Cruzeiro** Brazil
150 A2 **Cruzeiro do Sul** Brazil
 52 A2 **Crystal Brook** Austr.
139 D3 **Crystal City** U.S.A.
140 B1 **Crystal Falls** U.S.A.
103 E2 **Csongrád** Hungary
120 B2 **Cuando** *r.* Angola/Zambia
120 A2 **Cuangar** Angola
118 B3 **Cuango** *r.* Angola/Dem. Rep. of Congo
120 A1 **Cuanza** *r.* Angola
139 C3 **Cuatro Ciénegas** Mex.
144 B2 **Cuauhtémoc** Mex.
145 C3 **Cuautla** Mex.
146 B2 **Cuba** *country* West Indies
120 A2 **Cubal** Angola
120 A2 **Cubango** *r.* Angola/Namibia
150 A1 **Cúcuta** Col.
 73 B3 **Cuddalore** India
 73 B3 **Cuddapah** India
106 C1 **Cuéllar** Spain
120 A2 **Cuemba** Angola
150 A2 **Cuenca** Ecuador
107 C1 **Cuenca** Spain
107 C1 **Cuenca, Serranía de** *mts* Spain
145 C3 **Cuernavaca** Mex.
139 D3 **Cuero** U.S.A.
151 C3 **Cuiabá** Brazil
151 C3 **Cuiabá** *r.* Brazil
 96 A2 **Cuillin Sound** *sea chan.* U.K.
120 A1 **Cuilo** Angola
120 B2 **Cuito** *r.* Angola
120 A2 **Cuito Cuanavale** Angola
 60 B1 **Cukai** Malaysia
 53 C3 **Culcairn** Austr.
 53 C1 **Culgoa** Austr.
144 B2 **Culiacán** Mex.
 64 A1 **Culion** *i.* Phil.
107 C2 **Culiera** Spain
142 C2 **Cullman** U.S.A.
 97 C1 **Cullybackey** U.K.
151 C2 **Culuene** *r.* Brazil
150 B1 **Cumaná** Venez.
141 D3 **Cumberland** U.S.A.
140 B3 **Cumberland** *r.* U.S.A.
128 C2 **Cumberland Lake** Can.
127 G2 **Cumberland Peninsula** Can.
142 C1 **Cumberland Plateau** U.S.A.

127 G2 **Cumberland Sound** *sea chan.* Can.
 96 C3 **Cumbernauld** U.K.
135 B3 **Cummings** U.S.A.
 96 B3 **Cumnock** U.K.
144 B1 **Cumpas** Mex.
145 C3 **Cunduacán** Mex.
120 A2 **Cunene** *r.* Angola
108 A2 **Cuneo** Italy
 53 C1 **Cunnamulla** Austr.
108 A1 **Cuorgné** Italy
 96 C2 **Cupar** U.K.
147 D3 **Curaçao** *i.* Neth. Antilles
150 A2 **Curaray** *r.* Ecuador
153 A4 **Curicó** Chile
154 C3 **Curitiba** Brazil
 52 A2 **Curnamona** Austr.
 51 D3 **Currie** Austr.
 51 E2 **Curtis Island** Austr.
151 C2 **Curuá** *r.* Brazil
 60 B2 **Curup** Indon.
151 D2 **Cururupu** Brazil
155 D1 **Curvelo** Brazil
150 A3 **Cusco** Peru
139 D1 **Cushing** U.S.A.
134 D1 **Cut Bank** U.S.A.
 75 C2 **Cuttack** India
101 D1 **Cuxhaven** Ger.
 64 B1 **Cuyo Islands** Phil.
 Cuzco Peru *see* Cusco
119 C3 **Cyangugu** Rwanda
111 B3 **Cyclades** *is* Greece
129 C3 **Cypress Hills** Can.
 80 B2 **Cyprus** *country* Asia
102 C2 **Czech Republic** *country* Europe
103 D1 **Czersk** Pol.
103 D1 **Częstochowa** Pol.

D

 62 B1 **Đa, Sông** *r.* Vietnam
 69 D2 **Daban** China
114 A3 **Dabola** Guinea
 Dacca Bangl. *see* Dhaka
102 C2 **Dachau** Ger.
 70 A2 **Dachuan** China
 74 A2 **Dadu** Pak.
 64 B1 **Daet** Phil.
114 A3 **Dagana** Senegal
 64 B1 **Dagupan** Phil.
 74 B3 **Dahanu** India
 69 D2 **Da Hinggan Ling** *mts* China
116 C3 **Dahlak Archipelago** *is* Eritrea
100 C2 **Dahlem** Ger.
 60 B2 **Daik** Indon.
106 C2 **Daimiel** Spain
114 A3 **Dakar** Senegal
117 C4 **Daketa Shet'** *watercourse* Eth.
116 A2 **Dakhla Oasis** Egypt
 63 A3 **Đakoauk** India
 88 C3 **Dakol'ka** *r.* Belarus
109 D2 **Đakovica** Yugo.
109 C1 **Đakovo** Croatia
120 B2 **Dala** Angola
 68 C2 **Dalain Hob** China
 93 G3 **Dalälven** *r.* Sweden
111 C3 **Dalaman** Turkey
111 C3 **Dalaman** *r.* Turkey
 68 C2 **Dalandzadgad** Mongolia
 63 B2 **Đa Lat** Vietnam
 74 A2 **Dalbandin** Pak.
 98 C2 **Dalbeattie** U.K.
 51 E2 **Dalby** Austr.
143 C1 **Dale Hollow Lake** U.S.A.

 53 C3 **Dalgety** Austr.
139 C1 **Dalhart** U.S.A.
131 D2 **Dalhousie** Can.
 62 B1 **Dali** China
 70 C2 **Dalian** China
 96 C3 **Dalkeith** U.K.
139 D2 **Dallas** U.S.A.
128 A2 **Dall Island** U.S.A.
109 C2 **Dalmacija** *reg.* Croatia
 66 C2 **Dal'negorsk** Rus. Fed.
 66 B1 **Dal'nerechensk** Rus. Fed.
114 B4 **Daloa** Côte d'Ivoire
 51 D2 **Dalrymple, Mount** Austr.
 92 □A3 **Dalsmynni** Iceland
 75 C2 **Daltenganj** India
143 D2 **Dalton** U.S.A.
 60 B1 **Daludalu** Indon.
 92 □B2 **Dalvík** Iceland
 50 C1 **Daly** *r.* Austr.
 51 C1 **Daly Waters** Austr.
 74 B2 **Damān** India
 80 B2 **Damanhūr** Egypt
 59 C3 **Damar** *i.* Indon.
 80 B2 **Damascus** Syria
115 D3 **Damaturu** Nigeria
 76 B3 **Damāvand, Qolleh-ye** *mt.* Iran
 81 D2 **Damghan** Iran
101 D1 **Damme** Ger.
 75 B2 **Damoh** India
114 B4 **Damongo** Ghana
 59 C3 **Dampir, Selat** *sea chan.* Indon.
 75 D1 **Damxung** China
114 B4 **Danané** Côte d'Ivoire
 63 B2 **Đa Năng** Vietnam
141 E2 **Danbury** U.S.A.
 65 A1 **Dandong** China
146 B3 **Dangriga** Belize
 70 B2 **Dangshan** China
 89 E2 **Danilov** Rus. Fed.
 89 E2 **Danilovskaya Vozvyshennost'** *hills* Rus. Fed.
 70 B2 **Danjiangkou** China
 89 E3 **Dankov** Rus. Fed.
146 B3 **Danli** Hond.
101 E1 **Dannenberg (Elbe)** Ger.
 54 C2 **Dannevirke** N.Z.
 62 B2 **Dan Sai** Thai.
 Dantu China *see* Zhenjiang
110 A1 **Danube** *r.* Europe
140 B2 **Danville** *IL* U.S.A.
140 C3 **Danville** *KY* U.S.A.
141 D3 **Danville** *VA* U.S.A.
 71 A4 **Danzhou** China
 71 B3 **Daoxian** China
114 C3 **Dapaong** Togo
 68 C2 **Da Qaidam Zhen** China
 69 E1 **Daqing** China
 80 B2 **Dar'ā** Syria
 79 C2 **Dārāb** Iran
115 C1 **Daraj** Libya
 81 D2 **Dārān** Iran
 63 B2 **Đa Răng, Sông** *r.* Vietnam
 75 C2 **Darbhanga** India
119 D3 **Dar es Salaam** Tanz.
 74 B1 **Dargai** Pak.
 54 B1 **Dargaville** N.Z.
 53 C3 **Dargo** Austr.
 69 D1 **Darhan** Mongolia
150 A1 **Darién, Golfo del** *g.* Col.
 75 C2 **Dārjiling** India
 68 C2 **Darlag** China
 52 B2 **Darling** *r.* Austr.
 53 C1 **Darling Downs** *hills* Austr.
 50 A3 **Darling Range** *hills* Austr.
 98 C1 **Darlington** U.K.
 53 C2 **Darlington Point** Austr.
103 D1 **Darłowo** Pol.

101 D3 Darmstadt Ger.
115 E1 Darnah Libya
52 B2 Darnick Austr.
107 C3 Daroca Spain
99 D3 Dartford U.K.
99 A3 Dartmoor *hills* U.K.
131 D2 Dartmouth Can.
99 B3 Dartmouth U.K.
97 B1 Darty Mountains
        Rep. of Ireland
59 D3 Daru P.N.G.
50 C1 Darwin Austr.
76 B2 Dashkhovuz Turkm.
74 A2 Dasht r. Pak.
61 C1 Datadian Indon.
111 C3 Datça Turkey
70 B3 Datong China
64 B2 Datu Piang Phil.
74 B1 Daud Khel Pak.
88 B2 Daugava r. Latvia
88 C2 Daugavpils Latvia
100 C2 Daun Ger.
129 D2 Dauphin Can.
129 E2 Dauphin Lake Can.
73 B3 Davangere India
64 B2 Davao Phil.
64 B2 Davao Gulf Phil.
137 E2 Davenport U.S.A.
99 C2 Daventry U.K.
123 C2 Daveyton S. Africa
146 B4 David Panama
129 D2 Davidson Can.
126 E3 Davidson Lake Can.
135 B3 Davis U.S.A.
131 C1 Davis Inlet Can.
159 F3 Davis Sea Antarctica
160 P3 Davis Strait Can./Greenland
105 D2 Davos Switz.
79 C3 Dawqah Oman
126 B2 Dawson Can.
143 D2 Dawson U.S.A.
128 B2 Dawson Creek Can.
128 B2 Dawsons Landing Can.
68 C2 Dawu China
        Dawukou China *see*
        Shizuishan
104 B3 Dax France
68 C2 Daxue Shan *mts* China
71 B3 Dayong China
80 C2 Dayr az Zawr Syria
140 C3 Dayton U.S.A.
143 D3 Daytona Beach U.S.A.
122 B3 De Aar S. Africa
80 B2 Dead Sea *salt l.* Asia
71 B3 De'an China
152 B4 Deán Funes Arg.
128 B2 Dease Lake Can.
126 D2 Dease Strait Can.
135 C3 Death Valley *depr.* U.S.A.
104 C2 Deauville France
61 C1 Debak *Sarawak* Malaysia
109 D2 Debar Macedonia
103 E2 Debrecen Hungary
117 B3 Debre Markos Eth.
117 B3 Debre Tabor Eth.
117 B3 Debre Zeyit Eth.
142 C2 Decatur AL U.S.A.
140 B3 Decatur IL U.S.A.
73 B3 Deccan *plat.* India
102 C1 Děčín Czech Rep.
137 E2 Decorah U.S.A.
88 C2 Dedovichi Rus. Fed.
121 C2 Dedza Malawi
98 B2 Dee r. England/Wales U.K.
96 C2 Dee r. Scotland U.K.
53 D1 Deepwater Austr.
131 E2 Deer Lake Can.
134 D1 Deer Lodge U.S.A.
140 C2 Defiance U.S.A.
68 C2 Dêgê China

117 C4 Degeh Bur Eth.
102 C2 Deggendorf Ger.
91 E2 Degtevo Rus. Fed.
75 B1 Dehra Dun India
75 C2 Dehri India
69 E2 Dehui China
100 A2 Deinze Belgium
110 B1 Dej Romania
140 B2 De Kalb U.S.A.
78 A3 Dekemhare Eritrea
118 C3 Dekese Dem. Rep. Congo
135 C3 Delano U.S.A.
135 C3 Delano Peak U.S.A.
74 A1 Delārām Afgh.
123 C2 Delareyville S. Africa
129 D2 Delaronde Lake Can.
140 C2 Delaware U.S.A.
141 D3 Delaware r. U.S.A.
141 D3 Delaware state U.S.A.
141 D3 Delaware Bay U.S.A.
53 C3 Delegate Austr.
105 D2 Delémont Switz.
100 B1 Delft Neth.
100 C1 Delfzijl Neth.
121 D2 Delgado, Cabo c. Moz.
75 B2 Delhi India
60 B2 Deli i. Indon.
126 C2 Déline Can.
101 F2 Delitzsch Ger.
107 D2 Dellys Alg.
101 D1 Delmenhorst Ger.
109 B1 Delnice Croatia
83 L1 De-Longa, Ostrova is
        Rus. Fed.
129 D3 Deloraine Can.
111 B3 Delphi Greece
139 C3 Del Rio U.S.A.
136 B3 Delta CO U.S.A.
135 D3 Delta UT U.S.A.
126 B2 Delta Junction U.S.A.
109 D3 Delvinë Albania
118 C3 Demba Dem. Rep. Congo
117 B4 Dembi Dolo Eth.
89 D2 Demidov Rus. Fed.
138 B2 Deming U.S.A.
111 C3 Demirci Turkey
110 C2 Demirköy Turkey
102 C1 Demmin Ger.
142 C2 Demopolis U.S.A.
60 B2 Dempo, Gunung vol. Indon.
89 D2 Demyansk Rus. Fed.
122 B3 De Naawte S. Africa
117 C3 Denakil reg. Eritrea/Eth.
100 B1 Den Burg Neth.
100 B2 Dendermonde Belgium
70 A1 Dengkou China
70 B2 Dengzhou China
        Den Haag Neth. see
        The Hague
50 A2 Denham Austr.
100 B1 Den Helder Neth.
52 B3 Deniliquin Austr.
134 C2 Denio U.S.A.
137 D2 Denison IA U.S.A.
139 D2 Denison TX U.S.A.
111 C3 Denizli Turkey
53 D2 Denman Austr.
50 A3 Denmark Austr.
93 F4 Denmark country Europe
160 Q3 Denmark Strait
        Greenland/Iceland
61 C2 Denpasar Indon.
139 D2 Denton U.S.A.
50 A3 D'Entrecasteaux, Point
        Austr.
136 B3 Denver U.S.A.
75 C2 Deogarh Orissa India
74 B2 Deogarh Rajasthan India
75 C2 Deoghar India
83 K2 Deputatskiy Rus. Fed.

68 C3 Dêqên China
142 B2 De Queen U.S.A.
74 A2 Dera Bugti Pak.
74 B1 Dera Ghazi Khan Pak.
74 B1 Dera Ismail Khan Pak.
87 D4 Derbent Rus. Fed.
50 B1 Derby Austr.
99 C2 Derby U.K.
97 B2 Derg, Lough l.
        Rep. of Ireland
91 D1 Derhachi Ukr.
142 B2 De Ridder U.S.A.
91 D2 Derkul r. Rus. Fed./Ukr.
116 B3 Derudeb Sudan
122 B3 De Rust S. Africa
109 C2 Derventa Bos.-Herz.
98 C2 Derwent r. U.K.
98 B1 Derwent Water l. U.K.
77 C1 Derzhavinsk Kazakh.
152 B2 Desaguadero r. Bol.
129 D2 Deschambault Lake Can.
134 B1 Deschutes r. U.S.A.
117 B3 Desē Eth.
153 B5 Deseado Arg.
153 B5 Deseado r. Arg.
137 E2 Des Moines U.S.A.
137 E2 Des Moines r. U.S.A.
91 C1 Desna r. Rus. Fed./Ukr.
89 D3 Desnogorsk Rus. Fed.
101 F2 Dessau Ger.
126 B2 Destruction Bay Can.
128 C1 Detah Can.
101 D2 Detmold Ger.
140 C2 Detroit U.S.A.
137 D1 Detroit Lakes U.S.A.
100 B2 Deurne Neth.
110 B1 Deva Romania
100 C1 Deventer Neth.
96 C2 Deveron r. U.K.
103 D2 Devět Skal hill Czech Rep.
137 D1 Devil's Lake U.S.A.
128 A2 Devil's Paw mt. U.S.A.
99 C3 Devizes U.K.
74 B2 Devli India
110 C2 Devnya Bulg.
128 C2 Devon Can.
126 E1 Devon Island Can.
51 D4 Devonport Austr.
74 B2 Dewas India
137 F3 Dexter U.S.A.
70 A2 Deyang China
59 D3 Deyong, Tanjung pt Indon.
81 C2 Dezful Iran
70 B2 Dezhou China
78 B2 Dhahran Saudi Arabia
75 D2 Dhaka Bangl.
78 B3 Dhamār Yemen
75 C2 Dhamtari India
75 C2 Dhanbad India
75 C2 Dhankuta Nepal
62 A1 Dharmanagar India
75 C2 Dharmjaygarh India
73 B3 Dhārwād India
74 B2 Dhasa India
74 B3 Dhubāb Yemen
74 B2 Dhule India
144 A1 Diablo, Picacho del
        mt. Mex.
51 C2 Diamantina watercourse
        Austr.
155 D1 Diamantina Brazil
151 D3 Diamantina, Chapada plat.
        Brazil
151 C3 Diamantino Brazil
71 B3 Dianbai China
151 D3 Dianópolis Brazil
114 B4 Dianra Côte d'Ivoire
114 C3 Diapaga Burkina
79 C3 Dibā al Ḩiṣn U.A.E.
118 C3 Dibaya Dem. Rep. Congo

62 A1 **Dibrugarh** India
136 C1 **Dickinson** U.S.A.
142 C1 **Dickson** U.S.A.
　　　 Dicle r. Turkey see Tigris
105 D3 **Die** France
129 D2 **Diefenbaker, Lake** Can.
114 B3 **Diéma** Mali
62 A2 **Diên Châu** Vietnam
101 D1 **Diepholz** Ger.
104 C2 **Dieppe** France
115 D3 **Diffa** Niger
131 D2 **Digby** Can.
105 D3 **Digne-les-Bains** France
105 C2 **Digoin** France
64 D3 **Digos** Phil.
59 D3 **Digul** r. Indon.
　　　 Dihang r. China/India see
　　　 Brahmaputra
105 D2 **Dijon** France
117 C3 **Dikhil** Djibouti
111 C3 **Dikili** Turkey
100 A3 **Diksmuide** Belgium
115 D3 **Dikwa** Nigeria
117 B4 **Dīla** Eth.
59 C3 **Dili** East Timor
101 D2 **Dillenburg** Ger.
134 D1 **Dillon** U.S.A.
118 C4 **Dilolo** Dem. Rep. Congo
62 A1 **Dimapur** India
　　　 Dimashq Syria see Damascus
52 B3 **Dimboola** Austr.
110 C2 **Dimitrovgrad** Bulg.
87 D3 **Dimitrovgrad** Rus. Fed.
64 B1 **Dinagat** i. Phil.
104 B2 **Dinan** France
100 B2 **Dinant** Belgium
111 D3 **Dinar** Turkey
81 D2 **Dīnār, Kūh-e** mt. Iran
73 B3 **Dindigul** India
123 D1 **Dindiza** Moz.
101 E2 **Dingelstädt** Ger.
97 A2 **Dingle** Rep. of Ireland
97 A2 **Dingle Bay** Rep. of Ireland
96 B2 **Dingwall** U.K.
70 A2 **Dingxi** China
75 C2 **Dinngyè** China
154 B3 **Dionísio Cerqueira** Brazil
114 A3 **Diourbel** Senegal
64 B2 **Dipolog** Phil.
74 A1 **Dir** Pak.
51 D1 **Direction, Cape** Austr.
117 C4 **Dirê Dawa** Eth.
120 B2 **Dirico** Angola
50 A2 **Dirk Hartog Island** Austr.
53 C1 **Dirranbandi** Austr.
78 B3 **Dirs** Saudi Arabia
50 B2 **Disappointment, Lake**
　　　 salt flat Austr.
52 B3 **Discovery Bay** b. Austr.
143 E1 **Dismal Swamp** U.S.A.
99 D2 **Diss** U.K.
108 B3 **Dittaino** r. Sicily Italy
74 B2 **Diu** India
155 D3 **Divinópolis** Brazil
87 D4 **Divnoye** Rus. Fed.
114 B4 **Divo** Côte d'Ivoire
80 B2 **Divriği** Turkey
140 B2 **Dixon** U.S.A.
128 A2 **Dixon Entrance** sea chan.
　　　 Can./U.S.A.
80 C2 **Diyarbakır** Turkey
74 A2 **Diz** Pak.
115 D2 **Djado** Niger
115 D2 **Djado, Plateau du** Niger
118 B3 **Djambala** Congo
115 C2 **Djanet** Alg.
115 C1 **Djelfa** Alg.
118 B2 **Djéma** C.A.R.
114 B3 **Djenné** Mali
114 B3 **Djibo** Burkina

117 C3 **Djibouti** country Africa
117 C3 **Djibouti** Djibouti
114 C2 **Djougou** Benin
92 □C3 **Djúpivogur** Iceland
91 E1 **Dmitriyevka** Rus. Fed.
89 E3 **Dmitriyev-L'govskiy**
　　　 Rus. Fed.
89 E2 **Dmitrov** Rus. Fed.
　　　 Dnepr r. Rus. Fed. see Dnieper
89 D3 **Dnieper** r. Europe
　　　 Dnipro r. Ukr. see Dnieper
91 C2 **Dniprodzerzhyns'k** Ukr.
91 D2 **Dnipropetrovs'k** Ukr.
91 C2 **Dniprorudne** Ukr.
90 B2 **Dnister** r. Ukr.
88 C2 **Dno** Rus. Fed.
115 D4 **Doba** Chad
88 B2 **Dobele** Latvia
101 F2 **Döbeln** Ger.
59 C3 **Doberai, Jazirah** pen. Indon.
59 C3 **Dobo** Indon.
109 C2 **Doboj** Bos.-Herz.
110 C2 **Dobrich** Bulg.
89 F3 **Dobrinka** Rus. Fed.
89 E3 **Dobroye** Rus. Fed.
89 D3 **Dobrush** Belarus
155 E1 **Doce** r. Brazil
145 B2 **Doctor Arroyo** Mex.
144 B2 **Doctor Belisario**
　　　 Domínguez Mex.
111 C3 **Dodecanese** is Greece
　　　 Dodekanisos is Greece see
　　　 Dodecanese
136 C3 **Dodge City** U.S.A.
119 D3 **Dodoma** Tanz.
100 C2 **Doetinchem** Neth.
59 C3 **Dofa** Indon.
75 C1 **Dogai Coring** salt l. China
128 B2 **Dog Creek** Can.
67 B3 **Dōgo** i. Japan
115 C3 **Dogondoutchi** Niger
81 C2 **Doğubeyazıt** Turkey
79 C2 **Doha** Qatar
62 A2 **Doi Saket** Thai.
100 B1 **Dokkum** Neth.
88 C3 **Dokshytsy** Belarus
91 D2 **Dokuchayevs'k** Ukr.
59 D3 **Dolak, Pulau** i. Indon.
131 C2 **Dolbeau** Can.
104 B2 **Dol-de-Bretagne** France
105 D2 **Dole** France
99 B2 **Dolgellau** U.K.
89 E3 **Dolgorukovo** Rus. Fed.
89 E3 **Dolgoye** Rus. Fed.
108 B1 **Dolomiti** mts Italy
117 C4 **Dolo Odo** Eth.
126 D2 **Dolphin and Union Strait**
　　　 Can.
90 A2 **Dolyna** Ukr.
102 C2 **Domažlice** Czech Rep.
93 F3 **Dombås** Norway
103 D2 **Dombóvár** Hungary
128 B2 **Dome Creek** Can.
147 D3 **Dominica** country
　　　 West Indies
147 D3 **Dominican Republic** country
　　　 West Indies
89 E2 **Domodedovo** Rus. Fed.
111 B3 **Domokos** Greece
61 C2 **Dompu** Indon.
89 E3 **Don** r. Rus. Fed.
96 C2 **Don** r. U.K.
97 D1 **Donaghadee** U.K.
52 B3 **Donald** Austr.
　　　 Donau r. Austria/Ger. see
　　　 Danube
102 C2 **Donauwörth** Ger.
106 B2 **Don Benito** Spain
98 C2 **Doncaster** U.K.
120 A1 **Dondo** Angola

121 C2 **Dondo** Moz.
73 C4 **Dondra Head** hd Sri Lanka
97 B1 **Donegal** Rep. of Ireland
97 B1 **Donegal Bay** Rep. of Ireland
91 D2 **Donets'k** Ukr.
91 D2 **Donets'kyy Kryazh** hills
　　　 Rus. Fed./Ukr.
50 A2 **Dongara** Austr.
62 B1 **Dongchuan** China
71 A4 **Dongfang** China
66 B1 **Dongfanghong** China
58 B3 **Donggala** Indon.
65 A2 **Donggang** China
62 B2 **Đông Ha** Vietnam
　　　 Dong Hai sea N. Pacific
　　　 Ocean see East China Sea
62 B2 **Đông Hôi** Vietnam
118 B2 **Dongou** Congo
63 B2 **Dong Phraya Fai** mts Thai.
71 B3 **Dongshan** China
70 B2 **Dongsheng** China
70 C2 **Dongtai** China
71 B3 **Dongting Hu** l. China
　　　 Dong Ujimqin Qi China see
　　　 Uliastai
70 B2 **Dongying** China
54 B1 **Donnellys Crossing** N.Z.
107 C1 **Donostia - San Sebastián**
　　　 Spain
117 C4 **Dooxo Nugaaleed** val.
　　　 Somalia
99 B3 **Dorchester** U.K.
122 A1 **Dordabis** Namibia
104 B2 **Dordogne** r. France
100 B2 **Dordrecht** Neth.
123 C3 **Dordrecht** S. Africa
129 D2 **Doré Lake** l. Can.
101 D1 **Dorfmark** Ger.
114 B3 **Dori** Burkina
122 A3 **Doring** r. S. Africa
96 B2 **Dornoch** U.K.
96 B2 **Dornoch Firth** est. U.K.
89 D3 **Dorogobuzh** Rus. Fed.
90 B2 **Dorohoi** Romania
68 C1 **Döröö Nuur** salt l. Mongolia
92 G3 **Dorotea** Sweden
50 A2 **Dorre Island** Austr.
53 D2 **Dorrigo** Austr.
118 B2 **Dorsale Camerounaise**
　　　 slope Cameroon/Nigeria
100 C2 **Dortmund** Ger.
100 C2 **Dortmund-Ems-Kanal**
　　　 canal Ger.
153 B5 **Dos Bahías, Cabo** c. Arg.
101 F1 **Dosse** r. Ger.
114 C3 **Dosso** Niger
143 C2 **Dothan** U.S.A.
101 D1 **Dötlingen** Ger.
105 C1 **Douai** France
118 A2 **Douala** Cameroon
104 B2 **Douarnenez** France
114 B3 **Douentza** Mali
98 A1 **Douglas** Isle of Man
122 B2 **Douglas** S. Africa
128 A2 **Douglas** AK U.S.A.
138 B2 **Douglas** AZ U.S.A.
143 D2 **Douglas** GA U.S.A.
136 B2 **Douglas** WY U.S.A.
104 C1 **Doullens** France
154 B1 **Dourada, Serra** hills Brazil
154 B2 **Dourados** Brazil
154 B2 **Dourados, Serra dos** hills
　　　 Brazil
106 B1 **Douro** r. Port.
99 D3 **Dover** U.K.
141 D3 **Dover** U.S.A.
95 D3 **Dover, Strait of** France/U.K.
141 F1 **Dover-Foxcroft** U.S.A.
79 C2 **Dowlatābād** Bushehr Iran
79 C2 **Dowlatābād** Kermān Iran

97 D1	**Downpatrick** U.K.	
77 C3	**Dowshi** Afgh.	
67 B3	**Dōzen** *is* Japan	
130 C2	**Dozois, Réservoir** *resr* Can.	
154 B2	**Dracena** Brazil	
100 C1	**Drachten** Neth.	
110 B2	**Drăgăneşti-Olt** Romania	
110 B2	**Drăgăşani** Romania	
88 C3	**Drahichyn** Belarus	
123 C2	**Drakensberg** *mts*	
	Lesotho/S. Africa	
123 C2	**Drakensberg** *mts* S. Africa	
158 B8	**Drake Passage**	
	S. Atlantic Ocean	
111 B2	**Drama** Greece	
93 F4	**Drammen** Norway	
109 C3	**Drava** *r.* Europe	
128 C2	**Drayton Valley** Can.	
101 D2	**Dreieich** Ger.	
111 B3	**Drepano, Akra** *pt* Greece	
102 C1	**Dresden** Ger.	
104 C2	**Dreux** France	
100 B1	**Driemond** Neth.	
109 C2	**Drina** *r.* Bos.-Herz./Yugo.	
109 C2	**Drniš** Croatia	
110 B2	**Drobeta-Turnu Severin**	
	Romania	
101 D1	**Drochtersen** Ger.	
97 C2	**Drogheda** Rep. of Ireland	
90 A2	**Drohobych** Ukr.	
97 C1	**Dromore** U.K.	
74 B1	**Drosh** Pak.	
53 C3	**Drouin** Austr.	
128 C2	**Drumheller** Can.	
140 C1	**Drummond Island** U.S.A.	
131 C2	**Drummondville** Can.	
88 B3	**Druskininkai** Lith.	
91 D2	**Druzhkivka** Ukr.	
88 D2	**Druzhnaya Gorka** Rus. Fed.	
130 A2	**Dryden** Can.	
50 B1	**Drysdale** *r.* Austr.	
78 A2	**Dubā** Saudi Arabia	
79 C2	**Dubai** U.A.E.	
129 D1	**Dubawnt Lake** Can.	
	Dubayy U.A.E. *see* Dubai	
78 A2	**Dubbagh, Jabal ad** *mt.*	
	Saudi Arabia	
53 C2	**Dubbo** Austr.	
97 C2	**Dublin** Rep. of Ireland	
143 D2	**Dublin** U.S.A.	
90 B1	**Dubno** Ukr.	
141 D2	**Du Bois** U.S.A.	
114 A4	**Dubréka** Guinea	
109 C2	**Dubrovnik** Croatia	
90 B1	**Dubrovytsya** Ukr.	
89 D3	**Dubrowna** Belarus	
137 E2	**Dubuque** U.S.A.	
129 D2	**Duck Bay** Can.	
63 B2	**Đưc Trong** Vietnam	
101 E2	**Duderstadt** Ger.	
82 G2	**Dudinka** Rus. Fed.	
99 B2	**Dudley** U.K.	
106 B1	**Duero** *r.* Spain	
96 C2	**Dufftown** U.K.	
131 C1	**Dufreboy, Lac** *l.* Can.	
109 C2	**Dugi Rat** Croatia	
100 C2	**Duisburg** Ger.	
123 D1	**Duiwelskloof** S. Africa	
123 C3	**Dukathole** S. Africa	
79 C2	**Dukhān** Qatar	
89 D2	**Dukhovshchina** Rus. Fed.	
	Dukou China *see* Panzhihua	
88 C2	**Dūkštas** Lith.	
68 C2	**Dulan** China	
152 B4	**Dulce** *r.* Arg.	
100 C2	**Dülmen** Ger.	
110 C2	**Dulovo** Bulg.	
137 E1	**Duluth** U.S.A.	
64 B2	**Dumaguete** Phil.	
60 B1	**Dumai** Indon.	
64 B1	**Dumaran** *i.* Phil.	
142 B2	**Dumas** *AR* U.S.A.	
139 C1	**Dumas** *TX* U.S.A.	
96 B3	**Dumbarton** U.K.	
103 D2	**Ďumbier** *mt.* Slovakia	
96 C3	**Dumfries** U.K.	
55 J3	**Dumont d'Urville Sea**	
	Antarctica	
116 B1	**Dumyât** Egypt	
	Duna *r.* Hungary *see* Danube	
	Dunaj *r.* Slovakia *see* Danube	
103 D2	**Dunakeszi** Hungary	
	Dunărea *r.* Romania *see*	
	Danube	
110 C1	**Dunării, Delta** Romania	
103 D2	**Dunaújváros** Hungary	
	Dunav *r.* Yugo. *see* Danube	
90 B2	**Dunayivtsi** Ukr.	
96 C2	**Dunbar** U.K.	
96 C1	**Dunbeath** U.K.	
128 B3	**Duncan** Can.	
139 D2	**Duncan** U.S.A.	
96 C1	**Duncansby Head** U.K.	
97 C1	**Dundalk** Rep. of Ireland	
97 C2	**Dundalk Bay** Rep. of Ireland	
	Dundas Greenland *see*	
	Uummannaq	
123 D2	**Dundee** S. Africa	
96 C2	**Dundee** U.K.	
97 D1	**Dundrum Bay** U.K.	
54 B3	**Dunedin** N.Z.	
96 C2	**Dunfermline** U.K.	
97 C1	**Dungannon** U.K.	
74 B2	**Dungarpur** India	
97 C2	**Dungarvan** Rep. of Ireland	
99 D3	**Dungeness** *hd* U.K.	
97 C1	**Dungiven** U.K.	
53 D2	**Dungog** Austr.	
119 C2	**Dungu** Dem. Rep. Congo	
60 B1	**Dungun** Malaysia	
116 B2	**Dunqunab** Sudan	
69 E2	**Dunhua** China	
68 C2	**Dunhuang** China	
	Dunkerque France *see*	
	Dunkirk	
104 C1	**Dunkirk** France	
141 D2	**Dunkirk** U.S.A.	
97 C2	**Dún Laoghaire**	
	Rep. of Ireland	
97 D1	**Dunmurry** U.K.	
96 C1	**Dunnet Head** *hd* U.K.	
96 C3	**Duns** U.K.	
99 C3	**Dunstable** U.K.	
110 B2	**Dupnitsa** Bulg.	
136 C1	**Dupree** U.S.A.	
50 B1	**Durack** *r.* Austr.	
144 B2	**Durango** Mex.	
106 C1	**Durango** Spain	
136 B3	**Durango** U.S.A.	
139 D2	**Durant** U.S.A.	
153 C4	**Durazno** Uru.	
123 D2	**Durban** S. Africa	
104 C3	**Durban-Corbières** France	
122 A3	**Durbanville** S. Africa	
100 B2	**Durbuy** Belgium	
100 C2	**Düren** Ger.	
98 C1	**Durham** U.K.	
143 E1	**Durham** U.S.A.	
60 B1	**Duri** Indon.	
109 C2	**Durmitor** *mt.* Yugo.	
96 B1	**Durness** U.K.	
109 C2	**Durrës** Albania	
97 A3	**Dursey Island**	
	Rep. of Ireland	
111 C3	**Dursunbey** Turkey	
59 D3	**D'Urville, Tanjung** *pt* Indon.	
54 B2	**D'Urville Island** N.Z.	
71 A3	**Dushan** China	
77 C3	**Dushanbe** Tajik.	
100 C2	**Düsseldorf** Ger.	
71 A3	**Duyun** China	
91 D2	**Dvorichna** Ukr.	
74 A2	**Dwarka** India	
123 C1	**Dwarsberg** S. Africa	
134 C1	**Dworshak Reservoir** U.S.A.	
89 D3	**Dyat'kovo** Rus. Fed.	
96 C2	**Dyce** U.K.	
127 G2	**Dyer, Cape** Can.	
142 C1	**Dyersburg** U.S.A.	
103 D2	**Dyje** *r.* Austria/Czech Rep.	
103 D1	**Dylewska Góra** *hill* Pol.	
91 D2	**Dymytrov** Ukr.	
123 C3	**Dyoki** S. Africa	
87 E3	**Dyurtyuli** Rus. Fed.	
69 D2	**Dzamïn Üüd** Mongolia	
	Dzhambul Kazakh. *see* Taraz	
81 D1	**Dzhanga** Turkm.	
76 B2	**Dzhangala** Kazakh.	
91 C2	**Dzhankoy** Ukr.	
87 D4	**Dzharkurgan** Uzbek.	
77 C2	**Dzhizak** Uzbek.	
91 D3	**Dzhubga** Rus. Fed.	
83 K3	**Dzhugdzhur, Khrebet** *mts*	
	Rus. Fed.	
77 D2	**Dzhungarskiy Alatau,**	
	Khrebet *mts* China/Kazakh.	
76 C2	**Dzhusaly** Kazakh.	
103 E1	**Działdowo** Pol.	
69 D1	**Dzuunmod** Mongolia	
88 C3	**Dzyarzhynsk** Belarus	
88 C3	**Dzyatlavichy** Belarus	

E

131 E1	**Eagle** *r.* Can.	
134 C1	**Eagle Cap** *mt.* U.S.A.	
130 A2	**Eagle Lake** *l.* Can.	
134 B2	**Eagle Lake** *l.* U.S.A.	
139 C3	**Eagle Pass** U.S.A.	
126 B2	**Eagle Plain** Can.	
130 A1	**Ear Falls** Can.	
99 D3	**Eastbourne** U.K.	
156 C5	**East China Sea**	
	N. Pacific Ocean	
54 B1	**East Coast Bays** N.Z.	
99 D2	**East Dereham** U.K.	
129 D3	**Eastend** Can.	
148 B4	**Easter Island** *i.*	
	S. Pacific Ocean	
123 C3	**Eastern Cape** *prov.* S. Africa	
116 B2	**Eastern Desert** Egypt	
73 B3	**Eastern Ghats** *mts* India	
129 E2	**Easterville** Can.	
153 C6	**East Falkland** *i.* Falkland Is	
100 C1	**East Frisian Islands** *is* U.K.	
96 B3	**East Kilbride** U.K.	
99 C3	**Eastleigh** U.K.	
140 C2	**East Liverpool** U.S.A.	
123 C3	**East London** S. Africa	
130 C1	**Eastmain** Can.	
130 C1	**Eastmain** *r.* Can.	
143 D2	**Eastman** U.S.A.	
140 A3	**East St Louis** U.S.A.	
	East Siberian Sea	
	Rus. Fed. *see*	
	Vostochno-Sibirskoye More	
59 C3	**East Timor** *terr.* Asia	
140 A2	**Eau Claire** U.S.A.	
59 D2	**Eauripik** *atoll* Micronesia	
145 C2	**Ebano** Mex.	
99 B3	**Ebbw Vale** U.K.	
102 C1	**Eberswalde-Finow** Ger.	
109 C2	**Eboli** Italy	
118 B2	**Ebolowa** Cameroon	
107 D1	**Ebro** *r.* Spain	
107 C1	**Echarri-Aranaz** Spain	
114 C1	**Ech Chélif** Alg.	

144 A2 Echeverria, Pico *mt.* Mex.
129 E2 Echoing *r.* Can.
100 C3 Echternach Lux.
52 B2 Echuca Austr.
106 B2 Écija Spain
102 B1 Eckernförde Ger.
127 F2 Eclipse Sound *sea chan.* Can.
150 A2 Ecuador *country* S. America
116 C3 Ed Eritrea
117 A3 Ed Da'ein Sudan
117 B3 Ed Damazin Sudan
116 B3 Ed Damer Sudan
116 B3 Ed Debba Sudan
116 B3 Ed Dueim Sudan
51 D4 Eddystone Point Austr.
100 B1 Ede Neth.
118 B2 Edéa Cameroon
154 C1 Edéia Brazil
53 C3 Eden Austr.
98 B1 Eden *r.* U.K.
123 C2 Edenburg S. Africa
97 C2 Edenderry Rep. of Ireland
52 B2 Edenhope Austr.
111 B2 Edessa Greece
82 C1 Edgeøya *i.* Svalbard
139 D3 Edinburg U.S.A.
96 C3 Edinburgh U.K.
110 C2 Edirne Turkey
128 C2 Edmonton Can.
131 D2 Edmundston Can.
111 C3 Edremit Turkey
111 C3 Edremit Körfezi *b.* Turkey
128 C2 Edson Can.
119 C3 Edward, Lake
Dem. Rep. Congo/Uganda
139 C2 Edwards Plateau *TX* U.S.A.
100 C1 Eenrum Neth.
140 B3 Effingham U.S.A.
135 C3 Eğan Range *mts* U.S.A.
103 E2 Eger Hungary
93 E4 Egersund Norway
92 □C2 Egilsstaðir Iceland
80 B2 Eğirdir Turkey
80 B2 Eğirdir Gölü *l.* Turkey
104 C2 Égletons France
54 B1 Egmont, Mt *vol.* N.Z.
83 M2 Egvekinot Rus. Fed.
116 B2 Egypt *country* Africa
68 C2 Ehen Hudag China
100 C1 Eibergen Neth.
100 C2 Eifel *hills* Ger.
96 A2 Eigg *i.* U.K.
73 B4 Eight Degree Channel
India/Maldives
50 B1 Eighty Mile Beach Austr.
101 F2 Eilenburg Ger.
101 D2 Einbeck Ger.
100 B2 Eindhoven Neth.
153 F5 Eirunepé Brazil
120 B2 Eiseb *watercourse* Namibia
101 E2 Eisenach Ger.
102 C1 Eisenhüttenstadt Ger.
103 D2 Eisenstadt Austria
101 E2 Eisleben Lutherstadt Ger.
107 D2 Eivissa Spain
Eivissa *i.* Spain *see* Ibiza
107 C1 Ejea de los Caballeros
Spain
121 □D3 Ejeda Madag.
Ejin Qi China *see* Dalain Hob
93 H4 Ekenäs Fin.
77 D1 Ekibastuz Kazakh.
92 J2 Ekostrovskaya Imandra,
Ozero *l.* Rus. Fed.
93 F4 Eksjö Sweden
122 A2 Eksteenfontein S. Africa
130 B1 Ekwan *r.* Can.
62 A2 Ela Myanmar
80 A2 El 'Amiriya Egypt

123 C2 Elandsdoorn S. Africa
80 B2 El 'Arish Egypt
111 B3 Elassona Greece
80 B3 Elat Israel
80 B2 Elazığ Turkey
108 B2 Elba, Isola d' *i.* Italy
150 A1 El Banco Col.
109 D2 Elbasan Albania
150 B1 El Baúl Venez.
114 C1 El Bayadh Alg.
101 D1 Elbe *r.* Ger.
136 B3 Elbert, Mount U.S.A.
143 D2 Elberton U.S.A.
104 C2 Elbeuf France
80 B2 Elbistan Turkey
103 D1 Elbląg Pol.
87 D4 Elbrus *mt.* Rus. Fed.
Elburz Mountains Iran *see*
Alborz, Reshteh-ye
150 B1 El Callao Venez.
139 D3 El Campo U.S.A.
135 C4 El Centro U.S.A.
152 B2 El Cerro Bol.
107 C2 Elche Spain
107 C2 Elda Spain
137 E3 Eldon U.S.A.
144 B2 El Dorado Mex.
142 B2 El Dorado *AR* U.S.A.
137 D3 El Dorado *KS* U.S.A.
114 B2 El Eglab *plat.* Alg.
106 C2 El Ejido Spain
89 E2 Elektrostal' Rus. Fed.
150 A2 El Encanto Col.
146 C2 Eleuthera *i.* Bahamas
117 A3 El Fasher Sudan
144 B2 El Fuerte Mex.
117 A3 El Geneina Sudan
116 B3 El Geteina Sudan
96 C2 Elgin U.K.
140 B2 Elgin U.S.A.
80 B2 El Giza Egypt
115 C1 El Goléa Alg.
144 A1 El Golfo de Santa Clara
Mex.
119 D2 Elgon, Mount Uganda
80 A2 El Hammâm Egypt
114 A2 El Hammâmi *reg.* Maur.
114 A2 El Hierro *i.* Canary Is
145 C2 El Higo Mex.
114 C2 El Homr Alg.
El Iskandarîya Egypt *see*
Alexandria
87 D4 Elista Rus. Fed.
141 E2 Elizabeth U.S.A.
143 E1 Elizabeth City U.S.A.
140 B3 Elizabethtown U.S.A.
114 B1 El Jadida Morocco
103 E1 Ełk Pol.
139 D1 Elk City U.S.A.
128 C2 Elkford Can.
116 B2 El Khârga Egypt
140 B2 Elkhart U.S.A.
El Khartûm Sudan *see*
Khartoum
110 C2 Elkhovo Bulg.
140 D3 Elkins U.S.A.
128 C3 Elko Can.
134 C2 Elko U.S.A.
126 E1 Ellef Ringnes Island Can.
137 D1 Ellendale U.S.A.
134 B1 Ellensburg U.S.A.
54 B2 Ellesmere, Lake N.Z.
127 F1 Ellesmere Island Can.
98 B2 Ellesmere Port U.K.
126 E2 Ellice *r.* Can.
Ellice Islands *country*
S. Pacific Ocean *see* Tuvalu
123 C3 Elliotdale S. Africa
123 C1 Ellisras S. Africa

96 C2 Ellon U.K.
141 F2 Ellsworth U.S.A.
55 C2 Ellsworth Mountains
Antarctica
111 C3 Elmalı Turkey
80 B2 El Mansûra Egypt
115 C1 El Meghaïer Alg.
116 B2 ·El Minya Egypt
141 D2 Elmira U.S.A.
107 C2 El Moral Spain
101 D1 Elmshorn Ger.
117 A3 El Muglad Sudan
64 A1 El Nido Phil.
117 B3 El Obeid Sudan
144 B2 El Oro Mex.
115 C1 El Oued Alg.
138 A2 Eloy U.S.A.
138 B2 El Paso U.S.A.
144 B1 El Porvenir Mex.
107 D1 El Prat de Llobregat
Spain
El Qâhira Egypt *see* Cairo
139 D1 El Reno U.S.A.
145 B2 El Salado Mex.
144 B2 El Salto Mex.
146 B3 El Salvador *country*
Central America
145 B2 El Salvador Mex.
138 B3 El Sauz Mex.
144 A1 El Socorro Mex.
El Suweis Egypt *see* Suez
145 C2 El Temascal Mex.
150 B1 El Tigre Venez.
147 D4 El Tocuyo Venez.
116 B2 El Tûr Egypt
El Uqsur Egypt *see* Luxor
88 C2 Elva Estonia
106 B2 Elvas Port.
93 F3 Elverum Norway
119 E2 El Wak Kenya
99 D2 Ely U.K.
137 E1 Ely *MN* U.S.A.
135 D3 Ely *NV* U.S.A.
81 D2 Emāmrūd Iran
93 G4 Emån *r.* Sweden
76 B2 Emba Kazakh.
76 B2 Emba *r.* Kazakh.
123 C2 Embalenhle S. Africa
154 C1 Emboração, Represa de
resr Brazil
119 D3 Embu Kenya
100 C1 Emden Ger.
51 D2 Emerald Austr.
129 E3 Emerson Can.
111 C3 Emet Turkey
123 D2 eMgwenya S. Africa
123 D2 eMijindini S. Africa
115 D3 Emi Koussi *mt.* Chad
110 C2 Emine, Nos *pt* Bulg.
80 B2 Emirdağ Turkey
88 B2 Emmaste Estonia
100 B1 Emmeloord Neth.
100 C2 Emmelshausen Ger.
100 C1 Emmen Neth.
139 C3 Emory Peak U.S.A.
144 A2 Empalme Mex.
123 D2 Empangeni S. Africa
108 B2 Empoli Italy
137 D3 Emporia *KS* U.S.A.
141 D3 Emporia *VA* U.S.A.
100 C1 Ems *r.* Ger.
100 C1 Emsdetten Ger.
123 C2 Emzinoni S. Africa
59 D3 Enarotali Indon.
144 B2 Encarnación Mex.
152 C3 Encarnación Para.
155 D1 Encruzilhada Brazil
60 B1 Endau Malaysia
58 C3 Endeh Indon.
126 A2 Endicott Mountains U.S.A.

Enerhodar

91 C2 Enerhodar Ukr.
87 D3 Engel's Rus. Fed.
60 B2 Enggano i. Indon.
98 C2 England admin. div. U.K.
130 A1 English r. Can.
95 C4 English Channel
France/U.K.
139 D2 Enid U.S.A.
100 B1 Enkhuizen Neth.
93 G4 Enköping Sweden
108 B3 Enna Sicily Italy
129 C1 Ennadai Lake Can.
117 A3 En Nahud Sudan
115 E3 Ennedi, Massif mts Chad
53 C1 Enngonia Austr.
97 B2 Ennis Rep. of Ireland
139 D2 Ennis U.S.A.
97 C2 Enniscorthy Rep. of Ireland
97 C1 Enniskillen U.K.
97 B2 Ennistymon Rep. of Ireland
102 C2 Enns r. Austria
92 H2 Enontekiö Fin.
59 C3 Ensay Austr.
100 C1 Enschede Neth.
144 A1 Ensenada Mex.
70 A2 Enshi China
128 C1 Enterprise Can.
142 C2 Enterprise AL U.S.A.
134 C1 Enterprise OR U.S.A.
152 B3 Entre Rios Bol.
106 B2 Entroncamento Port.
115 C4 Enugu Nigeria
150 A2 Envira Brazil
135 D3 Ephraim U.S.A.
134 C1 Ephrata U.S.A.
105 D2 Épinal France
99 C3 Epsom U.K.
118 A2 Equatorial Guinea country
Africa
101 F3 Erbendorf Ger.
100 C3 Erbeskopf hill Ger.
81 C2 Erciş Turkey
65 B1 Erdao Jiang r. China
111 C2 Erdek Turkey
80 B2 Erdemli Turkey
152 C3 Erechim Brazil
69 D1 Ereentsav Mongolia
80 B2 Ereğli Konya Turkey
80 B1 Ereğli Zonguldak Turkey
69 D2 Erenhot China
Erevan Armenia see Yerevan
101 E2 Erfurt Ger.
80 B2 Ergani Turkey
114 B2 'Erg Chech des. Alg./Mali
115 D3 Erg du Ténéré des. Niger
111 C2 Ergene r. Turkey
140 C2 Erie U.S.A.
140 C2 Erie, Lake Can./U.S.A.
66 D2 Erimo-misaki c. Japan
116 B3 Eritrea country Africa
101 E3 Erlangen Ger.
50 C2 Erldunda Austr.
123 C2 Ermelo S. Africa
80 B2 Ermenek Turkey
111 B3 Ermoupoli Greece
73 B4 Ernakulam India
73 B3 Erode India
100 B2 Erp Neth.
114 B1 Er Rachidia Morocco
117 B3 Er Rahad Sudan
97 B1 Errigal hill Rep. of Ireland
97 A1 Erris Head hd Rep. of Ireland
109 D2 Ersekë Albania
91 E1 Ertil' Rus. Fed.
101 F2 Erzgebirge mts
Czech Rep./Ger.
80 B2 Erzincan Turkey
81 C2 Erzurum Turkey
93 E4 Esbjerg Denmark

135 D3 Escalante U.S.A.
144 B2 Escalón Mex.
140 B1 Escanaba U.S.A.
145 C3 Escárcega Mex.
107 C1 Escatrón Spain
100 A2 Escaut r. Belgium
101 E1 Eschede Ger.
100 B3 Esch-sur-Alzette Lux.
101 E2 Eschwege Ger.
100 C2 Eschweiler Ger.
135 C4 Escondido U.S.A.
144 B2 Escuinapa Mex.
145 C3 Escuintla Mex.
111 C3 Eşen Turkey
81 D2 Eşfahān Iran
123 D2 Esikhawini S. Africa
81 D1 Esk r. U.K.
131 D1 Esker Can.
92 □C2 Eskifjörður Iceland
93 G4 Eskilstuna Sweden
Eskimo Point Can. see
Arviat
80 B2 Eskişehir Turkey
81 C2 Eslāmābād-e Gharb Iran
111 C3 Esler Dağı mt. Turkey
111 C3 Eşme Turkey
150 A1 Esmeraldas Ecuador
79 D2 Espakeh Iran
104 C3 Espalion France
130 B2 Espanola Can.
138 B1 Espanola U.S.A.
50 B3 Esperance Austr.
144 B2 Esperanza Mex.
106 B2 Espichel, Cabo c. Port.
155 D1 Espinhaço, Serra do mts
Brazil
151 D3 Espinosa Brazil
144 A2 Espíritu Santo, Isla i. Mex.
49 H3 Espoo Fin.
153 A5 Esquel Arg.
114 B1 Essaouira Morocco
114 A2 Es Semara Western Sahara
100 C2 Essen Ger.
150 C1 Essequibo r. Guyana
83 L3 Esso Rus. Fed.
79 C2 Eştahbān Iran
151 E3 Estância Brazil
123 C2 Estcourt S. Africa
107 C1 Estella Spain
106 B2 Estepona Spain
106 C1 Esteras de Medinaceli
Spain
129 D2 Esterhazy Can.
152 B3 Esteros Para.
136 B2 Estes Park U.S.A.
129 D3 Estevan Can.
137 E2 Estherville U.S.A.
129 D2 Eston Can.
88 C2 Estonia country Europe
106 B1 Estrela, Serra da mts Port.
106 B2 Estremoz Port.
52 A1 Etadunna Austr.
104 C2 Étampes France
104 C1 Étaples France
75 B2 Etawah India
123 D2 eThandakukhanya S. Africa
117 B4 Ethiopia country Africa
109 C3 Etna, Monte vol. Sicily Italy
128 A2 Etolin Island i. U.S.A.
120 A2 Etosha Pan salt pan Namibia
100 C3 Ettelbruck Lux.
100 B2 Etten-Leur Neth.
99 D3 Eu France
53 C2 Euabalong Austr.
Euboea i. Greece see Evvoia
50 B3 Eucla Austr.
143 C2 Eufaula U.S.A.
139 D1 Eufaula Lake resr U.S.A.
134 B2 Eugene U.S.A.
144 A2 Eugenia, Punta pt Mex.
53 C1 Eulo Austr.

53 C2 Eumungerie Austr.
139 C2 Eunice U.S.A.
80 C2 Euphrates r. Asia
134 B2 Eureka CA U.S.A.
134 C1 Eureka MT U.S.A.
135 C3 Eureka NV U.S.A.
52 B2 Euriowie Austr.
53 C3 Euroa Austr.
106 B2 Europa Point Gibraltar
128 B2 Eutsuk Lake Can.
130 C1 Evans, Lac l. Can.
53 D1 Evans Head Austr.
127 F2 Evans Strait Can.
136 A2 Evanston U.S.A.
140 B3 Evansville U.S.A.
123 C2 Evaton S. Africa
79 C2 Evaz Iran
83 L2 Evensk Rus. Fed.
50 C2 Everard Range hills Austr.
75 C2 Everest, Mount China/Nepal
134 B1 Everett U.S.A.
100 A2 Evergem Belgium
143 D3 Everglades swamp U.S.A.
118 A2 Evinayong Equat. Guinea
93 E4 Evje Norway
106 B2 Évora Port.
104 C2 Évreux France
111 C2 Evros r. Greece/Turkey
111 B3 Evrotas r. Greece
80 B2 Evrychou Cyprus
111 B3 Evvoia i. Greece
119 E2 Ewaso Ngiro r. Kenya
152 B2 Exaltación Bol.
99 B3 Exe r. U.K.
99 B3 Exeter U.K.
99 B3 Exmoor hills U.K.
99 B3 Exmouth U.K.
50 A2 Exmouth Gulf Austr.
146 C2 Exuma Cays is Bahamas
91 D2 Eya r. Rus. Fed.
117 C4 Eyl Somalia
52 A1 Eyre, Lake salt flat Austr.
51 C3 Eyre Peninsula Austr.
94 B1 Eysturoy i. Faroe Is
123 D2 Ezakheni S. Africa
123 C2 Ezenzeleni S. Africa
70 B2 Ezhou China
86 E2 Ezhva Rus. Fed.
111 C3 Ezine Turkey

F

138 B2 Fabens U.S.A.
108 B2 Fabriano Italy
115 D3 Fachi Niger
114 B3 Fada-Ngourma Burkina
108 B2 Faenza Italy
59 C3 Fafanlap Indon.
110 B1 Făgăraş Romania
93 E3 Fagernes Norway
93 G4 Fagersta Sweden
153 B6 Fagnano, Lago l. Arg./Chile
114 B3 Faguibine, Lac l. Mali
92 □B3 Fagurhólsmýri Iceland
126 B2 Fairbanks U.S.A.
137 D2 Fairbury U.S.A.
135 B3 Fairfield U.S.A.
96 □ Fair Isle i. U.K.
137 E2 Fairmont MN U.S.A.
140 C3 Fairmont WV U.S.A.
128 C2 Fairview Can.
59 D2 Fais i. Micronesia
74 B1 Faisalabad Pak.
136 C1 Faith U.S.A.
75 C2 Faizabad India
59 C3 Fakfak Indon.
65 A1 Faku China

114 A4 Falaba Sierra Leone
139 D3 Falcon Lake l. Mex./U.S.A.
139 D3 Falfurrias U.S.A.
128 C2 Falher Can.
101 F2 Falkenberg Ger.
93 F4 Falkenberg Sweden
101 F1 Falkensee Ger.
96 C5 Falkirk U.K.
153 C6 Falkland Islands terr. S. Atlantic Ocean
93 F4 Falköping Sweden
135 C3 Fallon U.S.A.
141 E2 Fall River U.S.A.
137 D2 Falls City U.S.A.
99 A3 Falmouth U.K.
122 A3 False Bay S. Africa
93 F4 Falster i. Denmark
110 C1 Fălticeni Romania
93 G3 Falun Sweden
71 A3 Fangchenggang China
71 C3 Fangshan Taiwan
69 E1 Fangzheng China
108 B2 Fano Italy
62 B1 Fan Si Pan mt. Vietnam
119 C2 Faradje Dem. Rep. Congo
121 □D3 Farafangana Madag.
116 A2 Farafra Oasis Egypt
76 C3 Farāh Afgh.
114 A3 Faranah Guinea
78 B3 Farasān, Jazā'ir is Saudi Arabia
54 B2 Farewell, Cape N.Z.
137 D1 Fargo U.S.A.
137 E2 Faribault U.S.A.
141 E2 Farmington ME U.S.A.
138 B1 Farmington NM U.S.A.
141 D3 Farmville U.S.A.
99 C3 Farnborough U.K.
128 C2 Farnham, Mount Can.
128 A1 Faro Can.
106 B2 Faro Port.
88 A2 Fårö i. Sweden
94 B1 Faroe Islands terr. N. Atlantic Ocean
79 C2 Farrāshband Iran
Farvel, Kap c. Greenland see Nunap Isua
139 C2 Farwell U.S.A.
79 C2 Fāryāb Iran
79 C2 Fasā Iran
109 C2 Fasano Italy
90 B1 Fastiv Ukr.
75 B2 Fatehgarh India
75 C2 Fatehpur India
92 G2 Fauske Norway
92 □A3 Faxaflói b. Iceland
92 G3 Faxälven r. Sweden
115 D3 Faya Chad
142 B1 Fayetteville AR U.S.A.
143 E1 Fayetteville NC U.S.A.
142 C1 Fayetteville TN U.S.A.
74 B1 Fazilka India
114 A2 Fdérik Maur.
143 E2 Fear, Cape U.S.A.
54 C2 Featherston N.Z.
104 C2 Fécamp France
48 D2 Federated States of Micronesia country N. Pacific Ocean
102 C1 Fehmarn i. Ger.
101 F1 Fehrbellin Ger.
155 D2 Feia, Lagoa lag. Brazil
150 A2 Feijó Brazil
54 C2 Feilding N.Z.
151 E3 Feira de Santana Brazil
107 D2 Felanitx Spain
145 D3 Felipe C. Puerto Mex.
155 D1 Felixlândia Brazil
99 D3 Felixstowe U.K.
101 D2 Felsberg Ger.

108 B1 Feltre Italy
93 F3 Femunden l. Norway
71 B3 Fengcheng Jiangxi China
65 A1 Fengcheng Liaoning China
62 A1 Fengqing China
70 B2 Fengxian China
Fengxiang China see Lincang
71 C3 Fengyüan Taiwan
70 B1 Fengzhen China
105 D3 Feno, Capo di c. Corsica France
121 □D2 Fenoarivo Atsinanana Madag.
91 D2 Feodosiya Ukr.
108 A3 Fer, Cap de c. Alg.
77 C2 Fergana Uzbek.
137 D1 Fergus Falls U.S.A.
114 B4 Ferkessédougou Côte d'Ivoire
108 B2 Fermo Italy
131 D1 Fermont Can.
106 B1 Fermoselle Spain
97 B2 Fermoy Rep. of Ireland
143 D2 Fernandina Beach U.S.A.
154 B2 Fernandópolis Brazil
128 C3 Fernie Can.
108 B2 Ferrara Italy
154 B2 Ferreiros Brazil
108 A2 Ferro, Capo c. Sardinia Italy
106 B1 Ferrol Spain
100 B1 Ferwerd Neth.
114 B1 Fès Morocco
118 B3 Feshi Dem. Rep. Congo
137 E3 Festus U.S.A.
111 C3 Fethiye Turkey
96 □ Fetlar i. U.K.
130 C1 Feuilles, Rivière aux r. Can.
77 D3 Feyzābād Afgh.
Fez Morocco see Fès
121 □D3 Fianarantsoa Madag.
117 B4 Fichē Eth.
109 C2 Fier Albania
96 C2 Fife Ness pt U.K.
104 C3 Figeac France
106 B1 Figueira da Foz Port.
107 D1 Figueres Spain
114 B1 Figuig Morocco
49 F4 Fiji country S. Pacific Ocean
152 B3 Filadélfia Para.
55 O2 Filchner Ice Shelf Antarctica
98 C1 Filey U.K.
111 B3 Filippiada Greece
93 F4 Filipstad Sweden
96 C2 Findhorn r. U.K.
140 C2 Findlay U.S.A.
51 D4 Fingal Austr.
141 D2 Finger Lakes U.S.A.
92 I3 Finland country Europe
93 H4 Finland, Gulf of Europe
128 B2 Finlay r. Can.
53 C3 Finley Austr.
101 E2 Finne ridge Ger.
92 H2 Finnmarksvidda reg. Norway
92 G2 Finnsnes Norway
96 A2 Fionnphort U.K.
Firat r. Turkey see Euphrates
Firenze Italy see Florence
105 C2 Firminy France
75 B2 Firozabad India
74 B1 Firozpur India
79 C2 Fīrūzābād Iran
122 A2 Fish watercourse Namibia
122 B3 Fish r. S. Africa
99 A3 Fishguard U.K.
104 B2 Fismes France
106 B1 Fisterra, Cabo c. Spain
141 E2 Fitchburg U.S.A.
129 C2 Fitzgerald Can.

50 B1 Fitzroy Crossing Austr.
108 B2 Fivizzano Italy
119 C3 Fizi Dem. Rep. Congo
92 G3 Fjällsjälven r. Sweden
123 C3 Flagstaff S. Africa
138 A1 Flagstaff U.S.A.
130 C1 Flaherty Island Can.
98 C1 Flamborough Head hd U.K.
101 F1 Fläming hills Ger.
136 B2 Flaming Gorge Reservoir U.S.A.
134 D1 Flathead r. U.S.A.
134 D1 Flathead Lake U.S.A.
51 D1 Flattery, Cape Austr.
134 B1 Flattery, Cape U.S.A.
98 B2 Fleetwood U.K.
93 E4 Flekkefjord Norway
102 B1 Flensburg Ger.
104 B2 Flers France
51 D1 Flinders r. Austr.
50 A3 Flinders Bay Austr.
51 D3 Flinders Island Austr.
52 A2 Flinders Ranges mts Austr.
129 D2 Flin Flon Can.
140 C3 Flint U.S.A.
107 D1 Flix Spain
108 B2 Florac France
142 C2 Florence AL U.S.A.
138 A2 Florence AZ U.S.A.
134 B2 Florence OR U.S.A.
143 E2 Florence SC U.S.A.
150 A1 Florencia Col.
146 B3 Flores Guat.
58 C3 Flores i. Indon.
58 B3 Flores Sea Indon.
151 E2 Floresta Brazil
139 D3 Floresville U.S.A.
151 D2 Floriano Brazil
152 D3 Florianópolis Brazil
153 C4 Florida Uru.
143 D3 Florida state U.S.A.
143 D4 Florida, Straits of Bahamas/U.S.A.
111 B2 Florina Greece
93 E3 Florø Norway
129 D2 Foam Lake Can.
109 C2 Foča Bos.-Herz.
110 C1 Focșani Romania
71 B3 Fogang China
109 C2 Foggia Italy
131 E2 Fogo Island Can.
104 C3 Foix France
89 E3 Fokino Rus. Fed.
130 B2 Foleyet Can.
108 B2 Foligno Italy
99 D3 Folkestone U.K.
143 D2 Folkston U.S.A.
108 B2 Follonica Italy
129 C2 Fond-du-Lac Can.
129 D2 Fond du Lac r. Can.
140 B2 Fond du Lac U.S.A.
106 B1 Fondevila Spain
108 B2 Fondi Italy
146 B3 Fonseca, Golfo de b. Central America
150 B2 Fonte Boa Brazil
104 B2 Fontenay-le-Comte France
92 □C2 Fontur pt Iceland
53 C2 Forbes Austr.
101 E3 Forchheim Ger.
93 E3 Førde Norway
53 C1 Forbes Bridge Austr.
142 D2 Fordyce U.S.A.
142 C2 Forest U.S.A.
53 C3 Forest Hill Austr.
131 D2 Forestville Can.
96 C2 Forfar U.K.
134 B1 Forks U.S.A.
108 B2 Forlì Italy

Formentera

188

107 D2 Formentera i. Spain
107 D2 Formentor, Cap de c. Spain
155 C2 Formiga Brazil
152 C3 Formosa Arg.
Formosa country Asia see
Taiwan
154 C1 Formosa Brazil
96 C2 Forres U.K.
50 B3 Forrest Austr.
142 B1 Forrest City U.S.A.
51 D1 Forsayth Austr.
93 H3 Forssa Fin.
53 D2 Forster Austr.
136 B1 Forsyth U.S.A.
74 B2 Fort Abbas Pak.
130 B1 Fort Albany Can.
151 E2 Fortaleza Brazil
128 C2 Fort Assiniboine Can.
96 B2 Fort Augustus U.K.
134 D1 Fort Benton U.S.A.
135 B3 Fort Bragg U.S.A.
Fort Chimo Can. see Kuujjuaq
129 C2 Fort Chipewyan Can.
136 B2 Fort Collins U.S.A.
147 D3 Fort-de-France Martinique
137 E2 Fort Dodge U.S.A.
130 A2 Fort Frances Can.
Fort Franklin Can. see Déline
130 C1 Fort George Can.
126 C2 Fort Good Hope Can.
96 C2 Forth r. U.K.
96 C2 Forth, Firth of est. U.K.
152 C3 Fortín Madrejón Para.
143 D3 Fort Lauderdale U.S.A.
128 B1 Fort Liard Can.
128 C1 Fort Mackay Can.
129 C2 Fort McMurray Can.
126 C2 Fort McPherson Can.
136 C2 Fort Morgan U.S.A.
143 D3 Fort Myers U.S.A.
128 B2 Fort Nelson Can.
128 B2 Fort Nelson r. Can.
142 C2 Fort Payne U.S.A.
136 B1 Fort Peck U.S.A.
136 B1 Fort Peck Reservoir U.S.A.
143 D3 Fort Pierce U.S.A.
128 C1 Fort Providence Can.
129 D2 Fort Qu'Appelle Can.
128 C1 Fort Resolution Can.
130 C1 Fort Rupert Can.
128 B2 Fort St James Can.
128 B2 Fort St John Can.
128 C2 Fort Saskatchewan Can.
137 E3 Fort Scott U.S.A.
130 B1 Fort Severn Can.
76 B2 Fort-Shevchenko Kazakh.
128 B1 Fort Simpson Can.
129 C1 Fort Smith Can.
142 B1 Fort Smith U.S.A.
139 C2 Fort Stockton U.S.A.
138 C2 Fort Sumner U.S.A.
128 C2 Fort Vermilion Can.
142 C2 Fort Walton Beach U.S.A.
140 B2 Fort Wayne U.S.A.
96 B2 Fort William U.K.
139 D2 Fort Worth U.S.A.
126 B2 Fort Yukon U.S.A.
71 B3 Foshan China
92 F3 Fosna pen. Norway
93 E3 Fosnavåg Norway
92 □B3 Foss Iceland
92 □A2 Fossá Iceland
108 A2 Fossano Italy
53 C3 Foster Austr.
104 B2 Fougères France
96 □ Foula i. U.K.
111 C3 Fournoi i. Greece
114 A3 Fouta Djalon reg. Guinea
54 A3 Foveaux Strait N.Z.
136 C3 Fowler U.S.A.

50 C3 Fowlers Bay Austr.
128 C2 Fox Creek Can.
127 F2 Foxe Basin g. Can.
127 F2 Foxe Channel Can.
127 F2 Foxe Peninsula Can.
54 B2 Fox Glacier N.Z.
128 C2 Fox Lake Can.
128 A1 Fox Mountain Can.
54 C2 Foxton N.Z.
129 D2 Fox Valley Can.
97 C1 Foyle, Lough b.
Rep. of Ireland/U.K.
154 B3 Foz de Areia, Represa de
resr Brazil
120 A2 Foz do Cunene Angola
154 B3 Foz do Iguaçu Brazil
107 D1 Fraga Spain
154 C2 Franca Brazil
109 C2 Francavilla Fontana Italy
142 C2 France country Europe
118 B3 Franceville Gabon
137 D2 Francis Case, Lake U.S.A.
155 D1 Francisco Sá Brazil
120 B3 Francistown Botswana
128 B2 François Lake Can.
101 D2 Frankenberg (Eder) Ger.
101 D3 Frankenthal (Pfalz) Ger.
101 E2 Frankenwald mts Ger.
140 C3 Frankfort U.S.A.
101 D2 Frankfurt am Main Ger.
102 C1 Frankfurt an der Oder Ger.
101 E3 Fränkische Schweiz
reg. Ger.
141 D2 Franklin U.S.A.
126 C2 Franklin Bay Can.
134 C1 Franklin D. Roosevelt Lake
U.S.A.
128 B1 Franklin Mountains Can.
126 E2 Franklin Strait Can.
54 B2 Franz Josef Glacier N.Z.
Franz Josef Land is Rus. Fed.
see Zemlya Frantsa-Iosifa
108 A3 Frasca, Capo della c.
Sardinia Italy
128 B3 Fraser r. B.C. Can.
131 D1 Fraser r. Nfld. Can.
122 B3 Fraserburg S. Africa
96 C2 Fraserburgh U.K.
130 B2 Fraserdale Can.
51 E2 Fraser Island Austr.
128 B2 Fraser Lake Can.
153 C4 Fray Bentos Uru.
93 E4 Fredericia Denmark
139 D2 Frederick U.S.A.
139 D2 Fredericksburg TX U.S.A.
141 D3 Fredericksburg VA U.S.A.
128 A2 Frederick Sound sea chan.
U.S.A.
131 D2 Fredericton Can.
93 F4 Frederikshavn Denmark
Frederikshamn Fin. see Hamina
93 F4 Frederikstad Norway
140 B2 Freeport IL U.S.A.
139 D3 Freeport TX U.S.A.
146 C2 Freeport City Bahamas
139 D3 Freer U.S.A.
123 C2 Free State prov. S. Africa
114 A4 Freetown Sierra Leone
106 B2 Fregenal de la Sierra Spain
104 B2 Fréhel, Cap c. France
102 B2 Freiburg im Breisgau Ger.
102 C2 Freising Ger.
103 C2 Freistadt Austria
105 D3 Fréjus France
50 A3 Fremantle Austr.
137 D2 Fremont NE U.S.A.
140 C2 Fremont OH U.S.A.
151 C1 French Guiana terr.
S. America
134 E1 Frenchman r. U.S.A.

49 H5 French Polynesia terr.
S. Pacific Ocean
144 B2 Fresnillo Mex.
135 C3 Fresno U.S.A.
107 D2 Freu, Cap des c. Spain
105 D2 Freyming-Merlebach France
114 A3 Fria Guinea
152 B3 Frias Arg.
102 B2 Friedrichshafen Ger.
101 F1 Friesack Ger.
100 C1 Friesoythe Ger.
Frobisher Bay Can. see Iqaluit
127 G2 Frobisher Bay Can.
101 F2 Frohburg Ger.
87 D4 Frolovo Rus. Fed.
52 A2 Frome, Lake salt flat Austr.
52 A2 Frome Downs Austr.
100 C2 Fröndenberg Ger.
145 C3 Frontera Mex.
144 B1 Fronteras Mex.
108 B2 Frosinone Italy
92 E3 Frøya i. Norway
Frunze Kyrg. see Bishkek
105 D2 Frutigen Switz.
103 D2 Frýdek-Místek Czech Rep.
71 B3 Fu'an China
106 C1 Fuenlabrada Spain
152 C3 Fuerte Olimpo Para.
114 A2 Fuerteventura i. Canary Is
64 B1 Fuga i. Phil.
79 C2 Fujairah U.A.E.
67 C3 Fuji Japan
71 B3 Fujian prov. China
67 C3 Fujinomiya Japan
67 C3 Fuji-san vol. Japan
67 C3 Fukui Japan
67 B4 Fukuoka Japan
67 D3 Fukushima Japan
101 D2 Fulda Ger.
101 D2 Fulda r. Ger.
70 A3 Fuling China
137 E3 Fulton U.S.A.
105 C2 Fumay France
114 A1 Funchal Madeira
106 B1 Fundão Port.
131 D2 Fundy, Bay of g. Can.
70 B2 Funing Jiangsu China
71 A3 Funing Yunnan China
115 C3 Funtua Nigeria
79 C2 Fürgun, Küh-e mt. Iran
89 F2 Furmanov Rus. Fed.
155 C2 Furnas, Represa resr Brazil
51 D4 Furneaux Group is Austr.
100 C1 Fürstenau Ger.
101 E3 Fürth Ger.
66 D3 Furukawa Japan
127 F2 Fury and Hecla Strait Can.
65 A1 Fushun China
65 B1 Fusong China
79 C2 Fuwayriţ Qatar
70 B2 Fuyang China
69 E1 Fuyu China
68 B1 Fuyun China
71 B3 Fuzhou China
Fuzhou China see Linchuan
93 F4 Fyn i. Denmark
F.Y.R.O.M. country Europe
see Macedonia

G

117 C4 Gaalkacyo Somalia
120 A2 Gabela Angola
115 D1 Gabès Tunisia
115 D1 Gabès, Golfe de g. Tunisia
118 B3 Gabon country Africa
123 C1 Gaborone Botswana

110 C2 Gabrovo Bulg.
114 A3 Gabú Guinea-Bissau
73 B3 Gadag India
101 E1 Gadebusch Ger.
142 C2 Gadsden U.S.A.
110 C2 Găeşti Romania
108 B2 Gaeta Italy
143 D1 Gaffney U.S.A.
115 C1 Gafsa Tunisia
89 E2 Gagarin Rus. Fed.
114 B4 Gagnoa Côte d'Ivoire
131 D1 Gagnon Can.
81 C1 Gagra Georgia
122 A2 Gaiab watercourse Namibia
104 C3 Gaillac France
143 D3 Gainesville FL U.S.A.
143 D2 Gainesville GA U.S.A.
139 D2 Gainesville TX U.S.A.
98 C2 Gainsborough U.K.
52 A2 Gairdner, Lake salt flat Austr.
96 B2 Gairloch U.K.
119 E3 Galana r. Kenya
103 D2 Galanta Slovakia
148 C2 Galapagos Islands is
Pacific Ocean
96 C3 Galashiels U.K.
110 C1 Galaţi Romania
93 E3 Galdhøpiggen mt. Norway
145 B2 Galeana Mex.
128 C2 Galena Bay Can.
140 A2 Galesburg U.S.A.
122 B2 Galeshewe S. Africa
86 D3 Galich Rus. Fed.
116 B1 Galilee, Sea of Israel
142 C1 Gallatin U.S.A.
73 C4 Galle Sri Lanka
150 A1 Gallinas, Punta pt Col.
109 C2 Gallipoli Italy
Gallipoli Turkey see Gelibolu
92 H2 Gällivare Sweden
138 B1 Gallup U.S.A.
114 A2 Galtat Zemmour
Western Sahara
97 B2 Galtymore hill Rep. of Ireland
139 E3 Galveston U.S.A.
139 E3 Galveston Bay U.S.A.
97 B2 Galway Rep. of Ireland
97 B2 Galway Bay Rep. of Ireland
154 C1 Gamá Brazil
123 D3 Gamalakhe S. Africa
Gambia country Africa see
The Gambia
52 A3 Gambier Islands Austr.
131 E2 Gambo Can.
118 B3 Gamboma Congo
138 B1 Ganado U.S.A.
81 D3 Ganāveh Iran
81 C1 Gäncä Azer.
Gand Belgium see Gent
61 C2 Gandadiwata, Bukit
mt. Indon.
118 C3 Gandajika Dem. Rep. Congo
131 E2 Gander Can.
131 E2 Gander r. Can.
101 D1 Ganderkesee Ger.
107 D1 Gandesa Spain
74 B2 Gāndhīdhām India
74 B2 Gāndhīnagar India
74 B2 Gāndhī Sāgar resr India
107 C2 Gandia Spain
Ganga r. Bangl./India see
Ganges
153 B5 Gangán Arg.
74 B2 Ganganagar India
68 C2 Gangca China
75 C1 Gangdisê Shan mts China
75 D2 Ganges r. Bangl./India
105 C3 Ganges France
75 C2 Ganges, Mouths of the
Bangl./India

75 C2 Gangtok India
105 C2 Gannat France
136 B2 Gannett Peak U.S.A.
122 A3 Gansbaai S. Africa
70 A1 Gansu prov. China
71 B3 Ganzhou China
114 B3 Gao Mali
114 A3 Gaoual Guinea
70 B2 Gaoyou China
70 B2 Gaoyou Hu l. China
105 D3 Gap France
107 C2 Gap Carbon hd Alg.
75 C1 Gar China
53 C1 Garah Austr.
151 E2 Garanhuns Brazil
135 B2 Garberville U.S.A.
101 D1 Garbsen Ger.
154 C2 Garça Brazil
108 B1 Garda, Lago di l. Italy
101 E1 Gardelegen Ger.
136 C3 Garden City U.S.A.
129 E2 Garden Hill Can.
77 C3 Gardēz Afgh.
88 B2 Gargždai Lith.
75 C2 Garhchiroli India
123 C3 Gariep Dam resr S. Africa
122 A3 Garies S. Africa
119 D3 Garissa Kenya
102 C2 Garmisch-Partenkirchen Ger.
77 D3 Garmo, Qullai mt. Tajik.
52 B2 Garnpung Lake imp. l. Austr.
104 B3 Garonne r. France
117 C4 Garoowe Somalia
74 B2 Garoth India
118 B2 Garoua Cameroon
96 B2 Garry r. U.K.
126 E2 Garry Lake Can.
119 E3 Garsen Kenya
61 B2 Garut Indon.
140 B2 Gary U.S.A.
145 B2 Garza García Mex.
68 C2 Garzê China
104 B3 Gascony, Gulf of g.
France/Spain
50 A2 Gascoyne r. Austr.
115 D3 Gashua Nigeria
131 D2 Gaspé Can.
131 D2 Gaspé, Péninsule de Can.
143 E1 Gaston, Lake U.S.A.
143 D1 Gastonia U.S.A.
107 C2 Gata, Cabo de c. Spain
88 D2 Gatchina Rus. Fed.
98 C1 Gateshead U.K.
139 D2 Gatesville U.S.A.
130 C2 Gatineau r. Can.
53 D1 Gatton Austr.
129 E2 Gauer Lake Can.
93 E4 Gausta mt. Norway
123 C2 Gauteng prov. S. Africa
79 C2 Gāvbandī Iran
111 B3 Gavdos i. Greece
93 G3 Gävle Sweden
89 F2 Gavrilov Posad Rus. Fed.
89 E2 Gavrilov-Yam Rus. Fed.
62 A1 Gawai Myanmar
52 A2 Gawler Austr.
52 A2 Gawler Ranges hills Austr.
75 C2 Gaya India
114 C3 Gaya Niger
140 C1 Gaylord U.S.A.
86 E2 Gayny Rus. Fed.
116 B1 Gaza terr. Asia
80 B2 Gaza Gaza
76 C2 Gaz-Achak Turkm.
76 B3 Gazandzhyk Turkm.
80 B2 Gaziantep Turkey
114 B4 Gbarnga Liberia
103 D1 Gdańsk Pol.
88 A3 Gdańsk, Gulf of
Pol./Rus. Fed.

88 C2 Gdov Rus. Fed.
103 D1 Gdynia Pol.
116 B3 Gedaref Sudan
101 D2 Gedern Ger.
111 C3 Gediz r. Turkey
102 C1 Gedser Denmark*
100 B2 Geel Belgium
52 B3 Geelong Austr.
101 E1 Geesthacht Ger.
75 C1 Gê'gyai China
129 D2 Geikie r. Can.
93 E3 Geilo Norway
62 B1 Gejiu China
108 B3 Gela Sicily Italy
91 D3 Gelendzhik Rus. Fed.
111 C2 Gelibolu Turkey
100 C2 Gelsenkirchen Ger.
118 B2 Gemena Dem. Rep. Congo
111 C2 Gemlik Turkey
117 C4 Genalē Wenz r. Eth.
153 B4 General Acha Arg.
153 B4 General Alvear Arg.
153 C4 General Belgrano Arg.
144 B2 General Cepeda Mex.
153 B4 General Pico Arg.
153 B4 General Roca Arg.
64 B2 General Santos Phil.
141 D2 Genesee r. U.S.A.
141 D2 Geneseo U.S.A.
Geneva Switz. see Genève
141 D2 Geneva U.S.A.
Geneva, Lake France/Switz.
see Léman, Lac
105 D2 Genève Switz.
106 B2 Genil r. Spain
100 B2 Genk Belgium
108 A2 Genoa Italy
Genova Italy see Genoa
100 A2 Gent Belgium
101 F1 Genthin Ger.
50 A3 Geographe Bay Austr.
131 D1 George r. Can.
122 B3 George S. Africa
143 D3 George, Lake FL U.S.A.
141 E2 George, Lake NY U.S.A.
114 A3 Georgetown Gambia
151 C1 Georgetown Guyana
60 B1 George Town Malaysia
143 E2 Georgetown SC U.S.A.
139 D2 Georgetown TX U.S.A.
55 I2 George V Land reg.
Antarctica
81 C1 Georgia country Asia
143 D2 Georgia state U.S.A.
130 B2 Georgian Bay Can.
51 C2 Georgina watercourse
Austr.
77 E2 Georgiyevka Kazakh.
87 D4 Georgiyevsk Rus. Fed.
101 F2 Gera Ger.
151 D3 Geral de Goiás, Serra hills
Brazil
54 B2 Geraldine N.Z.
50 A2 Geraldton Austr.
80 B1 Gerede Turkey
74 A1 Gereshk Afgh.
135 C2 Gerlach U.S.A.
103 E2 Gerlachovský štit mt. Slovakia
102 C1 Germany country Europe
100 C2 Gerolstein Ger.
101 E3 Gerolzhofen Ger.
101 D2 Gersfeld (Rhön) Ger.
75 C1 Gêrzê China
141 D3 Gettysburg PA U.S.A.
137 D2 Gettysburg SD U.S.A.
109 D2 Gevgelija Macedonia
106 C1 Gexto Spain
111 C3 Geyikli Turkey
122 B2 Ghaap Plateau S. Africa
115 C1 Ghadāmis Libya

190 | Ghaghara

75 C2 Ghaghara r. India
114 B4 Ghana country Africa
120 B3 Ghanzi Botswana
115 C1 Ghardaïa Alg.
115 D1 Gharyān Libya
75 C2 Ghatal India
75 C2 Ghazipur India
77 C3 Ghazni Afgh.
Ghent Belgium see Gent
110 B1 Gherla Romania
105 D3 Ghisonaccia Corsica France
74 B2 Ghotāru India
74 A2 Ghotki Pak.
91 E3 Giaginskaya Rus. Fed.
97 C1 Giant's Causeway lava field U.K.
61 C2 Gianyar Indon.
109 C3 Giarre Sicily Italy
108 A1 Giaveno Italy
122 A2 Gibeon Namibia
106 B2 Gibraltar terr. Europe
106 B2 Gibraltar, Strait of Morocco/Spain
50 B2 Gibson Desert Austr.
68 C1 Gichgeniyn Nuruu mts Mongolia
117 B4 Gidolē Eth.
104 C2 Gien France
101 D2 Gießen Ger.
101 E1 Gifhorn Ger.
128 C2 Gift Lake Can.
67 C3 Gifu Japan
96 B3 Gigha i. U.K.
106 B1 Gijón Spain
138 A2 Gila r. U.S.A.
138 A2 Gila Bend U.S.A.
51 D1 Gilbert r. Austr.
Gilbert Islands country Pacific Ocean see Kiribati
134 D1 Gildford U.S.A.
116 A2 Gilf Kebir Plateau Egypt
53 C2 Gilgandra Austr.
74 B1 Gilgit Jammu and Kashmir
74 B1 Gilgit r. Jammu and Kashmir
53 C2 Gilgunnia Austr.
129 E2 Gillam Can.
136 B2 Gillette U.S.A.
99 D3 Gillingham U.K.
129 E2 Gimli Can.
117 C4 Ginir Eth.
109 C2 Ginosa Italy
53 C3 Gippsland reg. Austr.
74 A2 Girdar Dhor r. Pak.
80 B1 Giresun Turkey
107 D1 Girona Spain
96 B3 Girvan U.K.
54 C1 Gisborne N.Z.
93 F4 Gislaved Sweden
119 C3 Gitarama Rwanda
108 B2 Giulianova Italy
110 C2 Giurgiu Romania
110 C1 Giuvala, Pasul pass Romania
105 C2 Givors France
123 D1 Giyani S. Africa
80 B3 Giza Pyramids Egypt
109 D2 Gjirokastër Albania
126 E2 Gjoa Haven Can.
93 F3 Gjøvik Norway
131 E2 Glace Bay Can.
134 B1 Glacier Peak vol. U.S.A.
51 E2 Gladstone Austr.
92 □A2 Gláma mts Iceland
109 C2 Glamoč Bos.-Herz.
100 C3 Glan r. Ger.
97 B2 Glanaruddery Mountains Rep. of Ireland
96 B3 Glasgow U.K.
140 B3 Glasgow KY U.S.A.
136 B1 Glasgow MT U.S.A.

99 B3 Glastonbury U.K.
101 F2 Glauchau Ger.
86 E3 Glazov Rus. Fed.
89 E3 Glazunovka Rus. Fed.
96 B2 Glen Coe val. U.K.
138 A2 Glendale U.S.A.
53 D2 Glen Davis Austr.
136 C1 Glendive U.S.A.
83 B3 Glenelg r. Austr.
53 D1 Glen Innes Austr.
126 B2 Glennallen U.S.A.
96 C2 Glenrothes U.K.
141 E2 Glens Falls U.S.A.
96 C2 Glen Shee val. U.K.
97 B1 Glenties Rep. of Ireland
138 B2 Glenwood U.S.A.
136 B3 Glenwood Springs U.S.A.
103 D1 Gliwice Pol.
138 A2 Globe U.S.A.
103 D1 Głogów Pol.
92 F2 Glomfjord Norway
93 F4 Glomma r. Norway
53 D2 Gloucester Austr.
99 B3 Gloucester U.K.
101 F1 Glöwen Ger.
77 C1 Glubokoye Kazakh.
101 D1 Glückstadt Ger.
102 C2 Gmünd Austria
102 C2 Gmunden Austria
101 D1 Gnarrenburg Ger.
103 D1 Gniezno Pol.
109 D2 Gnjilane Yugo.
75 D2 Goalpara India
96 B3 Goat Fell hill U.K.
117 C4 Goba Eth.
120 A3 Gobabis Namibia
153 A5 Gobernador Gregores Arg.
69 D2 Gobi des. China/Mongolia
100 C2 Goch Ger.
122 A1 Gochas Namibia
74 B3 Godavari r. India
73 C3 Godavari, Mouths of the India
130 B2 Goderich Can.
74 B2 Godhra India
129 E2 Gods r. Can.
129 E2 Gods Lake l. Can.
Godwin-Austen, Mount China/Jammu and Kashmir see K2
130 C2 Goéland, Lac au l. Can.
131 D1 Goélands, Lac aux l. Can.
100 A2 Goes Neth.
154 C1 Goiandira Brazil
154 C1 Goiânia Brazil
154 B1 Goiás Brazil
154 B2 Goio-Erê Brazil
111 C3 Gökçeada i. Turkey
111 C3 Gökçedağ Turkey
121 B3 Gokwe Zimbabwe
93 E3 Gol Norway
62 A1 Golaghat India
111 C2 Gölcük Turkey
103 E1 Gołdap Pol.
101 F1 Goldberg Ger.
51 D1 Gold Coast Austr.
114 B4 Gold Coast coastal area Ghana
128 C2 Golden Can.
54 B2 Golden Bay N.Z.
128 B3 Golden Hinde mt. Can.
97 B2 Golden Vale lowland Rep. of Ireland
135 C3 Goldfield U.S.A.
128 B3 Gold River Can.
143 E1 Goldsboro U.S.A.
135 C4 Goleta U.S.A.
68 C2 Golmud China
81 D2 Golpāyegān Iran
96 C2 Golspie U.K.

119 C3 Goma Dem. Rep. Congo
75 C2 Gomati r. India
115 D3 Gombe Nigeria
115 D3 Gombi Nigeria
Gomel' Belarus see Homyel'
144 B2 Gómez Palacio Mex.
147 C3 Gonaïves Haiti
81 D2 Gonbad-e Kavus Iran
117 B3 Gonder Eth.
75 C2 Gondia India
111 C2 Gönen Turkey
115 D4 Gongola r. Nigeria
53 C2 Gongolon Austr.
145 C2 Gonzáles Mex.
139 D3 Gonzales U.S.A.
122 A3 Good Hope, Cape of S. Africa
134 D2 Gooding U.S.A.
136 C3 Goodland U.S.A.
53 C1 Goodooga Austr.
98 C2 Goole U.K.
53 C2 Goolgowi Austr.
52 A3 Goolwa Austr.
53 D1 Goondiwindi Austr.
134 B2 Goose Lake l. U.S.A.
102 B2 Göppingen Ger.
75 C2 Gorakhpur India
109 C2 Goražde Bos.-Herz.
111 C3 Gördes Turkey
89 D3 Gordeyevka Rus. Fed.
51 D4 Gordon, Lake Austr.
115 D4 Goré Chad
117 B4 Gorē Eth.
54 A3 Gore N.Z.
97 C2 Gorey Rep. of Ireland
81 C1 Gori Georgia
108 B1 Gorizia Italy
Gor'kiy Rus. Fed. see Nizhniy Novgorod
103 E2 Gorlice Pol.
103 C1 Görlitz Ger.
109 D2 Gornji Milanovac Yugo.
109 C2 Gornji Vakuf Bos.-Herz.
77 E1 Gorno-Altaysk Rus. Fed.
110 C2 Gornotrakiyska Nizina lowland Bulg.
77 E1 Gornyak Rus. Fed.
59 D3 Goroka P.N.G.
114 B3 Gorom Gorom Burkina
59 C2 Gorontalo Indon.
89 E3 Gorshechnoye Rus. Fed.
97 B2 Gorumna Island Rep. of Ireland
91 D3 Goryachiy Klyuch Rus. Fed.
103 D1 Gorzów Wielkopolski Pol.
53 D2 Gosford Austr.
66 D2 Goshogawara Japan
101 E2 Goslar Ger.
109 C2 Gospić Croatia
99 C3 Gosport U.K.
109 D2 Gostivar Macedonia
Göteborg Sweden see Gothenburg
101 E2 Gotha Ger.
93 F4 Gothenburg Sweden
136 C2 Gothenburg U.S.A.
93 G4 Gotland i. Sweden
111 B2 Gotse Delchev Bulg.
93 G4 Gotska Sandön i. Sweden
67 B4 Gōtsu Japan
101 D2 Göttingen Ger.
128 B2 Gott Peak Can.
100 B1 Gouda Neth.
114 A3 Goudiri Senegal
115 D3 Goudoumaria Niger
130 C2 Gouin, Réservoir resr Can.
53 C2 Goulburn Austr.
53 B3 Goulburn r. N.S.W. Austr.
53 B3 Goulburn r. Vic. Austr.

114 B3 **Goundam** Mali
107 D2 **Gouraya** Alg.
104 C3 **Gourdon** France
115 D3 **Gouré** Niger
122 B3 **Gourits** r. S. Africa
114 B3 **Gourma-Rharous** Mali
53 C3 **Gourock Range** mts Austr.
155 D1 **Governador Valadares** Brazil
143 E3 **Governor's Harbour** Bahamas
68 C2 **Govĭ Altayn Nuruu** mts Mongolia
75 C2 **Govind Ballash Pant Sägar** resr India
99 A3 **Gower** pen. U.K.
152 C3 **Goya** Arg.
81 C1 **Göyçay** Azer.
75 C1 **Gozha Co** salt l. China
122 B3 **Graaf-Reinet** S. Africa
101 E1 **Grabow** Ger.
109 C2 **Gračac** Croatia
87 E3 **Grachevka** Rus. Fed.
101 F2 **Gräfenhainichen** Ger.
53 D1 **Grafton** Austr.
137 D1 **Grafton** U.S.A.
139 D2 **Graham** U.S.A.
128 A2 **Graham Island** Can.
55 P3 **Graham Land** reg. Antarctica
123 C3 **Grahamstown** S. Africa
151 D2 **Grajaú** Brazil
111 B2 **Grámmos** mt. Greece
96 B2 **Grampian Mountains** U.K.
146 B3 **Granada** Nic.
106 C2 **Granada** Spain
141 E1 **Granby** Can.
114 A2 **Gran Canaria** i. Canary Is
152 B3 **Gran Chaco** reg. Arg./Para.
136 C1 **Grand** r. U.S.A.
146 C2 **Grand Bahama** i. Bahamas
131 E2 **Grand Bank** Can.
158 C2 **Grand Banks of Newfoundland** sea feature N. Atlantic Ocean
138 A1 **Grand Canyon** U.S.A.
138 A1 **Grand Canyon** gorge U.S.A.
146 B3 **Grand Cayman** i. Cayman Is
129 C2 **Grand Centre** Can.
134 C1 **Grand Coulee** U.S.A.
152 B2 **Grande** r. Bol.
154 B2 **Grande** r. Brazil
153 B6 **Grande, Bahía** b. Arg.
155 D2 **Grande, Ilha** i. Brazil
128 C2 **Grande Cache** Can.
121 D2 **Grande Comore** i. Comoros
128 C2 **Grande Prairie** Can.
115 D3 **Grand Erg de Bilma** des. Niger
114 B1 **Grand Erg Occidental** des. Alg.
115 C2 **Grand Erg Oriental** des. Alg.
131 D2 **Grande-Rivière** Can.
130 C1 **Grande Rivière de la Baleine** r. Can.
152 B4 **Grandes, Salinas** salt marsh Arg.
131 D2 **Grand Falls** N.B. Can.
131 E2 **Grand Falls** Nfld. Can.
128 C3 **Grand Forks** Can.
137 D1 **Grand Forks** U.S.A.
128 C1 **Grandin, Lac** l. Can.
137 D2 **Grand Island** U.S.A.
142 B3 **Grand Isle** U.S.A.
136 B3 **Grand Junction** U.S.A.
114 B4 **Grand-Lahou** Côte d'Ivoire
131 D2 **Grand Lake** l. N.B. Can.
131 E2 **Grand Lake** l. Nfld. Can.
137 E1 **Grand Marais** U.S.A.
106 B2 **Grândola** Port.
129 E2 **Grand Rapids** Can.

140 B2 **Grand Rapids** MI U.S.A.
137 E1 **Grand Rapids** MN U.S.A.
136 A2 **Grand Teton** mt. U.S.A.
147 C2 **Grand Turk** Turks and Caicos Is
134 C1 **Grangeville** U.S.A.
128 B2 **Granisle** Can.
134 E1 **Granite Peak** U.S.A.
108 B3 **Granitola, Capo** c. Sicily Italy
93 F4 **Gränna** Sweden
101 F1 **Gransee** Ger.
99 C2 **Grantham** U.K.
96 C2 **Grantown-on-Spey** U.K.
138 B1 **Grants** U.S.A.
134 B2 **Grants Pass** U.S.A.
104 B2 **Granville** France
129 D2 **Granville Lake** Can.
155 D1 **Grão Mogol** Brazil
123 D1 **Graskop** S. Africa
105 D3 **Grasse** France
107 D1 **Graus** Spain
92 F2 **Gravdal** Norway
104 B2 **Grave, Pointe de** pt France
129 D3 **Gravelbourg** Can.
130 C2 **Gravenhurst** Can.
53 D1 **Gravesend** Austr.
99 D3 **Gravesend** U.K.
105 D2 **Gray** France
103 D2 **Graz** Austria
146 C2 **Great Abaco** i. Bahamas
50 B3 **Great Australian Bight** g. Austr.
54 C1 **Great Barrier Island** N.Z.
51 D1 **Great Barrier Reef** Austr.
135 C3 **Great Basin** U.S.A.
126 D2 **Great Bear Lake** Can.
137 D3 **Great Bend** U.S.A.
63 A2 **Great Coco Island** Cocos Is
53 B3 **Great Dividing Range** mts Austr.
146 B2 **Greater Antilles** is Caribbean Sea
134 D1 **Great Falls** U.S.A.
123 C3 **Great Fish** r. S. Africa
123 C3 **Great Fish Point** S. Africa
147 C2 **Great Inagua** i. Bahamas
122 B3 **Great Karoo** plat. S. Africa
123 C3 **Great Kei** r. S. Africa
99 B2 **Great Malvern** U.K.
63 A3 **Great Nicobar** i. India
99 D2 **Great Ouse** r. U.K.
119 D3 **Great Rift Valley** Africa
119 D3 **Great Ruaha** r. Tanz.
134 D2 **Great Salt Lake** U.S.A.
135 D2 **Great Salt Lake Desert** U.S.A.
116 A2 **Great Sand Sea** des. Egypt/Libya
50 B2 **Great Sandy Desert** Austr.
128 C1 **Great Slave Lake** Can.
143 D1 **Great Smoky Mountains** U.S.A.
50 B2 **Great Victoria Desert** Austr.
70 B1 **Great Wall** China
99 D2 **Great Yarmouth** U.K.
106 B1 **Gredos, Sierra de** mts Spain
111 B3 **Greece** country Europe
136 C2 **Greeley** U.S.A.
82 F1 **Greem-Bell, Ostrov** i. Rus. Fed.
140 B3 **Green** r. KY U.S.A.
136 B3 **Green** r. WY U.S.A.
140 B2 **Green Bay** U.S.A.
140 B1 **Green Bay** b. U.S.A.
140 C3 **Greenbrier** r. U.S.A.
140 B3 **Greencastle** U.S.A.
143 D1 **Greeneville** U.S.A.
141 E2 **Greenfield** U.S.A.
129 D2 **Green Lake** Can.
127 I2 **Greenland** terr. N. America

160 R2 **Greenland Sea** Greenland/Svalbard
96 B3 **Greenock** U.K.
135 D3 **Green River** UT U.S.A.
136 B3 **Green River** WY U.S.A.
140 B3 **Greensburg** IN U.S.A.
141 D2 **Greensburg** PA U.S.A.
143 E2 **Green Swamp** U.S.A.
138 A2 **Green Valley** U.S.A.
114 B4 **Greenville** Liberia
142 C2 **Greenville** AL U.S.A.
142 B2 **Greenville** MS U.S.A.
143 E1 **Greenville** NC U.S.A.
143 D2 **Greenville** SC U.S.A.
139 D2 **Greenville** TX U.S.A.
53 D2 **Greenwell Point** Austr.
143 D2 **Greenwood** U.S.A.
50 B2 **Gregory, Lake** salt flat Austr.
51 D1 **Gregory Range** hills Austr.
102 C1 **Greifswald** Ger.
101 F2 **Greiz** Ger.
93 F4 **Grenå** Denmark
142 C2 **Grenada** U.S.A.
147 D3 **Grenada** country West Indies
104 C3 **Grenade** France
53 C2 **Grenfell** Austr.
129 D2 **Grenfell** Can.
105 D2 **Grenoble** France
51 D1 **Grenville, Cape** Austr.
134 B1 **Gresham** U.S.A.
100 C1 **Greven** Ger.
111 B2 **Grevena** Greece
100 C2 **Grevenbroich** Ger.
101 E1 **Grevesmühlen** Ger.
136 B2 **Greybull** U.S.A.
128 A1 **Grey Hunter Peak** Can.
131 E1 **Grey Islands** Can.
54 B2 **Greymouth** N.Z.
52 B1 **Grey Range** hills Austr.
97 C2 **Greystones** Rep. of Ireland
143 D2 **Griffin** U.S.A.
53 C2 **Griffith** Austr.
101 F2 **Grimma** Ger.
102 C1 **Grimmen** Ger.
98 C2 **Grimsby** U.K.
129 C2 **Grimshaw** Can.
92 0B2 **Grímsstaðir** Iceland
93 E4 **Grimstad** Norway
137 E2 **Grinnell** U.S.A.
123 C3 **Griqualand East** reg. S. Africa
122 B2 **Griqualand West** reg. S. Africa
127 F1 **Grise Fiord** Can.
96 C1 **Gritley** U.K.
123 C2 **Groblersdal** S. Africa
122 B2 **Groblershoop** S. Africa
104 B3 **Groix, Île de** i. France
100 C1 **Gronau (Westfalen)** Ger.
92 F3 **Grong** Norway
100 C1 **Groningen** Neth.
122 B2 **Grootdrink** S. Africa
51 C1 **Groote Eylandt** i. Austr.
120 A2 **Grootfontein** Namibia
122 A2 **Groot Karas Berg** plat. Namibia
122 B3 **Groot Swartberge** mts S. Africa
123 C3 **Groot Winterberg** mt. S. Africa
102 C2 **Großenlüder** Ger.
102 C2 **Großer Rachel** mt. Ger.
103 C2 **Grosser Speikkogel** mt. Austria
108 B2 **Grosseto** Italy
101 D3 **Groß-Gerau** Ger.
102 C2 **Großglockner** mt. Austria
100 C1 **Groß-Hesepe** Ger.
101 E2 **Großlohra** Ger.

Gross Ums

122 A1 **Gross Ums** Namibia
131 E1 **Groswater Bay** Can.
130 B2 **Groundhog** r. Can.
135 B3 **Grover Beach** U.S.A.
141 E2 **Groveton** U.S.A.
87 D2 **Groznyy** Rus. Fed.
109 C1 **Grubišno Polje** Croatia
103 D1 **Grudziądz** Pol.
122 A2 **Grünau** Namibia
92 □A3 **Grundarfjörður** Iceland
89 E3 **Gryazi** Rus. Fed.
89 F2 **Gryazovets** Rus. Fed.
103 D1 **Gryfice** Pol.
102 C1 **Gryfino** Pol.
146 C2 **Guacanayabo, Golfo de** b. Cuba
144 B2 **Guadalajara** Mex.
107 C1 **Guadalope** r. Spain
106 B2 **Guadalquivir** r. Spain
132 B4 **Guadalupe** i. Mex.
106 B2 **Guadalupe, Sierra de** mts Spain
138 C2 **Guadalupe Peak** U.S.A.
144 B2 **Guadalupe Victoria** Mex.
144 B2 **Guadalupe y Calvo** Mex.
106 C1 **Guadarrama, Sierra de** mts Spain
147 D3 **Guadeloupe** terr. West Indies
106 B2 **Guadiana** r. Port./Spain
106 C2 **Guadix** Spain
154 B2 **Guaíra** Brazil
147 C3 **Guajira, Península de la** pen. Col.
150 A2 **Gualaceo** Ecuador
59 D2 **Guam** terr. N. Pacific Ocean
144 B2 **Guamúchil** Mex.
144 B2 **Guanacevi** Mex.
151 D3 **Guanambi** Brazil
150 B1 **Guanare** Venez.
146 B2 **Guane** Cuba
70 A2 **Guang'an** China
71 B3 **Guangchang** China
71 B3 **Guangdong** prov. China
71 A3 **Guangxi** aut. reg. China
70 A2 **Guangyuan** China
71 B3 **Guangzhou** China
155 D1 **Guanhães** Brazil
147 D4 **Guanipa** r. Venez.
71 A3 **Guanling** China
65 A1 **Guanshui** China
Guansuo China see Guanling
147 C2 **Guantánamo** Cuba
150 B3 **Guaporé** r. Bol./Brazil
154 B3 **Guarapuava** Brazil
154 C3 **Guaraqueçaba** Brazil
155 C2 **Guaratinguetá** Brazil
106 B1 **Guarda** Port.
154 C1 **Guarda Mor** Brazil
106 C1 **Guardo** Spain
155 C2 **Guarujá** Brazil
144 B2 **Guasave** Mex.
146 A3 **Guatemala** country Central America
146 A3 **Guatemala** Guat.
150 B1 **Guaviare** r. Col.
155 C2 **Guaxupé** Brazil
150 A2 **Guayaquil** Ecuador
150 B3 **Guayaramerín** Bol.
144 A2 **Guaymas** Mex.
117 B3 **Guba** Eth.
86 E1 **Guba Dolgaya** Rus. Fed.
89 E3 **Gubkin** Rus. Fed.
115 C1 **Guelma** Alg.
114 A2 **Guelmine** Morocco
130 B2 **Guelph** Can.
145 C2 **Guémez** Mex.
104 C2 **Guéret** France
95 C4 **Guernsey** terr. Channel Is
144 A2 **Guerrero Negro** Mex.
131 D1 **Guers, Lac** l. Can.

70 B2 **Guichi** China
118 B2 **Guider** Cameroon
108 B2 **Guidonia-Montecelio** Italy
71 A3 **Guigang** China
100 A3 **Guignicourt** France
123 D1 **Guija** Moz.
99 C3 **Guildford** U.K.
71 B3 **Guilin** China
130 C1 **Guillaume-Delisle, Lac** l. Can.
106 B1 **Guimarães** Port.
114 A3 **Guinea** country Africa
112 D3 **Guinea, Gulf of** Africa
114 A3 **Guinea-Bissau** country Africa
104 B2 **Guingamp** France
104 B2 **Guipavas** France
154 B1 **Guiratinga** Brazil
150 B1 **Güiria** Venez.
100 A3 **Guise** France
64 B1 **Guiuan** Phil.
71 A3 **Guiyang** China
71 A3 **Guizhou** prov. China
74 B1 **Gujranwala** Pak.
74 B1 **Gujrat** Pak.
91 D2 **Gukovo** Rus. Fed.
76 B2 **Gulabe** Uzbek.
53 C2 **Gulargambone** Austr.
73 B3 **Gulbarga** India
88 C2 **Gulbene** Latvia
142 C2 **Gulfport** U.S.A.
69 E1 **Gulian** China
77 C2 **Gulistan** Uzbek.
Gulja China see Yining
129 D2 **Gull Lake** Can.
111 C3 **Güllük** Turkey
119 D2 **Gulu** Uganda
120 B2 **Gumare** Botswana
76 B3 **Gumdag** Turkm.
75 C2 **Gumla** India
100 C2 **Gummersbach** Ger.
74 B2 **Guna** India
53 C3 **Gundagai** Austr.
111 C3 **Güney** Turkey
118 B3 **Gungu** Dem. Rep. Congo
129 E2 **Gunisao** r. Can.
53 D2 **Gunnedah** Austr.
136 B3 **Gunnison** CO U.S.A.
135 D3 **Gunnison** UT U.S.A.
136 B3 **Gunnison** r. U.S.A.
73 B3 **Guntakal** India
60 A1 **Gunungsitoli** Indon.
60 A1 **Gunungtua** Indon.
102 C2 **Günzburg** Ger.
102 C2 **Gunzenhausen** Ger.
74 B2 **Gurgaon** India
151 D2 **Gurgueia** r. Brazil
150 B1 **Guri, Embalse de** resr Venez.
154 C1 **Gurinhatã** Brazil
151 D2 **Gurupi** r. Brazil
74 B2 **Gur Sikhar** mt. India
Gur'yev Kazakh. see Atyrau
115 C3 **Gusau** Nigeria
65 A2 **Gushan** China
74 A1 **Gushgy** Turkm.
70 B2 **Gushi** China
83 I3 **Gusinoozersk** Rus. Fed.
89 D2 **Gus'-Khrustal'nyy** Rus. Fed.
108 A3 **Guspini** Sardinia Italy
128 A2 **Gustavus** U.S.A.
101 F1 **Güstrow** Ger.
101 D2 **Gütersloh** Ger.
121 C2 **Gutu** Zimbabwe
75 D2 **Guwahati** India
150 C1 **Guyana** country S. America
Guyi China see Sanjiang
139 C1 **Guymon** U.S.A.
53 D2 **Guyra** Austr.
70 A2 **Guyuan** China

144 B1 **Guzmán** Mex.
144 B1 **Guzmán, Lago de** l. Mex.
74 A2 **Gwadar** Pak.
75 B2 **Gwalior** India
121 B3 **Gwanda** Zimbabwe
97 B1 **Gweebarra Bay** Rep. of Ireland
97 B1 **Gweedore** Rep. of Ireland
121 B2 **Gweru** Zimbabwe
115 D3 **Gwoza** Nigeria
53 D2 **Gwydir** r. Austr.
75 C2 **Gyangzê** China
75 C1 **Gyaring Co** l. China
68 C2 **Gyaring Hu** l. China
86 G1 **Gydanskiy Poluostrov** pen. Rus. Fed.
Gyêgu China see Yushu
51 E2 **Gympie** Austr.
103 D2 **Gyöngyös** Hungary
103 D2 **Győr** Hungary
129 E2 **Gypsumville** Can.
103 E2 **Gyula** Hungary
81 C1 **Gyumri** Armenia
76 B3 **Gyzylarbat** Turkm.

H

88 B2 **Haapsalu** Estonia
100 B1 **Haarlem** Neth.
101 C2 **Haarstrang** ridge Ger.
54 A2 **Haast** N.Z.
78 B3 **Habbān** Yemen
81 C2 **Habbāniyah, Hawr al** l. Iraq
67 C4 **Hachijō-jima** i. Japan
66 D2 **Hachinohe** Japan
121 C3 **Hacufera** Moz.
79 C2 **Hadd, Ra's al** pt Oman
96 C3 **Haddington** U.K.
115 D3 **Hadejia** Nigeria
93 E4 **Haderslev** Denmark
91 C1 **Hadyach** Ukr.
65 B2 **Haeju** N. Korea
65 B2 **Haeju-man** b. N. Korea
65 B3 **Haenam** S. Korea
78 B2 **Hafar al Bāṭin** Saudi Arabia
62 A1 **Haflong** India
92 □A3 **Hafnarfjörður** Iceland
78 A3 **Hagar Nish Plateau** Eritrea
100 C2 **Hagen** Ger.
101 E1 **Hagenow** Ger.
128 B2 **Hagensborg** Can.
141 D3 **Hagerstown** U.S.A.
93 F3 **Hagfors** Sweden
67 B4 **Hagi** Japan
62 B1 **Ha Giang** Vietnam
97 B2 **Hag's Head** hd Rep. of Ireland
119 D3 **Hai** Tanz.
62 B1 **Hai Duong** Vietnam
71 B3 **Haifeng** China
71 B3 **Haikou** China
78 B2 **Hā'il** Saudi Arabia
69 D1 **Hailar** China
92 H2 **Hailuoto** i. Fin.
70 B2 **Hainan** i. China
71 A4 **Hainan** prov. China
128 A2 **Haines** U.S.A.
128 A1 **Haines Junction** Can.
101 E2 **Hainich** ridge Ger.
101 E2 **Hainleite** ridge Ger.
62 B1 **Hai Phong** Vietnam
147 C3 **Haiti** country West Indies
116 B3 **Haiya** Sudan
103 E2 **Hajdúböszörmény** Hungary
78 B3 **Hajjah** Yemen
79 C2 **Hājjīābād** Iran
62 A1 **Haka** Myanmar
81 C1 **Hakkâri** Turkey

66 D2 **Hakodate** Japan
C1 **Halab** Syria *see* Aleppo
78 B2 **Halabān** Saudi Arabia
81 C2 **Halabja** Iraq
116 B2 **Halaib** Sudan
78 A2 **Halaib Triangle** *terr.*
　　　Egypt/Sudan
79 C3 **Halānīyāt, Juzur al** *is* Oman
78 A2 **Hālat 'Ammār** Saudi Arabia
68 C1 **Halban** Mongolia
101 E2 **Halberstadt** Ger.
64 B1 **Halcon, Mount** Phil.
93 F4 **Halden** Norway
101 E1 **Haldensleben** Ger.
75 B2 **Haldwani** India
79 C2 **Hāleh** Iran
54 A3 **Halfmoon Bay** N.Z.
131 D2 **Halifax** Can.
98 C2 **Halifax** U.K.
141 D3 **Halifax** U.S.A.
65 B3 **Halla-san** *mt.* S. Korea
127 F2 **Hall Beach** Can.
100 B2 **Halle** Belgium
102 C2 **Hallein** Austria
101 E2 **Halle (Saale)** Ger.
137 D1 **Hallock** U.S.A.
127 G2 **Hall Peninsula** Can.
50 B1 **Halls Creek** Austr.
59 C2 **Halmahera** *i.* Indon.
93 F4 **Halmstad** Sweden
67 B4 **Hamada** Japan
81 C2 **Hamadān** Iran
80 B2 **Hamāh** Syria
67 C4 **Hamamatsu** Japan
93 F3 **Hamar** Norway
116 B2 **Hamāta, Gebel** *mt.* Egypt
73 C4 **Hambantota** Sri Lanka
101 D1 **Hamburg** Ger.
78 A2 **Ḥamḍ, Wādī al** *watercourse*
　　　Saudi Arabia
78 B3 **Ḥamdah** Saudi Arabia
93 H3 **Hämeenlinna** Fin.
101 D1 **Hameln** Ger.
50 A2 **Hamersley Range** *mts* Austr.
65 B2 **Hamhŭng** N. Korea
68 C2 **Hami** China
116 B2 **Hamid** Sudan
52 B3 **Hamilton** Austr.
130 C2 **Hamilton** Can.
54 C1 **Hamilton** N.Z.
96 B3 **Hamilton** U.K.
142 C2 **Hamilton** *AL* U.S.A.
134 D1 **Hamilton** *MT* U.S.A.
140 C3 **Hamilton** *OH* U.S.A.
93 I3 **Hamina** Fin.
100 C2 **Hamm** Ger.
114 B2 **Hammada du Drâa** *plat.* Alg.
81 C2 **Ḥammār, Hawr al** *imp. l.* Iraq
101 D2 **Hammelburg** Ger.
92 G3 **Hammerdal** Sweden
92 H1 **Hammerfest** Norway
142 B2 **Hammond** U.S.A.
141 E3 **Hammonton** U.S.A.
79 C2 **Hāmūn-e Jaz Mūrīān**
　　　salt marsh Iran
74 A2 **Hamun-i-Lora** *dry lake* Pak.
74 A2 **Hamun-i-Mashkel**
　　　salt flat Pak.
78 A2 **Ḥanalc** Saudi Arabia
66 D3 **Hanamaki** Japan
101 D2 **Hanau** Ger.
70 B2 **Hancheng** China
140 B1 **Hancock** U.S.A.
70 B2 **Handan** China
135 C3 **Hanford** U.S.A.
68 C1 **Hangayn Nuruu** *mts*
　　　Mongolia
　　　Hanggin Houqi China *see*
　　　　Xamba
　　　Hangö Fin. *see* Hanko

70 C2 **Hangzhou** China
70 C2 **Hangzhou Wan** *b.* China
　　　Hanjia China *see* Pengshui
　　　Hanjiang China *see*
　　　　Yangzhou
93 H4 **Hanko** Fin.
135 D3 **Hanksville** U.S.A.
54 B2 **Hanmer Springs** N.Z.
129 C2 **Hanna** Can.
137 E3 **Hannibal** U.S.A.
101 D1 **Hannover** Ger.
101 D2 **Hannoversch Münden** Ger.
92 F3 **Hanöbukten** *b.* Sweden
62 B1 **Ha Nôi** Vietnam
　　　Hanoi Vietnam *see* Ha Nôi
130 B2 **Hanover** Can.
122 B3 **Hanover** S. Africa
93 E4 **Hanstholm** Denmark
88 C3 **Hantsavichy** Belarus
75 C2 **Hanumana** India
74 B2 **Hanumangarh** India
70 A2 **Hanzhong** China
92 H2 **Haparanda** Sweden
131 D1 **Hapert** Neth.
131 D1 **Happy Valley-Goose Bay**
　　　Can.
78 A2 **Haql** Saudi Arabia
79 B2 **Haradh** Saudi Arabia
88 C2 **Haradok** Belarus
78 B3 **Harajā** Saudi Arabia
121 C2 **Harare** Zimbabwe
79 C3 **Ḥarāsīs, Jiddat al** *des.*
　　　Oman
69 D1 **Har-Ayrag** Mongolia
69 E1 **Harbin** China
131 E2 **Harbour Breton** Can.
74 B2 **Harda Khās** India
100 C1 **Hardenberg** Neth.
100 B1 **Harderwijk** Neth.
122 A3 **Hardeveld** *mts* S. Africa
134 E1 **Hardin** U.S.A.
128 C1 **Hardisty Lake** Can.
100 C1 **Haren (Ems)** Ger.
117 C4 **Härer** Eth.
117 C4 **Hargeysa** Somalia
110 C1 **Harghita-Mădăraş, Vârful**
　　　mt. Romania
68 C2 **Har Hu** *l.* China
74 B1 **Haripur** Pak.
74 A1 **Hari Rūd** *r.* Afgh./Iran
100 B1 **Harlingen** Neth.
139 D3 **Harlingen** U.S.A.
99 D3 **Harlow** U.K.
134 E1 **Harlowton** U.S.A.
134 C2 **Harney Basin** U.S.A.
134 C2 **Harney Lake** U.S.A.
93 G3 **Härnösand** Sweden
69 E1 **Har Nur** China
68 C1 **Har Nuur** *l.* Mongolia
114 B4 **Harper** Liberia
101 D1 **Harpstedt** Ger.
130 C1 **Harricanaw** *r.* Can.
53 D2 **Harrington** Austr.
131 E1 **Harrington Harbour** Can.
96 A2 **Harris, Sound of**
　　　sea chan. U.K.
140 B3 **Harrisburg** *IL* U.S.A.
141 D2 **Harrisburg** *PA* U.S.A.
123 C2 **Harrismith** S. Africa
142 B1 **Harrison** U.S.A.
131 E1 **Harrison, Cape** Can.
126 E3 **Harrison Bay** U.S.A.
141 D3 **Harrisonburg** U.S.A.
137 E3 **Harrisonville** U.S.A.
98 C2 **Harrogate** U.K.
110 C2 **Hârşova** Romania
92 G2 **Harstad** Norway
122 B2 **Hartbees** *watercourse*
　　　S. Africa
103 D2 **Hartberg** Austria

141 E2 **Hartford** U.S.A.
99 A3 **Hartland Point** U.K.
98 C1 **Hartlepool** U.K.
128 B2 **Hartley Bay** Can.
123 B2 **Harts** *r.* S. Africa
143 D2 **Hartwell Reservoir** U.S.A.
68 C1 **Har Us Nuur** *l.* Mongolia
136 C1 **Harvey** U.S.A.
99 D3 **Harwich** U.K.
101 E2 **Harz** *hills* Ger.
73 B3 **Hassan** India
100 B2 **Hasselt** Belgium
115 C1 **Hassi Messaoud** Alg.
93 F4 **Hässleholm** Sweden
100 B2 **Hastière-Lavaux** Belgium
53 C3 **Hastings** Austr.
54 C1 **Hastings** N.Z.
99 D3 **Hastings** U.K.
137 E2 **Hastings** *MN* U.S.A.
137 D2 **Hastings** *NE* U.S.A.
　　　Hatay Turkey *see* Antakya
129 D2 **Hatchet Lake** Can.
52 B2 **Hatfield** Austr.
68 C1 **Hatgal** Mongolia
62 B2 **Ha Tinh** Vietnam
143 E1 **Hatteras, Cape** U.S.A.
142 C2 **Hattiesburg** U.S.A.
100 C2 **Hattingen** Ger.
63 B3 **Hat Yai** Thai.
117 C4 **Haud** *reg.* Eth.
93 E4 **Haugesund** Norway
93 E4 **Haukeligrend** Norway
92 I2 **Haukipudas** Fin.
54 C1 **Hauraki Gulf** N.Z.
114 B1 **Haut Atlas** *mts* Morocco
131 D2 **Hauterive** Can.
114 B1 **Hauts Plateaux** *plat.* Alg.
146 B2 **Havana** Cuba
99 C3 **Havant** U.K.
101 E1 **Havel** *r.* Ger.
101 F1 **Havelberg** Ger.
54 B2 **Havelock** N.Z.
54 C1 **Havelock North** N.Z.
99 A3 **Haverfordwest** U.K.
103 D2 **Havlíčkův Brod** Czech Rep.
92 H1 **Havøysund** Norway
111 C3 **Havran** Turkey
134 E1 **Havre** U.S.A.
131 D2 **Havre Aubert** Can.
131 D1 **Havre-St-Pierre** Can.
124 A5 **Hawaiian Islands**
　　　N. Pacific Ocean
98 B2 **Hawarden** U.K.
54 A2 **Hawea, Lake** N.Z.
54 B1 **Hawera** N.Z.
98 B1 **Hawes** U.K.
96 C3 **Hawick** U.K.
54 C1 **Hawke Bay** N.Z.
52 A2 **Hawker** Austr.
52 B1 **Hawkers Gate** Austr.
135 C3 **Hawthorne** U.S.A.
52 B2 **Hay** Austr.
128 C1 **Hay** *r.* Can.
134 C1 **Hayden** U.S.A.
129 E2 **Hayes** *r.* Man. Can.
126 F2 **Hayes** *r.* Nunavut Can.
79 C3 **Haymā'** Oman
111 C2 **Hayrabolu** Turkey
128 C1 **Hay River** Can.
137 D3 **Hays** U.S.A.
78 B3 **Hays** Yemen
90 B2 **Haysyn** Ukr.
99 C3 **Haywards Heath** U.K.
74 A1 **Hazarajat** *reg.* Afgh.
140 C3 **Hazard** U.S.A.
75 C2 **Hazārībāg** India
75 C2 **Hazaribagh Range** *mts*
　　　India
128 B2 **Hazelton** Can.
141 D2 **Hazleton** U.S.A.

53 C3 **Healesville** Austr.
130 B2 **Hearst** Can.
70 B2 **Hebei** prov. China
53 C1 **Hebel** Austr.
142 B1 **Heber Springs** U.S.A.
70 B2 **Hebi** China
131 D1 **Hebron** Can.
128 A2 **Hecate Strait** Can.
71 A3 **Hechi** China
93 F3 **Hede** Sweden
100 B1 **Heerenveen** Neth.
100 B1 **Heerhugowaard** Neth.
100 B2 **Heerlen** Neth.
80 B2 **Ḥefa** Israel
70 B2 **Hefei** China
70 B3 **Hefeng** China
69 E1 **Hegang** China
102 B1 **Heide** Ger.
122 A1 **Heide** Namibia
102 B2 **Heidelberg** Ger.
122 B3 **Heidelberg** S. Africa
102 B2 **Heilbronn** Ger.
69 E1 **Heilong Jiang** r. China/Rus. Fed.
93 I3 **Heinola** Fin.
92 F3 **Helagsfjället** mt. Sweden
142 B2 **Helena** AR U.S.A.
134 D1 **Helena** MT U.S.A.
96 B2 **Helensburgh** U.K.
102 B1 **Helgoland** i. Ger.
102 B1 **Helgoländer Bucht** b. Ger.
92 □A3 **Hella** Iceland
100 B2 **Hellevoetsluis** Neth.
107 C2 **Hellín** Spain
76 C3 **Helmand** r. Afgh.
101 E2 **Helmbrechts** Ger.
122 A2 **Helmeringhausen** Namibia
100 B2 **Helmond** Neth.
96 C1 **Helmsdale** U.K.
96 C1 **Helmsdale** r. U.K.
101 E1 **Helmstedt** Ger.
65 B1 **Helong** China
93 F4 **Helsingborg** Sweden
Helsingfors Fin. see **Helsinki**
93 F4 **Helsingør** Denmark
93 H3 **Helsinki** Fin.
97 C2 **Helvick Head** hd Rep. of Ireland
99 C3 **Hemel Hempstead** U.K.
101 D1 **Hemmoor** Ger.
92 F2 **Hemnesberget** Norway
70 B2 **Henan** prov. China
140 B3 **Henderson** KY U.S.A.
143 E1 **Henderson** NC U.S.A.
135 D3 **Henderson** NV U.S.A.
139 E2 **Henderson** TX U.S.A.
143 D1 **Hendersonville** U.S.A.
99 C3 **Hendon** U.K.
62 A1 **Hengduan Shan** mts China
100 C1 **Hengelo** Neth.
Hengnan China see **Hengyang**
70 B2 **Hengshui** China
71 A3 **Hengxian** China
71 B3 **Hengyang** China
Hengzhou China see **Hengxian**
91 C2 **Heniches'k** Ukr.
100 C2 **Hennef (Sieg)** Ger.
130 B1 **Henrietta Maria, Cape** Can.
139 D1 **Henryetta** U.S.A.
127 G2 **Henry Kater, Cape** Can.
101 D1 **Henstedt-Ulzburg** Ger.
120 A3 **Hentiesbaai** Namibia
62 A2 **Henzada** Myanmar
71 A3 **Hepu** China
76 C3 **Herāt** Afgh.
129 D2 **Herbert** Can.

101 D2 **Herbstein** Ger.
99 B2 **Hereford** U.K.
139 C2 **Hereford** U.S.A.
101 D1 **Herford** Ger.
100 C2 **Herkenbosch** Neth.
96 □ **Herma Ness** hd U.K.
122 A3 **Hermanus** S. Africa
53 C2 **Hermidale** Austr.
134 C1 **Hermiston** U.S.A.
59 D3 **Hermit Islands** P.N.G.
144 A2 **Hermosillo** Mex.
154 B3 **Hernandarias** Para.
100 C2 **Herne** Ger.
93 E4 **Herning** Denmark
99 C3 **Hertford** U.K.
123 C2 **Hertzogville** S. Africa
51 E2 **Hervey Bay** b. Austr.
101 F2 **Herzberg** Ger.
101 E3 **Herzogenaurach** Ger.
71 A3 **Heshan** China
128 A1 **Hess** r. Can.
101 D2 **Hessisch Lichtenau** Ger.
136 C1 **Hettinger** U.S.A.
101 E2 **Hettstedt** Ger.
101 D2 **Hexham** U.K.
71 B3 **Hexian** China
71 B3 **Heyuan** China
52 B3 **Heywood** Austr.
70 B2 **Heze** China
137 D3 **Hiawatha** U.S.A.
137 E1 **Hibbing** U.S.A.
54 C1 **Hicks Bay** N.Z.
66 D2 **Hidaka-sanmyaku** mts Japan
145 C2 **Hidalgo** Mex.
144 B2 **Hidalgo del Parral** Mex.
154 C1 **Hidrolândia** Brazil
High Atlas mts Morocco see **Haut Atlas**
134 B2 **High Desert** U.S.A.
128 C2 **High Level** Can.
143 E1 **High Point** U.S.A.
128 C2 **High Prairie** Can.
128 C2 **High River** Can.
129 D2 **Highrock Lake** Can.
99 C3 **High Wycombe** U.K.
88 B2 **Hiiumaa** i. Estonia
78 A2 **Hijaz** reg. Saudi Arabia
54 C1 **Hikurangi** mt. N.Z.
101 E2 **Hildburghausen** Ger.
101 E2 **Hilders** Ger.
101 D1 **Hildesheim** Ger.
100 C2 **Hillesheim** Ger.
140 C3 **Hillsboro** OH U.S.A.
139 D2 **Hillsboro** TX U.S.A.
53 C2 **Hillston** Austr.
143 D2 **Hilton Head Island** U.S.A.
100 B1 **Hilversum** Neth.
68 B2 **Himalaya** mts Asia
67 B4 **Himeji** Japan
123 C2 **Himeville** S. Africa
80 B2 **Ḩimş** Syria
51 D1 **Hinchinbrook Island** Austr.
74 A1 **Hindu Kush** mts Afgh./Pak.
143 D2 **Hinesville** U.S.A.
75 B2 **Hinganghat** India
74 A2 **Hīnīs** Turkey
92 G2 **Hinnøya** i. Norway
106 B2 **Hinojosa del Duque** Spain
128 C2 **Hinton** Can.
75 C2 **Hirakud Reservoir** India
66 D2 **Hirosaki** Japan
67 B4 **Hiroshima** Japan
101 E3 **Hirschaid** Ger.
101 E2 **Hirschberg** Ger.
105 C2 **Hirson** France
93 E4 **Hirtshals** Denmark
74 B2 **Hisar** India
147 C2 **Hispaniola** i. Caribbean Sea
81 C2 **Ḩīt** Iraq

67 D3 **Hitachi** Japan
67 D3 **Hitachinaka** Japan
92 E3 **Hitra** i. Norway
93 G4 **Hjälmaren** l. Sweden
129 D1 **Hjalmar Lake** Can.
93 F4 **Hjørring** Denmark
123 D2 **Hlabisa** S. Africa
92 □B2 **Hlíð** Iceland
91 C2 **Hlobyne** Ukr.
123 C2 **Hlohlowane** S. Africa
123 C2 **Hlotse** Lesotho
91 C1 **Hlukhiv** Ukr.
88 C2 **Hlybokaye** Belarus
114 C4 **Ho** Ghana
122 A1 **Hoachanas** Namibia
51 D4 **Hobart** Austr.
139 D1 **Hobart** U.S.A.
139 C2 **Hobbs** U.S.A.
93 E4 **Hobro** Denmark
117 C4 **Hobyo** Somalia
63 B2 **Hô Chi Minh** Vietnam
114 B3 **Hôd** reg. Maur.
103 E2 **Hódmezővásárhely** Hungary
100 B2 **Hoek van Holland** Neth.
65 B2 **Hoeyang** N. Korea
101 E2 **Hof** Ger.
101 E2 **Hofheim in Unterfranken** Ger.
92 □B3 **Höfn** Austurland Iceland
92 □A2 **Höfn** Vestfirðir Iceland
92 □B2 **Hofsjökull** ice cap Iceland
67 B4 **Hōfu** Japan
115 C2 **Hoggar** plat. Alg.
93 G4 **Högsby** Sweden
101 D2 **Hohe Rhön** mts Ger.
100 C2 **Hohe Venn** moorland Belgium
75 C1 **Hoh Xil Shan** mts China
63 B2 **Hôi An** Vietnam
62 A1 **Hojai** India
54 B2 **Hokitika** N.Z.
66 D2 **Hokkaidō** i. Japan
138 A2 **Holbrook** U.S.A.
137 D2 **Holdrege** U.S.A.
146 C2 **Holguín** Cuba
92 □B2 **Hóll** Iceland
Holland country Europe see **Netherlands**
140 B2 **Holland** U.S.A.
100 B1 **Hollum** Neth.
142 C2 **Holly Springs** U.S.A.
143 D3 **Hollywood** U.S.A.
92 F2 **Holm** Norway
100 C2 **Holman** Can.
92 H3 **Holmsund** Sweden
122 A2 **Holoog** Namibia
93 E4 **Holstebro** Denmark
143 D1 **Holston** r. U.S.A.
98 A2 **Holyhead** U.K.
98 C1 **Holy Island** England U.K.
98 A2 **Holy Island** Wales U.K.
136 C2 **Holyoke** U.S.A.
101 D2 **Holzminden** Ger.
62 A1 **Homalin** Myanmar
101 D2 **Homberg (Efze)** Ger.
114 B3 **Hombori** Mali
127 G2 **Home Bay** Can.
143 D3 **Homestead** U.S.A.
92 F3 **Hommelvik** Norway
89 D3 **Homyel'** Belarus
122 A3 **Hondeklipbaai** S. Africa
145 D3 **Hondo** r. Belize/Mex.
139 D3 **Hondo** U.S.A.
146 B3 **Honduras** country Central America
93 F3 **Hønefoss** Norway
135 B2 **Honey Lake** U.S.A.
104 C2 **Honfleur** France

62 B1 **Hông Gai** Vietnam
70 B3 **Honghu** China
71 A1 **Hongjiang** China
69 D3 **Hong Kong** China
71 B3 **Hong Kong**
 special admin. reg. China
65 B1 **Hongwŏn** N. Korea
70 B2 **Hongze Hu** *l.* China
66 D3 **Honjō** Japan
92 I1 **Honningsvåg** Norway
67 B3 **Honshū** *i.* Japan
134 B1 **Hood, Mount** *vol.* U.S.A.
50 A3 **Hood Point** Austr.
134 B1 **Hood River** U.S.A.
100 C1 **Hoogeveen** Neth.
100 C1 **Hoogezand-Sappemeer**
 Neth.
100 C2 **Hoog-Keppel** Neth. see
 Hoek van Holland
 Hook of Holland Neth. see
 Hoek van Holland
128 A2 **Hoonah** U.S.A.
100 B1 **Hoorn** Neth.
128 B3 **Hope** Can.
142 B2 **Hope** U.S.A.
83 N2 **Hope, Point** U.S.A.
131 D1 **Hopedale** Can.
131 D1 **Hope Mountains** Can.
52 B3 **Hopetoun** Austr.
122 B2 **Hopetown** S. Africa
141 D3 **Hopewell** U.S.A.
130 C1 **Hopewell Islands** Can.
50 B2 **Hopkins, Lake** *salt flat*
 Austr.
140 B3 **Hopkinsville** U.S.A.
134 B1 **Hoquiam** U.S.A.
81 C1 **Horasan** Turkey
93 F4 **Hörby** Sweden
89 D3 **Horki** Belarus
91 D2 **Horlivka** Ukr.
79 D2 **Hormak** Iran
79 C2 **Hormuz, Strait of**
 Iran/Oman
103 D2 **Horn** Austria
92 □A2 **Horn** *c.* Iceland
153 B6 **Horn, Cape** *c.* Chile
141 D2 **Hornell** U.S.A.
130 B2 **Hornepayne** Can.
98 C2 **Hornsea** U.K.
90 B2 **Horodenka** Ukr.
91 C1 **Horodnya** Ukr.
90 B2 **Horodok**
 Khmel'nyts'ka Oblast' Ukr.
90 A2 **Horodok** *L'vivs'ka Oblast'* Ukr.
90 A1 **Horokhiv** Ukr.
 Horqin Youyi Qianqi China
 see Ulanhot
131 E1 **Horse Islands** Can.
52 B3 **Horsham** Austr.
126 C2 **Horton** *r.* Can.
117 B4 **Hosa'ina** Eth.
74 A2 **Hoshab** Pak.
74 B1 **Hoshiarpur** India
77 E3 **Hotan** China
122 B2 **Hotazel** S. Africa
142 B2 **Hot Springs** *AR* U.S.A.
136 C2 **Hot Springs** *SD* U.S.A.
128 C1 **Hottah Lake** Can.
100 B2 **Houffalize** Belgium
70 B2 **Houma** China
142 B3 **Houma** U.S.A.
128 B2 **Houston** Can.
139 D3 **Houston** U.S.A.
122 B3 **Houwater** S. Africa
68 C1 **Hovd** Mongolia
99 C3 **Hove** U.K.
68 C1 **Hövsgöl Nuur** *l.* Mongolia
68 C1 **Hövüün** Mongolia
116 A3 **Howar, Wadi** *watercourse*
 Sudan
53 C3 **Howe, Cape** Austr.

53 C3 **Howlong** Austr.
101 D2 **Höxter** Ger.
96 C1 **Hoy** *i.* U.K.
93 E3 **Høyanger** Norway
102 C1 **Hoyerswerda** Ger.
109 C2 **Hradec Králové** Czech Rep.
91 C1 **Hrebinka** Ukr.
88 B3 **Hrodna** Belarus
62 A1 **Hsi-hseng** Myanmar
71 C3 **Hsinchu** Taiwan
71 C3 **Hsinying** Taiwan
62 A1 **Hsipaw** Myanmar
70 A2 **Huachi** China
150 A3 **Huacho** Peru
69 D2 **Huade** China
65 B1 **Huadian** China
70 B2 **Huaibei** China
71 A3 **Huaihua** China
70 B2 **Huainan** China
70 B2 **Huaiyang** China
70 B2 **Huaiyin** China
145 C3 **Huajuápan de León** Mex.
59 C3 **Huaki** Indon.
71 C3 **Hualien** Taiwan
150 A2 **Huallaga** *r.* Peru
120 A2 **Huambo** Angola
150 A3 **Huancayo** Peru
 Huangcaoba China see
 Xingyi
70 B2 **Huangchuan** China
 Huang Hai *sea* N. Pacific
 Ocean see Yellow Sea
70 B2 **Huang He** *r.* China
71 A4 **Huangliu** China
70 B2 **Huangshan** China
70 A2 **Huangtu Gaoyuan** *plat.*
 China
71 C3 **Huangyan** China
65 B1 **Huanren** China
150 A2 **Huánuco** Peru
152 B2 **Huanuni** Bol.
150 A2 **Huaráz** Peru
150 A3 **Huarmey** Peru
152 A3 **Huasco** Chile
152 A3 **Huasco** *r.* Chile
144 B2 **Huatabampo** Mex.
145 C3 **Huatusco** Mex.
71 A3 **Huayuan** China
70 B2 **Hubei** *prov.* China
73 B3 **Hubli** India
100 C2 **Hückelhoven** Ger.
98 C2 **Hucknall** U.K.
98 C2 **Huddersfield** U.K.
93 G3 **Hudiksvall** Sweden
141 E2 **Hudson** *r.* U.S.A.
129 D2 **Hudson Bay** Can.
127 F3 **Hudson Bay** *sea* Can.
128 B2 **Hudson's Hope** Can.
127 G2 **Hudson Strait** Can.
63 B2 **Huê** Vietnam
146 A3 **Huehuetenango** Guat.
144 B2 **Huehueto, Cerro**
 mt. Mex.
145 C2 **Huejutla** Mex.
106 B2 **Huelva** Spain
107 C2 **Huércal-Overa** Spain
107 C1 **Huesca** Spain
106 C2 **Huéscar** Spain
50 B3 **Hughes** Austr.
139 D2 **Hugo** U.S.A.
70 B1 **Huhhot** China
122 B2 **Huhudi** S. Africa
122 A2 **Huib-Hoch Plateau**
 Namibia
71 B3 **Huichang** China
65 B1 **Huich'ŏn** N. Korea
71 B3 **Huilai** China
120 A2 **Huila Plateau** Angola

62 B1 **Huili** China
65 B1 **Huinan** China
93 H3 **Huittinen** Fin.
145 C3 **Huixtla** Mex.
 Huiyang China see
 Huizhou
62 B1 **Huize** China
71 B3 **Huizhou** China
69 C1 **Hujirt** Mongolia
78 B2 **Hujr** Saudi Arabia
122 B1 **Hukuntsi** Botswana
78 B2 **Hulayfah** Saudi Arabia
66 B1 **Hulin** China
130 C2 **Hull** Can.
 Hulun China see Hailar
69 D1 **Hulun Nur** *l.* China
91 D2 **Hulyaypole** Ukr.
69 E1 **Huma** China
150 B2 **Humaitá** Brazil
122 B3 **Humansdorp** S. Africa
98 C2 **Humber** *est.* U.K.
126 D3 **Humboldt** Can.
142 C1 **Humboldt** U.S.A.
135 C2 **Humboldt** *r.* U.S.A.
103 E2 **Humenné** Slovakia
53 C3 **Hume Reservoir** Austr.
138 A1 **Humphreys Peak** U.S.A.
65 A1 **Hun** *r.* China
92 □A2 **Húnaflói** *b.* Iceland
71 B3 **Hunan** *prov.* China
65 C1 **Hunchun** China
110 B1 **Hunedoara** Romania
101 D2 **Hünfeld** Ger.
103 D2 **Hungary** *country* Europe
52 B1 **Hungerford** Austr.
65 B2 **Hüngnam** N. Korea
99 D2 **Hunstanton** U.K.
101 D1 **Hunte** *r.* Ger.
51 D4 **Hunter Islands** Austr.
99 C2 **Huntingdon** U.K.
140 B2 **Huntington** *IN* U.S.A.
140 C3 **Huntington** *WV* U.S.A.
54 C1 **Huntly** N.Z.
96 C2 **Huntly** U.K.
130 C2 **Huntsville** Can.
142 C2 **Huntsville** *AL* U.S.A.
139 D2 **Huntsville** *TX* U.S.A.
59 C3 **Huon Peninsula** P.N.G.
70 B2 **Huozhou** China
116 B2 **Hurghada** Egypt
137 D2 **Huron** U.S.A.
140 C2 **Huron, Lake** Can./U.S.A.
135 D3 **Hurricane** U.S.A.
92 □B3 **Húsavík** Iceland
110 C1 **Huşi** Romania
126 A2 **Huslia** U.S.A.
78 B3 **Husn Al 'Abr** Yemen
102 B1 **Husum** Ger.
69 C1 **Hutag** Mongolia
60 A1 **Hutanopan** Indon.
137 D3 **Hutchinson** U.S.A.
70 C2 **Huzhou** China
92 □C3 **Hvalnes** Iceland
92 □B3 **Hvannadalshnúkur** *vol.*
 Iceland
109 C2 **Hvar** *i.* Croatia
120 B2 **Hwange** Zimbabwe
136 C2 **Hyannis** U.S.A.
68 C1 **Hyargas Nuur** *salt l.*
 Mongolia
50 A3 **Hyden** Austr.
73 B3 **Hyderabad** India
74 A2 **Hyderabad** Pak.
105 D3 **Hyères** France
105 D3 **Hyères, Îles d'** *is* France
65 B1 **Hyesan** N. Korea
128 B2 **Hyland Post** Can.
67 B3 **Hyōno-sen** *mt.* Japan
99 D3 **Hythe** U.K.
93 H3 **Hyvinkää** Fin.

150 B2 **Iaco** r. Brazil
110 C2 **Ialomiţa** r. Romania
110 C1 **Ianca** Romania
110 C1 **Iaşi** Romania
64 A1 **Ibá** Phil.
115 C4 **Ibadan** Nigeria
150 A1 **Ibagué** Col.
150 A1 **Ibarra** Ecuador
78 B3 **Ibb** Yemen
100 C1 **Ibbenbüren** Ger.
115 C4 **Ibi** Nigeria
155 C1 **Ibiá** Brazil
155 D1 **Ibiraçu** Brazil
107 D2 **Ibiza** i. Spain
151 D3 **Ibotirama** Brazil
79 C2 **Ibrā'** Oman
79 C2 **Ibri** Oman
150 A3 **Ica** Peru
80 B2 **İçel** Turkey
92 □A3 **Iceland** country Europe
66 D3 **Ichinoseki** Japan
91 C1 **Ichnya** Ukr.
65 B2 **Ich'ŏn** N. Korea
139 E2 **Idabel** U.S.A.
134 D2 **Idaho** state U.S.A.
134 D2 **Idaho Falls** U.S.A.
100 C3 **Idar-Oberstein** Ger.
116 B2 **Idfu** Egypt
115 D2 **Idhān Awbārī** des. Libya
115 D2 **Idhān Murzūq** des. Libya
118 B3 **Idiofa** Dem. Rep. Congo
80 B2 **Idlib** Syria
158 B2 **Iepê** Brazil
100 A2 **Ieper** Belgium
119 D3 **Ifakara** Tanz.
121 □D3 **Ifanadiana** Madag.
115 C4 **Ife** Nigeria
114 C3 **Ifôghas, Adrar des** hills Mali
61 C1 **Igan** Sarawak Malaysia
154 C2 **Igarapava** Brazil
82 G2 **Igarka** Rus. Fed.
74 B3 **Igatpuri** India
81 C2 **Iğdır** Turkey
108 A3 **Iglesias** Sardinia Italy
127 F2 **Igloolik** Can.
Igluligaarjuk Can. see Chesterfield Inlet
130 A2 **Ignace** Can.
88 C2 **Ignalina** Lith.
110 C2 **İğneada** Turkey
111 B3 **Igoumenitsa** Greece
86 E3 **Igra** Rus. Fed.
86 F2 **Igrim** Rus. Fed.
154 B3 **Iguaçu** r. Brazil
154 B3 **Iguaçu Falls** Arg./Brazil
145 C3 **Iguala** Mex.
107 D1 **Igualada** Spain
154 C2 **Iguape** Brazil
154 B2 **Iguatemi** Brazil
154 B2 **Iguatemi** r. Brazil
151 E2 **Iguatu** Brazil
118 A3 **Iguéla** Gabon
119 D3 **Igunga** Tanz.
69 D2 **Ihbulag** Mongolia
121 □D3 **Ihosy** Madag.
92 I3 **Iisalmi** Fin.
115 C4 **Ijebu-Ode** Nigeria
100 B1 **IJmuiden** Neth.
100 B1 **IJssel** r. Neth.
100 B1 **IJsselmeer** l. Neth.
123 C2 **Ikageng** S. Africa
111 C3 **Ikaria** i. Greece
118 C3 **Ikela** Dem. Rep. Congo
110 B2 **Ikhtiman** Bulg.
67 A4 **Iki** i. Japan

121 □D3 **Ikongo** Madag.
65 B2 **Iksan** S. Korea
64 B1 **Ilagan** Phil.
81 C2 **Īlām** Iran
75 C2 **Ilam** Nepal
81 D3 **Ilawa** Pol.
79 C2 **Īlazārān, Kūh-e** mt. Iran
129 D2 **Île-à-la-Crosse** Can.
129 D2 **Île-à-la-Crosse, Lac** l. Can.
118 C3 **Ilebo** Dem. Rep. Congo
119 D2 **Ileret** Kenya
99 D3 **Ilford** U.K.
99 A3 **Ilfracombe** U.K.
155 D2 **Ilha Grande, Baía de** b. Brazil
154 B2 **Ilha Grande, Represa** resr Brazil
154 B2 **Ilha Solteira, Represa** resr Brazil
106 B1 **Ílhavo** Port.
151 E3 **Ilhéus** Brazil
64 B2 **Iligan** Phil.
152 A4 **Illapel** Chile
90 C2 **Illichivs'k** Ukr.
140 A3 **Illinois** r. U.S.A.
140 B3 **Illinois** state U.S.A.
90 B2 **Illintsi** Ukr.
115 C2 **Illizi** Alg.
89 D2 **Il'men', Ozero** l. Rus. Fed.
101 E2 **Ilmenau** Ger.
150 A3 **Ilo** Peru
64 B1 **Iloilo** Phil.
92 J3 **Ilomantsi** Fin.
115 C4 **Ilorin** Nigeria
53 D1 **Iluka** Austr.
127 H2 **Ilulissat** Greenland
67 A4 **Imari** Japan
117 C4 **Imī** Eth.
108 B2 **Imola** Italy
151 D2 **Imperatriz** Brazil
136 C2 **Imperial** U.S.A.
118 B2 **Impfondo** Congo
62 A1 **Imphal** India
111 C2 **İmroz** Turkey
150 B3 **Inambari** r. Peru
115 C2 **In Aménas** Alg.
59 C3 **Inanwatan** Indon.
92 I2 **Inari** Fin.
92 I2 **Inarijärvi** l. Fin.
67 D3 **Inawashiro-ko** l. Japan
80 B1 **İnce Burun** pt Turkey
65 B2 **Inch'ŏn** S. Korea
123 D2 **Incomati** r. Moz.
78 A3 **Inda Silasē** Eth.
144 B2 **Indé** Mex.
135 C3 **Independence** CA U.S.A.
137 E2 **Independence** IA U.S.A.
137 D3 **Independence** KS U.S.A.
137 E3 **Independence** MO U.S.A.
134 C2 **Independence Mountains** U.S.A.
76 B2 **Inderborskiy** Kazakh.
72 D2 **India** country Asia
141 D2 **Indiana** U.S.A.
140 B2 **Indiana** state U.S.A.
140 B3 **Indianapolis** U.S.A.
129 D2 **Indian Head** Can.
159 **Indian Ocean**
137 E2 **Indianola** IA U.S.A.
142 B2 **Indianola** MS U.S.A.
135 C3 **Indian Springs** U.S.A.
86 D2 **Indiga** Rus. Fed.
83 K2 **Indigirka** r. Rus. Fed.
109 D1 **Indija** Yugo.
135 C4 **Indio** U.S.A.
58 B3 **Indonesia** country Asia
74 B2 **Indore** India
61 B2 **Indramayu, Tanjung** pt Indon.
104 C2 **Indre** r. France

74 A2 **Indus** r. China/Pak.
74 A2 **Indus, Mouths of the** Pak.
80 B1 **İnebolu** Turkey
111 C2 **İnegöl** Turkey
144 B3 **Infiernillo, Presa** resr Mex.
53 D1 **Inglewood** Austr.
102 C2 **Ingolstadt** Ger.
75 C2 **Ingrāj Bāzār** India
123 D2 **Inhaca** Moz.
121 C3 **Inhambane** Moz.
97 A2 **Inishbofin** i. Rep. of Ireland
97 B2 **Inishmore** i. Rep. of Ireland
97 C1 **Inishowen** pen. Rep. of Ireland
54 B2 **Inland Kaikoura Range** mts N.Z.
102 C2 **Inn** r. Europe
127 G1 **Innaanganeq** c. Greenland
Inner Mongolia aut. reg. China see Nei Mongol Zizhiqu
96 B2 **Inner Sound** sea chan. U.K.
51 D1 **Innisfail** Austr.
102 C2 **Innsbruck** Austria
154 B1 **Inocência** Brazil
118 B3 **Inongo** Dem. Rep. Congo
103 D1 **Inowrocław** Pol.
114 C2 **In Salah** Alg.
62 A2 **Insein** Myanmar
86 F2 **Inta** Rus. Fed.
137 E1 **International Falls** U.S.A.
130 C1 **Inukjuak** Can.
126 C2 **Inuvik** Can.
96 B2 **Inveraray** U.K.
54 A3 **Invercargill** N.Z.
53 D1 **Inverell** Austr.
96 B2 **Invergordon** U.K.
128 C2 **Invermere** Can.
131 D2 **Inverness** Can.
96 B2 **Inverness** U.K.
96 C2 **Inverurie** U.K.
52 A3 **Investigator Strait** Austr.
77 E1 **Inya** Rus. Fed.
119 D3 **Inyonga** Tanz.
87 D3 **Inza** Rus. Fed.
111 B3 **Ioannina** Greece
137 D3 **Iola** U.S.A.
96 A2 **Iona** i. U.K.
111 B3 **Ionian Islands** Greece
109 C3 **Ionian Sea** Greece/Italy
Ionioi Nisoi is Greece see Ionian Islands
111 C3 **Ios** i. Greece
137 E2 **Iowa** state U.S.A.
137 E2 **Iowa City** U.S.A.
154 C1 **Ipameri** Brazil
155 D1 **Ipatinga** Brazil
81 C1 **Ipatovo** Rus. Fed.
123 C2 **Ipelegeng** S. Africa
150 A1 **Ipiales** Col.
154 B3 **Ipiranga** Brazil
60 B1 **Ipoh** Malaysia
154 B1 **Iporá** Brazil
118 C2 **Ippy** C.A.R.
111 C2 **Ipsala** Turkey
53 D1 **Ipswich** Austr.
99 D2 **Ipswich** U.K.
127 G2 **Iqaluit** Can.
152 A3 **Iquique** Chile
150 A2 **Iquitos** Peru
111 C3 **Irakleio** Greece
Iraklion Greece see Irakleio
73 D2 **Iran** country Asia
61 C1 **Iran, Pegunungan** mts Indon.
79 D2 **Īrānshahr** Iran
144 B2 **Irapuato** Mex.
81 C2 **Iraq** country Asia

154 B3 **Irati** Brazil
80 B2 **Irbid** Jordan
86 F3 **Irbit** Rus. Fed.
151 D3 **Irecê** Brazil
97 C2 **Ireland, Republic of** country
　　　Europe
118 C3 **Irema** Dem. Rep. Congo
76 D2 **Irgiz** Kazakh.
114 B3 **Irigui** reg. Mali/Maur.
119 D3 **Iringa** Tanz.
151 C2 **Iriri** r. Brazil
95 B3 **Irish Sea** Rep. of Ireland/U.K.
69 C1 **Irkutsk** Rus. Fed.
52 A2 **Iron Knob** Austr.
140 B1 **Iron Mountain** U.S.A.
140 A1 **Ironwood** U.S.A.
64 B1 **Irosin** Phil.
67 C4 **Irō-zaki** pt Japan
90 C1 **Irpin'** Ukr.
62 A2 **Irrawaddy** r. Myanmar
63 A2 **Irrawaddy, Mouths of the**
　　　Myanmar
86 F2 **Irtysh** r. Kazakh./Rus. Fed.
107 C1 **Irún** Spain
96 B3 **Irvine** U.K.
64 B2 **Isabela** Phil.
146 B3 **Isabela, Cordillera** mts Nic.
92 □A2 **Ísafjörður** Iceland
67 B4 **Isahaya** Japan
105 E2 **Isar** r. Ger.
96 □ **Isbister** U.K.
108 B2 **Ischia, Isola d'** i. Italy
67 C4 **Ise** Japan
118 C2 **Isengi** Dem. Rep. Congo
100 C2 **Iserlohn** Ger.
101 D1 **Isernhagen** Ger.
67 C4 **Ise-wan** b. Japan
114 C4 **Iseyin** Nigeria
　　　Isfahan Iran see **Eşfahān**
66 D2 **Ishikari-wan** b. Japan
77 D1 **Ishim** r. Kazakh./Rus. Fed.
66 D3 **Ishinomaki** Japan
67 D3 **Ishioka** Japan
140 B1 **Ishpeming** U.S.A.
111 C2 **Işıklar Dağı** mts Turkey
111 C3 **Işıklı** Turkey
123 D2 **Isipingo** S. Africa
119 C2 **Isiro** Dem. Rep. Congo
80 B2 **İskenderun** Turkey
82 G3 **Iskitim** Rus. Fed.
110 B2 **Iskūr** r. Bulg.
128 A2 **Iskut** r. Can.
74 B1 **Islamabad** Pak.
52 A2 **Island Lagoon** salt flat Austr.
129 E2 **Island Lake** l. Can.
54 B1 **Islands, Bay of** N.Z.
96 A3 **Islay** i. U.K.
94 A1 **Isle of Man** i. Irish Sea
116 B1 **Ismâ'ilîya** Egypt
109 C3 **Isola di Capo Rizzuto**
　　　Italy
110 C2 **Isperikh** Bulg.
80 B2 **Israel** country Asia
105 C2 **Issoire** France
111 C2 **İstanbul** Turkey
　　　İstanbul Boğazı str. Turkey
　　　see **Bosporus**
111 B3 **Istiaia** Greece
108 B1 **Istra** pen. Croatia
105 C3 **Istres** France
151 D3 **Itaberaba** Brazil
155 D1 **Itabira** Brazil
155 D2 **Itabirito** Brazil
151 E3 **Itabuna** Brazil
150 C2 **Itacoatiara** Brazil
154 B2 **Itaguajé** Brazil
154 B2 **Itaí** Brazil
154 B3 **Itaipu, Represa de** resr
　　　Brazil
151 C2 **Itaituba** Brazil

152 D3 **Itajaí** Brazil
155 C2 **Itajubá** Brazil
108 B2 **Italy** country Europe
155 D1 **Itamarandiba** Brazil
155 C1 **Itambacuri** Brazil
155 D1 **Itambé, Pico de** mt.
　　　Brazil
62 A1 **Itanagar** India
154 C2 **Itanhaém** Brazil
155 D1 **Itanhém** Brazil
155 D1 **Itaobim** Brazil
154 C1 **Itapajipe** Brazil
155 E1 **Itapebi** Brazil
155 D2 **Itapemirim** Brazil
155 D2 **Itaperuna** Brazil
155 D1 **Itapetinga** Brazil
154 C2 **Itapetininga** Brazil
154 C2 **Itapeva** Brazil
151 E3 **Itapicuru** r. Brazil
151 D2 **Itapicuru Mirim** Brazil
154 C1 **Itapuranga** Brazil
154 C2 **Itararé** Brazil
75 B2 **Itarsi** India
154 B1 **Itarumã** Brazil
155 D2 **Itaúna** Brazil
71 C3 **Itbayat** i. Phil.
141 D2 **Ithaca** U.S.A.
101 D1 **Ith Hils** ridge Ger.
118 C2 **Itimbiri** r.
　　　Dem. Rep. Congo
155 D1 **Itinga** Brazil
154 B1 **Itiquira** Brazil
154 A1 **Itiquira** r. Brazil
67 C4 **Itō** Japan
154 C2 **Itu** Brazil
150 A2 **Itui** r. Brazil
154 B2 **Ituiutaba** Brazil
119 C3 **Itula** Dem. Rep. Congo
154 C1 **Itumbiara** Brazil
154 B1 **Iturama** Brazil
101 D1 **Itzehoe** Ger.
83 N2 **Iul'tin** Rus. Fed.
154 B2 **Ivaí** r. Brazil
92 I2 **Ivalo** Fin.
88 C3 **Ivanava** Belarus
54 B2 **Ivanhoe** Austr.
90 B1 **Ivankiv** Ukr.
90 A2 **Ivano-Frankivs'k** Ukr.
89 F2 **Ivanovo** Rus. Fed.
88 C3 **Ivatsevichy** Belarus
111 C2 **Ivaylovgrad** Bulg.
86 F2 **Ivdel'** Rus. Fed.
154 B2 **Ivinheima** Brazil
154 B2 **Ivinheima** r. Brazil
127 H2 **Ivittuut** Greenland
　　　Ivory Coast country Africa
　　　see **Côte d'Ivoire**
108 A1 **Ivrea** Italy
111 C3 **İvrindi** Turkey
127 F2 **Ivujivik** Can.
67 D3 **Iwaki** Japan
67 B4 **Iwakuni** Japan
66 D2 **Iwamizawa** Japan
66 D2 **Iwanai** Japan
88 C3 **Iwye** Belarus
123 D3 **Ixopo** S. Africa
144 B2 **Ixtlán** Mex.
145 D2 **Izamal** Mex.
81 C1 **Izberbash** Rus. Fed.
86 E3 **Izhevsk** Rus. Fed.
86 E2 **Izhma** Rus. Fed.
89 E3 **Izmalkovo** Rus. Fed.
90 B2 **Izmayil** Ukr.
111 C3 **İzmir** Turkey
111 C3 **İznik Gölü** l. Turkey
145 C3 **Izúcar de Matamoros**
　　　Mex.
67 B3 **Izumo** Japan
90 B1 **Izyaslav** Ukr.
91 D2 **Izyum** Ukr.

106 C2 **Jabal, Bahr el** r.
　　　Sudan/Uganda see **White Nile**
75 B2 **Jabalón** r. Spain
75 B2 **Jabalpur** India
50 C1 **Jabiru** Austr.
109 C2 **Jablanica** Bos.-Herz.
151 E2 **Jaboatão** Brazil
154 C2 **Jaboticabal** Brazil
107 C1 **Jaca** Spain
145 C2 **Jacala** Mex.
151 C2 **Jacareacanga** Brazil
155 C2 **Jacareí** Brazil
155 D1 **Jacinto** Brazil
141 E1 **Jackman** U.S.A.
142 C2 **Jackson** AL U.S.A.
140 C2 **Jackson** MI U.S.A.
142 B2 **Jackson** MS U.S.A.
142 C1 **Jackson** TN U.S.A.
136 A2 **Jackson** WY U.S.A.
54 A2 **Jackson Head** hd N.Z.
142 B2 **Jacksonville** AR U.S.A.
143 D2 **Jacksonville** FL U.S.A.
140 A3 **Jacksonville** IL U.S.A.
143 E2 **Jacksonville** NC U.S.A.
139 D2 **Jacksonville** TX U.S.A.
147 C3 **Jacmel** Haiti
74 A2 **Jacobabad** Pak.
151 D3 **Jacobina** Brazil
131 D2 **Jacques Cartier, Mont**
　　　mt. Can.
151 D2 **Jacunda** Brazil
154 C2 **Jacupiranga** Brazil
109 C2 **Jadovnik** mt. Bos.-Herz.
150 A2 **Jaén** Peru
106 C2 **Jaén** Spain
52 A3 **Jaffa, Cape** Austr.
73 B4 **Jaffna** Sri Lanka
73 C3 **Jagdalpur** India
123 C2 **Jagersfontein** S. Africa
79 C2 **Jaghin** Iran
154 C2 **Jaguariaíva** Brazil
79 C2 **Jahrom** Iran
74 B2 **Jaipur** India
74 B2 **Jaisalmer** India
75 C2 **Jajarkot** Nepal
109 C2 **Jajce** Bos.-Herz.
60 B2 **Jakarta** Indon.
128 A1 **Jakes Corner** Can.
92 G2 **Jäkkvik** Sweden
92 H3 **Jakobstad** Fin.
77 D3 **Jalālābād** Kyrg.
77 D2 **Jalal-Abad** Kyrg.
74 B1 **Jalandhar** India
145 C3 **Jalapa Enríquez** Mex.
154 B2 **Jales** Brazil
74 B2 **Jalgaon** India
115 D4 **Jalingo** Nigeria
74 B1 **Jalna** India
144 B2 **Jalpa** Mex.
75 C2 **Jalpaiguri** India
145 C2 **Jalpan** Mex.
115 E2 **Jālū** Libya
146 B3 **Jamaica** country West Indies
146 C3 **Jamaica Channel**
　　　Haiti/Jamaica
75 C2 **Jamalpur** Bangl.
60 B2 **Jambi** Indon.
137 D2 **James** r. ND/SD U.S.A.
141 D3 **James** r. VA U.S.A.
130 B1 **James Bay** Can.
52 A2 **Jamestown** Austr.
137 D1 **Jamestown** ND U.S.A.
141 D2 **Jamestown** NY U.S.A.
74 B1 **Jammu** Jammu and Kashmir
74 B1 **Jammu and Kashmir** terr.
　　　Asia

74 B2 Jamnagar India
93 I3 Jämsä Fin.
75 C2 Jamshedpur India
75 C2 Jamuna r. Bangl.
75 C2 Janakpur Nepal
155 D1 Janaúba Brazil
78 D2 Jandaq Iran
140 B2 Janesville U.S.A.
84 C2 Jan Mayen i. Arctic Ocean
122 B3 Jansenville S. Africa
155 D1 Januária Brazil
74 B2 Jaora India
67 B4 Japan country Asia
156 C3 Japan, Sea of
        N. Pacific Ocean
150 B2 Japurá r. Brazil
154 C1 Jaraguá Brazil
154 B2 Jaraguari Brazil
152 C3 Jardim Brazil
69 D1 Jargalant Mongolia
103 D1 Jarocin Pol.
103 E1 Jarosław Pol.
92 F3 Järpen Sweden
70 A2 Jartai China
150 B3 Jarú Brazil
        Jarud China see Lubei
79 C2 Jāsk Iran
103 E2 Jasło Pol.
128 C2 Jasper Can.
140 B3 Jasper IN U.S.A.
139 E2 Jasper TX U.S.A.
103 D2 Jastrzębie-Zdrój Pol.
103 D2 Jászberény Hungary
154 B1 Jataí Brazil
74 A2 Jati Pak.
154 C2 Jaú Brazil
150 B2 Jaú r. Brazil
145 C2 Jaumave Mex.
75 C2 Jaunpur India
154 B1 Jauru Brazil
61 B2 Java i. Indon.
69 D1 Javarthushuu Mongolia
159 D4 Java Sea Indon.
        Jawa i. Indon. see Java
117 C4 Jawhar Somalia
103 D1 Jawor Pol.
103 D1 Jaworzno Pol.
59 D3 Jaya, Puncak mt. Indon.
59 D3 Jayapura Indon.
128 B1 Jean Marie River Can.
131 D1 Jeannin, Lac l. Can.
116 A3 Jebel Abyad Plateau
        Sudan
96 C3 Jedburgh U.K.
78 A2 Jeddah Saudi Arabia
101 E1 Jeetze r. Ger.
135 C3 Jefferson, Mount U.S.A.
137 E3 Jefferson City U.S.A.
88 C2 Jēkabpils Latvia
103 D1 Jelenia Góra Pol.
88 B2 Jelgava Latvia
61 C2 Jember Indon.
101 E2 Jena Ger.
80 B2 Jenin West Bank
142 B2 Jennings U.S.A.
151 D3 Jequié Brazil
155 D1 Jequitaí Brazil
155 D1 Jequitinhonha Brazil
155 E1 Jequitinhonha r. Brazil
147 C3 Jérémie Haiti
144 B2 Jerez Mex.
106 B2 Jerez de la Frontera Spain
109 D3 Jergucat Albania
115 C4 Jerid, Chott el salt l. Tunisia
134 D2 Jerome U.S.A.
95 C4 Jersey terr. Channel Is
151 D2 Jerumenha Brazil
80 B2 Jerusalem Israel/West Bank
53 D3 Jervis Bay Territory
        admin. div. Austr.

108 B1 Jesenice Slovenia
108 B2 Jesi Italy
101 F2 Jessen Ger.
75 C2 Jessore Bangl.
143 D2 Jesup U.S.A.
145 C3 Jesús Carranza Mex.
74 B2 Jhalawar India
74 B1 Jhang Pak.
75 B2 Jhansi India
75 C2 Jharsuguda India
74 B1 Jhelum Pak.
70 C2 Jiading China
69 E1 Jiamusi China
71 B3 Ji'an Jiangxi China
65 B1 Ji'an Jilin China
62 A1 Jianchuan China
        Jiandaoyu China see Zigui
70 B2 Jiangsu prov. China
71 B3 Jiangxi prov. China
70 A2 Jiangyou China
70 B3 Jianli China
71 B3 Jianyang Fujian China
70 A2 Jianyang Sichuan China
70 B2 Jiaohe China
70 C2 Jiaozhou China
70 B2 Jiaozuo China
70 C2 Jiaxing China
68 C2 Jiayuguan China
        Jiddah Saudi Arabia see
        Jeddah
92 G2 Jiehkkevarri mt. Norway
70 B2 Jiexiu China
68 C2 Jigzhi China
103 D2 Jihlava Czech Rep.
117 C4 Jijiga Eth.
69 E2 Jilib Somalia
117 C4 Jilib Somalia
65 B1 Jilin China
65 A1 Jilin Hada Ling mts China
117 B4 Jīma Eth.
144 B2 Jiménez Chihuahua Mex.
145 C2 Jiménez Tamaulipas Mex.
70 B2 Jinan China
70 B2 Jincheng China
53 C3 Jindabyne Austr.
103 D2 Jindřichův Hradec
        Czech Rep.
71 B3 Jingdezhen China
71 B3 Jinggangshan China
62 B1 Jinghong China
70 B2 Jingmen China
70 A2 Jingning China
70 A2 Jingsha China
70 A2 Jingtai China
71 A3 Jingxi China
65 B1 Jingyu China
70 A2 Jingyuan China
70 A2 Jingzhou China
71 B3 Jinhua China
70 B1 Jining Nei Mongol China
70 B2 Jining Shandong China
119 D2 Jinja Uganda
117 B4 Jinka Eth.
146 B3 Jinotepe Nic.
71 A3 Jinping China
        Jinsha Jiang r. China see
        Yangtze
70 B3 Jinshi China
70 C1 Jinxian China
150 B2 Jiparaná r. Brazil
79 C2 Jiroft Iran
71 A3 Jishou China
110 B2 Jiu r. Romania
70 A2 Jiuding Shan mt. China
70 B3 Jiujiang China
66 B1 Jixi China
78 B3 Jīzān Saudi Arabia
151 E2 João Pessoa Brazil
155 C1 João Pinheiro Brazil
74 B2 Jodhpur India

92 I3 Joensuu Fin.
67 C3 Jōetsu Japan
121 C3 Jofane Moz.
88 C2 Jõgeva Estonia
123 C2 Johannesburg S. Africa
134 C2 John Day U.S.A.
134 B1 John Day r. U.S.A.
128 C2 John d'Or Prairie Can.
143 E1 John H. Kerr Reservoir
        U.S.A.
96 C1 John o'Groats U.K.
143 D1 Johnson City U.S.A.
128 A1 Johnson's Crossing Can.
49 G2 Johnston Atoll
        N. Pacific Ocean
96 B3 Johnstone U.K.
141 D2 Johnstown U.S.A.
60 B1 Johor Bahru Malaysia
88 C2 Jõhvi Estonia
154 C3 Joinville Brazil
105 D2 Joinville France
92 G2 Jokkmokk Sweden
92 □B3 Jökulsá á Fjöllum r. Iceland
140 B2 Joliet U.S.A.
130 C2 Joliette Can.
64 B2 Jolo Phil.
64 B2 Jolo i. Phil.
61 C2 Jombang Indon.
75 C2 Jomsom Nepal
88 B2 Jonava Lith.
142 B1 Jonesboro AR U.S.A.
142 B2 Jonesboro LA U.S.A.
127 F1 Jones Sound sea chan. Can.
93 F4 Jönköping Sweden
131 C2 Jonquière Can.
145 C3 Jonuta Mex.
137 E3 Joplin U.S.A.
80 B2 Jordan country Asia
80 B2 Jordan r. Asia
136 B1 Jordan U.S.A.
134 C2 Jordan Valley U.S.A.
62 A1 Jorhat India
93 E4 Jørpeland Norway
115 C4 Jos Nigeria
145 C3 José Cardel Mex.
131 D1 Joseph, Lac l. Can.
50 B1 Joseph Bonaparte Gulf
        Austr.
115 C4 Jos Plateau Nigeria
93 E3 Jotunheimen mts Norway
122 B3 Joubertina S. Africa
123 C2 Jouberton S. Africa
93 I3 Joutseno Fin.
134 B1 Juan de Fuca Strait
        Can./U.S.A.
        Juanshui China see
        Tongcheng
145 B2 Juárez Mex.
151 D2 Juàzeiro Brazil
151 E2 Juàzeiro do Norte Brazil
117 B4 Juba Sudan
117 C5 Jubba r. Somalia
78 B2 Jubbah Saudi Arabia
107 C2 Júcar r. Spain
145 C3 Juchitán Mex.
102 C2 Judenburg Austria
101 D2 Jühnde Ger.
146 B3 Juigalpa Nic.
100 C1 Juist i. Ger.
155 D2 Juiz de Fora Brazil
150 A3 Juliaca Peru
75 C2 Jumla Nepal
74 B2 Junagadh India
139 D2 Junction U.S.A.
137 D3 Junction City U.S.A.
154 C2 Jundiaí Brazil
128 A2 Juneau U.S.A.
53 C2 Junee Austr.
105 D2 Jungfrau mt. Switz.
141 D2 Juniata r. U.S.A.

92 G3 Junsele Sweden
134 C2 Juntura U.S.A.
154 C2 Juquiá Brazil
117 A4 Jur r. Sudan
105 D2 Jura mts France/Switz.
96 B2 Jura i. U.K.
96 B3 Jura, Sound of
    sea chan. U.K.
88 B2 Jurbarkas Lith.
88 B2 Jūrmala Latvia
150 B2 Juruá r. Brazil
150 C2 Juruena r. Brazil
150 B2 Jutaí r. Brazil
101 F2 Jüterbog Ger.
70 B2 Juxian China
79 C2 Jüyom Iran
122 B1 Jwaneng Botswana
93 I3 Jyväskylä Fin.

K

74 B1 K2 mt. China/
    Jammu and Kashmir
119 C3 Kabalo Dem. Rep. Congo
119 C3 Kabare Dem. Rep. Congo
130 B2 Kabinakagami Lake Can.
118 C3 Kabinda Dem. Rep. Congo
118 B2 Kabo C.A.R.
120 B2 Kabompo Zambia
119 C3 Kabongo Dem. Rep. Congo
77 C3 Kābul Afgh.
64 B2 Kaburuang i. Indon.
121 B2 Kabwe Zambia
111 C2 Kaçanik Kosovo
72 A2 Kachchh, Gulf of India
83 I3 Kachug Rus. Fed.
81 C1 Kaçkar Dağı mt. Turkey
111 C2 Kadıköy Turkey
114 B3 Kadiolo Mali
73 B3 Kadmat i. India
121 B2 Kadoma Zimbabwe
63 A2 Kadonkani Myanmar
117 A3 Kaduqli Sudan
115 C3 Kaduna Nigeria
89 E2 Kaduy Rus. Fed.
86 E2 Kadzherom Rus. Fed.
114 A3 Kaédi Maur.
118 B1 Kaélé Cameroon
65 B2 Kaesŏng N. Korea
114 A3 Kaffrine Senegal
111 B3 Kafireas, Akra pt Greece
121 B2 Kafue Zambia
120 B2 Kafue r. Zambia
118 B2 Kaga Bandoro C.A.R.
83 K3 Kagal'nitskaya Rus. Fed.
67 B4 Kagoshima Japan
90 C2 Kaharlyk Ukr.
61 C2 Kahayan r. Indon.
118 B3 Kahemba Dem. Rep. Congo
101 E2 Kahla Ger.
79 C2 Kahnūj Iran
92 H2 Kahperusvaarat mts Fin.
80 B2 Kahramanmaraş Turkey
79 C2 Kahūrak Iran
59 C3 Kaiama Nigeria
115 C4 Kaiapoi N.Z.
59 C3 Kai Besar i. Indon.
70 B2 Kaifeng China
    Kaihua China see Wenshan
122 B2 Kaiingveld reg. S. Africa
59 C3 Kai Kecil i. Indon.
54 B2 Kaikohe N.Z.
114 A4 Kailahun Sierra Leone
23 Kaili China
59 C3 Kaimana Indon.
54 C1 Kaimana Mountains N.Z.
67 C4 Kainan Japan

115 C3 Kainji Reservoir Nigeria
54 B1 Kaipara Harbour N.Z.
74 B2 Kairana India
115 D1 Kairouan Tunisia
54 B1 Kaitaia N.Z.
54 C1 Kaitawa N.Z.
    Kaitong China see Tongyu
59 C3 Kaiwatu Indon.
65 A1 Kaiyuan Liaoning China
62 B1 Kaiyuan Yunnan China
92 I3 Kajaani Fin.
51 D2 Kajabbi Austr.
122 B2 Kakamas S. Africa
119 D2 Kakamega Kenya
91 C2 Kakhovka Ukr.
91 C2 Kakhovs'ke
    Vodoskhovyshche resr Ukr.
73 C3 Kākināda India
128 C1 Kakisa Can.
119 C3 Kakoswa Dem. Rep. Congo
126 B2 Kaktovik U.S.A.
    Kalaallit Nunaat terr.
    N. America see Greenland
59 C3 Kalabahi Indon.
120 B2 Kalabo Zambia
91 E1 Kalach Rus. Fed.
119 D2 Kalacha Dida Kenya
62 A1 Kaladan r. India/Myanmar
120 B3 Kalahari Desert Africa
92 H3 Kalajoki Fin.
111 B2 Kalamaria Greece
111 B3 Kalamata Greece
140 B2 Kalamazoo U.S.A.
111 B3 Kalampaka Greece
91 C2 Kalanchak Ukr.
63 B2 Kalasin Thai.
79 C2 Kalāt Iran
74 A2 Kalat Pak.
50 A2 Kalbarri Austr.
111 C3 Kale Turkey
80 B1 Kalecik Turkey
118 C3 Kalema Dem. Rep. Congo
119 C3 Kalémié Dem. Rep. Congo
62 A1 Kalemyo Myanmar
    Kalgan China see
    Zhangjiakou
50 B3 Kalgoorlie Austr.
109 C2 Kali Croatia
110 C2 Kaliakra, Nos pt Bulg.
61 C2 Kalimantan reg. Indon.
88 B3 Kaliningrad Rus. Fed.
91 D2 Kalininskaya Rus. Fed.
88 C3 Kalinkavichy Belarus
134 D1 Kalispell U.S.A.
103 D1 Kalisz Pol.
91 E2 Kalitva r. Rus. Fed.
92 H2 Kalix Sweden
92 H2 Kalixälven r. Sweden
111 C3 Kalkan Turkey
120 A3 Kalkfeld Namibia
92 I3 Kallavesi i. Fin.
92 F3 Kallsjön l. Sweden
93 G4 Kalmar Sweden
93 G4 Kalmarsund sea chan.
    Sweden
120 B2 Kalomo Zambia
128 B2 Kalone Peak Can.
75 B1 Kalpa India
73 B3 Kalpeni i. India
75 B2 Kalpi India
101 D1 Kaltenkirchen Ger.
89 E3 Kaluga Rus. Fed.
93 F4 Kalundborg Denmark
90 A2 Kalush Ukr.
89 E2 Kalyazin Rus. Fed.
111 C3 Kalymnos i. Greece
119 C3 Kama Dem. Rep. Congo
62 A2 Kama Myanmar
86 E3 Kama r. Rus. Fed.

66 D3 Kamaishi Japan
80 B2 Kaman Turkey
120 A2 Kamanjab Namibia
78 B3 Kamarān i. Yemen
74 A2 Kamarod Pak.
50 B3 Kambalda Austr.
119 C4 Kambove Dem. Rep. Congo
110 C2 Kamchiya r. Bulg.
110 B2 Kamenitsa mt. Bulg.
108 B2 Kamenjak, Rt pt Croatia
76 B1 Kamenka Kazakh.
91 D1 Kamenka Rus. Fed.
91 E2 Kamenolomni Rus. Fed.
83 M2 Kamenskoye Rus. Fed.
91 E2 Kamensk-Shakhtinskiy
    Rus. Fed.
86 F3 Kamensk-Ural'skiy
    Rus. Fed.
122 A3 Kamiesberge mts S. Africa
122 A3 Kamieskroon S. Africa
129 D1 Kamilukuak Lake l. Can.
119 C3 Kamina Dem. Rep. Congo
129 E1 Kaminak Lake Can.
90 A1 Kamin'-Kashyrs'kyy Ukr.
128 B2 Kamloops Can.
119 C3 Kamonia Dem. Rep. Congo
119 D2 Kampala Uganda
60 B1 Kampar r. Indon.
60 B1 Kampar Malaysia
100 B1 Kampen Neth.
119 C3 Kampene Dem. Rep. Congo
63 A2 Kamphaeng Phet Thai.
63 B2 Kâmpóng Cham Cambodia
63 B2 Kâmpóng Chhnăng
    Cambodia
    Kâmpóng Saôm Cambodia
    see Sihanoukville
63 B2 Kâmpóng Spoe Cambodia
63 B2 Kâmpôt Cambodia
129 D2 Kamsack Can.
86 E3 Kamskoye Vodokhranilishche
    resr Rus. Fed.
117 C4 Kamsuuma Somalia
90 B2 Kam"yanets'-Podil's'kyy Ukr.
90 A1 Kam"yanka-Buz'ka Ukr.
88 B3 Kamyanyets Belarus
91 D2 Kamyshevatskaya Rus. Fed.
87 D3 Kamyshin Rus. Fed.
135 D3 Kanab U.S.A.
118 C3 Kananga Dem. Rep. Congo
87 D3 Kanash Rus. Fed.
140 C3 Kanawha r. U.S.A.
67 C3 Kanazawa Japan
62 A1 Kanbalu Myanmar
63 A2 Kanchanaburi Thai.
73 B3 Kanchipuram India
77 C3 Kandahār Afgh.
86 C2 Kandalaksha Rus. Fed.
61 C2 Kandangan Indon.
74 A2 Kandhkot Pak.
114 C3 Kandi Benin
74 B2 Kandla India
53 C2 Kandos Austr.
121 □D2 Kandreho Madag.
73 C4 Kandy Sri Lanka
76 B2 Kandyagash Kazakh.
127 G1 Kane Bassin b. Greenland
91 D2 Kanevskaya Rus. Fed.
122 B1 Kang Botswana
127 H2 Kangaatsiaq Greenland
114 B3 Kangaba Mali
80 B2 Kangal Turkey
79 C2 Kangān Iran
60 B1 Kangar Malaysia
52 A3 Kangaroo Island Austr.
75 C2 Kangchenjunga mt.
    India/Nepal
65 B2 Kangdong N. Korea
61 C2 Kangean, Kepulauan is
    Indon.

Kangeq

200

127 I2	**Kangeq** c. Greenland	
127 I2	**Kangerlussuaq** inlet Greenland	
127 H2	**Kangerlussuaq** inlet Greenland	
127 H2	**Kangersuatsiaq** Greenland	
65 B1	**Kanggye** N. Korea	
131 D1	**Kangiqsualujjuaq** Can.	
127 G2	**Kangiqsujuaq** Can.	
127 G2	**Kangirsuk** Can.	
75 C2	**Kangmar** China	
65 B2	**Kangnŭng** S. Korea	
65 A1	**Kangping** China	
72 D2	**Kangto** mt. China/India	
62 A1	**Kani** Myanmar	
86 D2	**Kanin, Poluostrov** pen. Rus. Fed.	
86 D2	**Kanin Nos** Rus. Fed.	
91 C2	**Kaniv** Ukr.	
93 H3	**Kankaanpää** Fin.	
140 B2	**Kankakee** U.S.A.	
114 B3	**Kankan** Guinea	
75 C2	**Kanker** India	
	Kannur India see Cannanore	
115 C3	**Kano** Nigeria	
122 B3	**Kanonpunt** pt S. Africa	
67 B4	**Kanoya** Japan	
75 C2	**Kanpur** India	
136 C3	**Kansas** r. U.S.A.	
137 D3	**Kansas** state U.S.A.	
137 E3	**Kansas City** U.S.A.	
83 H3	**Kansk** Rus. Fed.	
114 C3	**Kantchari** Burkina	
91 D2	**Kantemirovka** Rus. Fed.	
97 B2	**Kanturk** Rep. of Ireland	
123 D2	**KaNyamazane** S. Africa	
71 C3	**Kaohsiung** Taiwan	
120 A2	**Kaokoveld** plat. Namibia	
114 A3	**Kaolack** Senegal	
120 B2	**Kaoma** Zambia	
118 C3	**Kapanga** Dem. Rep. Congo	
77 D2	**Kapchagay** Kazakh.	
77 D2	**Kapchagayskoye Vodokhranilishche** resr Kazakh.	
100 B2	**Kapellen** Belgium	
121 B2	**Kapiri Mposhi** Zambia	
127 H2	**Kapisillit** Greenland	
130 B1	**Kapiskau** r. Can.	
61 C1	**Kapit** Sarawak Malaysia	
63 A3	**Kapoe** Thai.	
117 B4	**Kapoeta** Sudan	
103 D2	**Kaposvár** Hungary	
61 B2	**Kapuas** r. Indon.	
52 A2	**Kapunda** Austr.	
130 B2	**Kapuskasing** Can.	
103 D2	**Kapuvár** Hungary	
88 C3	**Kapyl'** Belarus	
114 C4	**Kara** Togo	
111 C3	**Kara Ada** i. Turkey	
76 B2	**Kara-Bogaz Gol, Zaliv** b. Turkm.	
76 B2	**Karabogazkel'** Turkm.	
80 B1	**Karabük** Turkey	
76 C2	**Karabutak** Kazakh.	
110 C2	**Karacaköy** Turkey	
89 D3	**Karachev** Rus. Fed.	
74 A2	**Karachi** Pak.	
	Kara Deniz sea Asia/Europe see Black Sea	
77 D2	**Karaganda** Kazakh.	
77 D2	**Karagayly** Kazakh.	
83 L3	**Karaginskiy Zaliv** b. Rus. Fed.	
81 D2	**Karaj** Iran	
76 B2	**Karakalpakiya** Kazakh.	
64 B2	**Karakelong** i. Indon.	
77 D2	**Kara-Köl** Kyrg.	
77 D2	**Karakol** Kyrg.	
74 B1	**Karakoram** mts Asia	
76 B2	**Karakum, Peski** des. Kazakh.	
	Karakum Desert Turkm. see Karakumy, Peski	
76 C3	**Karakumy, Peski** des. Turkm.	
80 B2	**Karaman** Turkey	
77 E2	**Karamay** China	
54 B2	**Karamea** N.Z.	
54 B2	**Karamea Bight** b. N.Z.	
80 B2	**Karapınar** Turkey	
122 A2	**Karasburg** Namibia	
86 F1	**Kara Sea** sea Rus. Fed.	
92 I2	**Karasjok** Norway	
82 G3	**Karasuk** Rus. Fed.	
77 D2	**Karatau** Kazakh.	
77 C2	**Karatau, Khrebet** mts Kazakh.	
86 F2	**Karatayka** Rus. Fed.	
67 A4	**Karatsu** Japan	
60 B2	**Karawang** Indon.	
81 C2	**Karbalā'** Iraq	
103 E2	**Karcag** Hungary	
111 B3	**Karditsa** Greece	
88 B2	**Kärdla** Estonia	
122 B3	**Kareeberge** mts S. Africa	
75 B2	**Kareli** India	
74 B1	**Kargil** Jammu and Kashmir	
121 B2	**Kariba** Zimbabwe	
121 B2	**Kariba, Lake** resr Zambia/Zimbabwe	
61 B2	**Karimata, Pulau-pulau** is Indon.	
61 B2	**Karimata, Selat** str. Indon.	
73 B3	**Karimnagar** India	
61 C2	**Karimunjawa, Pulau-pulau** is Indon.	
91 C2	**Karkinits'ka Zatoka** g. Ukr.	
91 D2	**Karlivka** Ukr.	
109 C1	**Karlovac** Croatia	
102 C1	**Karlovy Vary** Czech Rep.	
93 F4	**Karlshamn** Sweden	
93 G4	**Karlskrona** Sweden	
102 B2	**Karlsruhe** Ger.	
93 F4	**Karlstad** Sweden	
101 D3	**Karlstadt** Ger.	
89 D3	**Karma** Belarus	
93 E4	**Karmøy** i. Norway	
75 D2	**Karnaphuli Reservoir** Bangl.	
74 B2	**Karnal** India	
110 C2	**Karnobat** Bulg.	
74 A2	**Karodi** Pak.	
121 B2	**Karoi** Zimbabwe	
121 C1	**Karonga** Malawi	
116 B3	**Karora** Eritrea	
111 C3	**Karpathos** i. Greece	
111 B3	**Karpenisi** Greece	
86 D2	**Karpogory** Rus. Fed.	
50 A2	**Karratha** Austr.	
81 C1	**Kars** Turkey	
88 C2	**Kārsava** Latvia	
77 C3	**Karshi** Uzbek.	
86 E2	**Karskiye Vorota, Proliv** str. Rus. Fed.	
	Karskoye More sea Rus. Fed. see Kara Sea	
101 E1	**Karstädt** Ger.	
111 C2	**Kartal** Turkey	
81 D3	**Kartaly** Rus. Fed.	
73 B3	**Karwar** India	
83 I3	**Karymskoye** Rus. Fed.	
111 B3	**Karystos** Greece	
80 A2	**Kaş** Turkey	
130 B1	**Kasabonika Lake** Can.	
118 C4	**Kasaji** Dem. Rep. Congo	
121 C2	**Kasama** Zambia	
120 B2	**Kasane** Botswana	
118 B3	**Kasangulu** Dem. Rep. Congo	
73 B3	**Kasaragod** India	
129 D1	**Kasba Lake** Can.	
120 B2	**Kasempa** Zambia	
119 C4	**Kasenga** Dem. Rep. Congo	
119 C3	**Kasese** Dem. Rep. Congo	
119 D2	**Kasese** Uganda	
81 D2	**Kāshān** Iran	
	Kashgar China see Kashi	
77 D3	**Kashi** China	
67 D3	**Kashima-nada** b. Japan	
89 E2	**Kashin** Rus. Fed.	
89 E3	**Kashira** Rus. Fed.	
89 E3	**Kashirskoye** Rus. Fed.	
67 C3	**Kashiwazaki** Japan	
76 B3	**Kāshmar** Iran	
74 A2	**Kashmor** Pak.	
119 C3	**Kashyukulu** Dem. Rep. Congo	
87 D3	**Kasimov** Rus. Fed.	
93 H3	**Kaskinen** Fin.	
119 C3	**Kasongo** Dem. Rep. Congo	
118 B3	**Kasongo-Lunda** Dem. Rep. Congo	
111 C3	**Kasos** i. Greece	
	Kaspiyskoye More sea Asia/Europe see Caspian Sea	
116 B3	**Kassala** Sudan	
101 D2	**Kassel** Ger.	
80 B1	**Kastamonu** Turkey	
111 B3	**Kastelli** Greece	
111 B2	**Kastoria** Greece	
89 D3	**Kastsyukovichy** Belarus	
119 D3	**Kasulu** Tanz.	
121 C2	**Kasungu** Malawi	
141 F1	**Katahdin, Mount** U.S.A.	
118 C3	**Katako-Kombe** Dem. Rep. Congo	
50 A3	**Katanning** Austr.	
63 A3	**Katchall** i. India	
111 B2	**Katerini** Greece	
128 A2	**Kate's Needle** mt. Can./U.S.A.	
121 C2	**Katete** Zambia	
62 A1	**Katha** Myanmar	
78 A2	**Katherîna, Gebel** mt. Egypt	
50 C1	**Katherine** r. Austr.	
74 B2	**Kathiawar** pen. India	
123 C2	**Kathlehong** S. Africa	
75 C2	**Kathmandu** Nepal	
122 B2	**Kathu** S. Africa	
74 B1	**Kathua** Jammu and Kashmir	
114 B3	**Kati** Mali	
75 C2	**Katihar** India	
54 C1	**Katikati** N.Z.	
123 C3	**Kati-Kati** S. Africa	
120 B2	**Katima Mulilo** Namibia	
111 B3	**Kato Achaïa** Greece	
53 D2	**Katoomba** Austr.	
103 D1	**Katowice** Pol.	
93 G4	**Katrineholm** Sweden	
115 C3	**Katsina** Nigeria	
115 C4	**Katsina-Ala** Nigeria	
77 C3	**Kattakurgan** Uzbek.	
93 F4	**Kattegat** str. Denmark/Sweden	
100 B1	**Katwijk aan Zee** Neth.	
93 H3	**Kauhajoki** Fin.	
88 B3	**Kaunas** Lith.	
115 C3	**Kaura-Namoda** Nigeria	
93 I3	**Kautokeino** Norway	
111 B2	**Kavala** Greece	
66 C2	**Kavalerovo** Rus. Fed.	
73 C3	**Kavali** India	
73 B3	**Kavaratti** i. India	
110 C2	**Kavarna** Bulg.	
81 D2	**Kavīr, Dasht-e** des. Iran	
67 C3	**Kawagoe** Japan	
54 B1	**Kawakawa** N.Z.	
67 C3	**Kawanishi** Japan	
130 C2	**Kawartha Lakes** Can.	
67 C3	**Kawasaki** Japan	
54 C1	**Kawerau** N.Z.	

63 A2 Kawkareik Myanmar
62 A1 Kawlin Myanmar
63 A2 Kawmapyin Myanmar
63 A2 Kawthaung Myanmar
77 D1 Kaxgar He r. China
114 B3 Kaya Burkina
61 C1 Kayan r. Indon.
136 B2 Kaycee U.S.A.
138 A1 Kayenta U.S.A.
114 A3 Kayes Mali
77 D2 Kaynar Kazakh.
80 B2 Kayseri Turkey
77 D1 Kazakhskiy Melkosopochnik plain Kazakh.
81 D1 Käzerün Iran
103 E2 Kazincbarcika Hungary
86 F2 Kazymskiy Mys Rus. Fed.
111 B3 Kea i. Greece
97 C1 Keady U.K.
137 D2 Kearney U.S.A.
138 A2 Kearny U.S.A.
116 A3 Kebkabiya Sudan
92 G2 Kebnekaise mt. Sweden
117 C4 K'ebrï Dehar Eth.
61 B2 Kebumen Indon.
128 B2 Kechika r. Can.
103 D2 Kecskemét Hungary
88 B2 Kédainiai Lith.
114 A3 Kédougou Senegal
103 D1 Kędzierzyn-Koźle Pol.
128 B1 Keele r. Can.
128 A1 Keele Peak mt. Can.
141 E2 Keene U.S.A.
122 A2 Keetmanshoop Namibia
129 E3 Keewatin Can.
111 B3 Kefallonia i. Greece
59 C3 Kefamenanu Indon.
92 □A3 Keflavík Iceland
77 D2 Kegen Kazakh.
128 C2 Keg River Can.
62 A1 Kehsi Mansam Myanmar
98 C2 Keighley U.K.
88 B2 Keila Estonia
122 B2 Keimoes S. Africa
92 I3 Keitele l. Fin.
52 B3 Keith Austr.
103 E2 Kékes mt. Hungary
60 B1 Kelang Malaysia
92 J2 Keles-Uayv, Gora hill Rus. Fed.
102 C2 Kelheim Ger.
80 B1 Kelkit r. Turkey
128 B1 Keller Lake l. Can.
134 C1 Kellogg U.S.A.
92 I2 Kelloselkä Fin.
97 C2 Kells Rep. of Ireland
88 B2 Kelmė Lith.
115 D4 Kelo Chad
128 C3 Kelowna Can.
96 C3 Kelso U.K.
134 B1 Kelso U.S.A.
60 B1 Keluang Malaysia
129 D2 Kelvington Can.
86 C2 Kem' Rus. Fed.
128 B2 Kemano Can.
111 C3 Kemer Turkey
82 G3 Kemerovo Rus. Fed.
92 H2 Kemi Fin.
92 I2 Kemijärvi Fin.
92 I2 Kemijoki r. Fin.
136 A2 Kemmerer U.S.A.
92 I3 Kempele Fin.
51 D2 Kempsey Austr.

130 C2 Kempt, Lac l. Can.
102 C2 Kempten (Allgäu) Ger.
123 C2 Kempton Park S. Africa
61 C2 Kemujan i. Indon.
129 D2 Kenaston Can.
98 B1 Kendal U.K.
59 C3 Kendari Indon.
61 C2 Kendawangan Indon.
115 D3 Kendégué Chad
75 C2 Kendujhargarh India
114 A4 Kenema Sierra Leone
118 B3 Kenge Dem. Rep. Congo
62 A1 Kengtung Myanmar
122 B2 Kenhardt S. Africa
114 B1 Kénitra Morocco
97 B3 Kenmare Rep. of Ireland
136 C1 Kenmare U.S.A.
97 A3 Kenmare River inlet Rep. of Ireland
100 C3 Kenn Ger.
137 E3 Kennett U.S.A.
134 C1 Kennewick U.S.A.
129 E3 Kenora Can.
140 B2 Kenosha U.S.A.
138 C2 Kent U.S.A.
77 C2 Kentau Kazakh.
140 B3 Kentucky r. U.S.A.
140 C3 Kentucky state U.S.A.
140 B3 Kentucky Lake U.S.A.
119 D2 Kenya country Africa
Kenya, Mount Kenya see Kirinyaga
117 E2 Keokuk U.S.A.
111 C3 Kepsut Turkey
52 B3 Kerang Austr.
91 D2 Kerch Ukr.
59 D3 Kerema P.N.G.
128 C3 Keremeos Can.
116 B3 Keren Eritrea
81 C2 Kerend Iran
159 C7 Kerguelen Plateau sea feature Indian Ocean
119 D3 Kericho Kenya
54 B1 Kerikeri N.Z.
60 B2 Kerinci, Gunung vol. Indon.
77 C3 Kerki Turkm.
111 A3 Kerkyra Greece
Kerkyra i. Greece see Corfu
116 B3 Kerma Sudan
79 C1 Kermän Iran
81 C2 Kermänshäh Iran
139 C2 Kermit U.S.A.
135 C3 Kern r. U.S.A.
100 C2 Kerpen Ger.
129 D2 Kerrobert Can.
139 D2 Kerrville U.S.A.
80 B2 Keryneia Cyprus
130 B1 Kesagami Lake Can.
111 C2 Keşan Turkey
67 D3 Kesennuma Japan
74 B2 Keshod India
100 C2 Kessel Neth.
98 B1 Keswick U.K.
103 D2 Keszthely Hungary
83 G2 Ket' r. Rus. Fed.
61 C2 Ketapang Indon.
128 A2 Ketchikan U.S.A.
134 D2 Ketchum U.S.A.
99 C2 Kettering U.K.
93 H3 Keuruu Fin.
100 C2 Kevelaer Ger.
140 B2 Kewanee U.S.A.
140 B1 Keweenaw Bay b. U.S.A.
140 B1 Keweenaw Peninsula U.S.A.
143 D3 Key Largo U.S.A.
141 D3 Keyser U.S.A.
123 C2 Kgotsong S. Africa
69 E1 Khabarovsk Rus. Fed.
80 B1 Khadyzhensk Rus. Fed.

62 A1 Khagrachari Bangl.
74 A2 Khairpur Pak.
122 B1 Khakhea Botswana
68 C1 Khamar-Daban, Khrebet mts Rus. Fed.
74 B2 Khambhat India
73 B3 Khambhat, Gulf of India
74 B2 Khamgaon India
78 B3 Khamir Yemen
78 B3 Khamis Mushayt Saudi Arabia
77 C3 Khänäbäd Afgh.
74 B2 Khandwa India
83 K2 Khandyga Rus. Fed.
74 B1 Khanewal Pak.
66 B2 Khanka, Lake China/Rus. Fed.
74 B2 Khanpur Pak.
77 D2 Khantau Kazakh.
83 H2 Khantayskoye, Ozero l. Rus. Fed.
86 F2 Khanty-Mansiysk Rus. Fed.
63 A2 Khao Chum Thong Thai.
63 A2 Khao Laem Reservoir Thai.
87 D4 Kharabali Rus. Fed.
75 C2 Kharagpur India
79 C2 Khärän r. Iran
91 D2 Kharkiv Ukr.
Khar'kov Ukr. see Kharkiv
110 C2 Kharmanli Bulg.
86 D3 Kharovsk Rus. Fed.
116 B3 Khartoum Sudan
87 D4 Khasav'yurt Rus. Fed.
79 D2 Khäsh Iran
78 A3 Khashm el Girba Sudan
78 A3 Khashm el Girba Dam Sudan
74 D2 Khäsi Hills India
110 C2 Khaskovo Bulg.
123 C3 Khayamnandi S. Africa
77 C2 Khayatbashi, Gora mt. Uzbek.
78 A2 Khaybar Saudi Arabia
122 A3 Khayelitsha S. Africa
62 B2 Khê Bo Vietnam
107 D2 Khemis Miliana Alg.
63 B2 Khemmarat Thai.
115 C1 Khenchela Alg.
81 D3 Kherämeh Iran
91 C2 Kherson Ukr.
83 H2 Kheta r. Rus. Fed.
69 D1 Khilok Rus. Fed.
89 E2 Khimki Rus. Fed.
89 E3 Khlevnoye Rus. Fed.
90 B2 Khmel'nyts'kyy Ukr.
76 B1 Khobda Kazakh.
89 E3 Khodzheyli Uzbek.
89 E3 Khokhol'skiy Rus. Fed.
74 B1 Khokhropar Pak.
89 D2 Kholm Rus. Fed.
89 D2 Kholm-Zhirkovskiy Rus. Fed.
79 C2 Khonj Iran
62 A2 Khon Kaen Thai.
62 A1 Khonsa India
86 E2 Khonuu Rus. Fed.
86 E2 Khoreyver Rus. Fed.
69 D1 Khorinsk Rus. Fed.
91 C2 Khorol Ukr.
81 C2 Khorramäbäd Iran
81 C2 Khorramshahr Iran
77 D3 Khorugh Tajik.
74 A1 Khowst Afgh.
62 A1 Khreum Myanmar
76 B1 Khromtau Kazakh.
90 B2 Khrystynivka Ukr.
77 D3 Khŭjand Tajik.
63 B2 Khu Khan Thai.
78 A2 Khulays Saudi Arabia
75 C2 Khulna Bangl.

81 D2 Khunsar Iran
79 B2 Khurays Saudi Arabia
74 B1 Khushab Pak.
90 A2 Khust Ukr.
123 C2 Khutsong S. Africa
74 A2 Khuzdar Pak.
79 C2 Khvormūj Iran
81 C2 Khvoy Iran
77 D3 Khyber Pass Afgh./Pak.
53 D2 Kiama Austr.
119 C3 Kiambi Dem. Rep. Congo
119 D3 Kibiti Tanz.
109 D2 Kičevo Macedonia
114 C3 Kidal Mali
99 B2 Kidderminster U.K.
114 A3 Kidira Senegal
54 C1 Kidnappers, Cape N.Z.
102 C1 Kiel Ger.
103 E1 Kielce Pol.
98 B1 Kielder Water resr U.K.
90 C1 Kiev Ukr.
114 A3 Kiffa Maur.
119 D3 Kigali Rwanda
119 C3 Kigoma Tanz.
88 B2 Kihnu i. Estonia
92 I2 Kiiminki Fin.
67 B4 Kii-suidō sea chan. Japan
109 D1 Kikinda Yugo.
119 C3 Kikondja Dem. Rep. Congo
59 D3 Kikori P.N.G.
59 D3 Kikori r. P.N.G.
118 B3 Kikwit Dem. Rep. Congo
65 B1 Kilchu N. Korea
118 B3 Kilembe Dem. Rep. Congo
139 E2 Kilgore U.S.A.
119 D3 Kilimanjaro vol. Tanz.
80 B2 Kılıs Turkey
90 B2 Kiliya Ukr.
97 D1 Kilkee Rep. of Ireland
96 E1 Kilkeel U.K.
97 C2 Kilkenny Rep. of Ireland
111 B2 Kilkis Greece
97 B1 Killala Bay Rep. of Ireland
97 B2 Killaloe Rep. of Ireland
129 C2 Killam Can.
97 B2 Killarney Rep. of Ireland
139 D2 Killeen U.S.A.
96 B2 Killin U.K.
97 B1 Killybegs Rep. of Ireland
96 B3 Kilmarnock U.K.
53 B3 Kilmore Austr.
119 D3 Kilosa Tanz.
97 B2 Kilrush Rep. of Ireland
119 C3 Kilwa Dem. Rep. Congo
119 D3 Kilwa Masoko Tanz.
119 D3 Kimambi Tanz.
52 A2 Kimba Austr.
136 C2 Kimball U.S.A.
128 C2 Kimberley Can.
122 B2 Kimberley S. Africa
50 B1 Kimberley Plateau Austr.
65 B1 Kimch'aek N. Korea
65 B2 Kimch'ŏn S. Korea
127 G2 Kimmirut Can.
89 E3 Kimovsk Rus. Fed.
118 B3 Kimpese Dem. Rep. Congo
89 E2 Kimry Rus. Fed.
61 C1 Kinabalu, Gunung mt. Sabah Malaysia
128 C2 Kinbasket Lake Can.
130 B2 Kincardine Can.
62 A1 Kinchang Myanmar
119 C3 Kinda Dem. Rep. Congo
98 C2 Kinder Scout hill U.K.
129 D2 Kindersley Can.
114 A3 Kindia Guinea
119 C3 Kindu Dem. Rep. Congo
86 D3 Kineshma Rus. Fed.
51 E2 Kingaroy Austr.

135 B3 King City U.S.A.
130 C1 King George Islands Can.
88 C2 Kingisepp Rus. Fed.
51 D3 King Island Austr.
50 B1 King Leopold Ranges hills Austr.
138 A1 Kingman U.S.A.
135 B3 Kings r. U.S.A.
52 A3 Kingscote Austr.
99 D2 King's Lynn U.K.
50 B1 King Sound b. Austr.
134 D2 Kings Peak U.S.A.
143 D1 Kingsport U.S.A.
130 C2 Kingston Can.
146 C3 Kingston Jamaica
141 E2 Kingston U.S.A.
52 A3 Kingston South East Austr.
98 C2 Kingston upon Hull U.K.
147 D3 Kingstown St Vincent
139 D3 Kingsville U.S.A.
99 B3 Kingswood U.K.
96 B2 Kingussie U.K.
126 E2 King William Island Can.
123 C3 King William's Town S. Africa
67 D3 Kinka-san i. Japan
93 F4 Kinna Sweden
97 B3 Kinsale Rep. of Ireland
118 B3 Kinshasa Dem. Rep. Congo
143 E1 Kinston U.S.A.
88 B2 Kintai Lith.
114 B4 Kintampo Ghana
96 B3 Kintyre pen. U.K.
130 C2 Kipawa, Lac l. Can.
83 I3 Kirensk Rus. Fed.
89 E3 Kireyevsk Rus. Fed.
Kirghizia country Asia see Kyrgyzstan
80 B2 Kırıkkale Turkey
89 E2 Kirillov Rus. Fed.
Kirin China see Jilin
119 D3 Kirinyaga mt. Kenya
89 D2 Kirishi Rus. Fed.
111 C3 Kırkağaç Turkey
96 C2 Kirkcaldy U.K.
96 B3 Kirkcudbright U.K.
92 J2 Kirkenes Norway
130 B2 Kirkland Lake Can.
137 E2 Kirksville U.S.A.
81 C2 Kirkūk Iraq
96 C1 Kirkwall U.K.
89 D3 Kirov Kaluzhskaya Oblast' Rus. Fed.
86 D3 Kirov Rus. Fed.
Kirovabad Azer. see Gäncä
86 E3 Kirovo-Chepetsk Rus. Fed.
91 C2 Kirovohrad Ukr.
86 C2 Kirovsk Rus. Fed.
91 D2 Kirovs'ke Ukr.
96 C2 Kirriemuir U.K.
86 E3 Kirs Rus. Fed.
74 A2 Kirthar Range mts Pak.
92 H2 Kiruna Sweden
67 C3 Kiryū Japan
89 E2 Kirzhach Rus. Fed.
119 C3 Kisangani Dem. Rep. Congo
118 B3 Kisantu Dem. Rep. Congo
60 A1 Kisaran Indon.
82 G3 Kiselevsk Rus. Fed.
75 C2 Kishanganj India
Kishinev Moldova see Chişinău
77 D1 Kishkenekol' Kazakh.
74 B1 Kishtwar Jammu and Kashmir
115 C4 Kisi Nigeria
119 D3 Kisii Kenya
103 D2 Kiskunfélegyháza Hungary

103 D2 Kiskunhalas Hungary
87 D4 Kislovodsk Rus. Fed.
117 C5 Kismaayo Somalia
119 D2 Kisoro Uganda
114 A4 Kissidougou Guinea
143 D3 Kissimmee U.S.A.
143 D3 Kissimmee, Lake U.S.A.
129 D2 Kississing Lake Can.
119 D3 Kisumu Kenya
114 B3 Kita Mali
66 D3 Kitakami Japan
66 D3 Kitakami-gawa r. Japan
67 B4 Kita-Kyūshū Japan
119 D2 Kitale Kenya
66 D2 Kitami Japan
130 B2 Kitchener Can.
93 J3 Kitee Fin.
119 D2 Kitgum Uganda
128 B2 Kitimat Can.
118 B3 Kitona Dem. Rep. Congo
119 D3 Kitunda Tanz.
128 B2 Kitwanga Can.
121 B2 Kitwe Zambia
101 E3 Kitzingen Ger.
92 I3 Kiuruvesi Fin.
119 C3 Kivu, Lake Dem. Rep. Congo/Rwanda
110 C2 Kıyıköy Turkey
86 E3 Kizel Rus. Fed.
111 C3 Kızılca Dağ mt. Turkey
87 D4 Kizlyar Rus. Fed.
92 I1 Kjøllefjord Norway
92 G2 Kjøpsvik Norway
102 C1 Kladno Czech Rep.
102 C2 Klagenfurt Austria
88 B2 Klaipėda Lith.
94 B1 Klaksvík Faroe Is
134 B1 Klamath r. U.S.A.
134 B2 Klamath Falls U.S.A.
134 B2 Klamath Mountains U.S.A.
102 C2 Klatovy Czech Rep.
122 A3 Klawer S. Africa
128 A2 Klawock U.S.A.
128 B2 Kleena Kleene Can.
122 B2 Kleinbegin S. Africa
122 A2 Kleinsee S. Africa
123 C2 Klerksdorp S. Africa
89 E3 Kletnya Rus. Fed.
100 C2 Kleve Ger.
89 D3 Klimavichy Belarus
89 D3 Klimovo Rus. Fed.
89 E2 Klimovsk Rus. Fed.
89 E2 Klin Rus. Fed.
101 F2 Klínovec mt. Czech Rep.
93 G4 Klintehamn Sweden
89 D3 Klintsy Rus. Fed.
109 C2 Ključ Bos.-Herz.
103 D1 Kłodzko Pol.
100 C1 Kloosterhaar Neth.
102 C2 Klosterneuburg Austria
101 E1 Klötze (Altmark) Ger.
103 D1 Kluczbork Pol.
128 A2 Klukwan U.S.A.
74 A2 Klupro Pak.
88 C3 Klyetsk Belarus
98 C1 Knaresborough U.K.
93 F3 Knästen hill Sweden
129 E2 Knee Lake Can.
101 E1 Knesebeck Ger.
101 E2 Knetzgau Ger.
109 C2 Knin Croatia
103 C2 Knittelfeld Austria
109 D2 Knjaževac Yugo.
100 A2 Knokke-Heist Belgium
143 D1 Knoxville U.S.A.
122 B3 Knysna S. Africa
67 C4 Kōbe Japan
København Denmark see Copenhagen
100 C2 Koblenz Ger.

59 C3 Kobroör *i.* Indon.
88 B3 Kobryn Belarus
109 D2 Kočani Macedonia
111 C2 Kocasu *r.* Turkey
75 C2 Koch Bihár India
Kochi India *see* Cochin
67 B4 Kōchi Japan
87 D4 Kochubey Rus. Fed.
75 C2 Kodarma India
117 B4 Kodok Sudan
90 B2 Kodyma Ukr.
111 C2 Kodzhaele *mt.* Bulg./Greece
122 A2 Koës Namibia
122 C2 Koffiefontein S. Africa
114 B4 Koforidua Ghana
67 C3 Kōfu Japan
131 D1 Kogaluk *r.* Can.
74 B1 Kohat Pak.
62 A1 Kohima India
88 C2 Kohtla-Järve Estonia
77 D2 Kokand Uzbek.
92 H3 Kokkola Fin.
140 B2 Kokomo U.S.A.
77 E2 Kokpekti Kazakh.
77 C1 Kokshetau Kazakh.
131 D1 Koksoak *r.* Can.
123 C3 Kokstad S. Africa
Koktokay China *see*
Fuyun
58 C3 Kolaka Indon.
86 C2 Kola Peninsula *pen.*
Rus. Fed.
92 H2 Kolari Fin.
114 A3 Kolda Senegal
93 E4 Kolding Denmark
107 D2 Koléa Alg.
86 D2 Kolguyev, Ostrov *i.*
Rus. Fed.
73 B3 Kolhapur India
88 B2 Kolkasrags *pt* Latvia
Kollam India *see* Quilon
Köln Ger. *see* Cologne
103 D1 Kołobrzeg Pol.
114 B3 Kolokani Mali
89 E2 Kolomna Rus. Fed.
90 B2 Kolomyya Ukr.
122 B2 Kolonkwane Botswana
82 G3 Kolpashevo Rus. Fed.
89 E1 Kolpny Rus. Fed.
Kol'skiy Poluostrov *pen.*
Rus. Fed. *see* Kola Peninsula
78 B3 Koluli Eritrea
119 C4 Kolwezi Dem. Rep. Congo
83 L2 Kolyma *r.* Rus. Fed.
83 L2 Kolymskaya Nizmennost'
lowland Rus. Fed.
83 M2 Kolymskiy, Khrebet *mts*
Rus. Fed.
67 C3 Komaki Japan
83 M3 Komandorskiye Ostrova *is*
Rus. Fed.
103 D2 Komárno Slovakia
123 D2 Komati *r.* Swaziland
67 C3 Komatsu Japan
119 C3 Kombe Dem. Rep. Congo
90 C2 Kominternivs'ke Ukr.
109 C2 Komiža Croatia
103 D2 Komló Hungary
118 B3 Komono Congo
111 C2 Komotini Greece
122 B3 Komsberg *mts* S. Africa
76 C1 Komsomolets Kazakh.
83 H1 Komsomolets, Ostrov *i.*
Rus. Fed.
89 F2 Komsomol'sk Rus. Fed.
91 C2 Komsomol's'k Ukr.
89 F2 Komsomol'skiy Rus. Fed.
69 E1 Komsomol'sk-na-Amure
Rus. Fed.
89 E2 Konakovo Rus. Fed.

75 C3 Kondagaon India
86 F2 Kondinskoye Rus. Fed.
119 D3 Kondoa Tanz.
86 C2 Kondopoga Rus. Fed.
89 E3 Kondrovo Rus. Fed.
127 I2 Kong Christian IX Land *reg.*
Greenland
127 I2 Kong Frederik VI Kyst
coastal area Greenland
65 B2 Kongju S. Korea
119 C3 Kongolo Dem. Rep. Congo
93 E4 Kongsberg Norway
93 F3 Kongsvinger Norway
77 D3 Kongur Shan *mt.* China
100 C2 Königswinter Ger.
103 D1 Konin Pol.
109 C2 Konjic Bos.-Herz.
122 A2 Konkiep *watercourse*
Namibia
91 C1 Konotop Ukr.
102 B2 Konstanz Ger.
115 C3 Kontagora Nigeria
63 B2 Kon Tum Vietnam
63 B2 Kontum, Plateau du
Vietnam
80 B2 Konya Turkey
100 C3 Konz Ger.
86 E3 Konzhakovskiy Kamen',
Gora *mt.* Rus. Fed.
134 C1 Kooskia U.S.A.
128 C3 Kootenay Lake Can.
122 B3 Kootjieskolk S. Africa
92 □B2 Kópasker Iceland
108 B1 Koper Slovenia
93 G4 Kopparberg Sweden
109 C2 Koprivnica Croatia
89 F3 Korablino Rus. Fed.
73 C3 Koraput India
101 D2 Korbach Ger.
109 D2 Korçë Albania
109 C2 Korčula Croatia
109 C2 Korčula *i.* Croatia
65 B1 Korea, North *country* Asia
65 B2 Korea, South *country* Asia
70 C2 Korea Bay *g.* China/N. Korea
65 B3 Korea Strait Japan/S. Korea
91 D2 Korenovsk Rus. Fed.
90 B1 Korets' Ukr.
111 C2 Körfez Turkey
114 B4 Korhogo Côte d'Ivoire
111 B3 Korinthiakos Kolpos
sea chan. Greece
111 B3 Korinthos Greece
103 D2 Kőris-hegy *hill* Hungary
109 D2 Koritnik *mt.* Albania
67 D3 Kōriyama Japan
80 B2 Korkuteli Turkey
68 B2 Korla China
103 D2 Körmend Hungary
114 B3 Koro Mali
131 D1 Koroc *r.* Can.
91 C1 Korocha Rus. Fed.
119 D3 Korogwe Tanz.
59 C2 Koror Palau
90 B1 Korosten' Ukr.
90 B1 Korostyshiv Ukr.
115 D3 Koro Toro Chad
91 C2 Korsun'-Shevchenkivs'kyy
Ukr.
103 E1 Korsze Pol.
100 A2 Kortrijk Belgium
83 L1 Koryakskaya, Sopka *vol.*
83 M2 Koryakskiy Khrebet *mts*
Rus. Fed.
86 D2 Koryazhma Rus. Fed.
65 B2 Koryŏng S. Korea
91 C1 Koryukivka Ukr.
111 C3 Kos Greece
111 C3 Kos *i.* Greece

65 B2 Kosan N. Korea
103 D1 Kościan Pol.
53 C3 Kosciuszko, Mount Austr.
81 B1 Kosh-Agach Rus. Fed.
103 E2 Košice Slovakia
92 H2 Koskullskulle Sweden
65 B2 Kosŏng N. Korea
109 D2 Kosovo *prov.* Yugo.
109 D2 Kosovska Mitrovica Yugo.
114 B4 Kossou, Lac de
l. Côte d'Ivoire
76 C1 Kostanay Kazakh.
110 B2 Kostenets Bulg.
123 C2 Koster S. Africa
117 B3 Kosti Sudan
86 C2 Kostomuksha Rus. Fed.
90 B1 Kostopil' Ukr.
89 F2 Kostroma Rus. Fed.
89 F2 Kostroma *r.* Rus. Fed.
102 C1 Kostrzyn Pol.
103 D1 Koszalin Pol.
103 D2 Kőszeg Hungary
74 B2 Kota India
60 B2 Kotaagung Indon.
61 C2 Kotabaru Indon.
61 C1 Kota Belud *Sabah*
Malaysia
60 B1 Kota Bharu Malaysia
60 B2 Kotabumi Indon.
61 C1 Kota Kinabalu *Sabah*
Malaysia
61 C1 Kota Samarahan *Sarawak*
Malaysia
86 D3 Kotel'nich Rus. Fed.
87 D4 Kotel'nikovo Rus. Fed.
83 K1 Kotel'nyy, Ostrov *i.*
Rus. Fed.
101 E2 Köthen (Anhalt) Ger.
93 I3 Kotka Fin.
86 D2 Kotlas Rus. Fed.
109 C2 Kotor Varoš Bos.-Herz.
87 D3 Kotovo Rus. Fed.
91 E1 Kotovsk Rus. Fed.
90 B2 Kotovs'k Ukr.
83 H2 Kotuy *r.* Rus. Fed.
100 A2 Koudekerke Neth.
114 B3 Koudougou Burkina
122 B3 Kougaberge *mts* S. Africa
118 B3 Koulamoutou Gabon
114 B3 Koulikoro Mali
114 A3 Koundâra Guinea
151 C1 Kourou Fr. Guiana
114 B3 Kouroussa Guinea
115 D3 Kousséri Cameroon
114 B3 Koutiala Mali
93 I3 Kouvola Fin.
92 J2 Kovdor Rus. Fed.
90 A1 Kovel' Ukr.
89 F2 Kovrov Rus. Fed.
54 B2 Kowhitirangi N.Z.
71 B3 Kowloon China
111 C3 Köyceğiz Turkey
86 D2 Koyda Rus. Fed.
126 A2 Koyukuk *r.* U.S.A.
111 B2 Kozani Greece
90 C1 Kozelets' Ukr.
89 E3 Kozel'sk Rus. Fed.
Kozhikode India *see* Calicut
90 B2 Kozyatyn Ukr.
63 A3 Krabi Thai.
63 A2 Kra Buri Thai.
63 B2 Krâchéh Cambodia
93 E4 Kragerø Norway
100 B1 Kraggenburg Neth.
109 D2 Kragujevac Yugo.
60 B2 Krakatau *i.* Indon.
103 D1 Kraków Pol.
91 D2 Kramators'k Ukr.
93 G3 Kramfors Sweden
111 B3 Kranidi Greece

86 E1 **Krasino** Rus. Fed.
88 C2 **Kräslava** Latvia
101 F2 **Kraslice** Czech Rep.
89 D3 **Krasnapollye** Belarus
89 D3 **Krasnaya Gora** Rus. Fed.
87 D3 **Krasnoarmeysk** Rus. Fed.
91 D2 **Krasnoarmiys'k** Ukr.
86 D2 **Krasnoborsk** Rus. Fed.
91 D2 **Krasnodar** Rus. Fed.
91 D2 **Krasnodon** Ukr.
88 C2 **Krasnogorodskoye**
       Rus. Fed.
91 D1 **Krasnogvardeyskoye**
       Rus. Fed.
91 C2 **Krasnohrad** Ukr.
91 C2 **Krasnohvardiys'ke** Ukr.
86 E3 **Krasnokamsk** Rus. Fed.
89 D2 **Krasnomayskiy** Rus. Fed.
91 C2 **Krasnoperekops'k** Ukr.
87 D3 **Krasnoslobodsk** Rus. Fed.
86 E3 **Krasnoufimsk** Rus. Fed.
83 H3 **Krasnoyarsk** Rus. Fed.
89 D2 **Krasnoye-na-Volge**
       Rus. Fed.
89 D3 **Krasnyy** Rus. Fed.
89 E2 **Krasnyy Kholm** Rus. Fed.
87 C4 **Krasnyy Luch** Ukr.
91 E2 **Krasnyy Sulin** Rus. Fed.
90 B2 **Krasyliv** Ukr.
100 C2 **Krefeld** Ger.
91 C2 **Kremenchuk** Ukr.
91 C2 **Kremenchuts'ka**
       Vodoskhovyshche *resr* Ukr.
103 D2 **Křemešník** *hill* Czech Rep.
91 D2 **Kreminna** Ukr.
103 D2 **Krems an der Donau** Austria
92 F2 **Kresttsy** Rus. Fed.
88 B2 **Kretinga** Lith.
100 C2 **Kreuzau** Ger.
100 C2 **Kreuztal** Ger.
118 A2 **Kribi** Cameroon
111 B3 **Krikellos** Greece
66 D1 **Kril'on, Mys** *c.* Rus. Fed.
73 C3 **Krishna** *r.* India
73 C3 **Krishna, Mouths of the**
       India
75 C2 **Krishnanagar** India
93 E4 **Kristiansand** Norway
93 F4 **Kristianstad** Sweden
92 E3 **Kristiansund** Norway
93 F4 **Kristinehamn** Sweden
      Kriti *i.* Greece *see* Crete
      Krivoy Rog Ukr. *see*
      Kryvyy Rih
109 C1 **Križevci** Croatia
108 B1 **Krk** *i.* Croatia
92 F3 **Krokom** Sweden
91 C1 **Krolevets'** Ukr.
101 D2 **Kronach** Ger.
63 B2 **Krŏng Kaôh Kŏng** Cambodia
127 I2 **Kronprins Frederik Bjerge**
       nunataks Greenland
123 C2 **Kroonstad** S. Africa
87 D4 **Kropotkin** Rus. Fed.
103 E2 **Krosno** Pol.
103 D1 **Krotoszyn** Pol.
60 B2 **Krui** Indon.
109 C2 **Krujë** Albania
111 C2 **Krumovgrad** Bulg.
      Krung Thep Thai. *see*
      Bangkok
88 C3 **Krupki** Belarus
109 D2 **Kruševac** Yugo.
101 E2 **Krušné Hory** *mts* Czech Rep.
128 A2 **Kruzof Island** U.S.A.
89 D3 **Krychaw** Belarus
91 D3 **Krymsk** Rus. Fed.
111 C3 **Krytiko Pelagos** *sea* Greece
91 C2 **Kryvyy Rih** Ukr.
114 B2 **Ksabi** Alg.

107 D2 **Ksar el Boukhari** Alg.
114 B1 **Ksar el Kebir** Morocco
89 E3 **Kshenskiy** Rus. Fed.
78 B2 **Kŭ', Jabal al** *hill*
       Saudi Arabia
61 C1 **Kuala Belait** Brunei
60 B1 **Kuala Kerai** Malaysia
60 B1 **Kuala Lipis** Malaysia
60 B1 **Kuala Lumpur** Malaysia
61 C2 **Kualapembuang** Indon.
60 B2 **Kuala Terengganu** Malaysia
60 B2 **Kualatungal** Indon.
61 C1 **Kuamut** *Sabah* Malaysia
65 A1 **Kuandian** China
60 B1 **Kuantan** Malaysia
91 D2 **Kuban'** *r.* Rus. Fed.
89 E2 **Kubenskoye, Ozero** *l.*
       Rus. Fed.
110 C2 **Kubrat** Bulg.
61 C1 **Kubuang** Indon.
61 C1 **Kuching** *Sarawak* Malaysia
109 C2 **Kuçovë** Albania
61 C2 **Kudus** Indon.
102 C2 **Kufstein** Austria
126 D2 **Kugluktuk** Can.
92 I3 **Kuhmo** Fin.
79 C2 **Kührän, Küh-e** *mt.* Iran
      Kuitin China *see* **Kuytun**
120 A2 **Kuito** Angola
128 A2 **Kuiu Island** U.S.A.
92 I2 **Kuivaniemi** Fin.
65 B2 **Kujang** N. Korea
109 D2 **Kukës** Albania
111 C3 **Kula** Turkey
75 D2 **Kula Kangri** *mt.* Bhutan
76 B2 **Kulandy** Kazakh.
88 B2 **Kuldiga** Latvia
122 B1 **Kule** Botswana
101 E2 **Kulmbach** Ger.
77 C3 **Kŭlob** Tajik.
76 B2 **Kul'sary** Kazakh.
77 D1 **Kulunda** Rus. Fed.
127 I2 **Kulusuk** Greenland
67 C3 **Kumagaya** Japan
67 B4 **Kumamoto** Japan
109 D2 **Kumanovo** Macedonia
114 B4 **Kumasi** Ghana
118 A2 **Kumba** Cameroon
78 B2 **Kumdah** Saudi Arabia
87 E3 **Kumertau** Rus. Fed.
65 B2 **Kumi** S. Korea
93 G4 **Kumla** Sweden
115 D3 **Kumo** Nigeria
62 A1 **Kumon Range** *mts*
       Myanmar
62 B2 **Kumphawapi** Thai.
      Kumul China *see* **Hami**
66 D2 **Kunashir, Ostrov** *i.* Rus. Fed.
61 C1 **Kundat** *Sabah* Malaysia
77 D2 **Kungei Alatau** *mts*
       Kazakh./Kyrg.
76 B2 **Kungrad** Uzbek.
93 F4 **Kungsbacka** Sweden
118 B2 **Kungu** Dem. Rep. Congo
86 E3 **Kungur** Rus. Fed.
62 A1 **Kunhing** Myanmar
77 D3 **Kunlun Shan** *mts* China
62 B1 **Kunming** China
65 B2 **Kunsan** S. Korea
50 B1 **Kununurra** Austr.
92 I3 **Kuopio** Fin.
109 C1 **Kupa** *r.* Croatia/Slovenia
59 C3 **Kupang** Indon.
88 B2 **Kupiškis** Lith.
111 C2 **Küplü** Turkey
128 A2 **Kupreanof Island** U.S.A.
91 D2 **Kup''yans'k** Ukr.
77 E2 **Kuqa** China
67 B4 **Kurashiki** Japan
67 B3 **Kurayoshi** Japan

89 E3 **Kurchatov** Rus. Fed.
110 C2 **Kürdzhali** Bulg.
67 B4 **Kure** Japan
88 B2 **Kuressaare** Estonia
86 F3 **Kurgan** Rus. Fed.
93 H3 **Kurikka** Fin.
156 C3 **Kuril Trench** *sea feature*
       N. Pacific Ocean
89 E3 **Kurkino** Rus. Fed.
117 B3 **Kurmuk** Sudan
73 B3 **Kurnool** India
67 D3 **Kuroiso** Japan
53 D2 **Kurri Kurri** Austr.
89 E3 **Kursk** Rus. Fed.
122 B2 **Kuruman** S. Africa
122 B2 **Kuruman** *watercourse*
       S. Africa
67 B4 **Kurume** Japan
83 I3 **Kurumkan** Rus. Fed.
73 C4 **Kurunegala** Sri Lanka
111 D3 **Kuşadası** Turkey
111 C3 **Kuşadası Körfezi** *b.* Turkey
111 C3 **Kuş Gölü** *l.* Turkey
91 D2 **Kushchevskaya** Rus. Fed.
66 D2 **Kushiro** Japan
76 C1 **Kushmurun** Kazakh.
75 C2 **Kushtia** Bangl.
66 D2 **Kushshro-ko** *l.* Japan
111 C3 **Kütahya** Turkey
81 C1 **K'ut'aisi** Georgia
109 C1 **Kutjevo** Croatia
103 D1 **Kutno** Pol.
118 B3 **Kutu** Dem. Rep. Congo
126 D2 **Kuujjua** *r.* Can.
131 D1 **Kuujjuaq** Can.
      Kuujjuarapik Can. *see*
      Poste-de-la-Baleine
92 I2 **Kuusamo** Fin.
120 A2 **Kuvango** Angola
89 D2 **Kuvshinovo** Rus. Fed.
78 B2 **Kuwait** *country* Asia
79 B2 **Kuwait** Kuwait
      Kuybyshev Rus. Fed. *see*
      Samara
91 D2 **Kuybysheve** Ukr.
87 D3 **Kuybyshevskoye**
       Vodokhranilishche *resr*
       Rus. Fed.
77 E2 **Kuytun** China
111 C3 **Kuyucak** Turkey
87 D3 **Kuznetsk** Rus. Fed.
90 B1 **Kuznetsovs'k** Ukr.
92 H1 **Kvalsund** Norway
123 D2 **KwaMashu** S. Africa
65 B2 **Kwangju** S. Korea
65 B1 **Kwanmo-bong** *mt.* N. Korea
123 C3 **Kwanobuhle** S. Africa
122 B3 **Kwanonzame** S. Africa
123 C3 **Kwatinidubu** S. Africa
123 C2 **KwaZamokhule** S. Africa
123 D2 **Kwazulu-Natal** *prov.* S. Africa
121 B2 **Kwekwe** Zimbabwe
118 B3 **Kwenge** *r.* Dem. Rep. Congo
103 D1 **Kwidzyn** Pol.
118 B3 **Kwilu** *r.* Angola/
       Dem. Rep. Congo
59 C3 **Kwoka** *mt.* Indon.
53 C3 **Kyabram** Austr.
62 A2 **Kyaikto** Myanmar
69 D1 **Kyakhta** Rus. Fed.
52 A2 **Kyancutta** Austr.
62 A1 **Kyaukpadaung** Myanmar
62 A2 **Kyaukpyu** Myanmar
88 B3 **Kybartai** Lith.
62 A2 **Kyebogyi** Myanmar
62 A2 **Kyeintali** Myanmar
74 B1 **Kyelang** India
      Kyiv Ukr. *see* Kiev
      Kyklades *is* Greece *see*
      Cyclades

129 D2 **Kyle** Can.
96 B2 **Kyle of Lochalsh** U.K.
100 C3 **Kyll** r. Ger.
111 B3 **Kyllíni** mt. Greece
111 B3 **Kymi** Greece
52 B3 **Kyneton** Austr.
119 D2 **Kyoga, Lake** Uganda
53 D1 **Kyogle** Austr.
65 B2 **Kyŏngju** S. Korea
67 C4 **Kyōto** Japan
111 B3 **Kyparissia** Greece
77 C1 **Kypshak, Ozero** salt l. Kazakh.
111 B3 **Kyra Panagia** i. Greece
77 D2 **Kyrgyzstan** country Asia
101 F1 **Kyritz** Ger.
92 H3 **Kyrönjoki** r. Fin.
86 E2 **Kyrta** Rus. Fed.
86 D2 **Kyssa** Rus. Fed.
111 B3 **Kythira** i. Greece
111 B3 **Kythnos** i. Greece
128 B2 **Kyuquot** Can.
67 B4 **Kyūshū** i. Japan
110 B2 **Kyustendil** Bulg.
90 C1 **Kyyivs'ke Vodoskhovyshche** resr Ukr.
92 H3 **Kyyjärvi** Fin.
68 C1 **Kyzyl** Rus. Fed.
76 C2 **Kyzylkum Desert** Kazakh./Uzbek.
77 C2 **Kyzylorda** Kazakh.

L

145 C3 **La Angostura, Presa de** resr Mex.
117 C4 **Laascaanood** Somalia
145 D3 **La Ascensión, Bahía de** b. Mex.
150 B1 **La Asunción** Venez.
114 A2 **Laâyoune** Western Sahara
87 K3 **Laba** r. Rus. Fed.
144 B2 **La Babia** Mex.
146 B3 **La Bahía, Islas de** is Hond.
131 D1 **La Baleine, Rivière à** r. Can.
62 A2 **La Banda** Arg.
104 B2 **La Baule-Escoublac** France
114 A3 **Labé** Guinea
128 A1 **Laberge, Lake** Can.
129 C2 **La Biche, Lac** l. Can.
87 D4 **Labinsk** Rus. Fed.
64 B1 **Labo** Phil.
144 B2 **La Boquilla, Presa de** resr Mex.
104 B3 **Labouheyre** France
131 D1 **Labrador** reg. Can.
131 D1 **Labrador City** Can.
158 C1 **Labrador Sea** Can./Greenland
150 B2 **Lábrea** Brazil
61 C1 **Labuan** Malaysia
60 B1 **Labuhanbilik** Indon.
59 C3 **Labuna** Indon.
63 A2 **Labutta** Myanmar
86 F2 **Labytnangi** Rus. Fed.
109 C2 **Laç** Albania
106 B1 **La Cabrera, Sierra de** mts Spain
105 C2 **La Capelle** France
131 D1 **Lac Bermen** l. Can.
73 B3 **Laccadive Islands** India
129 E2 **Lac du Bonnet** Can.
146 B3 **La Ceiba** Hond.
141 E1 **Lachute** Can.
103 D3 **La Ciotat** France
129 C2 **Lac La Biche** Can.

Lac la Martre Can. see Wha Ti
128 C2 **Lacombe** Can.
145 C3 **La Concordia** Mex.
108 A3 **Laconi** Sardinia Italy
141 E2 **Laconia** U.S.A.
104 B2 **La Coubre, Pointe de** pt France
128 C2 **La Crete** Can.
140 A2 **La Crosse** U.S.A.
144 B2 **La Cruz** Mex.
144 B2 **La Cuesta** Mex.
75 B1 **Ladakh Range** mts India
106 C1 **La Demanda, Sierra de** mts Spain
122 B3 **Ladismith** S. Africa
79 D2 **Lādīz** Iran
86 C2 **Ladoga, Lake** Rus. Fed.
Ladozhskoye Ozero l. Rus. Fed. see Ladoga, Lake
128 B3 **Ladysmith** Can.
123 C2 **Ladysmith** S. Africa
59 D3 **Lae** P.N.G.
62 B2 **Lae** Thai.
152 B3 **La Esmeralda** Bol.
93 F4 **Læsø** i. Denmark
143 C2 **La Fayette** U.S.A.
140 B2 **Lafayette** IN U.S.A.
142 B2 **Lafayette** LA U.S.A.
115 C4 **Lafia** Nigeria
104 B2 **La Flèche** France
143 D1 **La Follette** U.S.A.
131 C1 **Laforge** Can.
79 C2 **Lāft** Iran
108 A3 **La Galite** i. Tunisia
81 C1 **Lagan'** Rus. Fed.
118 B2 **Lagdo, Lac de** l. Cameroon
115 C1 **Laghouat** Alg.
155 D1 **Lagoa Santa** Brazil
114 A2 **La Gomera** i. Canary Is
147 C3 **La Gonâve, Île de** i. Haiti
114 C4 **Lagos** Nigeria
106 B2 **Lagos** Port.
134 C1 **La Grande** U.S.A.
130 C1 **La Grande 2, Réservoir** resr Can.
131 C1 **La Grande 4, Réservoir** resr Can.
130 C1 **La Grande 3, Réservoir** resr Can.
50 B1 **Lagrange** Austr.
143 C2 **La Grange** U.S.A.
150 B1 **La Gran Sabana** plat. Venez.
152 D3 **Laguna** Brazil
150 A2 **Lagunas** Peru
La Habana Cuba see Havana
61 C1 **Lahad Datu** Sabah Malaysia
104 B2 **La Hague, Cap de** c. France
60 B2 **Lahat** Indon.
78 B3 **Laḥij** Yemen
81 C2 **Lāhījān** Iran
100 C2 **Lahnstein** Ger.
74 B1 **Lahore** Pak.
74 A2 **Lahri** Pak.
93 I3 **Lahti** Fin.
115 D4 **Laï** Chad
53 D1 **Laidley** Austr.
104 C2 **L'Aigle** France
122 B3 **Laingsburg** S. Africa
92 H2 **Lainioälven** r. Sweden
115 C3 **L'Aïr, Massif de** mts Niger
96 B1 **Lairg** U.K.
108 B1 **Laives** Italy
70 B2 **Laiwu** China
70 C2 **Laiyang** China
70 B2 **Laizhou** China
70 B2 **Laizhou Wan** b. China
50 C1 **Lajamanu** Austr.
152 C3 **Lajes** Brazil
144 B2 **La Junta** Mex.

136 C3 **La Junta** U.S.A.
146 B2 **La Juventud, Isla de** i. Cuba
53 C2 **Lake Cargelligo** Austr.
53 D2 **Lake Cathie** Austr.
142 B2 **Lake Charles** U.S.A.
143 D2 **Lake City** FL U.S.A.
143 E2 **Lake City** SC U.S.A.
128 B3 **Lake Cowichan** Can.
128 A2 **Lake Havasu City** U.S.A.
143 D3 **Lakeland** U.S.A.
128 C2 **Lake Louise** Can.
134 B1 **Lake Oswego** U.S.A.
54 A2 **Lake Paringa** N.Z.
142 B2 **Lake Providence** U.S.A.
54 B2 **Lake Pukaki** N.Z.
53 C3 **Lakes Entrance** Austr.
134 B2 **Lakeview** U.S.A.
136 B3 **Lakewood** CO U.S.A.
141 E2 **Lakewood** NJ U.S.A.
143 D3 **Lake Worth** U.S.A.
74 A2 **Lakhpat** India
74 B1 **Lakki** Pak.
111 B3 **Lakonikos Kolpos** b. Greece
92 H1 **Lakselv** Norway
145 C3 **La Laguna, Picacho de** mt. Mex.
145 C3 **La Libertad** Guat.
106 B1 **Lalín** Spain
75 C2 **Lalitpur** India
129 D2 **La Loche** Can.
100 B2 **La Louvière** Belgium
108 A2 **La Maddalena** Sardinia Italy
131 D2 **La Madeleine, Îles de** is Can.
61 C1 **Lamag** Sabah Malaysia
La Manche str. France/U.K. see English Channel
136 C3 **Lamar** U.S.A.
79 C2 **Lamerd** Iran
108 A3 **La Marmora, Punta** mt. Sardinia Italy
128 C1 **La Martre, Lac** l. Can.
118 B3 **Lambaréné** Gabon
122 A3 **Lambert's Bay** S. Africa
106 B1 **Lamego** Port.
150 A3 **La Merced** Peru
52 B3 **Lameroo** Austr.
139 C2 **Lamesa** U.S.A.
111 B3 **Lamia** Greece
137 E2 **Lamoni** U.S.A.
62 A2 **Lampang** Thai.
139 D2 **Lampasas** U.S.A.
145 B2 **Lampazos** Mex.
99 A2 **Lampeter** U.K.
62 A2 **Lamphun** Thai.
119 E3 **Lamu** Kenya
107 D2 **La Nao, Cabo de** c. Spain
96 C3 **Lanark** U.K.
63 A2 **Lanbi Kyun** i. Myanmar
Lancang Jiang r. China see Mekong
98 B1 **Lancaster** U.K.
135 C4 **Lancaster** CA U.S.A.
140 C3 **Lancaster** OH U.S.A.
141 D2 **Lancaster** PA U.S.A.
143 D2 **Lancaster** SC U.S.A.
127 F2 **Lancaster Sound** str. Can.
Lanchow China see Lanzhou
102 C2 **Landeck** Austria
136 B2 **Lander** U.S.A.
99 A3 **Land's End** pt U.K.
102 C2 **Landshut** Ger.
93 F4 **Landskrona** Sweden
143 C2 **Lanett** U.S.A.
122 B3 **Langberg** mts S. Africa
137 D1 **Langdon** U.S.A.
93 F4 **Langeland** i. Denmark
101 D1 **Langen** Ger.
100 C1 **Langeoog** Ger.

100 C1 **Langeoog** i. Ger.
101 D2 **Langgöns** Ger.
92 □A3 **Langjökull** ice cap Iceland
105 C3 **Langogne** France
104 B3 **Langon** France
105 D2 **Langres** France
60 A1 **Langsa** Indon.
62 B1 **Lang Son** Vietnam
101 D1 **Langwedel** Ger.
129 C2 **Lanigan** Can.
153 A4 **Lanín, Volcán** vol. Arg./Chile
81 C2 **Länkäran** Azer.
104 B2 **Lannion** France
140 C2 **Lansing** U.S.A.
71 B3 **Lanxi** China
117 B4 **Lanya** Sudan
114 A2 **Lanzarote** i. Canary Is
70 A2 **Lanzhou** China
64 B1 **Laoag** Phil.
62 B1 **Lao Cai** Vietnam
70 B2 **Laohekou** China
Laojunmiao China see
Yumen
65 B1 **Laoling** China
65 B1 **Lao Ling** mts China
105 C2 **Laon** France
62 B2 **Laos** country Asia
71 B3 **Laotougou** China
154 C3 **Lapa** Brazil
114 A2 **La Palma** i. Canary Is
146 C4 **La Palma** Panama
150 B1 **La Paragua** Venez.
152 B2 **La Paz** Bol.
144 A2 **La Paz** Mex.
150 B2 **La Pedrera** Col.
66 D1 **La Pérouse Strait**
Japan/Rus. Fed.
145 C2 **La Pesca** Mex.
144 B2 **La Piedad** Mex.
154 C4 **La Plata** Arg.
154 C4 **La Plata, Río de** sea chan.
Arg./Uru.
93 I3 **Lappeenranta** Fin.
92 G2 **Lappland** reg. Europe
111 C2 **Lâpseki** Turkey
83 J1 **Laptev Sea** Rus. Fed.
Laptevykh, More sea
Rus. Fed. see Laptev Sea
92 H3 **Lapua** Fin.
152 B3 **La Quiaca** Arg.
79 C2 **Lär** Iran
114 B1 **Larache** Morocco
136 B2 **Laramie** U.S.A.
136 B2 **Laramie Mountains** U.S.A.
154 B3 **Laranjeiras do Sul** Brazil
59 C3 **Larantuka** Indon.
59 C3 **Larat** i. Indon.
107 D2 **Larba** Alg.
100 B3 **L'Ardenne, Plateau de**
Belgium
106 C1 **Laredo** Spain
139 D3 **Laredo** U.S.A.
96 B3 **Largs** U.K.
152 B3 **La Rioja** Arg.
111 B3 **Larisa** Greece
74 A2 **Larkana** Pak.
80 B2 **Larnaka** Cyprus
97 D1 **Larne** U.K.
100 B2 **La Roche-en-Ardenne**
Belgium
104 B2 **La Rochelle** France
104 B2 **La Roche-sur-Yon** France
107 C2 **La Roda** Spain
147 D3 **La Romana** Dom. Rep.
129 D2 **La Ronge** Can.
129 D2 **La Ronge, Lac** l. Can.
50 C1 **Larrimah** Austr.
55 P3 **Larsen Ice Shelf** Antarctica
93 F4 **Larvik** Norway
130 C2 **La Sarre** Can.

138 B2 **Las Cruces** U.S.A.
153 C4 **Las Flores** Arg.
153 B4 **Las Heras** Arg.
62 A1 **Lashio** Myanmar
109 C3 **La Sila** reg. Italy
152 B3 **Las Lomitas** Arg.
144 B2 **Las Nieves** Mex.
114 A2 **Las Palmas de Gran**
Canaria Canary Is
108 A2 **La Spezia** Italy
150 B3 **Las Piedras, Río de** r. Peru
153 B5 **Las Plumas** Arg.
129 D2 **Last Mountain Lake** Can.
152 B3 **Las Tórtolas, Cerro** mt.
Chile
118 B3 **Lastoursville** Gabon
109 C2 **Lastovo** i. Croatia
144 A2 **Las Tres Vírgenes, Volcán**
vol. Mex.
146 C2 **Las Tunas** Cuba
144 B2 **Las Varas** Chihuahua Mex.
144 B2 **Las Varas** Nayarit Mex.
138 B1 **Las Vegas** NM U.S.A.
135 C3 **Las Vegas** NV U.S.A.
131 E1 **La Tabatière** Can.
104 B3 **La Teste** France
108 B2 **Latina** Italy
147 D3 **La Tortuga, Isla** i. Venez.
64 B1 **La Trinidad** Phil.
89 E2 **Latskoye** Rus. Fed.
131 C2 **La Tuque** Can.
88 B2 **Latvia** country Europe
102 C1 **Lauchhammer** Ger.
101 E3 **Lauf an der Pegnitz** Ger.
105 D2 **Laufen** Switz.
51 D4 **Launceston** Austr.
99 A3 **Launceston** U.K.
62 A1 **Launggyaung** Myanmar
51 D1 **Laura** Austr.
142 C2 **Laurel** MS U.S.A.
134 E1 **Laurel** MT U.S.A.
109 C2 **Lauria** Italy
143 E2 **Laurinburg** U.S.A.
105 D2 **Lausanne** Switz.
61 C2 **Laut** i. Indon.
101 D2 **Lautersbach (Hessen)** Ger.
61 C2 **Laut Kecil, Kepulauan**
is Indon.
100 C1 **Lauwersmeer** l. Neth.
104 B2 **Laval** France
50 B2 **Laverton** Austr.
155 D2 **Lavras** Brazil
123 D2 **Lavumisa** Swaziland
61 C1 **Lawas** Sarawak Malaysia
62 A1 **Lawksawk** Myanmar
114 B3 **Lawra** Ghana
137 D3 **Lawrence** U.S.A.
142 C1 **Lawrenceburg** U.S.A.
139 D2 **Lawton** U.S.A.
78 A2 **Lawz, Jabal al** mt.
Saudi Arabia
93 F4 **Laxå** Sweden
109 D2 **Lazarevac** Yugo.
144 A1 **Lázaro Cárdenas** Baja
California Norte Mex.
144 B3 **Lázaro Cárdenas** Michoacán
Mex.
88 B3 **Lazdijai** Lith.
136 C2 **Lead** U.S.A.
129 D2 **Leader** Can.
136 B3 **Leadville** U.S.A.
Leaf Bay Can. see Tasiujaq
129 D2 **Leaf Rapids** Can.
97 B2 **Leane, Lough** l.
Rep. of Ireland
130 C1 **L'Eau Claire, Lac à l.** Can.
137 E3 **Leavenworth** U.S.A.
80 B2 **Lebanon** country Asia
137 E3 **Lebanon** MO U.S.A.
141 E2 **Lebanon** NH U.S.A.

134 B2 **Lebanon** OR U.S.A.
141 D2 **Lebanon** PA U.S.A.
89 E3 **Lebedyan'** Rus. Fed.
91 C1 **Lebedyn** Ukr.
104 C2 **Le Blanc** France
103 D1 **Lębork** Pol.
123 C1 **Lebowakgomo** S. Africa
106 B2 **Lebrija** Spain
153 A4 **Lebu** Chile
104 C3 **Le Bugue** France
109 C2 **Lecce** Italy
108 A1 **Lecco** Italy
102 C2 **Lech** r. Austria/Ger.
111 B3 **Lechaina** Greece
71 B3 **Lechang** China
102 B1 **Leck** Ger.
104 C3 **Lectoure** France
106 B1 **Ledesma** Spain
104 C2 **Le Dorat** France
128 C2 **Leduc** Can.
137 E1 **Leech Lake** U.S.A.
98 C2 **Leeds** U.K.
98 B2 **Leek** U.K.
100 C1 **Leer (Ostfriesland)** Ger.
143 D3 **Leesburg** U.S.A.
142 B2 **Leesville** U.S.A.
53 C2 **Leeton** Austr.
122 B3 **Leeu-Gamka** S. Africa
100 B1 **Leeuwarden** Neth.
50 A3 **Leeuwin, Cape** Austr.
147 D3 **Leeward Islands**
Caribbean Sea
111 B3 **Lefkáda** Greece
111 B3 **Lefkáda** i. Greece
Lefkosia Cyprus see Nicosia
64 B1 **Legaspi** Phil.
108 B1 **Legnago** Italy
103 D1 **Legnica** Pol.
75 B1 **Leh** Jammu and Kashmir
104 C2 **Le Havre** France
122 B1 **Lehututu** Botswana
74 B1 **Leiah** Pak.
103 D2 **Leibnitz** Austria
99 C2 **Leicester** U.K.
51 C1 **Leichhardt** r. Austr.
100 B1 **Leiden** Neth.
100 A2 **Leie** r. Belgium
52 A2 **Leigh Creek** Austr.
93 E3 **Leikanger** Norway
101 D1 **Leine** r. Ger.
97 C2 **Leinster** reg. Rep. of Ireland
101 F2 **Leipzig** Ger.
92 F2 **Leiranger** Norway
106 B2 **Leiria** Port.
93 E4 **Leirvik** Norway
97 C2 **Leixlip** Rep. of Ireland
71 B3 **Leiyang** China
71 B3 **Leizhou** China
71 A3 **Leizhou Bandao** pen. China
118 B3 **Lékana** Congo
100 B1 **Lelystad** Neth.
153 B6 **Le Maire, Estrecho de**
sea chan. Arg.
105 D2 **Léman, Lac** l. France/Switz.
104 C2 **Le Mans** France
137 D2 **Le Mars** U.S.A.
154 C2 **Leme** Brazil
80 B2 **Lemesos** Cyprus
101 D1 **Lemförde** Ger.
127 G2 **Lemieux Islands** Can.
136 C1 **Lemmon** U.S.A.
135 C3 **Lemoore** U.S.A.
131 D1 **Le Moyne, Lac** l. Can.
62 A1 **Lemro** r. Myanmar
109 C2 **Le Murge** hills Italy
83 J2 **Lena** r. Rus. Fed.
100 C1 **Lengerich** Ger.
71 B3 **Lengshuijiang** China
71 B3 **Lengshuitan** China
91 D2 **Lenine** Ukr.

Leningrad Rus. Fed. see
St Petersburg
91 D2 Leningradskaya Rus. Fed.
77 D3 Lenin Peak Kyrg./Tajik.
Leninsk Kazakh. see
Baykonur
89 E3 Leninskiy Rus. Fed.
100 A2 Lens Belgium
104 C1 Lens France
83 I2 Lensk Rus. Fed.
103 D2 Lenti Hungary
109 C3 Lentini Sicily Italy
114 B3 Léo Burkina
103 D2 Leoben Austria
99 B2 Leominster U.K.
144 B2 León Mex.
146 B3 León Nic.
106 B1 León Spain
122 A1 Leonardville Namibia
50 B2 Leonora Austr.
155 D2 Leopoldina Brazil
123 C1 Lephepe Botswana
123 C3 Lephoi S. Africa
71 B3 Leping China
105 C2 Le-Puy-en-Velay France
150 A2 Lérida Col.
106 C1 Lerma Spain
111 C3 Leros i. Greece
130 C1 Le Roy, Lac l. Can.
93 F4 Lerum Sweden
96 □ Lerwick U.K.
111 C3 Lesbos i. Greece
147 C3 Les Cayes Haiti
69 C3 Leshan China
86 D2 Leshukonskoye Rus. Fed.
109 C2 Leskovac Yugo.
104 B2 Lesneven France
89 E2 Lesnoye Rus. Fed.
83 H3 Lesosibirsk Rus. Fed.
123 C2 Lesotho country Africa
66 B1 Lesozavodsk Rus. Fed.
104 B2 Les Sables-d'Olonne France
147 D3 Lesser Antilles is
Caribbean Sea
128 C2 Lesser Slave Lake Can.
105 C3 Les Vans France
Lesvos i. Greece see Lesbos
103 D1 Leszno Pol.
99 C3 Letchworth U.K.
128 C3 Lethbridge Can.
150 C1 Lethem Guyana
59 C3 Leti, Kepulauan is Indon.
150 B2 Leticia Col.
123 C1 Lethakeng Botswana
104 C1 Le Touquet-Paris-Plage
France
99 D3 Le Tréport France
63 A2 Letsok-aw Kyun i. Myanmar
123 C2 Letsopa S. Africa
97 C1 Letterkenny Rep. of Ireland
105 C3 Leucate, Étang de l. France
60 A1 Leuser, Gunung mt. Indon.
100 B2 Leuven Belgium
111 B3 Levadeia Greece
92 F3 Levanger Norway
139 C2 Levelland U.S.A.
50 B1 Lévêque, Cape Austr.
100 C2 Leverkusen Ger.
103 D2 Levice Slovakia
54 C2 Levin N.Z.
131 C2 Lévis Can.
89 E3 Lev Tolstoy Rus. Fed.
99 D3 Lewes U.K.
96 A1 Lewis, Isle of i. U.K.
140 C3 Lewisburg U.S.A.
134 D1 Lewis Range mts U.S.A.
134 C1 Lewiston ID U.S.A.
141 E2 Lewiston ME U.S.A.
134 E1 Lewistown U.S.A.
140 C3 Lexington KY U.S.A.

136 D2 Lexington NE U.S.A.
141 D3 Lexington VA U.S.A.
64 B1 Leyte i. Phil.
109 C2 Lezhë Albania
89 F2 Lezhnevo Rus. Fed.
89 E3 L'gov Rus. Fed.
75 C2 Lhagoi Kangri mt. China
75 D2 Lhasa China
75 C2 Lhazê China
60 A1 Lhokseumawe Indon.
67 B3 Liancourt Rocks i.
N. Pacific Ocean
71 B3 Lianhua China
71 B3 Lianjiang China
70 C1 Lianshan China
70 B2 Lianyungang China
71 B3 Lianzhou China
65 A1 Liao r. China
70 B2 Liaocheng China
70 C1 Liaodong Bandao pen.
China
70 C1 Liaodong Wan b. China
70 C1 Liaoning prov. China
65 A1 Liaoyang China
65 B1 Liaoyuan China
128 E1 Liard r. Can.
134 C1 Libby U.S.A.
118 B2 Libenge Dem. Rep. Congo
136 C3 Liberal U.S.A.
103 D1 Liberec Czech Rep.
114 B4 Liberia country Africa
146 B3 Liberia Costa Rica
150 C1 Libertad Venez.
100 B3 Libin Belgium
104 B3 Libourne France
118 A2 Libreville Gabon
115 D2 Libya country Africa
115 E2 Libyan Desert Egypt/Libya
116 A1 Libyan Plateau Egypt
108 B3 Licata Sicily Italy
Licheng China see Lipu
121 C2 Lichinga Moz.
101 E2 Lichte Ger.
123 C2 Lichtenburg S. Africa
101 E2 Lichtenfels Ger.
88 C3 Lida Belarus
93 F4 Lidköping Sweden
50 C2 Liebig, Mount Austr.
105 D2 Liechtenstein country
Europe
100 B2 Liège Belgium
92 J3 Lieksa Fin.
119 C2 Lienart Dem. Rep. Congo
102 C2 Lienz Austria
88 B2 Liepāja Latvia
102 C2 Liezen Austria
97 C2 Liffey r. Rep. of Ireland
97 C1 Lifford Rep. of Ireland
53 C1 Lightning Ridge Austr.
121 C2 Ligonha r. Moz.
105 D3 Ligurian Sea France/Italy
119 C4 Likasi Dem. Rep. Congo
128 B2 Likely Can.
89 E2 Likhoslavl' Rus. Fed.
61 B1 Liku Indon.
105 D3 L'Île-Rousse Corsica France
71 B3 Liling China
93 F4 Lilla Edet Sweden
100 B3 Lille Belgium
105 C1 Lille France
93 E4 Lille Bælt sea chan.
Denmark
93 E3 Lillehammer Norway
93 F4 Lillestrøm Norway
128 B2 Lillooet Can.
121 C2 Lilongwe Malawi
64 B2 Liloy Phil.
150 A3 Lima Peru
140 C2 Lima U.S.A.
97 C1 Limavady U.K.

153 B4 Limay r. Arg.
101 F2 Limbach-Oberfrohna Ger.
88 B2 Limbaži Latvia
118 A2 Limbe Cameroon
100 D2 Limburg an der Lahn Ger.
122 B3 Lime Acres S. Africa
154 C2 Limeira Brazil
97 B2 Limerick Rep. of Ireland
93 E4 Limfjorden sea chan.
Denmark
111 C3 Limnos i. Greece
104 C2 Limoges France
146 B3 Limón Costa Rica
136 C3 Limon U.S.A.
104 C3 Limoux France
121 C3 Limpopo r. S. Africa/
Zimbabwe
64 A1 Linapacan i. Phil.
153 A4 Linares Chile
145 C2 Linares Mex.
106 C2 Linares Spain
62 B1 Lincang China
71 B3 Linchuan China
98 C2 Lincoln U.K.
140 B2 Lincoln IL U.S.A.
141 F1 Lincoln ME U.S.A.
137 D2 Lincoln NE U.S.A.
151 C1 Linden Guyana
142 C1 Linden U.S.A.
119 C2 Lindi r. Dem. Rep. Congo
119 D3 Lindi Tanz.
Lindisfarne i. U.K. see
Holy Island
80 A2 Lindos Greece
141 D2 Lindsay Can.
70 B2 Linfen China
64 B1 Lingayen Phil.
70 B2 Lingbao China
123 C3 Lingelethu S. Africa
123 C3 Lingelihle S. Africa
100 C1 Lingen (Ems) Ger.
60 B2 Lingga, Kepulauan is Indon.
71 A3 Lingshan China
71 A4 Lingshui China
114 A3 Linguère Senegal
155 D1 Linhares Brazil
70 A1 Linhe China
93 G4 Linköping Sweden
66 B1 Linkou China
70 B2 Linqing China
154 C2 Lins Brazil
136 C1 Linton U.S.A.
69 D2 Linxi China
69 C2 Linxia China
70 B2 Linyi Shandong China
70 B2 Linyi Shandong China
70 B2 Linying China
102 C2 Linz Austria
105 C3 Lion, Golfe du g. France
109 B3 Lipari Italy
108 B3 Lipari, Isole is Italy
89 E3 Lipetsk Rus. Fed.
110 B1 Lipova Romania
101 D2 Lippstadt Ger.
71 B3 Lipu China
76 C1 Lisakovsk Kazakh.
118 C2 Lisala Dem. Rep. Congo
Lisboa Port. see Lisbon
106 B2 Lisbon Port.
97 C1 Lisburn U.K.
97 B2 Liscannor Bay
Rep. of Ireland
104 C2 Lisieux France
99 A3 Liskeard U.K.
89 E3 Liski Rus. Fed.
53 D1 Lismore Austr.
97 C1 Lisnaskea U.K.
97 B2 Listowel Rep. of Ireland
71 A3 Litang Guangxi China
68 C2 Litang Sichuan China

140 B3 **Litchfield** *IL* U.S.A.
137 E1 **Litchfield** *MN* U.S.A.
53 D2 **Lithgow** Austr.
111 B3 **Lithino, Akra** *pt* Greece
88 B2 **Lithuania** *country* Europe
102 C1 **Litoměřice** Czech Rep.
146 C2 **Little Abaco** *i.* Bahamas
73 D3 **Little Andaman** *i.* India
137 E1 **Little Falls** U.S.A.
139 C2 **Littlefield** U.S.A.
99 C3 **Littlehampton** U.K.
122 A2 **Little Karas Berg** *plat.*
         Namibia
122 B3 **Little Karoo** *plat.* S. Africa
96 A2 **Little Minch** *sea chan.* U.K.
136 C1 **Little Missouri** *r.* U.S.A.
63 A3 **Little Nicobar** *i.* India
142 B2 **Little Rock** U.S.A.
141 E2 **Littleton** U.S.A.
70 B2 **Liujiachang** China
71 A3 **Liuzhou** China
88 C2 **Līvāni** Latvia
50 B1 **Liveringa** Austr.
138 C2 **Livermore, Mount** U.S.A.
131 D2 **Liverpool** Can.
98 B2 **Liverpool** U.K.
127 F2 **Liverpool** Can.
53 C2 **Liverpool Range** *mts* Austr.
134 D1 **Livingston** *MT* U.S.A.
139 E2 **Livingston** *TX* U.S.A.
139 D2 **Livingston, Lake** U.S.A.
120 B2 **Livingstone** Zambia
109 C2 **Livno** Bos.-Herz.
89 E3 **Livny** Rus. Fed.
140 C2 **Livonia** U.S.A.
108 B2 **Livorno** Italy
119 D3 **Liwale** Tanz.
70 B2 **Liyang** China
99 A4 **Lizard Point** U.K.
108 B1 **Ljubljana** Slovenia
93 G3 **Ljungan** *r.* Sweden
93 F4 **Ljungby** Sweden
93 G3 **Ljusdal** Sweden
93 G3 **Ljusnan** *r.* Sweden
99 B3 **Llandeilo** U.K.
99 B3 **Llandovery** U.K.
99 B2 **Llandrindod Wells** U.K.
98 B2 **Llandudno** U.K.
99 A3 **Llanelli** U.K.
98 A2 **Llangefni** U.K.
139 C2 **Llano Estacado** *plain* U.S.A.
150 B2 **Llanos** *reg.* Col./Venez.
107 D1 **Lleida** Spain
99 A2 **Lleyn Peninsula** U.K.
107 C2 **Llíria** Spain
106 C1 **Llodio** Spain
128 B2 **Lloyd George, Mount** Can.
129 D2 **Lloyd Lake** Can.
129 C2 **Lloydminster** Can.
152 B3 **Llullaillaco, Volcán** *vol.* Chile
123 C2 **Lobatse** Botswana
120 A2 **Lobito** Angola
101 F1 **Loburg** Ger.
96 B2 **Lochaber** *mts* U.K.
104 C2 **Loches** France
96 B2 **Lochgilphead** U.K.
96 B1 **Lochinver** U.K.
96 A2 **Lochmaddy** U.K.
52 A2 **Lochnagar** *mt.* U.K.
52 A2 **Lock** Austr.
96 C3 **Lockerbie** U.K.
139 D3 **Lockhart** U.S.A.
141 D2 **Lock Haven** U.S.A.
141 D2 **Lockport** U.S.A.
63 B2 **Lôc Ninh** Vietnam
105 C3 **Lodève** France
86 C2 **Lodeynoye Pole** Rus. Fed.
92 F2 **Lødingen** Norway
119 D2 **Lodwar** Kenya
103 D1 **Łódź** Pol.

62 B1 **Loei** Thai.
122 A3 **Loeriesfontein** S. Africa
92 F2 **Lofoten** *is* Norway
134 D2 **Logan** U.S.A.
126 B2 **Logan, Mount** Can.
140 B2 **Logansport** U.S.A.
108 B1 **Logatec** Slovenia
106 C1 **Logroño** Spain
101 D1 **Löhne** Ger.
101 D1 **Lohne (Oldenburg)** Ger.
62 A2 **Loikaw** Myanmar
62 A2 **Loi Lan** *mt.* Myanmar/Thai.
104 B2 **Loire** *r.* France
150 A2 **Loja** Ecuador
106 C2 **Loja** Spain
92 I2 **Lokan tekojärvi** *l.* Fin.
100 B2 **Lokeren** Belgium
122 B1 **Lokgwabe** Botswana
119 D2 **Lokichar** Kenya
119 D2 **Lokichokio** Kenya
89 D2 **Loknya** Rus. Fed.
115 C4 **Lokoja** Nigeria
89 D3 **Lokot'** Rus. Fed.
88 C2 **Loksa** Estonia
127 G2 **Loks Land** *i.* Can.
93 F4 **Lolland** *i.* Denmark
119 D3 **Lollondo** Tanz.
122 B2 **Lolwane** S. Africa
110 B2 **Lom** Bulg.
93 E3 **Lom** Norway
119 C2 **Lomami** *r.* Dem. Rep. Congo
153 C4 **Lomas de Zamora** Arg.
61 C2 **Lombok** *i.* Indon.
61 C2 **Lombok, Selat** *sea chan.*
         Indon.
114 C4 **Lomé** Togo
118 C3 **Lomela** *r.* Dem. Rep. Congo
100 B2 **Lommel** Belgium
96 B2 **Lomond, Loch** *l.* U.K.
88 C2 **Lomonosov** Rus. Fed.
135 B4 **Lompoc** U.S.A.
63 B2 **Lom Sak** Thai.
103 E1 **Łomża** Pol.
130 B2 **London** Can.
99 C3 **London** U.K.
140 C3 **London** U.S.A.
97 C1 **Londonderry** U.K.
50 B1 **Londonderry, Cape** Austr.
154 B2 **Londrina** Brazil
83 M2 **Longa, Proliv** *sea chan.*
         Rus. Fed.
61 C1 **Long Akah** *Sarawak* Malaysia
143 E2 **Long Bay** *b.* U.S.A.
135 C4 **Long Beach** U.S.A.
97 C2 **Longford** Rep. of Ireland
61 C2 **Longiram** Indon.
147 C2 **Long Island** Bahamas
130 C1 **Long Island** Can.
59 D3 **Long Island** P.N.G.
141 E2 **Long Island** U.S.A.
130 B2 **Longlac** Can.
130 B2 **Long Lake** *l.* Can.
136 B2 **Longmont** U.S.A.
140 C2 **Long Point** *pt* Can.
71 B3 **Longquan** China
131 E2 **Long Range Mountains**
         Can.
51 D2 **Longreach** Austr.
99 D2 **Long Stratton** U.K.
98 B1 **Longtown** U.K.
105 D2 **Longuyon** France
139 E2 **Longview** *TX* U.S.A.
134 B1 **Longview** *WA* U.S.A.
70 A2 **Longxi** China
71 B3 **Longxi Shan** *mt.* China
63 B2 **Long Xuyên** Vietnam
71 B3 **Longyan** China
82 C1 **Longyearbyen** Svalbard
102 B2 **Lons-le-Saunier** France
143 E2 **Lookout, Cape** U.S.A.

97 B2 **Loop Head** *hd*
         Rep. of Ireland
63 B2 **Lop Buri** Thai.
64 B1 **Lopez** Phil.
68 C2 **Lop Nur** *salt l.* China
118 B3 **Lopori** *r.* Dem. Rep. Congo
106 B2 **Lora del Río** Spain
140 C2 **Lorain** U.S.A.
74 A1 **Loralai** Pak.
107 C2 **Lorca** Spain
138 B2 **Lordsburg** U.S.A.
155 C2 **Lorena** Brazil
152 B2 **Loreto** Bol.
144 A2 **Loreto** Mex.
104 B2 **Lorient** France
96 B2 **Lorn, Firth of** *est.* U.K.
52 B3 **Lorne** Austr.
138 B1 **Los Alamos** U.S.A.
139 D3 **Los Aldamas** Mex.
153 A4 **Los Angeles** Chile
135 C4 **Los Angeles** U.S.A.
135 B3 **Los Banos** U.S.A.
152 B3 **Los Blancos** Arg.
153 A5 **Los Chonos, Archipiélago de**
         is Chile
91 E1 **Losevo** Rus. Fed.
108 B2 **Lošinj** *i.* Croatia
144 B2 **Los Mochis** Mex.
146 B4 **Los Mosquitos, Golfo de** *b.*
         Panama
118 B2 **Losombo** Dem. Rep. Congo
147 D3 **Los Roques, Islas** *is* Venez.
96 C2 **Lossiemouth** U.K.
150 B1 **Los Teques** Venez.
152 A4 **Los Vilos** Chile
104 C3 **Lot** *r.* France
96 C1 **Loth** U.K.
119 D2 **Lotikipi Plain** Kenya
118 C3 **Loto** Dem. Rep. Congo
89 E2 **Lotoshino** Rus. Fed.
62 B1 **Louang Namtha** Laos
62 B2 **Louangphrabang** Laos
118 B3 **Loubomo** Congo
104 B2 **Loudéac** France
71 B3 **Loudi** China
118 B3 **Loudima** Congo
114 A3 **Louga** Senegal
99 C2 **Loughborough** U.K.
97 B2 **Loughrea** Rep. of Ireland
105 D2 **Louhans** France
97 B2 **Louisburgh** Rep. of Ireland
142 B2 **Louisiana** *state* U.S.A.
123 C1 **Louis Trichardt** S. Africa
140 B3 **Louisville** *KY* U.S.A.
142 C2 **Louisville** *MS* U.S.A.
86 C2 **Loukhi** Rus. Fed.
130 C1 **Loups-Marins, Lacs des**
         lakes Can.
104 B3 **Lourdes** France
151 C1 **Lourenço** Brazil
106 B1 **Lousã** Port.
53 C2 **Louth** Austr.
98 C2 **Louth** U.K.
         Louvain Belgium *see* **Leuven**
89 D2 **Lovat'** *r.* Rus. Fed.
110 B2 **Lovech** Bulg.
136 B2 **Loveland** U.S.A.
135 C3 **Lovelock** U.S.A.
139 C2 **Lovington** U.S.A.
119 C3 **Lowa** Dem. Rep. Congo
141 E2 **Lowell** U.S.A.
128 C3 **Lower Arrow Lake** Can.
54 B2 **Lower Hutt** N.Z.
97 C1 **Lower Lough Erne** *l.* U.K.
128 B2 **Lower Post** Can.
99 D2 **Lowestoft** U.K.
103 D1 **Łowicz** Pol.
141 D2 **Lowville** U.S.A.
52 B2 **Loxton** Austr.
         Loyang China *see* **Luoyang**

89 D3 **Loyew** Belarus
92 F2 **Løypskardtinden** *mt.*
Norway
109 C2 **Loznica** Yugo.
91 D2 **Lozova** Ukr.
120 B2 **Luacano** Angola
70 B2 **Lu'an** China
120 A1 **Luanda** Angola
121 C2 **Luangwa** *r.* Zambia
121 B2 **Luanshya** Zambia
106 B1 **Luarca** Spain
120 B2 **Luau** Angola
120 A2 **Lubaczów** Pol.
120 A2 **Lubango** Angola
119 C3 **Lubao** Dem. Rep. Congo
103 E1 **Lubartów** Pol.
101 D2 **Lübbecke** Ger.
139 C2 **Lübbock** U.S.A.
101 E1 **Lübeck** Ger.
69 E2 **Lubei** China
87 E3 **Lubenka** Kazakh.
103 D1 **Lubin** Pol.
103 E1 **Lublin** Pol.
91 C1 **Lubny** Ukr.
61 C1 **Lubok Antu** *Sarawak*
Malaysia
101 E1 **Lübow** Ger.
101 E1 **Lübtheen** Ger.
119 C3 **Lubudi** Dem. Rep. Congo
60 D1 **Lubuklinggau** Indon.
119 C4 **Lubumbashi**
Dem. Rep. Congo
120 B2 **Lubungu** Zambia
119 C3 **Lubutu** Dem. Rep. Congo
120 A1 **Lucala** Angola
97 C2 **Lucan** Rep. of Ireland
120 B1 **Lucapa** Angola
96 B3 **Luce Bay** U.K.
154 B2 **Lucélia** Brazil
64 B1 **Lucena** Phil.
106 C2 **Lucena** Spain
103 D2 **Lučenec** Slovakia
109 C2 **Lucera** Italy
Lucerne Switz. *see* Luzern
101 E1 **Lüchow** Ger.
120 A2 **Lucira** Angola
101 F1 **Luckenwalde** Ger.
122 B2 **Luckhoff** S. Africa
75 C2 **Lucknow** India
120 B2 **Lucusse** Angola
Lüda China *see* Dalian
100 C2 **Lüdenscheid** Ger.
101 E1 **Lüder** Ger.
120 A3 **Lüderitz** Namibia
74 B1 **Ludhiana** India
140 B2 **Ludington** U.S.A.
99 B2 **Ludlow** U.K.
135 C4 **Ludlow** U.S.A.
110 C2 **Ludogorie** *reg.* Bulg.
93 G3 **Ludvika** Sweden
102 B2 **Ludwigsburg** Ger.
101 F1 **Ludwigsfelde** Ger.
101 D3 **Ludwigshafen am Rhein**
Ger.
101 E1 **Ludwigslust** Ger.
88 C2 **Ludza** Latvia
118 C3 **Luebo** Dem. Rep. Congo
120 A2 **Luena** Angola
70 A2 **Lüeyang** China
71 B3 **Lufeng** China
139 E2 **Lufkin** U.S.A.
88 C2 **Luga** Rus. Fed.
88 C2 **Luga** *r.* Rus. Fed.
105 D2 **Lugano** Switz.
121 C2 **Lugenda** *r.* Moz.
106 B1 **Lugo** Spain
110 B1 **Lugoj** Romania
91 D2 **Luhans'k** Ukr.
119 D3 **Luhombero** Tanz.
90 B1 **Luhyny** Ukr.

120 B2 **Luiana** Angola
118 C3 **Luilaka** *r.* Dem. Rep. Congo
105 D2 **Luino** Italy
92 I2 **Luiro** *r.* Fin.
118 C3 **Luiza** Dem. Rep. Congo
70 B2 **Lujiang** China
109 C2 **Lukavac** Bos.-Herz.
118 B3 **Lukenie** *r.* Dem. Rep. Congo
138 A2 **Lukeville** U.S.A.
89 E3 **Lukhovitsy** Rus. Fed.
103 E1 **Łuków** Pol.
120 B2 **Lukulu** Zambia
92 H2 **Luleå** Sweden
92 H2 **Luleälven** *r.* Sweden
110 C2 **Lüleburgaz** Turkey
70 B2 **Lüliang Shan** *mts* China
61 C2 **Lumajang** Indon.
75 C1 **Lumajangdong Co** *salt l.*
China
120 B2 **Lumbala Kaquengue** Angola
120 B2 **Lumbala N'guimbo** Angola
143 E2 **Lumberton** U.S.A.
61 C1 **Lumbis** Indon.
106 B1 **Lumbrales** Spain
63 B2 **Lumphät** Cambodia
129 D2 **Lumsden** Can.
54 A3 **Lumsden** N.Z.
93 F4 **Lund** Sweden
121 C2 **Lundazi** Zambia
99 A3 **Lundy Island** U.K.
101 E1 **Lüneburg** Ger.
101 E1 **Lüneburger Heide** *reg.* Ger.
100 C2 **Lünen** Ger.
105 D2 **Lunéville** France
120 B2 **Lunga** *r.* Zambia
114 A4 **Lungi** Sierra Leone
62 A1 **Lunglei** India
97 C2 **Lungnaquilla Mountain**
Rep. of Ireland
120 B2 **Lungwebungu** *r.* Zambia
74 B2 **Luni** *r.* India
88 C3 **Luninyets** Belarus
114 A4 **Lunsar** Sierra Leone
77 E2 **Luntai** China
71 A3 **Luodian** China
71 B3 **Luoding** China
70 B2 **Luohe** China
70 B2 **Luoyang** China
121 B2 **Lupane** Zimbabwe
71 A3 **Lupanshui** China
110 B1 **Lupeni** Romania
121 C2 **Lupilichi** Moz.
101 F2 **Luppa** Ger.
121 D2 **Lúrio** Moz.
121 D2 **Lúrio** *r.* Moz.
121 B2 **Lusaka** Zambia
118 C3 **Lusambo** Dem. Rep. Congo
109 C2 **Lushnjë** Albania
136 C2 **Lusk** U.S.A.
76 B3 **Lut, Dasht-e** *des.* Iran
101 F2 **Lutherstadt Wittenberg** Ger.
99 C3 **Luton** U.K.
61 C1 **Lutong** *Sarawak* Malaysia
129 C1 **Łutselk'e** Can.
90 B1 **Luts'k** Ukr.
122 B2 **Lutzputs** S. Africa
122 A3 **Lutzville** S. Africa
117 C4 **Luuq** Somalia
137 D2 **Luverne** U.S.A.
119 C3 **Luvua** *r.* Dem. Rep. Congo
123 D1 **Luvuvhu** *r.* S. Africa
119 D2 **Luwero** Uganda
59 C3 **Luwuk** Indon.
100 C3 **Luxembourg** *country* Europe
100 C3 **Luxembourg** Lux.
105 D2 **Luxeuil-les-Bains** France
123 C3 **Luxolweni** S. Africa
116 B2 **Luxor** Egypt
100 B2 **Luyksgestel** Neth.
86 D2 **Luza** Rus. Fed.

105 D2 **Luzern** Switz.
71 A3 **Luzhou** China
154 C1 **Luziânia** Brazil
151 D2 **Luzilândia** Brazil
64 B1 **Luzon** *i.* Phil.
71 C3 **Luzon Strait** Phil.
90 A2 **L'viv** Ukr.
L'vov Ukr. *see* L'viv
88 C3 **Lyakhavichy** Belarus
92 G3 **Lycksele** Sweden
123 D2 **Lydenburg** S. Africa
88 C3 **Lyel'chytsy** Belarus
88 C3 **Lyepyel'** Belarus
99 B3 **Lyme Bay** U.K.
141 D3 **Lynchburg** U.S.A.
129 D2 **Lynn Lake** Can.
129 D1 **Lynx Lake** Can.
105 C2 **Lyon** France
89 D2 **Lyozna** Belarus
86 E3 **Lys'va** Rus. Fed.
91 D2 **Lysychans'k** Ukr.
98 B2 **Lytham St Anne's** U.K.
88 C3 **Lyuban'** Belarus
89 E2 **Lyubertsy** Rus. Fed.
90 B1 **Lyubeshiv** Ukr.
89 F2 **Lyubim** Rus. Fed.
91 D2 **Lyubotyn** Ukr.
89 D2 **Lyubytino** Rus. Fed.
89 D3 **Lyudinovo** Rus. Fed.

M

80 B2 **Ma'an** Jordan
88 C2 **Maardu** Estonia
100 B2 **Maas** *r.* Neth.
100 B2 **Maaseik** Belgium
64 B1 **Maasin** Phil.
100 B2 **Maastricht** Neth.
121 C3 **Mabalane** Moz.
150 C1 **Mabaruma** Guyana
121 C3 **Mabote** Moz.
122 B2 **Mabule** Botswana
122 B1 **Mabutsane** Botswana
155 D2 **Macaé** Brazil
121 C2 **Macaloge** Moz.
126 E2 **MacAlpine Lake** Can.
151 C1 **Macapá** Brazil
150 A2 **Macará** Ecuador
155 D1 **Macarani** Brazil
61 C2 **Macassar Strait** Indon.
151 E2 **Macau** Brazil
71 B3 **Macau** *special admin. reg.*
China
123 D1 **Maccaretane** Moz.
98 B2 **Macclesfield** U.K.
50 B2 **Macdonald, Lake**
salt flat Austr.
50 C2 **Macdonnell Ranges**
mts Austr.
130 A1 **MacDowell Lake** Can.
106 B1 **Macedo de Cavaleiros**
Port.
52 B3 **Macedon** *mt.* Austr.
109 D2 **Macedonia** *country* Europe
151 E2 **Maceió** Brazil
108 B2 **Macerata** Italy
52 A2 **Macfarlane, Lake**
salt flat Austr.
97 B3 **Macgillycuddy's Reeks** *mts*
Rep. of Ireland
74 A2 **Mach** Pak.
155 C2 **Machado** Brazil
121 C3 **Machaila** Moz.
119 D3 **Machakos** Kenya
150 A2 **Machala** Ecuador
121 C3 **Machanga** Moz.
70 B2 **Macheng** China

141 F2 Machias U.S.A.
150 A1 Machiques Venez.
150 A3 Machupicchu Peru
123 D2 Macia Moz.
110 C1 Măcin Romania
53 D1 Macintyre r. Austr.
51 D2 Mackay Austr.
50 B2 Mackay, Lake salt flat Austr.
129 C1 MacKay Lake Can.
128 B2 Mackenzie Can.
128 A1 Mackenzie r. Can.
126 B2 Mackenzie Bay Can.
126 D1 Mackenzie King Island Can.
128 A1 Mackenzie Mountains Can.
128 B2 Macklin Can.
53 D2 Macksville Austr.
53 D1 Maclean Austr.
50 A2 MacLeod, Lake imp. l. Austr.
140 A2 Macomb U.S.A.
108 A2 Macomer Sardinia Italy
105 C2 Mâcon France
143 D2 Macon GA U.S.A.
137 E3 Macon MO U.S.A.
53 C2 Macquarie r. Austr.
52 D2 Macquarie Marshes Austr.
97 B3 Macroom Rep. of Ireland
52 A1 Macumba watercourse Austr.
145 C3 Macuspana Mex.
144 B2 Macuzari, Presa resr Mex.
123 D2 Madadeni S. Africa
121 □D3 Madagascar country Africa
115 D2 Madama Niger
111 B2 Madan Bulg.
59 D3 Madang P.N.G.
150 C2 Madeira r. Austr.
114 A1 Madeira terr.
N. Atlantic Ocean
144 B2 Madera Mex.
135 B3 Madera U.S.A.
73 B3 Madgaon India
118 B3 Madingou Congo
140 B3 Madison IN U.S.A.
137 D2 Madison SD U.S.A.
140 B2 Madison WI U.S.A.
140 C3 Madison WV U.S.A.
134 D1 Madison r. U.S.A.
140 B3 Madisonville U.S.A.
61 C2 Madiun Indon.
119 D2 Mado Gashi Kenya
68 C2 Madoi China
88 C2 Madona Latvia
78 A2 Madrakah Saudi Arabia
73 C3 Madras India
134 B2 Madras U.S.A.
145 C2 Madre, Laguna lag. Mex.
145 B3 Madre del Sur, Sierra
mts Mex.
144 B2 Madre Occidental, Sierra
mts Mex.
145 B2 Madre Oriental, Sierra
mts Mex.
106 C1 Madrid Spain
106 C1 Madridejos Spain
61 C2 Madura i. Indon.
61 C2 Madura, Selat sea chan.
Indon.
73 B4 Madurai India
67 C3 Maebashi Japan
62 A2 Mae Hong Son Thai.
62 A2 Mae Sariang Thai.
62 A2 Mae Suai Thai.
123 C2 Mafeteng Lesotho
119 D3 Mafia Island Tanz.
123 C2 Mafikeng S. Africa
119 D3 Mafinga Tanz.
154 C3 Mafra Brazil
83 L3 Magadan Rus. Fed.
153 A6 Magallanes, Estrecho de
sea chan. Chile
147 C4 Magangue Col.

144 A1 Magdalena Mex.
138 B2 Magdalena U.S.A.
144 A2 Magdalena, Bahía b. Mex.
101 E1 Magdeburg Ger.
97 C1 Magherafelt U.K.
87 E3 Magnitogorsk Rus. Fed.
142 B2 Magnolia U.S.A.
131 D1 Magpie, Lac l. Can.
114 A3 Magta' Lahjar Maur.
151 D2 Maguarinho, Cabo c. Brazil
123 D2 Magude Moz.
62 A1 Magwe Myanmar
81 C2 Mahābād Iran
74 B2 Mahajan India
74 B2 Mahajanga Madag.
61 C2 Mahakam r. Indon.
123 C1 Mahalapye Botswana
121 □D2 Mahalevona Madag.
75 C2 Mahanadi r. India
121 □D2 Mahanoro Madag.
63 B2 Maha Sarakham Thai.
121 □D2 Mahavavy r. Madag.
78 B2 Mahd adh Dhahab
Saudi Arabia
150 C1 Mahdia Guyana
74 B2 Mahesāna India
74 B2 Mahi r. India
54 C1 Mahia Peninsula N.Z.
89 D3 Mahilyow Belarus
107 D2 Mahón Spain
74 B2 Mahuva India
110 C2 Mahya Dağı mt. Turkey
129 D2 Maidstone Can.
99 D3 Maidstone U.K.
115 D3 Maiduguri Nigeria
75 C2 Maijdani India
101 D2 Main r. Ger.
118 B3 Mai-Ndombe, Lac l.
Dem. Rep. Congo
101 E3 Main-Donau-Kanal
canal Ger.
141 F1 Maine state U.S.A.
62 A1 Maingkwan Myanmar
96 C1 Mainland i. Scotland U.K.
96 □ Mainland i. Scotland U.K.
121 □D2 Maintirano Madag.
101 D2 Mainz Ger.
150 B1 Maiquetía Venez.
53 D2 Maitland N.S.W. Austr.
52 A2 Maitland S.A. Austr.
146 B3 Maíz, Islas del is Nic.
67 C3 Maizuru Japan
109 C2 Maja Jezercë mt. Albania
61 C2 Majene Indon.
Majorca i. Spain see
Mallorca
123 C2 Majwemasweu S. Africa
118 B3 Makabana Congo
58 B3 Makale Indon.
77 E2 Makanchi Kazakh.
109 C2 Makarska Croatia
Makassar Indon. see
Ujung Pandang
76 B2 Makat Kazakh.
123 D2 Makatini Flats lowland
S. Africa
114 A4 Makeni Sierra Leone
120 B3 Makgadikgadi salt pan
Botswana
87 D4 Makhachkala Rus. Fed.
76 B2 Makhambet Kazakh.
119 D3 Makindu Kenya
77 D1 Makinsk Kazakh.
91 D2 Makiyivka Ukr.
Makkah Saudi Arabia see
Mecca
131 E1 Makkovik Can.
103 E2 Makó Hungary
118 B2 Makokou Gabon
119 D3 Makongolosi Tanz.

122 B2 Makopong Botswana
79 D2 Makran reg. Iran/Pak.
89 E2 Maksatikha Rus. Fed.
81 C2 Mākū Iran
62 A1 Makum India
67 B4 Makurazaki Japan
115 C4 Makurdi Nigeria
92 G2 Malå Sweden
146 B4 Mala, Punta pt Panama
118 A2 Malabo Equat. Guinea
60 A1 Malacca, Strait of
Indon./Malaysia
134 D2 Malad City U.S.A.
88 C3 Maladzyechna Belarus
106 C2 Málaga Spain
117 B4 Malakal Sudan
61 C2 Malang Indon.
120 A1 Malanje Angola
93 G4 Mälaren l. Sweden
153 B4 Malargüe Arg.
80 B2 Malatya Turkey
121 C2 Malawi country Africa
Malawi, Lake Africa see
Nyasa, Lake
89 D2 Malaya Vishera Rus. Fed.
64 B2 Malaybalay Phil.
81 C2 Maläyer Iran
60 B1 Malaysia country Asia
81 C2 Malazgirt Turkey
103 D1 Malbork Pol.
101 F1 Malchin Ger.
100 A2 Maldegem Belgium
56 C5 Maldives country
Indian Ocean
153 C4 Maldonado Uru.
111 B3 Maleas, Akra pt Greece
103 D2 Malé Karpaty hills Slovakia
134 C2 Malheur Lake U.S.A.
114 B3 Mali country Africa
114 A3 Mali Guinea
58 C3 Malili Indon.
119 E3 Malindi Kenya
97 C1 Malin Head hd
Rep. of Ireland
97 B1 Malin More Rep. of Ireland
111 C2 Malkara Turkey
88 C3 Mal'kavichy Belarus
110 C2 Malko Tŭrnovo Bulg.
53 C3 Mallacoota Austr.
53 C3 Mallacoota Inlet b. Austr.
96 B2 Mallaig U.K.
129 E1 Mallery Lake Can.
107 D2 Mallorca i. Spain
97 B2 Mallow Rep. of Ireland
92 H2 Malmberget Sweden
100 C2 Malmédy Belgium
122 A3 Malmesbury S. Africa
93 F4 Malmö Sweden
62 B1 Malong China
118 C4 Malonga Dem. Rep. Congo
93 E3 Måløy Norway
89 E2 Maloyaroslavets Rus. Fed.
89 E2 Maloye Borisovo Rus. Fed.
85 E6 Malta country Europe
88 C2 Malta Latvia
134 E1 Malta U.S.A.
122 A1 Maltahöhe Namibia
98 C1 Malton U.K.
59 C3 Maluku is Indon.
93 F3 Malung Sweden
123 C2 Maluti Mountains Lesotho
73 B3 Malvan India
142 B2 Malvern U.S.A.
90 B1 Malyn Ukr.
83 L2 Malyy Anyuy r. Rus. Fed.
81 C1 Malyy Kavkaz mts Asia
83 K2 Malyy Lyakhovskiy, Ostrov i.
Rus. Fed.
123 C2 Mamafubedu S. Africa
119 C2 Mambasa Dem. Rep. Congo

118 B2 **Mambéré** r. C.A.R.
123 C2 **Mamelodi** S. Africa
150 B3 **Mamoré** r. Bol./Brazil
114 A3 **Mamou** Guinea
61 C2 **Mamuju** Indon.
114 B4 **Man** Côte d'Ivoire
150 B2 **Manacapuru** Brazil
107 D2 **Manacor** Spain
59 C2 **Manado** Indon.
146 B3 **Managua** Nic.
121 □D3 **Manakara** Madag.
78 B3 **Manākhah** Yemen
79 C2 **Manama** Bahrain
59 D3 **Manam Island** P.N.G.
121 □D3 **Mananara** r. Madag.
121 □D2 **Mananara Avaratra** Madag.
121 □D3 **Mananjary** Madag.
114 A3 **Manantali, Lac de** l. Mali
77 E2 **Manas Hu** l. China
59 C3 **Manatuto** East Timor
150 B2 **Manaus** Brazil
80 B2 **Manavgat** Turkey
98 B2 **Manchester** U.K.
141 E2 **Manchester** U.S.A.
121 □D3 **Mandabe** Madag.
93 E4 **Mandal** Norway
59 D3 **Mandala, Puncak** mt. Indon.
62 A1 **Mandalay** Myanmar
69 D1 **Mandalgovi** Mongolia
136 C1 **Mandan** U.S.A.
118 B1 **Mandara Mountains**
Cameroon/Nigeria
108 A3 **Mandas** Sardinia Italy
100 C2 **Manderscheid** Ger.
74 B1 **Mandi** India
114 B3 **Mandiana** Guinea
74 B1 **Mandi Burewala** Pak.
75 C2 **Mandla** India
121 □D2 **Mandritsara** Madag.
72 B2 **Mandsaur** India
50 A3 **Mandurah** Austr.
73 B3 **Mandya** India
108 B1 **Manerbio** Italy
90 B1 **Manevychi** Ukr.
109 C2 **Manfredonia** Italy
114 B3 **Manga** Burkina
118 B3 **Mangai** Dem. Rep. Congo
54 C1 **Mangakino** N.Z.
110 C2 **Mangalia** Romania
73 B3 **Mangalore** India
123 C2 **Mangaung** S. Africa
61 B2 **Manggar** Indon.
76 B2 **Mangistau** Kazakh.
68 C2 **Mangnai** China
121 C2 **Mangochi** Malawi
59 C3 **Mangole** i. Indon.
154 B3 **Mangueirinha** Brazil
69 E1 **Mangui** China
137 D3 **Manhattan** U.S.A.
121 C3 **Manhica** Moz.
155 D2 **Manhuaçu** Brazil
121 □D2 **Mania** r. Madag.
108 B1 **Maniago** Italy
150 B2 **Manicoré** Brazil
131 D2 **Manicouagan** r. Can.
131 D1 **Manicouagan, Réservoir**
resr Can.
79 B2 **Manīfah** Saudi Arabia
64 B1 **Manila** Phil.
53 D2 **Manilla** Austr.
111 C3 **Manisa** Turkey
140 B2 **Manistee** U.S.A.
129 E2 **Manitoba** prov. Can.
129 E2 **Manitoba, Lake** Can.
140 B1 **Manitou Islands** U.S.A.
130 B2 **Manitoulin Island** Can.
140 C2 **Manitowoc** U.S.A.
130 C2 **Maniwaki** Can.
150 A1 **Manizales** Col.
137 E2 **Mankato** U.S.A.

114 B4 **Mankono** Côte d'Ivoire
129 D3 **Mankota** Can.
73 C4 **Mankulam** Sri Lanka
74 B2 **Manmad** India
73 B4 **Mannar, Gulf of**
India/Sri Lanka
101 D3 **Mannheim** Ger.
128 C2 **Manning** Can.
52 A2 **Mannum** Austr.
129 C2 **Mannville** Can.
59 C3 **Manokwari** Indon.
119 C3 **Manono** Dem. Rep. Congo
63 A2 **Manoron** Myanmar
105 D3 **Manosque** France
131 C1 **Manouane, Lac** l. Can.
107 D1 **Manresa** Spain
121 B2 **Mansa** Zambia
127 F2 **Mansel Island** Can.
92 I2 **Mansel'kya** ridge
Fin./Rus. Fed.
53 C3 **Mansfield** Austr.
98 C2 **Mansfield** U.K.
142 B2 **Mansfield** LA U.S.A.
140 C2 **Mansfield** OH U.S.A.
141 D2 **Mansfield** PA U.S.A.
150 A2 **Manta** Ecuador
143 E1 **Manteo** U.S.A.
104 C2 **Mantes-la-Jolie** France
155 C2 **Mantiqueira, Serra da** mts
Brazil
108 B1 **Mantova** Italy
Mantua Italy see Mantova
151 C2 **Manuelzinho** Brazil
59 C3 **Manui** i. Indon.
54 B1 **Manukau** N.Z.
142 B2 **Many** U.S.A.
87 D4 **Manych-Gudilo, Ozero** l.
Rus. Fed.
119 D3 **Manyoni** Tanz.
106 C2 **Manzanares** Spain
144 B3 **Manzanillo** Mex.
69 D1 **Manzhouli** China
123 D2 **Manzini** Swaziland
115 D3 **Mao** Chad
59 D3 **Maoke, Pegunungan**
mts Indon.
123 C3 **Maokeng** S. Africa
65 A1 **Maokui Shan** mt. China
71 B3 **Maoming** China
121 C3 **Mapai** Moz.
75 C1 **Mapam Yumco** l. China
145 C3 **Mapastepec** Mex.
144 B2 **Mapimí** Mex.
144 B2 **Mapimí, Bolsón de**
des. Mex.
64 A2 **Mapin** i. Phil.
121 C3 **Mapinhane** Moz.
129 D3 **Maple Creek** Can.
121 C3 **Maputo** Moz.
123 D2 **Maputo** r. Moz./S. Africa
75 C2 **Maquan He** r. China
120 A1 **Maquela do Zombo**
Angola
153 B5 **Maquinchao** Arg.
137 E2 **Maquoketa** U.S.A.
150 B2 **Maraã** Brazil
151 D2 **Maraba** Brazil
151 C1 **Maracá, Ilha de** i. Brazil
150 A1 **Maracaibo** Venez.
150 A1 **Maracaibo, Lago de**
l. Venez.
154 A2 **Maracaju, Serra de** hills
Brazil
150 B1 **Maracay** Venez.
115 D2 **Marādah** Libya
115 C3 **Maradi** Niger
81 C2 **Marāgheh** Iran
151 D2 **Marajó, Baía de** est. Brazil
151 C2 **Marajó, Ilha de** i. Brazil
79 C2 **Marāki** Iran

119 D2 **Maralal** Kenya
50 C3 **Maralinga** Austr.
81 C2 **Marand** Iran
150 A2 **Marañón** r. Peru
130 B2 **Marathon** Can.
143 D4 **Marathon** U.S.A.
106 C2 **Marbella** Spain
50 A2 **Marble Bar** Austr.
123 C1 **Marble Hall** S. Africa
123 D3 **Marburg** S. Africa
101 D2 **Marburg an der Lahn** Ger.
99 D2 **March** U.K.
100 B2 **Marche-en-Famenne**
Belgium
106 B2 **Marchena** Spain
152 B4 **Mar Chiquita, Lago** l. Arg.
141 E2 **Marcy, Mount** U.S.A.
74 B1 **Mardan** Pak.
153 C4 **Mar del Plata** Arg.
81 C2 **Mardin** Turkey
96 B2 **Maree, Loch** l. U.K.
108 B3 **Marettimo, Isola** i. Sicily Italy
89 D2 **Marevo** Rus. Fed.
138 C2 **Marfa** U.S.A.
50 A3 **Margaret River** Austr.
147 D3 **Margarita, Isla de** i. Venez.
123 D3 **Margate** S. Africa
99 D3 **Margate** U.K.
119 C2 **Margherita Peak**
Dem. Rep. Congo/Uganda
76 C3 **Margo, Dasht-i** des. Afgh.
91 C2 **Marhanets'** Ukr.
62 A1 **Mari** Myanmar
152 B3 **María Elena** Chile
156 C5 **Mariana Trench** sea feature
N. Pacific Ocean
142 B2 **Marianna** AR U.S.A.
143 C2 **Marianna** FL U.S.A.
102 C2 **Mariánské Lázně**
Czech Rep.
144 B2 **Marías, Islas** is Mex.
78 B3 **Ma'rib** Yemen
109 C1 **Maribor** Slovenia
117 A4 **Maridi** watercourse Sudan
55 M2 **Marie Byrd Land** reg.
Antarctica
147 D3 **Marie-Galante** i. Guadeloupe
93 G3 **Mariehamn** Fin.
122 A1 **Mariental** Namibia
93 F4 **Mariestad** Sweden
143 D2 **Marietta** GA U.S.A.
140 C3 **Marietta** OH U.S.A.
105 D3 **Marignane** France
83 K3 **Marii, Mys** pt Rus. Fed.
88 B3 **Marijampolė** Lith.
154 C2 **Marília** Brazil
106 B1 **Marín** Spain
109 C3 **Marina di Gioiosa Ionica**
Italy
88 C3 **Mar"ina Horka** Belarus
140 B1 **Marinette** U.S.A.
154 B2 **Maringá** Brazil
106 B2 **Marinha Grande** Port.
140 B2 **Marion** IN U.S.A.
140 C2 **Marion** OH U.S.A.
143 E2 **Marion** SC U.S.A.
140 C3 **Marion** VA U.S.A.
143 D2 **Marion, Lake** U.S.A.
52 A2 **Marion Bay** Austr.
152 B3 **Mariscal Estigarribia** Para.
110 C2 **Maritsa** r. Bulg.
91 D2 **Mariupol'** Ukr.
117 C4 **Marka** Somalia
123 C1 **Marken** S. Africa
100 B1 **Markermeer** l. Neth.
83 I2 **Markha** r. Rus. Fed.
91 D2 **Markivka** Ukr.
142 B2 **Marksville** U.S.A.
101 D3 **Marktheidenfeld** Ger.
101 F2 **Marktredwitz** Ger.

Marl

212

100 C2 Marl Ger.
100 A3 Marle France
139 D2 Marlin U.S.A.
104 C3 Marmande France
111 C2 Marmara Denizi g. Turkey
111 C3 Marmaris Turkey
104 C2 Marne-la-Vallée France
121 □D2 Maroantsetra Madag.
101 E2 Maroldsweisach Ger.
121 □D2 Maromokotro mt. Madag.
121 C2 Marondera Zimbabwe
151 C1 Maroni r. Fr. Guiana
118 B1 Maroua Cameroon
121 □D2 Marovoay Madag.
140 E1 Marquette U.S.A.
117 A3 Marra, Jebel mt. Sudan
123 D2 Marracuene Moz.
114 B1 Marrakech Morocco
117 A3 Marra Plateau Sudan
52 A1 Marree Austr.
86 F2 Marresale Rus. Fed.
121 C2 Marromeu Moz.
121 C2 Marrupa Moz.
116 B2 Marsa Alam Egypt
115 D1 Marsa al Burayqah Libya
119 D2 Marsabit Kenya
108 B3 Marsala Sicily Italy
116 A1 Marsa Matrûh Egypt
101 D2 Marsberg Ger.
108 B2 Marsciano Italy
53 C2 Marsden Austr.
105 D3 Marseille France
137 D2 Marshall MN U.S.A.
137 E3 Marshall MO U.S.A.
139 E2 Marshall TX U.S.A.
49 E2 Marshall Islands country N. Pacific Ocean
137 E2 Marshalltown U.S.A.
140 A2 Marshfield U.S.A.
143 E3 Marsh Harbour Bahamas
142 B3 Marsh Island U.S.A.
88 A2 Märsta Sweden
63 A2 Martaban, Gulf of Myanmar
61 C2 Martapura Kalimantan Selatan Indon.
60 B2 Martapura Sumatera Indon.
141 E2 Martha's Vineyard i. U.S.A.
105 D2 Martigny Switz.
103 D2 Martin Slovakia
136 C2 Martin U.S.A.
145 C2 Martínez Mex.
147 D3 Martinique terr. West Indies
141 D3 Martinsburg U.S.A.
140 D3 Martinsville U.S.A.
54 C2 Marton N.Z.
107 D1 Martorell Spain
106 C2 Martos Spain
76 B1 Martuk Kazakh.
105 C3 Marvejols France
76 C3 Mary Turkm.
51 E2 Maryborough Austr.
122 B2 Marydale S. Africa
141 D3 Maryland state U.S.A.
137 D3 Marysville U.S.A.
137 E2 Maryville MO U.S.A.
143 D1 Maryville TN U.S.A.
119 D3 Masai Steppe plain Tanz.
119 D3 Masaka Uganda
65 B2 Masan S. Korea
119 D3 Masasi Tanz.
64 B1 Masbate Phil.
64 B1 Masbate i. Phil.
123 C2 Maseru Lesotho
76 B3 Mashhad Iran
123 C3 Masibambane S. Africa
79 C3 Masīlah, Wādī al watercourse Yemen
123 C2 Masilo S. Africa

119 D2 Masindi Uganda
79 C2 Masīrah i. Oman
79 C3 Masīrah, Gulf of b. Oman
81 C2 Masjed Soleymān Iran
97 B2 Mask, Lough l. Rep. of Ireland
121 □E2 Masoala, Tanjona c. Madag.
137 E2 Mason City U.S.A.
Masqat Oman see Muscat
108 B2 Massa Italy
141 E2 Massachusetts state U.S.A.
141 E2 Massachusetts Bay U.S.A.
121 C3 Massangena Moz.
120 A1 Massango Angola
116 B3 Massawa Eritrea
141 E2 Massena U.S.A.
105 C2 Massif Central mts France
140 C2 Massillon U.S.A.
114 B3 Massina Mali
123 D2 Massinga Moz.
123 D1 Massingir Moz.
78 A2 Mastābah Saudi Arabia
54 C2 Masterton N.Z.
74 A2 Mastung Pak.
78 A2 Mastūrah Saudi Arabia
88 B3 Masty Belarus
67 B4 Masuda Japan
Masuku Gabon see Franceville
121 C3 Masvingo Zimbabwe
118 B3 Matadi Dem. Rep. Congo
146 B3 Matagalpa Nic.
130 C2 Matagami Can.
130 C2 Matagami, Lac l. Can.
139 D3 Matagorda Island U.S.A.
120 A2 Matala Angola
114 A3 Matam Senegal
144 B2 Matamoros Coahuila Mex.
145 C2 Matamoros Tamaulipas Mex.
119 D3 Matandu r. Tanz.
131 D2 Matane Can.
146 B2 Matanzas Cuba
73 C4 Matara Sri Lanka
61 C2 Mataram Indon.
51 C1 Mataranka Austr.
107 D1 Mataró Spain
123 C3 Matatiele S. Africa
54 C1 Matawai N.Z.
152 B2 Mategua Bol.
145 C2 Matehuala Mex.
109 C2 Matera Italy
139 D3 Mathis U.S.A.
75 B2 Mathura India
64 B2 Mati Phil.
98 C2 Matlock U.K.
150 C3 Mato Grosso Brazil
154 B1 Mato Grosso, Planalto do plat. Brazil
123 D2 Matola Moz.
Matou China see Pingguo
67 B3 Matsue Japan
66 D2 Matsumae Japan
67 C4 Matsusaka Japan
71 C3 Matsu Tao i. Taiwan
67 B4 Matsuyama Japan
130 B1 Mattagami r. Can.
105 D2 Matterhorn mt. Italy/Switz.
134 C2 Matterhorn mt. U.S.A.
140 B3 Mattoon U.S.A.
121 C1 Maturín Venez.
123 C2 Matwabeng S. Africa
100 A2 Maubeuge France
104 C3 Maubourguet France
140 C2 Maumee r. U.S.A.
120 B2 Maun Botswana
62 A1 Maungdaw Myanmar
50 C2 Maurice, Lake salt flat Austr.
114 A3 Mauritania country Africa

113 H6 Mauritius country Indian Ocean
78 B2 Māwän, Khashm hill Saudi Arabia
118 B3 Mawanga Dem. Rep. Congo
70 B2 Mawei China
62 A1 Mawkmai Myanmar
62 A1 Mawlaik Myanmar
78 B2 Mawqaq Saudi Arabia
78 B3 Mawza Yemen
108 A3 Maxia, Punta mt. Sardinia Italy
83 J2 Maya r. Rus. Fed.
147 C2 Mayaguana i. Bahamas
96 B3 Maybole U.K.
104 B2 Mayenne France
104 B2 Mayenne r. France
128 C2 Mayerthorpe Can.
140 B3 Mayfield U.S.A.
87 D4 Maykop Rus. Fed.
126 B2 Mayo Can.
118 B3 Mayoko Congo
121 D2 Mayotte terr. Africa
83 J3 Mayskiy Rus. Fed.
140 C3 Maysville U.S.A.
118 B3 Mayumba Gabon
137 D1 Mayville U.S.A.
151 C2 Mazagão Brazil
104 C3 Mazamet France
72 A2 Mazar China
108 B3 Mazara del Vallo Sicily Italy
77 C3 Mazār-e Sharīf Afgh.
144 A2 Mazatán Mex.
146 A3 Mazatenango Guat.
144 B2 Mazatlán Mex.
88 B2 Mažeikiai Lith.
88 B2 Mazirbe Latvia
121 B3 Mazunga Zimbabwe
89 D3 Mazyr Belarus
123 D2 Mbabane Swaziland
118 B2 Mbaïki C.A.R.
121 C1 Mbala Zambia
119 D2 Mbale Uganda
118 B2 Mbalmayo Cameroon
118 B3 Mbandaka Dem. Rep. Congo
118 A2 Mbanga Cameroon
120 A1 M'banza Congo Angola
119 D3 Mbeya Tanz.
119 D4 Mbinga Tanz.
118 B2 Mbomo Congo
118 B2 Mbouda Cameroon
114 A3 Mbour Senegal
114 A3 Mbout Senegal
118 C3 Mbuji-Mayi Dem. Rep. Congo
119 D3 Mbuyuni Tanz.
139 D2 McAlester U.S.A.
139 D2 McAllen U.S.A.
128 B2 McBride Can.
134 C2 McCall U.S.A.
126 E2 McClintock Channel Can.
126 D2 McClure Strait Can.
142 B2 McComb U.S.A.
136 C2 McConaughy, Lake U.S.A.
136 C2 McCook U.S.A.
134 C2 McDermitt U.S.A.
134 D1 McDonald Peak U.S.A.
134 D1 McGuire, Mount U.S.A.
128 C2 McLennan Can.
128 B2 McLeod Lake Can.
134 B1 McMinnville OR U.S.A.
142 C1 McMinnville TN U.S.A.
137 D3 McPherson U.S.A.
123 C3 Mdantsane S. Africa
135 D3 Mead, Lake resr U.S.A.
129 D2 Meadow Lake Can.
140 C2 Meadville U.S.A.
66 D2 Meaken-dake vol. Japan
106 B1 Mealhada Port.
131 E1 Mealy Mountains Can.

128 C2 **Meander River** Can.
78 A2 **Mecca** Saudi Arabia
100 B2 **Mechelen** Belgium
100 B2 **Mechelen** Neth.
100 C2 **Meckenheim** Ger.
100 C2 **Meckenheim** Ger.
106 B1 **Meda** Port.
60 A1 **Meda** Indon.
153 B5 **Medanosa, Punta** pt Arg.
73 C4 **Medawachchiya** Sri Lanka
107 D2 **Médéa** Alg.
150 A1 **Medellín** Col.
115 D1 **Medenine** Tunisia
134 B2 **Medford** U.S.A.
110 C2 **Medgidia** Romania
110 B1 **Mediaş** Romania
136 B2 **Medicine Bow Mountains**
U.S.A.
136 B2 **Medicine Bow Peak** U.S.A.
129 C2 **Medicine Hat** Can.
137 D3 **Medicine Lodge** U.S.A.
155 D1 **Medina** Brazil
78 A2 **Medina** Saudi Arabia
106 C1 **Medinaceli** Spain
106 C1 **Medina del Campo** Spain
106 B1 **Medina de Rioseco** Spain
84 D6 **Mediterranean Sea**
129 C2 **Medley** Can.
87 E3 **Mednogorsk** Rus. Fed.
83 L2 **Medvezh'i, Ostrova** is
Rus. Fed.
86 C2 **Medvezh'yegorsk**
Rus. Fed.
50 A2 **Meekatharra** Austr.
136 B2 **Meeker** U.S.A.
75 B2 **Meerut** India
100 A2 **Meetkerke** Belgium
111 B3 **Megalopoli** Greece
131 C2 **Mégantic** Can.
75 C2 **Meghāsani** mt. India
80 A2 **Megisti** i. Greece
92 I1 **Mehamn** Norway
50 A2 **Meharry, Mount** Austr.
79 C2 **Mehrān** watercourse Iran
154 C1 **Meia Ponte** r. Brazil
118 B2 **Meiganga** Cameroon
65 B1 **Meihekou** China
Meijiang China see Ningdu
62 A1 **Meiktila** Myanmar
101 E2 **Meiningen** Ger.
102 C1 **Meißen** Ger.
71 B3 **Meizhou** China
152 B3 **Mejicana** mt. Arg.
152 A3 **Mejillones** Chile
117 B3 **Mek'elē** Eth.
114 C2 **Mekerrhane, Sebkha**
salt pan Alg.
114 B1 **Meknès** Morocco
63 B2 **Mekong** r. Asia
63 B3 **Mekong, Mouths of the**
Vietnam
60 B1 **Melaka** Malaysia
53 B3 **Melbourne** Austr.
143 D3 **Melbourne** U.S.A.
108 A2 **Mele, Capo** c. Italy
131 C1 **Mélèzes, Rivière aux** r. Can.
117 B3 **Melfi** Chad
109 C2 **Melfi** Italy
129 D2 **Melfort** Can.
92 F3 **Melhus** Norway
106 B1 **Melide** Spain
114 B1 **Melilla** N. Africa
91 D2 **Melitopol'** Ukr.
101 D1 **Melle** Ger.
93 F4 **Mellerud** Sweden
101 E2 **Mellrichstadt** Ger.
148 D2 **Mellum** i. Ger.
152 C4 **Melo** Uru.
115 C1 **Melrhir, Chott** salt l. Alg.
99 C2 **Melton Mowbray** U.K.

104 C2 **Melun** France
129 D2 **Melville** Can.
51 D1 **Melville, Cape** Austr.
131 E1 **Melville, Lake** Can.
50 C1 **Melville Island** Austr.
126 D1 **Melville Island** Can.
127 F2 **Melville Peninsula** Can.
102 C2 **Memmingen** Ger.
61 B1 **Mempawah** Indon.
80 B3 **Memphis** Egypt
142 B1 **Memphis** TN U.S.A.
139 C2 **Memphis** TX U.S.A.
91 C1 **Mena** Ukr.
142 B2 **Mena** U.S.A.
114 C3 **Ménaka** Mali
Mènam Khong r. Laos/Thai.
see Mekong
105 C2 **Mende** France
116 B3 **Mendefera** Eritrea
145 C2 **Méndez** Mex.
119 D2 **Mendi** Eth.
59 D3 **Mendi** P.N.G.
99 B3 **Mendip Hills** U.K.
153 B4 **Mendoza** Arg.
111 C3 **Menemen** Turkey
60 B2 **Menggala** Indon.
62 B1 **Mengzi** China
131 D1 **Menihek** Can.
52 B2 **Menindee** Austr.
52 B2 **Menindee Lake** Austr.
52 A3 **Meningie** Austr.
104 C2 **Mennecy** France
140 B1 **Menominee** U.S.A.
120 A2 **Menongue** Angola
107 D1 **Menorca** i. Spain
60 A2 **Mentawai, Kepulauan**
is Indon.
60 B2 **Mentok** Indon.
50 B2 **Menzies** Austr.
100 C1 **Meppel** Neth.
100 C1 **Meppen** Ger.
123 D1 **Mepuze** Moz.
123 C2 **Meqheleng** S. Africa
108 B1 **Merano** Italy
59 D3 **Merauke** Indon.
52 B2 **Merbein** Austr.
135 B3 **Merced** U.S.A.
152 C3 **Mercedes** Arg.
127 G2 **Mercy, Cape** Can.
139 C1 **Meredith, Lake** U.S.A.
91 D2 **Merefa** Ukr.
116 A3 **Merga Oasis** Sudan
63 A2 **Mergui** Myanmar
63 A2 **Mergui Archipelago** is
Myanmar
110 C2 **Meriç** r. Greece/Turkey
145 D2 **Mérida** Mex.
106 B2 **Mérida** Spain
150 A1 **Mérida** Venez.
142 C2 **Meridian** U.S.A.
53 C3 **Merimbula** Austr.
116 B3 **Merowe** Sudan
50 A3 **Merredin** Austr.
96 B3 **Merrick** hill U.K.
140 B1 **Merrill** U.S.A.
140 B2 **Merrillville** U.S.A.
128 B2 **Merritt** Can.
53 C2 **Merrygoen** Austr.
116 C3 **Mersa Fatma** Eritrea
100 C3 **Mersch** Lux.
101 E2 **Merseburg (Saale)** Ger.
98 B2 **Mersey** r. U.K.
60 B1 **Mersing** Malaysia
99 D3 **Mers-les-Bains** France
74 B2 **Merta** India
99 B3 **Merthyr Tydfil** U.K.
106 B2 **Mértola** Port.
119 D3 **Meru** vol. Tanz.
100 C3 **Merzig** Ger.
138 A2 **Mesa** U.S.A.

109 C2 **Mesagne** Italy
101 D2 **Meschede** Ger.
89 E3 **Meshchovsk** Rus. Fed.
91 E2 **Meshkovskaya** Rus. Fed.
111 B2 **Mesimeri** Greece
111 B3 **Mesolongi** Greece
121 D2 **Messalo** r. Moz.
109 C3 **Messina** Sicily Italy
123 D1 **Messina** S. Africa
109 C3 **Messina, Stretta di** str. Italy
111 B3 **Messiniakos Kolpos** b.
Greece
110 B2 **Mesta** r. Bulg.
150 B1 **Meta** r. Col./Venez.
127 G2 **Meta Incognita Peninsula**
Can.
152 B3 **Metán** Arg.
111 B3 **Methoni** Greece
109 C2 **Metković** Croatia
60 B2 **Metro** Indon.
117 B4 **Metu** Eth.
105 D2 **Metz** France
100 B2 **Meuse** r. Belgium/France
139 D2 **Mexia** U.S.A.
144 A1 **Mexicali** Mex.
144 A1 **Mexico** country
Central America
145 C3 **México** Mex.
137 E3 **México** U.S.A.
125 E5 **Mexico, Gulf of** Mex./U.S.A.
101 F1 **Meyenburg** Ger.
76 C3 **Meymaneh** Afgh.
86 D2 **Mezen'** Rus. Fed.
86 D2 **Mezen'** r. Rus. Fed.
86 E1 **Mezhdusharskiy, Ostrov**
i. Rus. Fed.
103 E2 **Mezőtúr** Hungary
144 B2 **Mezquitic** Mex.
88 C2 **Mežvidi** Latvia
121 C2 **Mfuwe** Zambia
123 D2 **Mhlume** Swaziland
74 B2 **Mhow** India
145 C3 **Miahuatlán** Mex.
106 B2 **Miajadas** Spain
143 D3 **Miami** FL U.S.A.
139 E1 **Miami** OK U.S.A.
143 D3 **Miami Beach** U.S.A.
81 C2 **Miandowāb** Iran
121 □D2 **Miandrivazo** Madag.
81 C2 **Mianeh** Iran
74 B1 **Mianwali** Pak.
70 A2 **Mianyang** China
121 □D2 **Miarinarivo** Madag.
87 F3 **Miass** Rus. Fed.
128 C2 **Mica Creek** Can.
103 E2 **Michalovce** Slovakia
140 B1 **Michigan** state U.S.A.
140 B2 **Michigan, Lake** U.S.A.
140 B2 **Michigan City** U.S.A.
130 B2 **Michipicoten Island** Can.
130 B2 **Michipicoten River** Can.
89 F3 **Michurinsk** Rus. Fed.
100 A2 **Middelburg** Neth.
123 C3 **Middelburg** E. Cape S. Africa
123 C2 **Middelburg** Mpumalanga
S. Africa
100 B2 **Middelharnis** Neth.
134 B2 **Middle Alkali Lake** U.S.A.
73 D3 **Middle Andaman** i. India
136 D2 **Middle Loup** r. U.S.A.
140 C3 **Middlesboro** U.S.A.
98 C1 **Middlesbrough** U.K.
141 E2 **Middletown** NY U.S.A.
140 C3 **Middletown** OH U.S.A.
78 B3 **Midi** Yemen
130 C2 **Midland** Can.
140 C2 **Midland** MI U.S.A.
139 C2 **Midland** TX U.S.A.
97 B3 **Midleton** Rep. of Ireland
94 B1 **Miðvágur** Faroe Is

109 D2 Midzhur *mt.* Bulg./Yugo.
103 E1 Mielec Pol.
110 C1 Miercurea-Ciuc Romania
106 B1 Mieres Spain
101 E1 Mieste Ger.
145 C3 Miguel Alemán, Presa
        resr Mex.
144 B2 Miguel Auza Mex.
144 B2 Miguel Hidalgo, Presa
        resr Mex.
63 A2 Migyaunglaung Myanmar
89 E3 Mikhaylov Rus. Fed.
        Mikhaylovgrad Bulg. *see*
        Montana
66 B2 Mikhaylovka Rus. Fed.
77 D1 Mikhaylovskiy Rus. Fed.
93 I3 Mikkeli Fin.
86 E2 Mikun' Rus. Fed.
67 C3 Mikuni-sanmyaku *mts* Japan
108 A1 Milan Italy
121 C2 Milange Moz.
        Milano Italy *see* Milan
111 C3 Milas Turkey
137 D1 Milbank U.S.A.
99 D2 Mildenhall U.K.
52 B2 Mildura Austr.
62 B1 Mile China
136 B1 Miles City U.S.A.
143 D3 Milford *DE* U.S.A.
135 D3 Milford *UT* U.S.A.
99 A3 Milford Haven U.K.
54 A2 Milford Sound N.Z.
107 D2 Miliana Alg.
116 B3 Milk, Wadi el *watercourse*
        Sudan
83 L3 Mil'kovo Rus. Fed.
129 C3 Milk River Can.
105 C3 Millau France
143 D2 Milledgeville U.S.A.
137 E1 Mille Lacs *lakes* U.S.A.
130 A2 Mille Lacs, Lac des *l.* Can.
137 D2 Miller U.S.A.
91 E2 Millerovo Rus. Fed.
52 A2 Millers Creek Austr.
52 B3 Millicent Austr.
141 F1 Millinocket U.S.A.
53 D1 Millmerran Austr.
98 B1 Millom U.K.
128 C1 Mills Lake Can.
111 B3 Milos *i.* Greece
89 E3 Miloslavskoye Rus. Fed.
91 E2 Milove Ukr.
52 B1 Milparinka Austr.
54 A3 Milton N.Z.
99 C2 Milton Keynes U.K.
140 B2 Milwaukee U.S.A.
104 B3 Mimizan France
118 B3 Mimongo Gabon
79 C2 Mīnāb Iran
58 C2 Minahasa, Semenanjung
        pen. Indon.
79 C2 Mina Jebel Ali U.A.E.
60 B1 Minas Indon.
153 C4 Minas Uru.
155 D1 Minas Novas Brazil
145 C3 Minatitlán Mex.
62 A1 Minbu Myanmar
64 B2 Mindanao *i.* Phil.
101 D1 Minden Ger.
142 B2 Minden *LA* U.S.A.
137 D2 Minden *NE* U.S.A.
64 B1 Mindoro *i.* Phil.
64 A1 Mindoro Strait Phil.
118 B3 Mindouli Congo
99 B3 Minehead U.K.
154 B1 Mineiros Brazil
139 D2 Mineral Wells U.S.A.
77 E3 Minfeng China
119 C4 Minga Dem. Rep. Congo
81 C1 Mingäçevir Azer.

131 D1 Mingan Can.
52 B2 Mingary Austr.
70 B2 Mingguang China
62 A1 Mingin Myanmar
107 C2 Minglanilla Spain
119 D4 Mingoyo Tanz.
69 E1 Mingshui China
71 B3 Mingxi China
73 B4 Minicoy *i.* India
50 A2 Minilya Austr.
131 D1 Minipi Lake Can.
130 A1 Miniss Lake Can.
115 C4 Minna Nigeria
137 E2 Minneapolis U.S.A.
129 E2 Minnedosa Can.
137 E2 Minnesota *r.* U.S.A.
137 E1 Minnesota *state* U.S.A.
106 B1 Miño *r.* Port./Spain
        Minorca *i.* Spain *see*
        Menorca
136 C1 Minot U.S.A.
88 C3 Minsk Belarus
103 E1 Mińsk Mazowiecki Pol.
131 D2 Minto Can.
130 C1 Minto, Lac *l.* Can.
70 A2 Minxian China
155 D1 Mirabela Brazil
155 D1 Miralta Brazil
111 C3 Mirampelou, Kolpos *b.*
        Greece
152 C3 Miranda Brazil
152 C2 Miranda *r.* Brazil
106 C1 Miranda de Ebro Spain
106 B1 Mirandela Port.
154 B2 Mirandópolis Brazil
79 C3 Mirbāt Oman
54 A3 Miri Sarawak Malaysia
153 C4 Mirim, Lagoa *l.* Brazil
79 D2 Mīrjāveh Iran
83 I2 Mirnyy Rus. Fed.
101 F1 Mirow Ger.
74 A2 Mirpur Khas Pak.
111 B3 Mirtoö Pelagos *sea* Greece
65 B2 Miryang S. Korea
75 C2 Mirzapur India
66 B1 Mishan China
146 B3 Miskitos, Cayos *is* Nic.
103 E2 Miskolc Hungary
59 C3 Misoöl *i.* Indon.
115 D1 Misrātah Libya
130 B1 Missinaibi *r.* Can.
130 B2 Missinaibi Lake Can.
128 B3 Mission Can.
130 B1 Missisa Lake Can.
142 C3 Mississippi *r.* U.S.A.
142 C2 Mississippi *state* U.S.A.
142 C3 Mississippi Delta U.S.A.
134 D1 Missoula U.S.A.
137 E3 Missouri *r.* U.S.A.
137 E3 Missouri *state* U.S.A.
131 C2 Mistassibi *r.* Can.
130 C1 Mistassini, Lac *l.* Can.
131 D1 Mistastin Lake Can.
103 D2 Mistelbach Austria
131 D1 Mistinibi, Lac *l.* Can.
130 C1 Mistissini Can.
51 D2 Mitchell Austr.
51 D1 Mitchell *r.* Austr.
137 D2 Mitchell U.S.A.
97 B2 Mitchelstown Rep. of Ireland
74 A2 Mithi Pak.
67 D3 Mito Japan
119 D3 Mitole Tanz.
53 D2 Mittagong Austr.
101 E2 Mittelhausen Ger.
101 D1 Mittellandkanal *canal* Ger.
101 F3 Mitterteich Ger.
145 A1 Mitú Col.
119 C4 Mitumba, Chaîne des *mts*
        Dem. Rep. Congo

119 C3 Mitumba, Monts *mts*
        Dem. Rep. Congo
118 B2 Mitzic Gabon
78 B2 Miyah, Wādi al *watercourse*
        Saudi Arabia
67 C4 Miyake-jima *i.* Japan
66 D3 Miyako Japan
76 B4 Miyakonojō Japan
87 B2 Miyaly Kazakh.
        Miyang China *see* Mile
67 B4 Miyazaki Japan
115 D1 Mizdah Libya
97 B3 Mizen Head *hd*
        Rep. of Ireland
90 A2 Mizhhir"ya Ukr.
93 G4 Mjölby Sweden
93 F3 Mjøsa *l.* Norway
119 D3 Mkomazi Tanz.
103 C1 Mladá Boleslav Czech Rep.
109 D2 Mladenovac Yugo.
103 E1 Mława Pol.
123 C3 Mlungisi S. Africa
90 B1 Mlyniv Ukr.
123 C2 Mmabatho S. Africa
123 C2 Mmathethe Botswana
135 E3 Moab U.S.A.
123 D2 Moamba Moz.
119 C3 Moba Dem. Rep. Congo
118 C2 Mobayi-Mbongo
        Dem. Rep. Congo
137 E3 Moberly U.S.A.
142 C2 Mobile U.S.A.
142 C2 Mobile Bay U.S.A.
136 C1 Mobridge U.S.A.
121 D2 Moçambique Moz.
62 B1 Móc Châu Vietnam
123 C1 Mochudi Botswana
121 D2 Mocimboa da Praia Moz.
150 A1 Mocoa Col.
154 C2 Mococa Brazil
144 B2 Mocorito Mex.
144 B1 Moctezuma *Chihuahua* Mex.
145 B2 Moctezuma *San Luis Potosí*
        Mex.
144 B2 Moctezuma *Sonora* Mex.
121 C2 Mocuba Moz.
105 D2 Modane France
122 B2 Modder *r.* S. Africa
108 B2 Modena Italy
135 B3 Modesto U.S.A.
53 C3 Moe Austr.
100 C2 Moers Ger.
96 C3 Moffat U.K.
        Mogadishu Somalia *see*
        Muqdisho
123 C1 Mogalakwena *r.* S. Africa
62 A1 Mogaung Myanmar
        Mogilev Belarus *see*
        Mahilyow
154 C2 Mogi-Mirim Brazil
83 I3 Mogocha Rus. Fed.
62 A1 Mogok Myanmar
103 D2 Mohács Hungary
123 C3 Mohale's Hoek Lesotho
107 D2 Mohammadia Alg.
141 E2 Mohawk *r.* U.S.A.
119 D3 Mohoro Tanz.
90 B2 Mohyliv Podil's'kyy Ukr.
110 C1 Moineşti Romania
92 F2 Mo i Rana Norway
104 C3 Moissac France
135 C3 Mojave U.S.A.
135 C3 Mojave Desert U.S.A.
62 B1 Mojiang China
154 C2 Moji das Cruzes Brazil
154 C2 Moji-Guaçu *r.* Brazil
54 B1 Mokau N.Z.
123 C2 Mokhotlong Lesotho
65 B3 Mokp'o S. Korea
145 C2 Molango Mex.

92 E3 **Molde** Norway
90 B2 **Moldova** *country* Europe
110 B1 **Moldoveanu, Vârful** *mt.*
　　　　Romania
90 B2 **Moldovei Centrale, Podişul**
　　　　plat. Moldova
123 C1 **Molepolole** Botswana
88 C1 **Molėtai** Lith.
109 C2 **Molfetta** Italy
107 C1 **Molina de Aragón** Spain
150 A3 **Mollendo** Peru
53 C2 **Molong** Austr.
122 B2 **Molopo** *watercourse*
　　　　Botswana/S. Africa
118 B2 **Moloundou** Cameroon
　　　　Maluku
59 C3 **Molucca Sea** Indon.
52 B2 **Momba** Austr.
119 D3 **Mombasa** Kenya
154 B1 **Mombuca, Serra da** *hills*
　　　　Brazil
93 F4 **Møn** *i.* Denmark
105 D3 **Monaco** *country* Europe
96 B2 **Monadhliath Mountains**
　　　　U.K.
97 C1 **Monaghan** Rep. of Ireland
89 D3 **Monastyrshchina** Rus. Fed.
90 B2 **Monastyryshche** Ukr.
66 D2 **Monbetsu** Japan
108 A1 **Moncalieri** Italy
86 F2 **Monchegorsk** Rus. Fed.
100 C2 **Mönchengladbach** Ger.
144 B2 **Monclova** Mex.
131 D2 **Moncton** Can.
106 B1 **Mondego** *r.* Port.
123 D2 **Mondlo** S. Africa
108 A2 **Mondovì** Italy
111 B3 **Monemvasia** Greece
66 D1 **Moneron, Ostrov** *i.* Rus. Fed.
137 E3 **Monett** U.S.A.
108 B1 **Monfalcone** Italy
106 B1 **Monforte** Spain
62 B1 **Mông Cai** Vietnam
62 B1 **Mong Lin** Myanmar
68 C1 **Mongolia** *country* Asia
62 A1 **Mong Pawk** Myanmar
62 A1 **Mong Ping** Myanmar
120 B2 **Mongu** Zambia
135 B3 **Monitor Range** *mts* U.S.A.
114 C4 **Mono** *r.* Togo
135 B3 **Mono Lake** U.S.A.
109 C2 **Monopoli** Italy
107 C1 **Monreal del Campo** Spain
142 B2 **Monroe** *LA* U.S.A.
140 B2 **Monroe** *WI* U.S.A.
137 F4 **Monroe City** U.S.A.
114 A4 **Monrovia** Liberia
100 A2 **Mons** Belgium
122 B3 **Montagu** S. Africa
109 C3 **Montalto** *mt.* Italy
110 B2 **Montana** Bulg.
134 E1 **Montana** *state* U.S.A.
104 C2 **Montargis** France
104 C3 **Montauban** France
141 E2 **Montauk Point** U.S.A.
123 C2 **Mont-aux-Sources** *mt.*
　　　　Lesotho
105 C2 **Montbard** France
105 D2 **Mont Blanc** *mt.* France/Italy
105 C2 **Montbrison** France
100 B3 **Montcornet** France
104 C3 **Mont-de-Marsan** France
104 C2 **Montdidier** France
151 C2 **Monte Alegre** Brazil
105 D3 **Monte-Carlo** Monaco
152 C4 **Monte Caseros** Arg.
146 C3 **Montego Bay** Jamaica

105 C3 **Montélimar** France
109 C2 **Montella** Italy
145 C2 **Montemorelos** Mex.
104 B2 **Montendre** France
109 C2 **Montenegro** *aut. rep.* Yugo.
121 C2 **Montepuez** Moz.
108 B2 **Montepulciano** Italy
135 B3 **Monterey** U.S.A.
135 B3 **Monterey Bay** U.S.A.
150 A1 **Montería** Col.
152 B2 **Montero** Bol.
145 B2 **Monterrey** Mex.
109 C2 **Montesano sulla**
　　　　Marcellana Italy
109 C2 **Monte Sant'Angelo** Italy
151 E3 **Monte Santo** Brazil
108 A2 **Monte Santu, Capo di** *c.*
　　　　Sardinia Italy
155 D1 **Montes Claros** Brazil
153 C4 **Montevideo** Uru.
137 D2 **Montevideo** U.S.A.
136 B3 **Monte Vista** U.S.A.
142 C2 **Montgomery** U.S.A.
105 D2 **Monthey** Switz.
142 B2 **Monticello** *AR* U.S.A.
135 E3 **Monticello** *UT* U.S.A.
104 C2 **Montignac** France
106 C2 **Montilla** Spain
131 D2 **Mont-Joli** Can.
130 C2 **Mont-Laurier** Can.
104 C2 **Montluçon** France
131 C2 **Montmagny** Can.
104 C2 **Montmorillon** France
51 D2 **Monto** Austr.
134 D2 **Montpelier** *ID* U.S.A.
141 E2 **Montpelier** *VT* U.S.A.
105 C3 **Montpellier** France
130 C2 **Montréal** Can.
129 D2 **Montreal Lake** Can.
129 D2 **Montreal Lake** *l.* Can.
99 D3 **Montreuil** France
105 D2 **Montreux** Switz.
96 C2 **Montrose** U.K.
136 B3 **Montrose** U.S.A.
147 D3 **Montserrat** *terr.* West Indies
62 A1 **Monywa** Myanmar
108 A1 **Monza** Italy
107 D1 **Monzón** Spain
123 C1 **Mookane** Botswana
53 B3 **Moonie** Austr.
53 C1 **Moonie** *r.* Austr.
52 A2 **Moonta** Austr.
50 A2 **Moore, Lake** *salt flat* Austr.
137 D1 **Moorhead** U.S.A.
53 C3 **Mooroopna** Austr.
122 A3 **Moorreesburg** S. Africa
130 B1 **Moose** *r.* Can.
130 B1 **Moose Factory** Can.
141 F1 **Moosehead Lake** Can.
129 D2 **Moose Jaw** Can.
137 E1 **Moose Lake** U.S.A.
129 D2 **Moosomin** Can.
130 B1 **Moosonee** Can.
52 B2 **Mootwingee** Austr.
123 C1 **Mopane** S. Africa
114 B3 **Mopti** Mali
150 A3 **Moquegua** Peru
93 F3 **Mora** Sweden
137 E1 **Mora** U.S.A.
75 B2 **Moradabad** India
121 □D2 **Moramanga** Madag.
103 D2 **Morarica** France
96 B2 **Moray Firth** *b.* U.K.
100 C3 **Morbach** Ger.
74 B2 **Morbi** India
104 B3 **Morcenx** France
69 E1 **Mordaga** China
129 E3 **Morden** Can.
91 E1 **Mordovo** Rus. Fed.
98 B1 **Morecambe** U.K.

98 B1 **Morecambe Bay** U.K.
53 C1 **Moree** Austr.
59 D3 **Morehead** P.N.G.
140 C3 **Morehead** U.S.A.
143 E2 **Morehead City** U.S.A.
145 B3 **Morelia** Mex.
107 C1 **Morella** Spain
106 B2 **Morena, Sierra** *mts* Spain
110 C2 **Moreni** Romania
128 A2 **Moresby, Mount** Can.
128 A2 **Moresby Island** Can.
142 B3 **Morgan City** U.S.A.
143 D1 **Morganton** U.S.A.
140 D3 **Morgantown** U.S.A.
105 D2 **Morges** Switz.
66 D2 **Mori** Japan
128 B2 **Morice Lake** Can.
66 D3 **Morioka** Japan
53 D2 **Morisset** Austr.
104 B2 **Morlaix** France
51 C1 **Mornington Island** Austr.
59 D3 **Morobe** P.N.G.
114 B1 **Morocco** *country* Africa
119 D3 **Morogoro** Tanz.
64 B2 **Moro Gulf** Phil.
122 B2 **Morokweng** S. Africa
121 □D3 **Morombe** Madag.
68 C1 **Mörön** Mongolia
121 □D3 **Morondava** Madag.
121 D2 **Moroni** Comoros
59 C2 **Morotai** *i.* Indon.
119 D2 **Moroto** Uganda
98 C1 **Morpeth** U.K.
154 C1 **Morrinhos** Brazil
129 E3 **Morris** Can.
137 D1 **Morris** U.S.A.
143 D1 **Morristown** U.S.A.
87 D3 **Morshanka** Rus. Fed.
154 B1 **Mortes, Rio das** *r.* Brazil
52 B3 **Mortlake** Austr.
53 D3 **Moruya** Austr.
96 B2 **Morvern** *reg.* U.K.
53 C3 **Morwell** Austr.
102 B2 **Mosbach** Ger.
89 E2 **Moscow** Rus. Fed.
134 C1 **Moscow** U.S.A.
100 C2 **Mosel** *r.* Ger.
105 D2 **Moselle** *r.* France
134 C1 **Moses Lake** U.S.A.
92 □A3 **Mosfellsbær** Iceland
55 B3 **Mosgiel** N.Z.
89 D2 **Moshenskoye** Rus. Fed.
119 D3 **Moshi** Tanz.
92 F2 **Mosjøen** Norway
　　　　Moskva Rus. Fed. *see*
　　　　Moscow
103 D2 **Mosonmagyaróvár** Hungary
93 F4 **Moss** Norway
122 B3 **Mossel Bay** S. Africa
122 B3 **Mossel Bay** *b.* S. Africa
118 B3 **Mossendjo** Congo
52 B2 **Mossgiel** Austr.
51 D1 **Mossman** Austr.
151 E2 **Mossoró** Brazil
53 D2 **Moss Vale** Austr.
102 C1 **Most** Czech Rep.
114 C1 **Mostaganem** Alg.
109 C2 **Mostar** Bos.-Herz.
152 C4 **Mostardas** Brazil
93 G4 **Motala** Sweden
96 C3 **Motherwell** U.K.
106 C2 **Motilla del Palancar** Spain
123 B1 **Motokwe** Botswana
106 C2 **Motril** Spain
110 B2 **Motru** Romania
145 B2 **Motul** Mex.
111 C3 **Moudros** Greece
118 B3 **Mouila** Gabon
52 B3 **Moulamein** Austr.
105 C2 **Moulins** France

63 A2 **Moulmein** Myanmar
143 D2 **Moultrie** U.S.A.
143 E2 **Moultrie, Lake** U.S.A.
140 B3 **Mound City** U.S.A.
115 D4 **Moundou** Chad
137 E3 **Mountain Grove** U.S.A.
142 B1 **Mountain Home** *AR* U.S.A.
134 C2 **Mountain Home** *ID* U.S.A.
143 D1 **Mount Airy** U.S.A.
52 A3 **Mount Barker** Austr.
53 C3 **Mount Beauty** Austr.
121 C2 **Mount Darwin** Zimbabwe
141 F2 **Mount Desert Island** U.S.A.
123 C3 **Mount Fletcher** S. Africa
123 C3 **Mount Frere** S. Africa
52 B3 **Mount Gambier** Austr.
59 D3 **Mount Hagen** P.N.G.
53 C2 **Mount Hope** Austr.
51 C2 **Mount Isa** Austr.
50 A2 **Mount Magnet** Austr.
52 B2 **Mount Manara** Austr.
54 C1 **Mount Maunganui** N.Z.
137 E2 **Mount Pleasant** *IA* U.S.A.
140 C2 **Mount Pleasant** *MI* U.S.A.
139 E2 **Mount Pleasant** *TX* U.S.A.
99 A3 **Mount's Bay** U.K.
134 B2 **Mount Shasta** U.S.A.
140 B3 **Mount Vernon** *IL* U.S.A.
140 C2 **Mount Vernon** *OH* U.S.A.
134 B1 **Mount Vernon** *WA* U.S.A.
51 D2 **Moura** Austr.
115 E3 **Mourdi, Dépression du** *depr.* Chad
97 C1 **Mourne Mountains** U.K.
100 A2 **Mouscron** Belgium
115 D3 **Moussoro** Chad
58 C2 **Moutong** Indon.
115 C2 **Mouydir, Monts du** *plat.* Alg.
100 B3 **Mouzon** France
97 B1 **Moy** *r.* Rep. of Ireland
117 B4 **Moyale** Eth.
123 C3 **Moyeni** Lesotho
77 D2 **Moyynty** Kazakh.
123 C3 **Mozambique** *country* Africa
113 G5 **Mozambique Channel** Africa
89 E2 **Mozhaysk** Rus. Fed.
119 D3 **Mpanda** Tanz.
121 C2 **Mpika** Zambia
121 C1 **Mporokoso** Zambia
123 C2 **Mpumalanga** *prov.* S. Africa
88 C2 **Mshinskaya** Rus. Fed.
107 D2 **M'Sila** Alg.
89 D2 **Msta** *r.* Rus. Fed.
89 D2 **Mstinskiy Most** Rus. Fed.
89 D3 **Mstsislaw** Belarus
89 E3 **Mtsensk** Rus. Fed.
119 E4 **Mtwara** Tanz.
118 B3 **Muanda** Dem. Rep. Congo
62 B2 **Muang Khammouan** Laos
63 B2 **Muang Không** Laos
62 B1 **Muang Ngoy** Laos
62 B1 **Muang Pakbeng** Laos
62 B2 **Muang Pakxan** Laos
62 B1 **Muang Sing** Laos
62 B2 **Muang Vangviang** Laos
62 B2 **Muang Xaignabouri** Laos
60 B1 **Muar** Malaysia
60 B2 **Muarabungo** Indon.
60 B2 **Muaradua** Indon.
61 C2 **Muaralaung** Indon.
60 A2 **Muarasiberut** Indon.
60 B2 **Muaratembesi** Indon.
61 C2 **Muarateweh** Indon.
119 D2 **Mubende** Uganda
115 D3 **Mubi** Nigeria
120 B2 **Muconda** Angola
155 E1 **Mucuri** Brazil
155 E1 **Mucuri** *r.* Brazil
66 A2 **Mudanjiang** China
66 A1 **Mudan Jiang** *r.* China

111 C2 **Mudanya** Turkey
101 E1 **Müden (Örtze)** Ger.
53 C2 **Mudgee** Austr.
63 A2 **Mudon** Myanmar
80 B1 **Mudurnu** Turkey
144 B2 **Mueda** Moz.
121 B2 **Mufulira** Zambia
120 B2 **Mufumbwe** Zambia
111 C3 **Muğla** Turkey
116 B2 **Muhammad Qol** Sudan
101 F2 **Mühlberg** Ger.
101 E2 **Mühlhausen (Thüringen)** Ger.
63 B3 **Mui Ca Mau** *c.* Vietnam
97 C2 **Muine Bheag** Rep. of Ireland
121 C2 **Muite** Moz.
65 B2 **Muju** S. Korea
90 A2 **Mukacheve** Ukr.
61 C1 **Mukah** *Sarawak* Malaysia
63 B2 **Mukdahan** Thai.
50 A3 **Mukinbudin** Austr.
58 B3 **Mukomuko** Indon.
121 C2 **Mulanje, Mount** Malawi
101 F2 **Mulde** *r.* Ger.
144 B2 **Mulegé** Mex.
139 C2 **Muleshoe** U.S.A.
106 C2 **Mulhacén** *mt.* Spain
100 C2 **Mülheim an der Ruhr** Ger.
105 D2 **Mulhouse** France
66 B1 **Muling** China
66 B1 **Muling** *r.* China
96 B2 **Mull** *i.* U.K.
53 C2 **Mullaley** Austr.
136 C2 **Mullen** U.S.A.
61 C1 **Muller, Pegunungan** *mts* Indon.
50 A2 **Mullewa** Austr.
97 C2 **Mullingar** Rep. of Ireland
96 B3 **Mull of Galloway** *c.* U.K.
96 B3 **Mull of Kintyre** *hd* U.K.
96 B3 **Mull of Oa** *hd* U.K.
120 B2 **Mulobezi** Zambia
74 B1 **Multan** Pak.
73 B3 **Mumbai** India
120 B2 **Mumbwa** Zambia
145 C2 **Muna** Mex.
101 E2 **Münchberg** Ger.
München Ger. *see* **Munich**
140 B2 **Muncie** U.S.A.
50 B3 **Mundrabilla** Austr.
119 C3 **Mungbere** Dem. Rep. Congo
75 C2 **Mungeli** India
53 C1 **Mungindi** Austr.
102 C2 **Munich** Ger.
155 D2 **Muniz Freire** Brazil
101 E1 **Münster** *Niedersachsen* Ger.
100 C2 **Münster** *Nordrhein-Westfalen* Ger.
97 B2 **Munster** *reg.* Rep. of Ireland
100 C2 **Münsterland** *reg.* Ger.
62 B1 **Muong Nhie** Vietnam
92 H2 **Muonio** Fin.
92 H2 **Muonioälven** *r.* Fin./Sweden
117 C4 **Muqdisho** Somalia
103 D2 **Mur** *r.* Austria
119 C3 **Muramvya** Burundi
119 D3 **Muranga** Kenya
81 B2 **Murat** *r.* Turkey
111 C2 **Muratlı** Turkey
50 A2 **Murchison** *watercourse* Austr.
107 C2 **Murcia** Spain
111 C2 **Mürefte** Turkey
110 B1 **Mureş** *r.* Romania
104 C3 **Muret** France
142 C1 **Murfreesboro** U.S.A.
77 C3 **Murghab** *r.* Afgh.
77 D3 **Murghob** Tajik.
155 D2 **Muriaé** Brazil

120 B1 **Muriege** Angola
101 F1 **Müritz** *l.* Ger.
86 C2 **Murmansk** Rus. Fed.
87 D3 **Murom** Rus. Fed.
66 D2 **Muroran** Japan
106 B1 **Muros** Spain
67 B4 **Muroto** Japan
67 B4 **Muroto-zaki** *pt* Japan
143 D1 **Murphy** U.S.A.
53 C1 **Murra Murra** Austr.
52 A3 **Murray** *r.* Austr.
128 B2 **Murray** *r.* Can.
140 B3 **Murray** U.S.A.
143 D2 **Murray, Lake** U.S.A.
52 A3 **Murray Bridge** Austr.
122 B3 **Murraysburg** S. Africa
52 B3 **Murrayville** Austr.
52 B2 **Murrumbidgee** *r.* Austr.
121 C2 **Murrupula** Moz.
53 D2 **Murrurundi** Austr.
109 C1 **Murska Sobota** Slovenia
54 C1 **Murupara** N.Z.
75 C2 **Murwara** India
53 D1 **Murwillumbah** Austr.
115 D2 **Murzūq** Libya
81 C2 **Muş** Turkey
110 B2 **Musala** *mt.* Bulg.
65 B1 **Musan** N. Korea
78 B3 **Musaymir** Yemen
79 C2 **Muscat** Oman
137 E2 **Muscatine** U.S.A.
50 C2 **Musgrave Ranges** *mts* Austr.
118 B3 **Mushie** Dem. Rep. Congo
60 B2 **Musi** *r.* Indon.
140 B2 **Muskegon** U.S.A.
139 D1 **Muskogee** U.S.A.
128 B2 **Muskwa** *r.* Can.
74 A1 **Muslimbagh** Pak.
78 A3 **Musmar** Sudan
119 D3 **Musoma** Tanz.
96 C3 **Musselburgh** U.K.
88 B2 **Mustjala** Estonia
53 D2 **Muswellbrook** Austr.
116 A2 **Mut** Egypt
121 C2 **Mutare** Zimbabwe
66 D2 **Mutsu** Japan
121 C2 **Mutuali** Moz.
92 I2 **Muurola** Fin.
70 A2 **Mu Us Shamo** *des.* China
120 A1 **Muxaluando** Angola
86 C2 **Muyezerskiy** Rus. Fed.
119 D3 **Muyinga** Burundi
76 B2 **Muynak** Uzbek.
74 B1 **Muzaffargarh** Pak.
75 C2 **Muzaffarnagar** India
75 C2 **Muzaffarpur** India
144 B2 **Múzquiz** Mex.
75 C1 **Muztag** *mt.* China
119 C3 **Mwanza** Dem. Rep. Congo
119 D3 **Mwanza** Tanz.
118 C3 **Mweka** Dem. Rep. Congo
121 B2 **Mwenda** Zambia
118 C3 **Mwene-Ditu** Dem. Rep. Congo
121 C2 **Mwenezi** Zimbabwe
119 C3 **Mweru, Lake** Dem. Rep. Congo/Zambia
118 C3 **Mwimba** Dem. Rep. Congo
120 B2 **Mwinilunga** Zambia
88 C3 **Myadzyel** Belarus
62 A2 **Myanaung** Myanmar
62 A1 **Myanmar** *country* Asia
63 A2 **Myaungmya** Myanmar
62 A1 **Myingyan** Myanmar
62 A1 **Myitkyina** Myanmar
91 C2 **Mykolayiv** Ukr.
111 C3 **Mykonos** Greece
111 C3 **Mykonos** *i.* Greece
86 E2 **Myla** Rus. Fed.
75 D2 **Mymensingh** Bangl.

62 A1 **Myohaung** Myanmar
65 B1 **Myŏnggan** N. Korea
88 C2 **Myory** Belarus
92 □B3 **Mýrdalsjökull** *ice cap* Iceland
91 C2 **Myrhorod** Ukr.
90 C2 **Myronivka** Ukr.
143 E2 **Myrtle Beach** U.S.A.
53 C3 **Myrtleford** Austr.
134 B2 **Myrtle Point** U.S.A.
89 E2 **Myshkin** Rus. Fed.
103 C1 **Myślibórz** Pol.
73 B3 **Mysore** India
83 N2 **Mys Shmidta** Rus. Fed.
63 B3 **My Tho** Vietnam
111 C3 **Mytilini** Greece
89 E3 **Mytishchi** Rus. Fed.
123 C3 **Mzamomhle** S. Africa
121 C2 **Mzimba** Malawi
121 C2 **Mzuzu** Malawi

N

97 C2 **Naas** Rep. of Ireland
122 A2 **Nababeep** S. Africa
87 E3 **Naberezhnyye Chelny** Rus. Fed.
59 D3 **Nabire** Indon.
80 B2 **Näblus** West Bank
123 C1 **Naboomspruit** S. Africa
121 D2 **Nacala** Moz.
63 A2 **Nachuge** India
139 E2 **Nacogdoches** U.S.A.
144 B1 **Nacozari de García** Mex.
74 B2 **Nadiad** India
90 A2 **Nadvirna** Ukr.
86 C2 **Nadvoitsy** Rus. Fed.
86 G2 **Nadym** Rus. Fed.
93 F4 **Næstved** Denmark
111 B3 **Nafpaktos** Greece
111 B3 **Nafplio** Greece
115 D1 **Nafūsah, Jabal** *hills* Libya
78 B4 **Nafy** Saudi Arabia
64 B1 **Naga** Phil.
130 B1 **Nagagami** *r.* Can.
67 C3 **Nagano** Japan
67 C3 **Nagaoka** Japan
75 C2 **Nagaon** India
74 B1 **Nagar** India
74 B2 **Nagar Parkar** Pak.
67 A4 **Nagasaki** Japan
67 B4 **Nagato** Japan
74 B2 **Nagaur** India
73 B4 **Nagercoil** India
74 A2 **Nagha Kalat** Pak.
74 B3 **Nagina** India
67 C3 **Nagoya** Japan
75 B2 **Nagpur** India
68 C2 **Nagqu** China
103 D2 **Nagyatád** Hungary
103 D2 **Nagykanizsa** Hungary
128 B1 **Nahanni Butte** Can.
76 A3 **Nahariyya** Israel
101 E1 **Nahrendorf** Ger.
153 A5 **Nahuel Huapi, Lago** *l.* Arg.
131 D1 **Nain** Can.
81 D2 **Nä'in** Iran
96 C2 **Nairn** U.K.
119 D3 **Nairobi** Kenya
119 D3 **Naivasha** Kenya
81 D2 **Najafäbäd** Iran
78 B2 **Najd** *reg.* Saudi Arabia
106 C1 **Nájera** Spain
65 C1 **Najin** N. Korea
78 B3 **Najrän** Saudi Arabia
        Nakambé *watercourse*
        Burkina/Ghana *see*
        White Volta

67 C3 **Nakatsugawa** Japan
78 A3 **Nakfa** Eritrea
66 B2 **Nakhodka** Rus. Fed.
63 B2 **Nakhon Pathom** Thai.
63 B2 **Nakhon Ratchasima** Thai.
63 B2 **Nakhon Sawan** Thai.
63 A3 **Nakhon Si Thammarat** Thai.
130 B1 **Nakina** Can.
121 C1 **Nakonde** Zambia
93 F4 **Nakskov** Denmark
119 D3 **Nakuru** Kenya
128 C2 **Nakusp** Can.
75 D2 **Nalbari** India
87 D4 **Nal'chik** Rus. Fed.
115 D1 **Nälüt** Libya
123 C2 **Namahadi** S. Africa
77 D2 **Namangan** Uzbek.
122 A2 **Namaqualand** *reg.* Namibia
122 A2 **Namaqualand** *reg.* S. Africa
51 E2 **Nambour** Austr.
53 D2 **Nambucca Heads** Austr.
65 B2 **Namch'ŏn** N. Korea
63 A2 **Nam Chon Reservoir** Thai.
75 D1 **Nam Co** *salt l.* China
62 B1 **Nam Đinh** Vietnam
120 A3 **Namib Desert** Namibia
120 A2 **Namibe** Angola
120 A3 **Namibia** *country* Africa
72 D2 **Namjagbarwa Feng** *mt.* China
59 C3 **Namlea** Indon.
53 C2 **Namoi** *r.* Austr.
134 C2 **Nampa** U.S.A.
114 B3 **Nampala** Mali
65 B2 **Namp'o** N. Korea
121 C2 **Nampula** Moz.
62 A1 **Namrup** India
92 F3 **Namsen** *r.* Norway
92 F3 **Namsos** Norway
63 A2 **Nam Tok** Thai.
83 J2 **Namtsy** Rus. Fed.
62 A1 **Namtu** Myanmar
100 B2 **Namur** Belgium
120 B2 **Namwala** Zambia
65 B2 **Namwŏn** S. Korea
62 A1 **Namya Ra** Myanmar
62 B2 **Nan** Thai.
128 B3 **Nanaimo** Can.
71 B3 **Nan'an** China
122 A1 **Nananib Plateau** Namibia
67 C3 **Nanao** Japan
71 B3 **Nanchang** *Jiangxi* China
71 B3 **Nanchang** *Jiangxi* China
70 A2 **Nanchong** China
63 A3 **Nancowry** *i.* India
105 D2 **Nancy** France
75 C1 **Nanda Devi** *mt.* India
71 A3 **Nandan** China
73 B3 **Nänded** India
74 B2 **Nandurbar** India
73 B3 **Nandyal** India
71 B3 **Nanfeng** China
118 B2 **Nanga Eboko** Cameroon
61 C2 **Nangahpinoh** Indon.
77 D3 **Nanga Parbat** *mt.*
        Jammu and Kashmir
61 C2 **Nangatayap** Indon.
70 B2 **Nangong** China
119 D3 **Nangulangwa** Tanz.
70 C2 **Nanhui** China
70 B2 **Nanjing** China
        Nanking China *see* **Nanjing**
120 A2 **Nankova** Angola
71 B3 **Nan Ling** *mts* China
71 A3 **Nanning** China
127 H2 **Nanortalik** Greenland
71 A3 **Nanpan Jiang** *r.* China
75 C2 **Nanpara** India
71 B3 **Nanping** China
69 E3 **Nansei-shotō** *is* Japan

104 B2 **Nantes** France
70 C2 **Nantong** China
141 F2 **Nantucket Island** U.S.A.
155 D1 **Nanuque** Brazil
64 B2 **Nanusa, Kepulauan** *is* Indon.
71 B3 **Nanxiong** China
70 B2 **Nanyang** China
70 B2 **Nanzhang** China
131 C1 **Naococane, Lac** *l.* Can.
74 A2 **Naokot** Pak.
135 B3 **Napa** U.S.A.
126 D2 **Napaktulik Lake** Can.
127 H2 **Napasoq** Greenland
54 C1 **Napier** N.Z.
108 B2 **Naples** Italy
143 D3 **Naples** U.S.A.
150 A2 **Napo** *r.* Ecuador
        Napoli Italy *see* **Naples**
114 B3 **Nara** Mali
93 I4 **Narach** Belarus
52 B3 **Naracoorte** Austr.
145 C2 **Naranjos** Mex.
63 B3 **Narathiwat** Thai.
105 C3 **Narbonne** France
63 A2 **Narcondam Island** India
127 C1 **Nares Strait** Can./Greenland
122 A1 **Narib** Namibia
87 D4 **Narimanov** Rus. Fed.
67 D3 **Narita** Japan
74 B2 **Narmada** *r.* India
74 B2 **Narnaul** India
108 B2 **Narni** Italy
90 B1 **Narodychi** Ukr.
89 E2 **Naro-Fominsk** Rus. Fed.
53 D3 **Narooma** Austr.
88 C3 **Narowlya** Belarus
53 C2 **Narrabri** Austr.
53 C2 **Narrandera** Austr.
53 C2 **Narromine** Austr.
88 C2 **Narva** Estonia
88 C2 **Narva Bay** Estonia/Rus. Fed.
92 G2 **Narvik** Norway
88 C2 **Narva**
        Vodokhranilishche *resr*
        Estonia/Rus. Fed.
86 E2 **Nar'yan-Mar** Rus. Fed.
77 D2 **Naryn** Kyrg.
74 B2 **Nashik** India
141 E2 **Nashua** U.S.A.
142 C1 **Nashville** U.S.A.
117 B4 **Nasir** Sudan
128 B2 **Nass** *r.* Can.
146 C2 **Nassau** Bahamas
116 B2 **Nasser, Lake** *resr* Egypt
93 F4 **Nässjö** Sweden
130 C1 **Nastapoca** *r.* Can.
130 C1 **Nastapoka Islands** Can.
120 B3 **Nata** Botswana
151 E2 **Natal** Brazil
131 D1 **Natashquan** Can.
131 D1 **Natashquan** *r.* Can.
142 B2 **Natchez** U.S.A.
142 B2 **Natchitoches** U.S.A.
53 C2 **Nathalia** Austr.
107 D1 **Nati, Punta** *pt* Spain
114 C3 **Natitingou** Benin
151 D3 **Natividade** Brazil
67 D3 **Natori** Japan
61 B1 **Natuna, Kepulauan** *is* Indon.
61 B1 **Natuna Besar** *i.* Indon.
120 A3 **Nauchas** Namibia
101 F1 **Nauen** Ger.
88 B2 **Naujoji Akmenė** Lith.
101 E2 **Naumburg (Saale)** Ger.
49 E3 **Nauru** *country*
        S. Pacific Ocean
145 C2 **Nautla** Mex.
88 C3 **Navahrudak** Belarus
106 B2 **Navalmoral de la Mata** Spain

106 B2 Navalvillar de Pela Spain
97 C2 Navan Rep. of Ireland
88 C2 Navapolatsk Belarus
83 M2 Navarin, Mys c. Rus. Fed.
153 B6 Navarino, Isla i. Chile
96 B1 Naver r. U.K.
89 D3 Navlya Rus. Fed.
110 C2 Năvodari Romania
77 C2 Navoi Uzbek.
144 B2 Navojoa Mex.
144 B2 Navolato Mex.
74 A2 Nawabshah Pak.
62 A1 Nawnghkio Myanmar
62 A1 Nawngleng Myanmar
81 C2 Naxçıvan Azer.
111 C3 Naxos i. Greece
144 B2 Nayar Mex.
66 D2 Nayoro Japan
80 B2 Nazareth Israel
144 B2 Nazas Mex.
144 B2 Nazas r. Mex.
150 A3 Nazca Peru
111 C3 Nazilli Turkey
117 B4 Nazrēt Eth.
79 C2 Nazwá Oman
121 B1 Nchelenge Zambia
122 B1 Ncojane Botswana
120 A1 N'dalatando Angola
118 C2 Ndélé C.A.R.
118 B3 Ndendé Gabon
115 D3 Ndjamena Chad
121 B2 Ndola Zambia
97 C1 Neagh, Lough l. U.K.
50 C2 Neale, Lake salt flat Austr.
111 B2 Nea Roda Greece
99 B3 Neath U.K.
53 C1 Nebine Creek r. Austr.
76 B3 Nebitdag Turkm.
150 B1 Neblina, Pico da mt. Brazil
89 D2 Nebolchi Rus. Fed.
136 C2 Nebraska state U.S.A.
137 D2 Nebraska City U.S.A.
108 B3 Nebrodi, Monti mts
   Sicily Italy
153 C4 Necochea Arg.
131 C1 Nedlouc, Lac l. Can.
135 D4 Needles U.S.A.
129 E2 Neepawa Can.
87 E3 Neftekamsk Rus. Fed.
82 F2 Nefteyugansk Rus. Fed.
120 A1 Negage Angola
117 B4 Negēlē Eth.
150 A2 Negra, Punta pt Peru
63 A2 Negrais, Cape Myanmar
153 B5 Negro r. Arg.
150 C2 Negro r. S. America
152 C4 Negro r. Uru.
106 B2 Negro, Cabo c. Morocco
64 B2 Negros i. Phil.
69 E1 Nehe China
70 D3 Neijiang China
129 D2 Neilburg Can.
70 A1 Nei Mongol Zizhiqu aut. reg.
   China
150 A1 Neiva Col.
129 E2 Nejanilini Lake Can.
117 B4 Nek'emtē Eth.
89 F2 Nekrasovskoye Rus. Fed.
89 D2 Nelidovo Rus. Fed.
73 B3 Nellore India
128 C3 Nelson Can.
129 E2 Nelson r. Can.
54 B2 Nelson N.Z.
52 B3 Nelson, Cape Austr.
53 D2 Nelson Bay Austr.
129 E2 Nelson House Can.
134 E1 Nelson Reservoir U.S.A.
123 D2 Nelspruit S. Africa
114 B3 Néma Maur.
88 B2 Neman Rus. Fed.

104 C2 Nemours France
66 D2 Nemuro Japan
90 B2 Nemyriv Ukr.
97 B2 Nenagh Rep. of Ireland
99 D2 Nene r. U.K.
69 E1 Nenjiang China
137 E3 Neosho U.S.A.
75 C2 Nepal country Asia
75 C2 Nepalganj Nepal
135 D3 Nephi U.S.A.
97 B1 Nephin hill Rep. of Ireland
97 B1 Nephin Beg Range hills
   Rep. of Ireland
131 D2 Nepisiguit r. Can.
119 C2 Nepoko r. Dem. Rep. Congo
104 C3 Nérac France
53 D1 Nerang Austr.
69 D1 Nerchinsk Rus. Fed.
89 F2 Nerekhta Rus. Fed.
109 C2 Neretva r. Bos.-Herz./Croatia
120 B2 Neriquinha Angola
88 B3 Neris r. Lith.
89 E2 Nerl' r. Rus. Fed.
86 F2 Nerokhi Rus. Fed.
154 C1 Nerópolis Brazil
83 J3 Neryungri Rus. Fed.
92 □C2 Neskaupstaður Iceland
96 B2 Ness, Loch l. U.K.
136 D3 Ness City U.S.A.
111 B2 Nestos r. Greece
100 B1 Netherlands country Europe
147 D3 Netherlands Antilles terr.
   West Indies
127 G2 Nettilling Lake Can.
101 F1 Neubrandenburg Ger.
105 D2 Neuchâtel Switz.
100 C2 Neuerburg Ger.
100 B3 Neufchâteau Belgium
105 D2 Neufchâteau France
104 C2 Neufchâtel-en-Bray France
101 D2 Neuhof Ger.
102 B1 Neumünster Ger.
102 B2 Neunkirchen Ger.
153 B4 Neuquén Arg.
153 B4 Neuquén r. Arg.
101 F1 Neuruppin Ger.
100 C2 Neuss Ger.
101 D1 Neustadt am Rübenberge
   Ger.
101 E3 Neustadt an der Aisch Ger.
101 F1 Neustrelitz Ger.
100 C2 Neuwied Ger.
137 E3 Nevada U.S.A.
135 C3 Nevada state U.S.A.
106 C2 Nevada, Sierra mts Spain
135 B2 Nevada, Sierra mts U.S.A.
88 C2 Nevel' Rus. Fed.
105 C2 Nevers France
53 C2 Nevertire Austr.
109 C2 Nevesinje Bos.-Herz.
87 D4 Nevinnomyssk Rus. Fed.
128 B2 New Aiyansh Can.
140 B3 New Albany U.S.A.
151 C1 New Amsterdam Guyana
141 E2 Newark NJ U.S.A.
140 C2 Newark OH U.S.A.
98 C2 Newark-on-Trent U.K.
141 E2 New Bedford U.S.A.
143 E1 New Bern U.S.A.
143 D2 Newberry U.S.A.
139 E2 New Boston U.S.A.
139 D3 New Braunfels U.S.A.
97 C2 Newbridge Rep. of Ireland
131 D2 New Brunswick prov. Can.
99 C3 Newbury U.K.
49 E4 New Caledonia terr.
   S. Pacific Ocean
53 D2 Newcastle Austr.
131 D2 Newcastle Can.
123 C2 Newcastle S. Africa

97 D1 Newcastle U.K.
140 C2 New Castle U.S.A.
136 C2 Newcastle U.S.A.
98 B2 Newcastle-under-Lyme U.K.
98 C1 Newcastle upon Tyne U.K.
97 B2 Newcastle West
   Rep. of Ireland
74 B2 New Delhi India
128 C3 New Denver Can.
53 D2 New England Range
   mts Austr.
131 E1 Newfoundland i. Can.
131 E1 Newfoundland prov. Can.
131 D2 New Glasgow Can.
59 D3 New Guinea i. Indon./P.N.G.
141 E2 New Hampshire state U.S.A.
141 E2 New Haven U.S.A.
128 B2 New Hazelton Can.
   New Hebrides country
   S. Pacific Ocean see Vanuatu
142 B2 New Iberia U.S.A.
141 E3 New Jersey state U.S.A.
130 C2 New Liskeard U.S.A.
50 A2 Newman Austr.
138 B2 New Mexico state U.S.A.
142 B3 New Orleans U.S.A.
140 C2 New Philadelphia U.S.A.
54 B1 New Plymouth N.Z.
99 C3 Newport England U.K.
99 B3 Newport Wales U.K.
142 B1 Newport AR U.S.A.
134 B2 Newport OR U.S.A.
141 E2 Newport RI U.S.A.
134 C1 Newport WA U.S.A.
141 D3 Newport News U.S.A.
143 E3 New Providence i. Bahamas
99 A3 Newquay U.K.
142 B2 New Roads U.S.A.
97 C2 New Ross Rep. of Ireland
97 C1 Newry U.K.
   New Siberia Islands
   Rus. Fed. see
   Novosibirskiye Ostrova
52 B2 New South Wales
   state Austr.
137 E2 Newton IA U.S.A.
137 D3 Newton KS U.S.A.
99 B3 Newton Abbot U.K.
96 B3 Newton Stewart U.K.
97 B2 Newtown Rep. of Ireland
99 B2 Newtown U.K.
136 C1 New Town U.S.A.
97 D1 Newtownabbey U.K.
97 D1 Newtownards U.K.
96 C3 Newtown St Boswells U.K.
97 C1 Newtownstewart U.K.
137 E2 New Ulm U.S.A.
141 E2 New York U.S.A.
141 D2 New York state U.S.A.
54 B2 New Zealand country
   Oceania
79 C2 Neyrīz Iran
76 B3 Neyshābūr Iran
145 C3 Nezahualcóyotl, Presa
   resr Mex.
61 B1 Ngabang Indon.
75 C2 Ngamring China
75 C1 Ngangla Ringco salt l. China
77 E3 Nganglong Kangri mt. China
75 C1 Nganglong Kangri mts
   China
75 C1 Ngangzê Co salt l. China
62 A2 Ngao Thai.
118 B2 Ngaoundéré Cameroon
54 C1 Ngaruawahia N.Z.
62 A2 Ngathangyaung Myanmar
118 B3 Ngo Congo
63 B2 Ngoc Linh mt. Vietnam
115 D4 Ngol Bembo Nigeria

68 C2 **Ngoring Hu** *l.* China
115 D3 **Ngourti** Niger
115 D3 **Nguigmi** Niger
59 D2 **Ngulu** *atoll* Micronesia
115 D3 **Nguru** Nigeria
123 D2 **Ngwelezana** S. Africa
121 C2 **Nhalalubue** Moz.
63 B2 **Nha Trang** Vietnam
52 B3 **Nhill** Austr.
123 D2 **Nhlangano** Swaziland
51 C1 **Nhulunbuy** Austr.
141 C2 **Niagara Falls** Can.
114 C3 **Niamey** Niger
119 C3 **Niangara** Dem. Rep. Congo
114 B3 **Niangay, Lac** *l.* Mali
60 A1 **Nias** *i.* Indon.
146 B3 **Nicaragua** *country*
       Central America
146 B3 **Nicaragua, Lago de** *l.* Nic.
105 D3 **Nice** France
73 D4 **Nicobar Islands** India
80 B2 **Nicosia** Cyprus
146 B4 **Nicoya, Golfo de** *b.*
       Costa Rica
88 B2 **Nida** Lith.
103 E1 **Nidzica** Pol.
102 B1 **Niebüll** Ger.
101 D2 **Niederau** Ger.
118 B2 **Niefang** Equat. Guinea
101 F1 **Niemegk** Ger.
101 D1 **Nienburg (Weser)** Ger.
100 B1 **Nieuwe-Niedorp** Neth.
151 C1 **Nieuw Nickerie** Suriname
122 A3 **Nieuwoudtville** S. Africa
100 A2 **Nieuwpoort** Belgium
80 B2 **Niğde** Turkey
115 D3 **Niger** *country* Africa
115 C4 **Niger** *r.* Africa
115 C4 **Niger, Mouths of the** Nigeria
115 C4 **Nigeria** *country* Africa
130 B2 **Nighthawk Lake** Can.
111 B2 **Nigrita** Greece
67 C3 **Niigata** Japan
67 B4 **Niihama** Japan
67 C4 **Nii-jima** *i.* Japan
67 C3 **Niitsu** Japan
100 B2 **Nijmegen** Neth.
100 C1 **Nijverdal** Neth.
92 J2 **Nikel'** Rus. Fed.
83 M3 **Nikol'skoye** Rus. Fed.
91 C2 **Nikopol'** Ukr.
80 B1 **Niksar** Turkey
79 D2 **Nikshahr** Iran
109 C2 **Nikšić** Yugo.
116 B1 **Nile** *r.* Africa
140 B2 **Niles** U.S.A.
74 B2 **Nimach** India
105 C3 **Nîmes** France
53 C3 **Nimmitabel** Austr.
117 B4 **Nimule** Sudan
53 C1 **Nindigully** Austr.
73 B4 **Nine Degree Channel**
       India
53 C3 **Ninety Mile Beach** Austr.
54 C1 **Ninety Mile Beach** N.Z.
70 C3 **Ningbo** China
71 B3 **Ningde** China
71 B3 **Ningdu** China
70 B2 **Ningguo** China
71 C3 **Ninghai** China
       Ningjiang China *see*
       Songyuan
68 C2 **Ningjing Shan** *mts* China
70 A2 **Ningxia** *aut. reg.* China
70 B2 **Ningyang** China
62 B1 **Ninh Binh** Vietnam
63 B2 **Ninh Hoa** Vietnam
66 D2 **Ninohe** Japan
137 D2 **Niobrara** *r.* U.S.A.
114 B3 **Niono** Mali

114 B3 **Nioro** Mali
104 B2 **Niort** France
129 D2 **Nipawin** Can.
130 B2 **Nipigon** Can.
130 B2 **Nipigon, Lake** Can.
131 D1 **Nipishish Lake** Can.
130 C2 **Nipissing, Lake** Can.
135 C3 **Nipton** U.S.A.
151 D3 **Niquelândia** Brazil
73 B3 **Nirmal** India
109 D2 **Niš** Yugo.
109 C2 **Nišava** *r.* Yugo.
108 B3 **Niscemi** *Sicily* Italy
67 B4 **Nishino-omote** Japan
155 D2 **Niterói** Brazil
96 C3 **Nith** *r.* U.K.
103 D2 **Nitra** Slovakia
49 G4 **Niue** *terr.* S. Pacific Ocean
92 H3 **Nivala** Fin.
100 B2 **Nivelles** Belgium
73 B3 **Nizamabad** India
87 E3 **Nizhnekamsk** Rus. Fed.
83 H3 **Nizhneudinsk** Rus. Fed.
82 G2 **Nizhnevartovsk** Rus. Fed.
89 F3 **Nizhniy Kislyay** Rus. Fed.
87 D3 **Nizhniy Lomov** Rus. Fed.
87 D3 **Nizhniy Novgorod**
       Rus. Fed.
86 E2 **Nizhniy Odes** Rus. Fed.
86 E3 **Nizhniy Tagil** Rus. Fed.
83 C2 **Nizhnyaya Tunguska** *r.*
       Rus. Fed.
91 C1 **Nizhyn** Ukr.
119 D3 **Njinjo** Tanz.
119 D3 **Njombe** Tanz.
121 C2 **Nkhotakota** Malawi
118 A2 **Nkongsamba** Cameroon
123 C3 **Nkululeko** S. Africa
123 C3 **Nkwenkwezi** S. Africa
67 B4 **Nobeoka** Japan
52 B1 **Noccundra** Austr.
144 A1 **Nogales** Mex.
138 A2 **Nogales** U.S.A.
104 C2 **Nogent-le-Rotrou** France
89 E2 **Noginsk** Rus. Fed.
74 B2 **Nohar** India
100 C3 **Nohfelden** Ger.
104 B2 **Noirmoutier, Île de** *i.* France
104 B2 **Noirmoutier-en-l'Île** France
67 C4 **Nojima-zaki** *c.* Japan
74 B2 **Nokha** India
93 H3 **Nokia** Fin.
74 A2 **Nok Kundi** Pak.
118 B2 **Nola** C.A.R.
86 D3 **Nolinsk** Rus. Fed.
123 C3 **Nomonde** S. Africa
123 D2 **Nondweni** S. Africa
62 B2 **Nong Khai** Thai.
52 A2 **Nonning** Austr.
144 B2 **Nonoava** Mex.
65 B2 **Nonsan** S. Korea
63 B2 **Nonthaburi** Thai.
122 B3 **Nonzwakazi** S. Africa
77 C3 **Norak** Tajik.
130 C2 **Noranda** Can.
82 C1 **Nordaustlandet** *i.* Svalbard
128 C2 **Nordegg** Can.
100 C1 **Norden** Ger.
83 H1 **Nordenshel'da, Arkhipelag**
       is Rus. Fed.
100 C1 **Norderney** Ger.
100 C1 **Norderney** *i.* Ger.
101 E1 **Norderstedt** Ger.
93 E3 **Nordfjordeid** Norway
101 E2 **Nordhausen** Ger.
101 D1 **Nordholz** Ger.
100 C1 **Nordhorn** Ger.
92 I1 **Nordkapp** *c.* Norway
92 F3 **Nordli** Norway
102 C2 **Nördlingen** Ger.

92 G3 **Nordmaling** Sweden
94 B1 **Norðoyar** *i.* Faroe Is
97 C2 **Nore** *r.* Rep. of Ireland
137 D2 **Norfolk** *NE* U.S.A.
141 D3 **Norfolk** *VA* U.S.A.
49 E4 **Norfolk Island** *terr.*
       S. Pacific Ocean
93 E3 **Norheimsund** Norway
82 G2 **Noril'sk** Rus. Fed.
139 D1 **Norman** U.S.A.
       Normandes, Îles *is*
       Europe *see* **Channel Islands**
51 D1 **Normanton** Austr.
93 G4 **Norrköping** Sweden
93 G4 **Norrtälje** Sweden
50 B3 **Norseman** Austr.
92 G3 **Norsjö** Sweden
50 C1 **Northallerton** U.K.
50 A2 **Northampton** Austr.
99 C2 **Northampton** U.K.
73 D3 **North Andaman** *i.* India
129 D2 **North Battleford** Can.
130 C2 **North Bay** Can.
130 C1 **North Belcher Islands** Can.
96 C2 **North Berwick** U.K.
       North Cape Norway *see*
       Nordkapp
54 B1 **North Cape** *c.* N.Z.
130 A1 **North Caribou Lake** Can.
143 E1 **North Carolina** *state* U.S.A.
130 B2 **North Channel** *lake channel*
       Can.
96 A3 **North Channel** U.K.
128 B3 **North Cowichan** Can.
136 C1 **North Dakota** *state* U.S.A.
99 C3 **North Downs** *hills* U.K.
143 E3 **Northeast Providence**
       Channel Bahamas
101 D2 **Northeim** Ger.
123 C1 **North** *prov.* S. Africa
122 A2 **Northern Cape** *prov.*
       S. Africa
129 E2 **Northern Indian Lake** Can.
97 C1 **Northern Ireland** *prov.* U.K.
48 D2 **Northern Mariana Islands**
       terr. N. Pacific Ocean
50 C1 **Northern Territory**
       admin. div. Austr.
96 C2 **North Esk** *r.* U.K.
137 E2 **Northfield** U.S.A.
99 D3 **North Foreland** *c.* U.K.
54 B1 **North Island** N.Z.
129 E2 **North Knife Lake** Can.
62 A1 **North Lakhimpur** India
136 C2 **North Platte** U.S.A.
136 C2 **North Platte** *r.* U.S.A.
96 C1 **North Ronaldsay** *i.* U.K.
94 D2 **North Sea** *sea* Europe
130 A1 **North Spirit Lake** *l.* Can.
53 D1 **North Stradbroke Island**
       Austr.
54 B1 **North Taranaki Bight**
       b. N.Z.
130 C1 **North Twin Island** Can.
98 B1 **North Tyne** *r.* U.K.
96 A2 **North Uist** *i.* U.K.
131 D2 **Northumberland Strait** Can.
122 C2 **North West** *prov.* S. Africa
50 A2 **North West Cape** Austr.
143 E3 **Northwest Providence**
       Channel Bahamas
131 E1 **North West River** Can.
128 B1 **Northwest Territories**
       admin. div. Can.
98 C1 **North York Moors** *moorland*
       U.K.
140 C3 **Norton** U.S.A.
121 C2 **Norton** Zimbabwe
140 C2 **Norwalk** U.S.A.
93 F3 **Norway** *country* Europe

129 E2 Norway House Can.
160 A3 Norwegian Sea
 N. Atlantic Ocean
99 D2 Norwich U.K.
141 E2 Norwich CT U.S.A.
141 D2 Norwich NY U.S.A.
66 D2 Noshiro Japan
91 C1 Nosivka Ukr.
122 B2 Nosop watercourse Africa
86 E2 Nossa Rus. Fed.
79 C2 Nosratābād Iran
 Nossob watercourse Africa
 see Nosop
121 □D2 Nosy Bé i. Madag.
121 □E2 Nosy Boraha i. Madag.
103 D1 Noteć r. Pol.
93 E4 Notodden Norway
67 C3 Noto-hantō pen. Japan
131 D2 Notre Dame, Monts
 mts Can.
131 E2 Notre Dame Bay Can.
130 C1 Nottaway r. Can.
99 C2 Nottingham U.K.
114 A2 Nouâdhibou Maur.
114 A3 Nouakchott Maur.
114 A3 Nouâmghâr Maur.
114 B3 Nouna Burkina
154 B3 Nova Esperança Brazil
155 D2 Nova Friburgo Brazil
109 C1 Nova Gradiška Croatia
154 C2 Nova Granada Brazil
155 D2 Nova Iguaçu Brazil
91 C2 Nova Kakhovka Ukr.
155 D1 Nova Lima Brazil
155 B2 Nova Londrina Brazil
91 C2 Nova Odesa Ukr.
150 B1 Nova Paraíso Brazil
131 D2 Nova Scotia prov. Can.
155 D1 Nova Venécia Brazil
83 K1 Novaya Sibir', Ostrov i.
 Rus. Fed.
86 E1 Novaya Zemlya is Rus. Fed.
103 D2 Nové Zámky Slovakia
91 C1 Novhorod-Sivers'kyy Ukr.
110 B2 Novi Iskŭr Bulg.
108 A2 Novi Ligure Italy
109 D2 Novi Pazar Yugo.
109 C1 Novi Sad Yugo.
87 D3 Novoanninskiy Rus. Fed.
150 B2 Novo Aripuanã Brazil
91 D2 Novoazovs'k Ukr.
91 D2 Novocherkassk Rus. Fed.
86 D2 Novodvinsk Rus. Fed.
152 C3 Novo Hamburgo Brazil
154 C2 Novo Horizonte Brazil
90 B1 Novohrad-Volyns'kyy Ukr.
103 D2 Novo Mesto Slovenia
91 D3 Novomikhaylovskiy
 Rus. Fed.
89 E3 Novomoskovsk Rus. Fed.
91 D2 Novomoskovs'k Ukr.
91 C1 Novomyrhorod Ukr.
91 C2 Novooleksiyivka Ukr.
91 D2 Novopskov Ukr.
91 D3 Novorossiysk Rus. Fed.
88 C2 Novorzhev Rus. Fed.
87 E3 Novosergiyevka Rus. Fed.
91 D2 Novoshakhtinsk Rus. Fed.
82 G3 Novosibirsk Rus. Fed.
83 K1 Novosibirskiye Ostrova is
 Rus. Fed.
89 E3 Novosil' Rus. Fed.
89 D2 Novosokol'niki Rus. Fed.
91 C2 Novotroyits'ke Ukr.
91 C2 Novoukrayinka Ukr.
90 A1 Novovolyns'k Ukr.
89 D3 Novozybkov Rus. Fed.
103 D2 Nový Jičín Czech Rep.
86 E2 Novyy Bor Rus. Fed.
91 D1 Novyy Oskol Rus. Fed.

86 G2 Novyy Port Rus. Fed.
82 G2 Novyy Urengoy Rus. Fed.
69 E1 Novyy Urgal Rus. Fed.
103 D1 Nowogard Pol.
53 D2 Nowra Austr.
81 D2 Now Shahr Iran
74 B1 Nowshera Pak.
103 E2 Nowy Dwór Pol.
103 E2 Nowy Targ Pol.
87 D2 Noyabr'sk Rus. Fed.
105 C2 Noyon France
121 C2 Nsanje Malawi
118 B3 Ntandembele
 Dem. Rep. Congo
119 D3 Ntungamo Uganda
79 C2 Nu'aym reg. Oman
116 B2 Nubian Desert Sudan
150 A3 Nudo Coropuna mt. Peru
129 E1 Nueltin Lake Can.
153 A5 Nueva Lubecka Arg.
144 B2 Nueva Rosita Mex.
144 B1 Nuevo Casas Grandes Mex.
144 B2 Nuevo Ideal Mex.
145 C2 Nuevo Laredo Mex.
117 C4 Nugaal watercourse Somalia
105 C2 Nuits-St-Georges France
62 A1 Nu Jiang r. China
76 B2 Nukus Uzbek.
50 B2 Nullagine Austr.
50 B3 Nullarbor Plain Austr.
115 D4 Numan Nigeria
67 C3 Numazu Japan
93 E3 Numedal val. Norway
59 C3 Numfoor i. Indon.
53 C3 Numurkah Austr.
127 J3 Nunap Isua c. Greenland
129 E1 Nunavut admin. div. Can.
99 C2 Nuneaton U.K.
116 B3 Nuñomoral Spain
108 A2 Nuoro Sardinia Italy
78 B2 Nuqrah Saudi Arabia
52 A2 Nuriootpa Austr.
92 I3 Nurmes Fin.
101 E3 Nürnberg Ger.
62 A1 Nu Shan mts China
74 A2 Nushki Pak.
127 H2 Nuuk Greenland
127 H2 Nuussuaq Greenland
127 H2 Nuussuaq pen. Greenland
78 A2 Nuweiba al Muzeina Egypt
122 B3 Nuweveldberge mts
 S. Africa
86 F2 Nyagan' Rus. Fed.
75 D1 Nyainqêntanglha Feng mt.
 China
75 D2 Nyainqêntanglha Shan mts
 China
117 A3 Nyala Sudan
75 C2 Nyalam China
86 D2 Nyandoma Rus. Fed.
118 B3 Nyanga r. Gabon
121 C2 Nyanga Zimbabwe
121 C1 Nyasa, Lake Africa
93 F4 Nyborg Denmark
92 I1 Nyborg Norway
93 G4 Nybro Sweden
119 D3 Nyeri Kenya
75 C1 Nyima China
68 C3 Nyingchi China
103 E2 Nyíregyháza Hungary
93 F4 Nykøbing Denmark
123 C1 Nylstroom S. Africa
53 C2 Nymagee Austr.
93 G4 Nynäshamn Sweden
53 C2 Nyngan Austr.
88 B3 Nyoman r. Belarus/Lith.
105 D3 Nyons France
86 E2 Nyrob Rus. Fed.
134 C2 Nyssa

119 C3 Nyunzu Dem. Rep. Congo
91 C2 Nyzhn'ohirs'kyy Ukr.
119 D3 Nzega Tanz.
114 B4 Nzérékoré Guinea
120 A1 N'zeto Angola

O

136 C2 Oahe, Lake U.S.A.
52 B2 Oakbank Austr.
142 B2 Oakdale U.S.A.
53 D1 Oakey Austr.
134 B1 Oak Harbor U.S.A.
140 C3 Oak Hill U.S.A.
135 B3 Oakland U.S.A.
50 B2 Oakover r. Austr.
134 B2 Oakridge U.S.A.
143 D1 Oak Ridge U.S.A.
54 B3 Oamaru N.Z.
64 B1 Oas Phil.
145 C3 Oaxaca Mex.
86 F2 Ob' r. Rus. Fed.
118 B2 Obala Cameroon
96 B2 Oban U.K.
106 B1 O Barco Spain
53 C2 Oberon Austr.
101 F3 Oberpfälzer Wald mts Ger.
101 F3 Oberviechtach Ger.
59 C3 Obi i. Indon.
151 C2 Óbidos Brazil
66 D2 Obihiro Japan
69 E1 Obluch'ye Rus. Fed.
89 E2 Obninsk Rus. Fed.
119 C2 Obo C.A.R.
117 C3 Obock Djibouti
118 B3 Obouya Congo
89 E3 Oboyan' Rus. Fed.
144 B2 Obregón, Presa resr Mex.
109 D2 Obrenovac Yugo.
87 E3 Obshchiy Syrt hills Rus. Fed.
86 G2 Obskaya Guba sea chan.
 Rus. Fed.
114 B4 Obuasi Ghana
90 C1 Obukhiv Ukr.
86 D2 Ob"yachevo Rus. Fed.
143 D3 Ocala U.S.A.
144 B2 Ocampo Mex.
106 C2 Ocaña Spain
150 A1 Occidental, Cordillera
 mts Col.
150 A3 Occidental, Cordillera
 mts Peru
141 D3 Ocean City U.S.A.
128 B2 Ocean Falls Can.
135 C4 Oceanside U.S.A.
91 C2 Ochakiv Ukr.
86 E3 Ocher Rus. Fed.
101 E3 Ochsenfurt Ger.
143 D2 Oconee r. U.S.A.
145 C3 Ocosingo Mex.
116 B2 Oda, Jebel mt. Sudan
66 D2 Ōdate Japan
67 C3 Odawara Japan
93 E3 Odda Norway
106 B2 Odemira Port.
111 C3 Ödemiş Turkey
93 F4 Odense Denmark
101 D3 Odenwald reg. Ger.
102 C1 Oderbucht Ger.
90 C2 Odesa Ukr.
139 C2 Odessa U.S.A.
114 B4 Odienné Côte d'Ivoire
103 D2 Odra r. Ger./Pol.
151 D2 Oeiras Brazil
100 D2 Oelde Ger.
136 C2 Oelrichs U.S.A.
101 F2 Oelsnitz Ger.

100 B1 Oenkerk Neth.
109 C2 Ofanto r. Italy
101 D2 Offenbach am Main Ger.
102 B2 Offenburg Ger.
117 C4 Ogadēn reg. Eth.
66 C3 Oga-hantō pen. Japan
67 C3 Ōgaki Japan
136 C2 Ogallala U.S.A.
115 C4 Ogbomoso Nigeria
134 D2 Ogden U.S.A.
141 D2 Ogdensburg U.S.A.
126 B2 Ogilvie r. Can.
126 B2 Ogilvie Mountains Can.
143 D2 Oglethorpe, Mount U.S.A.
130 B1 Ogoki r. Can.
130 B1 Ogoki Reservoir Can.
92 B2 Ogre Latvia
109 C1 Ogulin Croatia
140 B3 Ohio r. U.S.A.
140 C2 Ohio state U.S.A.
101 E2 Ohrdruf Ger.
109 D2 Ohrid Macedonia
151 C1 Oiapoque Brazil
141 D2 Oil City U.S.A.
100 A3 Oise r. France
67 B4 Ōita Japan
144 B2 Ojinaga Mex.
152 B3 Ojos del Salado, Nevado mt. Arg./Chile
89 F2 Oka r. Rus. Fed.
120 A3 Okahandja Namibia
120 A3 Okakarara Namibia
128 C3 Okanagan Can.
128 C3 Okanagan Lake Can.
134 C1 Okanogan U.S.A.
134 C1 Okanogan r. U.S.A.
74 B1 Okara Pak.
120 B2 Okavango r. Botswana/Namibia
120 B2 Okavango Delta swamp Botswana
67 C3 Okaya Japan
67 B4 Okayama Japan
67 C4 Okazaki Japan
143 D3 Okeechobee, Lake U.S.A.
143 D2 Okefenokee Swamp U.S.A.
99 A3 Okehampton U.K.
74 A2 Okha India
83 K3 Okha Rus. Fed.
75 C2 Okhaldhunga Nepal
83 K3 Okhotka r. Rus. Fed.
83 K3 Okhotsk Rus. Fed.
156 C2 Okhotsk, Sea of Japan/Rus. Fed.
91 C1 Okhtyrka Ukr.
69 E3 Okinawa i. Japan
67 B3 Oki-shotō is Japan
139 D1 Oklahoma state U.S.A.
139 D1 Oklahoma City U.S.A.
139 D1 Okmulgee U.S.A.
78 A2 Oko, Wadi watercourse Sudan
118 B3 Okondja Gabon
128 C2 Okotoks Can.
89 D3 Okovskiy Les for. Rus. Fed.
118 B3 Okoyo Congo
92 H1 Øksfjord Norway
62 A2 Oktwin Myanmar
86 D2 Oktyabr'skiy Arkhangel'skaya Oblast' Rus. Fed.
83 L3 Oktyabr'skiy Kamchatskaya Oblast' Rus. Fed.
87 E3 Oktyabr'skiy Respublika Bashkortostan Rus. Fed.
86 F2 Oktyabr'skoye Rus. Fed.
83 H1 Oktyabr'skoy Revolyutsii, Ostrov i. Rus. Fed.

89 D2 Okulovka Rus. Fed.
66 C2 Okushiri-tō i. Japan
93 G4 Öland i. Sweden
52 B2 Olary Austr.
153 B4 Olavarría Arg.
103 D1 Oława Pol.
108 A2 Olbia Sardinia Italy
126 B2 Old Crow Can.
101 D1 Oldenburg Ger.
102 C1 Oldenburg in Holstein Ger.
100 C1 Oldenzaal Neth.
97 B3 Old Head of Kinsale hd Rep. of Ireland
128 C2 Olds Can.
129 D2 Old Wives Lake Can.
141 D2 Olean U.S.A.
103 E1 Olecko Pol.
83 J2 Olekminsk Rus. Fed.
91 C2 Oleksandriya Ukr.
86 C2 Olenegorsk Rus. Fed.
83 I2 Olenek Rus. Fed.
83 I2 Olenek r. Rus. Fed.
89 D2 Olenino Rus. Fed.
90 B1 Olevs'k Ukr.
106 B2 Olhão Port.
122 A2 Olifants watercourse Namibia
123 D1 Olifants S. Africa
123 D1 Olifants r. Northern S. Africa
122 A3 Olifants r. W. Cape S. Africa
122 B2 Olifantshoek S. Africa
154 C2 Olímpia Brazil
151 E2 Olinda Brazil
123 C1 Oliphants Drift S. Africa
107 C2 Oliva Spain
155 D2 Oliveira Brazil
106 B2 Olivenza Spain
152 B3 Ollagüe Chile
150 A2 Olmos Peru
140 B3 Olney U.S.A.
103 D2 Olomouc Czech Rep.
64 B1 Olongapo Phil.
104 B3 Oloron-Ste-Marie France
107 D1 Olot Spain
69 D1 Olovyannaya Rus. Fed.
100 C2 Olpe Ger.
103 E1 Olsztyn Pol.
110 B2 Olt r. Romania
81 C1 Oltu Turkey
111 B3 Olympia Greece
134 B1 Olympia U.S.A.
111 B2 Olympos mt. Greece
134 B1 Olympus, Mount U.S.A.
83 M3 Olyutorskiy, Mys c. Rus. Fed.
97 C1 Omagh U.K.
137 D2 Omaha U.S.A.
79 C3 Oman country Asia
79 C2 Oman, Gulf of Asia
120 A3 Omaruru Namibia
120 B2 Omatako watercourse Namibia
116 B3 Omdurman Sudan
53 C3 Omeo Austr.
145 C3 Ometepec Mex.
78 A3 Om Hajēr Eritrea
128 B2 Omineca Mountains Can.
67 C3 Ōmiya Japan
100 C1 Ommen Neth.
83 L2 Omolon r. Rus. Fed.
100 B3 Omont France
82 F2 Omsk Rus. Fed.
83 L2 Omsukchan Rus. Fed.
110 C1 Omu, Vârful mt. Romania
67 A4 Ōmura Japan
141 D3 Onancock U.S.A.
140 C1 Onaping Lake Can.
131 C2 Onatchiway, Lac l. Can.
120 A2 Oncócua Angola

122 B3 Onderstedorings S. Africa
120 A2 Ondjiva Angola
86 C2 Onega Rus. Fed.
86 C2 Onega r. Rus. Fed.
86 C2 Onega, Lake l. Rus. Fed.
128 B2 One Hundred Mile House Can.
141 D2 Oneida Lake U.S.A.
137 D2 O'Neill U.S.A.
141 D2 Oneonta U.S.A.
110 C1 Oneşti Romania
Onezhskoye, Ozero l. Rus. Fed. see Onega, Lake
122 B2 Ongers watercourse S. Africa
65 B2 Ongjin N. Korea
73 C3 Ongole India
121 D3 Onilahy r. Madag.
115 C4 Onitsha Nigeria
122 A2 Onseepkans S. Africa
50 A2 Onslow Austr.
143 E2 Onslow Bay U.S.A.
130 A1 Ontario prov. Can.
134 C2 Ontario U.S.A.
141 D2 Ontario, Lake Can./U.S.A.
51 C2 Oodnadatta Austr.
Oostende Belgium see Ostend
100 B2 Oosterhout Neth.
100 A2 Oosterschelde est. Neth.
100 B1 Oost-Vlieland Neth.
128 B2 Ootsa Lake Can.
128 B2 Ootsa Lake l. Can.
118 C3 Opala Dem. Rep. Congo
130 C1 Opataca, Lac l. Can.
103 D1 Opava Czech Rep.
143 C2 Opelika U.S.A.
142 B2 Opelousas U.S.A.
130 C1 Opinaca, Réservoir resr Can.
131 C1 Opiscotéo, Lac l. Can.
88 C2 Opochka Rus. Fed.
144 A2 Opodepe Mex.
103 D1 Opole Pol.
76 B2 Opornyy Kazakh.
106 B1 Oporto Port.
54 C1 Opotiki N.Z.
93 E3 Oppdal Norway
54 B1 Opunake N.Z.
120 A2 Opuwo Namibia
110 B1 Oradea Romania
109 D2 Orahovac Yugo.
114 B1 Oran Alg.
152 B3 Orán Arg.
65 B1 Ŏrang N. Korea
53 C2 Orange Austr.
105 C3 Orange France
122 A2 Orange r. Namibia/S. Africa
139 E2 Orange U.S.A.
143 D2 Orangeburg U.S.A.
140 C2 Orangeville Can.
101 F1 Oranienburg Ger.
122 A2 Oranjemund Namibia
120 B3 Orapa Botswana
110 B1 Orăştie Romania
108 B2 Orbetello Italy
53 C3 Orbost Austr.
50 B1 Ord, Mount Austr.
106 B1 Ordes Spain
80 B1 Ordu Turkey
Ordzhonikidze Rus. Fed. see Vladikavkaz
91 C2 Ordzhonikidze Ukr.
93 G4 Örebro Sweden
134 B2 Oregon state U.S.A.
134 B1 Oregon City U.S.A.
87 C3 Orekhovo-Zuyevo Rus. Fed.
89 E3 Orel Rus. Fed.
83 K3 Orel', Ozero l. Rus. Fed.
135 D2 Orem U.S.A.

111 C3 **Ören** Turkey
87 E3 **Orenburg** Rus. Fed.
54 A3 **Orepuki** N.Z.
93 F4 **Öresund** str.
   Denmark/Sweden
99 D2 **Orford Ness** hd U.K.
111 C3 **Orhaneli** Turkey
111 C2 **Orhangazi** Turkey
83 I3 **Orhon Gol** r. Mongolia
152 B2 **Oriental, Cordillera** mts Bol.
150 A1 **Oriental, Cordillera** mts Col.
150 A3 **Oriental, Cordillera**
   mts Peru
107 C2 **Orihuela** Spain
91 D2 **Orikhiv** Ukr.
130 C2 **Orillia** Can.
150 B1 **Orinoco** r. Col./Venez.
150 B1 **Orinoco Delta** Venez.
93 H4 **Orissaare** Estonia
108 A3 **Oristano** Sardinia Italy
93 I3 **Orivesi** l. Fin.
151 C2 **Oriximiná** Brazil
145 C3 **Orizaba** Mex.
145 C3 **Orizaba, Pico de** vol. Mex.
92 E3 **Orkanger** Norway
93 F4 **Örkelljunga** Sweden
92 E3 **Orkla** r. Norway
96 C1 **Orkney Islands** is U.K.
154 C2 **Orlândia** Brazil
143 D3 **Orlando** U.S.A.
104 C2 **Orléans** France
74 A2 **Ormara** Pak.
64 B1 **Ormoc** Phil.
98 B2 **Ormskirk** U.K.
92 G3 **Örnsköldsvik** Sweden
114 B3 **Orodara** Burkina
134 C1 **Orofino** U.S.A.
   Oroqen Zizhiqi China see
   Alihe
64 B2 **Oroquieta** Phil.
108 A2 **Orosei** Sardinia Italy
108 A2 **Orosei, Golfo di** b. Sardinia
   Italy
103 E2 **Orosháza** Hungary
135 B3 **Oroville** U.S.A.
52 A2 **Orroroo** Austr.
89 D3 **Orsha** Belarus
87 E3 **Orsk** Rus. Fed.
93 E3 **Ørsta** Norway
106 B1 **Ortegal, Cabo** c. Spain
104 B3 **Orthez** France
106 B1 **Ortigueira** Spain
137 D1 **Ortonville** U.S.A.
83 J2 **Orulgan, Khrebet** mts
   Rus. Fed.
81 C2 **Orūmīyeh, Daryācheh-ye**
   salt l. Iran
152 B2 **Oruro** Bol.
108 B2 **Orvieto** Italy
146 B4 **Osa, Península de** pen.
   Costa Rica
137 E3 **Osage** r. U.S.A.
67 C4 **Ōsaka** Japan
101 E1 **Oschersleben (Bode)** Ger.
108 A2 **Oschiri** Sardinia Italy
89 E3 **Osetr** r. Rus. Fed.
77 D2 **Osh** Kyrg.
120 A2 **Oshakati** Namibia
130 C2 **Oshawa** Can.
66 C2 **Ō-shima** i. Japan
67 C3 **Ō-shima** i. Japan
140 B2 **Oshkosh** U.S.A.
81 C2 **Oshnoviyeh** Iran
115 C4 **Oshogbo** Nigeria
118 B3 **Oshwe** Dem. Rep. Congo
109 C1 **Osijek** Croatia
128 B2 **Osilinka** r. Can.
108 B2 **Osimo** Italy
123 D2 **Osizweni** S. Africa
137 E2 **Oskaloosa** U.S.A.

93 G4 **Oskarshamn** Sweden
89 E3 **Oskol** r. Rus. Fed.
93 F4 **Oslo** Norway
93 F4 **Oslofjorden** sea chan.
   Norway
80 B1 **Osmancık** Turkey
111 C2 **Osmaneli** Turkey
80 B2 **Osmaniye** Turkey
88 C2 **Os'mino** Rus. Fed.
100 D1 **Osnabrück** Ger.
153 A5 **Osorno** Chile
106 C1 **Osorno** Spain
128 C3 **Osoyoos** Can.
100 B2 **Oss** Neth.
51 D4 **Ossa, Mount** Austr.
83 L3 **Ossora** Rus. Fed.
89 D2 **Ostashkov** Rus. Fed.
101 D1 **Oste** r. Ger.
100 A2 **Ostend** Belgium
101 E1 **Osterburg (Altmark)** Ger.
93 F3 **Österdalälven** l. Sweden
101 D1 **Osterholz-Scharmbeck** Ger.
101 E2 **Osterode am Harz** Ger.
92 F3 **Östersund** Sweden
   Ostfriesische Inseln is Ger.
   see East Frisian Islands
100 C1 **Ostfriesland** reg. Ger.
93 G3 **Osthammar** Sweden
102 D2 **Ostrava** Czech Rep.
103 D1 **Ostróda** Pol.
89 E3 **Ostrogozhsk** Rus. Fed.
103 E1 **Ostrołęka** Pol.
101 F2 **Ostrov** Czech Rep.
88 C2 **Ostrov** Rus. Fed.
103 E1 **Ostrowiec Świętokrzyski**
   Pol.
103 E1 **Ostrów Mazowiecka** Pol.
103 D1 **Ostrów Wielkopolski** Pol.
110 B2 **Osŭm** r. Bulg.
67 B4 **Ōsumi-kaikyō** sea chan.
   Japan
67 B4 **Ōsumi-shotō** is Japan
106 B2 **Osuna** Spain
141 D2 **Oswego** U.S.A.
99 B2 **Oswestry** U.K.
67 C3 **Ōta** Japan
54 B3 **Otago Peninsula** N.Z.
54 C2 **Otaki** N.Z.
66 D2 **Otaru** Japan
120 A2 **Otavi** Namibia
134 C1 **Othello** U.S.A.
120 A3 **Otjiwarongo** Namibia
117 B3 **Otoro, Jebel** mt. Sudan
93 E4 **Otra** r. Norway
109 C2 **Otranto, Strait of**
   Albania/Italy
67 C3 **Ōtsu** Japan
93 E3 **Otta** Norway
130 C2 **Ottawa** Can.
130 C2 **Ottawa** r. Can.
140 B2 **Ottawa** IL U.S.A.
137 D3 **Ottawa** KS U.S.A.
130 B1 **Otter Rapids** Can.
100 B2 **Ottignies** Belgium
137 E2 **Ottumwa** U.S.A.
150 A2 **Otuzco** Peru
52 B3 **Otway, Cape** Austr.
142 B2 **Ouachita** r. U.S.A.
142 B2 **Ouachita, Lake** U.S.A.
142 B2 **Ouachita Mountains**
   U.S.A.
118 C2 **Ouadda** C.A.R.
115 D3 **Ouaddaï** reg. Chad
114 B3 **Ouagadougou** Burkina
114 B3 **Ouahigouya** Burkina
114 B3 **Oualâta** Maur.
118 C2 **Ouanda-Djallé** C.A.R.
114 B2 **Ouarâne** reg. Maur.
115 C1 **Ouargla** Alg.
114 B1 **Ouarzazate** Morocco

100 A2 **Oudenaarde** Belgium
122 B3 **Oudtshoorn** S. Africa
107 C2 **Oued Tlélat** Alg.
104 A2 **Ouessant, Île d'** i. France
118 B2 **Ouésso** Congo
114 B1 **Oujda** Morocco
107 D2 **Ouled Farès** Alg.
92 I2 **Oulu** Fin.
92 I3 **Oulujärvi** l. Fin.
108 A1 **Oulx** Italy
115 D3 **Oum-Chalouba** Chad
115 D3 **Oum-Hadjer** Chad
115 E3 **Ounianga Kébir** Chad
100 B2 **Oupeye** Belgium
100 C3 **Our, Vallée de l'** val.
   Ger./Lux.
106 B1 **Ourense** Spain
154 C2 **Ourinhos** Brazil
155 D2 **Ouro Preto** Brazil
100 B2 **Ourthe** r. Belgium
98 C2 **Ouse** r. U.K.
   Outaouais, Rivière des r.
   Can. see Ottawa
131 D2 **Outardes** r. Can.
131 D1 **Outardes Quatre, Réservoir**
   resr Can.
96 A2 **Outer Hebrides** is U.K.
120 A3 **Outjo** Namibia
129 D2 **Outlook** Can.
92 I3 **Outokumpu** Fin.
52 B3 **Ouyen** Austr.
106 B1 **Ovar** Port.
92 H2 **Överkalix** Sweden
135 D3 **Overton** U.S.A.
92 H2 **Övertorneå** Sweden
106 B1 **Oviedo** Spain
93 E3 **Øvre Ardal** Norway
93 E3 **Øvre Rendal** Norway
90 B1 **Ovruch** Ukr.
118 B3 **Owando** Congo
67 C4 **Owase** Japan
137 E2 **Owatonna** U.S.A.
140 B3 **Owensboro** U.S.A.
135 C3 **Owens Lake** U.S.A.
130 B2 **Owen Sound** Can.
115 C4 **Owerri** Nigeria
140 C2 **Owosso** U.S.A.
135 C3 **Owyhee** U.S.A.
134 C2 **Owyhee** r. U.S.A.
54 B2 **Oxford** N.Z.
99 C3 **Oxford** U.K.
142 C2 **Oxford** U.S.A.
129 E2 **Oxford Lake** Can.
52 B2 **Oxley** Austr.
   Ox Mountains
   Rep. of Ireland see
   Slieve Gamph
135 C4 **Oxnard** U.S.A.
67 C3 **Oyama** Japan
118 B2 **Oyem** Gabon
129 C2 **Oyen** Can.
105 D2 **Oyonnax** France
64 B2 **Ozamiz** Phil.
142 C2 **Ozark** U.S.A.
137 E3 **Ozark Plateau** U.S.A.
137 E3 **Ozarks, Lake of the**
   U.S.A.
83 L3 **Ozernovskiy** Rus. Fed.
88 B3 **Ozersk** Rus. Fed.
89 E3 **Ozery** Rus. Fed.
87 D3 **Ozinki** Rus. Fed.

P

127 H2 **Paamiut** Greenland
122 A3 **Paarl** S. Africa
103 D1 **Pabianice** Pol.

75 C2 **Pabna** Bangl.
74 A2 **Pab Range** *mts* Pak.
150 B1 **Pacaraima, Serra** *mts* Brazil
109 C3 **Pachino** *Sicily* Italy
145 C2 **Pachuca** Mex.
156 **Pacific Ocean**
103 D1 **Paczków** Pol.
60 B2 **Padang** Indon.
60 B2 **Padangpanjang** Indon.
60 A1 **Padangsidimpuan** Indon.
101 D2 **Paderborn** Ger.
Padova Italy *see* **Padua**
139 D3 **Padre Island** U.S.A.
52 B3 **Padthaway** Austr.
108 B1 **Padua** Italy
140 B3 **Paducah** *KY* U.S.A.
139 C2 **Paducah** *TX* U.S.A.
65 B1 **Paegam** N. Korea
65 B1 **Paekdu-san** *mt.*
China/N. Korea
65 A2 **Paengnyŏng-do** *i.* S. Korea
54 C1 **Paeroa** N.Z.
80 B2 **Pafos** Cyprus
109 C2 **Pag** Croatia
64 B2 **Pagadian** Phil.
60 B2 **Pagai Selatan** *i.* Indon.
60 B2 **Pagai Utara** *i.* Indon.
59 D1 **Pagan** *i.* N. Mariana Is
61 C2 **Pagatan** Indon.
138 A1 **Page** U.S.A.
88 B2 **Pagėgiai** Lith.
136 B3 **Pagosa Springs** U.S.A.
88 C2 **Paide** Estonia
93 I3 **Päijänne** *l.* Fin.
75 C2 **Paikü Co** *l.* China
138 A1 **Painted Desert** U.S.A.
96 B3 **Paisley** U.K.
92 H2 **Pajala** Sweden
150 C1 **Pakaraima Mountains**
Guyana
74 A2 **Pakistan** *country* Asia
62 A1 **Pakokku** Myanmar
88 B2 **Pakruojis** Lith.
103 D2 **Paks** Hungary
130 A1 **Pakwash Lake** Can.
63 B2 **Pakxé** Laos
115 D4 **Pala** Chad
60 B2 **Palabuhanratu, Teluk**
b. Indon.
111 C3 **Palaikastro** Greece
111 B3 **Palaiochora** Greece
122 B1 **Palamakoloi** Botswana
107 D1 **Palamós** Spain
83 L3 **Palana** Rus. Fed.
64 B1 **Palanan** Phil.
61 C2 **Palangkaraya** Indon.
74 B2 **Palanpur** India
120 B3 **Palapye** Botswana
83 L2 **Palatka** Rus. Fed.
143 D3 **Palatka** U.S.A.
59 C2 **Palau** *country*
N. Pacific Ocean
63 A2 **Palaw** Myanmar
64 A2 **Palawan** *i.* Phil.
93 H4 **Paldiski** Estonia
60 B2 **Palembang** Indon.
106 C1 **Palencia** Spain
145 C3 **Palenque** Mex.
108 B3 **Palermo** *Sicily* Italy
139 D2 **Palestine** U.S.A.
62 A1 **Paletwa** Myanmar
74 B2 **Pali** India
109 C2 **Palinuro, Capo** *c.* Italy
111 B3 **Paliouri, Akra** *pt* Greece
100 B3 **Paliseul** Belgium
92 I3 **Paljakka** *hill* Fin.
88 C2 **Palkino** Rus. Fed.
73 B4 **Palk Strait** India/Sri Lanka
54 C2 **Palliser, Cape** N.Z.
106 B2 **Palma del Río** Spain

107 D2 **Palma de Mallorca** Spain
154 B3 **Palmas** Brazil
114 B4 **Palmas, Cape** Liberia
154 C3 **Palmeira** Brazil
151 D2 **Palmeirais** Brazil
23 P2 **Palmer Land** *reg.* Antarctica
54 C2 **Palmerston North** N.Z.
109 C3 **Palmi** Italy
145 C2 **Palmillas** Mex.
150 A1 **Palmira** Col.
135 C4 **Palm Springs** U.S.A.
49 G3 **Palmyra Atoll**
N. Pacific Ocean
117 B3 **Paloich** Sudan
145 C3 **Palomares** Mex.
107 C2 **Palos, Cabo de** *c.* Spain
92 I3 **Paltamo** Fin.
58 B3 **Palu** Indon.
83 M2 **Palyavaam** *r.* Rus. Fed.
104 C3 **Pamiers** France
77 D3 **Pamir** *mts* Asia
143 E1 **Pamlico Sound** *sea chan.*
U.S.A.
152 B2 **Pampa Grande** Bol.
153 B4 **Pampas** *reg.* Arg.
150 A1 **Pamplona** Col.
107 C1 **Pamplona** Spain
111 D2 **Pamukova** Turkey
60 B2 **Panaitan** *i.* Indon.
73 B3 **Panaji** India
146 B4 **Panama** *country*
Central America
146 C4 **Panamá** Panama
146 C4 **Panamá, Golfo de** *g.*
Panama
146 C4 **Panama Canal** Panama
142 C2 **Panama City** U.S.A.
135 C3 **Panamint Range** *mts*
U.S.A.
61 B1 **Panarik** Indon.
64 B1 **Panay** *i.* Phil.
109 D2 **Pančevo** Yugo.
64 B1 **Pandan** Phil.
75 C2 **Pandaria** India
73 B3 **Pandharpur** India
88 B2 **Panevėžys** Lith.
61 C2 **Pangkalanbuun** Indon.
60 A1 **Pangkalansusu** Indon.
60 B2 **Pangkalpinang** Indon.
127 G2 **Pangnirtung** Can.
86 G2 **Pangody** Rus. Fed.
89 F3 **Panino** Rus. Fed.
74 B2 **Panipat** India
74 A2 **Panjgur** Pak.
65 C1 **Pan Ling** *mts* China
74 B2 **Panna** India
50 A2 **Pannawonica** Austr.
154 B2 **Panorama** Brazil
65 B1 **Panshi** China
145 C2 **Pánuco** Mex.
71 A3 **Panxian** China
62 B1 **Panzhihua** China
109 C3 **Paola** Italy
63 B2 **Paôy Pêt** Cambodia
103 D2 **Pápa** Hungary
54 B1 **Papakura** N.Z.
145 C2 **Papantla** Mex.
100 C1 **Papenburg** Ger.
59 D3 **Papua, Gulf of** P.N.G.
59 D3 **Papua New Guinea** *country*
Oceania
62 A2 **Papun** Myanmar
154 C1 **Paraburdoo** Austr.
154 C1 **Paracatu** Brazil
155 C1 **Paracatu** *r.* Brazil
52 A2 **Parachilna** Austr.
109 D2 **Paraćin** Yugo.
155 D1 **Pará de Minas** Brazil
135 B3 **Paradise** U.S.A.
142 B1 **Paragould** U.S.A.

151 C3 **Paraguai** *r.* Brazil
152 C3 **Paraguay** *r.* Arg./Para.
152 C3 **Paraguay** *country*
S. America
155 D2 **Paraíba do Sul** *r.* Brazil
154 B1 **Paraíso** Brazil
145 C3 **Paraíso** Mex.
114 C4 **Parakou** Benin
151 C1 **Paramaribo** Suriname
83 L3 **Paramushir, Ostrov** *i.*
Rus. Fed.
152 B4 **Paraná** Arg.
154 A3 **Paraná** *r.* S. America
154 B1 **Paranaíba** Brazil
154 B2 **Paranaíba** *r.* Brazil
154 B2 **Paranaguá** Brazil
154 B2 **Paranapanema** *r.* Brazil
154 B2 **Paranapiacaba, Serra** *mts*
Brazil
154 B2 **Paranavaí** Brazil
54 B2 **Paraparaumu** N.Z.
155 D2 **Parati** Brazil
154 B1 **Paraúna** Brazil
105 C2 **Paray-le-Monial** France
73 B3 **Parbhani** India
101 E1 **Parchim** Ger.
155 E1 **Pardo** *r.* Bahia Brazil
154 B2 **Pardo** *r.* Mato Grosso do Sul
Brazil
154 C2 **Pardo** *r. São Paulo* Brazil
103 D1 **Pardubice** Czech Rep.
150 B3 **Parecis, Serra dos** *hills*
Brazil
130 C2 **Parent, Lac** *l.* Can.
58 B3 **Parepare** Indon.
89 D2 **Parfino** Rus. Fed.
111 B3 **Parga** Greece
109 C3 **Parghelia** Italy
147 D3 **Paria, Gulf of**
Trin. and Tob./Venez.
150 B1 **Parima, Serra** *mts* Brazil
151 C2 **Parintins** Brazil
104 C2 **Paris** France
142 C1 **Paris** *TN* U.S.A.
139 D2 **Paris** *TX* U.S.A.
93 H3 **Parkano** Fin.
138 A2 **Parker** U.S.A.
140 C3 **Parkersburg** U.S.A.
53 C2 **Parkes** Austr.
140 A1 **Park Falls** U.S.A.
137 D1 **Park Rapids** U.S.A.
108 B2 **Parma** Italy
151 D2 **Parnaíba** Brazil
151 D2 **Parnaíba** *r.* Brazil
111 B3 **Parnassós** *mt.* Greece
54 B2 **Parnassus** N.Z.
111 B3 **Parnon** *mts* Greece
88 B2 **Pärnu** Estonia
65 B2 **P'aro-ho** *l.* S. Korea
52 B2 **Paroo** *watercourse* Austr.
76 C3 **Paropamisus** *mts* Afgh.
111 C3 **Paros** *i.* Greece
144 B2 **Parras** Mex.
126 C2 **Parry, Cape** Can.
126 D1 **Parry Islands** Can.
130 B2 **Parry Sound** Can.
137 D3 **Parsons** U.S.A.
101 D2 **Partenstein** Ger.
104 B2 **Parthenay** France
97 B2 **Partry Mountains**
Rep. of Ireland
151 C2 **Paru** *r.* Brazil
135 C4 **Pasadena** U.S.A.
62 A2 **Pasawng** Myanmar
142 C2 **Pascagoula** U.S.A.
110 C1 **Pașcani** Romania
134 C1 **Pasco** U.S.A.
102 C1 **Pasewalk** Ger.
129 D2 **Pasfield Lake** Can.
60 B1 **Pasir Putih** Malaysia

74 A2 **Pasni** Pak.
153 A5 **Paso Río Mayo** Arg.
135 B3 **Paso Robles** U.S.A.
155 D2 **Passa Tempo** Brazil
102 C2 **Passau** Ger.
152 C3 **Passo Fundo** Brazil
152 B3 **Passos** Brazil
88 C2 **Pastavy** Belarus
150 A2 **Pastaza** r. Peru
150 A1 **Pasto** Col.
61 C2 **Pasuruan** Indon.
88 B2 **Pasvalys** Lith.
153 A6 **Patagonia** reg. Arg.
75 C2 **Patan** Nepal
54 B1 **Patea** N.Z.
141 E2 **Paterson** U.S.A.
Pathein Myanmar see
    Bassein
136 B2 **Pathfinder Reservoir** U.S.A.
61 C2 **Pati** Indon.
62 A1 **Pätkai Bum** mts
    India/Myanmar
111 C3 **Patmos** i. Greece
75 C2 **Patna** India
81 C2 **Patnos** Turkey
154 B3 **Pato Branco** Brazil
152 C4 **Patos, Lagoa dos** l. Brazil
155 C1 **Patos de Minas** Brazil
152 B4 **Patquía** Arg.
111 B3 **Patra** Greece
75 C2 **Patratu** India
154 C1 **Patrocínio** Brazil
63 B3 **Pattani** Thai.
63 B2 **Pattaya** Thai.
128 B2 **Pattullo, Mount** Can.
129 D2 **Patuanak** Can.
144 B3 **Pátzcuaro** Mex.
104 B3 **Pau** France
104 B2 **Pauillac** France
62 A1 **Pauk** Myanmar
151 D2 **Paulistana** Brazil
151 E2 **Paulo Afonso** Brazil
123 D2 **Paulpietersburg** S. Africa
139 D2 **Pauls Valley** U.S.A.
62 A2 **Paungde** Myanmar
155 D1 **Pavão** Brazil
108 A1 **Pavia** Italy
88 B2 **Pāvilosta** Latvia
110 C2 **Pavlikeni** Bulg.
77 D1 **Pavlodar** Kazakh.
91 D2 **Pavlohrad** Ukr.
91 E1 **Pavlovsk** Rus. Fed.
91 D2 **Pavlovskaya** Rus. Fed.
60 B2 **Payakumbuh** Indon.
134 C2 **Payette** U.S.A.
134 C2 **Payette** r. U.S.A.
86 F2 **Pay-Khoy, Khrebet** hills
    Rus. Fed.
152 C4 **Paysandú** Uru.
81 C1 **Pazar** Turkey
110 B2 **Pazardzhik** Bulg.
111 C3 **Pazarköy** Turkey
108 B1 **Pazin** Croatia
63 A2 **Pe** Myanmar
128 C2 **Peace** r. Can.
128 C2 **Peace River** Can.
135 E3 **Peale, Mount** U.S.A.
142 C2 **Pearl** r. U.S.A.
139 D3 **Pearsall** U.S.A.
102 C2 **Pebane** Moz.
109 D2 **Peć** Yugo.
155 D1 **Peçanha** Brazil
86 E2 **Pechora** Rus. Fed.
86 E2 **Pechora** r. Rus. Fed.
88 C2 **Pechory** Rus. Fed.
139 C2 **Pecos** U.S.A.
139 C3 **Pecos** r. U.S.A.
103 D2 **Pécs** Hungary
155 D1 **Pedra Azul** Brazil
154 C2 **Pedregulho** Brazil

151 D2 **Pedreiras** Brazil
73 C4 **Pedro, Point** Sri Lanka
151 D2 **Pedro Afonso** Brazil
154 B1 **Pedro Gomes** Brazil
152 B3 **Pedro Juan Caballero** Para.
96 C3 **Peebles** U.K.
143 E2 **Pee Dee** r. U.S.A.
126 C2 **Peel** r. Can.
98 A1 **Peel Isle of Man
128 C2 **Peerless Lake** Can.
54 B2 **Pegasus Bay** N.Z.
101 E3 **Pegnitz** Ger.
62 A2 **Pegu** Myanmar
62 A2 **Pegu Yoma** mts Myanmar
153 B4 **Pehuajó** Arg.
101 E1 **Peine** Ger.
88 C2 **Peipus, Lake**
    Estonia/Rus. Fed.
111 B3 **Peiraias** Greece
154 B2 **Peixe** r. Brazil
61 B2 **Pekalongan** Indon.
60 B1 **Pekan** Malaysia
60 B1 **Pekanbaru** Indon.
    Peking China see **Beijing**
130 B2 **Pelee Island** Can.
59 C3 **Peleng** i. Indon.
92 I2 **Pelkosenniemi** Fin.
122 A2 **Pella** S. Africa
59 D3 **Pelileuhu Islands** P.N.G.
92 H2 **Pello** Fin.
128 A1 **Pelly** r. Can.
127 F2 **Pelly Bay** Can.
128 A1 **Pelly Mountains** Can.
152 C4 **Pelotas** Brazil
152 C3 **Pelotas, Rio das** r. Brazil
141 F1 **Pemadumcook Lake** U.S.A.
61 B1 **Pemangkat** Indon.
60 A1 **Pematangsiantar** Indon.
121 D2 **Pemba** Moz.
120 B2 **Pemba** Zambia
119 D3 **Pemba Island** Tanz.
128 B2 **Pemberton** Can.
137 D1 **Pembina** r. U.S.A.
130 C2 **Pembroke** Can.
99 A3 **Pembroke** U.K.
106 C1 **Peña Cerredo** mt. Spain
145 C2 **Peña Nevada, Cerro**
    mt. Mex.
154 B2 **Penápolis** Brazil
106 B1 **Peñaranda de Bracamonte**
    Spain
107 C1 **Peñarroya** mt. Spain
106 B2 **Peñarroya-Pueblonuevo**
    Spain
106 B1 **Peñas, Cabo de** c. Spain
153 A5 **Penas, Golfo de** g. Chile
106 B1 **Peña Ubiña** mt. Spain
134 C1 **Pendleton** U.S.A.
128 B2 **Pendleton Bay** Can.
134 C1 **Pend Oreille Lake** U.S.A.
74 B3 **Penganga** r. India
123 D1 **Penge** S. Africa
70 C2 **Penglai** China
71 A3 **Pengshui** China
106 A2 **Peniche** Port.
98 B1 **Penicuik** U.K.
108 B2 **Penne** Italy
98 B1 **Pennines** hills U.K.
141 D2 **Pennsylvania** state U.S.A.
127 G2 **Penny Icecap** Can.
141 F2 **Penobscot** r. U.S.A.
52 B3 **Penola** Austr.
50 C3 **Penong** Austr.
98 B1 **Penrith** U.K.
142 C2 **Pensacola** U.S.A.
55 Q1 **Pensacola Mountains**
    Antarctica
61 C1 **Pensiangan** Sabah Malaysia
128 C3 **Penticton** Can.
96 C1 **Pentland Firth** sea chan. U.K.

99 B2 **Penygadair** hill U.K.
87 D3 **Penza** Rus. Fed.
99 A3 **Penzance** U.K.
140 B2 **Peoria** U.S.A.
107 C1 **Perales del Alfambra** Spain
51 E2 **Percy Isles** Austr.
86 F2 **Peregrebnoye** Rus. Fed.
150 A1 **Pereira** Col.
154 B2 **Pereira Barreto** Brazil
90 A2 **Peremyshlyany** Ukr.
89 E2 **Pereslavl'-Zalesskiy**
    Rus. Fed.
91 C1 **Pereyaslav-Khmel'nyts'kyy**
    Ukr.
153 B4 **Pergamino** Arg.
92 H3 **Perhonjoki** r. Fin.
131 C1 **Péribonca, Lac** l. Can.
152 B3 **Perico** Arg.
144 B2 **Pericos** Mex.
104 C2 **Périgueux** France
147 C4 **Perija, Sierra de** mts Venez.
153 A5 **Perito Moreno** Arg.
101 E1 **Perleberg** Ger.
86 E3 **Perm'** Rus. Fed.
52 A2 **Pernatty Lagoon** salt flat
    Austr.
105 C2 **Péronne** France
145 C3 **Perote** Mex.
104 C3 **Perpignan** France
99 A3 **Perranporth** U.K.
143 D2 **Perry** FL U.S.A.
143 D2 **Perry** GA U.S.A.
137 E2 **Perry** IA U.S.A.
139 C1 **Perryton** U.S.A.
137 F3 **Perryville** U.S.A.
91 D2 **Pershore** U.K.
91 D2 **Pershotravens'k** Ukr.
50 A3 **Perth** Austr.
96 C2 **Perth** U.K.
105 D3 **Pertuis** France
108 A2 **Pertusato, Capo** c. Corsica
    France
150 A2 **Peru** country S. America
147 H4 **Peru-Chile Trench**
    sea feature S. Pacific Ocean
108 B2 **Perugia** Italy
154 C2 **Peruíbe** Brazil
100 A2 **Péruwelz** Belgium
90 C2 **Pervomays'k** Ukr.
91 C2 **Pervomays'ke** Ukr.
89 F3 **Pervomayskiy** Rus. Fed.
91 D2 **Pervomays'kyy** Ukr.
108 B2 **Pesaro** Italy
108 B2 **Pescara** Italy
108 B2 **Pescara** r. Italy
74 B1 **Peshawar** Pak.
109 D2 **Peshkopi** Albania
109 C1 **Pesnica** Slovenia
89 E2 **Pestovo** Rus. Fed.
144 B3 **Petatlán** Mex.
140 B2 **Petenwell Lake** U.S.A.
52 A2 **Peterborough** Austr.
130 C2 **Peterborough** Can.
99 C2 **Peterborough** U.K.
96 D2 **Peterhead** U.K.
50 B2 **Petermann Ranges**
    mts Austr.
129 D2 **Peter Pond Lake** Can.
128 A2 **Petersburg** AK U.S.A.
141 D3 **Petersburg** VA U.S.A.
101 D1 **Petershagen** Ger.
131 D1 **Petit Lac Manicouagan**
    l. Can.
131 E1 **Petit Mécatina** r. Can.
145 D2 **Peto** Mex.
140 C1 **Petoskey** U.S.A.
80 B2 **Petra** Jordan
66 B2 **Petra Velikogo, Zaliv** b.
    Rus. Fed.
111 B2 **Petrich** Bulg.

151 D2 Petrolina Brazil
77 C1 Petropavlovsk Kazakh.
83 L3 Petropavlovsk-Kamchatskiy Rus. Fed.
110 B1 Petroşani Romania
89 F3 Petrovskoye Rus. Fed.
86 C2 Petrozavodsk Rus. Fed.
123 C2 Petrusburg S. Africa
123 C2 Petrus Steyn S. Africa
122 B3 Petrusville S. Africa
89 E2 Petushki Rus. Fed.
60 A1 Peureula Indon.
83 M2 Pevek Rus. Fed.
102 B2 Pforzheim Ger.
102 C2 Pfunds Austria
101 D3 Pfungstadt Ger.
123 C2 Phahameng S. Africa
123 D1 Phalaborwa S. Africa
74 B2 Phalodi India
63 A3 Phangnga Thai.
63 B2 Phan Rang Vietnam
63 B2 Phan Thiêt Vietnam
63 B3 Phatthalung Thai.
62 A2 Phayao Thai.
129 D2 Phelps Lake Can.
143 C2 Phenix City U.S.A.
63 A2 Phet Buri Thai.
63 B2 Phichit Thai.
141 D3 Philadelphia U.S.A.
136 C2 Philip U.S.A.
100 B2 Philippeville Belgium
100 A2 Philippine Neth.
64 B1 Philippines country Asia
64 B1 Philippine Sea N. Pacific Ocean
126 B2 Philip Smith Mountains U.S.A.
122 B3 Philipstown S. Africa
53 C3 Phillip Island Austr.
137 D3 Phillipsburg U.S.A.
123 C2 Phiritona S. Africa
63 B2 Phitsanulok Thai.
63 B2 Phnom Penh Cambodia see Phnum Pénh
63 B2 Phnum Pénh Cambodia
138 A2 Phoenix U.S.A.
63 B2 Phon Thai.
62 B1 Phôngsali Laos
62 B2 Phrae Thai.
63 A3 Phuket Thai.
63 B2 Phumi Sâmraông Cambodia
123 C2 Phuthaditjhaba S. Africa
108 A1 Piacenza Italy
108 B2 Pianosa, Isola i. Italy
110 C1 Piatra Neamţ Romania
151 D2 Piauí r. Brazil
108 B1 Piave r. Italy
117 B4 Pibor r. Sudan
117 B4 Pibor Post Sudan
142 C2 Picayune U.S.A.
152 B3 Pichanal Arg.
144 A2 Pichilingue Mex.
98 C1 Pickering U.K.
130 A1 Pickle Lake Can.
152 B2 Picos Brazil
153 B5 Pico Truncado Arg.
53 D2 Picton Austr.
145 C3 Piedras Negras Guat.
145 B2 Piedras Negras Mex.
93 I3 Pieksämäki Fin.
92 I3 Pielinen l. Fin.
136 C2 Pierre U.S.A.
105 C3 Pierrelatte France
123 D2 Pietermaritzburg S. Africa
123 C1 Pietersburg S. Africa
110 B1 Pietrosa mt. Romania
128 C2 Pigeon Lake Can.
153 B4 Pigüé Arg.
92 I3 Pihtipudas Fin.
145 C3 Pijijiapan Mex.

136 C3 Pikes Peak U.S.A.
122 A3 Piketberg S. Africa
140 C3 Pikeville U.S.A.
103 D1 Piła Pol.
153 C4 Pilar r. Brazil
152 C3 Pilar Para.
53 C2 Pilliga Austr.
154 C1 Pilões, Serra dos mts Brazil
150 B3 Pimenta Bueno Brazil
153 C4 Pinamar Arg.
80 B2 Pınarbaşı Turkey
146 B2 Pinar del Río Cuba
103 E1 Pińczów Pol.
151 D2 Pindaré r. Brazil
111 B2 Pindos mts Greece
142 B2 Pine Bluff U.S.A.
50 C1 Pine Creek Austr.
136 B2 Pinedale U.S.A.
86 D2 Pinega Rus. Fed.
129 D2 Pinehouse Lake Can.
111 B3 Pineios r. Greece
128 C1 Pine Point Can.
136 C2 Pine Ridge U.S.A.
123 D2 Pinetown S. Africa
70 B2 Pingdingshan China
70 A2 Pingguo China
71 B3 Pingjiang China
70 A2 Pingliang China
71 C3 P'ingtung Taiwan
71 A3 Pingxiang Guangxi China
71 B3 Pingxiang Jiangxi China
70 B2 Pingyin China
151 D2 Pinheiro Brazil
101 D1 Pinneberg Ger.
145 C3 Pinotepa Nacional Mex.
88 C3 Pinsk Belarus
135 D3 Pioche U.S.A.
119 C3 Piodi Dem. Rep. Congo
103 E1 Pionki Pol.
103 D1 Piotrków Trybunalski Pol.
137 D2 Pipestone U.S.A.
131 C2 Pipmuacan, Réservoir resr Can.
154 C2 Piquiri r. Brazil
154 C1 Piracanjuba Brazil
154 C2 Piracicaba Brazil
155 D1 Piracicaba r. Brazil
154 C2 Piraçununga Brazil
154 C2 Piraí do Sul Brazil
154 C2 Pirajuí Brazil
154 B1 Piranhas Brazil
151 E2 Piranhas r. Brazil
154 C1 Pirapora Brazil
154 C2 Pires do Rio Brazil
154 C1 Piripiri Brazil
59 C3 Piru Indon.
108 B2 Pisa Italy
152 A2 Pisagua Chile
150 A3 Pisco Peru
102 C2 Písek Czech Rep.
79 D2 Pīshīn Iran
145 D2 Pisté Mex.
109 C2 Pisticci Italy
108 B2 Pistoia Italy
106 C1 Pisuerga r. Spain
134 B2 Pit r. U.S.A.
154 B2 Pitanga Brazil
155 D1 Pitangui Brazil
49 H6 Pitcairn Islands terr. S. Pacific Ocean
92 H2 Piteå Sweden
92 H2 Piteälven r. Sweden
110 B2 Piteşti Romania
75 C2 Pithoragarh India
96 C2 Pitlochry U.K.
128 B2 Pitt Island Can.
137 E3 Pittsburg U.S.A.
141 D2 Pittsburgh U.S.A.
141 E2 Pittsfield U.S.A.
53 D1 Pittsworth Austr.

155 C2 Piumhí Brazil
150 A2 Piura Peru
90 C2 Pivdennyy Buh r. Ukr.
131 E2 Placentia Can.
135 B3 Placerville U.S.A.
146 C2 Placetas Cuba
139 C2 Plainview U.S.A.
154 C1 Planaltina Brazil
142 B2 Plaquemine U.S.A.
106 B1 Plasencia Spain
147 C4 Plato Col.
137 D2 Platte r. U.S.A.
141 E2 Plattsburgh U.S.A.
101 F1 Plau Ger.
101 F2 Plauen Ger.
101 F1 Plauer See l. Ger.
89 E3 Plavsk Rus. Fed.
63 B2 Plây Cu Vietnam
129 E2 Playgreen Lake Can.
153 B4 Plaza Huincul Arg.
139 D3 Pleasanton U.S.A.
54 B2 Pleasant Point N.Z.
104 C2 Pleaux France
130 B1 Pledger Lake Can.
54 C1 Plenty, Bay of g. N.Z.
136 C1 Plentywood U.S.A.
83 H2 Plesetsk Rus. Fed.
131 C1 Plétipi, Lac l. Can.
100 C2 Plettenberg Ger.
122 B3 Plettenberg Bay S. Africa
110 B2 Pleven Bulg.
109 C2 Pljevlja Yugo.
109 C2 Ploče Croatia
103 D1 Płock Pol.
109 C2 Pločno mt. Bos.-Herz.
104 B2 Ploemeur France
110 C2 Ploieşti Romania
89 F2 Ploskoye Rus. Fed.
110 B2 Plovdiv Bulg.
88 B2 Plungė Lith.
88 C3 Plyeshchanitsy Belarus
147 D3 Plymouth Montserrat
99 A3 Plymouth U.K.
140 B2 Plymouth U.S.A.
88 C2 Plyussa Rus. Fed.
102 C2 Plzeň Czech Rep.
114 B3 Pô Burkina
108 B1 Po r. Italy
77 E2 Pobedy, Pik mt. China/Kyrg.
142 B1 Pocahontas U.S.A.
134 D2 Pocatello U.S.A.
90 B1 Pochayiv Ukr.
89 D3 Pochep Rus. Fed.
89 D3 Pochinok Rus. Fed.
145 C3 Pochutla Mex.
141 D3 Pocomoke City U.S.A.
155 C2 Poços de Caldas Brazil
89 D2 Poddor'ye Rus. Fed.
91 D1 Podgorenskiy Rus. Fed.
109 C2 Podgorica Yugo.
82 G3 Podgornoye Rus. Fed.
83 H2 Podkamennaya Tunguska r. Rus. Fed.
89 E2 Podol'sk Rus. Fed.
109 D2 Podujevo Yugo.
122 A2 Pofadder S. Africa
89 D3 Pogar Rus. Fed.
109 D2 Pogradec Albania
65 B2 Pohang S. Korea
110 B2 Poiana Mare Romania
118 B3 Poie Dem. Rep. Congo
118 B3 Pointe-Noire Congo
126 B2 Point Lake Can.
140 C3 Point Pleasant U.S.A.
104 C2 Poitiers France
74 B2 Pokaran India
75 C2 Pokhara Nepal
83 J2 Pokrovsk Rus. Fed.
91 D2 Pokrovskoye Rus. Fed.

138 A1 Polacca U.S.A.
106 B1 Pola de Lena Spain
103 D1 Poland country Europe
88 C2 Polatsk Belarus
77 C3 Pol-e Khomrī Afgh.
61 C2 Polewali Indon.
118 B2 Poli Cameroon
102 C1 Police Pol.
109 C2 Policoro Italy
105 D2 Poligny France
64 B1 Polillo Islands Phil.
90 B1 Polis'ke Ukr.
103 D1 Polkowice Pol.
109 C3 Pollino, Monte mt. Italy
91 D2 Polohy Ukr.
90 B1 Polonne Ukr.
134 D1 Polson U.S.A.
91 C2 Poltava Ukr.
66 B2 Poltavka Rus. Fed.
91 D2 Poltavskaya Rus. Fed.
88 C2 Põlva Estonia
111 B2 Polygyros Greece
106 B2 Pombal Port.
108 B2 Pomezia Italy
92 I2 Pomokaira reg. Fin.
110 C2 Pomorie Bulg.
102 C1 Pomorska, Zatoka b. Pol.
155 D1 Pompéu Brazil
139 D1 Ponca City U.S.A.
147 D3 Ponce Puerto Rico
73 B3 Pondicherry India
127 F2 Pond Inlet Can.
106 B1 Ponferrada Spain
117 A4 Pongo watercourse Sudan
123 D2 Pongola r. S. Africa
128 C2 Ponoka Can.
154 B3 Ponta Grossa Brazil
154 C1 Pontalina Brazil
105 D2 Pont-à-Mousson France
105 D2 Pontarlier France
102 B2 Pontcharra France
142 B2 Pontchartrain, Lake U.S.A.
106 B2 Ponte de Sor Port.
129 D3 Ponteix Can.
150 C3 Pontes-e-Lacerda Brazil
106 B1 Pontevedra Spain
140 B2 Pontiac IL. U.S.A.
140 C2 Pontiac MI U.S.A.
61 B2 Pontianak Indon.
104 B2 Pontivy France
151 C1 Pontoetoe Suriname
129 E2 Ponton Can.
99 B3 Pontypool U.K.
108 B2 Ponziane, Isole is Italy
99 C3 Poole U.K.
Poona India see Pune
52 B2 Pooncarie Austr.
152 B2 Poopó, Lago de l. Bol.
150 A1 Popayán Col.
83 I2 Popigay r. Rus. Fed.
52 B2 Popiltah Austr.
129 E2 Poplar r. Can.
137 E3 Poplar Bluff U.S.A.
118 B3 Popokabaka
         Dem. Rep. Congo
110 C2 Popovo Bulg.
103 E2 Poprad Slovakia
151 D3 Porangatu Brazil
74 A2 Porbandar India
111 C3 Poreč Croatia
93 H3 Pori Fin.
54 B2 Porirua N.Z.
88 C2 Porkhov Rus. Fed.
104 B2 Pornic France
83 K3 Poronaysk Rus. Fed.
111 B3 Poros Greece
93 E4 Porsgrunn Norway
97 C1 Portadown U.K.
97 D1 Portaferry U.K.

140 B2 Portage U.S.A.
129 E3 Portage la Prairie Can.
128 B3 Port Alberni Can.
106 B2 Portalegre Port.
139 C2 Portales U.S.A.
128 A2 Port Alexander U.S.A.
128 B2 Port Alice Can.
134 B1 Port Angeles U.S.A.
51 D4 Port Arthur Austr.
139 E3 Port Arthur U.S.A.
96 A3 Port Askaig U.K.
52 A2 Port Augusta Austr.
147 C3 Port-au-Prince Haiti
131 E1 Port aux Choix Can.
73 D3 Port Blair India
52 B3 Port Campbell Austr.
54 B3 Port Chalmers N.Z.
143 D3 Port Charlotte U.S.A.
147 C3 Port-de-Paix Haiti
128 A2 Port Edward Can.
155 D1 Porteirinha Brazil
151 C2 Portel Brazil
130 B2 Port Elgin Can.
123 C3 Port Elizabeth S. Africa
96 A3 Port Ellen U.K.
98 A1 Port Erin Isle of Man
122 A3 Porterville S. Africa
135 C3 Porterville U.S.A.
52 B3 Port Fairy Austr.
54 C1 Port Fitzroy N.Z.
118 A3 Port-Gentil Gabon
115 C4 Port Harcourt Nigeria
128 B2 Port Hardy Can.
         Port Harrison Can. see
         Inukjuak
131 D2 Port Hawkesbury Can.
50 A2 Port Hedland Austr.
99 A2 Porthmadog U.K.
131 E1 Port Hope Simpson Can.
140 C2 Port Huron U.S.A.
106 B2 Portimão Port.
53 C2 Portland N.S.W. Austr.
52 B3 Portland Vic. Austr.
141 E2 Portland ME U.S.A.
134 B1 Portland OR U.S.A.
128 A2 Portland Canal inlet Can.
97 C2 Portlaoise Rep. of Ireland
139 D3 Port Lavaca U.S.A.
52 A2 Port Lincoln Austr.
114 A4 Port Loko Sierra Leone
53 D2 Port Macquarie Austr.
128 B2 Port McNeill Can.
131 D2 Port-Menier Can.
59 D3 Port Moresby P.N.G.
96 A1 Port Nis U.K.
122 A2 Port Nolloth S. Africa
         Port-Nouveau-Québec Can.
         see Kangiqsualujjuaq
         Porto Port. see Oporto
150 B2 Porto Acre Brazil
152 C4 Porto Alegre Brazil
151 C3 Porto Artur Brazil
151 C3 Porto dos Gaúchos Óbidos
         Brazil
150 C3 Porto Esperidião Brazil
108 B2 Portoferraio Italy
151 C2 Porto Franco Brazil
147 D3 Port of Spain Trin. and Tob.
108 B1 Portogruaro Italy
108 B2 Portomaggiore Italy
154 B2 Porto Mendes Brazil
152 C3 Porto Murtinho Brazil
151 D3 Porto Nacional Brazil
114 C4 Porto-Novo Benin
154 B2 Porto Primavera, Represa
         resr Brazil
151 C2 Porto Santana Brazil
155 E1 Porto Seguro Brazil
108 B2 Porto Tolle Italy
108 A2 Porto Torres Sardinia Italy

105 D3 Porto-Vecchio Corsica
         France
150 B2 Porto Velho Brazil
150 A2 Portoviejo Ecuador
52 B3 Port Phillip Bay Austr.
52 A2 Port Pirie Austr.
96 A2 Portree U.K.
128 B3 Port Renfrew Can.
97 C1 Portrush U.K.
116 B1 Port Said Egypt
143 C3 Port St Joe U.S.A.
123 C3 Port St Johns S. Africa
123 D3 Port Shepstone S. Africa
99 C3 Portsmouth U.K.
141 E2 Portsmouth NH U.S.A.
140 C3 Portsmouth OH U.S.A.
141 D3 Portsmouth VA U.S.A.
97 C1 Portstewart U.K.
116 B3 Port Sudan Sudan
142 C3 Port Sulphur U.S.A.
99 B3 Port Talbot U.K.
106 B2 Portugal country Europe
97 B2 Portumna Rep. of Ireland
105 C3 Port-Vendres France
93 I3 Porvoo Fin.
65 B2 Poryŏng S. Korea
152 C3 Posadas Arg.
89 E2 Poshekhon'ye Rus. Fed.
92 I2 Posio Fin.
58 C3 Poso Indon.
151 D3 Posse Brazil
101 E2 Pößneck Ger.
139 C2 Post U.S.A.
130 C1 Poste-de-la-Baleine Can.
122 B2 Postmasburg S. Africa
109 C2 Posušje Bos.-Herz.
139 E1 Poteau U.S.A.
109 C2 Potenza Italy
123 C1 Potgietersrus S. Africa
151 D2 Poti r. Brazil
81 C1 P'ot'i Georgia
115 D3 Potiskum Nigeria
141 D3 Potomac, South Branch
         r. U.S.A.
152 B2 Potosí Bol.
64 B1 Pototan Phil.
138 C3 Potrero del Llano Mex.
101 F1 Potsdam Ger.
141 E2 Potsdam U.S.A.
141 D2 Pottstown U.S.A.
141 D2 Pottsville U.S.A.
131 E2 Pouch Cove Can.
141 E2 Poughkeepsie U.S.A.
98 B2 Poulton-le-Fylde U.K.
155 C2 Pouso Alegre Brazil
63 B2 Poŭthisăt Cambodia
103 D2 Považská Bystrica Slovakia
109 C2 Povlen mt. Yugo.
106 B1 Póvoa de Varzim Port.
136 B2 Powell U.S.A.
135 D3 Powell, Lake resr U.S.A.
128 B3 Powell River Can.
154 B1 Poxoréu Brazil
         Poyang China see Boyang
71 B3 Poyang Hu l. China
109 D2 Požarevac Yugo.
145 C2 Poza Rica Mex.
109 C1 Požega Croatia
109 D2 Požega Yugo.
79 D2 Pozm Tīāb Iran
103 D1 Poznań Pol.
106 C2 Pozoblanco Spain
108 B2 Pozzuoli Italy
60 B2 Prabumulih Indon.
102 C2 Prachatice Czech Rep.
63 A2 Prachuap Khiri Khan Thai.
155 E1 Prado Brazil
102 C1 Prague Czech Rep.
         Praha Czech Rep. see
         Prague

139 C2 Prairie Dog Town Fork
　　　 r. U.S.A.
140 A2 Prairie du Chien U.S.A.
60 A1 Prapat Indon.
154 C1 Prata Brazil
105 E3 Prato Italy
137 D3 Pratt U.S.A.
61 C2 Praya Indon.
63 B2 Preǎh Vihéar Cambodia
89 F2 Prechistoye Rus. Fed.
129 D2 Preeceville Can.
88 C2 Preiļi Latvia
53 C2 Premer Austr.
105 C2 Prémery France
101 F1 Premnitz Ger.
102 C1 Prenzlau Ger.
63 A2 Preparis Island Cocos Is
63 A2 Preparis North Channel
　　　 Cocos Is
63 A2 Preparis South Channel
　　　 Cocos Is
103 D2 Přerov Czech Rep.
138 A2 Prescott U.S.A.
109 D2 Preševo Yugo.
152 B3 Presidencia Roque Sáenz
　　　 Peña Arg.
151 D2 Presidente Dutra Brazil
154 B3 Presidente Epitácio Brazil
154 B2 Presidente Prudente Brazil
138 C3 Presidio U.S.A.
103 E2 Prešov Slovakia
141 F1 Presque Isle U.S.A.
101 F2 Pressel Ger.
98 B2 Preston U.K.
134 D2 Preston U.S.A.
96 B3 Prestwick U.K.
155 C1 Preto *r.* Brazil
123 C2 Pretoria S. Africa
111 B3 Preveza Greece
63 B2 Prey Vêng Cambodia
109 C2 Priboj Yugo.
135 D3 Price U.S.A.
88 B3 Prienai Lith.
122 B2 Prieska S. Africa
103 D2 Prievidza Slovakia
109 C2 Prijedor Bos.-Herz.
76 A2 Prikaspiyskaya
　　　 Nizmennost' *lowland*
　　　 Kazakh./Rus. Fed.
109 D2 Prilep Macedonia
91 D2 Primorsko-Akhtarsk
　　　 Rus. Fed.
129 D2 Primrose Lake Can.
129 D2 Prince Albert Can.
122 B3 Prince Albert S. Africa
126 D2 Prince Albert Peninsula
　　　 Can.
122 B3 Prince Albert Road S. Africa
126 C2 Prince Alfred, Cape Can.
122 A3 Prince Alfred Hamlet
　　　 S. Africa
127 F2 Prince Charles Island Can.
55 E2 Prince Charles Mountains
　　　 Antarctica
131 D2 Prince Edward Island
　　　 prov. Can.
128 B2 Prince George Can.
126 E2 Prince of Wales Island Can.
128 A2 Prince of Wales Island
　　　 U.S.A.
126 D2 Prince of Wales Strait Can.
126 D1 Prince Patrick Island Can.
126 E2 Prince Regent Inlet
　　　 sea chan. Can.
128 A2 Prince Rupert Can.
51 D1 Princess Charlotte Bay
　　　 Austr.
128 B3 Princess Royal Island Can.
128 B3 Princeton Can.
134 B2 Prineville U.S.A.

90 B1 Pripet *r.* Belarus/Ukr.
90 A1 Pripet Marshes Belarus/Ukr.
109 D2 Priština Yugo.
101 F1 Pritzwalk Ger.
109 C2 Privlaka Croatia
89 F2 Privolzhsk Rus. Fed.
109 D2 Prizren Yugo.
151 C1 Professor van Blommestein
　　　 Meer *resr* Suriname
145 D2 Progreso Mex.
81 C1 Prokhladnyy Rus. Fed.
109 D2 Prokuplje Yugo.
126 C3 Prophet *r.* Can.
128 B2 Prophet River Can.
51 D2 Proserpine Austr.
63 B3 Protvino Rus. Fed.
110 C2 Provadiya Bulg.
141 E2 Providence U.S.A.
146 B3 Providencia, Isla de *i.*
　　　 Caribbean Sea
83 N2 Provideniya Rus. Fed.
135 D2 Provo U.S.A.
129 C2 Provost Can.
154 B3 Prudentópolis Brazil
126 B2 Prudhoe Bay U.S.A.
100 C2 Prüm Ger.
105 D3 Prunelli-di-Fiumorbo
　　　 Corsica France
103 E1 Pruszków Pol.
110 C1 Prut *r.* Europe
91 C1 Pryluky Ukr.
91 D2 Prymors'k Ukr.
139 D1 Pryor U.S.A.
　　　 Prypyats' *r.* Belarus *see* Pripet
103 E2 Przemyśl Pol.
111 C3 Psara *i.* Greece
81 C1 Psebay Rus. Fed.
91 D3 Pshekha *r.* Rus. Fed.
88 C2 Pskov Rus. Fed.
88 C2 Pskov, Lake
　　　 Estonia/Rus. Fed.
111 B2 Ptolemaïda Greece
109 C1 Ptuj Slovenia
150 A2 Pucallpa Peru
71 B3 Pucheng China
65 B2 Puch'ŏn S. Korea
103 D1 Puck Pol.
92 I2 Pudasjärvi Fin.
86 C2 Pudozh Rus. Fed.
　　　 Puducheri India *see*
　　　 Pondicherry
145 C3 Puebla Mex.
136 C3 Pueblo U.S.A.
153 B4 Puelén Arg.
106 C2 Puente-Genil Spain
153 A5 Puerto Aisén Chile
152 B2 Puerto Alegre Bol.
145 C3 Puerto Ángel Mex.
146 B4 Puerto Armuelles Panama
150 B1 Puerto Ayacucho Venez.
146 B3 Puerto Cabezas Nic.
150 B1 Puerto Carreño Col.
153 A5 Puerto Cisnes Chile
144 A2 Puerto Cortés Mex.
145 C3 Puerto Escondido Mex.
152 B2 Puerto Frey Bol.
150 B1 Puerto Inírida Col.
153 B5 Puerto Isabel Bol.
150 A2 Puerto Leguízamo Col.
144 A2 Puerto Libertad Mex.
106 C2 Puertollano Spain
153 B5 Puerto Madryn Arg.
150 B3 Puerto Maldonado Peru
153 A5 Puerto Montt Chile
153 A6 Puerto Natales Chile
150 B1 Puerto Nuevo Col.
141 A1 Puerto Peñasco Mex.
152 C3 Puerto Pinasco Para.
150 B1 Puerto Plata Dom. Rep.
150 A2 Puerto Portillo Peru

64 A2 Puerto Princesa Phil.
147 D3 Puerto Rico *terr.* West Indies
158 B3 Puerto Rico Trench
　　　 sea feature Caribbean Sea
153 B6 Puerto Santa Cruz Arg.
144 B2 Puerto Vallarta Mex.
87 D3 Pugachev Rus. Fed.
74 B2 Pugal India
54 B2 Pukaki, Lake N.Z.
129 C2 Pukatawagan Can.
65 B1 Pukchin N. Korea
65 B1 Pukch'ŏng N. Korea
54 B1 Pukekohe N.Z.
65 B1 Puksubaek-san *mt.* N. Korea
108 B2 Pula Croatia
108 A3 Pula *Sardinia* Italy
152 B3 Pulacayo Bol.
92 I3 Pulkkila Fin.
134 C1 Pullman U.S.A.
64 B1 Pulog, Mount Phil.
150 A2 Puná, Isla *i.* Ecuador
54 B2 Punakaiki N.Z.
123 D1 Punda Maria S. Africa
73 B3 Pune India
65 B1 P'ungsan N. Korea
121 C2 Púnguè *r.* Moz.
153 B4 Punta Alta Arg.
153 A6 Punta Arenas Chile
108 A2 Punta Balestrieri *mt.*
　　　 Sardinia Italy
146 B3 Puntarenas Costa Rica
150 A1 Punto Fijo Venez.
92 I3 Puolanka Fin.
70 B3 Puqi China
82 G2 Pur *r.* Rus. Fed.
75 C3 Puri India
100 B1 Purmerend Neth.
75 C2 Pūrnia India
75 C2 Puruliya India
150 B2 Purus *r.* Peru
61 B2 Purwakarta Indon.
65 B1 Puryŏng N. Korea
65 B2 Pusan S. Korea
88 C2 Pustoshka Rus. Fed.
62 A1 Putao Myanmar
71 B3 Putian China
　　　 Puting China *see* De'an
61 C2 Puting, Tanjung *pt* Indon.
101 F1 Putlitz Ger.
58 A2 Putrajaya Malaysia
102 C1 Puttgarden Ger.
150 A2 Putumayo *r.* Col.
61 C1 Putusibau Indon.
91 C1 Putyvl' Ukr.
127 F2 Puvurnituq Can.
70 B2 Puyang China
104 C3 Puylaurens France
99 A2 Pwllheli U.K.
62 A1 Pyapon Myanmar
82 G2 Pyasina *r.* Rus. Fed.
87 D4 Pyatigorsk Rus. Fed.
91 C2 P''yatykhatky Ukr.
62 A2 Pyè Myanmar
88 C3 Pyetrykaw Belarus
93 H3 Pyhäjärvi *l.* Fin.
92 H3 Pyhäjoki *r.* Fin.
92 I3 Pyhäsalmi Fin.
62 A2 Pyinmana Myanmar
62 A1 Pyôksŏng N. Korea
65 B2 P'yŏnggang N. Korea
65 B2 P'yŏngyang N. Korea
135 C2 Pyramid Lake U.S.A.
107 D1 Pyrenees *mts* Europe
111 B3 Pyrgos Greece
91 C1 Pyryatyn Ukr.
103 C1 Pyrzyce Pol.
88 C2 Pytalovo Rus. Fed.
62 A2 Pyu Myanmar
111 B3 Pyxaria *mt.* Greece

Q

127 G1	**Qaanaaq** Greenland
123 C3	**Qacha's Nek** Lesotho
69 D2	**Qagan Nur** China
68 C2	**Qaidam Pendi** basin China
74 A1	**Qalāt** Afgh.
78 B3	**Qal'at Bishah** Saudi Arabia
129 E1	**Qamanirjuaq Lake** l. Can.
	Qamanittuaq Can. see Baker Lake
78 B3	**Qam Hadīl** Saudi Arabia
78 B2	**Qaryat al Ulyā** Saudi Arabia
127 H2	**Qasigiannguit** Greenland
79 D2	**Qaşr-e-Qand** Iran
81 C2	**Qaşr-e Shīrīn** Iran
127 H2	**Qassimiut** Greenland
78 B3	**Qa'tabah** Yemen
79 C2	**Qatar** country Asia
116 A2	**Qattâra Depression** Egypt
81 C1	**Qazax** Azer.
81 C1	**Qazimämmäd** Azer.
81 C2	**Qäzvīn** Iran
116 B2	**Qena** Egypt
127 H2	**Qeqertarsuaq** i. Greenland
127 H2	**Qeqertarsuatsiaat** Greenland
127 H2	**Qeqertarsuup Tunua** b. Greenland
79 C2	**Qeshm** Iran
70 A3	**Qianjiang** Chongqing China
70 B2	**Qianjiang** Hubei China
65 A1	**Qian Shan** mts China
70 C2	**Qidong** China
68 B2	**Qiemo** China
71 A3	**Qijiang** China
68 C2	**Qijiaojing** China
127 G2	**Qikiqtarjuaq** Can.
74 A2	**Qila Ladgasht** Pak.
68 C2	**Qilian Shan** mts China
127 I2	**Qillak** i. Greenland
70 B3	**Qimen** China
127 G1	**Qimusseriarsuaq** b. Greenland
70 C2	**Qingdao** China
68 C2	**Qinghai** prov. China
68 C2	**Qinghai Hu** salt l. China
68 C2	**Qinghai Nanshan** mts China
71 B3	**Qingyuan** Guangdong China
65 A1	**Qingyuan** Liaoning China
68 B2	**Qing Zang Gaoyuan** plat. China
70 B2	**Qingzhou** China
70 B2	**Qinhuangdao** China
70 A2	**Qin Ling** mts China
	Qinting China see Lianhua
70 B2	**Qinyang** China
71 A3	**Qinzhou** China
71 B4	**Qionghai** China
68 C2	**Qionglai Shan** mts China
71 B4	**Qiongshan** China
69 E1	**Qiqihar** China
79 C2	**Qīr** Iran
66 B1	**Qitaihe** China
70 B2	**Qixian** China
	Qogir Feng mt. China/Jammu and Kashmir see K2
81 D2	**Qom** Iran
81 D2	**Qomishêh** Iran
	Qomolangma Feng mt. China/Nepal see Everest, Mount
	Ooqek China see Tacheng
100 C1	**Quakenbrück** Ger.
63 B2	**Quang Ngai** Vietnam
63 B2	**Quang Tri** Vietnam
71 B3	**Quanzhou** Fujian China
71 B3	**Quanzhou** Guangxi China
108 A3	**Quartu Sant'Elena** Sardinia Italy

138 A2	**Quartzsite** U.S.A.
81 C1	**Quba** Azer.
53 C3	**Queanbeyan** Austr.
131 C2	**Québec** Can.
130 C1	**Québec** prov. Can.
101 E2	**Quedlinburg** Ger.
128 A2	**Queen Charlotte** Can.
128 A2	**Queen Charlotte Islands** Can.
128 B2	**Queen Charlotte Sound** sea chan. Can.
128 B2	**Queen Charlotte Strait** Can.
126 D1	**Queen Elizabeth Islands** Can.
126 E2	**Queen Maud Gulf** Can.
55 B2	**Queen Maud Land** reg. Antarctica
55 N1	**Queen Maud Mountains** Antarctica
52 B1	**Queensland** state Austr.
51 D4	**Queenstown** Austr.
54 A3	**Queenstown** N.Z.
123 C3	**Queenstown** S. Africa
121 C2	**Quelimane** Moz.
138 B2	**Quemado** U.S.A.
154 B2	**Querência do Norte** Brazil
145 B2	**Querétaro** Mex.
101 E2	**Querfurt** Ger.
128 B2	**Quesnel** Can.
128 B2	**Quesnel Lake** Can.
74 A1	**Quetta** Pak.
64 A2	**Quezon** Phil.
64 B1	**Quezon City** Phil.
120 A2	**Quibala** Angola
150 A1	**Quibdó** Col.
104 B2	**Quiberon** France
104 C3	**Quillan** France
153 C4	**Quilmes** Arg.
73 B4	**Quilon** India
51 D2	**Quilpie** Austr.
153 A4	**Quilpué** Chile
120 A1	**Quimbele** Angola
152 B3	**Quimili** Arg.
104 B2	**Quimper** France
104 B2	**Quimperlé** France
137 E3	**Quincy** IL U.S.A.
141 E2	**Quincy** MA U.S.A.
63 B2	**Qui Nhon** Vietnam
107 C1	**Quinto** Spain
53 D2	**Quionga** Moz.
121 C3	**Quissico** Moz.
120 A2	**Quitapa** Angola
150 A2	**Quito** Ecuador
151 E2	**Quixadá** Brazil
71 A3	**Qujing** China
52 A2	**Quorn** Austr.
79 C2	**Qurayat** Oman
77 C3	**Qürghonteppa** Tajik.
116 B2	**Quseir** Egypt
71 B3	**Quzhou** China

R

103 D2	**Raab** r. Austria
92 H3	**Raahe** Fin.
100 C1	**Raalte** Neth.
61 C2	**Raas** i. Indon.
61 C2	**Raba** Indon.
114 B1	**Rabat** Morocco
78 A2	**Rābigh** Saudi Arabia
90 B2	**Rābnița** Moldova
131 E2	**Race, Cape** Can.
142 B3	**Raceland** U.S.A.
63 B3	**Rach Gia** Vietnam
140 B2	**Racine** U.S.A.
78 B3	**Radā'** Yemen
110 C1	**Rădăuți** Romania

140 B3	**Radcliff** U.S.A.
74 B2	**Radhanpur** India
130 C1	**Radisson** Can.
103 E1	**Radom** Pol.
103 D1	**Radomsko** Pol.
90 B1	**Radomyshl'** Ukr.
109 D2	**Radoviš** Macedonia
88 B2	**Radviliškis** Lith.
78 A2	**Raḍwá, Jabal** mt. Saudi Arabia
90 B1	**Radyvyliv** Ukr.
75 C2	**Rae Bareli** India
128 C1	**Rae-Edzo** Can.
128 C1	**Rae Lakes** Can.
100 C2	**Raeren** Belgium
54 C1	**Raetihi** N.Z.
152 B4	**Rafaela** Arg.
118 C2	**Rafaï** C.A.R.
78 B2	**Raffā'** Saudi Arabia
79 C1	**Rafsanjān** Iran
64 B2	**Ragang, Mount** vol. Phil.
109 B3	**Ragusa** Sicily Italy
59 C3	**Raha** Indon.
88 D3	**Rahachow** Belarus
74 B2	**Rahimyar Khan** Pak.
73 B3	**Raichur** India
75 C2	**Raigarh** India
74 B2	**Rainbow Lake** Can.
134 B1	**Rainier, Mount** vol. U.S.A.
130 A2	**Rainy Lake** Can.
129 E3	**Rainy River** Can.
75 C2	**Raipur** India
93 H3	**Raisio** Fin.
73 C3	**Rajahmundry** India
61 C1	**Rajang** r. Sarawak Malaysia
74 B2	**Rajanpur** Pak.
73 B4	**Rajapalaiyam** India
74 B2	**Rajasthan Canal** India
74 B2	**Rajgarh** India
74 B2	**Rajkot** India
74 B2	**Rajpur** India
75 C2	**Rajshahi** Bangl.
54 B2	**Rakaia** r. N.Z.
90 A2	**Rakhiv** Ukr.
91 D1	**Rakitnoye** Rus. Fed.
88 C2	**Rakke** Estonia
88 C2	**Rakvere** Estonia
143 E1	**Raleigh** U.S.A.
74 B2	**Ramgarh** India
81 C2	**Rāmhormoz** Iran
78 B3	**Ramlat Dahm** des. Saudi Arabia/Yemen
	Ramlat Rabyânah des. Libya see Rebiana Sand Sea
110 C1	**Râmnicu Sărat** Romania
110 B1	**Râmnicu Vâlcea** Romania
89 E3	**Ramon'** Rus. Fed.
123 C1	**Ramotswa** Botswana
75 B2	**Rampur** India
62 A2	**Ramree Island** Myanmar
98 A1	**Ramsey** Isle of Man
99 D3	**Ramsgate** U.K.
75 C2	**Ranaghat** India
61 C1	**Ranau** Sabah Malaysia
153 A4	**Rancagua** Chile
75 C2	**Ranchi** India
93 F4	**Randers** Denmark
54 B2	**Rangiora** N.Z.
54 C1	**Rangitaiki** r. N.Z.
	Rangoon Myanmar see Yangôn
75 C2	**Rangpur** Bangl.
129 E1	**Rankin Inlet** Can.
53 C2	**Rankin's Springs** Austr.
96 B2	**Rannoch Moor** moorland U.K.
74 B2	**Rann of Kachchh** marsh India
63 A3	**Ranong** Thai.
59 C3	**Ransiki** Indon.

61 C2 **Rantaupanjang** Indon.
60 A1 **Rantauprapat** Indon.
92 I2 **Ranua** Fin.
78 B2 **Ranyah, Wādī** *watercourse*
 Saudi Arabia
136 C2 **Rapid City** U.S.A.
88 B2 **Rapla** Estonia
74 A2 **Rapur** India
153 B5 **Rasa, Punta** *pt* Arg.
79 C2 **Ra's al Khaymah** U.A.E.
117 B3 **Ras Dashen** *mt.* Eth.
88 B2 **Raseiniai** Lith.
81 C2 **Rasht** Iran
74 A2 **Ras Koh** *mt.* Pak.
88 C2 **Rasony** Belarus
87 D3 **Rasskazovo** Rus. Fed.
79 C2 **Ras Tannūrah** Saudi Arabia
101 D1 **Rastede** Ger.
93 F3 **Rätan** Sweden
74 B2 **Ratangarh** India
63 A2 **Rat Buri** Thai.
62 A1 **Rathedaung** Myanmar
101 F1 **Rathenow** Ger.
97 C1 **Rathlin Island** U.K.
74 B2 **Ratlam** India
73 B3 **Ratnagiri** India
73 C4 **Ratnapura** Sri Lanka
90 A1 **Ratne** Ukr.
138 C1 **Raton** U.S.A.
96 D2 **Rattray Head** *hd* U.K.
101 E1 **Ratzeburg** Ger.
92 □B2 **Raufarhöfn** Iceland
54 C1 **Raukumara Range** *mts* N.Z.
93 H3 **Rauma** Fin.
61 C2 **Raung, Gunung** *vol.* Indon.
75 C2 **Raurkela** India
134 D1 **Ravalli** U.S.A.
81 C2 **Rāvansar** Iran
108 B2 **Ravenna** Italy
102 B2 **Ravensburg** Ger.
74 B1 **Ravi** *r.* Pak.
74 B1 **Rawalpindi** Pak.
103 D1 **Rawicz** Pol.
50 B3 **Rawlinna** Austr.
136 B2 **Rawlins** U.S.A.
153 B5 **Rawson** Arg.
73 C3 **Rāyagarha** India
69 E1 **Raychikhinsk** Rus. Fed.
78 B3 **Raydah** Yemen
87 E3 **Rayevskiy** Rus. Fed.
134 B1 **Raymond** U.S.A.
53 D2 **Raymond Terrace** Austr.
139 D3 **Raymondville** U.S.A.
145 C2 **Rayón** Mex.
63 B2 **Rayong** Thai.
78 A2 **Rayyis** Saudi Arabia
104 B2 **Raz, Pointe du** *pt* France
81 C2 **Razāzah, Buḩayrat ar** *l.* Iraq
110 C2 **Razgrad** Bulg.
110 C2 **Razim, Lacul** *lag.* Romania
110 B2 **Razlog** Bulg.
104 B2 **Ré, Île de** *i.* France
99 C3 **Reading** U.K.
141 D2 **Reading** U.S.A.
115 E2 **Rebiana Sand Sea** *des.*
 Libya
66 D1 **Rebun-tō** *i.* Japan
50 B3 **Recherche, Archipelago of**
 the *is* Austr.
89 D3 **Rechytsa** Belarus
151 E2 **Recife** Brazil
123 C3 **Recife, Cape** S. Africa
100 C2 **Recklinghausen** Ger.
152 C3 **Reconquista** Arg.
142 B2 **Red** *r.* U.S.A.
131 E1 **Red Bay** Can.
135 B2 **Red Bluff** U.S.A.
98 C1 **Redcar** U.K.
51 D2 **Redcliff** Can.
52 B2 **Red Cliffs** Austr.

128 C2 **Red Deer** Can.
126 D3 **Red Deer** *r.* Can.
129 D2 **Red Deer Lake** Can.
134 B2 **Redding** U.S.A.
99 C2 **Redditch** U.K.
137 D2 **Redfield** U.S.A.
130 A1 **Red Lake** Can.
137 E1 **Red Lakes** U.S.A.
134 E1 **Red Lodge** U.S.A.
134 B2 **Redmond** U.S.A.
137 D2 **Red Oak** U.S.A.
106 B2 **Redondo** Port.
159 B2 **Red Sea** Africa/Asia
128 B1 **Redstone** *r.* Can.
137 E2 **Red Wing** U.S.A.
137 D2 **Redwood Falls** U.S.A.
97 C2 **Ree, Lough** *l.* Rep. of Ireland
134 B2 **Reedsport** U.S.A.
54 B2 **Reefton** N.Z.
102 C2 **Regen** Ger.
155 E1 **Regência** Brazil
102 C2 **Regensburg** Ger.
114 C2 **Reggane** Alg.
109 C3 **Reggio di Calabria** Italy
108 B2 **Reggio nell'Emilia** Italy
110 B1 **Reghin** Romania
129 D2 **Regina** Can.
122 A1 **Rehoboth** Namibia
101 D2 **Reichenbach** Ger.
143 E1 **Reidsville** U.S.A.
99 C3 **Reigate** U.K.
105 C2 **Reims** France
101 E1 **Reinbek** Ger.
129 D2 **Reindeer** *r.* Can.
129 E2 **Reindeer Island** Can.
129 D2 **Reindeer Lake** Can.
92 F2 **Reine** Norway
100 C3 **Reinsfeld** Ger.
123 C2 **Reitz** S. Africa
122 B2 **Reivilo** S. Africa
129 D1 **Reliance** Can.
107 D2 **Relizane** Alg.
79 C2 **Remeshk** Iran
105 D2 **Remiremont** France
100 C2 **Remscheid** Ger.
102 B1 **Rendsburg** Ger.
141 D1 **Renfrew** Can.
60 B2 **Rengat** Indon.
90 B2 **Reni** Ukr.
52 B2 **Renmark** Austr.
100 D2 **Rennerod** Ger.
104 B2 **Rennes** France
129 D1 **Rennie Lake** Can.
108 B2 **Reno** *r.* Italy
135 C3 **Reno** U.S.A.
70 A3 **Renshou** China
140 B2 **Rensselaer** U.S.A.
75 C2 **Renukut** India
54 B2 **Renwick** N.Z.
58 B3 **Reo** Indon.
136 D3 **Republican** *r.* U.S.A.
127 F2 **Repulse Bay** Can.
150 A2 **Requena** Peru
107 C2 **Requena** Spain
154 B2 **Reserva** Brazil
152 C3 **Resistencia** Arg.
110 B1 **Reşiţa** Romania
126 F2 **Resolute Bay** Can.
127 G2 **Resolution Island** Can.
105 C2 **Rethel** France
111 B3 **Rethymno** Greece
113 H6 **Réunion** *terr.* Indian Ocean
107 D1 **Reus** Spain
102 B2 **Reutlingen** Ger.
128 C2 **Revelstoke** Can.
144 A3 **Revillagigedo, Islas** *is* Mex.
128 A2 **Revillagigedo Island** U.S.A.
75 C2 **Rewa** India
134 D2 **Rexburg** U.S.A.
92 □A3 **Reykjanestá** *pt* Iceland

92 □A3 **Reykjavík** Iceland
145 C2 **Reynosa** Mex.
88 C2 **Rēzekne** Latvia
 Rhein *r.* Ger. *see* Rhine
100 C1 **Rheine** Ger.
101 F1 **Rheinsberg** Ger.
100 C2 **Rhin** *r.* France *see* Rhine
101 F1 **Rhine** *r.* Europe
140 B1 **Rhinelander** U.S.A.
101 F1 **Rhinluch** *marsh* Ger.
101 F1 **Rhinow** Ger.
141 E2 **Rhode Island** *state* U.S.A.
111 C3 **Rhodes** Greece
111 C3 **Rhodes** *i.* Greece
110 B2 **Rhodope Mountains**
 Bulg./Greece
105 C3 **Rhône** *r.* France/Switz.
 Rhuthun U.K. *see* Ruthin
98 B2 **Rhyl** U.K.
154 C1 **Rianópolis** Brazil
60 B1 **Riau, Kepulauan** *is* Indon.
106 B1 **Ribadeo** Spain
106 B1 **Ribadesella** Spain
154 B2 **Ribas do Rio Pardo** Brazil
121 C2 **Ribáuè** Moz.
98 B2 **Ribble** *r.* U.K.
154 C2 **Ribeira** *r.* Brazil
154 C2 **Ribeirão Preto** Brazil
104 C2 **Ribérac** France
152 B2 **Riberalta** Bol.
102 C1 **Ribnitz-Damgarten** Ger.
140 A1 **Rice Lake** U.S.A.
123 D2 **Richards Bay** S. Africa
126 B2 **Richardson Mountains** Can.
135 D3 **Richfield** U.S.A.
134 C1 **Richland** U.S.A.
140 A2 **Richland Center** U.S.A.
53 D2 **Richmond** *N.S.W.* Austr.
51 D2 **Richmond** *Qld* Austr.
54 B2 **Richmond** N.Z.
122 B3 **Richmond** S. Africa
98 C1 **Richmond** U.K.
140 C3 **Richmond** *IN* U.S.A.
140 C3 **Richmond** *KY* U.S.A.
141 D3 **Richmond** *VA* U.S.A.
130 C2 **Rideau Lakes** Can.
135 C3 **Ridgecrest** U.S.A.
102 C1 **Riesa** Ger.
100 D1 **Rieste** Ger.
123 B2 **Riet** *r.* S. Africa
101 D2 **Rietberg** Ger.
108 B2 **Rieti** Italy
136 B3 **Rifle** U.S.A.
88 B2 **Riga** Latvia
88 B2 **Riga, Gulf of** Estonia/Latvia
79 C2 **Rīgān** Iran
134 D2 **Rigby** U.S.A.
131 E1 **Rigolet** Can.
93 H3 **Riihimäki** Fin.
108 B1 **Rijeka** Croatia
134 C2 **Riley** U.S.A.
78 B2 **Rimah, Wādī al** *watercourse*
 Saudi Arabia
103 E2 **Rimavská Sobota** Slovakia
128 C2 **Rimbey** Can.
108 B2 **Rimini** Italy
131 D2 **Rimouski** Can.
93 F3 **Ringebu** Norway
93 E4 **Ringkøbing** Denmark
92 G2 **Ringvassøy** *i.* Norway
101 D1 **Rinteln** Ger.
150 A2 **Riobamba** Ecuador
150 B3 **Rio Branco** Brazil
154 C3 **Rio Branco do Sul** Brazil
154 C2 **Rio Brilhante** Brazil
154 C2 **Rio Claro** Brazil
153 B4 **Río Colorado** Arg.
153 B4 **Río Cuarto** Arg.
155 D2 **Rio de Janeiro** Brazil
153 B6 **Río Gallegos** Arg.

153 B6	Rio Grande Arg.
152 C4	Rio Grande Brazil
144 B2	Rio Grande Mex.
139 D3	Rio Grande r. Mex./U.S.A.
139 D3	Rio Grande City U.S.A.
150 A1	Riohacha Col.
150 A2	Rioja Peru
145 D2	Rio Lagartos Mex.
105 C2	Riom France
152 B2	Rio Mulatos Bol.
154 C3	Rio Negro Brazil
155 D1	Rio Pardo de Minas Brazil
138 B1	Rio Rancho U.S.A.
150 A2	Rio Tigre Ecuador
154 B1	Rio Verde Brazil
145 C2	Rio Verde Mex.
154 B1	Rio Verde de Mato Grosso Brazil
90 C1	Ripky Ukr.
98 C2	Ripley U.K.
107 D1	Ripoll Spain
98 C1	Ripon U.K.
66 D1	Rishiri-tō i. Japan
93 E4	Riser Norway
122 B2	Ritchie U.K.
63 A2	Ritchie's Archipelago is India
134 C1	Ritzville U.S.A.
153 B3	Rivadavia Arg.
108 B1	Riva del Garda Italy
146 B3	Rivas Nic.
152 C4	Rivera Uru.
129 D2	Riverhurst Can.
98 B2	Riverina reg. Austr.
122 B3	Riversdale S. Africa
135 C4	Riverside U.S.A.
136 B2	Riverton U.S.A.
131 D2	Riverview Can.
104 C3	Rivesaltes France
131 D2	Rivière-du-Loup Can.
90 B1	Rivne Ukr.
54 B2	Riwaka N.Z.
78 B2	Riyadh Saudi Arabia
81 C1	Rize Turkey
70 B2	Rizhao China
105 C2	Roanne France
141 D3	Roanoke U.S.A.
143 E1	Roanoke r. U.S.A.
143 E1	Roanoke Rapids U.S.A.
52 A3	Robe Austr.
101 F1	Röbel Ger.
92 H3	Robertsfors Sweden
122 A3	Robertson S. Africa
114 A4	Robertsport Liberia
128 C2	Roberval Can.
50 A2	Robinson Range hills Austr.
52 B2	Robinvale Austr.
129 D2	Roblin Can.
128 C2	Robson, Mount Can.
108 B3	Rocca Busambra mt. Sicily Italy
153 C4	Rocha Uru.
98 B2	Rochdale U.K.
154 B1	Rochedo Brazil
100 B2	Rochefort Belgium
104 B2	Rochefort France
137 E2	Rochester MN U.S.A.
141 E2	Rochester NH U.S.A.
141 D2	Rochester NY U.S.A.
140 B2	Rockford U.S.A.
51 E2	Rockhampton Austr.
143 D2	Rock Hill U.S.A.
50 A3	Rockingham Austr.
140 A2	Rock Island U.S.A.
136 B3	Rock Springs MT U.S.A.
133 C3	Rocksprings U.S.A.
136 B2	Rock Springs WY U.S.A.
136 C3	Rocky Ford U.S.A.
143 E1	Rocky Mount U.S.A.
128 C2	Rocky Mountain House Can.

124 D3	Rocky Mountains U.S.A.
100 B3	Rocroi France
102 C1	Rødbyhavn Denmark
131 E1	Roddickton Can.
104 C3	Rodez France
89 F2	Rodniki Rus. Fed.
	Rodos Greece see Rhodes
	Rodos i. Greece see Rhodes
50 A2	Roebourne Austr.
50 B1	Roebuck Bay Austr.
123 C1	Roedtan S. Africa
100 B2	Roermond Neth.
100 A2	Roeselare Belgium
127 F2	Roes Welcome Sound sea chan. Can.
142 B1	Rogers U.S.A.
122 B3	Roggeveldberge esc. S. Africa
92 G2	Rognan Norway
134 B2	Rogue r. U.S.A.
88 B2	Roja Latvia
60 B1	Rokan r. Indon.
88 C2	Rokiškis Lith.
90 B1	Rokytne Ukr.
154 B2	Rolândia Brazil
137 E3	Rolla U.S.A.
51 D2	Roma Austr.
59 C3	Roma i. Indon.
	Roma Italy see Rome
123 C2	Roma Lesotho
139 D3	Roma U.S.A.
143 E2	Romain, Cape U.S.A.
110 C1	Roman Romania
110 B1	Romania country Europe
91 C3	Roman-Kosh mt. Ukr.
69 D1	Romanovka Rus. Fed.
105 D2	Rombas France
64 B1	Romblon Phil.
108 B2	Rome Italy
143 C2	Rome GA U.S.A.
141 D2	Rome NY U.S.A.
99 D3	Romford U.K.
105 C2	Romilly-sur-Seine France
91 C1	Romny Ukr.
104 C2	Romorantin-Lanthenay France
99 C3	Romsey U.K.
96 □	Ronas Hill hill U.K.
151 D3	Roncador, Serra do hills Brazil
106 B2	Ronda Spain
154 B2	Rondon Brazil
154 B1	Rondonópolis Brazil
74 B1	Rondu Jammu and Kashmir
71 A3	Rong'an China
71 A3	Rongjiang China
62 A1	Rongklang Range mts Myanmar
	Rongmei China see Hefeng
93 F4	Rønne Denmark
55 P2	Ronne Ice Shelf Antarctica
101 D1	Ronnenberg Ger.
100 A2	Ronse Belgium
75 B2	Roorda huizum Neth.
100 B2	Roorkee India
100 B2	Roosendaal Neth.
135 E2	Roosevelt U.S.A.
55 K2	Roosevelt Island Antarctica
128 B2	Roosevelt, Mount Can.
104 B3	Roquefort France
150 B1	Roraima, Mount Guyana
93 F3	Røros Norway
153 B4	Rosario Arg.
144 A1	Rosario Baja California Norte Mex.
144 B2	Rosario Sinaloa Mex.
144 B2	Rosario Sonora Mex.
151 C3	Rosário Oeste Brazil
144 A2	Rosarito Mex.
109 C3	Rosarno Italy

104 B2	Roscoff France
97 B2	Roscommon Rep. of Ireland
97 C2	Roscrea Rep. of Ireland
147 D3	Roseau Dominica
137 D1	Roseau U.S.A.
134 B2	Roseburg U.S.A.
139 D3	Rosenberg U.S.A.
101 D1	Rosengarten Ger.
102 C2	Rosenheim Ger.
129 D2	Rosetown Can.
122 A2	Rosh Pinah Namibia
110 C2	Roșiori de Vede Romania
93 F4	Roskilde Denmark
89 D3	Roslavl' Rus. Fed.
109 C3	Rossano Italy
97 B1	Rossan Point Rep. of Ireland
55 K1	Ross Ice Shelf Antarctica
131 D2	Rossignol, Lake Can.
128 C3	Rossland Can.
97 C2	Rosslare Rep. of Ireland
114 A3	Rosso Maur.
105 D3	Rosso, Capo c. Corsica France
99 B3	Ross-on-Wye U.K.
91 D1	Rossosh' Rus. Fed.
128 A1	Ross River Can.
55 K2	Ross Sea Antarctica
92 F2	Røssvatnet l. Norway
79 C2	Rostāq Iran
129 D2	Rosthern Can.
102 C1	Rostock Ger.
89 E2	Rostov Rus. Fed.
91 D2	Rostov-na-Donu Rus. Fed.
92 H2	Rosvik Sweden
138 C2	Roswell U.S.A.
59 D2	Rota i. N. Mariana Is
59 C3	Rote i. Indon.
101 D1	Rotenburg (Wümme) Ger.
102 C2	Roth Ger.
98 C1	Rothbury U.K.
98 C2	Rotherham U.K.
96 C3	Rothesay U.K.
53 C2	Roto Austr.
105 D3	Rotondo, Monte mt. Corsica France
54 C1	Rotorua N.Z.
54 C1	Rotorua, Lake N.Z.
101 E2	Rottenbach Ger.
102 C2	Rottenmann Austria
100 B2	Rotterdam Neth.
102 B2	Rottweil Ger.
105 C1	Roubaix France
104 C2	Rouen France
	Roulers Belgium see Roeselare
53 D2	Round Mountain mt. Austr.
131 E2	Round Pond l. Can.
139 D2	Round Rock U.S.A.
134 E1	Roundup U.S.A.
96 C1	Rousay i. U.K.
130 C2	Rouyn Can.
92 I2	Rovaniemi Fin.
91 D2	Roven'ki Rus. Fed.
91 D2	Roven'ky Ukr.
108 B1	Rovereto Italy
63 B2	Rôviĕng Tbong Cambodia
108 B1	Rovigo Italy
108 B1	Rovinj Croatia
53 C1	Rowena Austr.
64 B2	Roxas Mindanao Phil.
64 B1	Roxas Mindoro Phil.
64 A1	Roxas Palawan Phil.
64 B1	Roxas Panay Phil.
52 A2	Roxby Downs Austr.
138 C1	Roy U.S.A.
140 B1	Royale, Isle i. U.S.A.
104 B2	Royan France
99 C2	Royston U.K.
90 C2	Rozdil'na Ukr.
91 C2	Rozdol'ne Ukr.

100 B3 Rozoy-sur-Serre France
87 D1 Rtishchevo Rus. Fed.
54 C1 Ruapehu, Mount *vol.* N.Z.
54 A3 Ruapuke Island N.Z.
78 B3 Rubʿ al Khālī *des.*
       Saudi Arabia
91 D2 Rubizhne Ukr.
77 E1 Rubtsovsk Rus. Fed.
135 C2 Ruby Mountains U.S.A.
66 C2 Rudnaya Pristanʾ
       Rus. Fed.
89 D3 Rudnya Rus. Fed.
76 C1 Rudnyy Kazakh.
82 E1 Rudolʾfa, Ostrov *i.*
       Rus. Fed.
101 E2 Rudolstadt Ger.
119 D3 Rufiji *r.* Tanz.
153 B4 Rufino Arg.
121 B2 Rufunsa Zambia
70 C2 Rugao China
99 C2 Rugby U.K.
136 C1 Rugby U.S.A.
102 C1 Rügen *i.* Ger.
101 E2 Ruhla Ger.
88 B2 Ruhnu *i.* Estonia
100 C2 Ruhr *r.* Ger.
71 C3 Ruiʾan China
138 B2 Ruidoso U.S.A.
144 B2 Ruiz Mex.
119 D3 Rukwa, Lake Tanz.
96 A2 Rum *i.* U.K.
109 C1 Ruma Yugo.
78 B2 Rumāh Saudi Arabia
117 A4 Rumbek Sudan
105 D2 Rumilly France
50 C1 Rum Jungle Austr.
54 B2 Runanga N.Z.
98 B2 Runcorn U.K.
120 A2 Rundu Namibia
68 B2 Ruoqiang China
130 C1 Rupert *r.* Can.
130 C1 Rupert Bay Can.
121 C2 Rusape Zimbabwe
110 C2 Ruse Bulg.
77 D3 Rushon Tajik.
136 C2 Rushville U.S.A.
53 C3 Rushworth Austr.
129 D2 Russell Can.
54 B1 Russell N.Z.
142 C2 Russellville AL U.S.A.
142 B1 Russellville AR U.S.A.
140 B3 Russellville KY U.S.A.
101 D2 Rüsselsheim Ger.
82 D3 Russian Federation *country*
       Asia/Europe
123 C2 Rustenburg S. Africa
142 B2 Ruston U.S.A.
98 B2 Ruthin U.K.
141 E2 Rutland U.S.A.
75 B1 Rutog China
119 E4 Ruvuma *r.* Moz./Tanz.
79 C2 Ruweis U.A.E.
77 C1 Ruzayevka Kazakh.
87 D3 Ruzayevka Rus. Fed.
119 D3 Rwanda *country* Africa
89 E3 Ryazanʾ Rus. Fed.
89 F3 Ryazhsk Rus. Fed.
86 C2 Rybachiy, Poluostrov *pen.*
       Rus. Fed.
89 E2 Rybinsk Rus. Fed.
89 E2 Rybinskoye
       Vodokhranilishche *resr*
       Rus. Fed.
103 D1 Rybnik Pol.
89 E3 Rybnoye Rus. Fed.
99 D3 Rye U.K.
89 D3 Rylʾsk Rus. Fed.
67 C3 Ryōtsu Japan
       Ryukyu Islands Japan *see*
       Nansei-shotō

103 E1 Rzeszów Pol.
89 D2 Rzhev Rus. Fed.

S

79 C2 Saʾādatābād Iran
101 E2 Saale *r.* Ger.
101 E2 Saalfeld Ger.
102 B2 Saarbrücken Ger.
88 B2 Saaremaa *i.* Estonia
92 I2 Saarenkylä Fin.
93 I3 Saarijärvi Fin.
102 B2 Saarlouis Ger.
80 B2 Sabʿ Ābār Syria
107 D1 Sabadell Spain
61 C1 Sabah *state* Malaysia
61 C2 Sabalana *i.* Indon.
155 D1 Sabará Brazil
108 B2 Sabaudia Italy
115 D2 Sabhā Libya
123 D2 Sabie r. Moz./S. Africa
145 B2 Sabinas Mex.
145 B2 Sabinas Hidalgo Mex.
131 D2 Sable, Cape Can.
143 D3 Sable, Cape U.S.A.
131 E2 Sable Island Can.
106 B1 Sabugal Port.
78 B3 Şabyā Saudi Arabia
76 B3 Sabzevār Iran
120 A2 Sachanga Angola
130 A1 Sachigo Lake *l.* Can.
65 B3 Sachʾon S. Korea
126 C2 Sachs Harbour Can.
135 B3 Sacramento U.S.A.
138 B2 Sacramento Mountains
       U.S.A.
135 B2 Sacramento Valley U.S.A.
123 C3 Sada S. Africa
107 C1 Sádaba Spain
78 B3 Saʾdah Yemen
62 A1 Sadiya India
67 C3 Sadoga-shima *i.* Japan
107 D2 Sa Dragonera *i.* Spain
93 F4 Säffle Sweden
138 B2 Safford U.S.A.
99 D2 Saffron Walden U.K.
86 B1 Safi Morocco
89 D2 Safonovo
       Arkhangelʾskaya Oblastʾ
       Rus. Fed.
89 D2 Safonovo
       Smolenskaya Oblastʾ
       Rus. Fed.
78 B2 Safrāʾ as Sark *esc.*
       Saudi Arabia
75 C2 Saga China
67 B4 Saga Japan
62 A1 Sagaing Myanmar
67 C3 Sagamihara Japan
75 B2 Sagar India
140 C2 Saginaw U.S.A.
140 C2 Saginaw Bay U.S.A.
106 B2 Sagres Port.
146 B2 Sagua la Grande Cuba
141 F1 Saguenay *r.* Can.
107 C2 Sagunto Spain
76 B2 Sagyndyk, Mys *pt* Kazakh.
106 B1 Sahagún Spain
114 C3 Sahara *des.* Africa
       Sahara el Gharbīya *des.*
       Egypt *see* Western Desert
       Sahara el Sharqīya *des.*
       Egypt *see* Eastern Desert
       Saharan Atlas *mts* Alg. *see*
       Atlas Saharien
75 B2 Saharanpur India
75 C2 Saharsa India

144 B2 Sahuayo Mex.
78 B2 Şāḩūq *reg.* Saudi Arabia
80 B2 Saïda Lebanon
75 C2 Saidpur Bangl.
       Saigon Vietnam *see*
       Hồ Chi Minh
62 A1 Saiha India
69 D2 Saihan Tal China
67 B4 Saiki Japan
93 I3 Saimaa *l.* Fin.
144 B2 Sain Alto Mex.
96 C3 St Abb's Head *hd* U.K.
99 C3 St Albans U.K.
99 B3 St Alban's Head *hd* U.K.
96 C2 St Andrews U.K.
100 B2 St Anthonis Neth.
131 E1 St Anthony Can.
134 D2 St Anthony U.S.A.
52 B3 St Arnaud Austr.
131 E1 St-Augustin Can.
131 E1 St-Augustin r. Can.
143 D3 St Augustine U.S.A.
99 A3 St Austell U.K.
104 C2 St-Avertin France
98 B1 St Bees Head *hd* U.K.
105 D3 St-Bonnet-en-Champsaur
       France
99 A3 St Bride's Bay U.K.
104 B2 St-Brieuc France
130 C2 St Catharines Can.
99 C3 St Catherine's Point U.K.
137 E3 St Charles U.S.A.
140 C2 St Clair, Lake Can./U.S.A.
105 D2 St-Claude France
137 E1 St Cloud U.S.A.
140 A1 St Croix r. U.S.A.
147 D3 St Croix Island *i.*
       Virgin Is (U.S.A.)
105 C2 St-Dizier France
131 D2 Ste-Anne-des-Monts Can.
105 D2 Ste-Égrève France
126 B2 St Elias Mountains Can.
131 D1 Ste Marguerite r. Can.
129 E2 Ste Rose du Lac Can.
104 B2 Saintes France
105 C2 St-Étienne France
108 A2 St-Florent Corsica France
105 C2 St-Flour France
136 C3 St Francis U.S.A.
105 D2 St Gallen Switz.
104 C3 St-Gaudens France
53 C1 St George Austr.
135 D3 St George U.S.A.
143 D3 St George Island U.S.A.
131 C2 St-Georges Can.
147 D3 St George's Grenada
97 C3 St George's Channel
       Rep. of Ireland/U.K.
112 C5 St Helena *terr.*
       S. Atlantic Ocean
122 A3 St Helena S. Africa
122 A3 St Helena Bay *b.* S. Africa
98 B2 St Helens U.K.
134 B1 St Helens, Mount *vol.* U.S.A.
95 C4 St Helier Channel Is
100 B2 St-Hubert Belgium
141 E1 St-Hyacinthe Can.
140 C1 St Ignace U.S.A.
130 B2 St Ignace Island Can.
99 A3 St Ives U.K.
128 A2 St James, Cape Can.
131 C2 St-Jean, Lac *l.* Can.
104 B2 St-Jean-d'Angély France
104 B2 St-Jean-de-Monts France
104 D2 St-Jean-sur-Richelieu Can.
141 E1 St-Jérôme Can.
135 C1 St Joe *r.* U.S.A.
131 D2 St John Can.
141 F1 St John *r.* Can.
147 D3 St John's Antigua

131 E2	St John's Can.
138 B2	St Johns U.S.A.
141 E2	St Johnsbury U.S.A.
137 E3	St Joseph U.S.A.
130 A1	St Joseph, Lake Can.
130 B2	St Joseph Island Can.
104 C2	St-Junien France
94 B2	St Kilda i. U.K.
147 D3	St Kitts and Nevis country West Indies
100 A2	St-Laureins Belgium
	St-Laurent, Golfe du Can. see St Lawrence, Gulf of
151 C1	St-Laurent-du-Maroni Fr. Guiana
131 D2	St Lawrence inlet Can.
131 D2	St Lawrence, Gulf of Can.
83 N2	St Lawrence Island U.S.A.
104 B2	St-Lô France
114 A3	St Louis Senegal
137 E3	St Louis U.S.A.
137 E1	St Louis r. U.S.A.
147 D3	St Lucia country West Indies
123 D2	St Lucia Estuary S. Africa
147 D3	St Maarten i. West Indies
104 B2	St-Malo France
104 B2	St-Malo, Golfe de g. France
122 A3	St Martin, Cap S. Africa
141 D2	St Marys U.S.A.
130 C2	St Maurice r. Can.
105 D2	St Moritz Switz.
104 B2	St-Nazaire France
100 B2	St-Niklaas Belgium
104 C1	St-Omer France
129 C2	St Paul Can.
137 E2	St Paul U.S.A.
137 E2	St Peter U.S.A.
95 C4	St Peter Port Channel Is
89 D2	St Petersburg Rus. Fed.
143 D3	St Petersburg U.S.A.
131 E2	St-Pierre St Pierre and Miquelon
131 E2	St Pierre and Miquelon terr. N. America
104 B2	St-Pierre-d'Oléron France
105 C2	St-Pourçain-sur-Sioule France
131 D2	St Quentin Can.
105 C2	St-Quentin France
131 D2	St Siméon Can.
129 C2	St Theresa Point Can.
130 B2	St Thomas Can.
105 D3	St-Tropez France
105 D3	St-Tropez, Cap de c. France
57 C6	St Veit an der Glan Austria
52 A3	St Vincent, Gulf Austr.
147 D3	St Vincent and the Grenadines i. West Indies
100 C2	St-Vith Belgium
129 C2	St Walburg Can.
100 C3	St Wendel Ger.
104 C2	St-Yrieix-la-Perche France
59 D1	Saipan i. N. Mariana Is
152 B2	Sajama, Nevado mt. Bol.
122 B2	Sak watercourse S. Africa
67 C4	Sakai Japan
67 B4	Sakaide Japan
78 B2	Sakākah Saudi Arabia
136 C1	Sakakawea, Lake U.S.A.
111 D2	Sakarya Turkey
111 D2	Sakarya r. Turkey
66 C3	Sakata Japan
65 C1	Sakchu N. Korea
83 K3	Sakhalin i. Rus. Fed.
123 C2	Sakhile S. Africa
81 C1	Şäki Azer.
88 B3	Šakiai Lith.
69 E3	Sakishima-shotō is Japan
62 B2	Sakon Nakhon Thai.
122 B3	Sakrivier S. Africa

67 D3	Sakura Japan
91 C2	Saky Ukr.
93 G4	Sala Sweden
130 C2	Salaberry-de-Valleyfield Can.
88 B2	Salacgrīva Latvia
109 C2	Sala Consilina Italy
135 C4	Salada, Laguna salt l. Mex.
152 B4	Salado r. Arg.
145 C2	Salado r. Mex.
114 B4	Salaga Ghana
122 B1	Salajwe Botswana
115 D3	Salal Chad
78 A2	Salālā Sudan
79 C3	Şalālah Oman
145 B2	Salamanca Mex.
106 B1	Salamanca Spain
106 B1	Salas Spain
59 C3	Salawati i. Indon.
58 C3	Salayar i. Indon.
148 B4	Sala y Gómez, Isla i. S. Pacific Ocean
104 C2	Salbris France
88 C3	Šalčininkai Lith.
106 C1	Saldaña Spain
122 A3	Saldanha S. Africa
88 B2	Saldus Latvia
53 C3	Sale Austr.
86 F2	Salekhard Rus. Fed.
73 B3	Salem India
137 E3	Salem MO U.S.A.
134 B2	Salem OR U.S.A.
96	Salem U.K.
109 B2	Salerno Italy
98 B2	Salford U.K.
151 E2	Salgado r. Brazil
103 D2	Salgótarján Hungary
151 E2	Salgueiro Brazil
136 B3	Salida U.S.A.
111 C3	Salihli Turkey
88 C3	Salihorsk Belarus
121 C2	Salima Malawi
121 C2	Salimo Moz.
137 D3	Salina U.S.A.
108 B3	Salina, Isola i. Italy
145 C3	Salina Cruz Mex.
155 D1	Salinas Brazil
144 B2	Salinas Mex.
135 B3	Salinas U.S.A.
151 D2	Salinópolis Brazil
99 C3	Salisbury U.K.
141 D3	Salisbury MD U.S.A.
143 D1	Salisbury NC U.S.A.
151 D2	Salitre r. Brazil
92 I2	Salla Fin.
127 F2	Salluit Can.
75 C2	Sallyana Nepal
81 C2	Salmās Iran
134 D1	Salmon U.S.A.
134 C1	Salmon r. U.S.A.
128 C2	Salmon Arm Can.
134 C2	Salmon River Mountains U.S.A.
100 C3	Salmtal Ger.
93 H3	Salo Fin.
87 D4	Sal'sk Rus. Fed.
122 B3	Salt watercourse S. Africa
138 A2	Salt r. U.S.A.
152 B3	Salta Arg.
145 B2	Saltillo Mex.
134 D2	Salt Lake City U.S.A.
154 C2	Salto Brazil
152 C4	Salto Uru.
155 E1	Salto da Divisa Brazil
154 B2	Salto del Guairá Para.
135 C4	Salton Sea salt l. U.S.A.
143 D2	Saluda U.S.A.
108 A2	Saluzzo Italy
151 E3	Salvador Brazil

79 C2	Salwah Saudi Arabia
62 A2	Salween r. Myanmar
81 C2	Salyan Azer.
102 C2	Salzburg Austria
101 E1	Salzgitter Ger.
101 D2	Salzkotten Ger.
101 E1	Salzwedel Ger.
144 B1	Samalayuca Mex.
66 D2	Samani Japan
64 B1	Samar i. Phil.
87 E3	Samara Rus. Fed.
61 C2	Samarinda Indon.
77 C3	Samarkand Uzbek.
81 C2	Sāmarrā' Iraq
81 C1	Şamaxı Azer.
119 C3	Samba Dem. Rep. Congo
61 C1	Sambaliung mts Indon.
75 C2	Sambalpur India
61 C2	Sambar, Tanjung pt Indon.
61 B1	Sambas Indon.
121 □E2	Sambava Madag.
90 A2	Sambir Ukr.
153 C4	Samborombón, Bahía b. Arg.
65 B2	Samch'ŏk S. Korea
81 C2	Samdi Dag mt. Turkey
119 D3	Same Tanz.
78 B2	Samirah Saudi Arabia
65 B1	Samjiyŏn N. Korea
49 G4	Samoa country S. Pacific Ocean
109 C1	Samobor Croatia
111 C3	Samos i. Greece
111 C2	Samothraki Greece
111 C2	Samothraki i. Greece
61 C2	Sampit Indon.
119 C3	Sampwe Dem. Rep. Congo
139 E2	Sam Rayburn Reservoir U.S.A.
80 B1	Samsun Turkey
81 C1	Samtredia Georgia
63 B3	Samui, Ko i. Thai.
63 B2	Samut Songkhram Thai.
114 B3	San Mali
78 B3	Şan'ā' Yemen
118 A2	Sanaga r. Cameroon
81 C2	Sanandaj Iran
146 B3	San Andrés, Isla de i. Caribbean Sea
138 B2	San Andres Mountains U.S.A.
145 C3	San Andrés Tuxtla Mex.
139 C2	San Angelo U.S.A.
139 D3	San Antonio U.S.A.
135 C4	San Antonio, Mount U.S.A.
107 D2	San Antonio Abad Spain
152 B3	San Antonio de los Cobres Arg.
153 B5	San Antonio Oeste Arg.
108 B2	San Benedetto del Tronto Italy
144 A3	San Benedicto, Isla i. Mex.
135 C4	San Bernardino U.S.A.
135 C4	San Bernardino Mountains U.S.A.
143 C3	San Blas, Cape U.S.A.
152 B2	San Borja Bol.
144 B2	San Buenaventura Mex.
64 B1	San Carlos Phil.
147 D4	San Carlos Venez.
153 A5	San Carlos de Bariloche Arg.
147 C4	San Carlos del Zulia Venez.
135 C4	San Clemente Island U.S.A.
104 C2	Sancoins France
150 A1	San Cristóbal Venez.
145 C3	San Cristóbal de las Casas Mex.
146 C2	Sancti Spíritus Cuba
123 D1	Sand r. S. Africa

61 C1	**Sandakan** *Sabah* Malaysia	
93 E3	**Sandane** Norway	
111 B2	**Sandanski** Bulg.	
96 C1	**Sanday** *i.* U.K.	
139 C2	**Sanderson** U.S.A.	
150 B3	**Sandia** Peru	
135 C4	**San Diego** U.S.A.	
80 B2	**Sandıklı** Turkey	
93 E4	**Sandnes** Norway	
92 F2	**Sandnessjøen** Norway	
118 C3	**Sandoa** Dem. Rep. Congo	
103 E1	**Sandomierz** Pol.	
89 E2	**Sandovo** Rus. Fed.	
62 A2	**Sandoway** Myanmar	
94 B1	**Sandoy** *i.* Faroe Is	
134 C1	**Sandpoint** U.S.A.	
71 B3	**Sandu** China	
94 B1	**Sandur** Faroe Is	
140 C2	**Sandusky** U.S.A.	
122 A3	**Sandveld** *mts* S. Africa	
93 F4	**Sandvika** Norway	
93 G3	**Sandviken** Sweden	
131 E1	**Sandwich Bay** Can.	
129 D2	**Sandy Bay** Can.	
51 E2	**Sandy Cape** Austr.	
130 A1	**Sandy Lake** Can.	
130 A1	**Sandy Lake** *l.* Can.	
144 A1	**San Felipe** *Baja California Norte* Mex.	
145 B2	**San Felipe** *Guanajuato* Mex.	
150 B1	**San Felipe** Venez.	
144 A2	**San Fernando** *Baja California Norte* Mex.	
145 C2	**San Fernando** *Tamaulipas* Mex.	
64 B1	**San Fernando** *Luzon* Phil.	
64 B1	**San Fernando** *Luzon* Phil.	
106 B2	**San Fernando** Spain	
147 D3	**San Fernando** Trin. and Tob.	
150 B1	**San Fernando de Apure** Venez.	
143 D3	**Sanford** *FL* U.S.A.	
141 E2	**Sanford** *ME* U.S.A.	
152 B4	**San Francisco** Arg.	
135 B3	**San Francisco** U.S.A.	
107 D2	**San Francisco Javier** Spain	
74 B3	**Sangamner** India	
83 J2	**Sangar** Rus. Fed.	
108 A3	**San Gavino Monreale** *Sardinia* Italy	
101 E2	**Sangerhausen** Ger.	
61 C1	**Sanggau** Indon.	
118 B3	**Sangha** *r.* Congo	
109 C3	**San Giovanni in Fiore** Italy	
64 B2	**Sangir** *i.* Indon.	
59 C2	**Sangir, Kepulauan** *is* Indon.	
65 B2	**Sangju** S. Korea	
61 C1	**Sangkulirang** Indon.	
73 B3	**Sangli** India	
118 B2	**Sangmélima** Cameroon	
121 C3	**Sango** Zimbabwe	
105 D2	**San Gottardo, Passo del** *pass* Switz.	
136 B3	**Sangre de Cristo Range** *mts* U.S.A.	
75 C2	**Sangsang** China	
144 A2	**San Hipólito, Punta** *pt* Mex.	
144 A2	**San Ignacio** Mex.	
130 C1	**Sanikiluaq** Can.	
71 A3	**Sanjiang** China	
135 B3	**San Joaquín** *r.* U.S.A.	
153 B5	**San Jorge, Golfo de** *g.* Arg.	
146 B4	**San José** Costa Rica	
64 B1	**San Jose** *Luzon* Phil.	
64 B1	**San Jose** *Mindoro* Phil.	
135 B3	**San Jose** U.S.A.	
144 A2	**San José, Isla** *i.* Mex.	
144 B2	**San José de Bavicora** Mex.	
64 B1	**San Jose de Buenavista** Phil.	

144 A2	**San José de Comondú** Mex.	
144 B2	**San José del Cabo** Mex.	
150 A1	**San José del Guaviare** Col.	
152 B4	**San Juan** Arg.	
146 B3	**San Juan** *r.* Costa Rica/Nic.	
147 D3	**San Juan** Puerto Rico	
135 D3	**San Juan** *r.* U.S.A.	
107 D2	**San Juan Bautista** Spain	
145 C3	**San Juan Bautista Tuxtepec** Mex.	
134 B1	**San Juan Islands** U.S.A.	
144 B2	**San Juanito** Mex.	
136 B3	**San Juan Mountains** U.S.A.	
153 B5	**San Julián** Arg.	
75 C2	**Sankh** *r.* India	
	Sankt-Peterburg Rus. Fed. *see* St Petersburg	
80 B2	**Şanlıurfa** Turkey	
138 B3	**San Lorenzo** Mex.	
106 B2	**Sanlúcar de Barrameda** Spain	
144 B2	**San Lucas** Mex.	
153 B4	**San Luis** Arg.	
145 B2	**San Luis de la Paz** Mex.	
138 A2	**San Luisito** Mex.	
135 B3	**San Luis Obispo** U.S.A.	
145 B2	**San Luis Potosí** Mex.	
144 A1	**San Luis Río Colorado** Mex.	
139 D3	**San Marcos** U.S.A.	
108 B2	**San Marino** *country* Europe	
108 B2	**San Marino** San Marino	
144 B2	**San Martín de Bolaños** Mex.	
153 A5	**San Martín de los Andes** Arg.	
153 B5	**San Matías, Golfo** *g.* Arg.	
70 B2	**Sanmenxia** China	
146 B3	**San Miguel** El Salvador	
152 B3	**San Miguel de Tucumán** Arg.	
145 C3	**San Miguel Sola de Vega** Mex.	
71 B3	**Sanming** China	
153 B4	**San Nicolás de los Arroyos** Arg.	
135 C4	**San Nicolas Island** U.S.A.	
123 C2	**Sannieshof** S. Africa	
103 E2	**Sanok** Pol.	
64 B1	**San Pablo** Phil.	
144 B2	**San Pablo Balleza** Mex.	
152 B3	**San Pedro** Arg.	
114 B4	**San-Pédro** Côte d'Ivoire	
144 A2	**San Pedro** Mex.	
138 A2	**San Pedro** *watercourse* U.S.A.	
106 B2	**San Pedro, Sierra de** *mts* Spain	
144 B2	**San Pedro de las Colonias** Mex.	
146 B3	**San Pedro Sula** Hond.	
108 A3	**San Pietro, Isola di** *i.* *Sardinia* Italy	
144 A1	**San Quintín, Cabo** *c.* Mex.	
153 B4	**San Rafael** Arg.	
108 A2	**San Remo** Italy	
146 B3	**San Salvador** El Salvador	
152 B3	**San Salvador de Jujuy** Arg.	
109 C2	**San Severo** Italy	
109 C2	**Sanski Most** Bos.-Herz.	
152 B2	**Santa Ana** Bol.	
146 B3	**Santa Ana** El Salvador	
144 A1	**Santa Ana** Mex.	
135 C4	**Santa Ana** U.S.A.	
144 B2	**Santa Bárbara** Mex.	
135 C4	**Santa Barbara** U.S.A.	
154 B2	**Santa Bárbara, Serra de** *hills* Brazil	
152 B3	**Santa Catalina** Chile	
150 B2	**Santa Clara** Col.	

146 C2	**Santa Clara** Cuba	
135 C4	**Santa Clarita** U.S.A.	
109 C3	**Santa Croce, Capo** *c.* *Sicily* Italy	
153 B6	**Santa Cruz** *r.* Arg.	
152 B2	**Santa Cruz** Bol.	
64 B1	**Santa Cruz** Phil.	
135 B3	**Santa Cruz** U.S.A.	
145 C3	**Santa Cruz Barillas** Guat.	
155 E1	**Santa Cruz Cabrália** Brazil	
107 C2	**Santa Cruz de Moya** Spain	
114 A2	**Santa Cruz de Tenerife** Canary Is	
135 C4	**Santa Cruz Island** U.S.A.	
152 B4	**Santa Fé** Arg.	
138 B1	**Santa Fe** U.S.A.	
154 B1	**Santa Helena de Goiás** Brazil	
153 B4	**Santa Isabel** Arg.	
154 B1	**Santa Luisa, Serra de** *hills* Brazil	
152 C3	**Santa Maria** Brazil	
144 B1	**Santa María** *r.* Mex.	
135 B4	**Santa Maria** U.S.A.	
123 D2	**Santa Maria, Cabo de** *c.* Moz.	
106 B2	**Santa Maria, Cabo de** *c.* Port.	
151 D2	**Santa Maria das Barreiras** Brazil	
109 C3	**Santa Maria di Leuca, Capo** *c.* Italy	
150 A1	**Santa Marta** Col.	
135 C4	**Santa Monica** U.S.A.	
151 D3	**Santana** Brazil	
106 C1	**Santander** Spain	
108 A3	**Sant'Antioco** *Sardinia* Italy	
108 A3	**Sant'Antioco, Isola di** *i.* *Sardinia* Italy	
151 C2	**Santarém** Brazil	
106 B2	**Santarém** Port.	
154 B1	**Santa Rita do Araguaia** Brazil	
153 B4	**Santa Rosa** Arg.	
152 C3	**Santa Rosa** Brazil	
135 B3	**Santa Rosa** *CA* U.S.A.	
138 C2	**Santa Rosa** *NM* U.S.A.	
146 B3	**Santa Rosa de Copán** Hond.	
135 B4	**Santa Rosa Island** U.S.A.	
144 A2	**Santa Rosalía** Mex.	
152 C3	**Santiago** Brazil	
153 A4	**Santiago** Chile	
147 C3	**Santiago** Dom. Rep.	
144 B2	**Santiago** Mex.	
146 B4	**Santiago** Panama	
64 B1	**Santiago** Phil.	
106 B1	**Santiago de Compostela** Spain	
144 B2	**Santiago Ixcuintla** Mex.	
144 B2	**Santiago Papasquiaro** Mex.	
107 D1	**Sant Jordi, Golf de** *g.* Spain	
155 D2	**Santo Amaro de Campos** Brazil	
155 C2	**Santo André** Brazil	
152 C3	**Santo Ângelo** Brazil	
154 B2	**Santo Antônio da Platina** Brazil	
151 E3	**Santo Antônio de Jesus** Brazil	
150 B2	**Santo Antônio do Içá** Brazil	
155 C2	**Santo Antônio do Monte** Brazil	
147 D3	**Santo Domingo** Dom. Rep.	
138 B1	**Santo Domingo Pueblo** U.S.A.	
111 C3	**Santorini** *i.* Greece	
155 C2	**Santos** Brazil	
152 C3	**Santo Tomé** Arg.	
153 A5	**San Valentín, Cerro** *mt.* Chile	

146 B3 San Vicente El Salvador
144 A1 San Vicente Mex.
150 A3 San Vicente de Cañete Peru
108 B2 San Vincenzo Italy
108 B3 San Vito, Capo c. Sicily Italy
71 A4 Sanya China
155 C2 São Bernardo do Campo Brazil
152 C3 São Borja Brazil
154 C3 São Carlos Brazil
153 D1 São Félix Mato Grosso Brazil
151 C2 São Félix Pará Brazil
155 D2 São Fidélis Brazil
155 D1 São Francisco Brazil
151 E3 São Francisco r. Brazil
154 C3 São Francisco, Ilha de i. Brazil
154 C3 São Francisco do Sul Brazil
152 C4 São Gabriel Brazil
155 D2 São Gonçalo Brazil
155 C1 São Gotardo Brazil
155 D2 São João da Barra Brazil
155 C2 São João da Boa Vista Brazil
106 B1 São João da Madeira Port.
155 D1 São João do Paraíso Brazil
155 D2 São João Nepomuceno Brazil
154 C2 São Joaquim da Barra Brazil
154 C2 São José do Rio Preto Brazil
155 C3 São José dos Campos Brazil
154 C3 São José dos Pinhais Brazil
155 C2 São Lourenço Brazil
151 C2 São Luís Brazil
154 C2 São Manuel Brazil
154 C1 São Marcos r. Brazil
151 D2 São Marcos, Baía de b. Brazil
155 E1 São Mateus Brazil
155 C2 São Paulo Brazil
151 D2 São Raimundo Nonato Brazil
155 C1 São Romão Brazil
155 C2 São Sebastião, Ilha do i. Brazil
154 C2 São Sebastião do Paraíso Brazil
154 B1 São Simão Brazil
154 B1 São Simão, Barragem de resr Brazil
59 C2 Sao-Siu Indon.
155 D2 São Tomé, Cabo de c. Brazil
112 D3 São Tomé and Principe country Africa
155 C2 São Vicente Brazil
106 B3 São Vicente, Cabo de c. Port.
59 C3 Saparua Indon.
89 F3 Sapozhok Rus. Fed.
66 D2 Sapporo Japan
109 C2 Sapri Italy
81 C3 Saqqez Iran
81 D3 Sarāb Iran
63 B2 Sara Buri Thai.
109 C2 Sarajevo Bos.-Herz.
76 B1 Saraktash Rus. Fed.
141 E2 Saranac Lake U.S.A.
109 D3 Sarandë Albania
64 B2 Sarangani Islands Phil.
87 E3 Saransk Rus. Fed.
87 E3 Sarapul Rus. Fed.
143 D3 Sarasota U.S.A.
90 B2 Sarata Ukr.
136 B2 Saratoga U.S.A.
141 E2 Saratoga Springs U.S.A.
61 C1 Saratok Sarawak Malaysia

87 D3 Saratov Rus. Fed.
79 D2 Saravan Iran
63 B2 Saravan Laos
61 C1 Sarawak state Malaysia
110 C2 Saray Turkey
111 C3 Sarayköy Turkey
79 D2 Sarbāz Iran
74 B2 Sardarshahr India
Sardegna i. Italy see Sardinia
108 A2 Sardinia i. Italy
92 G2 Sarektjåkkå mt. Sweden
77 C3 Sar-e Pol Afgh.
158 B3 Sargasso Sea Atlantic Ocean
74 B1 Sargodha Pak.
115 D4 Sarh Chad
79 D2 Sarhad reg. Iran
81 D2 Sārī Iran
111 C3 Sarigöl Turkey
81 C1 Sarıkamış Turkey
61 C1 Sarikei Sarawak Malaysia
51 D2 Sarina Austr.
115 D2 Sarīr Tibesti des. Libya
65 B2 Sariwŏn N. Korea
111 C2 Sarıyer Turkey
77 D2 Sarkand Kazakh.
111 C2 Şarköy Turkey
59 D3 Sarmi Indon.
140 C2 Sarnia Can.
90 B1 Sarny Ukr.
60 B2 Sarolangun Indon.
111 B3 Saronikos Kolpos g. Greece
111 C2 Saros Körfezi b. Turkey
87 D3 Sarova Rus. Fed.
105 D2 Sarrebourg France
106 B1 Sarria Spain
107 C1 Sarrión Spain
105 D3 Sartène Corsica France
103 D2 Sárvár Hungary
76 B2 Sarykamyshkoye Ozero salt l. Turkm./Uzbek.
77 D2 Saryozek Kazakh.
77 D2 Saryshagan Kazakh.
82 F3 Sarysu watercourse Kazakh.
77 D3 Sary-Tash Kyrg.
75 C2 Sasaram India
67 A4 Sasebo Japan
129 D2 Saskatchewan prov. Can.
129 D2 Saskatchewan r. Can.
129 D2 Saskatoon Can.
83 I2 Saskylakh Rus. Fed.
123 C2 Sasolburg S. Africa
87 D3 Sasovo Rus. Fed.
114 B4 Sassandra Côte d'Ivoire
108 A2 Sassari Sardinia Italy
102 C1 Sassnitz Ger.
114 A3 Satadougou Mali
123 D1 Satara S. Africa
75 C2 Satna India
74 B2 Satpura Range mts India
63 B2 Sattahip Thai.
110 B1 Satu Mare Romania
63 B3 Satun Thai.
144 B2 Saucillo Mex.
93 E4 Sauda Norway
92 □B2 Sauðárkrókur Iceland
78 B2 Saudi Arabia country Asia
105 C3 Saugues France
105 C2 Saulieu France
130 B2 Sault Ste Marie Can.
140 C1 Sault Ste Marie U.S.A.
77 C1 Saumalkol' Kazakh.
59 C3 Saumlakki Indon.
104 B2 Saumur France
120 B1 Saurimo Angola
102 D2 Sava r. Europe
91 E1 Savala r. Rus. Fed.
143 D2 Savannah GA U.S.A.
142 C1 Savannah TN U.S.A.
143 D2 Savannah r. U.S.A.
63 B2 Savannakhét Laos

130 A1 Savant Lake l. Can.
111 C3 Savaştepe Turkey
89 F2 Savino Rus. Fed.
86 D2 Savinskiy Rus. Fed.
108 A2 Savona Italy
93 I3 Savonlinna Fin.
92 I2 Savukoski Fin.
74 B2 Sawai Madhopur India
62 A2 Sawankhalok Thai.
136 B3 Sawatch Range mts U.S.A.
53 D2 Sawtell Austr.
59 C3 Sawu Sea Indon.
79 C3 Sayhūt Yemen
69 D2 Saynshand Mongolia
141 D2 Sayre U.S.A.
144 B3 Sayula Jalisco Mex.
145 C3 Sayula Veracruz Mex.
128 B2 Sayward Can.
89 E2 Sazonovo Rus. Fed.
114 B2 Sbaa Alg.
98 B1 Scafell Pike hill U.K.
109 C3 Scalea Italy
96 C1 Scapa Flow inlet U.K.
130 C2 Scarborough Can.
147 D3 Scarborough Trin. and Tob.
98 C1 Scarborough U.K.
64 A1 Scarborough Shoal sea feature Phil.
96 A2 Scarinish U.K.
Scarpanto i. Greece see Karpathos
105 D2 Schaffhausen Switz.
100 B1 Schagen Neth.
102 C2 Schärding Austria
100 A2 Scharendijke Neth.
101 D1 Scharhörn sea feature Ger.
101 D1 Scheeßel Ger.
131 D1 Schefferville Can.
135 D3 Schell Creek Range mts U.S.A.
141 E2 Schenectady U.S.A.
101 E3 Scheßlitz Ger.
100 C1 Schiermonnikoog i. Neth.
108 B1 Schio Italy
101 F2 Schkeuditz Ger.
101 E1 Schladen Ger.
101 E2 Schleiz Ger.
102 B1 Schleswig Ger.
101 D2 Schloß Holte-Stukenbrock Ger.
101 D2 Schlüchtern Ger.
101 E2 Schlüsselfeld Ger.
100 C1 Schmallenberg Ger.
101 D1 Schneverdingen Ger.
101 E1 Schönebeck (Elbe) Ger.
101 D1 Schöningen Ger.
100 B2 Schoonhoven Neth.
59 D3 Schouten Islands P.N.G.
102 C2 Schwandorf Ger.
61 C2 Schwaner, Pegunungan mts Indon.
101 E1 Schwarzenbek Ger.
101 F2 Schwarzenberg Ger.
122 A2 Schwarzrand mts Namibia
102 C2 Schwaz Austria
102 C1 Schwedt an der Oder Ger.
101 E2 Schweinfurt Ger.
101 E1 Schwerin Ger.
101 E1 Schweriner See l. Ger.
105 D2 Schwyz Switz.
108 B3 Sciacca Sicily Italy
95 B4 Scilly, Isles of U.K.
140 C3 Scioto r. U.S.A.
136 B1 Scobey U.S.A.
53 D2 Scone Austr.
55 R3 Scotia Ridge sea feature S. Atlantic Ocean
158 C8 Scotia Sea S. Atlantic Ocean
96 C2 Scotland admin. div. U.K.
128 B2 Scott, Cape Can.

123 D3	**Scottburgh** S. Africa	
136 C3	**Scott City** U.S.A.	
136 C3	**Scottsbluff** U.S.A.	
142 C2	**Scottsboro** U.S.A.	
96 B1	**Scourie** U.K.	
141 D2	**Scranton** U.S.A.	
98 C2	**Scunthorpe** U.K.	
105 E2	**Scuol** Switz.	
129 E2	**Seal** r. Can.	
122 B3	**Seal, Cape** S. Africa	
52 B3	**Sea Lake** Austr.	
139 D3	**Sealy** U.S.A.	
142 B1	**Searcy** U.S.A.	
98 B1	**Seascale** U.K.	
134 B1	**Seattle** U.S.A.	
141 E2	**Sebago Lake** U.S.A.	
144 A2	**Sebastián Vizcaíno, Bahía** b. Mex.	
110 B1	**Sebeş** Romania	
60 B2	**Sebesi** i. Indon.	
88 C2	**Sebezh** Rus. Fed.	
80 B1	**Şebinkarahisar** Turkey	
143 D3	**Sebring** U.S.A.	
128 B3	**Sechelt** Can.	
150 A2	**Sechura** Peru	
73 B3	**Secunderabad** India	
137 E3	**Sedalia** U.S.A.	
105 C2	**Sedan** France	
54 B2	**Seddon** N.Z.	
138 A2	**Sedona** U.S.A.	
101 E2	**Seeburg** Ger.	
101 E1	**Seehausen (Altmark)** Ger.	
122 A2	**Seeheim** Namibia	
104 C2	**Sées** France	
101 E2	**Seesen** Ger.	
101 E1	**Seevetal** Ger.	
114 A4	**Sefadu** Sierra Leone	
123 C1	**Sefare** Botswana	
60 B1	**Segamat** Malaysia	
86 C2	**Segezha** Rus. Fed.	
114 B3	**Ségou** Mali	
106 C1	**Segovia** Spain	
115 C2	**Séguédine** Niger	
114 B4	**Séguéla** Côte d'Ivoire	
139 D3	**Seguin** U.S.A.	
107 C2	**Segura** r. Spain	
106 C2	**Segura, Sierra de** mts Spain	
120 B3	**Sehithwa** Botswana	
93 H3	**Seinäjoki** Fin.	
104 C2	**Seine** r. France	
104 B2	**Seine, Baie de** b. France	
103 E1	**Sejny** Pol.	
60 B2	**Sekayu** Indon.	
114 B4	**Sekondi** Ghana	
59 C3	**Selaru** i. Indon.	
61 C2	**Selatan, Tanjung** pt Indon.	
126 A2	**Selawik** U.S.A.	
98 C2	**Selby** U.K.	
120 B3	**Selebi-Phikwe** Botswana	
105 D2	**Sélestat** France	
92 □A3	**Selfoss** Iceland	
114 A3	**Sélibabi** Maur.	
138 A1	**Seligman** U.S.A.	
116 A2	**Selima Oasis** Sudan	
111 C3	**Selimiye** Turkey	
114 B3	**Sélingué, Lac de** l. Mali	
83 C4	**Selizharovo** Rus. Fed.	
93 E4	**Seljord** Norway	
129 E2	**Selkirk** Can.	
96 C3	**Selkirk** U.K.	
128 C2	**Selkirk Mountains** Can.	
142 C2	**Selma** AL U.S.A.	
135 C3	**Selma** CA U.S.A.	
89 D3	**Sel'tso** Rus. Fed.	
150 A2	**Selvas** reg. Brazil	
134 C1	**Selway** r. U.S.A.	
129 D1	**Selwyn Lake** Can.	
128 A1	**Selwyn Mountains** Can.	
51 C2	**Selwyn Range** hills Austr.	
60 B2	**Semangka, Teluk** b. Indon.	
61 C2	**Semarang** Indon.	
61 B1	**Sematan** Sarawak Malaysia	
118 B2	**Sembé** Congo	
81 C2	**Şemdinli** Turkey	
91 C1	**Semenivka** Ukr.	
86 D3	**Semenov** Rus. Fed.	
61 C2	**Semeru, Gunung** vol. Indon.	
89 E3	**Semiluki** Rus. Fed.	
136 B2	**Seminoe Reservoir** U.S.A.	
139 C2	**Seminole** U.S.A.	
143 D2	**Seminole, Lake** U.S.A.	
77 E1	**Semipalatinsk** Kazakh.	
61 C1	**Semitau** Indon.	
81 D2	**Semnān** Iran	
61 C1	**Semporna** Sabah Malaysia	
105 C2	**Semur-en-Auxois** France	
150 B2	**Sena Madureira** Brazil	
120 B2	**Senanga** Zambia	
67 B4	**Sendai** Kagoshima Japan	
67 D3	**Sendai** Miyagi Japan	
114 A3	**Senegal** country Africa	
114 A3	**Sénégal** r. Maur./Senegal	
102 C1	**Senftenberg** Ger.	
119 D3	**Sengerema** Tanz.	
151 D3	**Senhor do Bonfim** Brazil	
108 B2	**Senigallia** Italy	
109 B2	**Senj** Croatia	
92 G2	**Senja** i. Norway	
122 B2	**Senlac** S. Africa	
104 C2	**Senlis** France	
63 B2	**Senmonorom** Cambodia	
117 B3	**Sennar** Sudan	
130 C2	**Senneterre** Can.	
123 C3	**Senqu** r. Lesotho	
105 C2	**Sens** France	
109 D1	**Senta** Yugo.	
128 B2	**Sentinel Peak** Can.	
75 B2	**Seoni** India	
65 B2	**Seoul** S. Korea	
155 D2	**Sepetiba, Baía de** b. Brazil	
59 D3	**Sepik** r. P.N.G.	
61 C1	**Sepinang** Indon.	
131 D1	**Sept-Îles** Can.	
59 C3	**Seram** i. Indon.	
59 C3	**Seram Sea** Indon.	
59 C3	**Serang** Indon.	
109 D2	**Serbia** aut. rep. Yugo.	
89 E3	**Serebryanyye Prudy** Rus. Fed.	
60 B1	**Seremban** Malaysia	
119 D3	**Serengeti Plain** Tanz.	
87 D3	**Sergach** Rus. Fed.	
89 E2	**Sergiyev Posad** Rus. Fed.	
61 C1	**Seria** Brunei	
61 C1	**Serian** Sarawak Malaysia	
111 B3	**Serifos** i. Greece	
80 B2	**Serik** Turkey	
59 C3	**Sermata, Kepulauan** is Indon.	
86 F3	**Serov** Rus. Fed.	
120 B3	**Serowe** Botswana	
106 B2	**Serpa** Port.	
89 E3	**Serpukhov** Rus. Fed.	
154 B1	**Serranópolis** Brazil	
100 A3	**Serre** r. France	
111 B2	**Serres** Greece	
151 E3	**Serrinha** Brazil	
155 D1	**Sêrro** Brazil	
154 C2	**Sertãozinho** Brazil	
61 C2	**Seruyan** r. Indon.	
68 C2	**Sêrxu** China	
120 A2	**Sesfontein** Namibia	
108 B2	**Sessa Aurunca** Italy	
107 D2	**Ses Salines, Cap de** c. Spain	
108 A2	**Sestri Levante** Italy	
105 C3	**Sète** France	
155 D1	**Sete Lagoas** Brazil	
92 G2	**Setermoen** Norway	
93 E4	**Setesdal** r. Norway	
115 C1	**Sétif** Alg.	
67 B4	**Seto-naikai** sea Japan	
114 B1	**Settat** Morocco	
98 B1	**Settle** U.K.	
106 B2	**Setúbal** Port.	
106 B2	**Setúbal, Baía de** b. Port.	
130 A1	**Seul, Lac** l. Can.	
76 A2	**Sevan, Lake** Armenia	
	Sevana Lich l. Armenia see **Sevan, Lake**	
91 C3	**Sevastopol'** Ukr.	
105 C3	**Sévérac-le-Château** France	
130 B1	**Severn** r. Can.	
122 B2	**Severn** S. Africa	
99 B3	**Severn** r. U.K.	
86 D2	**Severnaya Dvina** r. Rus. Fed.	
83 H1	**Severnaya Zemlya** is Rus. Fed.	
86 D2	**Severnyy** Nenetskiy Avtonomnyy Okrug Rus. Fed.	
86 F2	**Severnyy** Respublika Komi Rus. Fed.	
86 C2	**Severodvinsk** Rus. Fed.	
86 C2	**Severomorsk** Rus. Fed.	
91 D3	**Severskaya** Rus. Fed.	
135 D3	**Sevier** r. U.S.A.	
135 D3	**Sevier Lake** U.S.A.	
	Sevilla Spain see **Seville**	
106 B2	**Seville** Spain	
128 A2	**Sewell Inlet** Can.	
128 C2	**Sexsmith** Can.	
144 B2	**Sextin** r. Mex.	
86 G1	**Seyakha** Rus. Fed.	
113 H4	**Seychelles** country Indian Ocean	
92 □C2	**Seyðisfjörður** Iceland	
91 C1	**Seym** r. Rus. Fed./Ukr.	
81 C2	**Seymchan** Rus. Fed.	
53 C3	**Seymour** Austr.	
140 B3	**Seymour** IN U.S.A.	
139 D2	**Seymour** TX U.S.A.	
105 C2	**Sézanne** France	
111 B3	**Sfakia** Greece	
110 C1	**Sfântu Gheorghe** Romania	
115 D1	**Sfax** Tunisia	
	's-Gravenhage Neth. see **The Hague**	
96 A2	**Sgurr Alasdair** hill U.K.	
70 A2	**Shaanxi** prov. China	
91 D2	**Shabel'sk** Rus. Fed.	
77 D3	**Shache** China	
55 R1	**Shackleton Range** Antarctica	
99 B3	**Shaftesbury** U.K.	
75 C2	**Shahdol** India	
77 C3	**Shah Fuladi** mt. Afgh.	
75 B2	**Shahjahanpur** India	
81 D2	**Shahr-e Kord** Iran	
82 C2	**Shakhovskaya** Rus. Fed.	
77 C3	**Shakhrisabz** Uzbek.	
91 E2	**Shakhty** Rus. Fed.	
86 D3	**Shakhun'ya** Rus. Fed.	
66 D2	**Shakotan-misaki** c. Japan	
68 C2	**Shaluli Shan** mts China	
129 E2	**Shamattawa** Can.	
139 C1	**Shamrock** U.S.A.	
68 C2	**Shandan** China	
70 B2	**Shandong** prov. China	
70 C2	**Shandong Bandao** pen. China	
121 B2	**Shangani** r. Zimbabwe	
70 C2	**Shanghai** China	
70 C2	**Shanghai** mun. China	
71 B3	**Shanghang** China	
70 B2	**Shangqiu** China	
71 B3	**Shangrao** China	
70 B2	**Shangshui** China	
70 C2	**Shangyu** China	
69 E1	**Shangzhi** China	
70 A2	**Shangzhou** China	

97 B2 Shannon *r.* Rep. of Ireland
97 B2 Shannon, Mouth of the
        Rep. of Ireland
71 B3 Shantou China
70 B2 Shanxi *prov.* China
71 B3 Shaoguan China
71 B3 Shaowu China
70 C2 Shaoxing China
71 B3 Shaoyang China
116 C2 Shaqrā' Saudi Arabia
90 B2 Sharhorod Ukr.
71 C2 Sharjah U.A.E.
88 C2 Sharkawshchyna Belarus
50 A2 Shark Bay Austr.
78 A2 Sharm el Sheikh Egypt
140 C2 Sharon U.S.A.
86 D3 Shar'ya Rus. Fed.
121 B3 Shashe *r.*
        Botswana/Zimbabwe
117 B4 Shashemenë Eth.
134 B2 Shasta, Mount *vol.* U.S.A.
134 B2 Shasta Lake U.S.A.
89 E2 Shatura Rus. Fed.
129 D3 Shaunavon Can.
140 B2 Shawano U.S.A.
131 C2 Shawinigan Can.
139 D1 Shawnee U.S.A.
50 B2 Shay Gap Austr.
89 E3 Shchekino Rus. Fed.
89 E2 Shchelkovo Rus. Fed.
89 E3 Shchigry Rus. Fed.
91 C1 Shchors Ukr.
88 B3 Shchuchyn Belarus
89 D1 Shebekino Rus. Fed.
77 C3 Sheberghān Afgh.
140 B2 Sheboygan U.S.A.
91 D3 Shebsh *r.* Rus. Fed.
97 C2 Sheelin, Lough *l.*
        Rep. of Ireland
98 C2 Sheffield U.K.
89 E2 Sheksna Rus. Fed.
89 E2 Sheksninskoye
        Vodokhranilishche *resr*
        Rus. Fed.
83 M2 Shelagskiy, Mys *pt* Rus. Fed.
131 D2 Shelburne Can.
134 D1 Shelby U.S.A.
140 B3 Shelbyville IN U.S.A.
142 C1 Shelbyville TN U.S.A.
83 L2 Shelikhova, Zaliv *g.* Rus. Fed.
129 D2 Shellbrook Can.
134 B1 Shelton U.S.A.
137 D2 Shenandoah U.S.A.
141 D3 Shenandoah *r.* U.S.A.
141 D3 Shenandoah Mountains
        U.S.A.
118 A2 Shendam Nigeria
86 D2 Shenkursk Rus. Fed.
65 A1 Shenyang China
71 B3 Shenzhen China
90 B1 Shepetivka Ukr.
53 C3 Shepparton Austr.
99 D3 Sheppey, Isle of *i.* U.K.
131 D2 Sherbrooke N.S. Can.
131 C2 Sherbrooke Que. Can.
116 B3 Shereiq Sudan
136 B2 Sheridan U.S.A.
139 D2 Sherman U.S.A.
100 B2 's-Hertogenbosch Neth.
96 □ Shetland Islands *is* U.K.
76 B2 Shetpe Kazakh.
        Shevchenko Kazakh. *see*
        Aktau
137 D1 Sheyenne *r.* U.S.A.
79 B3 Shibām Yemen
66 D2 Shibetsu Japan
71 B3 Shicheng China
96 B2 Shiel, Loch *l.* U.K.
77 E2 Shihezi China
        Shijiao China *see* Fogang

70 B2 Shijiazhuang China
74 A2 Shikarpur Pak.
67 B4 Shikoku *i.* Japan
66 D2 Shikotsu-ko *l.* Japan
86 D2 Shilega Rus. Fed.
75 C2 Shiliguri India
75 D2 Shillong India
89 F3 Shilovo Rus. Fed.
117 C3 Shimbiris *mt.* Somalia
67 C3 Shimizu Japan
73 B3 Shimoga India
67 B4 Shimonoseki Japan
96 B1 Shin, Loch *l.* U.K.
67 C4 Shingū Japan
123 D1 Shingwedzi S. Africa
123 D1 Shingwedzi *r.* S. Africa
119 D3 Shinyanga Tanz.
67 C4 Shiono-misaki *c.* Japan
138 B1 Shiprock U.S.A.
71 A3 Shiqian China
70 A2 Shiquan China
        Shiquanhe China *see* Gar
        Shiquan He *r.* China/Pak. *see*
        Indus
67 C3 Shirane-san *mt.* Japan
81 D3 Shīrāz Iran
66 D2 Shiretoko-misaki *c.* Japan
74 B2 Shiriya-zaki *c.* Japan
74 B2 Shiv India
75 B2 Shivpuri India
70 B2 Shiyan China
70 A2 Shizuishan China
67 C4 Shizuoka Japan
89 D3 Shklow Belarus
109 C2 Shkodër Albania
83 H1 Shmidta, Ostrov *i.* Rus. Fed.
135 C3 Shoshone U.S.A.
135 C3 Shoshone Mountains *mts*
        U.S.A.
123 C1 Shoshong Botswana
91 C1 Shostka Ukr.
70 B2 Shouxian China
138 A2 Show Low U.S.A.
91 C2 Shpola Ukr.
142 B2 Shreveport U.S.A.
99 B2 Shrewsbury U.K.
62 A1 Shuangjiang China
87 E4 Shubarkuduk Kazakh.
116 B1 Shubrā el Kheima Egypt
89 D2 Shugozero Rus. Fed.
120 B2 Shumba Zimbabwe
110 C2 Shumen Bulg.
88 C2 Shumilina Belarus
89 D3 Shumyachi Rus. Fed.
126 A2 Shungnak U.S.A.
78 B3 Shuqrah Yemen
89 F2 Shushkodom Rus. Fed.
81 C2 Shushtar Iran
128 C2 Shuswap Lake Can.
89 F2 Shuya Rus. Fed.
89 F2 Shuyskoye Rus. Fed.
62 A1 Shwebo Myanmar
62 A1 Shwedwin Myanmar
62 A2 Shwegyin Myanmar
77 C2 Shymkent Kazakh.
91 C2 Shyroke Ukr.
59 C3 Sia Indon.
74 A2 Siahan Range *mts* Pak.
74 B1 Sialkot Pak.
64 B2 Siargao *i.* Phil.
88 B2 Šiauliai Lith.
109 C2 Šibenik Croatia
60 A2 Siberut *i.* Indon.
74 A2 Sibi Pak.
110 B1 Sibiu Romania
60 A1 Sibolga Indon.
62 A1 Sibsagar India
61 C1 Sibu Sarawak Malaysia
118 B2 Sibut C.A.R.
64 B1 Sibuyan *i.* Phil.

64 B1 Sibuyan Sea Phil.
128 C2 Sicamous Can.
63 A3 Sichon Thai.
70 A2 Sichuan *prov.* China
70 A2 Sichuan Pendi *basin* China
105 D3 Sicié, Cap *c.* France
        Sicilia *i.* Italy *see* Sicily
108 B3 Sicilian Channel Italy/Tunisia
108 B3 Sicily *i.* Italy
150 A3 Sicuani Peru
74 B2 Siddhapur India
111 C3 Sideros, Akra *pt* Greece
107 D2 Sidi Aïssa Alg.
107 D2 Sidi Ali Alg.
114 B1 Sidi Bel Abbès Alg.
114 A2 Sidi Ifni Morocco
60 A1 Sidikalang Indon.
96 C2 Sidlaw Hills U.K.
99 B3 Sidmouth U.K.
134 B1 Sidney U.S.A.
136 C1 Sidney MT U.S.A.
136 C2 Sidney NE U.S.A.
140 C2 Sidney OH U.S.A.
143 D2 Sidney Lanier, Lake U.S.A.
154 B2 Sidrolândia Brazil
103 E1 Siedlce Pol.
100 C2 Sieg *r.* Ger.
100 D2 Siegen Ger.
63 B2 Siĕmréab Cambodia
108 B2 Siena Italy
103 D1 Sieradz Pol.
153 B5 Sierra Grande Arg.
114 A4 Sierra Leone *country* Africa
144 B2 Sierra Mojada Mex.
138 A2 Sierra Vista U.S.A.
105 D2 Sierre Switz.
111 B3 Sifnos *i.* Greece
107 C2 Sig Alg.
127 H2 Sigguup Nunaa *pen.*
        Greenland
103 E2 Sighetu Marmaţiei Romania
110 B1 Sighişoara Romania
60 A1 Sigli Indon.
92 □B2 Siglufjörður Iceland
102 B2 Sigmaringen Ger.
100 B3 Signy-l'Abbaye France
106 C1 Sigüenza Spain
114 B3 Siguiri Guinea
88 B2 Sigulda Latvia
63 B2 Sihanoukville Cambodia
92 I3 Siilinjärvi Fin.
81 C2 Siirt Turkey
60 B2 Sijunjung Indon.
74 B2 Sikar India
114 B3 Sikasso Mali
137 F3 Sikeston U.S.A.
66 B2 Sikhote-Alin' *mts* Rus. Fed.
111 C3 Sikinos *i.* Greece
144 B2 Silao Mex.
75 D2 Silchar India
75 C2 Siletiteniz, Ozero *salt l.*
        Kazakh.
75 C2 Sigarhi Nepal
80 B2 Silifke Turkey
75 C1 Siling Co *salt l.* China
110 C2 Silistra Bulg.
80 A1 Silivri Turkey
93 F3 Siljan *l.* Sweden
93 E4 Silkeborg Denmark
88 C2 Sillamäe Estonia
142 B1 Siloam Springs U.S.A.
123 D2 Silobela S. Africa
88 B2 Šilutė Lith.
81 C2 Silvan Turkey
138 B2 Silver City U.S.A.
136 B3 Silverton U.S.A.
62 B1 Simao China
130 C2 Simard, Lac *l.* Can.
111 C3 Simav Turkey
111 C3 Simav Dağları *mts* Turkey

118 C2 Simba Dem. Rep. Congo
141 D2 Simcoe, Lake Can.
60 A1 Simeulue i. Indon.
91 C3 Simferopol' Ukr.
110 B1 Şimleu Silvaniei Romania
100 C3 Şimmern (Hunsrück) Ger.
129 D2 Simonhouse Can.
51 C2 Simpson Desert Austr.
93 F4 Simrishamn Sweden
60 A1 Sinabang Indon.
116 B2 Sinai pen. Egypt
71 A3 Sinan China
65 B2 Sinanju N. Korea
62 A1 Sinbo Myanmar
150 A1 Sincelejo Col.
111 C3 Sındırgı Turkey
86 E2 Sindor Rus. Fed.
111 C3 Sinekçi Turkey
106 B2 Sines Port.
106 B2 Sines, Cabo de c. Port.
75 C2 Singahi India
60 B1 Singapore country Asia
61 C2 Singaraja Indon.
119 D3 Singida Tanz.
62 A1 Singkaling Hkamti Myanmar
61 B1 Singkawang Indon.
60 A1 Singkil Indon.
53 D2 Singleton Austr.
62 A1 Singu Myanmar
108 A2 Siniscola Sardinia Italy
109 C2 Sinj Croatia
116 B3 Sinkat Sudan
            Sinkiang aut. reg. China see
            Xinjiang Uygur Zizhiqu
80 B1 Sinop Turkey
65 B1 Sinp'o N. Korea
61 C1 Sintang Indon.
139 D3 Sinton U.S.A.
65 A1 Sinŭiju N. Korea
103 D2 Siófok Hungary
105 D2 Sion Switz.
137 D2 Sioux Center U.S.A.
137 D2 Sioux City U.S.A.
137 D2 Sioux Falls U.S.A.
130 A1 Sioux Lookout Can.
65 A1 Siping China
129 E2 Sipiwesk Lake Can.
60 A2 Sipura i. Indon.
93 E4 Sira r. Norway
            Siracusa Italy see Syracuse
51 C1 Sir Edward Pellew Group
            is Austr.
116 B1 Sirhān, Wādī an
            watercourse Saudi Arabia
79 C2 Sirik Iran
62 B2 Siri Kit Dam Thai.
128 B1 Sir James MacBrien,
            Mount Can.
79 C2 Sirjan Iran
81 C2 Şırnak Turkey
74 B2 Sirohi India
74 B2 Sirsa India
115 D1 Sirte Libya
115 D1 Sirte, Gulf of Libya
88 B2 Širvintos Lith.
145 C2 Sisal Mex.
122 B2 Sishen S. Africa
81 C2 Sisian Armenia
129 D2 Sisipuk Lake Can.
63 B2 Sisŏphŏn Cambodia
105 D3 Sisteron France
75 C2 Sitapur India
123 D2 Siteki Swaziland
128 A2 Sitka U.S.A.
62 A2 Sittang r. Myanmar
100 B2 Sittard Neth.
62 A1 Sittwe Myanmar
61 C2 Situbondo Indon.
80 B2 Sivas Turkey
111 C3 Sivaslı Turkey

80 B2 Siverek Turkey
80 B2 Sivrihisar Turkey
116 A2 Siwa Egypt
74 B1 Siwalik Range mts
            India/Nepal
105 C3 Six-Fours-les-Plages France
70 B2 Sixian China
123 C2 Siyabuswa S. Africa
93 F4 Sjælland i. Denmark
109 D2 Sjenica Yugo.
92 G2 Sjøvegan Norway
91 C2 Skadovs'k Ukr.
93 F4 Skagen Denmark
93 E4 Skagerrak str.
            Denmark/Norway
134 B1 Skagit r. U.S.A.
128 A2 Skagway U.S.A.
74 B1 Skardu Jammu and Kashmir
103 E1 Skarżysko-Kamienna Pol.
103 D2 Skawina Pol.
128 B2 Skeena r. Can.
128 B2 Skeena Mountains Can.
98 D2 Skegness U.K.
92 H3 Skellefteå Sweden
92 H3 Skellefteälven r. Sweden
97 C2 Skerries Rep. of Ireland
111 B3 Skiathos i. Greece
97 B3 Skibbereen Rep. of Ireland
92 □B2 Skiðadals-jökull glacier
            Iceland
98 B1 Skiddaw hill U.K.
93 E4 Skien Norway
103 E1 Skierniewice Pol.
115 C1 Skikda Alg.
52 B3 Skipton Austr.
98 B2 Skipton U.K.
93 E4 Skive Denmark
92 H1 Skjervøy Norway
111 B3 Skopelos i. Greece
89 E3 Skopin Rus. Fed.
109 D2 Skopje Macedonia
93 F4 Skövde Sweden
141 F2 Skowhegan U.S.A.
88 B2 Skrunda Latvia
128 A1 Skukum, Mount Can.
123 D1 Skukuza S. Africa
88 B2 Skuodas Lith.
96 A2 Skye i. U.K.
111 B3 Skyros Greece
111 B3 Skyros i. Greece
93 F4 Slagelse Denmark
97 C2 Slaney r. Rep. of Ireland
88 C2 Slantsy Rus. Fed.
109 C1 Slatina Croatia
110 B2 Slatina Romania
129 C1 Slave r. Can.
114 C4 Slave Coast Africa
128 C2 Slave Lake Can.
82 G3 Slavgorod Rus. Fed.
109 C1 Slavonski Brod Croatia
90 B1 Slavuta Ukr.
90 C1 Slavutych Ukr.
91 D2 Slavyansk-na-Kubani
            Rus. Fed.
89 D3 Slawharad Belarus
103 D1 Sławno Pol.
97 A2 Slea Head hd Rep. of Ireland
130 C1 Sleeper Islands Can.
97 D1 Slieve Donard hill U.K.
97 B1 Slieve Gamph hills
            Rep. of Ireland
97 B1 Sligo Rep. of Ireland
97 B1 Sligo Bay Rep. of Ireland
93 G4 Slite Sweden
110 C2 Sliven Bulg.
110 C2 Slobozia Romania
128 C3 Slocan Can.
88 C3 Slonim Belarus
100 B1 Sloten Neth.
99 C3 Slough U.K.

103 D2 Slovakia country Europe
108 B1 Slovenia country Europe
91 D2 Slov'yans'k Ukr.
90 B1 Sluch r. Ukr.
103 D1 Słupsk Pol.
88 C3 Slutsk Belarus
97 A2 Slyne Head hd
            Rep. of Ireland
131 D1 Smallwood Reservoir Can.
88 C3 Smalyavichy Belarus
88 C3 Smarhon' Belarus
129 D2 Smeaton Can.
109 D2 Smederevo Yugo.
109 D2 Smederevska Palanka
            Yugo.
91 C2 Smila Ukr.
88 C2 Smiltene Latvia
128 B2 Smithers Can.
143 E1 Smithfield U.S.A.
141 D3 Smith Mountain Lake
            U.S.A.
130 C2 Smiths Falls Can.
137 D3 Smoky Hills U.S.A.
92 E3 Smøla i. Norway
89 D3 Smolensk Rus. Fed.
110 B2 Smolyan Bulg.
130 B2 Smooth Rock Falls Can.
            Smyrna Turkey see İzmir
92 □B3 Snæfell mt. Iceland
98 A1 Snaefell hill Isle of Man
132 B2 Snake r. U.S.A.
134 D2 Snake River Plain U.S.A.
128 C1 Snare Lake Can.
100 B1 Sneek Neth.
97 B3 Sneem Rep. of Ireland
122 B3 Sneeuberge mts S. Africa
108 B1 Snežnik mt. Slovenia
91 C2 Snihurivka Ukr.
93 E3 Snøhetta mt. Norway
129 D1 Snowbird Lake l. Can.
98 A2 Snowdon mt. U.K.
            Snowdrift Can. see Łutselk'e
129 C1 Snowdrift r. Can.
138 A2 Snowflake U.S.A.
129 D2 Snow Lake Can.
52 A2 Snowtown Austr.
53 C3 Snowy r. Austr.
53 C3 Snowy Mountains Austr.
139 C2 Snyder U.S.A.
121 □D2 Soalala Madag.
117 B4 Sobat r. Sudan
100 C3 Sobernheim Ger.
89 F2 Sobinka Rus. Fed.
151 D3 Sobradinho, Barragem de
            resr Brazil
151 D2 Sobral Brazil
87 C4 Sochi Rus. Fed.
65 B2 Sŏch'ŏn S. Korea
150 A1 Socorro Col.
138 B2 Socorro U.S.A.
144 A3 Socorro, Isla i. Mex.
56 B4 Socotra i. Yemen
63 B3 Soc Trăng Vietnam
106 C2 Socuéllamos Spain
92 I2 Sodankylä Fin.
134 D2 Soda Springs U.S.A.
93 G3 Söderhamn Sweden
93 G4 Södertälje Sweden
116 A3 Sodiri Sudan
117 B4 Sodo Eth.
93 G3 Södra Kvarken str.
            Fin./Sweden
100 C1 Soest Ger.
110 B2 Sofia Bulg.
            Sofiya Bulg. see Sofia
68 C2 Sog China
93 E3 Sognefjorden inlet Norway
111 D3 Söğüt Turkey
116 B2 Sohâg Egypt
100 B2 Soignies Belgium

105 C2 **Soissons** France
90 A1 **Sokal'** Ukr.
111 C3 **Söke** Turkey
81 C1 **Sokhumi** Georgia
114 C4 **Sokodé** Togo
89 F2 **Sokol** Rus. Fed.
101 F2 **Sokolov** Czech Rep.
115 C3 **Sokoto** Nigeria
115 C3 **Sokoto** r. Nigeria
90 B2 **Sokyryany** Ukr.
73 B3 **Solāpur** India
135 B3 **Soledad** U.S.A.
89 F2 **Soligalich** Rus. Fed.
99 C2 **Solihull** U.K.
86 E3 **Solikamsk** Rus. Fed.
87 E3 **Sol'-Iletsk** Rus. Fed.
100 C2 **Solingen** Ger.
92 G3 **Sollefteå** Sweden
93 G4 **Sollentuna** Sweden
101 D2 **Solling** hills Ger.
89 E2 **Solnechnogorsk** Rus. Fed.
60 B2 **Solok** Indon.
49 E3 **Solomon Islands** country
S. Pacific Ocean
105 D3 **Solothurn** Switz.
101 D1 **Soltau** Ger.
89 D1 **Sol'tsy** Rus. Fed.
96 C3 **Solway Firth** est. U.K.
120 B2 **Solwezi** Zambia
111 C3 **Soma** Turkey
117 C4 **Somalia** country Africa
120 B1 **Sombo** Angola
109 C1 **Sombor** Yugo.
144 B2 **Sombrerete** Mex.
140 C3 **Somerset** U.S.A.
123 C3 **Somerset East** S. Africa
126 E2 **Somerset Island** Can.
122 A3 **Somerset West** S. Africa
101 E2 **Sömmerda** Ger.
75 C2 **Son** r. India
93 E4 **Sønderborg** Denmark
101 E2 **Sondershausen** Ger.
Søndre Strømfjord inlet
Greenland see
Kangerlussuaq
62 B1 **Sông Da, Hô** resr Vietnam
119 D4 **Songea** Tanz.
65 B1 **Sŏnggan** N. Korea
65 B1 **Songhua Hu** resr China
Sŏngjin N. Korea see
Kimch'aek
63 B3 **Songkhla** Thai.
69 E1 **Songling** China
65 B2 **Sŏngnam** S. Korea
65 B2 **Sŏngnim** N. Korea
120 A1 **Songo** Angola
121 C2 **Songo** Moz.
69 E1 **Songyuan** China
Sonid Youqi China see
Saihan Tal
89 E2 **Sonkovo** Rus. Fed.
62 B1 **Son La** Vietnam
74 A2 **Sonmiani** Pak.
101 E2 **Sonneberg** Ger.
144 A2 **Sonora** r. Mex.
135 B3 **Sonora** CA U.S.A.
139 C2 **Sonora** TX U.S.A.
138 A2 **Sonoyta** Mex.
117 A4 **Sopo** watercourse Sudan
103 D2 **Sopron** Hungary
108 B2 **Sora** Italy
130 C2 **Sorel** Can.
51 D4 **Sorell** Austr.
106 C1 **Soria** Spain
76 B2 **Sor Mertvyy Kultuk** dry lake
Kazakh.
90 B2 **Soroca** Moldova
154 C3 **Sorocaba** Brazil
87 E3 **Sorochinsk** Rus. Fed.
59 D2 **Sorol** atoll Micronesia

59 C3 **Sorong** Indon.
119 D2 **Soroti** Uganda
92 H1 **Sørøya** i. Norway
92 G2 **Sorsele** Sweden
64 B1 **Sorsogon** Phil.
86 C2 **Sortavala** Rus. Fed.
92 G2 **Sortland** Norway
65 B2 **Sŏsan** S. Korea
123 C2 **Soshanguve** S. Africa
86 E2 **Sosnogorsk** Rus. Fed.
86 D2 **Sosnovka** Rus. Fed.
88 C2 **Sosnovyy Bor** Rus. Fed.
103 D1 **Sosnowiec** Pol.
91 D2 **Sosyka** r. Rus. Fed.
145 C2 **Soto la Marina** Mex.
118 B2 **Souanké** Congo
104 C3 **Souillac** France
Sŏul S. Korea see Seoul
104 B2 **Soulac-sur-Mer** France
104 B3 **Soulom** France
80 B2 **Soûr** Lebanon
107 D2 **Sour el Ghozlane** Alg.
129 D3 **Souris** Man. Can.
131 D2 **Souris** P.E.I. Can.
129 E3 **Souris** r. Can.
151 E2 **Sousa** Brazil
115 D1 **Sousse** Tunisia
104 B3 **Soustons** France
122 B3 **South Africa, Republic of**
country Africa
99 C3 **Southampton** U.K.
127 F2 **Southampton Island** Can.
73 D3 **South Andaman** i. India
52 A1 **South Australia** state Austr.
130 B2 **South Baymouth** Can.
140 B2 **South Bend** U.S.A.
143 D2 **South Carolina** state U.S.A.
156 B4 **South China Sea**
N. Pacific Ocean
136 C2 **South Dakota** state U.S.A.
99 C3 **South Downs** hills U.K.
129 D2 **Southend** Can.
99 D3 **Southend-on-Sea** U.K.
54 B2 **Southern Alps** mts N.Z.
50 A3 **Southern Cross** Austr.
129 E2 **Southern Indian Lake** Can.
159 **Southern Ocean**
143 E1 **Southern Pines** U.S.A.
96 B3 **Southern Uplands** hills U.K.
149 F6 **South Georgia and South
Sandwich Islands** terr.
S. Atlantic Ocean
96 A2 **South Harris** pen. U.K.
129 E1 **South Henik Lake** l. Can.
54 B2 **South Island** N.Z.
135 B3 **South Lake Tahoe** U.S.A.
128 B1 **South Nahanni** r. Can.
55 Q4 **South Orkney Islands**
S. Atlantic Ocean
136 C2 **South Platte** r. U.S.A.
98 B2 **Southport** U.K.
143 E2 **Southport** U.S.A.
96 C1 **South Ronaldsay** i. U.K.
123 D3 **South Sand Bluff** pt
S. Africa
129 D2 **South Saskatchewan** r. Can.
129 E2 **South Seal** r. Can.
55 P3 **South Shetland Islands**
Antarctica
98 C1 **South Shields** U.K.
54 B1 **South Taranaki Bight** b. N.Z.
130 C1 **South Twin Island** Can.
96 A2 **South Uist** i. U.K.
53 D2 **South West Rocks** Austr.
99 D2 **Southwold** U.K.
109 C3 **Soverato** Italy
88 B2 **Sovetsk** Rus. Fed.
86 F2 **Sovetskiy** Rus. Fed.

91 C2 **Sovyets'kyy** Ukr.
123 C2 **Soweto** S. Africa
66 D1 **Sōya-misaki** c. Japan
90 C1 **Sozh** r. Europe
110 C2 **Sozopol** Bulg.
106 C1 **Spain** country Europe
99 C2 **Spalding** U.K.
135 D2 **Spanish Fork** U.S.A.
97 B2 **Spanish Point**
Rep. of Ireland
108 B3 **Sparagio, Monte** mt. Sicily
Italy
135 C3 **Sparks** U.S.A.
140 A2 **Sparta** U.S.A.
143 D2 **Spartanburg** U.S.A.
111 B3 **Sparti** Greece
109 C3 **Spartivento, Capo** c. Italy
89 D3 **Spas-Demensk** Rus. Fed.
89 F2 **Spas-Klepiki** Rus. Fed.
66 B2 **Spassk-Dal'niy** Rus. Fed.
89 F3 **Spassk-Ryazanskiy**
Rus. Fed.
111 B3 **Spatha, Akra** pt Greece
136 C2 **Spearfish** U.S.A.
139 C1 **Spearman** U.S.A.
137 D2 **Spencer** U.S.A.
52 A2 **Spencer Gulf** est. Austr.
98 C1 **Spennymoor** U.K.
54 B2 **Spenser Mountains** N.Z.
101 D3 **Spessart** reg. Ger.
96 C2 **Spey** r. U.K.
102 B2 **Speyer** Ger.
100 C1 **Spiekeroog** i. Ger.
100 B2 **Spijkenisse** Neth.
128 C2 **Spirit River** Can.
103 D2 **Spišská Nová Ves** Slovakia
82 C1 **Spitsbergen** i. Svalbard
102 C2 **Spittal an der Drau** Austria
109 C2 **Split** Croatia
129 E2 **Split Lake** Can.
129 E2 **Split Lake** l. Can.
134 C1 **Spokane** U.S.A.
140 A1 **Spooner** U.S.A.
102 C1 **Spree** r. Ger.
122 A2 **Springbok** S. Africa
131 E2 **Springdale** Can.
142 B1 **Springdale** U.S.A.
101 D1 **Springe** Ger.
138 C1 **Springer** U.S.A.
138 B2 **Springerville** U.S.A.
136 C3 **Springfield** CO U.S.A.
140 B3 **Springfield** IL U.S.A.
141 E2 **Springfield** MA U.S.A.
137 E3 **Springfield** MO U.S.A.
140 C3 **Springfield** OH U.S.A.
134 B2 **Springfield** OR U.S.A.
123 C3 **Springfontein** S. Africa
131 D2 **Springhill** Can.
143 D3 **Spring Hill** U.S.A.
54 B2 **Springs Junction** N.Z.
98 D2 **Spurn Head** hd U.K.
128 B3 **Squamish** Can.
109 C3 **Squillace, Golfo di** g. Italy
Srbija aut. rep. Yugo. see
Serbia
110 C2 **Sredets** Bulg.
83 L3 **Sredinnyy Khrebet** mts
Rus. Fed.
83 L2 **Srednekolymsk** Rus. Fed.
89 E3 **Sredne-Russkaya
Vozvyshennost'** hills
Rus. Fed.
83 I2 **Sredne-Sibirskoye
Ploskogor'ye** plat. Rus. Fed.
110 B2 **Srednogorie** Bulg.
69 D1 **Sretensk** Rus. Fed.
61 C1 **Sri Aman** Sarawak Malaysia
73 B4 **Sri Jayewardenepura Kotte**
Sri Lanka
73 C3 **Srikakulam** India

73 C4 Sri Lanka country Asia
74 B1 Srinagar Jammu and Kashmir
73 B3 Srivardhan India
101 D1 Stade Ger.
101 E1 Stadensen Ger.
100 C1 Stadskanaal Neth.
101 D2 Stadtallendorf Ger.
101 D1 Stadthagen Ger.
101 E2 Staffelstein Ger.
99 B2 Stafford U.K.
99 C3 Staines U.K.
91 D2 Stakhanov Ukr.
Stalingrad Rus. Fed. see Volgograd
103 E1 Stalowa Wola Pol.
99 C3 Stamford U.K.
141 E2 Stamford CT U.S.A.
139 D2 Stamford TX U.S.A.
122 A1 Stampriet Namibia
92 F2 Stamsund Norway
123 C2 Standerton S. Africa
140 C2 Standish U.S.A.
123 D2 Stanger S. Africa
153 C6 Stanley Falkland Is
136 C1 Stanley U.S.A.
83 I3 Stanovoye Nagor'ye mts Rus. Fed.
83 J3 Stanovoy Khrebet mts Rus. Fed.
53 D1 Stansthorpe Austr.
103 E1 Starachowice Pol.
Stara Planina mts Bulg./Yugo. see Balkan Mountains
89 D2 Staraya Russa Rus. Fed.
89 D2 Staraya Toropa Rus. Fed.
110 C2 Stara Zagora Bulg.
103 D1 Stargard Szczeciński Pol.
142 C2 Starkville U.S.A.
91 D2 Starobil's'k Ukr.
89 D3 Starodub Rus. Fed.
103 D1 Starogard Gdański Pol.
90 B2 Starokostyantyniv Ukr.
91 D2 Staromins'kaya Rus. Fed.
91 D2 Staroshcherbinovskaya Rus. Fed.
91 D2 Starotitarovskaya Rus. Fed.
89 F3 Staroyur'yevo Rus. Fed.
99 B3 Start Point U.K.
88 C3 Staryya Darohi Belarus
89 E3 Staryy Oskol Rus. Fed.
101 E2 Staßfurt Ger.
141 D2 State College U.S.A.
143 D2 Statesboro U.S.A.
143 D1 Statesville U.S.A.
93 E4 Stavanger Norway
87 D4 Stavropol' Rus. Fed.
87 D4 Stavropol'skaya Vozvyshennost' hills Rus. Fed.
52 B3 Stawell Austr.
123 C2 Steadville S. Africa
136 B2 Steamboat Springs U.S.A.
101 E2 Stedten Ger.
128 C2 Steen River Can.
134 C2 Steens Mountain U.S.A.
100 C1 Steenwijk Neth.
126 D2 Stefansson Island Can.
101 E3 Steigerwald Ger.
129 E3 Steinbach Can.
100 C1 Steinfurt Ger.
120 A3 Steinhausen Namibia
92 F3 Steinkjer Norway
122 A3 Steinkopf S. Africa
122 B2 Stella S. Africa
105 D2 Stenay France
101 E1 Stendal Ger.
Stepanakert Azer. see Xankändi

131 E2 Stephenville Can.
139 D2 Stephenville U.S.A.
122 B3 Sterling S. Africa
136 C2 Sterling CO U.S.A.
140 B2 Sterling IL U.S.A.
87 E3 Sterlitamak Rus. Fed.
101 E1 Sternberg Ger.
128 C2 Stettler Can.
140 C2 Steubenville U.S.A.
99 C3 Stevenage U.K.
129 E2 Stevenson Lake Can.
126 B2 Stevens Village U.S.A.
128 B2 Stewart Can.
126 B2 Stewart r. Can.
54 A3 Stewart Island N.Z.
127 F2 Stewart Lake Can.
102 C2 Steyr Austria
123 B3 Steytlerville S. Africa
128 A2 Stikine r. Can.
128 A2 Stikine Plateau Can.
122 B3 Stilbaai S. Africa
139 D1 Stillwater U.S.A.
109 D2 Stip Macedonia
96 C2 Stirling U.K.
92 F3 Stjørdalshalsen Norway
103 D2 Stockerau Austria
93 G4 Stockholm Sweden
98 B2 Stockport U.K.
135 B3 Stockton U.S.A.
98 C1 Stockton-on-Tees U.K.
63 B2 Stœng Trêng Cambodia
96 B1 Stoer, Point of U.K.
98 B2 Stoke-on-Trent U.K.
109 C2 Stolac Bos.-Herz.
100 C2 Stolberg (Rheinland) Ger.
88 C3 Stolin Belarus
101 F2 Stollberg Ger.
101 D1 Stolzenau Ger.
96 C2 Stonehaven U.K.
129 E2 Stonewall Can.
129 D2 Stony Rapids Can.
92 G2 Storavan l. Sweden
93 F3 Store Bælt sea chan. Denmark
92 F3 Støren Norway
92 F2 Storforshei Norway
126 D2 Storkerson Peninsula Can.
137 D2 Storm Lake U.S.A.
93 E3 Stornosa mt. Norway
96 A1 Stornoway U.K.
86 E2 Storozhevsk Rus. Fed.
90 B2 Storozhynets' Ukr.
92 F3 Storsjön l. Sweden
92 H2 Storslett Norway
92 G2 Storuman Sweden
99 C3 Stour r. England U.K.
99 C2 Stour r. England U.K.
130 A1 Stout Lake Can.
88 C3 Stowbtsy Belarus
97 C1 Strabane U.K.
102 C2 Strakonice Czech Rep.
102 C1 Stralsund Ger.
122 A3 Strand S. Africa
93 E3 Stranda Norway
97 D1 Strangford Lough inlet U.K.
96 B3 Stranraer U.K.
105 D2 Strasbourg France
140 C2 Stratford Can.
54 B1 Stratford N.Z.
139 C1 Stratford U.S.A.
99 C2 Stratford-upon-Avon U.K.
128 C2 Strathmore Can.
96 C2 Strathspey val. U.K.
102 C2 Straubing Ger.
51 D1 Streaky Bay Austr.
140 B2 Streator U.S.A.
110 B2 Strehaia Romania
111 B2 Strimonas r. Greece
153 B5 Stroeder Arg.
101 D1 Ströhen Ger.
109 C3 Stromboli, Isola i. Italy

96 C1 Stromness U.K.
92 G3 Strömsund Sweden
96 C1 Stronsay i. U.K.
53 D2 Stroud Austr.
99 B3 Stroud U.K.
100 C1 Strücklingen (Saterland) Ger.
109 D2 Struga Macedonia
88 C2 Strugi-Krasnyye Rus. Fed.
122 B3 Struis Bay S. Africa
109 D2 Strumica Macedonia
122 B2 Strydenburg S. Africa
90 A2 Stryy Ukr.
128 B2 Stuart Lake Can.
130 A1 Stull Lake Can.
89 E3 Stupino Rus. Fed.
140 B2 Sturgeon Bay U.S.A.
130 C2 Sturgeon Falls Can.
130 A2 Sturgeon Lake Can.
140 B2 Sturgis MI U.S.A.
136 C2 Sturgis SD U.S.A.
50 B1 Sturt Creek watercourse Austr.
52 B1 Sturt Stony Desert Austr.
123 C3 Stutterheim S. Africa
102 B2 Stuttgart Ger.
142 B2 Stuttgart U.S.A.
92 □A2 Stykkishólmur Iceland
90 B1 Styr r. Belarus/Ukr.
155 D1 Suaçuí Grande r. Brazil
116 B3 Suakin Sudan
78 A3 Suara, Mount Eritrea
110 C1 Subotica Yugo.
110 C1 Suceava Romania
97 B2 Suck r. Rep. of Ireland
152 B2 Sucre Bol.
154 B2 Sucuriú r. Brazil
89 E2 Suda Rus. Fed.
91 C3 Sudak Ukr.
117 B3 Sudan country Africa
130 B2 Sudbury Can.
117 A4 Sudd swamp Sudan
89 F2 Sudislavl' Rus. Fed.
89 F2 Sudogda Rus. Fed.
94 B1 Suðuroy i. Faroe Is
107 C2 Sueca Spain
116 B2 Suez Egypt
116 B2 Suez, Gulf of Egypt
80 B2 Suez Canal Egypt
141 D3 Suffolk U.S.A.
79 C2 Şuḩār Oman
69 D1 Sühbaatar Mongolia
101 E2 Suhl Ger.
109 C1 Suhopolje Croatia
70 B2 Suide China
70 A2 Suining China
70 B2 Suiping China
70 B2 Suizhou China
74 B2 Sujangarh India
74 B1 Sujanpur India
74 A2 Sujawal Pak.
60 B2 Sukabumi Indon.
61 B2 Sukadana Indon.
89 B1 Sukhinichi Rus. Fed.
89 F2 Sukhona r. Rus. Fed.
62 A2 Sukhothai Thai.
74 A2 Sukkur Pak.
89 E2 Sukromny Rus. Fed.
59 C3 Sula, Kepulauan is Indon.
74 A1 Sulaiman Ranges mts Pak.
58 C3 Sulawesi i. Indon.
150 A2 Sullana Peru
137 E3 Sullivan U.S.A.
139 D2 Sulphur Springs U.S.A.
64 B2 Sulu Archipelago is Phil.
64 A2 Sulu Sea N. Pacific Ocean
101 E3 Sulzbach-Rosenberg Ger.
79 C2 Sumāil Oman

Sumatera

60 A1 **Sumatera** i. Indon.
58 C3 **Sumatra** i. Indon. *see*
    Sumatera
58 C3 **Sumba** i. Indon.
61 C2 **Sumbawa** i. Indon.
61 C2 **Sumbawabesar** Indon.
119 D3 **Sumbawanga** Tanz.
120 A2 **Sumbe** Angola
96 □ **Sumburgh** U.K.
96 □ **Sumburgh Head** hd U.K.
61 C2 **Sumenep** Indon.
67 D4 **Sumisu-jima** i. Japan
131 D2 **Summerside** Can.
140 C3 **Summersville** U.S.A.
128 B2 **Summit Lake** Can.
103 D2 **Šumperk** Czech Rep.
81 C1 **Sumqayıt** Azer.
143 D2 **Sumter** U.S.A.
91 C1 **Sumy** Ukr.
75 D2 **Sunamganj** Bangl.
65 B2 **Sunan** N. Korea
79 C2 **Şunaynah** Oman
52 B3 **Sunbury** Austr.
141 D2 **Sunbury** U.S.A.
65 B2 **Sunch'ŏn** N. Korea
65 B3 **Sunch'ŏn** S. Korea
123 C2 **Sun City** S. Africa
60 B2 **Sunda, Selat** str. Indon.
136 C2 **Sundance** U.S.A.
75 C2 **Sundarbans** reg. Bangl./India
98 C1 **Sunderland** U.K.
128 C2 **Sundre** Can.
93 G3 **Sundsvall** Sweden
123 D3 **Sundumbili** S. Africa
60 B2 **Sungailiat** Indon.
60 B2 **Sungaipenuh** Indon.
60 B1 **Sungai Petani** Malaysia
80 B1 **Sungurlu** Turkey
93 E3 **Sunndalsøra** Norway
134 C1 **Sunnyside** U.S.A.
135 B3 **Sunnyvale** U.S.A.
83 I2 **Suntar** Rus. Fed.
74 A2 **Suntsar** Pak.
114 B4 **Sunyani** Ghana
82 D2 **Suoyarvi** Rus. Fed.
138 A2 **Superior** AZ U.S.A.
137 D2 **Superior** NE U.S.A.
140 A1 **Superior** WI U.S.A.
140 B1 **Superior, Lake** Can./U.S.A.
89 D3 **Suponevo** Rus. Fed.
81 C2 **Süq ash Shuyūkh** Iraq
70 B2 **Suqian** China
78 A2 **Süq Suwayq** Saudi Arabia
79 C2 **Şūr** Oman
74 A2 **Surab** Pak.
61 C2 **Surabaya** Indon.
61 C2 **Surakarta** Indon.
74 B2 **Surat** India
74 B2 **Suratgarh** India
63 A3 **Surat Thani** Thai.
89 D3 **Surazh** Rus. Fed.
109 D2 **Surdulica** Yugo.
74 B2 **Surendranagar** India
82 F2 **Surgut** Rus. Fed.
64 B2 **Surigao** Phil.
63 B2 **Surin** Thai.
151 C1 **Suriname** country S. America
    Surt Libya *see* Sirte
    Surt, Khalīj g. Libya *see*
    Sirte, Gulf of
60 B2 **Surulangun** Indon.
89 F2 **Susanino** Rus. Fed.
135 B2 **Susanville** U.S.A.
80 B1 **Suşehri** Turkey
131 D2 **Sussex** Can.
101 D1 **Süstedt** Ger.
100 C1 **Sustrum** Ger.
83 K2 **Susuman** Rus. Fed.
111 C3 **Susurluk** Turkey
75 B1 **Sutak** Jammu and Kashmir

122 B3 **Sutherland** S. Africa
99 C2 **Sutton Coldfield** U.K.
66 D2 **Suttsu** Japan
89 E3 **Suvorov** Rus. Fed.
103 E1 **Suwałki** Pol.
63 B2 **Suwannaphum** Thai.
143 D3 **Suwannee** r. U.S.A.
    Suweis, Qanâ el canal Egypt
    see Suez Canal
65 B2 **Suwŏn** S. Korea
79 C2 **Sūzā** Iran
89 F2 **Suzdal'** Rus. Fed.
70 B2 **Suzhou** Anhui China
70 C2 **Suzhou** Jiangsu China
67 C3 **Suzu** Japan
67 C3 **Suzu-misaki** pt Japan
82 B1 **Svalbard** terr. Arctic Ocean
91 D2 **Svatove** Ukr.
63 B2 **Svay Riĕng** Cambodia
93 F3 **Sveg** Sweden
88 C2 **Švenčionys** Lith.
93 F4 **Svendborg** Denmark
    Sverdlovsk Rus. Fed. *see*
    Yekaterinburg
109 D2 **Sveti Nikole** Macedonia
88 B3 **Svetlogorsk** Rus. Fed.
88 B3 **Svetlyy** Rus. Fed.
93 I3 **Svetogorsk** Rus. Fed.
110 C2 **Svilengrad** Bulg.
110 B2 **Svinecea Mare, Vârful** mt.
    Romania
110 C2 **Svishtov** Bulg.
103 D2 **Svitavy** Czech Rep.
91 C2 **Svitlovods'k** Ukr.
69 E1 **Svobodnyy** Rus. Fed.
92 F2 **Svolvær** Norway
88 C3 **Svyetlahorsk** Belarus
143 D2 **Swainsboro** U.S.A.
120 A3 **Swakopmund** Namibia
52 B3 **Swan Hill** Austr.
128 C2 **Swan Hills** Can.
129 D2 **Swan Lake** l. Can.
129 D2 **Swan River** Can.
53 D2 **Swansea** Austr.
99 B3 **Swansea** U.K.
123 C2 **Swartruggens** S. Africa
    Swatow China *see* Shantou
123 D2 **Swaziland** country Africa
93 G3 **Sweden** country Europe
139 C2 **Sweetwater** U.S.A.
136 B2 **Sweetwater** r. U.S.A.
122 B3 **Swellendam** S. Africa
103 D1 **Świdnica** Pol.
103 D1 **Świdwin** Pol.
103 D1 **Świebodzin** Pol.
103 D1 **Świecie** Pol.
129 D2 **Swift Current** Can.
97 C1 **Swilly, Lough** inlet
    Rep. of Ireland
99 C3 **Swindon** U.K.
102 C1 **Świnoujście** Pol.
105 D2 **Switzerland** country Europe
97 C2 **Swords** Rep. of Ireland
88 C3 **Syanno** Belarus
89 D2 **Sychevka** Rus. Fed.
53 D2 **Sydney** Austr.
131 D2 **Sydney** Can.
131 D2 **Sydney Mines** Can.
91 D2 **Syeverodonets'k** Ukr.
86 E2 **Syktyvkar** Rus. Fed.
142 C2 **Sylacauga** U.S.A.
75 D2 **Sylhet** Bangl.
102 B1 **Sylt** i. Ger.
111 C3 **Symi** i. Greece
91 D2 **Synel'nykove** Ukr.
109 C3 **Syracuse** Sicily Italy
136 C3 **Syracuse** KS U.S.A.
141 D2 **Syracuse** NY U.S.A.
77 C2 **Syrdar'ya** r. Asia
80 B2 **Syria** country Asia

63 A2 **Syriam** Myanmar
    Syrian Desert Asia *see*
    Bādiyat ash Shām
111 B3 **Syros** i. Greece
87 D3 **Syzran'** Rus. Fed.
102 C1 **Szczecin** Pol.
103 D1 **Szczecinek** Pol.
103 E1 **Szczytno** Pol.
103 E2 **Szeged** Hungary
103 D2 **Székesfehérvár** Hungary
103 E2 **Szekszárd** Hungary
103 E2 **Szentes** Hungary
103 D2 **Szentgotthárd** Hungary
103 D2 **Szigetvár** Hungary
103 E2 **Szolnok** Hungary
103 D2 **Szombathely** Hungary

T

78 B2 **Tābah** Saudi Arabia
76 B3 **Tabas** Iran
81 D3 **Tābask, Kūh-e** mt. Iran
150 B2 **Tabatinga** Brazil
114 B2 **Tabelbala** Alg.
129 C3 **Taber** Can.
102 C2 **Tábor** Czech Rep.
119 D3 **Tabora** Tanz.
114 B4 **Tabou** Côte d'Ivoire
81 C2 **Tabrīz** Iran
78 A2 **Tabūk** Saudi Arabia
77 E2 **Tacheng** China
102 C2 **Tachov** Czech Rep.
64 B1 **Tacloban** Phil.
150 A3 **Tacna** Peru
134 B1 **Tacoma** U.S.A.
152 C4 **Tacuarembó** Uru.
138 B3 **Tacupeto** Mex.
117 C3 **Tadjoura** Djibouti
80 B2 **Tadmur** Syria
129 E2 **Tadoule Lake** Can.
65 B2 **Taebaek** S. Korea
65 B3 **Taejŏn** S. Korea
65 B2 **Taejong** S. Korea
65 B2 **T'aepaek** S. Korea
107 C1 **Tafalla** Spain
152 B3 **Tafí Viejo** Arg.
79 D2 **Taftān, Kūh-e** mt. Iran
91 D2 **Taganrog** Rus. Fed.
91 D2 **Taganrog, Gulf of**
    Rus. Fed./Ukr.
62 A1 **Tagaung** Myanmar
64 B1 **Tagaytay City** Phil.
64 B2 **Tagbilaran** Phil.
64 B1 **Tagudin** Phil.
64 B2 **Tagum** Phil.
106 B2 **Tagus** r. Port./Spain
60 B1 **Tahan, Gunung** mt. Malaysia
115 C2 **Tahat, Mont** mt. Alg.
69 E1 **Tahe** China
139 E1 **Tahlequah** U.S.A.
135 B3 **Tahoe, Lake** U.S.A.
135 B3 **Tahoe City** U.S.A.
128 D2 **Tahoe Lake** Can.
115 C3 **Tahoua** Niger
79 C2 **Tahrūd** Iran
128 B3 **Tahsis** Can.
70 B2 **Tai'an** China
    Taibus Qi China *see*
    Baochang
71 C3 **T'aichung** Taiwan
54 C1 **Taihape** N.Z.
70 C2 **Tai Hu** l. China
52 A3 **Tailem Bend** Austr.
71 C3 **T'ainan** Taiwan
155 D1 **Taiobeiras** Brazil
71 C3 **T'aipei** Taiwan
60 B1 **Taiping** Malaysia

71 B3 **Taishan** China
153 A5 **Taitao, Península de** *pen.* Chile
71 C3 **T'aitung** Taiwan
92 I2 **Taivalkoski** Fin.
92 H2 **Taivaskero** *hill* Fin.
71 C3 **Taiwan** *country* Asia
71 B3 **Taiwan Strait** China/Taiwan
70 B2 **Taiyuan** China
70 B2 **Taizhou** *Jiangsu* China
71 C3 **Taizhou** *Zhejiang* China
78 B3 **Ta'izz** Yemen
75 B2 **Taj Mahal** India
Tajo *r.* Port. *see* **Tagus**
58 A1 **Tak** Thai.
54 C1 **Takaka** N.Z.
67 B4 **Takamatsu** Japan
67 C3 **Takaoka** Japan
54 B1 **Takapuna** N.Z.
67 C3 **Takasaki** Japan
122 B1 **Takatokwane** Botswana
67 C3 **Takayama** Japan
67 C3 **Takefu** Japan
60 A1 **Takengon** Indon.
63 B2 **Takêv** Cambodia
63 B2 **Ta Khmau** Cambodia
66 D2 **Takikawa** Japan
128 B2 **Takla Lake** Can.
128 B2 **Takla Landing** Can.
77 E3 **Taklimakan Shamo** *des.* China
128 A2 **Taku** *r.* Can./U.S.A.
63 A3 **Takua Pa** Thai.
115 C4 **Takum** Nigeria
88 C3 **Talachyn** Belarus
74 B1 **Talagang** Pak.
150 A2 **Talara** Peru
74 A2 **Talar-i-Band** *mts* Pak.
59 C2 **Talaud, Kepulauan** *is* Indon.
106 C2 **Talavera de la Reina** Spain
153 A4 **Talca** Chile
153 A4 **Talcahuano** Chile
89 E2 **Taldom** Rus. Fed.
77 D2 **Taldykorgan** Kazakh.
59 C3 **Taliabu** *i.* Indon.
64 B1 **Talisay** Phil.
61 C2 **Taliwang** Indon.
81 C2 **Tall 'Afar** Iraq
143 D2 **Tallahassee** U.S.A.
88 B2 **Tallinn** Estonia
142 B2 **Tallulah** U.S.A.
104 B2 **Talmont-St-Hilaire** France
90 C2 **Tal'ne** Ukr.
117 B3 **Talodi** Sudan
91 E1 **Talovaya** Rus. Fed.
126 E2 **Taloyoak** Can.
88 B2 **Talsi** Latvia
152 A3 **Taltal** Chile
129 C1 **Taltson** *r.* Can.
60 A1 **Talu** Indon.
53 C1 **Talwood** Austr.
114 B4 **Tamale** Ghana
115 C2 **Tamanrasset** Alg.
99 A3 **Tamar** *r.* U.K.
144 C3 **Tamazunchale** Mex.
114 A3 **Tambacounda** Senegal
61 B1 **Tambelan, Kepulauan** *is* Indon.
91 E1 **Tambov** Rus. Fed.
145 C2 **Tamiahua, Laguna de** *lag.* Mex.
143 D3 **Tampa** U.S.A.
143 D3 **Tampa Bay** U.S.A.
93 H3 **Tampere** Fin.
145 C2 **Tampico** Mex.
69 D1 **Tamsagbulag** Mongolia
102 C2 **Tamsweg** Austria
53 D2 **Tamworth** Austr.
99 C2 **Tamworth** U.K.

119 E3 **Tana** *r.* Kenya
67 C4 **Tanabe** Japan
92 I1 **Tana Bru** Norway
117 B3 **T'ana Hāyk'** *l.* Eth.
61 C2 **Tanahgrogot** Indon.
58 C3 **Tanahjampea** *i.* Indon.
50 C1 **Tanami Desert** Austr.
126 A2 **Tanana** U.S.A.
108 A1 **Tanaro** *r.* Italy
65 B1 **Tanch'ŏn** N. Korea
64 B2 **Tandag** Phil.
110 C2 **Ţăndărei** Romania
153 C4 **Tandil** Arg.
74 A2 **Tando Adam** Pak.
74 A2 **Tando Muhammad Khan** Pak.
114 B2 **Tanezrouft** *reg.* Alg./Mali
119 D3 **Tanga** Tanz.
119 C3 **Tanganyika, Lake** Africa
Tanger Morocco *see* **Tangier**
101 E1 **Tangermünde** Ger.
75 C1 **Tanggula Shan** *mts* China
114 B1 **Tangier** Morocco
75 C1 **Tangra Yumco** *salt l.* China
70 B2 **Tangshan** China
68 C2 **Taniantaweng Shan** *mts* China
59 C3 **Tanimbar, Kepulauan** *is* Indon.
64 B2 **Tanjay** Phil.
60 A1 **Tanjungbalai** Indon.
60 B2 **Tanjungkarang-Telukbetung** Indon.
61 B2 **Tanjungpandan** Indon.
60 B1 **Tanjungpinang** Indon.
61 C1 **Tanjungredeb** Indon.
61 C1 **Tanjungselor** Indon.
74 B1 **Tank** Pak.
115 C3 **Tanout** Niger
75 C2 **Tansen** Nepal
116 B1 **Tanta** Egypt
119 D3 **Tanzania** *country* Africa
69 E1 **Taonan** China
138 B1 **Taos** U.S.A.
114 B2 **Taoudenni** Mali
88 C2 **Tapa** Estonia
145 C3 **Tapachula** Mex.
151 C2 **Tapajós** *r.* Brazil
60 A1 **Tapaktuan** Indon.
145 C3 **Tapanatepec** Mex.
150 B2 **Tapauá** Brazil
114 B4 **Tapeta** Liberia
74 B2 **Tāpi** *r.* India
141 D3 **Tappahannock** U.S.A.
150 B2 **Tapurucuara** Brazil
154 B1 **Taquari** *r.* Brazil
154 A1 **Taquari** *r.* Brazil
154 B1 **Taquari, Serra do** *hills* Brazil
154 C2 **Taquaritinga** Brazil
115 D4 **Taraba** *r.* Nigeria
Ţarābulus Libya *see* **Tripoli**
61 C1 **Tarakan** Indon.
88 A3 **Taran, Mys** *pt* Rus. Fed.
Taranaki, Mount *vol.* N.Z. *see* **Egmont, Mt**
106 C1 **Tarancón** Spain
109 C2 **Taranto** Italy
109 C2 **Taranto, Golfo di** *g.* Italy
150 A2 **Tarapoto** Peru
91 E2 **Tarasovskiy** Rus. Fed.
150 A2 **Tarauacá** Brazil
150 B2 **Tarauacá** *r.* Brazil
77 D2 **Taraz** Kazakh.
107 C1 **Tarazona** Spain
77 E2 **Tarbagatay, Khrebet** *mts* Kazakh.
96 C2 **Tarbert** *Scotland* U.K.
96 B3 **Tarbert** *Scotland* U.K.
104 C3 **Tarbes** France
96 B2 **Tarbet** U.K.

51 C3 **Tarcoola** Austr.
53 D2 **Taree** Austr.
110 C2 **Târgovişte** Romania
110 B1 **Târgu Jiu** Romania
110 B1 **Târgu Mureş** Romania
110 C1 **Târgu Neamţ** Romania
79 C2 **Tarīf** U.A.E.
152 B3 **Tarija** Bol.
79 B3 **Tarīm** Yemen
77 E2 **Tarim He** *r.* China
77 E3 **Tarim Pendi** *basin* China
59 D3 **Taritatu** *r.* Indon.
82 G2 **Tarko-Sale** Rus. Fed.
114 B4 **Tarkwa** Ghana
64 B1 **Tarlac** Phil.
93 F3 **Tärnaby** Sweden
77 C3 **Tarnak** *r.* Afgh.
110 B1 **Târnăveni** Romania
103 E1 **Tarnobrzeg** Pol.
103 E1 **Tarnów** Pol.
114 B1 **Taroudannt** Morocco
108 B2 **Tarquinia** Italy
107 D1 **Tarragona** Spain
107 D1 **Tàrrega** Spain
80 B2 **Tarsus** Turkey
152 B3 **Tartagal** Arg.
104 B3 **Tartas** France
88 C2 **Tartu** Estonia
80 B2 **Ţarţūs** Syria
155 D1 **Tarumirim** Brazil
89 E3 **Tarusa** Rus. Fed.
108 B1 **Tarvisio** Italy
Tashi Chho Bhutan *see* **Thimphu**
81 D3 **Tashk, Daryācheh-ye** *l.* Iran
77 C2 **Tashkent** Uzbek.
131 D1 **Tasiujaq** Can.
77 E2 **Taskesken** Kazakh.
54 B2 **Tasman Bay** N.Z.
51 D4 **Tasmania** *state* Austr.
54 B2 **Tasman Mountains** N.Z.
156 D8 **Tasman Sea** S. Pacific Ocean
115 C2 **Tassili du Hoggar** *plat.* Alg.
115 C2 **Tassili n'Ajjer** *plat.* Alg.
103 D2 **Tatabánya** Hungary
90 B2 **Tatarbunary** Ukr.
83 K3 **Tatarskiy Proliv** *str.* Rus. Fed.
67 C4 **Tateyama** Japan
128 C1 **Tathlina Lake** Can.
78 B3 **Tathlith** Saudi Arabia
78 B2 **Tathlith, Wādī** *watercourse* Saudi Arabia
53 C3 **Tathra** Austr.
62 A1 **Tatkon** Myanmar
128 B2 **Tatla Lake** Can.
74 A2 **Tatta** Pak.
154 C2 **Tatuí** Brazil
139 C2 **Tatum** U.S.A.
81 C2 **Tatvan** Turkey
151 D2 **Taua** Brazil
155 C2 **Taubaté** Brazil
101 D3 **Tauberbischofsheim** Ger.
54 C1 **Taumarunui** N.Z.
62 A1 **Taunggyi** Myanmar
62 A2 **Taungup** Myanmar
99 B3 **Taunton** U.K.
100 C2 **Taunus** *hills* Ger.
54 C1 **Taupo** N.Z.
54 C1 **Taupo, Lake** N.Z.
88 B2 **Tauragė** Lith.
54 C1 **Tauranga** N.Z.
111 C3 **Tavas** Turkey
86 F3 **Tavda** Rus. Fed.
106 B2 **Tavira** Port.
93 A3 **Tavistock** U.K.
63 A2 **Tavoy** Myanmar
111 C3 **Tavşanlı** Turkey
99 A3 **Taw** *r.* U.K.

Tawas City

242

140 C2 Tawas City U.S.A.
61 C1 Tawau Sabah Malaysia
64 A2 Tawitawi i. Phil.
145 C3 Taxco Mex.
77 D3 Taxkorgan China
96 C2 Tay r. U.K.
96 B2 Tay, Firth of est. U.K.
96 B2 Tay, Loch l. U.K.
128 B2 Taylor Can.
139 D2 Taylor U.S.A.
140 B3 Taylorville U.S.A.
78 A2 Taymá' Saudi Arabia
83 H2 Taymura r. Rus. Fed.
83 H2 Taymyr, Ozero l. Rus. Fed.
83 G2 Taymyr, Poluostrov pen. Rus. Fed.
63 B2 Tây Ninh Vietnam
64 A1 Taytay Phil.
82 C2 Taz r. Rus. Fed.
114 B1 Taza Morocco
129 D2 Tazin Lake Can.
86 G2 Tazovskaya Guba sea chan. Rus. Fed.
81 C1 T'bilisi Georgia
91 E2 Tbilisskaya Rus. Fed.
118 B3 Tchibanga Gabon
118 B2 Tcholliré Cameroon
103 D1 Tczew Pol.
144 B2 Teacapán Mex.
54 A3 Te Anau N.Z.
54 A3 Te Anau, Lake N.Z.
145 C3 Teapa Mex.
54 C1 Te Awamutu N.Z.
115 C1 Tébessa Alg.
60 B2 Tebingtinggi Sumatera Indon.
60 A1 Tebingtinggi Sumatera Indon.
114 B4 Techiman Ghana
144 B3 Tecomán Mex.
144 B2 Tecoripa Mex.
145 B3 Técpan Mex.
144 B2 Tecuala Mex.
110 C1 Tecuci Romania
76 C3 Tedzhen Turkm.
76 C3 Tedzhen r. Turkm.
68 C1 Teeli Rus. Fed.
98 C1 Tees r. U.K.
111 C3 Tefenni Turkey
61 B2 Tegal Indon.
146 B3 Tegucigalpa Hond.
115 C4 Teguidda-n-Tessoumt Niger
114 B4 Téhini Côte d'Ivoire
81 D2 Tehrān Iran
145 C3 Tehuacán Mex.
145 C3 Tehuantepec, Golfo de g. Mex.
145 C3 Tehuantepec, Istmo de isth. Mex.
99 A2 Teifi r. U.K.
Tejo r. Spain see Tagus
145 B3 Tejupilco Mex.
54 B2 Tekapo, Lake N.Z.
145 D2 Tekax Mex.
116 B3 Tekezē Wenz r. Eritrea/Eth.
111 C2 Tekirdağ Turkey
54 C1 Te Kuiti N.Z.
75 C2 Tel r. India
81 C1 T'elavi Georgia
80 B2 Tel Aviv-Yafo Israel
145 D2 Telchac Puerto Mex.
128 A2 Telegraph Creek Can.
154 B2 Telêmaco Borba Brazil
99 B2 Telford U.K.
60 A2 Telo Indon.
86 E2 Tel'pos-Iz, Gora mt. Rus. Fed.
88 B2 Telšiai Lith.
60 B1 Teluk Anson Malaysia
61 B2 Telukbatang Indon.
60 A1 Telukdalam Indon.
130 C2 Temagami Lake Can.
61 C2 Temanggung Indon.

123 C2 Temba S. Africa
60 B2 Tembilahan Indon.
120 A1 Tembo Aluma Angola
99 B2 Teme r. U.K.
60 D1 Temerloh Malaysia
77 D1 Temirtau Kazakh.
53 C2 Temora Austr.
139 D2 Temple U.S.A.
97 C2 Templemore Rep. of Ireland
145 C2 Tempoal Mex.
91 D2 Temryuk Rus. Fed.
153 A4 Temuco Chile
54 B2 Temuka N.Z.
145 C2 Tenabo Mex.
73 C3 Tenali India
63 A2 Tenasserim Myanmar
99 A3 Tenby U.K.
117 C3 Tendaho Eth.
105 D3 Tende France
108 A2 Tende, Col de pass France/Italy
Ten Degree Channel India
67 D4 Tendō Japan
114 B3 Tenenkou Mali
115 C2 Ténéré du Tafassâsset des. Niger
114 A2 Tenerife i. Canary Is
107 D2 Ténès Alg.
61 C2 Tengah, Kepulauan is Indon.
62 A1 Tengchong China
61 C2 Tenggarong Indon.
70 A2 Tengger Shamo des. China
71 B3 Tengxian China
119 C3 Tenke Dem. Rep. Congo
114 B3 Tenkodogo Burkina
51 C1 Tennant Creek Austr.
142 C1 Tennessee r. U.S.A.
142 C1 Tennessee state U.S.A.
145 C3 Tenosique Mex.
53 D1 Tenterfield Austr.
154 B2 Teodoro Sampaio Brazil
155 D1 Teófilo Otôni Brazil
145 C3 Teopisca Mex.
144 B2 Tepache Mex.
54 B1 Te Paki N.Z.
144 B3 Tepalcatepec Mex.
144 B2 Tepatitlán Mex.
144 B2 Tepehuanes Mex.
109 D2 Tepelenë Albania
144 B2 Tepic Mex.
102 C1 Teplice Czech Rep.
89 E3 Teploye Rus. Fed.
144 B2 Tequila Mex.
108 B2 Teramo Italy
89 E3 Terbuny Rus. Fed.
90 B2 Terebovlya Ukr.
87 D4 Terek r. Rus. Fed.
151 D2 Teresina Brazil
154 C2 Teresópolis Brazil
63 A3 Teressa Island India
80 B1 Terme Turkey
77 C3 Termez Uzbek.
108 B3 Termini Imerese Sicily Italy
145 C3 Términos, Laguna de lag. Mex.
109 B2 Termoli Italy
59 C2 Ternate Indon.
100 A2 Terneuzen Neth.
108 B2 Terni Italy
90 B2 Ternopil' Ukr.
128 B2 Terrace Can.
130 B2 Terrace Bay Can.
122 B2 Terra Firma S. Africa
140 B3 Terre Haute U.S.A.
131 E2 Terrenceville Can.
100 B1 Terschelling i. Neth.
108 A3 Tertenia Sardinia Italy
107 C1 Teruel Spain
92 H2 Tervola Fin.
109 C2 Tešanj Bos.-Herz.

116 B3 Teseney Eritrea
66 D2 Teshio-gawa r. Japan
128 A1 Teslin Can.
128 A1 Teslin Lake Can.
154 B1 Tesouro Brazil
115 C3 Tessaoua Niger
121 C2 Tete Moz.
90 C1 Teteriv r. Ukr.
101 F1 Teterow Ger.
90 B2 Tetiyiv Ukr.
114 B1 Tétouan Morocco
109 D2 Tetovo Macedonia
152 B3 Teuco r. Arg.
144 B2 Teul de González Ortega Mex.
101 D1 Teutoburger Wald hills Ger.
108 B2 Tevere r. Italy
54 A3 Teviot N.Z.
51 D2 Tewantin Austr.
54 C2 Te Wharau N.Z.
139 E2 Texarkana U.S.A.
53 D1 Texas Austr.
139 D2 Texas state U.S.A.
139 E3 Texas City U.S.A.
100 B1 Texel i. Neth.
139 D2 Texoma, Lake U.S.A.
123 C2 Teyateyaneng Lesotho
89 F2 Teykovo Rus. Fed.
89 F2 Teza r. Rus. Fed.
75 D2 Tezpur India
62 A1 Tezu India
129 E1 Tha-anne r. Can.
123 C2 Thabana-Ntlenyana mt. Lesotho
123 C2 Thaba Putsoa mt. Lesotho
123 C1 Thabazimbi S. Africa
123 C2 Thabong S. Africa
63 A2 Thagyettaw Myanmar
62 B1 Thai Binh Vietnam
63 B2 Thailand country Asia
61 B2 Thailand, Gulf of Asia
62 B1 Thai Nguyên Vietnam
63 A3 Thalang Thai.
74 B1 Thal Desert Pak.
101 E2 Thale (Harz) Ger.
62 B2 Tha Li Thai.
123 C1 Thamaga Botswana
116 C3 Thamar, Jabal mt. Yemen
79 C3 Thamarit Oman
130 B2 Thames r. Can.
54 C1 Thames N.Z.
99 D3 Thames est. U.K.
99 D3 Thames r. U.K.
63 A2 Thanbyuzayat Myanmar
62 B2 Thanh Hoa Vietnam
73 B3 Thanjavur India
74 A2 Thano Bula Khan Pak.
62 B1 Than Uyen Vietnam
74 A2 Thar Desert India/Pak.
52 B1 Thargomindah Austr.
62 A2 Tharrawaddy Myanmar
81 C2 Tharthār, Buhayrat ath l. Iraq
111 B3 Thasos i. Greece
62 B1 Thât Khê Vietnam
62 A2 Thaton Myanmar
62 A1 Thaungdut Myanmar
62 A2 Thayetmyo Myanmar
62 A1 Thazi Myanmar
146 C2 The Bahamas country West Indies
98 B1 The Cheviot hill U.K.
134 B1 The Dalles U.S.A.
99 C2 The Fens reg. U.K.
114 A3 The Gambia country Africa
116 B2 The Great Oasis Egypt
79 C2 The Gulf Asia
100 B1 The Hague Neth.
129 E1 Thelon r. Can.
101 E2 Themar Ger.

96 A1 **The Minch** sea chan. U.K.
150 B2 **Theodore Roosevelt** r. Brazil
129 D2 **The Pas** Can.
111 B2 **Thermaïkos Kolpos** g. Greece
136 B2 **Thermopolis** U.S.A.
53 C3 **The Rock** Austr.
130 B2 **Thessalon** Can.
111 B2 **Thessaloniki** Greece
99 D2 **Thetford** U.K.
131 C2 **Thetford Mines** Can.
62 A1 **The Triangle** mts Myanmar
131 D1 **Thévenet, Lac** l. Can.
99 D2 **The Wash** b. U.K.
139 D2 **The Woodlands** U.S.A.
142 B3 **Thibodaux** U.S.A.
129 E2 **Thicket Portage** Can.
137 D1 **Thief River Falls** U.S.A.
105 C2 **Thiers** France
119 D3 **Thika** Kenya
73 B4 **Thiladhunmathee Atoll** Maldives
75 C2 **Thimphu** Bhutan
105 D2 **Thionville** France
Thira i. Greece see Santorini
98 C1 **Thiruvananthapuram** India see Trivandrum
93 E4 **Thisted** Denmark
129 E1 **Thlewiaza** r. Can.
62 A2 **Thoen** Thai.
123 D1 **Thohoyandou** S. Africa
101 E1 **Thomasburg** Ger.
97 C3 **Thomastown** Rep. of Ireland
143 D2 **Thomasville** U.S.A.
100 C2 **Thommen** Belgium
129 E2 **Thompson** Can.
128 E3 **Thompson** r. U.S.A.
134 C1 **Thompson Falls** U.S.A.
128 B2 **Thompson Sound** Can.
96 C3 **Thornhill** U.K.
55 C2 **Thorshavnheiane** reg. Antarctica
104 B2 **Thouars** France
128 C2 **Three Hills** Can.
63 A2 **Three Pagodas Pass** Myanmar/Thai.
114 B4 **Three Points, Cape** Ghana
63 B2 **Thu Dâu Môt** Vietnam
100 B2 **Thuin** Belgium
121 B3 **Thuli** Zimbabwe
130 B2 **Thunder Bay** Can.
63 A3 **Thung Song** Thai.
101 E2 **Thüringer Becken** reg. Ger.
101 E2 **Thüringer Wald** mts Ger.
97 C2 **Thurles** Rep. of Ireland
96 C1 **Thurso** U.K.
96 C1 **Thurso** r. U.K.
151 D2 **Tianguá** Brazil
70 B2 **Tianjin** China
70 B2 **Tianjin** mun. China
71 A3 **Tianlin** China
70 B2 **Tianmen** China
70 A2 **Tianshui** China
154 B2 **Tibagi** r. Brazil
118 B2 **Tibati** Cameroon
Tiberias, Lake l. Israel see Galilee, Sea of
115 D2 **Tibesti** mts Chad
Tibet aut. reg. China see Xizang Zizhiqu
Tibet, Plateau of China see Qing Zang Gaoyuan
52 B1 **Tibooburra** Austr.
144 A2 **Tiburón, Isla** i. Mex.
114 B3 **Tichît** Maur.
114 A2 **Tichla** Western Sahara
145 D2 **Ticul** Mex.
114 A3 **Tidjikja** Maur.
100 B2 **Tiel** Neth.

65 A1 **Tieling** China
100 A2 **Tielt** Belgium
100 B2 **Tienen** Belgium
68 B2 **Tien Shan** mts China/Kyrg.
Tientsin China see Tianjin
93 G3 **Tierp** Sweden
145 C3 **Tierra Blanca** Mex.
145 C3 **Tierra Colorada** Mex.
153 B6 **Tierra del Fuego, Isla Grande de** i. Arg./Chile
154 C2 **Tietê** Brazil
Tiflis Georgia see T'bilisi
143 D2 **Tifton** U.S.A.
90 B2 **Tighina** Moldova
131 D2 **Tignish** Can.
150 A2 **Tigre** r. Ecuador/Peru
81 C2 **Tigris** r. Asia
145 C2 **Tihuatlán** Mex.
144 A1 **Tijuana** Mex.
91 E2 **Tikhoretsk** Rus. Fed.
89 D2 **Tikhvin** Rus. Fed.
89 D2 **Tikhvinskaya Gryada** ridge Rus. Fed.
54 C1 **Tikokino** N.Z.
81 C2 **Tikrīt** Iraq
83 J2 **Tiksi** Rus. Fed.
100 B2 **Tilburg** Neth.
152 B3 **Tilcara** Arg.
52 B1 **Tilcha** Austr.
114 C3 **Tillabéri** Niger
134 B1 **Tillamook** U.S.A.
63 A3 **Tillanchong Island** India
111 C3 **Tilos** i. Greece
52 B2 **Tilpa** Austr.
86 F2 **Til'tim** Rus. Fed.
89 E3 **Tim** Rus. Fed.
86 D2 **Timanskiy Kryazh** ridge Rus. Fed.
54 B2 **Timaru** N.Z.
91 D2 **Timashevsk** Rus. Fed.
114 B3 **Timbedgha** Maur.
50 C1 **Timber Creek** Austr.
Timbuktu Mali see Tombouctou
114 C2 **Timimoun** Alg.
110 B1 **Timiş** r. Romania
110 B1 **Timişoara** Romania
130 B2 **Timmins** Can.
89 E2 **Timokhino** Rus. Fed.
151 D2 **Timon** Brazil
59 C3 **Timor** i. Indon.
58 C3 **Timor Sea** Austr./Indon.
93 G3 **Timrå** Sweden
114 B2 **Tindouf** Alg.
75 C2 **Tingri** China
93 F4 **Tingsryd** Sweden
59 D2 **Tinian** i. N. Mariana Is
153 B3 **Tinogasta** Arg.
111 C3 **Tinos** Greece
111 C3 **Tinos** i. Greece
115 C2 **Tinrhert, Plateau du** Alg.
62 A1 **Tinsukia** India
107 D2 **Tipasa** Alg.
97 C2 **Tipperary** Rep. of Ireland
109 C2 **Tirana** Albania
Tiranë Albania see Tirana
108 B1 **Tirano** Italy
90 B2 **Tiraspol** Moldova
111 C3 **Tire** Turkey
96 A2 **Tiree** i. U.K.
74 B1 **Tirich Mir** mt. Pak.
73 B3 **Tiruchchirāppalli** India
73 B4 **Tirunelveli** India
73 B3 **Tirupati** India
73 B3 **Tiruppattur** India
73 B3 **Tiruppur** India
109 D1 **Tisa** r. Europe
129 D2 **Tisdale** Can.
107 D2 **Tissemsilt** Alg.
152 B2 **Titicaca, Lago** l. Bol./Peru

75 C2 **Titlagarh** India
110 C2 **Titu** Romania
143 D3 **Titusville** U.S.A.
99 B3 **Tiverton** U.K.
108 B2 **Tivoli** Italy
79 C2 **Tiwi** Oman
145 D2 **Tizimín** Mex.
107 D2 **Tizi Ouzou** Alg.
114 B2 **Tiznit** Morocco
145 C3 **Tlacotalpán** Mex.
144 B2 **Tlahualilo** Mex.
145 C3 **Tlapa** Mex.
145 C3 **Tlaxcala** Mex.
145 C3 **Tlaxiaco** Mex.
114 B1 **Tlemcen** Alg.
123 C1 **Tlokweng** Botswana
128 B2 **Toad River** Can.
121 □D2 **Toamasina** Madag.
60 A1 **Toba, Danau** l. Indon.
74 A1 **Toba and Kakar Ranges** mts Pak.
147 D3 **Tobago** i. Trin. and Tob.
59 C2 **Tobelo** Indon.
130 B2 **Tobermory** Can.
96 A2 **Tobermory** U.K.
129 D2 **Tobin Lake** l. Can.
60 B2 **Toboali** Indon.
76 C1 **Tobol** r. Kazakh./Rus. Fed.
86 F3 **Tobol'sk** Rus. Fed.
151 D2 **Tocantinópolis** Brazil
151 D2 **Tocantins** r. Brazil
143 D2 **Toccoa** U.S.A.
108 A1 **Toce** r. Italy
152 A3 **Tocopilla** Chile
53 C3 **Tocumwal** Austr.
144 A2 **Todos Santos** Mex.
128 B3 **Tofino** Can.
96 □ **Toft** U.K.
59 C3 **Togian, Kepulauan** is Indon.
114 C4 **Togo** country Africa
74 B2 **Tohana** India
126 B2 **Tok** U.S.A.
116 B3 **Tokar** Sudan
Tokara-rettō is Japan
91 E1 **Tokarevka** Rus. Fed.
49 G3 **Tokelau** terr. S. Pacific Ocean
77 D2 **Tokmak** Kyrg.
91 D2 **Tokmak** Ukr.
54 C1 **Tokoroa** N.Z.
68 B2 **Toksun** China
67 B4 **Tokushima** Japan
67 C3 **Tōkyō** Japan
121 □D3 **Tôlañaro** Madag.
154 B2 **Toledo** Brazil
106 C2 **Toledo** Spain
140 C2 **Toledo** U.S.A.
106 C2 **Toledo, Montes de** mts Spain
142 B2 **Toledo Bend Reservoir** U.S.A.
121 □D3 **Toliara** Madag.
58 C2 **Tolitoli** Indon.
108 B1 **Tolmezzo** Italy
104 B3 **Tolosa** Spain
145 C3 **Toluca** Mex.
87 D3 **Tol'yatti** Rus. Fed.
140 A2 **Tomah** U.S.A.
66 D2 **Tomakomai** Japan
106 B2 **Tomar** Port.
103 E1 **Tomaszów Lubelski** Pol.
103 E1 **Tomaszów Mazowiecki** Pol.
144 B3 **Tomatlán** Mex.
142 C2 **Tombigbee** r. U.S.A.
155 D2 **Tombos** Brazil
114 B3 **Tombouctou** Mali
120 A2 **Tombua** Angola
123 C1 **Tom Burke** S. Africa
53 C2 **Tomingley** Austr.
58 C3 **Tomini, Teluk** g. Indon.

Tomislavgrad

244

109 C2 **Tomislavgrad** Bos.-Herz.
50 A2 **Tom Price** Austr.
82 G3 **Tomsk** Rus. Fed.
93 F4 **Tomtabacken** hill Sweden
145 C3 **Tonalá** Mex.
150 B2 **Tonantins** Brazil
59 C2 **Tondano** Indon.
49 G4 **Tonga** country
S. Pacific Ocean
71 B3 **Tongcheng** China
70 A2 **Tongchuan** China
71 A3 **Tongdao** China
65 B2 **Tongduch'ŏn** S. Korea
100 B2 **Tongeren** Belgium
65 B2 **Tonghae** S. Korea
62 B1 **Tonghai** China
65 B1 **Tonghua** China
65 B2 **Tongjosŏn-man** b. N. Korea
62 B1 **Tongking, Gulf of**
China/Vietnam
69 E2 **Tongliao** China
70 B2 **Tongling** China
52 B2 **Tongo** Austr.
71 A3 **Tongren** China
96 B1 **Tongshan** China see Xuzhou
71 A4 **Tongshi** China
Tongtian He r. China see
Yangtze
96 B1 **Tongue** U.K.
65 B3 **T'ongyŏng** S. Korea
69 E2 **Tongyu** China
65 A1 **Tongyuanpu** China
74 B2 **Tonk** India
63 B2 **Tônlé Sab** l. Cambodia
135 C3 **Tonopah** U.S.A.
93 F4 **Tønsberg** Norway
135 D2 **Tooele** U.S.A.
52 B3 **Tooleybuc** Austr.
53 D1 **Toowoomba** Austr.
137 D3 **Topeka** U.S.A.
144 B2 **Topia** Mex.
144 B2 **Topolobampo** Mex.
86 C2 **Topozero, Ozero** l. Rus. Fed.
134 B1 **Toppenish** U.S.A.
111 C3 **Torbalı** Turkey
76 B3 **Torbat-e Ḥeydarīyeh** Iran
76 C3 **Torbat-e Jām** Iran
106 C1 **Tordesillas** Spain
107 C1 **Tordesilos** Spain
107 D1 **Torelló** Spain
101 F2 **Torgau** Ger.
100 A2 **Torhout** Belgium
154 B1 **Torixoreu** Brazil
106 B1 **Tormes** r. Spain
92 H2 **Torneälven** r. Sweden
127 G3 **Torngat Mountains** Can.
92 H2 **Tornio** Fin.
106 B1 **Toro** Spain
130 C2 **Toronto** Can.
119 D2 **Tororo** Uganda
80 B2 **Toros Dağları** mts Turkey
99 B3 **Torquay** U.K.
106 B2 **Torrão** Port.
106 B1 **Torre** mt. Port.
107 D1 **Torreblanca** Spain
106 B1 **Torre de Moncorvo** Port.
106 C1 **Torrelavega** Spain
106 C2 **Torremolinos** Spain
52 A2 **Torrens, Lake** salt flat Austr.
107 C2 **Torrent** Spain
144 B2 **Torreón** Mex.
106 B2 **Torres Novas** Port.
106 B2 **Torres Vedras** Port.
107 C2 **Torrevieja** Spain
96 B2 **Torridon** U.K.
106 C2 **Torrijos** Spain
141 E2 **Torrington** CT U.S.A.
136 C2 **Torrington** WY U.S.A.
107 D1 **Torroella de Montgrí** Spain

94 B1 **Tórshavn** Faroe Is
108 A3 **Tortoli** Sardinia Italy
107 D1 **Tortosa** Spain
103 D1 **Toruń** Pol.
97 B1 **Tory Island** Rep. of Ireland
89 D2 **Torzhok** Rus. Fed.
122 B2 **Tosca** S. Africa
89 D2 **Tosno** Rus. Fed.
152 B3 **Tostado** Arg.
101 D1 **Tostedt** Ger.
80 B1 **Tosya** Turkey
86 D3 **Tot'ma** Rus. Fed.
67 B3 **Tottori** Japan
114 B4 **Touba** Côte d'Ivoire
114 B1 **Toubkal, Jbel** mt.
Morocco
122 B3 **Tougan** Burkina
115 C1 **Touggourt** Alg.
105 D2 **Toul** France
71 C3 **Touliu** Taiwan
105 D3 **Toulon** France
104 C3 **Toulouse** France
62 A2 **Toungoo** Myanmar
105 C2 **Tournai** Belgium
105 C2 **Tournus** France
151 E2 **Touros** Brazil
104 C2 **Tours** France
115 D2 **Toussidé, Pic** mt. Chad
122 B3 **Touwsrivier** S. Africa
66 D2 **Towada** Japan
134 D1 **Townsend** U.S.A.
51 D1 **Townsville** Austr.
77 E2 **Toxkan He** r. China
66 D2 **Tōya-ko** l. Japan
67 C3 **Toyama** Japan
67 C3 **Toyota** Japan
115 C1 **Tozeur** Tunisia
81 C1 **Tqvarch'eli** Georgia
80 B2 **Trâblous** Lebanon
80 B1 **Trabzon** Turkey
106 B2 **Trafalgar, Cabo** c. Spain
128 C3 **Trail** Can.
88 B3 **Trakai** Lith.
97 B2 **Tralee** Rep. of Ireland
97 C2 **Tramore** Rep. of Ireland
63 A3 **Trang** Thai.
59 C3 **Trangan** i. Indon.
55 I2 **Transantarctic Mountains**
Antarctica
Transylvanian Alps mts
Romania see
Carpaţii Meridionali
108 B3 **Trapani** Sicily Italy
53 C3 **Traralgon** Austr.
63 B2 **Trat** Thai.
102 C2 **Traunstein** Ger.
140 B2 **Traverse City** U.S.A.
103 D2 **Třebíč** Czech Rep.
109 C2 **Trebinje** Bos.-Herz.
103 E2 **Trebišov** Slovakia
109 C1 **Trebnje** Slovenia
153 C4 **Treinta-y-Tres** Uru.
153 B5 **Trelew** Arg.
93 F4 **Trelleborg** Sweden
130 C2 **Tremblant, Mont** hill Can.
109 C2 **Tremiti, Isole** is Italy
134 D2 **Tremonton** U.S.A.
107 D1 **Tremp** Spain
103 D2 **Trenčín** Slovakia
153 B4 **Trenque Lauquén** Arg.
98 C2 **Trent** r. U.K.
108 B1 **Trento** Italy
141 D2 **Trenton** U.S.A.
137 E2 **Trenton** MO U.S.A.
141 E2 **Trenton** NJ U.S.A.
131 E2 **Trepassey** Can.
153 B4 **Tres Arroyos** Arg.
155 C2 **Três Corações** Brazil
154 B2 **Três Lagoas** Brazil
153 A5 **Tres Lagos** Arg.

155 C1 **Três Marias, Represa** resr
Brazil
155 C2 **Três Pontas** Brazil
153 B5 **Tres Puntas, Cabo** c. Arg.
155 C2 **Três Rios** Brazil
101 F1 **Treuenbrietzen** Ger.
108 A1 **Treviglio** Italy
108 B1 **Treviso** Italy
99 A3 **Trevose Head** hd U.K.
109 C3 **Tricase** Italy
73 B3 **Trichur** India
53 C2 **Trida** Austr.
100 C3 **Trier** Ger.
108 B1 **Trieste** Italy
108 B1 **Triglav** mt. Slovenia
59 D3 **Trikora, Puncak** mt. Indon.
97 C2 **Trim** Rep. of Ireland
73 C4 **Trincomalee** Sri Lanka
154 C1 **Trindade** Brazil
152 B2 **Trinidad** Bol.
147 D3 **Trinidad** i. Trin. and Tob.
136 C3 **Trinidad** U.S.A.
147 D3 **Trinidad and Tobago**
country West Indies
131 E2 **Trinity Bay** Can.
111 B3 **Tripoli** Greece
Tripoli Lebanon see Trâblous
115 D1 **Tripoli** Libya
149 G5 **Tristan da Cunha** i.
S. Atlantic Ocean
73 B4 **Trivandrum** India
108 B2 **Trivento** Italy
103 D2 **Trnava** Slovakia
109 C2 **Trogir** Croatia
109 C2 **Troia** Italy
100 C3 **Troisdorf** Ger.
131 C2 **Trois-Rivières** Can.
86 E2 **Troitsko-Pechorsk** Rus. Fed.
151 C2 **Trombetas** r. Brazil
123 C3 **Trompsburg** S. Africa
92 G2 **Tromsø** Norway
92 F3 **Trondheim** Norway
128 C2 **Trout Lake** Can.
128 B1 **Trout Lake** l. N.W.T. Can.
130 A1 **Trout Lake** l. Ont. Can.
99 B3 **Trowbridge** U.K.
142 C2 **Troy** AL U.S.A.
141 E2 **Troy** NY U.S.A.
105 C2 **Troyes** France
109 D2 **Trstenik** Yugo.
89 D3 **Trubchevsk** Rus. Fed.
106 B1 **Truchas** Spain
79 C2 **Trucial Coast** U.A.E.
146 B3 **Trujillo** Hond.
150 A2 **Trujillo** Peru
106 B2 **Trujillo** Spain
147 C4 **Trujillo** Venez.
142 B1 **Trumann** U.S.A.
131 D2 **Truro** Can.
99 A3 **Truro** U.K.
138 B2 **Truth or Consequences**
U.S.A.
103 D1 **Trutnov** Czech Rep.
93 F3 **Trysil** Norway
103 D1 **Trzebiatów** Pol.
68 B1 **Tsagaannuur** Mongolia
121 C2D2 **Tsaratanana, Massif du**
mts Madag.
110 C2 **Tsarevo** Bulg.
122 A2 **Tses** Namibia
122 B1 **Tsetseng** Botswana
68 C1 **Tsetserleg** Mongolia
122 B1 **Tshabong** Botswana
122 B1 **Tshane** Botswana
91 D2 **Tshchikskoye**
Vodokhranilishche resr
Rus. Fed.
118 B3 **Tshela** Dem. Rep. Congo
118 C3 **Tshikapa** Dem. Rep. Congo
118 C3 **Tshikapa** r. Dem. Rep. Congo

123 D1 Tshipise S. Africa
118 C3 Tshitanzu Dem. Rep. Congo
118 C3 Tshuapa r. Dem. Rep. Congo
87 D4 Tsimlyanskoye
Vodokhranilishche resr
Rus. Fed.
Tsingtao China see Qingdao
Tsining China see Jining
121 □D2 Tsiroanomandidy Madag.
123 C3 Tsomo S. Africa
67 C4 Tsu Japan
67 C3 Tsuchiura Japan
66 D2 Tsugarū-kaikyō str. Japan
120 A2 Tsumeb Namibia
122 A1 Tsumis Park Namibia
120 B2 Tsumkwe Namibia
67 C3 Tsuruga Japan
66 C3 Tsuruoka Japan
67 A4 Tsushima is Japan
Tsushima-kaikyō str.
Japan/S. Korea see
Korea Strait
67 B3 Tsuyama Japan
123 C2 Tswelelang S. Africa
91 C2 Tsyurupyns'k Ukr.
Tthenaagoo Can. see
Nahanni Butte
59 C3 Tual Indon.
97 B2 Tuam Rep. of Ireland
91 C3 Tuapse Rus. Fed.
54 A3 Tuatapere N.Z.
138 A1 Tuba City U.S.A.
61 C2 Tuban Indon.
152 D3 Tubarão Brazil
102 B2 Tübingen Ger.
115 E1 Tubruq Libya
144 A1 Tubutama Mex.
152 C2 Tucavaca Bol.
128 B1 Tuchitua Can.
138 A2 Tucson U.S.A.
139 C1 Tucumcari U.S.A.
150 B1 Tucupita Venez.
151 D2 Tucuruí Brazil
151 D2 Tucuruí, Represa resr Brazil
107 C1 Tudela Spain
106 B1 Tuela r. Port.
77 C2 Tuensang India
123 D2 Tugela r. S. Africa
64 B1 Tuguegarao Phil.
106 B1 Tui Spain
59 C3 Tukangbesi, Kepulauan
is Indon.
126 C2 Tuktoyaktuk Can.
88 B2 Tukums Latvia
145 C2 Tula Mex.
89 E3 Tula Rus. Fed.
145 C2 Tulancingo Mex.
135 C3 Tulare U.S.A.
138 B2 Tularosa U.S.A.
110 C1 Tulcea Romania
90 B2 Tul'chyn Ukr.
129 E1 Tulemalu Lake Can.
139 C2 Tulia U.S.A.
142 C1 Tullahoma U.S.A.
97 C2 Tullamore Rep. of Ireland
104 C2 Tulle France
139 D1 Tully Austr.
139 D1 Tulsa U.S.A.
150 A1 Tumaco Col.
123 C2 Tumahole S. Africa
93 G4 Tumba Sweden
118 B3 Tumba, Lac l.
Dem. Rep. Congo
53 C3 Tumbarumba Austr.
150 A2 Tumbes Peru
128 B2 Tumbler Ridge Can.
52 A2 Tumby Bay Austr.
65 B1 Tumen China
150 B1 Tumereng Guyana
64 A2 Tumindao i. Phil.

74 A2 Tump Pak.
151 C1 Tumucumaque, Serra hills
Brazil
53 C3 Tumut Austr.
99 D3 Tunbridge Wells, Royal U.K.
80 B2 Tunceli Turkey
53 D2 Tuncurry Austr.
119 D4 Tundthe r.
110 C2 Tundzha r. Bulg.
128 B1 Tungsten Can.
115 D1 Tunis Tunisia
115 C1 Tunisia country Africa
150 A1 Tunja Col.
92 F3 Tunnsjøen l. Norway
Tunxi China see Huangshan
154 B2 Tupã Brazil
154 C1 Tupaciguara Brazil
142 C2 Tupelo U.S.A.
152 B3 Tupiza Bol.
83 H2 Tura Rus. Fed.
86 F3 Tura r. Rus. Fed.
78 B2 Turabah Saudi Arabia
83 J3 Turana, Khrebet mts
Rus. Fed.
54 C1 Turangi N.Z.
76 B2 Turan Lowland Asia
78 A2 Turayf Saudi Arabia
88 B2 Turba Estonia
74 A2 Turbat Pak.
150 A1 Turbo Col.
110 B1 Turda Romania
Turfan China see Turpan
76 C2 Turgay Kazakh.
111 C3 Turgutlu Turkey
80 B1 Turhal Turkey
107 C2 Turia r. Spain
108 A1 Turin Italy
86 F3 Turinsk Rus. Fed.
90 A1 Turiys'k Ukr.
119 D2 Turkana, Lake salt l.
Eth./Kenya
77 C2 Turkestan Kazakh.
80 B2 Turkey country Asia
76 B2 Turkmenbashi Turkm.
76 B2 Turkmenistan country Asia
147 C2 Turks and Caicos Islands
terr. West Indies
93 H3 Turku Fin.
135 B3 Turlock U.S.A.
54 C2 Turnagain, Cape N.Z.
100 B2 Turnhout Belgium
129 D2 Turnor Lake Can.
110 B2 Turnu Măgurele Romania
68 B2 Turpan China
77 D2 Turugart Pass China/Kyrg.
142 C2 Tuscaloosa U.S.A.
142 C2 Tuskegee U.S.A.
73 B4 Tuticorin India
120 B3 Tutume Botswana
49 F3 Tuvalu country
S. Pacific Ocean
78 B2 Tuwayq, Jabal hills
Saudi Arabia
78 B2 Tuwayq, Jabal mts
Saudi Arabia
78 A2 Tuwwal Saudi Arabia
144 B2 Tuxpan Nayarit Mex.
145 C2 Tuxpan Veracruz Mex.
145 C3 Tuxtla Gutiérrez Mex.
62 B1 Tuyên Quang Vietnam
63 B2 Tuy Hoa Vietnam
80 B2 Tuz Gölü salt l. Turkey
81 C2 Tuz Khurmātū Iraq
109 C2 Tuzla Bos.-Herz.
91 E2 Tuzlov r. Rus. Fed.
89 E2 Tver' Rus. Fed.
98 B1 Tweed r. U.K.
122 A2 Twee Rivier Namibia
135 C4 Twentynine Palms U.S.A.
131 E2 Twillingate Can.

134 D2 Twin Falls U.S.A.
137 E1 Two Harbors U.S.A.
129 C2 Two Hills Can.
139 D2 Tyler U.S.A.
83 J3 Tynda Rus. Fed.
93 F3 Tynset Norway
111 B3 Tyrnavos Greece
52 B3 Tyrrell, Lake dry lake Austr.
108 B2 Tyrrhenian Sea France/Italy
76 B2 Tyub-Karagan, Mys pt
Kazakh.
87 E3 Tyul'gan Rus. Fed.
86 F3 Tyumen' Rus. Fed.
83 J2 Tyung r. Rus. Fed.
99 A3 Tywi r. U.K.
123 D1 Tzaneen S. Africa

U

120 B2 Uamanda Angola
150 B2 Uaupés Brazil
155 D2 Ubá Brazil
155 D1 Ubaí Brazil
151 E3 Ubaitaba Brazil
118 B3 Ubangi r. C.A.R./
Dem. Rep. Congo
67 B4 Ube Japan
106 C2 Úbeda Spain
154 C1 Uberaba Brazil
154 C1 Uberlândia Brazil
123 D2 Ubombo S. Africa
63 B2 Ubon Ratchathani Thai.
119 C3 Ubundu Dem. Rep. Congo
150 A2 Ucayali r. Peru
74 B2 Uch Pak.
77 E2 Ucharal Kazakh.
66 D2 Uchiura-wan b. Japan
83 J3 Uchur r. Rus. Fed.
128 B3 Ucluelet Can.
74 B2 Udaipur India
91 C1 Uday r. Ukr.
93 F4 Uddevalla Sweden
92 G2 Uddjaure l. Sweden
100 B2 Uden Neth.
74 B1 Udhampur
Jammu and Kashmir
108 B1 Udine Italy
89 E2 Udomlya Rus. Fed.
62 B2 Udon Thani Thai.
73 B3 Udupi India
83 K3 Udyl', Ozero l. Rus. Fed.
67 C3 Ueda Japan
58 C3 Uekuli Indon.
118 C2 Uele r. Dem. Rep. Congo
101 E1 Uelzen Ger.
119 C2 Uere r. Dem. Rep. Congo
87 E3 Ufa Rus. Fed.
119 D3 Ugalla r. Tanz.
119 D2 Uganda country Africa
89 E2 Uglich Rus. Fed.
89 D2 Uglovka Rus. Fed.
89 D3 Ugra Rus. Fed.
103 D2 Uherské Hradiště
Czech Rep.
101 E2 Uichteritz Ger.
96 A2 Uig U.K.
120 A1 Uíge Angola
65 B2 Üijŏngbu S. Korea
135 D2 Uinta Mountains U.S.A.
120 A3 Uis Mine Namibia
65 B2 Ŭisŏng S. Korea
123 C3 Uitenhage S. Africa
100 C1 Uithuizen Neth.
74 B2 Ujjain India
58 B3 Ujung Pandang Indon.
89 F3 Ukholovo Rus. Fed.
62 A1 Ukhrul India

86 E2 **Ukhta** Rus. Fed.
135 B3 **Ukiah** U.S.A.
127 H2 **Ukkusissat** Greenland
88 B2 **Ukmergė** Lith.
90 C2 **Ukraine** *country*
Europe
69 D1 **Ulaanbaatar** Mongolia
68 C1 **Ulaangom** Mongolia
Ulan Bator Mongolia *see*
Ulaanbaatar
Ulanhad China *see* Chifeng
69 E1 **Ulanhot** China
87 D4 **Ulan-Khol** Rus. Fed.
69 D1 **Ulan-Ude** Rus. Fed.
75 D1 **Ulan Ul Hu** *l.* China
65 B2 **Ulchin** S. Korea
Uleåborg Fin. *see* Oulu
88 C2 **Ülenurme** Estonia
73 B3 **Ulhasnagar** India
69 D1 **Uliastai** China
68 C1 **Uliastay** Mongolia
59 D2 **Ulithi** *atoll* Micronesia
53 D3 **Ulladulla** Austr.
96 B2 **Ullapool** U.K.
98 B1 **Ullswater** *l.* U.K.
65 C2 **Ullŭng-do** *i.* S. Korea
102 B2 **Ulm** Ger.
65 B2 **Ulsan** S. Korea
96 □ **Ulsta** U.K.
97 C1 **Ulster** *reg.*
Rep. of Ireland/U.K.
52 B3 **Ultima** Austr.
111 C3 **Ulubey** Turkey
111 C2 **Uludağ** *mt.* Turkey
123 D2 **Ulundi** S. Africa
77 E2 **Ulungur Hu** *l.* China
Uluru *hill* Austr. *see*
Ayers Rock
98 B1 **Ulverston** U.K.
87 D4 **Ul'yanovsk** Rus. Fed.
136 C3 **Ulysses** U.S.A.
90 C2 **Uman'** Ukr.
86 C2 **Umba** Rus. Fed.
59 D3 **Umboi** i. P.N.G.
92 H3 **Umeå** Sweden
92 H3 **Umeälven** *r.* Sweden
157 I2 **Umiiviip Kangertiva** *inlet*
Greenland
126 D2 **Umingmaktok** Can.
123 D2 **Umlazi** S. Africa
117 A3 **Umm Keddada** Sudan
78 A2 **Umm Lajj** Saudi Arabia
117 B3 **Umm Ruwaba** Sudan
115 E1 **Umm Sa'ad** Libya
134 B2 **Umpqua** *r.* U.S.A.
120 A2 **Umpulo** Angola
123 C3 **Umtata** S. Africa
154 B2 **Umuarama** Brazil
109 C1 **Una** *r.* Bos.-Herz./Croatia
155 E1 **Una** Brazil
154 C1 **Unaí** Brazil
78 B2 **'Unayzah** Saudi Arabia
136 C1 **Underwood** U.S.A.
89 D3 **Unecha** Rus. Fed.
53 C2 **Ungarie** Austr.
52 A2 **Ungarra** Austr.
127 G3 **Ungava, Péninsule d'**
pen. Can.
127 G3 **Ungava Bay** Can.
65 C1 **Unggi** N. Korea
90 B2 **Ungheni** Moldova
Unguja *i.* Tanz. *see*
Zanzibar Island
154 B3 **União da Vitória** Brazil
150 B2 **Unini** *r.* Brazil
142 C1 **Union City** U.S.A.
122 B3 **Uniondale** S. Africa
141 D3 **Uniontown** U.S.A.
79 C2 **United Arab Emirates**
country Asia

95 C3 **United Kingdom** *country*
Europe
132 D3 **United States of America**
country N. America
129 D2 **Unity** Can.
96 □ **Unst** i. U.K.
101 E2 **Unstrut** *r.* Ger.
89 E3 **Upa** *r.* Rus. Fed.
119 C3 **Upemba, Lac** *l.*
Dem. Rep. Congo
122 B2 **Upington** S. Africa
134 B2 **Upper Alkali Lake** U.S.A.
128 C2 **Upper Arrow Lake** Can.
134 B2 **Upper Klamath Lake** U.S.A.
128 B1 **Upper Liard** Can.
97 C1 **Upper Lough Erne** *l.* U.K.
93 G4 **Uppsala** Sweden
78 B2 **'Uqlat aş Şuqūr**
Saudi Arabia
Urad Qianqi China *see*
Xishanzui
76 B2 **Ural** *r.* Kazakh./Rus. Fed.
53 D2 **Uralla** Austr.
Ural Mountains Rus. Fed.
see Ural'skiy Khrebet
76 B1 **Ural'sk** Kazakh.
87 E3 **Ural'skiy Khrebet** *mts*
Rus. Fed.
119 D3 **Urambo** Tanz.
53 C3 **Urana** Austr.
129 D2 **Uranium City** Can.
66 F2 **Uray** Rus. Fed.
98 C1 **Ure** *r.* U.K.
86 D3 **Uren'** Rus. Fed.
144 A2 **Ures** Mex.
76 C2 **Urgench** Uzbek.
100 B1 **Urk** Neth.
111 C3 **Urla** Turkey
109 D2 **Uroševac** Yugo.
144 B2 **Uruáchic** Mex.
151 D3 **Uruaçu** Brazil
144 B3 **Uruapan** Mex.
150 A3 **Urubamba** *r.* Peru
151 C2 **Urucara** Brazil
151 D2 **Uruçuí** Brazil
151 C2 **Urucurituba** Brazil
152 C3 **Uruguaiana** Brazil
153 C4 **Uruguay** *country* S. America
Urumchi China *see* Ürümqi
68 B2 **Ürümqi** China
53 D2 **Urunga** Austr.
110 C2 **Urziceni** Romania
67 B4 **Usa** Japan
86 E2 **Usa** *r.* Rus. Fed.
111 C3 **Uşak** Turkey
82 G1 **Ushakova, Ostrov** *i.*
Rus. Fed.
77 D2 **Ushtobe** Kazakh.
153 B6 **Ushuaia** Arg.
86 E2 **Usinsk** Rus. Fed.
88 C3 **Uskhodni** Belarus
89 E3 **Usman'** Rus. Fed.
86 D2 **Ussel** France
104 C2 **Ussel** France
86 B2 **Ussuriysk** Rus. Fed.
108 B3 **Ustica, Isola di** *i.* Sicily Italy
83 H3 **Ust'-Ilimsk** Rus. Fed.
86 E2 **Ust'-Ilych** Rus. Fed.
103 D1 **Ustka** Pol.
83 L3 **Ust'-Kamchatsk** Rus. Fed.
77 E2 **Ust'-Kamenogorsk** Kazakh.
86 F2 **Ust'-Kara** Rus. Fed.
86 E2 **Ust'-Kulom** Rus. Fed.
83 I3 **Ust'-Kut** Rus. Fed.
91 D2 **Ust'-Labinsk** Rus. Fed.
88 C2 **Ust'-Luga** Rus. Fed.
86 E2 **Ust'-Nem** Rus. Fed.
83 K2 **Ust'-Nera** Rus. Fed.
83 K2 **Ust'-Omchug** Rus. Fed.
83 H3 **Ust'-Ordynskiy** Rus. Fed.

86 E2 **Ust'-Tsil'ma** Rus. Fed.
86 D2 **Ust'-Ura** Rus. Fed.
76 B2 **Ustyurt Plateau**
Kazakh./Uzbek.
89 E2 **Ustyuzhna** Rus. Fed.
89 D2 **Usvyaty** Rus. Fed.
135 D3 **Utah** *state* U.S.A.
135 D2 **Utah Lake** U.S.A.
93 I4 **Utena** Lith.
141 D2 **Utica** U.S.A.
107 C2 **Utiel** Spain
128 C2 **Utikuma Lake** Can.
100 B1 **Utrecht** Neth.
106 B2 **Utrera** Spain
92 I2 **Utsjoki** Fin.
67 C3 **Utsunomiya** Japan
87 D4 **Utta** Rus. Fed.
62 B2 **Uttaradit** Thai.
127 G1 **Uummannaq** Greenland
127 H2 **Uummannaq Fjord** *inlet*
Greenland
93 H3 **Uusikaupunki** Fin.
139 D3 **Uvalde** U.S.A.
119 D3 **Uvinza** Tanz.
68 C1 **Uvs Nuur** *salt l.* Mongolia
67 B4 **Uwajima** Japan
78 A2 **'Uwayriḍ, Ḥarrat al** *lava field*
Saudi Arabia
116 A2 **Uweinat, Jebel** *mt.* Sudan
83 H3 **Uyar** Rus. Fed.
115 C4 **Uyo** Nigeria
152 B3 **Uyuni, Salar de** *salt flat* Bol.
76 C2 **Uzbekistan** *country* Asia
104 C2 **Uzerche** France
105 C3 **Uzès** France
90 C1 **Uzh** *r.* Ukr.
90 A2 **Uzhhorod** Ukr.
109 C2 **Užice** Yugo.
89 E3 **Uzlovaya** Rus. Fed.
111 C3 **Üzümlü** Turkey
111 C2 **Uzunköprü** Turkey

V

123 B2 **Vaal** *r.* S. Africa
123 C2 **Vaal Dam** S. Africa
123 C1 **Vaalwater** S. Africa
92 H3 **Vaasa** Fin.
103 D2 **Vác** Hungary
152 C3 **Vacaria** Brazil
154 B2 **Vacaria, Serra** *hills* Brazil
135 B3 **Vacaville** U.S.A.
74 B2 **Vadodara** India
92 I1 **Vadsø** Norway
105 D2 **Vaduz** Liechtenstein
94 B1 **Vágar** *i.* Faroe Is
94 B1 **Vágur** Faroe Is
103 D2 **Váh** *r.* Slovakia
88 B2 **Vaida** Estonia
136 B3 **Vail** U.S.A.
79 C2 **Vakīlābād** Iran
108 B1 **Valdagno** Italy
89 D2 **Valday** Rus. Fed.
89 D2 **Valdayskaya**
Vozvyshennost' *hills*
Rus. Fed.
106 B2 **Valdecañas, Embalse de**
resr Spain
93 G4 **Valdemarsvik** Sweden
105 D2 **Val-de-Meuse** France
106 C2 **Valdepeñas** Spain
153 B5 **Valdés, Península** *pen.* Arg.
153 A4 **Valdivia** Chile
130 C2 **Val-d'Or** Can.
143 D2 **Valdosta** U.S.A.
128 C2 **Valemount** Can.
105 C3 **Valence** France

107 C2 **Valencia** Spain
150 B1 **Valencia** Venez.
107 C2 **Valencia, Golfo de** g. Spain
100 A2 **Valenciennes** France
136 C2 **Valentine** U.S.A.
64 B1 **Valenzuela** Phil.
150 A1 **Valera** Venez.
109 C2 **Valjevo** Yugo.
88 C2 **Valka** Latvia
93 H3 **Valkeakoski** Fin.
100 B2 **Valkenswaard** Neth.
91 D2 **Valky** Ukr.
55 D2 **Valkyrie Dome** ice feature
Antarctica
145 D2 **Valladolid** Mex.
106 C1 **Valladolid** Spain
107 C2 **Vall de Uxó** Spain
93 E4 **Valle** Norway
145 C2 **Vallecillos** Mex.
150 B1 **Valle de la Pascua** Venez.
150 A1 **Valledupar** Col.
145 C2 **Valle Hermoso** Mex.
135 B3 **Vallejo** U.S.A.
152 A3 **Vallenar** Chile
137 C2 **Valley City** U.S.A.
134 B2 **Valley Falls** U.S.A.
128 C2 **Valleyview** Can.
107 D1 **Valls** Spain
88 C2 **Val Marie** Can.
88 C2 **Valmiera** Latvia
88 C3 **Valozhyn** Belarus
154 B2 **Valparaíso** Brazil
153 A4 **Valparaíso** Chile
105 C3 **Valréas** France
59 D3 **Vals, Tanjung** c. Indon.
74 B3 **Valsād** India
122 B2 **Valspan** S. Africa
91 D1 **Valuyki** Rus. Fed.
106 B2 **Valverde del Camino** Spain
81 C2 **Van** Turkey
141 F1 **Van Buren** U.S.A.
128 B3 **Vancouver** Can.
134 B1 **Vancouver** U.S.A.
128 B3 **Vancouver Island** Can.
140 B3 **Vandalia** U.S.A.
123 C2 **Vanderbijlpark** S. Africa
128 B2 **Vanderhoof** Can.
88 C2 **Vändra** Estonia
93 F4 **Vänern** l. Sweden
93 F4 **Vänersborg** Sweden
121 □D3 **Vangaindrano** Madag.
81 C2 **Van Gölü** salt l. Turkey
138 C2 **Van Horn** U.S.A.
59 D3 **Vanimo** P.N.G.
83 K3 **Vanino** Rus. Fed.
104 B2 **Vannes** France
59 D3 **Van Rees, Pegunungan**
mts Indon.
122 A3 **Vanrhynsdorp** S. Africa
93 H3 **Vantaa** Fin.
49 E4 **Vanuatu** country
S. Pacific Ocean
140 C2 **Van Wert** U.S.A.
122 B3 **Vanwyksvlei** S. Africa
122 B2 **Van Zylsrus** S. Africa
75 C2 **Varanasi** India
92 I1 **Varangerfjorden** sea chan.
Norway
92 I1 **Varanger Halvøya** pen.
Norway
109 C1 **Varaždin** Croatia
93 F4 **Varberg** Sweden
109 D2 **Vardar** r. Macedonia
93 E4 **Varde** Denmark
92 J1 **Vardø** Norway
100 D1 **Varel** Ger.
88 B3 **Varėna** Lith.
108 A1 **Varese** Italy
155 C2 **Varginha** Brazil
93 I3 **Varkaus** Fin.

110 C2 **Varna** Bulg.
93 F4 **Värnamo** Sweden
155 D1 **Várzea da Palma** Brazil
86 C2 **Varzino** Rus. Fed.
Vasa Fin. see **Vaasa**
88 C2 **Vasknarva** Estonia
110 C1 **Vaslui** Romania
93 G4 **Västerås** Sweden
93 G3 **Västerdalälven** r. Sweden
88 A2 **Västerhaninge** Sweden
93 G4 **Västervik** Sweden
108 B2 **Vasto** Italy
90 C1 **Vasyl'kiv** Ukr.
104 C2 **Vatan** France
108 B2 **Vatican City** Europe
92 □B3 **Vatnajökull** ice cap Iceland
110 C1 **Vatra Dornei** Romania
93 F4 **Vättern** l. Sweden
138 B2 **Vaughn** U.S.A.
105 C3 **Vauvert** France
88 B3 **Vawkavysk** Belarus
93 F4 **Växjö** Sweden
86 E1 **Vaygach, Ostrov** i. Rus. Fed.
101 D1 **Vechta** Ger.
110 C2 **Vedea** r. Romania
100 C1 **Veendam** Neth.
100 B1 **Veenendaal** Neth.
129 C2 **Vegreville** Can.
106 B2 **Vejer de la Frontera** Spain
93 E4 **Vejle** Denmark
109 D2 **Velbŭzhdki Prokhod** pass
Macedonia
100 B2 **Veldhoven** Neth.
109 B2 **Velebit** mts Croatia
100 C2 **Velen** Ger.
109 C1 **Velenje** Slovenia
109 D2 **Veles** Macedonia
106 C2 **Vélez-Málaga** Spain
155 D1 **Velhas** r. Brazil
109 D2 **Velika Plana** Yugo.
88 C2 **Velikaya** r. Rus. Fed.
89 D2 **Velikiye Luki** Rus. Fed.
89 D2 **Velikiy Novgorod**
Rus. Fed.
86 D2 **Velikiy Ustyug** Rus. Fed.
110 C2 **Veliko Tŭrnovo** Bulg.
108 B2 **Veli Lošinj** Croatia
89 D2 **Velizh** Rus. Fed.
86 D2 **Vel'sk** Rus. Fed.
101 F1 **Velten** Ger.
91 D1 **Velykyy Burluk** Ukr.
108 B2 **Venafro** Italy
154 C2 **Venceslau Bráz** Brazil
104 C2 **Vendôme** France
89 E3 **Venev** Rus. Fed.
Venezia Italy see **Venice**
150 B1 **Venezuela** country
S. America
150 A1 **Venezuela, Golfo de**
g. Venez.
108 B1 **Venice** Italy
143 D3 **Venice** U.S.A.
108 B1 **Venice, Gulf of** Europe
100 C2 **Venlo** Neth.
100 B1 **Venray** Neth.
88 B2 **Venta** r. Latvia/Lith.
88 B2 **Venta** Lith.
123 C3 **Venterstad** S. Africa
99 C3 **Ventnor** U.K.
88 B2 **Ventspils** Latvia
135 C4 **Ventura** U.S.A.
139 C3 **Venustiano Carranza, Presa**
resr Mex.
107 C2 **Vera** Spain
145 C3 **Veracruz** Mex.
74 B2 **Veraval** India
108 A1 **Verbania** Italy
108 A1 **Vercelli** Italy
105 D3 **Vercors** reg. France
92 F3 **Verdalsøra** Norway

154 B1 **Verde** r. Goiás Brazil
154 B2 **Verde** r. Mato Grosso do Sul
Brazil
144 B2 **Verde** r. Mex.
138 A2 **Verde** r. U.S.A.
155 D1 **Verde Grande** r. Brazil
101 D1 **Verden (Aller)** Ger.
154 B1 **Verdinho, Serra do** mts
Brazil
108 A2 **Verdon** r. France
105 D2 **Verdun** France
123 C2 **Vereeniging** S. Africa
106 B1 **Verín** Spain
91 D3 **Verkhnebakanskiy** Rus. Fed.
92 J2 **Verkhnetulomskiy** Rus. Fed.
91 E1 **Verkhniy Mamon** Rus. Fed.
89 E3 **Verkhov'ye** Rus. Fed.
90 A2 **Verkhovyna** Ukr.
83 J2 **Verkhoyanskiy Khrebet** mts
Rus. Fed.
129 C2 **Vermilion** Can.
137 E2 **Vermillion** U.S.A.
130 A2 **Vermillion Bay** Can.
141 E2 **Vermont** state U.S.A.
135 E2 **Vernal** U.S.A.
128 C2 **Vernon** Can.
139 D2 **Vernon** U.S.A.
143 D3 **Vero Beach** U.S.A.
111 B2 **Veroia** Greece
108 B1 **Verona** Italy
104 C2 **Versailles** France
123 D2 **Vertou** France
123 D2 **Verulam** S. Africa
100 B2 **Verviers** Belgium
105 C2 **Vervins** France
105 D3 **Vescovato** Corsica France
87 E3 **Veselaya, Gora** mt.
Rus. Fed.
91 C2 **Vesele** Ukr.
105 D2 **Vesoul** France
92 F2 **Vesterålen** is Norway
92 F2 **Vestfjorden** sea chan.
Norway
94 B1 **Vestmanna** Faroe Is
93 E3 **Vestnes** Norway
108 B2 **Vesuvio** vol. Italy
89 E2 **Ves'yegonsk** Rus. Fed.
93 G4 **Vetlanda** Sweden
86 D3 **Vetluga** Rus. Fed.
100 A2 **Veurne** Belgium
105 D2 **Vevey** Switz.
91 D1 **Veydelevka** Rus. Fed.
80 B1 **Vezirköprü** Turkey
151 D2 **Viana** Brazil
106 B1 **Viana do Castelo** Port.
Viangchan Laos see
Vientiane
62 B1 **Viangphoukha** Laos
154 C1 **Vianópolis** Brazil
108 B2 **Viareggio** Italy
93 E4 **Viborg** Denmark
109 C3 **Vibo Valentia** Italy
107 D1 **Vic** Spain
145 C3 **Vicente Guerrero** Mex.
108 B1 **Vicenza** Italy
105 C2 **Vichy** France
142 B2 **Vicksburg** U.S.A.
155 D2 **Viçosa** Brazil
52 A3 **Victor Harbor** Austr.
50 C1 **Victoria** r. Austr.
52 B3 **Victoria** state Austr.
128 B3 **Victoria** Can.
153 A4 **Victoria** Chile
119 D3 **Victoria, Lake** Africa
52 B2 **Victoria, Lake** Austr.
62 A1 **Victoria, Mount** Myanmar
59 D3 **Victoria, Mount** P.N.G.
120 B2 **Victoria Falls** waterfall
Zambia/Zimbabwe

126 D2 **Victoria Island** Can.
50 C1 **Victoria River Downs** Austr.
122 B3 **Victoria West** S. Africa
135 C4 **Victorville** U.S.A.
110 D2 **Videle** Romania
92 □A2 **Viðidalsá** Iceland
153 B5 **Viedma** Arg.
153 A5 **Viedma, Lago** l. Arg.
100 B3 **Vielsalm** Belgium
101 E2 **Vienenburg** Ger.
103 D2 **Vienna** Austria
105 C2 **Vienne** France
105 C2 **Vienne** r. France
62 B2 **Vientiane** Laos
100 C2 **Viersen** Ger.
104 C2 **Vierzon** France
144 B2 **Viesca** Mex.
109 C2 **Vieste** Italy
62 B2 **Vietnam** country Asia
62 B1 **Viêt Tri** Vietnam
64 B1 **Vigan** Phil.
108 A1 **Vigevano** Italy
106 B1 **Vigo** Spain
73 C3 **Vijayawada** India
92 □B3 **Vík** Iceland
129 C2 **Viking** Can.
106 B2 **Vila Franca de Xira** Port.
106 B1 **Vilagarcía de Arousa** Spain
106 B1 **Vilalba** Spain
106 B1 **Vila Nova de Gaia** Port.
107 D1 **Vilanova i la Geltrú** Spain
106 B1 **Vila Real** Port.
106 B1 **Vilar Formoso** Port.
152 D2 **Vila Velha** Brazil
150 A3 **Vilcabamba, Cordillera**
     mts Peru
92 G3 **Vilhelmina** Sweden
150 B3 **Vilhena** Brazil
88 C2 **Viljandi** Estonia
88 B3 **Vilkaviškis** Lith.
83 H1 **Vil'kitskogo, Proliv** str.
     Rus. Fed.
144 B1 **Villa Ahumada** Mex.
106 B1 **Villablino** Spain
102 C2 **Villach** Austria
144 A2 **Villa Constitución** Mex.
144 B2 **Villa de Cos** Mex.
152 B4 **Villa Dolores** Arg.
145 C3 **Villa Flores** Mex.
145 C2 **Villagrán** Mex.
145 C3 **Villahermosa** Mex.
144 A2 **Villa Insurgentes** Mex.
152 B4 **Villa María** Arg.
152 B3 **Villa Montes** Bol.
144 B2 **Villanueva** Mex.
106 B2 **Villanueva de la Serena**
     Spain
106 C2 **Villanueva de los Infantes**
     Spain
152 C3 **Villa Ocampo** Arg.
108 A3 **Villaputzu** Sardinia Italy
106 C2 **Villarrobledo** Spain
152 B3 **Villa Unión** Arg.
144 B2 **Villa Unión** Durango Mex.
144 B2 **Villa Unión** Sinaloa Mex.
150 A1 **Villavicencio** Col.
152 B3 **Villazón** Bol.
107 C2 **Villena** Spain
104 C3 **Villeneuve-sur-Lot** France
142 B2 **Ville Platte** U.S.A.
105 C2 **Villeurbanne** France
102 B2 **Villingen** Ger.
88 C3 **Vilnius** Lith.
91 C2 **Vil'nohirs'k** Ukr.
91 D2 **Vil'nyans'k** Ukr.
100 B2 **Vilvoorde** Belgium
88 C3 **Vileyka** Belarus
83 J2 **Vilyuy** r. Rus. Fed.
93 G4 **Vimmerby** Sweden

153 A4 **Viña del Mar** Chile
107 D1 **Vinaròs** Spain
140 B3 **Vincennes** U.S.A.
55 G3 **Vincennes Bay** Antarctica
141 D3 **Vineland** U.S.A.
62 B2 **Vinh** Vietnam
63 B2 **Vinh Long** Vietnam
139 D1 **Vinita** Latvia
90 B2 **Vinnytsya** Ukr.
55 C2 **Vinson Massif** mt Antarctica
93 E3 **Vinstra** Norway
108 B1 **Vipiteno** Italy
64 B1 **Virac** Phil.
129 D3 **Virden** Can.
104 B2 **Vire** France
120 A2 **Virei** Angola
155 D1 **Virgem da Lapa** Brazil
138 A1 **Virgin** r. U.S.A.
123 C2 **Virginia** S. Africa
137 E1 **Virginia** state U.S.A.
141 D3 **Virginia** state U.S.A.
141 D3 **Virginia Beach** U.S.A.
135 C3 **Virginia City** U.S.A.
147 D3 **Virgin Islands (U.K.)** terr.
     West Indies
147 D3 **Virgin Islands (U.S.A.)** terr.
     West Indies
63 B2 **Virôchey** Cambodia
109 C1 **Virovitica** Croatia
100 B3 **Virton** Belgium
88 C2 **Virtsu** Estonia
109 C2 **Vis** i. Croatia
88 C2 **Visaginas** Lith.
135 C3 **Visalia** U.S.A.
74 B2 **Visavadar** India
64 B1 **Visayan Sea** Phil.
93 G4 **Visby** Sweden
126 D2 **Viscount Melville Sound**
     sea chan. Can.
151 D2 **Viseu** Brazil
106 B1 **Viseu** Port.
73 C3 **Vishakhapatnam** India
88 C2 **Viški** Latvia
109 C2 **Visoko** Bos.-Herz.
108 B2 **Viterbo** Italy
83 I3 **Vitim** r. Rus. Fed.
155 D2 **Vitória** Brazil
151 D3 **Vitória da Conquista** Brazil
106 C1 **Vitoria-Gasteiz** Spain
104 B2 **Vitré** France
105 C2 **Vitry-le-François** France
89 D3 **Vitsyebsk** Belarus
105 D2 **Vittel** France
108 B3 **Vittoria** Sicily Italy
108 B1 **Vittorio Veneto** Italy
106 B1 **Viveiro** Spain
144 A2 **Vizcaíno, Sierra** mts Mex.
110 C2 **Vize** Turkey
73 C3 **Vizianagaram** India
100 B2 **Vlaardingen** Neth.
87 D4 **Vladikavkaz** Rus. Fed.
89 F2 **Vladimir** Rus. Fed.
66 B2 **Vladivostok** Rus. Fed.
109 D2 **Vlasotince** Yugo.
100 B1 **Vlieland** i. Neth.
100 A1 **Vlissingen** Neth.
109 C2 **Vlorë** Albania
102 C2 **Vöcklabruck** Austria
101 D2 **Vogelsberg** hills Ger.
119 D3 **Voi** Kenya
105 D2 **Voiron** France
131 D1 **Voisey Bay** Can.
109 C1 **Vojvodina** prov. Yugo.
92 J3 **Voknavolok** Rus. Fed.
     Volcano Bay b. Japan see
     Uchiura-wan
89 E2 **Volga** Rus. Fed.
89 F2 **Volga** r. Rus. Fed.
87 D4 **Volgodonsk** Rus. Fed.
87 D4 **Volgograd** Rus. Fed.

89 D2 **Volkhov** Rus. Fed.
89 D1 **Volkhov** r. Rus. Fed.
101 E2 **Volkstedt** Ger.
91 D2 **Volnovakha** Ukr.
90 B2 **Volochys'k** Ukr.
91 D2 **Volodars'ke** Ukr.
90 B1 **Volodars'k-Volyns'kyy** Ukr.
90 B1 **Volodymyrets'** Ukr.
90 A1 **Volodymyr-Volyns'kyy** Ukr.
89 E2 **Vologda** Rus. Fed.
89 E2 **Volokolamsk** Rus. Fed.
91 D1 **Volokonovka** Rus. Fed.
111 B3 **Volos** Greece
88 C2 **Volosovo** Rus. Fed.
89 D2 **Volot** Rus. Fed.
89 E3 **Volovo** Rus. Fed.
87 D3 **Vol'sk** Rus. Fed.
114 C4 **Volta, Lake** resr Ghana
155 D2 **Volta Redonda** Brazil
87 D4 **Volzhskiy** Rus. Fed.
92 □C2 **Vopnafjörður** Iceland
88 C3 **Voranava** Belarus
86 F2 **Vorkuta** Rus. Fed.
88 B2 **Vormsi** i. Estonia
89 E3 **Voronezh** Rus. Fed.
89 E3 **Voronezh** r. Rus. Fed.
91 E1 **Vorontsovka** Rus. Fed.
91 C2 **Vorskla** r. Rus. Fed.
88 C2 **Võrtsjärv** l. Estonia
88 C2 **Võru** Estonia
122 B3 **Vosburg** S. Africa
105 D2 **Vosges** mts France
89 E2 **Voskresensk** Rus. Fed.
93 E3 **Voss** Norway
83 K2 **Vostochno-Sibirskoye More**
     sea Rus. Fed.
83 H3 **Vostochnyy Sayan** mts
     Rus. Fed.
86 E3 **Votkinsk** Rus. Fed.
154 C2 **Votuporanga** Brazil
100 B3 **Vouziers** France
92 J2 **Voynitsa** Rus. Fed.
91 C2 **Voznesens'k** Ukr.
93 E4 **Vrådal** Norway
66 B2 **Vrangel'** Rus. Fed.
83 N2 **Vrangelya, Ostrov** i.
     Rus. Fed.
109 D2 **Vranje** Yugo.
110 C2 **Vratnik** pass Bulg.
110 B2 **Vratsa** Bulg.
109 C1 **Vrbas** r. Bos.-Herz.
109 C1 **Vrbas** Yugo.
122 A3 **Vredenburg** S. Africa
122 A3 **Vredendal** S. Africa
100 B3 **Vresse** Belgium
109 D1 **Vršac** Yugo.
122 B2 **Vryburg** S. Africa
123 D2 **Vryheid** S. Africa
89 D1 **Vsevolozhsk** Rus. Fed.
109 D2 **Vučitrn** Yugo.
109 C1 **Vukovar** Croatia
86 E2 **Vuktyl'** Rus. Fed.
123 C2 **Vukuzakhe** S. Africa
109 B3 **Vulcano, Isola** i. Italy
63 B2 **Vung Tau** Vietnam
74 B2 **Vyara** India
     Vyatka Rus. Fed. see Kirov
89 D2 **Vyaz'ma** Rus. Fed.
93 I3 **Vyborg** Rus. Fed.
88 C2 **Vyerkhnyadzvinsk** Belarus
87 D3 **Vyksa** Rus. Fed.
90 B2 **Vylkove** Ukr.
90 A2 **Vynohradiv** Ukr.
89 D2 **Vypolzovo** Rus. Fed.
89 D2 **Vyritsa** Rus. Fed.
91 D2 **Vyselki** Rus. Fed.
90 C1 **Vyshhorod** Ukr.
89 D2 **Vyshniy-Volochek** Rus. Fed.
103 D2 **Vyškov** Czech Rep.
86 C2 **Vytegra** Rus. Fed.

W

114 B3 **Wa** Ghana
100 B2 **Waal** r. Neth.
100 B2 **Waalwijk** Neth.
128 C2 **Wabasca** r. Can.
128 C2 **Wabasca-Desmarais** Can.
140 B3 **Wabash** r. U.S.A.
117 C4 **Wabē Gestro** r. Eth.
117 C4 **Wabē Shebelē Wenz** r. Eth.
129 E2 **Wabowden** Can.
143 D3 **Waccasassa Bay** U.S.A.
101 D2 **Wächtersbach** Ger.
139 D2 **Waco** U.S.A.
74 A2 **Wad** Pak.
115 D2 **Waddān** Libya
100 B1 **Waddeneilanden** is Neth.
100 B1 **Waddenzee** sea chan. Neth.
128 B2 **Waddington, Mount** Can.
100 B1 **Waddinxveen** Neth.
129 D2 **Wadena** Can.
137 D1 **Wadena** U.S.A.
116 B2 **Wadi Halfa** Sudan
116 B3 **Wad Medani** Sudan
70 C2 **Wafangdian** China
100 B2 **Wageningen** Neth.
127 F2 **Wager Bay** Can.
53 C3 **Wagga Wagga** Austr.
137 D2 **Wahoo** U.S.A.
137 D1 **Wahpeton** U.S.A.
54 B2 **Waiau** r. N.Z.
59 C3 **Waigeo** i. Indon.
58 B3 **Waikabubak** Indon.
52 A2 **Waikerie** Austr.
54 B2 **Waimate** N.Z.
75 B3 **Wainganga** r. India
58 C3 **Waingapu** Indon.
129 C2 **Wainwright** Can.
54 C1 **Waiouru** N.Z.
54 B2 **Waipara** N.Z.
54 C1 **Waipawa** N.Z.
54 B2 **Wairau** r. N.Z.
54 C1 **Wairoa** N.Z.
54 B2 **Waitaki** r. N.Z.
54 B1 **Waitara** N.Z.
54 B1 **Waiuku** N.Z.
119 E2 **Wajir** Kenya
67 C3 **Wakasa-wan** b. Japan
54 A3 **Wakatipu, Lake** N.Z.
129 D2 **Wakaw** Can.
67 C4 **Wakayama** Japan
136 D3 **WaKeeney** U.S.A.
54 B2 **Wakefield** N.Z.
98 C2 **Wakefield** U.K.
66 D1 **Wakkanai** Japan
123 D3 **Wakkerstroom** S. Africa
103 D1 **Wałbrzych** Pol.
53 D2 **Walcha** Austr.
100 C1 **Walchum** Ger.
103 D1 **Wałcz** Pol.
99 B2 **Wales** admin. div. U.K.
53 C2 **Walgett** Austr.
119 C3 **Walikale** Dem. Rep. Congo
135 C3 **Walker Lake** l. U.S.A.
52 A2 **Wallaroo** Austr.
98 B2 **Wallasey** U.K.
134 C1 **Walla Walla** U.S.A.
101 D3 **Walldürn** Ger.
122 A2 **Wallendbeen** Austr.
49 F4 **Wallis and Futuna Islands** terr. S. Pacific Ocean
96 □ **Walls** U.K.
98 B1 **Walney, Isle of** i. U.K.
99 C2 **Walsall** U.K.
136 C3 **Walsenburg** U.S.A.
101 D1 **Walsrode** Ger.
143 D2 **Walterboro** U.S.A.
120 A3 **Walvis Bay** Namibia

119 C2 **Wamba** Dem. Rep. Congo
52 B1 **Wanaaring** Austr.
54 A3 **Wanaka** N.Z.
54 A2 **Wanaka, Lake** N.Z.
130 B2 **Wanapitei Lake** Can.
154 B3 **Wanda** Arg.
66 B1 **Wanda Shan** mts China
62 A1 **Wanding** China
54 C1 **Wanganui** N.Z.
53 C3 **Wangaratta** Austr.
100 C1 **Wangerooge** i. Ger.
65 B3 **Wangqing** China
62 A1 **Wan Hsa-la** Myanmar
71 B4 **Wanning** China
100 B2 **Wanroij** Neth.
99 C3 **Wantage** U.K.
70 A2 **Wanxian** China
70 A2 **Wanyuan** China
73 B3 **Warangal** India
101 D2 **Warburg** Ger.
50 B2 **Warburton** Austr.
52 A1 **Warburton** watercourse Austr.
75 B2 **Wardha** India
96 C1 **Ward Hill** U.K.
128 B2 **Ware** Can.
101 F1 **Waren** Ger.
100 C2 **Warendorf** Ger.
53 D1 **Warialda** Austr.
122 A2 **Warmbad** Namibia
135 C3 **Warm Springs** U.S.A.
134 C2 **Warner Lakes** U.S.A.
143 D2 **Warner Robins** U.S.A.
152 B2 **Warnes** Bol.
52 B3 **Warracknabeal** Austr.
53 C2 **Warrego** r. Austr.
53 C2 **Warren** Austr.
142 B2 **Warren** AR U.S.A.
140 C2 **Warren** OH U.S.A.
141 D2 **Warren** PA U.S.A.
97 C1 **Warrenpoint** U.K.
137 E3 **Warrensburg** U.S.A.
122 B2 **Warrenton** S. Africa
115 C4 **Warri** Nigeria
98 B2 **Warrington** U.K.
52 B3 **Warrnambool** Austr.
103 E1 **Warsaw** Pol.
Warszawa Pol. see Warsaw
103 C1 **Warta** r. Pol.
53 D1 **Warwick** Austr.
99 C2 **Warwick** U.K.
135 C3 **Wasco** U.S.A.
136 C1 **Washburn** U.S.A.
141 D3 **Washington** DC U.S.A.
137 E2 **Washington** IA U.S.A.
140 B3 **Washington** IN U.S.A.
137 E3 **Washington** MO U.S.A.
143 E1 **Washington** NC U.S.A.
140 C2 **Washington** PA U.S.A.
134 B1 **Washington** state U.S.A.
141 E2 **Washington, Mount** U.S.A.
140 C3 **Washington Court House** U.S.A.
74 A2 **Washuk** Pak.
130 C1 **Waskaganish** Can.
129 E2 **Waskaiowaka Lake** Can.
122 A2 **Wasser** Namibia
130 C2 **Waswanipi, Lac** l. Can.
58 C3 **Watampone** Indon.
141 E2 **Waterbury** U.S.A.
129 D2 **Waterbury Lake** Can.
97 C2 **Waterford** Rep. of Ireland
97 C2 **Waterford Harbour** Rep. of Ireland
137 E2 **Waterloo** U.S.A.
123 C1 **Waterpoort** S. Africa
141 D2 **Watertown** NY U.S.A.
137 D2 **Watertown** SD U.S.A.
140 B2 **Watertown** WI U.S.A.
141 F2 **Waterville** U.S.A.

99 C3 **Watford** U.K.
136 C1 **Watford City** U.S.A.
129 D2 **Wathaman** r. Can.
139 D1 **Watonga** U.S.A.
129 D2 **Watrous** Can.
119 C2 **Watsa** Dem. Rep. Congo
140 B2 **Watseka** U.S.A.
118 C3 **Watsi Kengo** Dem. Rep. Congo
128 B1 **Watson Lake** Can.
135 B3 **Watsonville** U.S.A.
59 C3 **Watubela, Kepulauan** is Indon.
59 D3 **Wau** P.N.G.
117 A4 **Wau** Sudan
53 D2 **Wauchope** Austr.
140 B2 **Waukegan** U.S.A.
139 D2 **Waurika** U.S.A.
140 B2 **Wausau** U.S.A.
99 D2 **Waveney** r. U.K.
141 E2 **Waverly** U.S.A.
143 D2 **Waycross** U.S.A.
137 D2 **Wayne** U.S.A.
143 D2 **Waynesboro** GA U.S.A.
141 D3 **Waynesboro** VA U.S.A.
143 D1 **Waynesville** U.S.A.
74 B1 **Wazirabad** Pak.
98 C1 **Wear** r. U.K.
139 D2 **Weatherford** U.S.A.
134 B2 **Weaverville** U.S.A.
130 B1 **Webequie** Can.
117 C4 **Webi Shabeelle** r. Somalia
137 D1 **Webster** U.S.A.
137 E2 **Webster City** U.S.A.
55 Q2 **Weddell Sea** Antarctica
100 B2 **Weert** Neth.
53 C2 **Wee Waa** Austr.
100 C2 **Wegberg** Ger.
103 E1 **Węgorzewo** Pol.
101 F3 **Weiden in der Oberpfalz** Ger.
70 B2 **Weifang** China
70 C2 **Weihai** China
53 C1 **Weilmoringle** Austr.
101 E2 **Weimar** Ger.
70 A2 **Weinan** China
51 D1 **Weipa** Austr.
53 C1 **Weir** r. Austr.
140 C2 **Weirton** U.S.A.
62 B1 **Weishan** China
101 E2 **Weißenfels** Ger.
102 C2 **Weißkugel** mt. Austria/Italy
101 F1 **Wejherowo** Pol.
140 C3 **Welch** U.S.A.
117 B3 **Weldiya** Eth.
123 C2 **Welkom** S. Africa
99 C2 **Welland** r. U.K.
51 C1 **Wellesley Islands** Austr.
53 C2 **Wellington** Austr.
54 B2 **Wellington** N.Z.
122 A3 **Wellington** S. Africa
137 D3 **Wellington** U.S.A.
153 A5 **Wellington, Isla** i. Chile
53 C3 **Wellington, Lake** Austr.
128 B2 **Wells** Can.
99 B3 **Wells** U.K.
134 D2 **Wells** U.S.A.
50 B2 **Wells, Lake** salt flat Austr.
54 B1 **Wellsford** N.Z.
98 D2 **Wells-next-the-Sea** U.K.
102 C2 **Wels** Austria
99 B2 **Welshpool** U.K.
123 C2 **Wembesi** S. Africa
51 C1 **Wemindji** Can.
134 B1 **Wenatchee** U.S.A.
71 B4 **Wenchang** China
114 B4 **Wenchi** Ghana
70 C2 **Wendeng** China
101 E1 **Wendisch Evern** Ger.
117 B4 **Wendo** Eth.

134 D2 Wendover U.S.A.
71 B3 Wengyuan China
71 C3 Wenling China
71 A3 Wenshan China
52 B2 Wentworth Austr.
71 C3 Wenzhou China
123 C2 Wepener S. Africa
122 B2 Werda Botswana
101 F2 Werdau Ger.
101 F1 Werder Ger.
101 F3 Wernberg-Köblitz Ger.
101 E2 Wernigerode Ger.
101 D2 Werra r. Ger.
53 D2 Werris Creek Austr.
101 D3 Wertheim Ger.
100 C2 Wesel Ger.
101 E1 Wesendorf Ger.
101 D1 Weser r. Ger.
101 D1 Weser sea chan. Ger.
51 C1 Wessel, Cape Austr.
51 C1 Wessel Islands Austr.
123 C2 Wesselton S. Africa
80 B2 West Bank terr. Asia
140 B2 West Bend U.S.A.
99 C2 West Bromwich U.K.
100 C2 Westerburg Ger.
100 C1 Westerholt Ger.
50 B2 Western Australia
        state Austr.
122 B3 Western Cape prov. S. Africa
116 A2 Western Desert des. Egypt
73 B3 Western Ghats mts India
114 A2 Western Sahara terr. Africa
        Western Samoa country
        S. Pacific Ocean see Samoa
100 A2 Westerschelde est. Neth.
100 C1 Westerstede Ger.
100 C2 Westerwald hills Ger.
153 B6 West Falkland i. Falkland Is
140 B3 West Frankfort U.S.A.
147 D2 West Indies N. America
96 A1 West Loch Roag b. U.K.
128 C2 Westlock Can.
100 B2 Westmalle Belgium
142 B1 West Memphis U.S.A.
140 C3 Weston U.S.A.
99 B3 Weston-super-Mare U.K.
143 D3 West Palm Beach U.S.A.
137 E3 West Plains U.S.A.
137 D2 West Point U.S.A.
54 B2 Westport N.Z.
97 B2 Westport Rep. of Ireland
129 D2 Westray Can.
96 C1 Westray i. U.K.
100 B1 West-Terschelling Neth.
97 B1 West Town Rep. of Ireland
140 C3 West Virginia state U.S.A.
53 C2 West Wyalong Austr.
134 D2 West Yellowstone U.S.A.
59 C3 Wetar i. Indon.
128 C2 Wetaskiwin Can.
101 D2 Wetzlar Ger.
59 D3 Wewak P.N.G.
97 C2 Wexford Rep. of Ireland
129 D2 Weyakwin Can.
129 D2 Weyburn Can.
101 D1 Weyhe Ger.
99 B3 Weymouth U.K.
54 C1 Whakatane N.Z.
129 E1 Whale Cove Can.
96 □ Whalsay i. U.K.
54 B1 Whangarei N.Z.
98 C2 Wharfe r. U.K.
139 D3 Wharton U.S.A.
128 C1 Wha Ti Can.
136 B2 Wheatland U.S.A.
138 B1 Wheeler Peak NM U.S.A.
135 D3 Wheeler Peak NV U.S.A.
140 C2 Wheeling U.S.A.
98 B1 Whernside hill U.K.
128 B2 Whistler Can.
98 C1 Whitby U.K.
142 B2 White r. U.S.A.
50 B2 White, Lake salt flat Austr.
131 E2 White Bay Can.
136 C1 White Butte mt. U.S.A.
52 B2 White Cliffs Austr.
128 C2 Whitecourt Can.
134 D1 Whitefish U.S.A.
98 B1 Whitehaven U.K.
97 D1 Whitehead U.K.
128 A1 Whitehorse Can.
142 B3 White Lake l. U.S.A.
135 C3 White Mountain Peak U.S.A.
116 B3 White Nile r. Sudan/Uganda
86 C2 White Sea Rus. Fed.
134 D1 White Sulphur Springs
        U.S.A.
143 E2 Whiteville U.S.A.
114 B3 White Volta watercourse
        Burkina/Ghana
138 B2 Whitewater Baldy
        mt. U.S.A.
130 B1 Whitewater Lake Can.
129 D2 Whitewood Can.
96 B3 Whithorn U.K.
54 C1 Whitianga N.Z.
135 C3 Whitney, Mount U.S.A.
51 D1 Whitsunday Island Austr.
52 A2 Whyalla Austr.
62 A1 Wiang Phran Thai.
100 A2 Wichelen Belgium
139 D3 Wichita U.S.A.
139 D1 Wichita Falls U.S.A.
96 C1 Wick U.K.
138 A2 Wickenburg U.S.A.
97 C2 Wicklow Rep. of Ireland
97 D2 Wicklow Head hd
        Rep. of Ireland
97 C2 Wicklow Mountains
        Rep. of Ireland
98 B2 Widnes U.K.
101 D1 Wiehengebirge hills Ger.
100 C2 Wiehl Ger.
103 D1 Wieluń Pol.
        Wien Austria see Vienna
103 D2 Wiener Neustadt Austria
100 B1 Wieringerwerf Neth.
100 D2 Wiesbaden Ger.
100 C1 Wiesmoor Ger.
103 D1 Wieżyca hill Pol.
99 C3 Wight, Isle of i. U.K.
96 B3 Wigtown U.K.
100 B2 Wijchen Neth.
52 B2 Wilcannia Austr.
123 C3 Wild Coast S. Africa
123 C2 Wilge r. S. Africa
100 D1 Wilhelmshaven Ger.
141 D2 Wilkes-Barre U.S.A.
55 H3 Wilkes Land reg. Antarctica
129 D2 Wilkie Can.
138 B2 Willcox U.S.A.
100 B2 Willebroek Belgium
147 D3 Willemstad Neth. Antilles
52 B3 William, Mount Austr.
52 A1 William Creek Austr.
138 A1 Williams U.S.A.
141 D3 Williamsburg U.S.A.
128 B2 Williams Lake Can.
140 C3 Williamson U.S.A.
141 D2 Williamsport U.S.A.
143 E1 Williamston U.S.A.
122 B3 Williston S. Africa
136 C1 Williston U.S.A.
128 B2 Williston Lake Can.
135 B3 Willits U.S.A.
137 D1 Willmar U.S.A.
122 B3 Willowmore S. Africa
123 C3 Willowvale S. Africa
50 B2 Wills, Lake salt flat Austr.
52 A3 Willunga Austr.
52 A2 Wilmington Austr.
141 D3 Wilmington DE U.S.A.
143 E2 Wilmington NC U.S.A.
100 D2 Wilnsdorf Ger.
143 E1 Wilson U.S.A.
53 C3 Wilson's Promontory
        pen. Austr.
100 B3 Wiltz Lux.
50 B2 Wiluna Austr.
99 C3 Winchester U.K.
140 C3 Winchester KY U.S.A.
141 D3 Winchester VA U.S.A.
98 B1 Windermere l. U.K.
120 A3 Windhoek Namibia
137 D2 Windom U.S.A.
51 D2 Windorah Austr.
136 B2 Wind River Range
        mts U.S.A.
53 D2 Windsor Austr.
130 B2 Windsor Can.
147 D3 Windward Islands
        Caribbean Sea
147 C3 Windward Passage
        Cuba/Haiti
137 D3 Winfield U.S.A.
100 A2 Wingene Belgium
53 D2 Wingham Austr.
130 B1 Winisk Can.
130 B1 Winisk r. Can.
130 B1 Winisk Lake Can.
63 A2 Winkana Myanmar
129 E3 Winkler Can.
114 B4 Winneba Ghana
140 B2 Winnebago, Lake U.S.A.
134 C2 Winnemucca U.S.A.
136 C2 Winner U.S.A.
142 B2 Winnfield U.S.A.
137 E1 Winnibigoshish, Lake U.S.A.
129 E3 Winnipeg Can.
129 E2 Winnipeg r. Can.
129 D2 Winnipeg, Lake Can.
129 D2 Winnipegosis, Lake Can.
141 E2 Winnipesaukee, Lake U.S.A.
142 B2 Winnsboro U.S.A.
137 E2 Winona MN U.S.A.
142 C2 Winona MS U.S.A.
100 C1 Winschoten Neth.
101 D1 Winsen (Aller) Ger.
101 E1 Winsen (Luhe) Ger.
138 A1 Winslow U.S.A.
143 D1 Winston-Salem U.S.A.
101 D2 Winterberg Ger.
143 D3 Winter Haven U.S.A.
100 C2 Winterswijk Neth.
105 D2 Winterthur Switz.
51 D2 Winton Austr.
54 A3 Winton N.Z.
52 A2 Wirrabara Austr.
99 D2 Wisbech U.K.
140 A2 Wisconsin r. U.S.A.
140 B2 Wisconsin state U.S.A.
140 B2 Wisconsin Rapids U.S.A.
103 D1 Wisła r. Pol.
101 E1 Wismar Ger.
123 C2 Witbank S. Africa
98 D2 Withernsea U.K.
100 B1 Witmarsum Neth.
99 C3 Witney U.K.
123 D2 Witrivier S. Africa
101 E1 Wittenberge Ger.
101 E1 Wittenburg Ger.
101 E1 Wittingen Ger.
100 C3 Wittlich Ger.
100 C1 Wittmund Ger.
101 F1 Wittstock Ger.
120 A3 Witvlei Namibia
101 D2 Witzenhausen Ger.
103 D1 Władysławowo Pol.
103 D1 Włocławek Pol.

53 C3 **Wodonga** Austr.
59 C3 **Wokam** *i.* Indon.
99 C3 **Woking** U.K.
101 F2 **Wolfen** Ger.
101 E1 **Wolfenbüttel** Ger.
101 D2 **Wolfhagen** Ger.
136 B1 **Wolf Point** U.S.A.
101 E1 **Wolfsburg** Ger.
100 C3 **Wolfstein** Ger.
131 D2 **Wolfville** Can.
102 C1 **Wolgast** Ger.
102 C1 **Wolin** Pol.
129 D2 **Wollaston Lake** Can.
129 D2 **Wollaston Lake** *l.* Can.
126 D2 **Wollaston Peninsula** Can.
53 D2 **Wollongong** Austr.
101 E2 **Wolmirsleben** Ger.
101 E1 **Wolmirstedt** Ger.
100 E1 **Wolvega** Neth.
99 B2 **Wolverhampton** U.K.
65 B2 **Wŏnju** S. Korea
128 B2 **Wonowon** Can.
65 B2 **Wŏnsan** N. Korea
53 C3 **Wonthaggi** Austr.
52 A2 **Woocalla** Austr.
51 C1 **Woodah, Isle** *i.* Austr.
99 D2 **Woodbridge** U.K.
136 B3 **Woodland Park** U.S.A.
50 C2 **Woodroffe, Mount** Austr.
51 C1 **Woods, Lake** *salt flat* Austr.
129 E3 **Woods, Lake of the**
Can./U.S.A.
53 C3 **Woods Point** Austr.
131 D2 **Woodstock** *N.B.* Can.
140 C2 **Woodstock** *Ont.* Can.
54 C2 **Woodville** N.Z.
139 D1 **Woodward** U.S.A.
53 D2 **Woolgoolga** Austr.
52 A2 **Woomera** Austr.
140 C2 **Wooster** U.S.A.
122 A3 **Worcester** S. Africa
99 B2 **Worcester** U.K.
141 E2 **Worcester** U.S.A.
102 C2 **Wörgl** Austria
98 B1 **Workington** U.K.
98 C2 **Worksop** U.K.
136 B2 **Worland** U.S.A.
101 D3 **Worms** Ger.
99 C3 **Worthing** U.K.
137 D2 **Worthington** U.S.A.
58 C3 **Wotu** Indon.
59 C3 **Wowoni** *i.* Indon.
Wrangel Island Rus. Fed.
see Vrangelya, Ostrov
128 B2 **Wrangell** U.S.A.
96 B1 **Wrath, Cape** U.K.
136 C2 **Wray** U.S.A.
122 A2 **Wreck Point** S. Africa
98 B2 **Wrexham** U.K.
136 B2 **Wright** U.S.A.
63 A2 **Wrightmyo** India
128 B1 **Wrigley** Can.
103 D1 **Wrocław** Pol.
103 D1 **Września** Pol.
70 B2 **Wu'an** China
70 A2 **Wudu** China
70 A2 **Wuhai** China
70 B2 **Wuhan** China
70 B2 **Wuhu** China
Wujin China *see* Changzhou
115 C4 **Wukari** Nigeria
62 B1 **Wuliang Shan** *mts* China
59 C3 **Wuliaru** *i.* Indon.
71 A3 **Wumeng Shan** *mts* China
130 B1 **Wunnummin Lake** Can.
101 F2 **Wunsiedel** Ger.
101 D1 **Wunstorf** Ger.
62 A1 **Wuntho** Myanmar
100 C2 **Wuppertal** Ger.
122 A3 **Wuppertal** S. Africa

101 E2 **Wurzbach** Ger.
101 D3 **Würzburg** Ger.
101 F2 **Wurzen** Ger.
68 C2 **Wuwei** China
70 A2 **Wuxi** *Chongqing* China
70 C2 **Wuxi** *Jiangsu* China
Wuxing China *see* Huzhou
71 A3 **Wuxuan** China
Wuyang China *see* Zhenyuan
69 E1 **Wuyiling** China
71 B3 **Wuyishan** China
71 B3 **Wuyi Shan** *mts* China
70 A1 **Wuyuan** China
70 A2 **Wuzhong** China
71 B3 **Wuzhou** China
53 C2 **Wyangala Reservoir** Austr.
52 B3 **Wycheproof** Austr.
99 B3 **Wye** *r.* U.K.
50 B1 **Wyndham** Austr.
142 B1 **Wynne** U.S.A.
129 D2 **Wynyard** Can.
136 B2 **Wyoming** *state* U.S.A.
103 E1 **Wyszków** Pol.
140 C3 **Wytheville** U.S.A.

X

117 D3 **Xaafuun** Somalia
121 C3 **Xai-Xai** Moz.
70 A1 **Xamba** China
62 B1 **Xam Hua** Laos
120 A2 **Xangongo** Angola
81 C2 **Xankändi** Azer.
111 B2 **Xanthi** Greece
150 B3 **Xapuri** Brazil
107 C2 **Xàtiva** Spain
Xiaguan China *see* Dali
71 B3 **Xiamen** China
70 A2 **Xi'an** China
70 A3 **Xianfeng** China
70 B2 **Xiangfan** China
Xiangjiang China *see*
Huichang
62 B2 **Xiangkhoang** Laos
71 B3 **Xiangtan** China
Xiangyang China *see*
Xiangfan
70 B2 **Xiantao** China
70 A2 **Xianyang** China
70 B2 **Xiaogan** China
69 E1 **Xiao Hinggan Ling** *mts*
China
70 C2 **Xiaoshan** China
62 B1 **Xichang** China
145 C2 **Xicohténcatl** Mex.
70 A2 **Xifeng** *Gansu* China
71 A3 **Xifeng** *Guizhou* China
75 C2 **Xigazê** China
83 I4 **Xilinhot** China
70 B2 **Xincai** China
68 C2 **Xinghai** China
70 B2 **Xinghua** China
71 B3 **Xingning** China
70 A2 **Xingping** China
70 B2 **Xingtai** China
151 C2 **Xingu** *r.* Brazil
71 A3 **Xingyi** China
71 B3 **Xinhua** China
68 C2 **Xining** China
75 C1 **Xinjiang Uygur Zizhiqu**
aut. reg. China
Xinjing China *see* Jingxi
65 A1 **Xinmin** China
71 B3 **Xinning** China
70 B2 **Xintai** China
70 B2 **Xinxiang** China
70 B2 **Xinyang** China

71 B3 **Xinyu** China
70 B2 **Xinzhou** *Shanxi* China
69 D2 **Xinzhou** *Shanxi* China
106 B1 **Xinzo de Limia** Spain
Xiongshan China *see*
Zhenghe
68 C2 **Xiqing Shan** *mts* China
151 D3 **Xique Xique** Brazil
71 A3 **Xishanzui** China
71 A3 **Xiushan** China
71 B3 **Xiuying** China
70 B2 **Xixia** China
75 C1 **Xizang Zizhiqu** *aut. reg.*
China
71 A3 **Xuanwei** China
70 B2 **Xuanzhou** China
70 B2 **Xuchang** China
Xucheng China *see* Xuwen
117 C4 **Xuddur** Somalia
Xujiang China *see*
Guangchang
71 B3 **Xun Jiang** *r.* China
71 B3 **Xunwu** China
71 B3 **Xuwen** China
71 A3 **Xuyong** China
70 B2 **Xuzhou** China

Y

117 B4 **Yabēlo** Eth.
69 D1 **Yablonovyy Khrebet** *mts*
Rus. Fed.
143 D1 **Yadkin** *r.* U.S.A.
75 C2 **Yadong** China
89 E2 **Yagnitsa** Rus. Fed.
118 B1 **Yagoua** Cameroon
128 C3 **Yahk** Can.
144 B2 **Yahualica** Mex.
80 B2 **Yahyalı** Turkey
67 C4 **Yaizu** Japan
134 B1 **Yakima** U.S.A.
114 B3 **Yako** Burkina
66 D2 **Yakumo** Japan
126 B3 **Yakutat** U.S.A.
83 J2 **Yakutsk** Rus. Fed.
91 C2 **Yakymivka** Ukr.
63 A3 **Yala** Thai.
53 C3 **Yallourn** Austr.
111 C2 **Yalova** Turkey
91 C3 **Yalta** Ukr.
65 A1 **Yalu Jiang** *r.* China/N. Korea
67 D3 **Yamagata** Japan
67 B4 **Yamaguchi** Japan
86 F1 **Yamal, Poluostrov** *pen.*
Rus. Fed.
53 D1 **Yamba** Austr.
117 A4 **Yambio** Sudan
110 C2 **Yambol** Bulg.
86 G2 **Yamburg** Rus. Fed.
62 A1 **Yamethin** Myanmar
114 B4 **Yamoussoukro** Côte d'Ivoire
90 B2 **Yampil'** Ukr.
75 C2 **Yamuna** *r.* India
75 D2 **Yamzho Yumco** *l.* China
83 K2 **Yana** *r.* Rus. Fed.
70 A2 **Yan'an** China
150 A3 **Yanaoca** Peru
78 A2 **Yanbu' al Baḥr** Saudi Arabia
70 C2 **Yancheng** China
50 A3 **Yanchep** Austr.
70 B2 **Yangcheng** China
70 B2 **Yangchun** China
65 B2 **Yangdok** N. Korea
62 A2 **Yangôn** Myanmar
70 B2 **Yangquan** China
71 B3 **Yangshuo** China

70 C3 **Yangtze** r. China
69 E2 **Yangtze, Mouths of the**
China
70 B2 **Yangzhou** China
65 B1 **Yanji** China
137 D2 **Yankton** U.S.A.
83 K2 **Yano-Indigirskaya**
Nizmennost' lowland
Rus. Fed.
83 K2 **Yanskiy Zaliv** g. Rus. Fed.
53 C1 **Yantabulla** Austr.
70 C2 **Yantai** China
118 B2 **Yaoundé** Cameroon
59 D2 **Yap** i. Micronesia
59 D3 **Yapen** i. Indon.
59 D3 **Yapen, Selat** sea chan. Indon.
144 A2 **Yaqui** r. Mex.
51 E2 **Yaraka** Austr.
86 D3 **Yaransk** Rus. Fed.
78 B3 **Yarim** Yemen
77 D3 **Yarkant He** r. China
75 D2 **Yarlung Zangbo** r. China
131 D2 **Yarmouth** Can.
86 F2 **Yarongo** Rus. Fed.
89 E2 **Yaroslavl'** Rus. Fed.
66 B2 **Yaroslavskiy** Rus. Fed.
53 C3 **Yarram** Austr.
89 D2 **Yartsevo** Rus. Fed.
89 E3 **Yasnogorsk** Rus. Fed.
63 B2 **Yasothon** Thai.
53 C2 **Yass** Austr.
111 C3 **Yatağan** Turkey
129 E1 **Yathkyed Lake** Can.
67 B4 **Yatsushiro** Japan
150 B2 **Yavari** r. Brazil/Peru
75 B2 **Yavatmāl** India
90 A2 **Yavoriv** Ukr.
67 B4 **Yawatahama** Japan
81 D2 **Yazd** Iran
142 B2 **Yazoo City** U.S.A.
111 B3 **Ydra** i. Greece
85 A2 **Ye** Myanmar
77 D3 **Yecheng** China
144 B2 **Yécora** Mex.
89 E3 **Yefremov** Rus. Fed.
89 E2 **Yegor'yevsk** Rus. Fed.
117 B4 **Yei** Sudan
86 F3 **Yekaterinburg** Rus. Fed.
89 E3 **Yelets** Rus. Fed.
114 A3 **Yélimané** Mali
96 □ **Yell** i. U.K.
128 C1 **Yellowknife** Can.
Yellow River r. China see
Huang He
69 E2 **Yellow Sea** N. Pacific Ocean
136 C1 **Yellowstone** r. U.S.A.
136 A2 **Yellowstone Lake** U.S.A.
88 C3 **Yel'sk** Belarus
78 B3 **Yemen** country Asia
86 E2 **Yemva** Rus. Fed.
91 D2 **Yenakiyeve** Ukr.
62 A1 **Yenangyaung** Myanmar
62 B1 **Yên Bai** Vietnam
114 B4 **Yendi** Ghana
111 C3 **Yenice** Turkey
111 C3 **Yenifoça** Turkey
68 C1 **Yenisey** r. Rus. Fed.
53 C2 **Yenval** Austr.
99 B3 **Yeovil** U.K.
51 E2 **Yeppoon** Austr.
83 I2 **Yerbogachen** Rus. Fed.
81 C1 **Yerevan** Armenia
77 D1 **Yereymentau** Kazakh.
87 D3 **Yershov** Rus. Fed.
65 B2 **Yesan** S. Korea
77 C1 **Yesil'** Kazakh.
111 C3 **Yeşilova** Turkey
99 A3 **Yes Tor** hill U.K.
53 D1 **Yetman** Austr.
62 A1 **Yeu** Myanmar

104 B2 **Yeu, Île d'** i. France
91 C2 **Yevpatoriya** Ukr.
91 D2 **Yeysk** Rus. Fed.
88 C2 **Yezyaryshcha** Belarus
71 A3 **Yibin** China
70 B2 **Yichang** China
69 E1 **Yichun** Heilong. China
71 B3 **Yichun** Jiangxi China
110 C2 **Yıldız Dağları** mts Turkey
80 B2 **Yıldızeli** Turkey
71 A3 **Yinchuan** China
65 B1 **Yingchengzi** China
71 B3 **Yingde** China
70 C1 **Yingkou** China
70 B2 **Yingshan** Hubei China
70 A2 **Yingshan** Sichuan China
71 B3 **Yingtan** China
71 E2 **Yining** China
117 B4 **Yirga Alem** Eth.
70 B2 **Yishui** China
68 C2 **Yiwu** China
71 B3 **Yiyang** China
71 A3 **Yizhou** China
92 I1 **Yli-Kitka** l. Fin.
92 H2 **Ylitornio** Fin.
92 H3 **Ylivieska** Fin.
61 C2 **Yogyakarta** Indon.
118 B2 **Yoko** Cameroon
67 C3 **Yokohama** Japan
67 D3 **Yola** Nigeria
67 D3 **Yonezawa** Japan
71 B3 **Yong'an** China
71 B3 **Yongchun** China
70 A2 **Yongdeng** China
65 B2 **Yŏngdŏk** S. Korea
71 C3 **Yongkang** China
62 B1 **Yongsheng** China
71 B3 **Yongzhou** China
150 A1 **Yopal** Col.
50 A3 **York** Austr.
98 C2 **York** U.K.
137 D2 **York** NE U.S.A.
141 D3 **York** PA U.S.A.
51 D1 **York, Cape** Austr.
52 A3 **Yorke Peninsula** Austr.
52 A3 **Yorketown** Austr.
98 C2 **Yorkshire Wolds** hills U.K.
129 D2 **Yorkton** Can.
87 D3 **Yoshkar-Ola** Rus. Fed.
97 C3 **Youghal** Rep. of Ireland
53 C2 **Young** Austr.
52 A2 **Younghusband Peninsula**
Austr.
140 C2 **Youngstown** U.S.A.
114 B3 **Youvarou** Mali
77 E2 **Youyi Feng** mt.
China/Rus. Fed.
80 B2 **Yozgat** Turkey
134 B2 **Yreka** U.S.A.
Yr Wyddfa mt. U.K. see
Snowdon
105 C2 **Yssingeaux** France
93 F4 **Ystad** Sweden
Ysyk-Köl salt l. Kyrg. see Balykchy
77 D2 **Ysyk-Köl** salt l. Kyrg.
92 □A3 **Ytri-Rangá** r. Iceland
62 B1 **Yuanjiang** China
62 B1 **Yuan Jiang** r. China
62 B1 **Yuanmou** China
135 B3 **Yuba City** U.S.A.
67 D2 **Yūbari** Japan
145 C3 **Yucatán** pen. Mex.
146 B2 **Yucatan Channel** Cuba/Mex.
70 B2 **Yuci** China
50 C2 **Yuendumu** Austr.
71 B3 **Yueyang** China
86 F2 **Yugorsk** Rus. Fed.
109 D2 **Yugoslavia** country Europe
83 L2 **Yukagirskoye Ploskogor'ye**
plat. Rus. Fed.

126 A2 **Yukon** r. Can./U.S.A.
128 A1 **Yukon Territory**
admin. div. Can.
71 B3 **Yulin** Guangxi China
70 A2 **Yulin** Shaanxi China
62 B1 **Yulongxue Shan** mt. China
138 A2 **Yuma** AZ U.S.A.
136 C2 **Yuma** CO U.S.A.
68 C2 **Yumen** China
80 B2 **Yunak** Turkey
70 B2 **Yuncheng** China
71 B3 **Yunfu** China
62 B1 **Yunnan** prov. China
52 A2 **Yunta** Austr.
70 B2 **Yunyang** China
150 A2 **Yurimaguas** Peru
77 E2 **Yurungkax He** r. China
71 C3 **Yü Shan** mt. Taiwan
68 C2 **Yushu** China
Yushuwan China see
Huaihua
81 C1 **Yüsufeli** Turkey
77 C3 **Yutian** China
62 B1 **Yuxi** China
66 D2 **Yuzhno-Kuril'sk** Rus. Fed.
83 K3 **Yuzhno-Sakhalinsk**
Rus. Fed.
91 C2 **Yuzhnoukrayinsk** Ukr.
104 C2 **Yvetot** France

Z

100 B1 **Zaandam** Neth.
69 D1 **Zabaykal'sk** Rus. Fed.
78 B3 **Zabīd** Yemen
76 C3 **Zābol** Iran
79 D2 **Zāboli** Iran
144 B3 **Zacapu** Mex.
144 B2 **Zacatecas** Mex.
145 C3 **Zacatepec** Mex.
145 C3 **Zacatlán** Mex.
111 B3 **Zacharo** Greece
144 B2 **Zacoalco** Mex.
145 C2 **Zacualtipán** Mex.
109 C2 **Zadar** Croatia
63 A3 **Zadetkyi Kyun** i. Myanmar
89 E3 **Zadonsk** Rus. Fed.
106 B2 **Zafra** Spain
80 B2 **Zagazig** Egypt
109 C1 **Zagreb** Croatia
81 C2 **Zagros, Kūhhā-ye** mts Iran
79 D2 **Zāhedān** Iran
80 B2 **Zahlé** Lebanon
78 B3 **Zahrān** Saudi Arabia
Zaire country Africa see
Congo, Democratic
Republic of
109 D2 **Zaječar** Yugo.
89 E3 **Zakharovo** Rus. Fed.
81 C2 **Zākhō** Iraq
111 B3 **Zakynthos** Greece
111 B3 **Zakynthos** i. Greece see
Zante
103 D2 **Zalaegerszeg** Hungary
110 B1 **Zalău** Romania
78 B2 **Zalim** Saudi Arabia
117 A3 **Zalingei** Sudan
78 A2 **Zalmā, Jabal az** mt.
Saudi Arabia
128 C2 **Zama City** Can.
Zambeze r. Moz. see
Zambezi
120 B2 **Zambezi** Zambia
120 C2 **Zambezi** r. Zambia
120 B2 **Zambia** country Africa
64 B2 **Zamboanga** Phil.
64 B2 **Zamboanga Peninsula** Phil.

106 B1 **Zamora** Spain
144 B3 **Zamora de Hidalgo** Mex.
103 E1 **Zamość** Pol.
75 B1 **Zanda** China
100 B2 **Zandvliet** Belgium
140 C3 **Zanesville** U.S.A.
81 C2 **Zanjān** Iran
111 B3 **Zante** i. Greece
119 D3 **Zanzibar** Tanz.
119 D3 **Zanzibar Island** Tanz.
89 E3 **Zaokskiy** Rus. Fed.
115 C2 **Zaouatallaz** Alg.
70 B2 **Zaozhuang** China
89 D2 **Zapadnaya Dvina** r. Europe
89 D2 **Zapadnaya Dvina** Rus. Fed.
68 B1 **Zapadnyy Sayan** reg.
Rus. Fed.
139 D3 **Zapata** U.S.A.
92 J2 **Zapolyarnyy** Rus. Fed.
91 D2 **Zaporizhzhya** Ukr.
101 E2 **Zappendorf** Ger.
80 B2 **Zara** Turkey
145 B2 **Zaragoza** Mex.
107 C1 **Zaragoza** Spain
76 B3 **Zarand** Iran
76 C3 **Zaranj** Afgh.
88 C2 **Zarasai** Lith.
89 E3 **Zaraysk** Rus. Fed.
150 B1 **Zaraza** Venez.
115 C3 **Zaria** Nigeria
90 B1 **Zarichne** Ukr.
81 D3 **Zarqān** Iran
66 B2 **Zarubino** Rus. Fed.
103 D1 **Żary** Pol.
115 D1 **Zarzis** Tunisia
75 B1 **Zaskar Mountains** India
123 C3 **Zastron** S. Africa
69 E1 **Zavitinsk** Rus. Fed.
103 D1 **Zawiercie** Pol.
77 E2 **Zaysan, Ozero** i. Kazakh.
68 C3 **Zayü** China
90 B1 **Zdolbuniv** Ukr.
       Zealand i. Denmark see
       Sjælland
100 A2 **Zeebrugge** Belgium
123 C2 **Zeerust** S. Africa
50 C2 **Zeil, Mount** Austr.
101 F2 **Zeitz** Ger.
88 B3 **Zelenogradsk** Rus. Fed.
82 E1 **Zemlya Aleksandry** i.
       Rus. Fed.
82 E1 **Zemlya Frantsa-Iosifa** is
       Rus. Fed.
82 F1 **Zemlya Vil'cheka** i.
       Rus. Fed.
107 D2 **Zemmora** Alg.
145 C3 **Zempoaltépetl, Nudo de**
       mt. Mex.
65 B1 **Zengfeng Shan** mt. China
105 D2 **Zermatt** Switz.
91 E2 **Zernograd** Rus. Fed.
101 E2 **Zeulenroda** Ger.
101 D1 **Zeven** Ger.
100 C2 **Zevenaar** Neth.
83 J3 **Zeya** Rus. Fed.
79 C2 **Zeydābād** Iran
83 J3 **Zeyskoye**
       Vodokhranilishche resr
       Rus. Fed.
103 D1 **Zgierz** Pol.
75 C2 **Zhabdün** China
88 B3 **Zhabinka** Belarus
76 A2 **Zhalpaktal** Kazakh.
77 C1 **Zhaltyr** Kazakh.
76 B2 **Zhanaozen** Kazakh.
       Zhangde China see Anyang
70 B1 **Zhangjiakou** China
71 B3 **Zhangping** China
71 B3 **Zhangshu** China
68 C2 **Zhangye** China

71 B3 **Zhangzhou** China
71 B3 **Zhanjiang** China
71 B3 **Zhao'an** China
71 B3 **Zhaoqing** China
71 A3 **Zhaotong** China
75 C1 **Zhari Namco** salt l. China
77 E2 **Zharkent** Kazakh.
89 D2 **Zharkovskiy** Rus. Fed.
77 E2 **Zharma** Kazakh.
90 C2 **Zhashkiv** Ukr.
71 C3 **Zhejiang** prov. China
82 F1 **Zhelaniya, Mys** c. Rus. Fed.
89 E3 **Zheleznogorsk** Rus. Fed.
70 A2 **Zhenba** China
71 A3 **Zheng'an** China
71 B3 **Zhenghe** China
70 B2 **Zhengzhou** China
70 B2 **Zhenjiang** China
71 A3 **Zhenyuan** China
91 E1 **Zherdevka** Rus. Fed.
86 D2 **Zheshart** Rus. Fed.
77 C2 **Zhezkazgan**
       Karagandinskaya Oblast'
       Kazakh.
77 C2 **Zhezkazgan**
       Karagandinskaya Oblast'
       Kazakh.
83 J2 **Zhigansk** Rus. Fed.
       Zhi Qu r. China see Yangtze
76 C1 **Zhitikara** Kazakh.
88 D3 **Zhlobin** Belarus
90 B2 **Zhmerynka** Ukr.
74 A1 **Zhob** Pak.
83 L1 **Zhokhova, Ostrov** i.
       Rus. Fed.
62 A1 **Zhongdian** China
       Zhonghe China see Xiushan
70 A2 **Zhongning** China
71 B3 **Zhongshan** China
       Zhongshan China see
       Lupanshui
70 A2 **Zhongwei** China
       Zhongxin China see
       Zhongdian
70 B2 **Zhoukou** China
70 C2 **Zhoushan** China
91 C2 **Zhovti Vody** Ukr.
65 A2 **Zhuanghe** China
70 B2 **Zhucheng** China
89 D3 **Zhukovka** Rus. Fed.
89 E2 **Zhukovskiy** Rus. Fed.
70 B2 **Zhumadian** China
       Zhuoyang China see Suiping
71 B3 **Zhuzhou** Hunan China
71 B3 **Zhuzhou** Hunan China
90 A2 **Zhydachiv** Ukr.
88 C3 **Zhytkavichy** Belarus
90 B1 **Zhytomyr** Ukr.
103 D2 **Žiar nad Hronom** Slovakia
70 B2 **Zibo** China
103 D1 **Zielona Góra** Pol.
62 A1 **Zigaing** Myanmar
71 A3 **Zigong** China
70 B2 **Zigui** China
114 A3 **Ziguinchor** Senegal
144 B3 **Zihuatanejo** Mex.
103 D2 **Žilina** Slovakia
83 H3 **Zima** Rus. Fed.
145 C2 **Zimapán** Mex.
121 C3 **Zimbabwe** country Africa
114 A4 **Zimmi** Sierra Leone
110 C2 **Zimnicea** Romania
115 C3 **Zinder** Niger
78 B3 **Zinjibār** Yemen
103 D2 **Zirc** Hungary
62 A1 **Ziro** India
79 C2 **Zir Rūd** Iran
103 D2 **Zistersdorf** Austria
145 B3 **Zitácuaro** Mex.
103 C1 **Zittau** Ger.

87 E3 **Zlatoust** Rus. Fed.
103 D2 **Zlín** Czech Rep.
89 D3 **Zlynka** Rus. Fed.
89 E3 **Zmiyevka** Rus. Fed.
91 D2 **Zmiyiv** Ukr.
89 E3 **Znamenka** Orlovskaya Oblast'
       Rus. Fed.
91 E1 **Znamenka**
       Tambovskaya Oblast'
       Rus. Fed.
91 C2 **Znam"yanka** Ukr.
103 D2 **Znojmo** Czech Rep.
91 D1 **Zolochiv** Kharkiv's'ka Oblast'
       Ukr.
90 A2 **Zolochiv** L'vivs'ka Oblast' Ukr.
91 C2 **Zolotonosha** Ukr.
89 E3 **Zolotukhino** Rus. Fed.
121 C2 **Zomba** Malawi
60 B1 **Zonguldak** Turkey
105 D3 **Zonza** Corsica France
114 B4 **Zorzor** Liberia
115 D2 **Zouar** Chad
114 A2 **Zouérat** Maur.
109 D1 **Zrenjanin** Yugo.
89 D1 **Zubtsov** Rus. Fed.
105 D2 **Zug** Switz.
81 C1 **Zugdidi** Georgia
106 B2 **Zújar** r. Spain
100 C2 **Zülpich** Ger.
121 C2 **Zumbo** Moz.
145 C3 **Zumpango** Mex.
138 B1 **Zuni Mountains** U.S.A.
71 A3 **Zunyi** China
109 C1 **Županja** Croatia
105 D2 **Zürich** Switz.
100 C1 **Zutphen** Neth.
115 D1 **Zuwārah** Libya
90 C2 **Zvenyhorodka** Ukr.
121 C3 **Zvishavane** Zimbabwe
103 D2 **Zvolen** Slovakia
109 C2 **Zvornik** Bos.-Herz.
114 B4 **Zwedru** Liberia
123 C3 **Zwelitsha** S. Africa
103 D2 **Zwettl** Austria
101 F2 **Zwickau** Ger.
100 C1 **Zwolle** Neth.
83 L2 **Zyryanka** Rus. Fed.